D0942586

Frommer's®

Honduras

2nd Edition

by Nicholas Gill

Here's what the critics say about Frommer's:

"Amazingly easy to use. Very portable, very complete."
—BOOKLIST

"Detailed, accurate, and easy-to-read information for all price ranges."
—GLAMOUR MAGAZINE

"Hotel information is close to encyclopedic."
—DES MOINES SUNDAY REGISTER

"Frommer's Guides have a way of giving you a real feel for a place."
—KNIGHT RIDDER NEWSPAPERS

917.283

John Wiley & Sons Canada, Ltd.

ABOUT THE AUTHOR

Writer and photographer **Nicholas Gill** is based in Lima, Peru, and Brooklyn, New York. His work regularly appears in publications such as the *New York Times, Condé Nast Traveler, National Geographic Traveler,* and *Afar.* He has also contributed to *Frommer's Chile* and South and Central American guides. Visit his personal website, www.nicholasgill.com, for more information or his blog on Latin American food, drink, and travel, www.newworldreview.com.

Published by:

JOHN WILEY & SONS CANADA, LTD.

6045 Freemont Blvd.
Mississauga, ON L5R 4J3

Copyright © 2011 John Wiley & Sons Canada, Ltd. All rights reserved. No part of this work covered by the copyright, herein may be reproduced or used in any form or by any means—graphic, electronic or mechanical—without prior written permission of the publisher. Any request for photocopying, or other reprographic copying of any part of this book shall be directed in writing to The Canadian Copyright Licensing Agency (Access Copyright). For an Access Copyright license, visit www.accesscopyright.ca or call toll free, 1-800-893-5777.

Wiley and the Wiley Publishing logo are trademarks or registered trademarks of John Wiley & Sons, Inc. and/or its affiliates. Frommer's is a trademark or registered trademark of Arthur Frommer. Used under license. All other trademarks are the property of their respective owners. John Wiley & Sons, Inc. is not associated with any product or vendor mentioned in this book.

ISBN 978-1-118-07275-2

Editor: Gene Shannon
Developmental Editor: William Travis
Production Editor: Pamela Vokey
Editorial Assistant: Jeremy Hanson-Finger
Project Coordinator: Kristie Rees
Cartographer: Lohnes + Wright
Production by Wiley Indianapolis Composition Services

Front cover photo: Roatan, Islas de la Bahia, Honduras © Greg Johnston / Lonely Planet Images
Back cover photo: Roatan: Ocelot on tree branch © Tier Und Naturfotografie J & C Sohns / Getty Images

For reseller information, including discounts and premium sales, please call our sales department: Tel. 416-646-7992. For press review copies, author interviews, or other publicity information, please contact our publicity department: Tel. 416-646-4582; Fax: 416-236-4448.

Wiley also publishes its books in a variety of electronic formats. Some content that appears in print may not be available in electronic formats.

Manufactured in the United States

1 2 3 4 5 RRD 12 11 10 09 08

CONTENTS

List of Maps vi

1 THE BEST OF HONDURAS 1

The Best Travel Experiences 2
The Best Culinary Experiences 2
The Best Small Towns 3
The Best Health & Spa Retreats 4
The Best Markets & Shopping 5
The Best Beaches 6
The Best Adventure Activities 7
The Best Wildlife Watching 7
The Most Intriguing Historical Sites 8
The Best Family Activities 8
The Best Splurge Hotels 9
The Best Hotels that Won't Empty Your Wallet 10

2 HONDURAS IN DEPTH 11

Honduras Today 12
DATELINE 14
Looking Back: Honduran History 14
Honduras in Pop Culture 20
Eating & Drinking 22
When to Go 25
HONDURAS CALENDAR OF EVENTS 25
Lay of the Land 26
GENERAL RESOURCES FOR GREEN TRAVEL 28
Responsible Travel 29

3 THE HONDURAS ACTIVE VACATION PLANNER 31

Honduras's Top National Parks & Bio-Reserves 31
Activities A to Z 34
HEALTH, SAFETY & ETIQUETTE IN THE WILDERNESS 39
Organized Adventure Trips 42
FROMMERS.COM: THE COMPLETE TRAVEL RESOURCE 44
Ecologically Oriented Volunteer & Study Programs 44

4 SUGGESTED ITINERARIES IN HONDURAS 45

The Regions in Brief 45

The Best of Honduras in 1 Week 47

The Best of Honduras in 2 Weeks 48

The Best of Honduras for Families 51

The Ultimate Bay Islands Dive Trip 52

La Mosquitia & Beyond 54

The Adrenaline-Pumping Adventure Vacation 56

Best of Tegucigalpa & the South 58

5 TEGUCIGALPA 60

Orientation 60

NEIGHBORHOODS IN BRIEF 64

Getting Around 64

FAST FACTS: TEGUCIGALPA 65

Where to Stay 66

Where to Eat 69

What to See & Do 73

A HOLY CELEBRATION 76

Side Trips from Tegucigalpa 76

6 SOUTHERN HONDURAS 82

Yuscaran 82

Danlí 84

CIGAR FACTORY TOURS IN DANLÍ 86

Choluteca 86

Isla del Tigre 88

7 WESTERN HONDURAS 92

San Pedro Sula 92

FAST FACTS: SAN PEDRO SULA 96

PARQUE NACIONAL EL CUSUCO 98

Lago de Yojoa 105

FAST FACTS: LAGO DE YOJOA 106

Highway CA 5 to Copán Ruínas 111

Comayagua 113

Copán Ruínas & Copán 117

Santa Rosa de Copán 131

Gracias 134

NATIONAL HERO: LEMPIRA 135

La Ruta Lenca 140

8 THE NORTH COAST 146

Puerto Cortes 146

Omoa 150

Tela 153

La Ceiba 162

FAST FACTS: LA CEIBA 165

Sambo Creek 172

Pico Bonito National Park 174

Cayos Cochinos 178

Trujillo 180

9 THE BAY ISLANDS 186

Roatán 187

SCUBA DIVING IN ROATÁN 193

VISITING ROATÁN BY CRUISESHIP 195

CRUISE SHIP SHORE EXCURSIONS 196

DIVING OPERATORS IN ROATÁN 200

PIRATES OF THE BAY ISLANDS 213

Utila 214

ISLAND SLANG 215

THE WORLD'S WHALE SHARK HEADQUARTERS 219

TOP FIVE DIVE SITES IN UTILA 220

HOUSE OR CONDO RENTAL ON UTILA 223

Guanaja 226

DIVE SITES IN GUANAJA 231

10 LA MOSQUITIA 234

Essentials 235

Batalla 236

Palacios 238

Laguna de Ibans 239

Reserva de la Biosfera del Río Plátano 242

RAFTING DOWN THE RÍO PLÁTANO 244

Brus Laguna 245

THE LOST CITIES OF THE RAINFOREST 246

Laguna de Caratasca & Eastern La Mosquitia 249

11 OLANCHO 253

Juticalpa 254

Catacamas 257

Gualaco 260

El Carbon 261

La Union 261

Yoro 262

THE RAIN OF FISH 263

12 PLANNING YOUR TRIP TO HONDURAS 264

Getting There 265

Getting Around 267

Tips on Accommodations 268

HEALTH 268

FAST FACTS: HONDURAS 271

Airline websites 279

13 USEFUL TERMS & PHRASES 281

Glossary of Spanish-Language Terms 281

Common Honduran Words & Phrases 285

14 HONDURAN WILDLIFE 286

Fauna 286

Flora 295

Index 298

General Index 298

Accommodations Index 307

Restaurants Index 309

LIST OF MAPS

Looking Back at Honduras 17
Honduras in 1 Week 48
Honduras in 2 Weeks 49
Honduras for Families 52
Ultimate Bay Islands Dive Trip 53
La Mosquitia & Beyond 55
The Adrenaline-Pumping Adventure Vacation 57
Tegucigalpa & the South 59
Tegucigalpa 61
Southern Honduras 83
Western Honduras 93
San Pedro Sula 97
Copán 119
Copán Ruínas 121
The North Coast 147
Tela 155
La Ceiba 163
The Bay Islands 189
Roatán 191
Utila 217
Guanaja 229
La Mosquitia 237
Olancho 255

ACKNOWLEDGMENTS

At Frommer's, I'd like to thank Gene Shannon for his guidance on this project and Jen Reilly for her continued support. As always, thanks to my wife Claudia and family for their love. In Honduras, there are so many people who gave their time that without their help this book would not have been possible. In Gracias, Cinia Molina at Posada de Don Juan for her selfless advice and recommendations. Howard Rosenzweig at Casa de Café in Copan was another enormous help. On Roatán, I'd especially like to thank Kent at Blue Bahia for his smoked wahoo salad and Rick at Infinity Bay for support. On Utila, all help from Utopia Dive Village was extremely appreciated, as is from everyone at Utila Lodge and the Whale Shark Research and Oceanic Research Center and for Vern Fine for making the trip between the islands so much easier for a guidebook writer. On the Rio Cangrejal, everyone at Omega Lodge, Casa Verde, and Villas Pico Bonito. At Lago de Yojoa, brewer Robert Dale and bird guru Malcolm Gladwell at D&D Brewery for always being able to provide a nice pint and set of binoculars just when I need them the most.

HOW TO CONTACT US

In researching this book, we discovered many wonderful places—hotels, restaurants, shops, and more. We're sure you'll find others. Please tell us about them, so we can share the information with your fellow travelers in upcoming editions. If you were disappointed with a recommendation, we'd love to know that, too. Please write to:

Frommer's Honduras, 2nd Edition

John Wiley & Sons Canada, Ltd. • 6045 Freemont Blvd. • Mississauga, ON L5R 4J3

ADVISORY & DISCLAIMER

Travel information can change quickly and unexpectedly, and we strongly advise you to confirm important details locally before traveling, including information on visas, health and safety, traffic and transport, accommodation, shopping and eating out. We also encourage you to stay alert while traveling and to remain aware of your surroundings. Avoid civil disturbances, and keep a close eye on cameras, purses, wallets and other valuables.

While we have endeavored to ensure that the information contained within this guide is accurate and up-to-date at the time of publication, we make no representations or warranties with respect to the accuracy or completeness of the contents of this work and specifically disclaim all warranties, including without limitation warranties of fitness for a particular purpose. We accept no responsibility or liability for any inaccuracy or errors or omissions, or for any inconvenience, loss, damage, costs or expenses of any nature whatsoever incurred or suffered by anyone as a result of any advice or information contained in this guide.

The inclusion of a company, organization or Website in this guide as a service provider and/or potential source of further information does not mean that we endorse them or the information they provide. Be aware that information provided through some Websites may be unreliable and can change without notice. Neither the publisher or author shall be liable for any damages arising herefrom.

OTHER GREAT GUIDES FOR YOUR TRIP:

Frommer's Nicaragua & El Salvador

Frommer's Central America

Frommer's Guatemala

FROMMER'S STAR RATINGS, ICONS & ABBREVIATIONS

Every hotel, restaurant, and attraction listing in this guide has been ranked for quality, value, service, amenities, and special features using a **star-rating system.** In country, state, and regional guides, we also rate towns and regions to help you narrow down your choices and budget your time accordingly. Hotels and restaurants are rated on a scale of zero (recommended) to three stars (exceptional). Attractions, shopping, nightlife, towns, and regions are rated according to the following scale: zero stars (recommended), one star (highly recommended), two stars (very highly recommended), and three stars (must-see).

In addition to the star-rating system, we also use **seven feature icons** that point you to the great deals, in-the-know advice, and unique experiences that separate travelers from tourists. Throughout the book, look for:

special finds—those places only insiders know about

fun facts—details that make travelers more informed and their trips more fun

kids—best bets for kids and advice for the whole family

special moments—those experiences that memories are made of

overrated—places or experiences not worth your time or money

insider tips—great ways to save time and money

great values—where to get the best deals

The following abbreviations are used for credit cards:

AE	American Express	DISC	Discover	V	Visa
DC	Diners Club	MC	MasterCard		

TRAVEL RESOURCES AT FROMMERS.COM

Frommer's travel resources don't end with this guide. **Frommers.com** has travel information on more than 4,000 destinations. We update features regularly, giving you access to the most current trip-planning information and the best airfare, lodging, and car-rental bargains. You can also listen to podcasts, connect with other Frommers.com members through our active reader forums, share your travel photos, read blogs from guidebook editors and fellow travelers, and much more.

THE BEST OF HONDURAS

1

Here, you'll find one of the least explored and most adventurous destinations anywhere in Central America. Honduras offers up a little bit of everything: Caribbean beaches and spectacular coral reefs surrounding the Bay Islands; lost Maya ruins like Copán; indigenous cultures like the Lenca or Pech; colonial mountain retreats like Gracias; rainforest canopy tours; colorful festivals; and more types of birds and wildlife than your local zoo.

Honduras' capital, Tegucigalpa, is a contrast of past and present, dancing between colonial churches and a pulsating set of modern restaurants and nightlife. San Pedro Sula is the country's commercial center, with shopping malls and American-style amenities, but still within earshot of national parks and beaches. La Ceiba on the North Coast plays a backdrop to Pico Bonito National Park and Garífuna villages, while the century-old buildings in the sleepy backwater of Tela recall the city's days as a capital of banana production.

Soak in natural hot springs in the jungle-clad mountains near Copán and Gracias in the western reaches of the country, then stop by a coffee plantation or cigar factory to pick your senses back up. Tiny coastal villages and Spanish forts dot the north coast of the country, from Trujillo to Puerto Cortés. Just off shore are the Bay Islands of Roatán, Utila, and Guanaja—three unspoiled Caribbean paradises of swaying palms, sandy white beaches, and clean coral reefs.

From a refreshing bowl of ceviche to a simple bean and cheese baleada at a street-side stall, culinary gems are everywhere in Honduras. The western part of the country loves their chuletas, or pork chops, while beachside seafood shacks on the North Coast are fond of serving tapado, a hearty coconut and seafood stew, and garlic shrimp served with rice and banana. Cool off from the heat with mango juice or, better yet, a Monkey La-La, a creamy cocktail made on the Bay Islands.

Before dawn, hard-core (some might say loco) birders are crawling through the cloud forest mud of Celaque, La Tigre, or Cerro Azul Meámbar national parks to listen for the first calls of quetzals, toucans, motmots, and trogons. Down on the coast, canals through patches of mangroves, in places like La Mosquitia's Rio Platano reserve or Cuero y Salado near La Ceiba, reveal abundant wildlife ranging from howler monkeys and manatees to crocodiles and iguanas. In the dense forests of Pico Bonito, endangered species are as common as eco-lodges and adventure tour operators.

THE best TRAVEL EXPERIENCES

- **Semana Santa** (Comayagua): No festival or celebration in Honduras compares in magnitude and passion to Holy Week in Comayagua. This is a big deal here. Elaborate sawdust carpets called *alfombras*—built during the night and trampled apart the next day—are only a glimpse of what is to come. Expect nothing less than vivacious daily processions and hordes of pilgrims showing their devotion from Palm Sunday to Easter Sunday. See p. 114.
- **Diving in the Bay Islands:** Sharing the world's second-largest barrier reef with Belize, the Bay Islands of Honduras provide not only one of the most superb underwater experiences available, but also one of the cheapest when compared to the certification and rates of the rest of the world. With dive shops on every corner, it is hard not to strap on a tank and mask. If you prefer to go sans scuba gear, there are always glass-bottom boats, submarines, snorkeling with whale sharks, and a dolphin-training program. See p. 193.
- **Bird-watching:** Trogons, motmots, tanagers, scarlet macaws, boat-billed herons, resplendent quetzals, and toucans are only a small fraction the avian life you will encounter in places such as Lancetilla, Lago de Yojoa, Pico Bonito, Cerro Azul, and Celaque. Some areas of the country have recorded as many as 400 species, a good reason why birders in the know have been flocking to Honduras for years. See p. 35.
- **Traveling in La Mosquitia:** Rich with wildlife and home to ethnic groups like the Miskito, Pech, Garífuna, and Tawahkas, Central America's largest tract of rainforest is nothing less than spectacular. Community-based tourism initiatives, run directly in the indigenous villages themselves, assist in your exploration of the swamps, wetlands, grasslands, lagoons, and beaches. If you have a couple of weeks, sign up for a 10- to 14-day rafting expedition on the Río Plátano or Río Patuca. See chapter 11.
- **Seeing the still-smoking Flor de Copán Factory** (Western Honduras): The *Flor de Copán* tobacco factory is world renowned for its production of fine cigars like the Don Melo line. A tour here involves a walkthrough of the factory's heady drying and de-veining rooms and witnessing firsthand the country's most skilled rollers at work. Even if you hate smoking, this is a great chance to mingle with real Hondurans, outside the standard tourist industry. See p. 132.
- **Become a dolphin trainer** (the Bay Islands): Sign up with Anthony's Key Resort on Roatán for full hands-on training to become a bona fide dolphin trainer via their 7-day Dolphin Training 101 course. On Bailey's Key, a private key near the resort, professional trainers will lead you in a course on bottlenose dolphin behavior, anatomy, and physiology. If you just have a day, a swim, snorkel, or dive with these mischievous mammals can be had. See p. 194.

THE best CULINARY EXPERIENCES

- **Hacienda San Lucas** (Western Honduras): On a hillside overlooking the Copán valley, this rustic 100-year-old family-owned hacienda dishes out an authentic

Maya Chortí five-course candlelight dinner focusing on fresh, local ingredients and revived recipes that are prepared with traditional tools. Their tamales, *ticucos,* corn chowder, and fire-roasted chicken with *Maya adobo* sauce—like mole, minus the chocolate—have been celebrated widely by the international media. If you're really into it, the staff will even bring you into the kitchen to make authentic Honduran tamales. See p. 128.

- **Eating a baleada** (the North Coast): The Honduran version of the taco, or *pupusa,* is a corn tortilla with refried black beans and fresh cream. It is the country's iconic snack food and is served in street side stalls and sit-down restaurants almost anywhere you go for less than the price of a local phone call. Spice it up with eggs, chicken, avocado, *loroco,* or anything else your stomach is growling for. See chapter 8.
- **Lenca recipes at Rinconcito Graciano** (Western Honduras): Lenca recipes passed down through generations not only have been preserved, but also use mostly organic ingredients from local farmers at this small Gracias restaurant in the colonial heart of the city. Many of the dishes, which are served on locally made clay plates, such as *chorocos* (a type of tamale from San Manuel de Colohete) and *lengua de res* (tongue) are rarely found outside of local homes in the region. The owner is heavily involved with preservation of the colonial history and Lenca culture, and is a driving force behind tourism in the region. See p. 138.
- **Garífuna-style dining** (the North Coast): Step into almost any Garífuna village, like Travesia or Sambo Creek, and look for the simple thatched-roof eateries, usually right on the beach, for what will likely be an entire afternoon or evening of food and drinks. Try *tapado*—a seafood stew that combines fish, shrimp, green plantains, *achiote,* and herbs with coconut milk—or *dulce de coco*—shredded coconut cooked in sugar, formed into bars, and sold by the bag. See chapter 8.
- **Lago de Yojoa fish shack strip** (Western Honduras): The dozens of nearly identical shacks right on the highway with carbon-copy menus and stellar views of the lake and mountains are the unequivocal favorite rest stops for Hondurans traveling between San Pedro Sula and Tegucigalpa. Each serves fresh fish—often fried whole—caught right from the lake and dished out with a side of plantains. See p. 110.
- **Beer and birds at D&D Brewery** (Western Honduras): Sick of not being able to find a decent pint in Honduras? American Robert Dale decided to brew his own. Now, you can drink blueberry soda or a porter at the only microbrewery in the country and chat about the toucans and motmots you spotted earlier that day. Hungry? Try their real American breakfasts, pancakes, burgers, burritos, pork chops, and a few Honduran staples. See p. 110.

THE best SMALL TOWNS

- **Miami** (the North Coast): This Miami is about as far away from South Beach as you can imagine. Set on a narrow sandbar between the Caribbean and the Los Micos lagoon in Parque Nacional Jeannette Kawas/Punta Sal, this Garífuna village, just a small collection of thatched huts, has remained unchanged for a couple of hundred years. Get there while you can, though, as development around Tela Bay is a serious threat to the way of life of this and other communities nearby. See p. 155.
- **Raista/Belén** (La Mosquitia): These two side-by-side Miskito communities, set on a small strip of land between the Laguna de Ibas and the Caribbean, have become

an unlikely base for exploring the Mosquito Coast. Their very center is a grassy strip of land flanked by houses that serves as a grazing area for horses, a soccer field, and an airstrip. With two good yet surprisingly cheap and unknown eco-lodges, deserted beaches, and boat access to explore the monkey- and caiman-rich creeks of Parú, Ilbila, and Banaka, you won't be short on things to do. See p. 240.

- **Santa Lucía and Valle de Ángeles** (Tegucigalpa): These two laidback 16th-century villages, in the mountains near Tegucigalpa, are lined with small handicraft shops, country-style restaurants, outdoor cafes, leafy cobblestone plazas, and colonial churches. Come during the week, and you will have the place to yourself. Come on the weekends for a rush of *capitalinos* getting out of the city for some fresh air. See p. 80.
- **Amapala** (Southern Honduras): With the port that once drove this town on Isla del Tigre moved to the mainland, a renewed interest in tourism has sprung up in this sleepy fishing village, where you can see as far away as El Salvador and Nicaragua. A homestay program with local families, a few simple hotels, all the seafood you can handle, and the only good Pacific beaches in Honduras are all waiting to be discovered. See p. 89.
- **Gracias** (Western Honduras): While fast food chains and tour buses are blanketing Antigua, in nearby Guatemala, Gracias (once the capital of Central America) is still quaint and tranquil, and locals have yet to trade their cowboy hats for North Face jackets. Ongoing restorations are beautifying the city and nearby villages by the day, and expanded hotel options and even a new hot springs facility—the area's second—add to the attractions. Don't forget that Gracias is also the jumping-off point for the colonial churches and traditional culture along the La Ruta Lenca and the cloud forests of Parque Nacional Celaque. See p. 134.
- **East Harbour** (the Bay Islands): Sometimes just called Utila town, the Bay Islands' main population center is an eclectic mishmash of tourist services, dive shops, and typical island architecture. For the backpacker on a budget, this is paradise: cheap accommodations, basement prices for a dive certification, and a nightlife scene that rages well into the night every day of the week. Some stay for weeks, others for months. Some tend bar or become dive masters, and never leave. See p. 214.

THE best HEALTH & SPA RETREATS

- **Hacienda San Lucas** (Western Honduras): Yoga and meditation retreats draw power from the ancient stones of the Maya ruins not far from Hacienda San Lucas. A new gazebo with sweeping views of the Copán Valley below was built in 2007 specifically to enhance spiritual and health elements at the rustic lodge—and it has worked, though the fine cuisine, cozy accommodations, and abundance of orchids and trees don't exactly hurt the cause. See p. 125.
- **Sante Wellness Center** (the Bay Islands): Not far from Parrot Tree Plantation on Roatán, this is the most complete wellness center in all of Honduras. The Sante Wellness Center has not only daily yoga classes and a certified massage school, but also the finest selection of services this side of the reef. Need examples? Try a Chocolate Fondue Massage and Body Wrap, Salt Glow, European Facial, or Noni Wrap. See p. 210.

- **A raw food and yoga rainforest retreat** (the North Coast): Casa Verde in the Rio Cangrejal area of Pico Bonito National Park is the first of its kind in Honduras. Sign up by the week or the month, and learn to eat right, improve your yoga skills, and live a healthier lifestyle. See p. 177.
- **Thermal baths in Gracias** (Western Honduras): As long as you can appreciate steaming hot water, it won't matter whether you visit the public hot springs just outside of town or Posada de Don Juan's nicer, private facilities. It's still a long way from feeling touristy, and you will likely share hot springs in Gracias with only a handful of friendly locals. ***Note:*** Most rewarding after an intense hike in Celaque National Park. See p. 136.
- **Utopia Village spa or yoga retreats** (the Bay Islands): Isolated on Utila's rather lonely southwestern shore, this funky hotel opened in 2007 and gave the island something that it has long lacked: an element of luxury. Apart from having one of the top diving operations on the island, they opened the first full-scale spa on the island and occasionally organize yoga retreats. See p. 221.
- **Luna Jaguar Hot Springs Resort** (Western Honduras): In the hills outside of Copán, this fantasy-like hot springs and ultimate relaxation park might be a bit too recreated for some, but you cannot deny the pleasure of soaking in dozens of steamy pools all with different temperatures and surrounded by tropical green foliage. For added relief, take a massage in their thatched building overlooking a series of misty waterfalls and pools. See p. 123.

THE best MARKETS & SHOPPING

- **Guamilito Market** (Western Honduras): Products from around the country, as well as El Salvador and Guatemala, fill up literally hundreds of small stalls in the legendary San Pedro shopping stop. You'll find everything from hammocks, T-shirts, and Lenca pottery to cigars, Maya figurines, jewelry, coffee, Garífuna coconut carvings, and women making tortillas. See p. 99.
- **Valle de Ángeles** (Tegucigalpa): With dozens of craft shops selling handicrafts from around the country and the region, this idyllic mountain town is your one-stop Honduras shop. When not daydreaming in a sidewalk cafe, gallery hop for everything from leather belts to oversized Honduran hammocks to fine silver jewelry. See p. 77.
- **Yaba Ding Ding** (the Bay Islands): Next to HB Warren in Coxen Hole is one of the best craft shops in all of Honduras. The store stocks one of the most complete collections of Honduran crafts, including Lenca pottery, straw baskets, weavings from the highlands, Garífuna art, and more. See p. 192.
- **Handicraft markets** (Western Honduras): In Copán Ruínas, the options are plenty for handicraft shopping, thanks to numerous small artisan markets and craft co-ops sprinkled all over the cobblestone center. You'll find ceramic masks, stone imitations of Maya statues, trendy home accessories, jade jewelry, carved wood chests, hammocks, and multicolored woven pants that no one should ever wear. See p. 112.
- **Ceramics on La Ruta Lenca** (Western Honduras): The black-and-white ceramic bowls, plates, pots, and cups of the Lencas are sold throughout the country and are one of the favorite artisan wares to bring back home. The pottery is designed

using pre-Columbian techniques that have changed little over the centuries and created by many of the same families who pass down their methods. See p. 140.

- **A North Coast Handicraft Co-op** (the North Coast): Trujillo's Made in Honduras is a cooperative of more than 80 artisans who come from mostly rural villages from all over Honduras. Find *tuno* tree bark paintings, coffee, and jewelry. Displays in the store describe how most items were made, by which family, and where. See p. 183.

THE best BEACHES

- **West Bay Beach, Roatán** (the Bay Islands): The crystal clear water and powdery white sand on this end of Roatán have led many to call this one of the top beaches in the entire Caribbean—which is not exactly a place without competition. While new hotels are creeping in all the time, they rarely top two levels, and there still is not a single 500-room mega-resort to eat away all the tropical charm. Don't forget your snorkel gear; the world's second-largest barrier reef is just off shore. See p. 205.
- **Tela Bay** (the North Coast): In town, the best of the public beaches are in front of the Telamar and Ensenada beach resorts, but the more desolate ones near Sambo Creek and Punta Sal are hard not to like. Major development plans are in store here that could turn Tela Bay into the next Cancun, which is hard to say if it will be a good thing or a bad thing. It will be a few years before any noticeable difference can be seen, so for the time being, these waters are a bargain. See p. 157.
- **The Mosquito Coast** (La Mosquitia): Hundreds of miles of white sandy beach and not a soul in sight. Can this be real? It is, and with absolutely no development anytime soon—not even a hint—you can rest assured that for at least the next decade, the secret will be safe and sound. See p. 240.
- **Playa Negra, Isla del Tigre** (Southern Honduras): This black sand beach on Isla del Tigre—and all beaches on Isla del Tigre, for that matter—is practically deserted these days, though that doesn't have to be a bad thing. While everyone is flocking to the Caribbean coast, go Pacific for an unadulterated taste of the salty air. See p. 89.
- **Cayos Cochinos** (the North Coast): Tiny, cartoonish islands with little more than one palm tree and a spit of sand are surrounded by pristine coral reefs and jaw-dropping clear waters. Just one eco-friendly resort, a small Garífuna village, and a couple of forested hills holding a very rare species of snake are all the civilization you will find. There might not be a beach bar blasting Jimmy Buffett and selling frothy brews in sight, but it's a small tradeoff for paradise. See p. 178.
- **West End, Guanaja** (the Bay Islands): You have to go to the very corner of the second-largest and most-undeveloped of the Bay Islands to find this remarkable beach, though it is well worth the trip, even if you aren't staying in the one small hotel that sits here. Caribbean pine and the occasional sound of a coconut falling into the perfectly blue water will likely be your only company. See p. 229.
- **Water Cay, Utila** (the Bay Islands): This uninhabited coral cay, a tiny paradise of golden sand and crystal-clear water, is the best beach on the Bay Island of Utila. A short boat ride from town, it's the perfect place for a moment of rest after an exhausting series of dives. There are no facilities here, but if you didn't pack a lunch, you can literally swim over to Jewel and Pigeon Cay. See p. 218.

THE best ADVENTURE ACTIVITIES

- **Rafting the Río Plátano** (La Mosquitia): One of the all-time great journeys of Central America. This 10- to 12-day trip starts high in the mountains of Olancho and ends at the Caribbean coast, covering the length of a UNESCO biosphere reserve that few have visited. Class III–IV rapids, scarlet macaws, the occasional tapir, and Pech and Miskito villages are only part of the journey. This is one you will never forget. See p. 244.
- **Hiking in Celaque National Park** (Western Honduras): The elusive resplendent quetzal is not all you might see in one of the most prime pieces of cloud forest in Central America. If you're lucky, the occasional monkey or jaguar might make an appearance, but orchids, flowers, and lush green foliage are more dependable and worth the trip alone. Most come for an intense day hike, though those with a sturdy set of legs will not regret a 2-day trip to Cerro Las Minas, the highest point in Honduras. See p. 139.
- **Climbing La Picucha** (Olancho): The highest point of Sierra de Agalta National Park takes 4 to 5 days, making it one of the most difficult hikes in Honduras. Your prize will be a well-marked trail all to yourself, with waterfalls, unspoiled primary forests, and an abundance of rare flora and fauna for you to marvel at. See p. 258.
- **Intense rapids on Río Cangrejal** (the North Coast): These class III–V rapids are the premier whitewater trips in the country and are one of the most accessible routes you can find. Both safety standards and adrenaline are high, and a handful of companies offer the trip daily from their small lodges in and around Pico Bonito National Park. See p. 175.
- **The trails around Las Marías** (La Mosquitia): Hire a Pech guide to lead you on this 3-day hike up the perfect conical mountain of Pico Dama or just on a day trip to see mysterious petroglyphs. High chances of seeing wildlife and interactions with unspoiled Indian villages are a big part of the lure. See p. 243.

THE best WILDLIFE WATCHING

- **Río Plátano Biosphere Reserve** (La Mosquitia): One of the most remote and inaccessible reserves in Central America has preserved the array of diverse creatures better than most. Whether you take a *pipante* (dugout canoe) to Las Marías or raft here from Olancho, those with good eyes and guides will spot tapirs, jaguars, anteaters, spider monkeys, iguanas, scarlet macaws, harpy eagles, toucans, and much, much more. See p. 242.
- **Lancetilla Botanical Garden** (the North Coast): Bird-watchers are in paradise at Lancetilla, a onetime banana research facility founded by William Popenoe of United Fruit in 1925 and now one of the world's largest botanical gardens. More than 350 species of birds frolic in the citrus groves, bamboo groves, and primary forests. See p. 156.
- **Lago de Yojoa** (Western Honduras): Two national parks (Santa Bárbara and Cerro Azul Meámbar), with an enormous range of tropical birds, mammals, and plants, sit on both sides of this sparkling lake in the center of the country. The lake itself

is rich with wildlife, including several types of toucans, woodpeckers, herons, kingfishers, otters, bats, and lizards. See p. 105.

- **Cuero y Salado Reserve** (the North Coast): While not always easy to find, manatees are the main attraction at this mangrove-lined river reserve near La Ceiba. On any given day, though, an early-morning canoe ride will put you in touch with caimans, howler monkeys, kingfishers, and boat-billed herons. See p. 166.
- **Whale sharks off Utila** (the Bay Islands): During select months every year, the waters off Utila become ground zero for whale sharks, not to mention whale shark enthusiasts. The deep waters on the north side of the island make it one of the best places in the world to see these bus-sized creatures, a big reason why two whale shark research facilities are located here. See p. 218.

THE most INTRIGUING HISTORICAL SITES

- **Copán** (Western Honduras): Often referred to as the Paris of the Maya world, these majestic ruins will take you through a dramatic journey of the Maya civilization. The secret to understanding the Copán ruins is a large square block of carved stone known as the Altar Q, which represents the dynastic lineage of 16 kings whose rule spanned nearly 4 centuries. See p. 117.
- **Walpaulban Sirpi** (La Mosquitia): Not far from Las Marías, numerous petroglyphs are carved into stones that date back thousands of years and are believed to be from the Paya culture. Some, including Walpaulban Sirpi, are found right in the Río Plátano. They aren't easy to reach, though. You'll need to traverse 5 hours upstream in a pole-propelled dugout canoe, or *pipante,* to get there—or visit near the end of a long rafting trip. See p. 243.
- **William Walker's grave** (the North Coast): In the old Trujillo cemetery in the center of town sits the remains of William Walker, the American adventurer who launched several invasions of Central American nations and was shot by firing squad in Trujillo in 1860. Check out his epitaph, which still reads: *Fusilado.* See p. 181.
- **Los Naranjos Eco-Archeological Park** (Western Honduras): What exactly is an eco-archeological park? It is a place with both archeological remains and protected natural land. Los Naranjos is both a small Lenca site, with a few mounds that date back to approximately 700 B.C., as well as a great place for bird-watching along the lush green shores of Lago de Yojoa. Facilities on-site exist for both types of visitors: an archeological museum with historical details and artifacts, and a tower where you can relax with your binoculars. See p. 106.
- **El Puente** (Western Honduras): Near the town of La Entrada outside of Copán sits this rarely visited archeological complex. A couple of pyramids and the encroaching jungle make it seem not all that different from Copán; just a bit smaller and without the madding crowds. See p. 130.

THE best FAMILY ACTIVITIES

- **Chiminike** (Tegucigalpa): The modish children's museum in the capital isn't shy about making sure kids are entertained: a human body room complete with fart sounds, a crawl through an intestinal tract, and a graffiti-prone VW Beetle. The kids might not realize it, but every quirk is part of the museum's ingenious learning process. See p. 74.

- **Dolphin Summer Scuba Camp** (the Bay Islands): During the summer months at Anthony's Key Resort on Roatán, small groups of children ages 5 to 14 can learn about bottlenose dolphins through various encounters, feeding, and training sessions, while also practicing their snorkel or dive skills. Accompanying parents aren't left out, though; they can go off with their peers on diving or snorkel trips. See p. 194.
- **Take a canopy tour:** In the past few years, the number of zip-line operators has exploded in Honduras, and more than a dozen are in operation now. From the waterfall at Pulhapanzak, to the Garífuna village of Sambo Creek, to the Caribbean island of Roatán, you can glide from platform to platform surrounded by dense jungle or breathtaking views. See p. 36.
- **Garífuna or Miskito dance performances** (the Bay Islands, La Mosquitia): Though some performances are aimed at cruise ship passengers, the lively dance tradition for the Garífuna population of Roatán still exists, especially during holiday and festival times. Along the Mosquito Coast, tourist-hungry Miskito villages have been known to occasionally set up nighttime performances. See p. 241.
- **Macaw Mountain** (Western Honduras): A walk through this lushly forested, fun-filled private compound near Copán is just what a child needs to take his or her mind off boring ruins and museums. Photo ops with a few friendly birds on your head and shoulders are a must for families. See p. 123.

THE best SPLURGE HOTELS

- **Pico Bonito Lodge** (the North Coast; ✆ **888/428-0221;** www.picobonito.com): While you can see wildly biodiverse Parque Nacional Pico Bonito near La Ceiba a number of ways, few would argue against a stay at luxurious Pico Bonito Lodge, which has a butterfly farm, its own set of trails, a resort-style pool, spa facilities, and a gourmet restaurant. Guided hikes bring you through former cacao fields, across several levels of tropical forest, and to much-needed soaks in swimming holes and at waterfalls. See p. 176.
- **Hotel Telamar** (the North Coast; ✆ **504/2269-4414;** www.hoteltelamar.com): This neighborhood of pastel-colored stilted villas was once owned by Tela Railroad Company executives on one of Tela's best beaches. With the addition of a few posh buildings with hotel-style rooms, several restaurants, and a 90m-long (395-ft.) pool, complete with waterfalls and slides, it was transformed into Tela's first resort. Even the old villas have been remodeled and are rented out by the day or week. The combination of history and luxury has never been better. See p. 158.
- **Infinity Bay** (the Bay Islands; ✆ **504/2445-5016;** www.infinitybay.com): If the hotel's massive infinity pool doesn't put a twinkle in your eye, the intoxicatingly turquoise water on the best stretch of beach in the country surely will. This condo-resort is the most upscale that West Bay Beach, or anywhere on Roatán for that matter, has seen. When Phase II is completed, they'll add a full-service spa and another restaurant. See p. 206.
- **Palmetto Bay Plantation** (the Bay Islands; ✆ 504/9991-0811; www.palmettobay plantation.com): Isolated on a stretch of Roatán's loneliest shore, this hotel gave

the island one of its first tastes of the worldly exotic, with the Balinese-style eco-friendly beach houses. This notion was pushed further with the filming of *Temptation Island International.* See p. 210.

- **Portal del Angel** (Tegucigalpa; © **504/2239-6538;** www.portaldelangelhn.com): This place has buckets of style, maybe more than anywhere else in the country. Right in the Zona Viva, near the best restaurants in the capital, the opulent boutique digs are adorned with marble pillars, wrought-iron balconies, and parquet floors, and appointed with handmade furniture. It is much more than just a nice change from the business-leisure hotels that dominate Tegus. See p. 66.
- **Real Intercontinental** (Tegucigalpa; © **504/2290-2700;** www.ichotelsgroup.com): Of the major business hotels in Tegucigalpa and San Pedro Sula, the Real Intercontinental is tops. Modern, tech-friendly facilities, trendy lounges and restaurants that are centers of cool in the city, a pleasant pool area, and a great location make the 157-room property superb. See p. 67.

THE best HOTELS THAT WON'T EMPTY YOUR WALLET

- **Casa de Café** (Western Honduras; © **504/2651-4620;** www.casadecafecopan.com): Casa de Café's rotating breakfasts, clean and comfortable rooms, and lovely views make it one of my favorite hotels in Honduras. Their new boutique hotel a few blocks away, Terramaya, and adjacent rental houses could also qualify. See p. 126.
- **Hotel Gran Central** (the North Coast; © **504/2448-1099;** www.hotelgrancentral.com): A blend of tropical and colonial chic sets this restored colonial building in Tela apart from its rivals. Black-and-white checkerboard tiles paired with hand-painted designs on the walls give a welcome air of class and style for a price that's hard to beat. See p. 160.
- **Casa Alemania** (the North Coast; © **504/2434-4466;** www.trujillohonduras.com): German food and beer are on hand from owners Gunter and Paula at this intimate hotel right on the Trujillo beach front. The 10 rooms are beyond comfortable and have all the amenities that you'll find at the Hilton. They even have dorm-style beds and camping space for those on a tight budget. See p. 183.
- **Posada de Don Juan** (Western Honduras; © **504/2656-1020;** www.posadadedonjuanhotel.com): With recent renovations, this boutique colonial inn has left no questions about which is the top hotel in Gracias. In 2008, they doubled in size, added a pool and Jacuzzi in a colonial courtyard, and built their own hot springs facility outside of the city. See p. 137.
- **West Bay B&B** (the Bay Islands; © **504/2445-5080;** www.westbaybedandbreakfast.com): For the price of the rooms here, which are new and surprisingly upscale, you wouldn't be able to buy dinner at one of the nearby resorts. If you don't mind a 5-minute walk to the top beach in the country, you will be rewarded with spacious, comfortable rooms. See p. 206.
- **Yamari Savannah Cabañas** (La Mosquitia; © **504/2443-8009;** www.larutamoskitia.com): A stay in this true solar-powered eco-lodge in the wilderness, about an hour from Brus Laguna, costs just $10 a night. It's set in one of La Mosquitia's bizarre savannahs, where you will bird-watch by kayak, inner tube, or traditional Cayucos canoe. Drop these same stilted cabins into Brazil, and you are looking to pay 10 times the price. See p. 248.

HONDURAS IN DEPTH

Honduras has unjustly been overshadowed by its neighbors for decades. For some time, divers have passed over Honduras to go to Belize, nature and beach lovers have traveled to Costa Rica, and culture and history buffs have headed to Guatemala and Mexico. This is beginning to change, though, as more and more tourists are coming to realize that all of these attractions can be found in Honduras, and that even though large crowds and over-development threaten other Central American countries, Honduras is still practically untouched and unscathed, with more cloud forests and unexplored tracts of wilderness than anywhere in the region.

Much of it may still be taken up by banana cultivation, but few other countries in the world today can lay claim to such lush natural beauty. About the size of Tennessee, Honduras is home to 20 national parks, a couple of biosphere reserves, and nearly 100 other protected ecological areas. Cultural diversity is also abundant here. The country has almost 8 million people, mostly mestizos (mixed descendents of the Spanish and Ameri-Indians), as well as another 10% divided among eight main indigenous groups: the Lencas, the Chortís, the Tolupan, the Garinagu, the Miskitos, the Pech, the Tawahkas, and the Bay Islanders. Several of the groups have maintained many of their cultural traditions, even with the overwhelming forces from the outside.

Adventure has been woven into the very fabric of this country over the past 400 years. Christopher Columbus set foot on the Bay Islands and the North Coast on his fourth and final voyage to the Americas in 1502, but that may be the most boring tale. Consider also that the country's history involves pirates raiding gold from Spanish ships and hiding the booty in caves on the Bay Islands, archeologists searching for Maya ruins and crystal skulls, and a North American named William Walker launching a raid on the country with his own small army. Throw in conquistadors, indigenous warriors, multinational fruit corporations, whale sharks, and indigenous land rights, and you have one of the most exciting environments on the planet.

While political instability in 2009 put a temporary hold on most developments that were already underway, things are slowly coming back together. Until just a few years ago, Honduras's tourist infrastructure had been limited, but the country is in the midst of a tourism revolution, and there's no telling exactly what the future has in store—only that you can expect more variety, better hotels, and a far greater range of wild and wonderful tours and attractions than has ever existed here before.

HONDURAS TODAY

The Honduras of today is a place bursting with energy and excitement. Luxury ecolodges near La Ceiba can now compete with anyplace else in Central America, and beach resorts are set to turn Tela Bay into a major getaway. Cruise landings on the Bay Islands are expected to explode in the next decade as the ports are now expanded. The Maya ruins of Copán are luring more and more visitors from countries to the north. Even La Mosquitia, traditionally one of the least accessible and most unorganized places in the Americas, is turning to community-based tours and excelling at them.

While the major metropolitan areas are becoming more modern, some creative small rural towns and indigenous villages are finding ways to earn an income through tourism while not sacrificing their ways of life. Honduras is one of the most ethnically diverse places in Latin America, and any brief journey through the country will make you well aware of this. The cultural makeup of every region is a little different. The vast majority (an estimated 85% to 90%) of Honduras's 7.8 million or so people are ***mestizos*** or Ladinos, which means they are of mixed American Indian and Spanish descent. The *mestizo* population therefore dominates the country's cities and the economic and political landscape of the country.

There are also eight other major ethnic groups that are concentrated in various regions around the country, the largest being the **Lenca,** who reside in the southwest, particularly the mountains and valleys near Gracias, and number around 100,000 in Honduras. The Lencas are descended from Chibcha-speaking Indians who came to Honduras from Colombia and Venezuela several thousand years ago. Nearby in the Copán Valley and along the border with Guatemala the **Chortí-Maya** are another indigenous group numbering between 4,000 and 5,000. They are the descendents of the ancient Mayas.

The second-largest ethnic group in the country is the **Garífuna,** descendents of Carib and Arawak Indians who mixed with escaped African slaves and now populate the entire North Coast and the Bay Islands and number around 95,000. The British forcibly transplanted the Garífuna from the Cayman Islands to the island of Roatán in 1787, and from there, they moved to other islands and to the mainland. The Garífuna still populate the Bay Islands, though they share the land with the **Bay Islanders**—another ethnic group descended from pirates and blacks from elsewhere in the Caribbean—and an increasing number of North Americans who are buying property and calling the islands home.

In the department of Yoro in the central highlands, the **Tolupan** inhabit scattered communities isolated among the mountains. Three other indigenous groups can be found in the La Mosquitia (Mosquito Coast) region of the country. The lack of roads and transportation in this region has allowed the small pockets of **Miskitos, Pech,** and **Tawahkas** to maintain their cultural identities far better than most other indigenous groups in Central America, who have sometimes been engulfed by mainstream society. While the Miskitos are not a straight indigenous group—rather a cultural mishmash of an unknown tribe, English pirates, and escaped African slaves—the Pech and Tawahkas have remained practically unchanged since pre-conquest days, though the always-encroaching forces of development are rapidly marching their way.

It happens so much in Latin America that it has become cliché: Punctuality is not one of the qualities that most Hondurans are better known for. Things move a bit slower here. If you agree to meet someone, don't expect them to be exactly on time. In general, tour companies are fairly prompt, but I would allow some leeway. The

The Legacy of Hurricane Mitch

In October 1998, the most powerful Atlantic hurricane ever recorded at the time, Hurricane Mitch, decimated the country. Wind speeds as high as 288kmph (179 mph) caused billions of dollars in damage throughout the country. In the end, more than 6,000 people were killed and more than 1.5 million people were displaced, 70% of roads and bridges were destroyed, 70% of all crops were lost, and entire towns were destroyed by this storm. Relief poured in from the world community, although funds quickly dried up or never materialized (such as $640 million from various European organizations). Though the country has by now mostly recovered from the hurricane and is more or less back to normal, to this day, many economic woes are still blamed on Mitch, and long-term effects will continue to linger for many years.

same goes for buses. While larger bus companies will stick to their departure times, smaller and more rural buses may wait until the bus is full before leaving.

Roman Catholicism is—and has been since the arrival of the Spanish—the major religion here and covers as much as 95% of the population. While there is separation of church and state, Catholic teachings are part of the national school curriculum. In the 1960s and '70s, priests became quite vocal against abuses by the Honduran military and general exploitation of the public by the government, and some were deported or had their churches shut down. In 1975, right-wing attacks against the priests reached a boiling point when a group of Olancho landowners killed 14 people, including two priests.

Protestant churches, especially evangelical, have undergone a tremendous growth in Honduras since the 1980s. Denominations such as Methodist, Church of God, Seventh Day Adventist, and Assemblies of God are among the most popular and can be found in all parts of the country. In La Mosquitia, the Moravian church has one of the strongest followings. The Christian sect, which was formed in the 1400s in what is today the Czech Republic, arrived on the scene in 1928 when the national government paid little or no attention to the region. They opened health clinics—including the one in Ahuas that is still the best in the region—and schools. There are now more than 100 congregations spread throughout the region, though in 1999 there was a split in the church between reformers and traditionalists, so some communities have two Moravian churches.

Since the turn of the millennium, one significant development has been a push to increase the number of tourists entering the country. While diving has always attracted visitors, tourism marketing strategies have begun to branch out and focus on ecotourism, cultural tourism, beaches, bird-watching, cigar factory tours, coffee tastings, and a range of interesting little diversions that the country has kept locked away for so long.

Honduras is becoming known as a safe, fashionable, and still undiscovered alternative to what some might say are an overdeveloped Costa Rica and Yucatán. Before the world economic collapse and the country's constitutional crisis, more than 1.5 million people were coming to Honduras annually, a rate that was increasing at 15% to 20% annually. While those numbers dropped off considerably during the past two years, significant investment in projects, such as the one at Los Micos Lagoon (that hopes to turn Tela Bay into the next great Central American beach destination), and the expansion of cruise facilities on Roatán should help see those numbers come back to where they were and continue to increase considerably over the next few decades.

Still, much of the development remains concentrated on a few small pockets, and it will be some time before it spills over onto the rest of the country. Some travelers fear the Honduras they once knew will disappear—and to some extent, that is true—but there are plenty of positives to help ease the transition.

LOOKING BACK: HONDURAN HISTORY

Early History

Prior to the arrival of the Spanish, the Mayas, who drifted down from Mexico and Guatemala to settle in the highlands and valleys throughout the western half of the country, inhabited Honduras. In A.D. 426, they founded the city-state of Copán, considered one of the intellectual capitals of the Maya for its rich architecture and design— until around A.D. 800, when the Maya civilization mysteriously began to collapse. While pockets of the Mayas' descendents remained in the region after this collapse, other indigenous groups—such as the Lencas, the Miskito, and the Pech—eventually developed, as well.

Spanish Conquest

On July 30, 1502, during his fourth and final voyage to the Americas, Christopher Columbus reached the pine-covered island of Guanaja, becoming the first European to set foot on Honduran soil. Eventually, Columbus would set sail for the northern mainland coast, stopping in Trujillo on August 14 and soon after in Puerto Castilla, where the first Catholic Mass in Honduras took place. The Honduran coast was ignored for several decades until after Hernán Cortés's conquest of the Aztecs, when the Spanish exploration of the mainland began. In 1523, conquistador Gil Gonzáles de Avila reached the Golfo de Fonseca, but was quickly captured a year later by rival Spaniard Cristóbal de Olid, who founded the colony of Triunfo de la Cruz. Olid's

DATELINE

A.D. 500–A.D. 1000	Maya civilization flourishes.
200–899	Maya Classical Period; Copán at its peak.
900	Copán is abandoned.
1502	Columbus sails along the coast of Honduras.
1525	Spain begins conquest of Honduras, which is accomplished only in 1539 after bitter struggles with the native population and rivals representing Spanish power centers in Mexico, Panama, and Hispaniola.
1537	The Spanish kill Lenca Indian chieftain Lempira.
1600s	Northern coast falls to British buccaneers; British protectorate is established over the coast until 1860, while the Spanish concentrate on the inland area.
1797	Approximately 5,000 Garífuna from the island of San Vicente are dropped on Roatán.
1821	Honduras gains independence from Spain but joins the Mexican Empire the following year.
1823	Honduras joins the United Provinces of Central America,

soldiers turned on him, though, and he was swiftly executed. Cortés learned of the power struggle and sent trusted Francisco de las Casas to intervene and establish a colony at Trujillo in 1525.

In the 1530s, gold and silver were discovered in the country's western highlands, and an influx of Spaniards quickly arrived on the scene, leading to the founding of the cities of San Pedro de Puerto Caballos, now San Pedro Sula, and Gracias a Dios. In answer to this, a Lenca chief named Lempira unified rival tribes to launch attacks on the Spanish from his fort at Cerquín. The Spanish waged a fierce assault on the fort for more than 6 months but to no avail. So the Spanish initiated peace talks with Lempira, only to murder him upon his arrival. After his death, significant resistance from the native groups was slowed and eventually stopped.

The Spanish, now that they were in full control of the territory, proceeded to decimate the native population via enslavement and harsh treatment—they wiped out as much as 95% of the indigenous population within a few decades. To make up for the labor shortage, African slaves were brought in during the 1540s. For the next few centuries, more colonies were founded, and a provincial capital was established in Gracias a Dios, though it was quickly moved to Comayagua. Mining fuelled the economy until the collapse of silver prices forced the Spaniards to turn to agricultural endeavors such as tobacco farming and raising cattle.

Pirates & The Garífuna

During the 1600s, the Spanish began looting the riches of the South American continent and would send ships up the Central American coast on their return to Spain. French and English pirates, like the legendary Henry Morgan and John Coxen, began using the Bay Islands as their base for expeditions to plunder these Spanish ships and they set up semi-permanent settlements there. When war erupted between England and Spain in 1739, the British took control over the islands and established a fort at Port Royal in Roatán. The treaty of Aix-la-Chapelle returned the islands to Spain, though the British reclaimed them during another war in 1779; in 1797, descendents of Carib Indians and African slaves from the Cayman Islands, called the Garífuna, were dumped in Roatán by the British. More waves of Garífuna arrived from the

which also include Costa Rica, El Salvador, Guatemala, and Nicaragua.

1838 Honduras becomes an independent nation.

1859 American William Walker invades Nicaragua.

1859 The Bay Islands are ceded to Honduras by the British.

1860 William Walker is executed.

1880 The capital moves from Comayagua to Tegucigalpa.

1913 The United Fruit Company controls ¾ of banana exports.

1969 The Soccer War breaks out with El Salvador. The war lasts 5 days, killing more than 2,000 Hondurans.

1971 Hurricane Edith destroys nearly every house at Cape Gracias.

1974 Hurricane Fifi kills 5,000.

1980 Copán becomes a UNESCO World Heritage site.

1982 U.S.-backed Nicaraguan Contras attempt to bring down Nicaragua's Sandinista government from Honduran territory.

continues

Caymans in the 1830s and began permanent settlements on the islands, as well as along the north coast of the mainland.

Independence

On September 15, 1821, Honduras declared independence from Spain, along with the Central American territories of Guatemala, El Salvador, Costa Rica, and Nicaragua. After a brief period as part of independent Mexico, it joined the United Provinces of Central America in 1823. Infighting among the provinces brought upon the collapse of this federation in 1838, however, leaving the members to form independent countries. On November 15 of that year, most of current-day Honduras became a separate nation. The Bay Islands gained sovereignty from Britain in 1859.

Over the next 150 years, the country was plagued by political unrest that saw various rebellions, civil wars, coups, rigged elections, invasions, and changes of government, most of which occurred during the 20th century. In one of the more unusual events, American William Walker attempted to conquer Central America with his own army, going as far as taking over Nicaragua in 1856, before being sent back by joint Central American forces. In 1860 he returned, landing in Trujillo, but didn't get very far. He was executed that same year.

The Banana Republic

In the early 19th century, U.S. companies such as the Tela Railroad Company, a subsidiary of United Fruit (now Chiquita), and Standard Fruit (now Dole) established banana plantations of vast tracts of land along the North Coast and held sway over politics in the country. Bananas became the chief product in the country, accounting for as much as 80% of exports in 1929. The bribing of politicians and unjust labor practices marred the industry for much of the 20th century and kept the country from developing its own business elite, which led to a two-month strike by plantation workers in 1954.

In 1956, the country's first military coup took place. A new constitution put the control of the military in the hands of the top general, not in the president, and thus began a period of military rule of the country. In 1963, only days before the next

1982–83 Political unrest leads General Alvarez to detain trade union activists and create Death Squads.

1984 U.S.-run training camps for Salvadoran counter-revolutionaries are shut down.

1990 The last remaining Nicaraguan Contras leave Honduras.

1998 Hurricane Mitch devastates Honduras.

2003 Congress sends troops to Iraq. A free trade agreement with the U.S. is formed, along with Guatemala, El Salvador, and Nicaragua.

2005 Manuel Zelaya of the Liberal Party is elected president.

2006 The Central American Free Trade Agreement (CAFTA) goes into effect.

2009 In June, after an attempt to alter the constitution, president Manuel Zelaya is removed from office and sent into exile. President of the Congress Roberto Micheletti is sworn in as interim president. In November, conservative Porfirio Lobo Sosa is elected the new President, and he is sworn in to office 2 months later.

Looking Back at Honduras

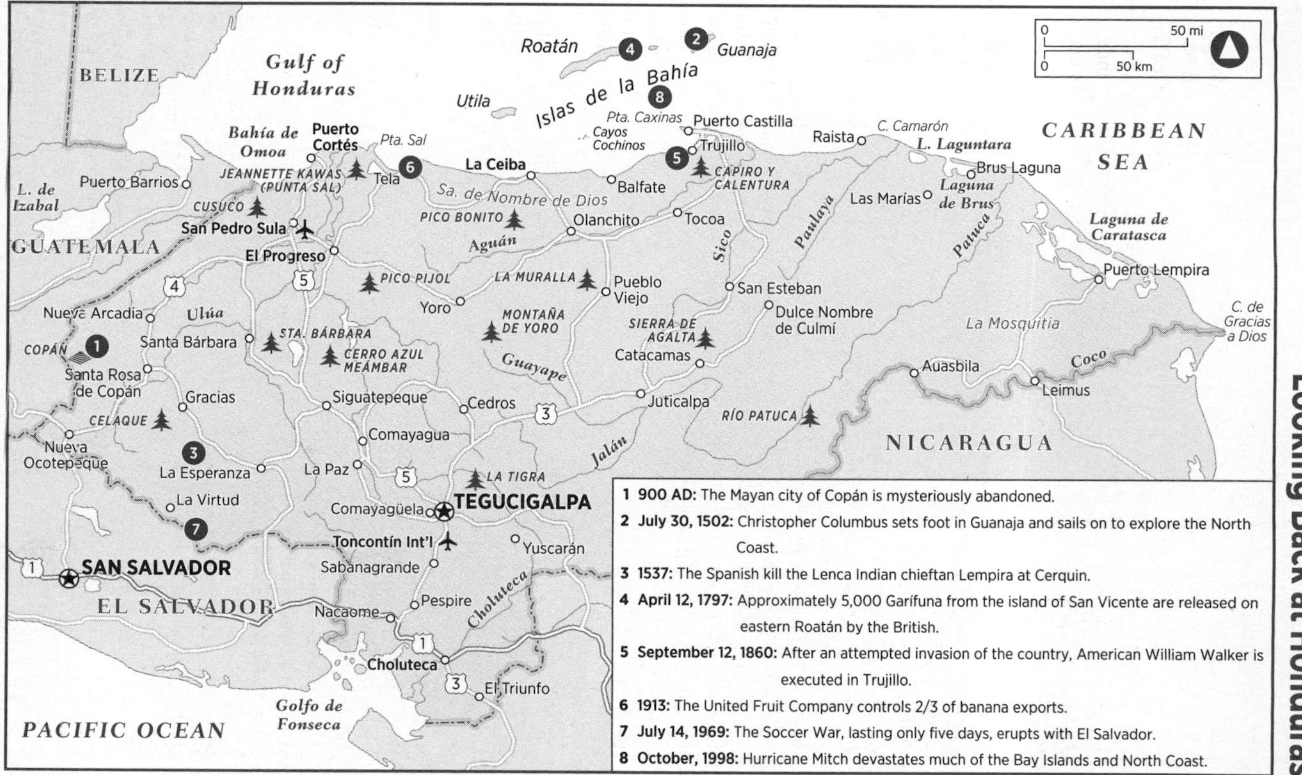

The Maya Calendar

We now live in the fourth world, according to the *Popol Vuh,* the sacred Maya book of creation myths and predictions, and the first three creation attempts have failed. The book predicts that this age will end on December 21, 2012. Doesn't that signify the start of the apocalypse? Not necessarily. New Age scholars have a wide range of theories on what exactly will occur or what the Maya had in mind. Some say it is nothing less than the end of the world, while others are more optimistic and foresee a day of positive human evolution. Hotels around Copán, the Bay Islands, and major Maya ceremonial sites in Guatemala are already booking up for this date and are planning all sorts of special events.

The origin of the date comes from the Maya Calendar, a time-tracking system so accurate that other Mesoamerican societies, including the Aztecs and Toltecs, adopted it. Even today, many Chortí Maya communities in the Copán Valley and elsewhere in Central America do not follow the standard Gregorian calendar like the rest of society.

The Maya Calendar is a system of several calendars that can be combined in varying ways. Astronomical calculations in each calendar predict the cycles of the sun, moon, and Venus, which indicated how the Maya had a sophisticated knowledge of mathematics and astronomy unknown to their old-world contemporaries. Each day has a hieroglyphic representation composed of numbers and pictographs, many of which can by found at most ancient Maya sites.

The calendar uses three different dating systems—the Tzolkin, Haab, and Long Count:

- **The Tzolkin Calendar:** This calendar of 260 days was created by multiplying 20 by 13. The numerical system was founded on a base-20 system (as opposed to our own base-10 system). Some think this came from the number of human fingers and toes, and that 13 symbolized the number of levels in the Upper World, where the gods lived. Another theory is that 260 days came from the approximate length of human pregnancy, and that midwives developed the calendar to coordinate with expected births. The Maya believed that each day of the Tzolkin had a character that influenced events. A priest read the calendar to predict a baby's future, and children were often named according to the day they were born.
- **The Haab Calendar:** The Haab was the Maya solar calendar made up of 18 months of 20 days each, plus a period of 5 unnamed days at the end of the year known as the Wayeb, which adds up to a 365-day cycle. It was thought that if an event occurred one day during a specific Haab cycle, a similar event was likely to occur on that same day in the next Haab cycle.
- **The Long Count Calendar:** This calendar can be used to describe any date in the future and was used only by priests and royalty. It tracked longer periods of time, and was based on the number of days since a mythical starting point (Aug 11, 3114 B.C.). In yet another layer of complexity, the Tzolkin combines with the Haab to form a synchronized cycle of 52 years, called the Calendar Round.

election, the military, headed by Colonel López Arellano, seized power and canceled the election. Two years later, Arellano was elected on his own and then served a 6-year term. A year after the next election he again took control during another military coup. When it was discovered that Arellano took a $1.25-million bribe from the United Brands Fruit Company, previously known as United Fruit, he was removed from office. In his place came General Juan Alberto Melgar Castro, whose reign was rocked by a scandal involving using the military for drug trafficking. Next came General Policarpo Paz García, who would return the country to civilian rule in 1980 with the election of a president and congress.

The Soccer War & Civil Unrest

During the end of the 19th century and much of the 20th century, the two main political parties in Honduras, liberals (who preferred a free market economy like in the U.S.) and conservatives (who desired an aristocratic-style regime), wrestled power from each other again and again. From 1821 to 1982, the Constitution was rewritten an astounding 17 times. Political conflict was not all internal, however. In 1969, more than 300,000 undocumented Salvadorans were believed to be living in Honduras and the government and private groups increasingly sought to blame them for the country's economic woes. During a World Cup preliminary match in Tegucigalpa a disturbance broke out between fans on both sides, followed by a more intense incident during the next game in San Salvador. Salvadorans living in Honduras began to be harassed and even killed, leading to a mass exodus from the country. On June 27, 1969, Honduras broke off diplomatic relations with El Salvador, and on July 14, the Salvadoran air force began an assault on Honduras and took control of the city of Nueva Ocotepeque, marking the start of what would be called the Soccer War. Though the war ended up lasting only 5 days and ended in a stalemate of sorts, in the end, between 60,000 and 130,000 Salvadorans were expelled or fled from Honduras, and more than 2,000 people, mostly Hondurans, were killed. While a peace treaty was signed in 1980, the subject is still touchy on both sides and even to this day relations remain strained.

Civil wars broke out in every country neighboring Honduras in the late 1970s and '80s. El Salvador, Guatemala, and Nicaragua all saw wide-scale political upheaval, assassinations, and all-out civil unrest. To the surprise of many, Honduras, despite its shaky governments, scandals, and economic problems, escaped any major turmoil during this period—the one exception being protests over U.S. military involvement in the country.

During the 1980s, the U.S. provided aid to the country in exchange for using it as a base for counter-insurgency movements (led by the CIA-trained group the Contras) against the Sandinistas in Nicaragua. Student and opposition leaders in Honduras organized massive protests against the U.S. military influence, to which the Honduran military responded by kidnapping and killing protestors. The protests only grew, however, and eventually the country was forced to reexamine its policies on U.S. operations in Honduras—especially after it was revealed in 1986 that the Reagan Administration had sold arms to Iran to support the anti-Sandinistas in Honduras. In 1988, the military agreement with the U.S. was not renewed, and the Nicaraguan Contras ended up leaving the country entirely by 1990, when the Contra War concluded.

The Modern Economy

During the late 1980s and into the 1990s, struggles to maintain the value of the lempira against the dollar resulted in rapid inflation. Because wages remained the same, many Hondurans simply became poorer than they already were. When Carlos Roberto Flores Facussé became president in 1988, he initiated wide-scale currency reforms and took steps to modernize the economy. Things looked like they were about to change for the better. And then came Hurricane Mitch. Killing thousands and displacing more than a million, Mitch was not a disaster that the country could

Impressions

"Here was the flora of the tropics in its rankest and most prodigal growth. Spaces here and there had been wrested from the jungle and planted with bananas and cane and orange groves. The rest was a riot of wild vegetation, the monkeys, tapirs, jaguars, alligators and prodigious reptiles and insects. Where no road was a cut a serpent could scarcely make its way through the tangle of vines and creepers."

—O. Henry, *Cabbages and King*

overcome quickly. The infrastructure of many towns and villages was forever changed, and the effects still continue to linger.

In 2006, Manuel Zelaya Rosales, a rancher from the Olancho town of Juticalpa, was elected president after promises of doubling the police force, re-educating gang members, and lowering petroleum prices. Soon after, the Central America and Dominican Republic Free Trade Agreement, CAFTA-DR, went into effect in Honduras amid wide-scale protests throughout Central America. Elsewhere, corruption, scandals, and growing concerns over the economy marred the first years of Zelaya's presidency. Rising food and energy costs led Zelaya to turn to controversial Venezuelan President Hugo Chavez for help. In 2008, he famously called on the United States to legalize drugs in order to prevent violence and murders that are the result of the drug trade in Honduras. In 2009, Zelaya raised the monthly minimum wage from $157 to $289, an approximately 60% hike. The intention was to help eliminate poverty in the country; however, the motion backfired, and many employers were forced to lay off workers they could not afford to pay. Zelaya's presidency was marked by low approval ratings and frequent clashes with many business leaders, who are generally pro-U.S.

In June of 2009, after an attempt to alter presidential term limits, Zelaya was ousted—in his pajamas—by a military coup and exiled to Costa Rica, much to the surprise of the world community. President of the Congress Roberto Micheletti, of Zelaya's own party, was immediately sworn in as interim president. Zelaya snuck back into the country briefly, holing himself up in the Brazilian Embassy until January before being transferred to the Dominican Republic. In November of 2009, conservative Porfirio Lobo Sosa was elected the new President. At first, international leaders were hesitant to support the new government amid the confusion of Zelaya's ouster, though most eventually came around.

HONDURAS IN POP CULTURE

Books

While Honduras has often been overshadowed by the impressive arts emerging from neighboring countries, the country's vibrant and diverse population has a number of achievements in the fine arts. The country has been blessed with many gifted writers, including journalist Rafael Heliodoro Valle, poet Juan Ramón Molina, and novelist Ramón Amaya Amador. The very first novel published by a Honduran was by a female. Lucila Gamero de Medina, born in Danlí, wrote *Blanco Olmedo* in 1903, which was followed by several other novels, such as *Amalia Montiel.*

As Honduras became a center of banana production and the number of textile factories increased, so did the journalistic attempts at exposing them. *Banana Cultures: Agriculture, Consumption, and Environmental Change in Honduras and the*

United States (University of Texas Press, 2006), by John Soluri, covers the history and growth of Honduras's banana industry along with the consumer mass market in the United States, while Ramón Amaya Amador's novel *Prisión Verde* (Editorial Baktun, 1983) gives an unsettling account of life on a banana plantation through the eyes of a worker. Peter Chapman's *Bananas! How The United Fruit Company Shaped the World* (Canongate U.S., 2008) details how United Fruit set the precedent for the institutionalized power and the company's influence in shaping several Latin American nations.

Several well-known writers from abroad have also found comfort here. William Sydney Porter, aka O. Henry, spent a year or so in Trujillo and Roatán while escaping embezzlement charges in the U.S. The influence of his time in Honduras was seen by coining the term "Banana Republic" and writing *Cabbages and Kings* (Doubleday, 1904), a collection of stories revolving around the fictitious Central American town of Coralio, Anchuria. *The Mosquito Coast* (Houghton Mifflin, 1982), the novel by Paul Theroux (later turned into a 1986 movie starring Harrison Ford, River Phoenix, and Helen Mirren), takes an egotistical inventor, Allie Fox, who is disgusted with American society, along with his wife and four children, from the United States to the north coast of Honduras. With a local family, they set up their own society in the jungle while battling Christian missionaries, guerillas, and the harsh environment of La Mosquitia. Peter Matthiessen's *Far Tortuga* (Vintage, 1988) follows a group of turtle hunters from Roatán to the waters neighboring the Mosquito Coast of Honduras and Nicaragua. Poetic and by no means a traditional novel, the story is highly recommended.

Having hosted countless adventurers, Honduras has provided a backdrop for a plethora of excellent travelogues. Theodore Morde, who possibly had ties to the CIA and claimed to have found a lost city in La Mosquitia, wrote the somewhat strange travelogue *Lost City of the Monkey God.* In *Roatán Odyssey* (Patricia J. Mills, 2007), Anne Jennings Brown details her life as she moved to Roatán with her then husband, the adventurer Howard Jennings, who eventually attempts to kill her in the jungles of Ecuador while searching for Inca gold.

Cultural insights into the history and people of the country have been told through a number of interesting books. Medea Benjamin's *Don't Be Afraid, Gringo: A Honduran Woman Speaks From the Heart: The Story of Elvia Alvarado* (Harper Perennial, 1989) is the story of a poverty-stricken peasant in rural Honduras that's a favorite read of many volunteers and Peace Corps workers. *And the Sea Shall Hide Them* (Nightengale Press, 2005) by Utila-born author William Jackson, recounts the tale of the murders of 10 crew members aboard the ship *Olympia* as it made its way from East Harbour to Roatán in 1905. *Enrique's Journey* (Random House, 2006), by Sonia Nazario, details the true story of a 16-year-old Honduran boy who goes to find his mother, who left him to live in the United States. It's a gripping account of the immigrant experience in Central America and there's even talk of turning it into an HBO series.

For those looking to get more in-depth information on the Maya civilization, there are several excellent options. Older but still relevant, John Louis Stevenson's *Incidents of Travel in Central America, Chiapas, and Yucatan* (Volumes I and II), first published in 1841, describes dozens of Maya sites as they were being rediscovered, including Copán. *The Maya* (Thames and Hudson, 2005), by Michael D. Coe, is a good primer on the history of the civilization. *A Forest of Kings: The Untold Story of the Ancient Maya* (Harper Perennial, 1992), by David Freidel and Linda Schele, creates one of the most realistic accounts of what life was actually like in the Maya world. *Maya Art and Architecture* (Thames and Hudson, 1999), by Mary Ellen Miller, explores the aesthetic beauty in the pyramids and stelae throughout the Maya world.

While there is yet to be a proper wildlife guide to Honduras, those wanting more background on the avian life in the country will want to pick up a copy of *A Guide to the Birds of Mexico and Northern Central America,* by Steve N. G. Howell and Sophie Webb (Oxford University Press, 1995). *Adventures in Nature: Honduras* (Avalon Travel Publishing, 1997), by Ron Mader and Jim Gollin, thoroughly details the protected areas of Honduras and the wildlife found within them.

Art

Honduras does have a thriving folk art scene. Best known are the country's primitivist painters, such as José Antonio Velásquez (1906–83) and Pablo Zelaya Sierra (1896–1933). The Lencas are also known throughout Central America for their pottery and ceramics. There are several methods that are highly regional. In La Paz, black-and-white and zoomorphic forms play predominantly in the designs, while in La Campa, the ceramics are known for the use of red engobe clay. Finally, the artisans in Valle del Ángeles are prized for their wood and leather work, while the Santa Bárbara area is known for producing excellent junco-palm hats, baskets, and mats.

Music

Along the North Coast and Bay Islands, the Garífuna have won acclaim for their dance and music, particularly ***punta,*** or *bangidy,* an intense dance performed by pairs amid the beats of drums, maracas, and other instruments. *Punta* has probably caught on more on the international scene than any other form of Honduran music. Top albums include Aurelio Martinez's *Garífuna Soul* and the late Andy Palacios's critically acclaimed Wátina. Ceibeño Guillermo Anderson has a growing following on the world music circuit, as well. The musician fuses Honduran Garífuna rhythms, such as *parranda* and *punta,* with better-known reggae, salsa, and other Caribbean styles, and frequently sings about the protection of the natural environment. While musicians in both La Ceiba and San Pedro Sula are peddlers of Latin America's ever-present pop, rock, rap, reggae mix of reggaeton, none has particularly caught on outside of their local followings.

EATING & DRINKING

Let's speak bluntly: Honduras is not known for its cuisine. It does not have the creative culinary background and diverse regional plates that, say, Mexico or Peru has. Yet, if you look around and even go off the beaten track a bit, there are some absolute gastronomic gems. The national dish of Honduras is a mountain of food, the *plato típico:* a heaping, carb overload of beef, plantains, beans, marinated cabbage, fresh cream, and tortillas. *Anafres,* a refried black bean and cheese fondue served in a clay pot accompanied by tortilla chips, is the favorite appetizer in the country. Sometimes chorizo is added. Like tacos in Mexico or *pupusas* in El Salvador, the *baleada*—a folded wheat flour tortilla filled with beans, crumbled cheese, and sour cream, and sometimes beef, chicken, or pork—is a snack food found everywhere in the country, including in fast food restaurants, street-side stalls, and many typical restaurants. In the highlands, *chuletas de cerdo,* or pork chops, are on most restaurant menus, as are steaks and other beef dishes. In freshwater lakes on the mainland, especially Lago de Yojoa, fish—usually tilapia or sea bass—are fried whole and served with plantains. The term *"estilo de Yojoa"* can be seen all over the country and generally signifies a fish fried in its entirety. *Pollo frito,* or fried chicken, is another extremely common meal and can be found across the country.

Breakfast, Lunch & Dinner

Hondurans like to eat. They eat three meals a day, and none of them are light. A typical breakfast, or *desayuno,* is filling. Eggs (usually *revueltos,* or scrambled), a slice of fried ham, thick tortillas, cheese, refried beans, and plantains are served with fresh-squeezed juice and coffee. A morning meal on the run might just consist of a corn tamale and cup of coffee. Cereal is catching on in parts of the country, as well. Lunch, *almuerzo,* is generally served between noon and 2pm, and for most, it's the biggest meal of the day. The *plato típico* is what many see every day, though most restaurants have a variety of options, including the *plato del día,* a set menu with a main course and several sides, much like the *plato típico* but smaller. Dinner, or *cena,* is served between 6pm and 8pm, and for many is the lightest meal. It might be a sandwich or *baleada,* or even just a *licuado,* a sort of fruit shake. Almost every meal is served with rice, refried beans, and a basket of warm tortillas.

Fast Food

Sadly, multinational fast food chains dominate the landscape of many Honduran cities. American fast and casual chains like McDonald's and Applebee's can be found in and surrounding malls, which are also widespread, across the country and along most major highways. Many American-style grills, usually run by expats, can also be found in major tourist areas and generally have a mix of both Honduran and international dishes. Greasy, fried potato chips and other snacks are common; however, a more local flavor is a bag of *tajadas,* or fried plantain chips served with a slice of lime and salsa.

Garífuna Cooking

On the North Coast and the Bay Islands, Garífuna restaurants—often just beachside *champas,* which are thatched-roof wooden shacks often on stilts—are well known for their *tapado,* a seafood stew made with sweet potatoes, malanga, yucca, and plantains. *Pescado al ajillo,* grilled fish in garlic sauce, along with ceviche, conch, and stews, are made with coconut milk and served with cassava bread, and shrimp in a dozen preparations are also enjoyed along the coast. *Pan de coco,* or coconut bread, is served with every Garífuna meal.

Honduras's Favorite Snack: The *Baleada*

In El Salvador, there are *pupusas.* In Mexico, there are tacos. In Honduras, there are *baleadas.* The simple version consists of a corn tortilla that has been put on a grill, which kind of tastes at times like—as much as I hate to say it—a thinner version of one of Taco Bell's *chalupa* shells. It's slathered in refried black beans and a bit of fresh cream and grated farmer's cheese, then folded over. It's the any-time-of-day snack. You can have one for breakfast and they add eggs. On a 10-day rafting trip on the Río Plátano, my guide served them with whatever meal he could get away with. In San Pedro Sula, which has more fast food joints than anywhere I have ever been, a few chains—such as Baleada Express and Super Baleadas—serve up massive *baleadas* filled with anything you want: avocado, sausage, plantains, bell peppers, onions, chilies, pork, jalapenos, and more.

Lencan Cooking

While the Lencas are the largest indigenous group in Honduras, their unique recipes are almost entirely contained along the Lenca Trail near Gracias. Tamales, steamed corn dough stuffed with different ingredients, are big here. *Ticucos,* a tamale with legumes, beans, and the herb *loroco,* are common, while a tamale called *chorocos* can be found only in San Manuel de Colohete. Different types of chorizos, *pollo en crema de locro* (chicken in loroco cream) and *lengua de res* (beef tongue), are standard plates. Only one formal restaurant I know of serves a wide range of traditional Lenca recipes: the outstanding and mostly organic Rinconcito Graciano (see p. 138) in Gracias. Elsewhere, you can find these dishes in family homes and small eateries along the trail.

Non-Alcoholic Beverages

As you may have guessed, coffee is consumed throughout the country. Coffee is one of the major cash crops of Honduras and production is concentrated in Olancho, in the Copán Valley, in the South, east of Tegucigalpa, and also along the North Coast. Larger operations, such as Café Copán, export around the world, while smaller gourmet and organic brands, such as Café Welchez, cater mostly to tourists. Nearly all coffee served in Honduras is freshly brewed, and Nescafe is nowhere to be found. It is almost always served black with too much sugar—at least, in my humble opinion. The restaurant chain Espresso Americano is a U.S.-based chain that has become the unofficial Honduran alternative to Starbucks, although it is considerably cheaper. Inside, you will find a range of common coffee drinks, like cappuccinos and macchiatos, as well as pastries and light snacks.

To help combat the heat or just to fill your belly between meals, there is nothing better than a *licuado,* a blended milk and fruit shake. *Aguas,* or *refrescos,* are also common and blend fruit with purified water. *Horchata* is a sweet milk-and-rice drink, sort of like a hot rice pudding, that can be found in the western part of the country.

Alcohol

Beer is probably the libation of choice at bars and restaurants across the country. While you can find standard international brands such as Heineken and Budweiser almost everywhere, most opt for the local brands, all brewed by the same company: Cervecería Nacional. The two most common are the light, smooth Port Royal, a pilsner in a green bottle, and Salva Vida (Life Saver), a lager served in a brown bottle. Imperial, also a lager, is the heaviest of the three and is the choice beer of the south and Olancho. The indie facility at D&D Brewery at Lago de Yojoa is the first microbrewery in the country and serves several different brews, though it can be found on tap only at the brewery and in one restaurant in Copán.

Guifiti, a traditional drink that combines alcohol with medicinal plants, is consumed at festivals and to cure ailments in Garífuna communities on the Bay Islands and along the North Coast. The country's favorite spirit is the *rotgut aguardiente,* sometimes called *guaro.* The town of Yuscarán south of Tegucigalpa is the main production center and home of the El Buen Gusto factory.

In the Bay Islands and all along the Caribbean coast, rum is the drink of choice. There are no major Honduran rum producers; however, Nicaragua's excellent Flor de Caña can be found everywhere, and they have a distillery on this side of the border.

Wine, while obviously not produced in Honduras, is becoming more and more common among the middle classes, and you'll find a growing number of wine bars and expanded wine lists at restaurants.

WHEN TO GO

High tourist season in Honduras is during national holidays and the dry season, running roughly from January to June. Rain can occur anytime during the year, and flooding in the highlands can completely shut down roads and transportation at any time. For the Bay Islands, you should book well in advance during Semana Santa (Easter week) and Christmas/New Year's, though the weather tends to be nice much of the year (with occasional rain). The best months for spotting whale sharks are March and April, when rates also tend to go up. In La Mosquitia, the drier months (Feb–May and Aug–Nov) are easiest for travel.

Weather

Honduras lies completely within the tropics. Temperatures range from hot and humid on the Caribbean coast (75°–93°F/24°–34°C), to mild and even cool in highland areas (61°–68°F/16°–20°C), to hot and dry along the southern Pacific coast (82°–90°F/28°–32°C). Seasonal temperatures don't vary drastically, and the change mostly relates to elevation. The amount of precipitation does vary, though. May to November is typically considered the rainy season for the interior, while September to January brings the rains for the North Coast, Bay Islands, and La Mosquitia. Hurricane season runs from August to November, although most, not all, hurricanes are a minor inconvenience.

Tegucigalpa's Average Daytime Temperature & Rainfall

	JAN	FEB	MAR	APR	MAY	JUNE	JULY	AUG	SEPT	OCT	NOV	DEC
Temp. °F	68	70	73	75	75	72	73	72	72	70	69	68
Temp. °C	20	21	23	24	24	22	23	22	22	21	21	20
Rainfall (in.)	0.3	0.2	0.3	1.3	6.0	6.3	3.2	3.5	7.3	5.3	1.5	0.5

La Ceiba's Average Daytime Temperature & Rainfall

	JAN	FEB	MAR	APR	MAY	JUNE	JULY	AUG	SEPT	OCT	NOV	DEC
Temp. °F	75	76	77	80	82	84	82	82	80	80	77	76
Temp. °C	23	24	25	27	28	29	28	28	27	27	25	24
Rainfall (in.)	13.1	10.5	7.2	3.7	3.6	5.5	6.0	6.6	7.9	15.5	15.5	15.8

Roatán's Average Daytime Temperature & Rainfall

	JAN	FEB	MAR	APR	MAY	JUNE	JULY	AUG	SEPT	OCT	NOV	DEC
Temp. °F	80	81	82	83	86	86	86	86	87	88	86	80
Temp. °C	27	27	28	28	30	30	30	30	31	31	30	27
Rainfall (in.)	8.6	4.7	3.2	2.3	2.7	5.8	10.4	6.9	6.1	17.8	16.4	14.0

Honduras Calendar of Events

For an exhaustive list of events beyond those listed here, check http://events.frommers.com, where you'll find a searchable, up-to-the-minute roster of what's happening in cities all over the world.

FEBRUARY

Feria de la Virgen de Suyapa, Tegucigalpa. A holiday revered by Catholics throughout the country. The week surrounding February 3, the day Pope Pius XII selected as the Saint's Feast Day, honors the statue with processions and Mass at the Basílica de Suyapa and other churches around the country. Early February.

MARCH

Semana Santa, Comayagua. Holy Week celebrations in Comayagua are the peak of Catholicism in Honduras and feature a week of elaborate processions that reenact the Easter story with bright costumes and colorful *alfombras,* which are sawdust carpets that are designed on the night before and trampled apart in the morning. A smaller festival occurs in Santa Rosa de Copán. Late March.

APRIL

Garífuna Day, the Bay Islands and North Coast. Dancing, drinking *Guifiti,* music, and other cultural feats take place from April 12 to 16 to celebrate the arrival of the Garífuna on Roatán in 1797, particularly in the town of Punta Gorda. Mid-April.

MAY

Feria de San Isidro, La Ceiba. Hundreds of thousands of revelers flock to this North Coast town for the Honduran version of Carnaval. Here, parades march through the downtown streets, the constant beating of drums is everywhere, and all-night partying occurs on the beaches. The week preceding the third Saturday of May.

JUNE

Feria Juniana, San Pedro Sula. San Pedro comes alive for numerous live music and cultural performances that take place in the streets, including a lively parade down Avenida Circunvalación on June 29. This one is more modern and commercialized than some of the events in rural destinations. Last week of June.

JULY

Garífuna Festival, Bajamar. One of the most vibrant cultural festivals in the entire country occurs in the tiny Garífuna community of Bajamar near Puerto Cortés on the North Coast. The festival, which attracts Garífuna from neighboring villages and around the country, runs for several weeks. July 9 through 24.

AUGUST

Sun Jam Festival, Water Cay, Utila. On a select weekend each August, partygoers descend upon the tiny tropical island of Water Cay near Utila for an all night rave and party featuring electronic music. The crowd is limited to 1,500, so buy your tickets in advance. One weekend in early to mid August.

SEPTEMBER

Independence Day, national. Independence day in Honduras is a lighthearted affair. There are three days of parades, pageants, dances, and contests that culminate on September 15, which is the actual day of Independence. September 13 through 15.

LAY OF THE LAND

Geologically, Honduras is one of the most interesting places in Central America. Even within specific regions the types of landscapes can vary drastically. Tracts of forests and mountains separated by fertile valleys dominate much of the mainland of the country, while low-lying tropical forests and clean, sandy beaches feature prominently on both coasts and islands.

Running like a spine down the middle of the country, the Sierra de Agalta mountain range in Olancho splits the country almost in half. On one side is where nearly the entire population of the country lives, and is home to all major cities, such as the capital of Tegucigalpa, the commercial center of San Pedro Sula, and North Coast transport hubs of Puerto Cortés, Tela, and La Ceiba. Here is also where you will find the tallest mountains, farmland, and numerous tracts of cloud, temperate, and tropical forests.

On the other side of the range is quite the contrast. Roads and large cities are unheard of and are replaced by the long rivers, dense mangroves, immense rainforests, and lonely savannahs of La Mosquitia. Mountains are more like hills here and nearly all villages sit clustered together along the coast.

Coastlines are a mix of reef-studded bays, mangrove forests, and sandy beaches, which all make for fine diving, wildlife watching, and swimming. Along the 500-mile (805km) North Coast, one of the agricultural powerhouses of the country, jagged peaks and cloud forests of the Merendón Mountain Range battle it out with fruit farms and lush jungle at sea level, while the 100km (62-mile) Pacific coastline is a mishmash of canals and arid hills. On the Bay Islands and Cayos Cochinos, beaches and mangroves cling to the shorelines, while significant deposits of coral reef sit just offshore. Most of the islands in the country have some form of elevated land, though the rise is relatively minor when compared to the rest of the country.

Conservation

Beginning with Parque Nacional La Tigra in 1982, Honduras has become one of the most protected nations in Latin America and has a proud tradition of environmentalism and conservation, though government officials and corporations with deep pockets have frequently hindered projects. Two biosphere reserves—Tawahka Asangni and Río Plátano—and 20 national parks stand out alongside more than 100 smaller reserves and protected areas that have helped preserve some of the largest and most diverse tracts of land in the region and the array of rare wildlife that inhabits them. Major highlights for visitors are the 36 protected tracts of cloud forests found in the country.

All is not ideal in the country, though. Enforcing the borders and boundaries of protected areas has become a serious issue in recent years. While conservation and environmental awareness are increasing in some parks, such as Celaque and Pico Bonito, others like La Muralla are unsupervised, and facilities are slowly falling into a state of disarray. Indigenous groups have not fared well, either. Many have seen their lands taken away and are pushed further and further into the fringes of the land as modern ways of life exert their steady hand. Poachers and drug smugglers often infiltrate remote regions of some of the lesser-visited parks, which tend to be home to some of the greatest biodiversity. The growth of tourism in every corner of the country is a positive sign, and communities in and around some of the protected areas are quickly learning just how valuable these new foreign visitors can be.

Natural Resources

The range of flora and fauna found in Honduras is hard to fathom. More than 800 species of birds alone have been recorded here, many of which are endemic to the country. Mammals are numerous, as well, with more than 300 species represented, including manatees, jaguars, tapirs, monkeys, ocelots, and peccaries. Reptiles and amphibians? There is no shortage of those, either: caimans, iguanas, snakes, frogs, and toads. Insects and butterflies? Don't even get me started. I could go on for days.

Off the north shore, the coral reef that surrounds the Bay Islands is home to 96% of all aquatic species found in the Caribbean. Exploitation of marine life and overfishing is of concern. There's a ban on fishing within 8km (5 miles) of any low-tide mark; however, commercial fishing boats ignore the rules and are rarely fined for it,

GENERAL RESOURCES FOR green travel

The following websites provide valuable wide-ranging information on sustainable travel. For a list of even more sustainable resources, as well as tips and explanations on how to travel greener, visit www.frommers.com/planning.

- **Responsible Travel** (www.responsibletravel.com) is a great source of sustainable travel ideas; the site is run by a spokesperson for ethical tourism in the travel industry. **Sustainable Travel International** (www.sustainabletravelinternational.org) promotes ethical tourism practices and manages an extensive directory of sustainable properties and tour operators around the world.
- In the U.K., **Tourism Concern** (www.tourismconcern.org.uk) works to reduce social and environmental problems connected to tourism. The **Association of Independent Tour Operators (AITO;** www.aito.co.uk) is a group of specialist operators leading the field in making holidays sustainable.
- In Canada, **www.greenlivingonline.com** offers extensive content on how to travel sustainably, including a travel and transport section and profiles of the best green shops and services in Toronto, Vancouver, and Calgary.
- In Australia, the national body that sets guidelines and standards for ecotourism is **Ecotourism Australia** (www.ecotourism.org.au). **The Green Directory** (www.thegreendirectory.com.au), **Green Pages** (www.thegreenpages.com.au), and **Eco Directory** (www.ecodirectory.com.au) offer sustainable travel tips and directories of green businesses.
- **Carbonfund** (www.carbonfund.org), **TerraPass** (www.terrapass.org), and **Carbon Neutral** (www.carbonneutral.org) provide info on "carbon offsetting," or offsetting the greenhouse gas emitted during flights.
- **Greenhotels** (www.greenhotels.com) recommends green-rated member hotels around the world that fulfill the company's stringent environmental requirements. **Environmentally Friendly Hotels** (www.environmentallyfriendlyhotels.com) offers more green accommodation ratings. The **Hotel Association of Canada** (www.hacgreenhotels.com) has a Green Key Eco-Rating Program, which audits the environmental performance of Canadian hotels, motels, and resorts.
- **Sustain Lane** (www.sustainlane.com) lists sustainable eating and drinking choices around the U.S.; also visit **www.eatwellguide.org** for tips on eating sustainably in the U.S. and Canada.
- For information on animal-friendly issues throughout the world, visit **Tread Lightly** (www.treadlightly.org). For information about the ethics of swimming with dolphins, visit the **Whale and Dolphin Conservation Society** (www.wdcs.org).
- **Volunteer International** (www.volunteerinternational.org) has a list of questions to help you determine the intentions and the nature of a volunteer program. For general info on volunteer travel, visit **www.volunteerabroad.org.**

which seriously hurts the small-scale fisherman, such as the Garífuna who fish according to traditional means, and throws off the balance of the extremely delicate ecosystems in a number of lagoons and reserves.

The forest cover in Honduras—a significant portion of which is valuable pine and mahogany—is the densest in Central America. However, deforestation has been occurring in recent years at a shocking rate, as almost 2% of total forest cover is being cut down (half of which is being done illegally) on an annual basis. The United States is the largest buyer of the wood, and a significant amount of the illegal wood makes its way tax-free into the American market, some of which reports have traced to stores such as Home Depot. Logging companies have frequently entered into national parks in Olancho, and COHDEFOR, the agency that is supposed to regulate the forests, has been subject to corruption investigations on numerous occasions. New forestry laws have been proposed in Congress for several years, but bribes and big businesses have hampered passing them. Environmental groups such as the Olancho Environmentalist Movement (MAO) and the Campamento Environmentalist Movement have been met with threats, and members have even been killed on several occasions.

RESPONSIBLE TRAVEL

Honduras has lagged behind its Central American neighbors like Costa Rica in sustainable tourism—though admittedly, the country is a leader in the green game. The infrastructure and the money just haven't been there. High energy prices, especially in rural areas, have not made things easy, but poor planning and government mismanagement have also caused serious ecological problems. Even current tourism projects, such as the one at Los Micos Lagoon near Tela, have caused environmentalists to worry.

There is a glimmer of hope, however. On the local level and with the help of international NGOs and devoted conservationists, things are just now starting to swing the other way.

Perhaps the most important project is going on in the most desolate place. In La Mosquitia, the organization La Ruta Moskitia (an alliance of five indigenous communities) and RARE (an international conservation organization) have designed a community-based tourism project to address poverty alleviation and biodiversity conservation in the Río Plátano Biosphere Reserve. They work directly with local villagers to train them as guides and help launch new tours and eco-lodges. Many of the villages even accept seasonal volunteers to help protect the nests of leatherback turtles and other rare species that call the region their home.

In Pico Bonito National Park, including the parts along the Río Cangrejal, new eco-lodges, tour operators, and conservation-minded individuals are grouping together and working with local villages in the park and NGOs. Other projects like these, almost entirely organized and operated without government assistance, are occurring in places such as Utila, Lago de Yojoa, Copán, and beyond. It makes you wonder just what could be done if the government stepped in. As these small hotels gain worldwide recognition, choosing to stay there over the larger chain hotels makes an important statement to other hotels in the area that are increasingly following their example.

On the Bay Islands, the increasing number of resorts and passing cruise ships are contributing to the damage of the Bay Islands' reef system. Organizations such as the Roatán Marine Park (www.roatanmarinepark.com) are becoming increasingly important in helping visitors understand just how delicate the reef system is. On Utila, the

Whale Shark and Oceanic Research Center (www.wsorc.org) encourages sustainable viewing of whale sharks by limiting the number of boats and the distance from a confirmed whale shark sighting. Divers in the Bay Islands can do their part by ensuring that their dive operators are following basic guidelines. It's also a good idea to question your hotel as to whether they treat their own wastewater and have a system in place for recycling.

At present, no sustainable tourism organizations focus specifically on Honduras. So, to plan the most ecologically friendly Honduras vacation, you should do your best to control your impact on the environment by reusing water bottles (better yet, bring your own and make sure you refill from safe sources), avoiding plastic bags, walking and using mass transportation when possible, and not disturbing flora and fauna. It's important to not buy gifts made from protected species such as black coral, which is often sold as jewelry on the Bay Islands. You'll also want to avoid eating iguana, which pops up on restaurant menus along the North Coast rather often, as you will not be able to guarantee it is not a protected species of the reptile, of which there are many.

To find out which hotels and tour operators are eco-friendly, refer to the "Green Resources" box, p. 28. While they don't focus specifically on Honduras, most of them cover the country in some way.

THE HONDURAS ACTIVE VACATION PLANNER

3

While Costa Rica and, to some extent, Guatemala, Nicaragua, and Panama get all the attention, Honduras has quietly crept out of nowhere to become one of Central America's adventure tourism hot-spots. It's not just diving anymore. You can take a canopy tour, windsurf, protect a turtle habitat, or go bird-watching.

An infinite number of ways to plan an active vacation in Honduras exist. This chapter lays out your options, from tour operators who run multi-activity package tours that often include stays at eco-lodges, to the best places in Honduras to pursue active endeavors (with listings of tour operators, guides, and outfitters that specialize in each), to an overview of the country's national parks and bio-reserves. I also list some language learning and volunteer travel options for those of you with a little more time on your hands and a desire to actively assist Honduras in the maintenance and preservation of its natural wonders.

HONDURAS'S TOP NATIONAL PARKS & BIO-RESERVES

Honduras is one of the most ecologically protected nations in Latin America. Twenty national parks and two biosphere reserves are paired with dozens of smaller reserves, which have helped to preserve the region's most mountainous and forested country and the thousands of rare species that live within it. While enforcement of the borders has been an issue in recent years, few countries can compete with the ongoing level of commitment environmentalists have shown here. Some of the most important parks and reserves are listed below by region.

Southern Honduras

Parque Nacional La Tigra ★ The first protected area in Honduras sits amazingly only 26km (16 miles) northeast of sprawling Tegucigalpa. The former logging site and home of the El Rosario Mining Company has been protected since 1982 and the 238 sq. km (92 sq. miles) of cloud forests, home to quetzals and slews of mammals, are well on their way to recovery. See p. 76.

Refugio de Vida Silvestre Ojochal Just 13km (8 miles) from the Nicaraguan border, near San Marcos de Colón, the rare dry tropical forests and patches of cloud forests are rarely visited, though a few decent trails intersect the park. See p. 87.

Western Honduras

Parque Nacional El Cusuco The Merendón Mountain Range, just off the coast and 45km (28 miles) west of San Pedro Sula, is the setting for this pristine tract of cloud forest. The bird life, for those who don't mind the difficulty in getting here, is spectacular. Apart from a healthy population of quetzals, visitors will find toucans, hummingbirds, and parrots. See p. 98.

Parque Nacional Cerro Azul Meámbar ★★ Bordering the east side of Lago de Yojoa, this 478-sq.-km (185-sq.-mile) park runs from a base of coffee plantations and tropical and pine forests to a height of 2,047m (6,716 ft.), where the cloud forests are found. The infrastructure is good, but it is constantly improving, giving greater access to hundreds of bird species and more than 50 species of mammals. See p. 106.

Parque Nacional Montaña de Santa Bárbara The second-highest peak in the country, at 2,744m (9,003 ft.), is found within this mostly cloud-forest park on the western side of Lago de Yojoa. While there is no infrastructure, the bird life is spectacular—more than 400 species, like trogons, toucans, and woodpeckers, as well as the occasional troop of monkeys and other mammals. See p. 107.

Parque Nacional Montaña de Celaque ★★★ The sloping pine and cloud forests—one of the largest and most unspoiled in Central America—of Celaque, 9km (5½ miles) west of Gracias, are the starting point for 11 rivers that supply fresh water as far away as El Salvador. While quetzals are frequently spotted, the park also holds almost 50 species of mammals, like jaguars, monkeys, and pumas. Improving trail conditions are helping to open up the park, though few travelers make it this way. See p. 139.

The North Coast

Jardín Botánico Lancetilla ★★ American botanist William Popenoe, hired by United Fruit in 1926 to research bananas and disease treatment on the plantations, established this facility, which the Honduran government took control over in 1974. Sitting 5km (3 miles) north of Tela, the garden is now the second largest tropical botanical garden in the world, spanning roughly 1,680 hectares (4,151 acres) and containing more than 1,200 species of plants and almost 400 species of birds. See p. 156.

Parque Nacional Jeannette Kawas/Punta Sal ★★★ Sitting on a peninsula in the western corner of Tela Bay, 16km (10 miles) west of Tela, this 782 sq. km (302 sq. mile) park is one of the country's finest. The beaches, pristine coral reefs, and lush green jungle hold an incredible array of species like marine turtles, dolphins, manatees, caimans, ocelots, peccaries, and monkeys. From November to February, the park becomes an important stop for tens of thousands of migratory birds. The Garífuna village of Miami, one of the most traditional in the country, sits within the park, just before the Los Micos Lagoon meets the Caribbean Sea. Tensions between environmentalists and business owners have been ongoing for several years, as the Los Micos Lagoon Golf & Beach Resort project, which some fear will turn Tela Bay into the next Cancun, has taken off. The park was renamed in honor of Honduran activist and President of PROLANSATE Jeannette Kawas Fernández, who was killed after establishing the park amid controversy from business groups. See p. 156.

Refugio de Vida Silvestre Punta Izopo ★ While the ecosystem of Punta Izopo—which covers the eastern point of Tela Bay—is quite similar to that of Jeannette Kawas, it is much less accessible. The wildlife reserve sits 12km (7½ miles) east of Tela, where the Lean and Hicaque rivers meet the ocean, but not before getting lost in a web of canals and almost impenetrable mangrove forests. Caimans, manatees, turtles, monkeys, and plenty of bird species can be spotted in the park. See p. 157.

Refugio Nacional de Vida Silvestre Cuero y Salado ★★★ This huge, wildlife-rich estuary, 30km (19 miles) west of La Ceiba, where three rivers—the Cuero, Salado, and San Juan—meet the Caribbean, is one of the most important natural reserves in the country. Mangroves and low-lying tropical forests intersected by canals contain nearly 200 species of birds, as well as an abundance of mammals like sloths, ocelots, otters, and howler and white-faced monkeys, plus the extremely rare West Indian manatee. See p. 166.

Pico Bonito National Park ★★★ The jewel of the national park system, the more than 100,000-hectare (247,105-acre) Pico Bonito National Park, south of La Ceiba, contains seven different ecosystems. As it climbs from sea level to the 2,436m (7,992-ft.) jagged mountain the park is named after, the degree of biodiversity becomes almost bewildering. Two main access points, one at Pico Bonito Lodge and the other along the Rio Cangrejal, allow visitors to enter a rainforest cartoon of waterfalls, crystalline pools, and misty green trails. The list of creatures here is nothing short of a dream: 400 species of birds, jaguars, ocelots, tapirs, pumas, deer, and white-faced and spider monkeys, not to mention countless species of reptiles, amphibians, and butterflies. To get these results, much of the interior of the park is off-limits to visitors. See p. 174.

Parque Nacional Marino Cayos Cochinos ★★★ It's almost comical how perfect these two small islands and 13 coral cays are. Some hold just a patch of palm trees ringed by white sand and crystalline water. The 489-sq.-km (189-sq.-mile) reserve, 30km (19 miles) northeast of La Ceiba, protects not just the land, but also the pristine coral and flourishing marine life below. See p. 178.

Parque Nacional Capiro y Calentura This 4,500-hectare (11,120-acre) national park, 3km (1¾ miles) south of Trujillo, holds one 1,235m-high (4,052-ft.) mountain and several zones of tropical forest. Toucans, macaws, and the occasional monkey are only a fraction of the wildlife found within. See p. 182.

Refugio de Vida Silvestre Guaimoreto Just 5km (3 miles) east of Trujillo sits a large tract of mangrove forest, similar to Cuero y Salado. Inside the forest is one big lagoon with a flurry of canals leading off it that are home to caimans, monkeys, and a seasonal flock of migratory birds from November to February. See p. 182.

Bay Islands

Sandy Bay & West End Marine Park This collection of protected coral reefs, seagrass beds, and mangrove forests was started and maintained by concerned divers. It sits just off the north shore of Roatán. See p. 194.

Reserva Marina Turtle Harbour In the wild mangrove jungles on the north shore of Utila, this marine reserve was initiated to protect the hawksbill sea turtles that nest here. See p. 220.

La Mosquitia

Reserva de la Biosfera del Río Plátano ★★★ This 525,000 hectares (1.3 million acres) of wetlands, beaches, pine savannas, tropical forests, and rivers—stretching from Olancho to the Caribbean Sea—is like a mini Amazon, and is one of the world's great natural reserves. Few places on Earth are so dynamic and the biodiversity here is jaw dropping, which is why UNESCO named it a World Heritage site in 1980. Baird's tapirs, jaguars, giant anteaters, spider monkeys, white-tailed deer, white-lipped peccaries, river otters, turtles, iguanas, and a list of avian species that is fast approaching 400 all make their home here. It's not just the wildlife, though. The indigenous Pech and Miskitos also inhabit the park. Community-based ecotourism projects with the help of an international NGO have begun to take off and make access here relatively easy. Still, the best way to visit is on 10-day rafting trips down the Río Plátano from Olancho. See p. 242.

Reserva de la Biosfera del Tawahka Asangni ★★★ This 230,000-hectare (568,342-acre) reserve, southeast of Puerto Lempira along the Nicaragua border, is even more isolated than the Río Plátano Biosphere Reserve. It was established in 1999 and surrounds the highly threatened Tawahka indigenous group, who number fewer than 1,000 and live in only a handful of communities along the Patuca and Wampú rivers. See p. 251.

Olancho

Monumento Nacional El Boquerón ★ Two river canyons and one mountain can be found in this 4,000-hectare (9,884-acre) reserve, between Catacamas and Juticalpa, that was the original site of the first Spanish settlement in Olancho, San Jorge de Olancho. Vast tracts of primary and secondary forests and, to a lesser extent, cloud forests can be found here. See p. 256.

Parque Nacional Sierra de Agalta ★★ The 27,000-hectare (66,718-acre) national park in the Sierra de Agalta National Park that separates Olancho from La Mosquitia holds within it one of the largest—and mostly unexplored—tracts of virgin cloud forests in all of Central America. A range of microclimates reveal a wealth of species, including more than 400 species of birds and 61 species of mammals. The popular hiking mountain Pico La Picucha and the Talgua caves can also be found within the park. See p. 257.

Parque Nacional La Muralla Once the premier national park in Honduras, a lack of security on the roads leading here and a lack of control of loggers within the park has caused La Muralla, 14km (8¾ miles) from La Unión, to lose funding. Still, birders will appreciate the frequent sightings of quetzals and toucanets that live in the cloud and pine forests within the park. See p. 262.

Parque Nacional Pico Pijol This 11,206-hectare (27,691-acre) reserve, 3km (1¾ miles) south of Yoro, was created to protect four rivers that are an important water source for San Pedro Sula. While it lacks facilities—there are, at last count, zero—above 1,800m (5,906 ft.), the cloud forests here are unspoiled and crawling with wildlife. See p. 262.

ACTIVITIES A TO Z

Adventure activities and tourism, by their very nature, carry certain risks and dangers. Over the years, there have been several deaths and dozens of minor injuries in activities ranging from mountain biking to whitewater rafting to canopy tours. Regulation is lacking in Honduras for many activities; therefore, I try to list only the most reputable and safest of companies. Some may carry higher fees than others, though any tour operator that is offering questionable prices should be questioned. Often, tour operators will try to cut corners to give the lowest price, but when a problem occurs, they shut down and then open again under another name. Obviously, I don't list those. If you ever have any doubt as to the safety of the guide, equipment, or activity, it's better to be safe than sorry. Moreover, know your limits and abilities, and don't try to exceed them.

Archeological Digs & Research

If archeological discoveries are what you had in mind in a Honduras vacation, there are numerous ongoing excavations at any given time in Western Honduras. Keep in mind that most digs involve long hot days under the sun and working in the dirt. They are far from an Indiana Jones experience. Most sites relate to the Mayas; however, some focus on other pre-Columbian cultures. These kinds of trips are popular with college students looking for course credit, as well as retirees and general history buffs.

Several organizations focus on this type of volunteer work. Try the **Maya Research Program** (www.mayaresearchprogram.org), which organizes digs in various Central American countries, including several sites in Western Honduras.

Another option is the **Archeological Institute of America** (AIA; ✆ **800/748-6262;** www.archaeological.org), which organizes excavations and programs all over the world.

Biking

Honduras has everything you need for an excellent biking trip: good dirt roads, logging trails, rolling hills, fine scenery, and loads of places to go. The only problem is, not many are doing it. Full-day and half-day mountain biking tours are becoming increasingly common in the La Ceiba area and Copán, though the sport is still in its relative infancy.

Jungle River Tours (✆ **504/2440-1268;** www.jungleriverlodge.com) and **Omega Tours** (✆ **504/2440-0334;** www.omegatours.info) run downhill mountain biking trips in and around Pico Bonito National Park.

Bird-Watching

Honduras is a bird-watcher's paradise, with hundreds of species to spot (approximately 800 have been recorded). In places such as Lancetilla and Lago de Yojoa, the number of different recorded species at either location is closing in on an astounding 400 species. The 30-plus tracts of cloud forests, including Montaña de Celaque National Park and La Tigra National Park, are rarely explored and are full of hummingbirds and the usually hard to spot resplendent quetzal.

Rare species found in the country include motmots, jacamars, woodpeckers, macaws, harpy eagles, kingfishers, trogons, herons, owls, and tanagers. I've been all over Latin America, and there is nowhere I have seen toucans on such a regular basis as I have here at maybe six relatively easy-to-reach spots. Birders will delight in much-sought-after species—the great potoo, keel-billed motmot, and maroon-chested ground dove are all found here.

Malcolm Glasgow (✆ **504/2994-9719;** www.dd-brewery.org), who knows bird life on and around Lago de Yojoa better than almost anyone, runs a range of extremely popular half-day and day tours on the lake for L250 per person, and two-day trips to Santa Bárbara National Park for L1,000 per person, including transport and rustic accommodation. Minimum two people; prices drop for larger groups. In Copán, owner of the Alas Encantadas butterfly farm and lodge **Roberto Gallardo** (✆ **504/2651-4133**), who has written several books on Honduran birds and wildlife, runs specialty bird-watching trips, as well.

Victor Emanuel Nature Tours (✆ **800/328-8326;** www.ventbird.com) leads bird-watching trips to Honduras with some of the foremost authorities in the field, while staying at top nature lodges.

Wings (✆ **888/293-6443;** www.wingsbirds.com) is a well-respected birding operator that has been running tours for more than 3 decades.

In addition to these companies, many environmental organizations, including the **National Audubon Society** (✆ **800/967-7425** or 212/979-8947; www.audubon.org), periodically offer organized trips to Honduras.

Canopy/Zip-Line Tours

For some reason, canopy tours (sometimes called zip-line tours) have caught on wildly in Honduras. They offer a unique and exhilarating way to experience the rainforest. By bringing you to the treetops, you get to see the place where two-thirds of all rainforest species live—although most are frightened off by gringos flying through the air on a regular basis.

Most of the tours consist of strapping yourself in a climbing harness and walking to a platform approximately 30m (98 ft.) above the forest floor. Usually 10 to 20 platforms connected by metal cables form a course. With the help of a guide, you will attach your harness to the cable and jump, flying through the air to the next platform, where another guide is waiting. There are canopy tours in the country in almost every major tourist destination (Copán, Pulhapanzak Falls, Roatán, La Ceiba, Sambo Creek, Omoa), and more are popping up all the time. There's little regulation of the tours, so be sure you feel confident in the course and the safety standards before setting off. The operators listed below are recommended.

ROATÁN

- **Gumbalimba Park:** ✆ **504/2445-1033;** www.gumbalimbapark.com
- **South Shore Canopy Tour:** www.southshorecanopy.com
- **Pirates of the Caribbean Canopy:** ✆ **504/2455-7576;** www.roatanpiratescanopy.com
- **Palmetto Ridge Canopy:** ✆ **504/2445-7853;** www.tropicalrez.com

OMOA

- **Rawacala:** ✆ **504/2556-9466;** www.bttours.net

LA CEIBA

- **Jungle River Tours:** ✆ **504/2440-1268;** www.jungleriverlodge.com

Cigar Factory Tours

After the 1959 Communist Revolution, Cuban cigar makers began to flood into Honduras for what they saw as soil and weather conditions that were comparable to those of Cuba. Honduras is one of the world's premier cigar production centers. While there are a few exceptions, most cigar production in Honduras centers on two areas: Santa Rosa de Copán in the west and Danlí in the southeast. You can usually walk up to a cigar factory and arrange a brief tour. Most are free, and you just need to give a small tip to the host. Photos and videos are usually not allowed.

Camacho Cigars (✆ **305/2592-0722**; www.camachocigars.com), based outside of Danlí, runs the most formal cigar tours in the country on select dates throughout the year. From their Camp Camacho in the Valle de Jamastrán, the company holds in-depth, 3-day "seed to store" seminars for consumers and retailers that include all meals and accommodations.

Diving & Snorkeling

Honduras is one of the world's great dive destinations. The world's second-largest barrier reef runs along the Bay Islands and the Caribbean coast.

The Bay Islands, just 48km (30 miles) off the coast, are renowned as one of the cheapest diving destinations in the world, at less than L760 per dive on Roatán and even less on Utila and Guanaja. Almost every hotel on the Bay Island has its own dive master or gets special rates with a preferred dive center. Most will offer a range of courses, from basic certifications to master and instructor development courses. Nitrox is widely available, and world-class recompression chambers can be found on both Utila and Roatán. Diving is more or less concentrated here, but a few other locations, such as Omoa and the Cayos Cochinos, also have excellent diving and can arrange certification courses.

ROATÁN

- **Anthony's Key Resort:** ✆ 954/929-0090; www.anthonyskey.com
- **Bananarama Dive Resort:** ✆ 504/2445-5005; www.bananaramadive.com
- **Coconut Tree Divers:** ✆ 504/2445-4081; www.coconuttreedivers.com
- **Coco View Resort:** ✆ 504/2911-7371; www.cocoviewresort.com
- **Fantasy Island Resort:** ✆ 504/2455-7499; www.fantasyislandresort.com
- **Native Sons:** ✆ 504/2445-4003; www.nativesonsroatan.com
- **Octopus Dive School:** ✆ 504/2403-8071; www.roatan-octopusdiveschool.com
- **Reef Gliders:** ✆ 504/2403-8243; www.reefgliders.com
- **Sueno del Mar Dive Center:** ✆ 800/298-9009 in the U.S.; www.suenodelmar.com
- **Roatán Shark Dive:** ✆ 504/2445-1283; www.sharkdiveroatan.com

GUANAJA

- **Nautilus:** ✆ 952/953-4124; www.usdivetravel.com

UTILA

- **Alton's Dive Center:** ✆ 504/2425-3704; www.diveinutila.com
- **Bay Islands College of Diving:** ✆ 504/2425-3291; www.dive-utila.com
- **Captain Morgan's Dive Shop:** ✆ 504/2425-3349; www.divingutila.com
- **Deep Blue Divers:** ✆ 504/2425-3211; www.deepblueutila.com
- **Utila Dive Center:** ✆ 504/2425-3350; www.utiladivecenter.com
- **Utila Water Sports:** ✆ 504/2425-3264; www.utilawatersports.com
- **Utopia Dive Village:** ✆ 504/3344-9387; www.utopiadivevillage.com

CAYOS COCHINOS

- **Plantation Beach Resort:** ✆ 504/3371-7556; www.plantationbeachresort.com

FOREIGN-BASED DIVE OPERATORS

Maduro Dive (**✆ 800/327-6709;** www.madurodive.com), a Miami-based dive specialty operator, runs dive packages to the Bay Islands and other exotic destinations around the world. **Uncommon Adventures** (**✆ 800/390-9675;** www.uncommonadventures.com) has a range of dive tours and kayaking trips, mostly based on the Bay Islands.

Dolphin Training

Only in Honduras can you find a program like this accessible by tourists. **Anthony's Key Resort** (**✆ 504/2445-3008;** www.anthonyskey.com), with the help of the Roatán Institute for Marine Sciences, organizes short-term dolphin-training programs, where you can work with the training staff in 1-day, 2-day, or weeklong sessions. There's even a Dolphin Scuba Camp for children held throughout the summer.

Fishing

While only insiders know it, Honduras has long been a top fishing spot. The Bay Islands and Brus Laguna, two completely different settings, have been luring some of the world's top anglers for years, long before luxury facilities were here. While the Bay Islands are best for deep-sea sport fishing for marlin and bone fishing off the reef, Brus Laguna is home to massive tarpon from the lagoon.

Early Bird Fishing Charters (✆ 504/2445-3019; www.earlybirdfishingcharters.com), a member of the conservation-minded Fishermens Association of Roatán, leads frequent excursions from the West End to waters all around the island. Prices begin at $400 for a half-day tour with 1 to 4 people.

Pescado Roatán (✆ 504/9930-6139; www.pescadoroatan.com) is a fly and deep-sea fishing specialist using top quality equipment. **Fly Fish Guanaja** (**✆ 970/708-0626;** www.flyfishguanaja.com) has all-inclusive 7-day saltwater fly-fishing trips from Roatán, including round-trip airfare, for $3,000.

Team Marin Fishing (**✆ 504/9987-0875;** www.teammarinhondurasfishing.com) is the best operator in the Brus Laguna area. Their all-inclusive tours include fishing, meals, round-trip airline tickets from La Ceiba, a local guide in La Ceiba, a local English-speaking fishing guide for all fishing excursions, boat transport, and airport transfers. Tours start at $889 per person, based on double occupancy, for a 3-night/4 day excursion.

Golf

There are now several golf courses operating in Honduras, though many are small and private. The oldest is the 9-hole **Villa Elena Country Club** (**✆ 504/2224-0400**), 9km (5½ miles) north of Tegucigalpa on the road to San Pedro Sula. The best course by far is the Pete Dye–designed **Black Pearl Golf Club** (**✆ 504/3318-2146;** www.blackpearlgolf.com), Roatán's first course. The 18-hole, par-72 resort course measures 7,057 yards and is located at the Pristine Bay resort. Near Tela, the **Los Micos Beach & Golf Resort,** an 18-hole Gary Player–designed course, should be operating by 2012.

Hiking

While facilities are not always maintained outside of top trails, Honduras has an excellent array of hiking routes. Most trails, especially the more remote sections, are very rarely visited, and therefore, your chances of seeing rare wildlife increase dramatically.

HEALTH, SAFETY & ETIQUETTE IN THE wilderness

While most tours and adventure activities are relatively safe, serious risks are involved for careless participants. But a little common sense is all you need. Risks most often occur when someone tries to extend their efforts beyond their physical capabilities. Know your limits. The sometimes extreme heat and wild temperature shifts found in Honduras can take their toll on a body rather quickly. Heavy downpours can occur at any time, thus dropping the temperatures and making rainforest paths beyond slippery. Rain gear is essential in Honduras, as is sunscreen. Have dry clothes ready, too, for the end of your excursion.

When hiking through the jungle—there's real, genuine, wild jungle here—and the backcountry, there are general precautions to take. Chances are you won't see many snakes, if any, but if you do, don't encourage one to bite you. Stay calm, don't make any sudden movements, and don't touch it. You are not a crocodile hunter, so don't act like one. If you swim in lagoons and near mangrove forests, just remember that healthy populations of critters—from otters to caimans—inhabit most of them. Ask locals where it is safe to swim. Also, avoid swimming in major rivers unless a guide or local operator can vouch for their safety. Be careful with ocean currents, as well.

Bugs and bug bites will probably be your greatest health concern in the Honduran wilderness, and even they aren't as big a problem as you might expect. Even in La Mosquitia, there aren't that many mosquitoes. Mostly, bugs are an inconvenience, although mosquitoes can carry malaria or dengue. Strong repellent and proper clothing minimize both the danger and the inconvenience; you might also want to bring along some cortisone or Benadryl cream to soothe itching. At the beaches, especially on the Bay Islands and the North Coast, you'll probably be bitten by *pirujas* (sand fleas or no-see-ums). These nearly invisible insects leave an irritating welt. Try not to scratch because this can lead to open sores and infections. Pirujas are most active at sunrise and sunset, so you might want to cover up or avoid the beaches at these times.

The slogan "Leave nothing but footprints; take nothing but memories" certainly applies here, though if you can avoid leaving footprints, even better. Much of the Honduran wilderness holds an array of rare and little-known flora and fauna. Some of it is highly endangered and even endemic to the specific mountain or tract of forest. Do not cut or uproot plants or flowers. Pack out everything you pack in, and please do not litter. Take photos and nothing else.

Rarely will you encounter another hiker here. It's not because the trails are disappointing, it's simply because no one has discovered the country yet. Drop 10 of the top trails in Honduras in Costa Rica, and each would have an airstrip and a luxury tent camp before you could snap a photo.

Some of the best hikes in the country include the 2-day hike to Montaña de Celaque National Park near Gracias, the 2- to 4-day hikes at Pico La Picucha in Olancho, and a number of 2- to 4-day hikes around the town of Las Marías in the Río Plátano Biosphere Reserve. Other good trails can be found in Olancho destinations like La Muralla National Park, in Pico Bonito National Park, La Tigra National Park, and several others in all parts of the country.

La Moskitia Ecoaventuras (© **504/2440-2124;** www.lamoskitiaecoaventuras.com), run by naturalist Jorge Salaverri, one of the most respected promoters of ecotourism in the country, offers a wide variety of hikes in Pico Bonito National Park, all over Olancho, La Mosquitia, and beyond.

La Ruta Moskitia (© **504/2443-1276;** www.larutamoskitia.com), the 100% community-owned and -operated programs, lead a range of day hikes and multiday hikes from La Mosquitia destinations, especially Las Marías.

Colosuca-Celaque (© **504/2656-0627**), in Gracias, arranges treks to Montaña de Celaque National Park, and shorter and less intense day hikes along La Ruta Lenca.

Jungle Expedition (© **504/9762-6620;** www.junglexpedition.org), based in San Pedro Sula, runs various hikes in nearby Parque Nacional Cusuco.

Base Camp Adventures (© **504/2651-4695;** www.basecamphonduras.com), in Copan, offers 2-, 4-, and 6- to 8-hour hikes to isolated Chortí villages and to waterfalls.

Horseback Riding

As roads are poor outside of big cities, the horse is a main method of transportation in places such as Olancho, La Mosquitia, and the mountains in the west of the country. And though much of Honduras is horse and cowboy country, the activity is only partly opening up to tourism. Riding tours, which generally only last ½ to 1 day, are run from Copán, La Ceiba, and La Mosquitia, as well as less frequently from locations such as Utila and mountain villages near Tegucigalpa.

MC Tours (© **504/2651-4453;** www.mctours-honduras.com), **Yaragua** (© **504/2651-4147;** www.yaragua.com), and **Xukpi** (© **504/2651-4435**) all lead short horse-riding tours in and around Copán, usually to Chortí Maya communities.

Omega Tours (© **504/2440-0334;** www.omegatours.info) in La Ceiba has one of the largest varieties of tours on horseback on the North Coast, ranging from 6-hour beach rides to multiday trips through Pico Bonito National Park.

Red Ridge Stables (© **504/2390-4812**), in East Harbour on Utila, has 2-hour rides to Pumpkin Hill Beach, freshwater caves, and other destinations on the island. Trips run $35 for a 2-hour ride.

Kayaking

The North Coast of Honduras and the Bay Islands dominate the kayaking scene in the country. Extended multiday trips that hop around the Cayos Cochinos and shorter day trips exploring mangrove forests are increasingly showing up on the itineraries of local tour operators.

Half Moon Bay Kayak Co. (© **650/773-6101** in the U.S.; www.hmbkayak.com) runs 8-day sea kayaking trips in Guanaja, based at Graham's Place, for $1,500 per person, not including airfare.

Utila Water Sports (© **504/2425-3264;** www.utilawatersports.com), on Utila, rents kayaks so you can explore the mangroves and canals that cover much of the island.

Kayak Utila (no phone; www.kayakutila.com) rents sit-on-top kayaks to explore the mangrove channels on Utila.

La Moskitia Ecoaventuras (© **504/2550-2124;** www.lamoskitiaecoaventuras.com) runs day trips to the Cacao lagoon near La Ceiba.

Language Immersion

While Honduras is not nearly as popular with language travelers as neighboring Guatemala, the practice of language immersion is growing steadily. Many North American, Australian, and European students, retirees, business people, and general travelers choose to study Spanish in Latin America because of low prices and the option of homestays with local families. Many feel that the on-the-ground practice they receive in everyday interactions with native speakers helps considerably when learning. Countless programs exist in the country, but most are found in Copán, La Ceiba, San Pedro Sula, and other large population centers.

Central America Spanish School (© **504/2440-1707;** www.ca-spanish.com) has the most programs in the country, with classroom locations in La Ceiba, Utila, Roatán, and Copán. They can arrange homestays with local families, as well as combine your studies with additional activities, such as dive certifications.

In Copán, your best options are **Ixbalanque** (© **504/2651-4321;** www.ixbalanque.com) and **Guacamaya** (© **504/2651-4360;** www.guacamaya.com), which have similar facilities and prices. Both arrange and encourage homestays.

Spa & Yoga Retreats

Honduras still has a long way to go in terms of attracting health travelers compared to neighbors such as Costa Rica. Still, there are decent wellness retreats in a few parts of the country and a few blips on the radar for what is on the way.

The mountains in the west, once the land of the Mayas, are the center of spiritual and wellness tourism in the country. The **Hacienda San Lucas** (see p. 125), near Copán, often holds comprehensive yoga and spiritual-cleansing retreats led by internationally renowned names in the field, while the hills outside of Copán and the Gracias area are becoming more and more known for their hot springs. American Wendy Green has Ashtanga yoga classes open to the public at her riverside studio, **Casa Verde** (no phone; www.wendygreenyoga.com) near La Ceiba in the Rio Cangrejal sector of Parque Nacional Pico Bonito, and also organizes intensive raw-food and wellness retreats. **Earth Mama's** (© **504/9607-0704;** www.earthmamasroatan.com) on Roatán's West End also offers daily yoga sessions. Near Tegucigalpa, **Yoga's Garden Spa** (© **504/2236-9139;** www.yogasgardenspa.com) holds regular yoga, Pilates, tai chi, and belly-dancing classes, as well as offers full spa services.

On the Bay Islands, several resorts have added spas, and in recent years, the range of treatments and services has grown significantly. Most of the best spas are concentrated on Roatán such as Barefoot Cay, Baan Suerte, and Sante Spa, though Utopia Village on Utila also offers wellness packages.

Expect all this to change, though, when several new major luxury resorts and spas are built on the Bay Islands in the next couple of years.

Volunteer & Working Trips

Honduras and Latin America, in general, are great places to devote your time and goodwill. Most volunteer programs fall in one of three categories: those that help rural communities, those that protect the environment, and those that preserve and collect data on historical sites. Most programs have a fee that will cover your food or lodging. **Volunteer Honduras** (www.volunteerhonduras.org) is a good place to start looking and a great resource for those thinking about volunteering in Honduras.

NPH International (✆ **504/2224-0573;** www.nph.org) is a group of orphanages scattered throughout the Americas, including one near Tegucigalpa. A variety of long-term volunteers are always needed, ranging from doctors to English teachers and speech pathologists.

Proniño Honduras (✆ 504/2647-3424; www.pronino.org) and **The Friends of El Hogar** (www.foeh.org.uk) work with street children in northern Honduras to help them end drug addiction and focus on long-term education.

Children of the Light (✆ **504/3304-1414;** www.thechildrenofthelight.org), a Christian organization, has built a school and has organized other community outreach projects for street children in the region.

Whitewater Rafting

With some of the longest rivers and unexplored whitewater in Central America, Honduras is quickly earning a name for itself in the rafting world. The Rio Cangrejal (Class III–V), which runs through Pico Bonito National Park, is one of the best whitewater rivers in Central America for both the scenery and the quality of the rapids. Other rivers—mostly in Olancho and La Mosquitia—such as the Río Plátano (Class II–IV), Río Patuca (Class II), and Río Sico (Class II–IV), have quality rapids, as well, though they are multiday adventures, and rapids may appear on only part of the route.

The following operators all lead trips on the Río Cangrejal and multiday trips in the Río Plátano Biosphere Reserve. Some will run trips in the Río Patuca, as well:

- **Garífuna Tours:** ✆ **504/2440-3252;** www.garifunatours.com
- **Jungle River Tours:** ✆ **504/2440-1268;** www.jungleriverlodge.com
- **La Moskitia Ecoaventuras:** ✆ **504/2550-2124;** www.lamoskitiaecoaventuras.com
- **Omega Tours:** ✆ **504/2440-0334;** www.omegatours.info

Wind & Kite Surfing

Strong coastal winds and sheltered bays give much of the North Coast and the Bay Islands excellent wind- and kite-surfing conditions. Neither sport has caught on to a mass audience yet, but a few dedicated operators are helping to change that.

Kite Honduras (✆ **504/3312-8439;** www.kitehonduras.com), on Roatán, has beginner to advanced lessons using IKO instruction methods, with board rentals and repairs, as well as customized trips for advanced riders. **Wind Surf Honduras** (✆ **504/2445-3292;** www.windsurfhonduras.com) has the largest collection of board rentals in Honduras and gives lessons ranging from $40 for 1½ hours to $110 for 6 hours.

ORGANIZED ADVENTURE TRIPS

Honduran Tour Agencies

While many international tour operators run tours to Honduras, they are almost always contracted out through local operators, such as those mentioned here. Booking directly will save you a bundle. A bundle! Most are based in La Ceiba, Copán, or San Pedro Sula, but have offices in other parts of the country and the U.S., as well. Most operators include lodging and airfare, though it depends on the package you buy. In most instances, they all provide regional flights and lodging.

Arrecife Tours (✆ **504/2516-0955;** www.arrecifetours.com) runs complete package tours of Honduras, covering the most visited sites, from their U.S. and Honduras offices.

Garífuna Tours (✆ **504/2440-3252;** www.garifunatours.com) is one of the most popular group adventure tour operations in the country. While they specialize in daylong trips to the national parks along the North Coast near La Ceiba and Tela, they also run package tours to the Bay Islands and Copán.

Roatán Charters (✆ **800/282-8932;** www.roatan.com) is a one-stop shop for almost any tour, regional flight, or hotel in Honduras or Belize, though they focus mostly on the Bay Islands.

Jungle River Tours (✆ **504/2440-1268;** www.jungleriverlodge.com) is a budget operator that focuses on adventure activities such as rafting, kayaking, and hiking in select destinations along the North Coast.

La Moskitia Ecoaventuras (✆ **504/2414-5798;** www.lamoskitiaecoaventuras.com) is run by internationally known naturalist Jorge Salaverri, who has worked tirelessly to promote ecotourism in the country and helped set up several of the national parks and involve the local communities. They offer everything from 10- to 14-day rafting trips in the Río Plátano Biosphere Reserve and explorations in even more remote parts of La Mosquitia to day hikes and kayak trips in national parks along the North Coast.

La Ruta Moskitia (✆ **504/2406-6782;** www.larutamoskitia.com) is a grassroots tourism initiative that arranges a wide variety of day tours and guided 4- to 9-day excursions with cultural groups in La Mosquitia.

MC Tours (✆ **504/2651-4453;** www.mctours-honduras.com) is one of the largest operators in the country and offers a range of tours covering nearly every major tourist destination.

Omega Tours (✆ **504/2440-0334;** www.omegatours.info) gives a range of adventure tours, like rafting trips on the Río Plátano, and multi-activity tours from their lodge along the Río Cangrejal. They have the most complete horseback-riding excursions among all of the tour operators.

For more information on escorted general-interest tours, including questions to ask before booking your trip, see www.frommers.com/planning.

U.S. & International-Based Adventure Tour Operators

These agencies and operators specialize in well-organized and coordinated tours that cover your entire stay. Many travelers prefer to have everything arranged and confirmed before arriving in Honduras, and this is a good idea for first-timers and during the high season. Most of these operators, however, are not cheap, with 10-day tours generally costing in the neighborhood of $1,800 to $3,000 per person, not including airfare.

Gap Adventures (✆ **800/708-7761;** www.gapadventures.com) has adventure and leisure tours in more than 100 countries, including Honduras.

Journey Latin America (✆ **020/8747-8315;** www.journeylatinamerica.co.uk) is a specialty travel agency focusing on all Latin American destinations. They have several trips in Honduras covering the Bay Islands, Copán, and the North Coast, which can all be booked in conjunction with trips elsewhere in the region.

Mesoamerican Ecotourism Alliance/MEA (✆ **800/682-0584;** www.travelwithmea.org) offers a handful of very specific, all-inclusive, multiday tours in Honduras that explore many of the top and most remote national parks in the country.

Mountain Travel Sobek (✆ **888/831-7526;** www.mtsobek.com), an off-the-beaten-track adventure travel operator that is no stranger to luxury, has 7- to 9-day trips that begin and end in San Pedro Sula and take in both the reef and rainforest.

Overseas Adventure Travel (✆ **800/493-6824;** www.oattravel.com) offers good-value natural history and "soft adventure" itineraries with optional add-on excursions. Tours are limited to 16 people and are guided by naturalists. All accommodations are in small hotels, lodges, or tent camps. Their Honduras itineraries are usually part of larger Central America tours that take in several countries over several weeks.

ECOLOGICALLY ORIENTED VOLUNTEER & STUDY PROGRAMS

Many international organizations can help get you involved with protecting the vast wilderness within Honduras.

Earthwatch (✆ **800/776-0188;** www.earthwatch.org) has volunteering trips throughout the country that help conserve natural sites such as turtle nesting areas and the coral reef surrounding the Bay Islands.

Guaruma (✆ **504/2406-6782;** www.guaruma.org) is a Honduras-based nonprofit organization that helps promote environmental awareness and conservation in the Rio Cangrejal watershed on the eastern edge of Pico Bonito National Park.

Sustainable Harvest International (✆ **919/942-2221;** www.sustainableharvest.org) teaches rural communities about sustainable agriculture, solar energy systems, organic growing techniques, and irrigation systems. In Honduras, the program is in operation with rural communities near Santa Barbara.

Honduras Coral Reef Fund (✆ **504/2442-2670;** www.cayoscochinos.org) leads all scientific research on the Cayos Cochinos, from surveying the reef to protecting sea-turtle nesting sites. Occasionally, they will accept volunteers.

frommers.com: THE COMPLETE TRAVEL RESOURCE

Planning a trip or just returned? Head to **Frommers.com,** voted Best Travel Site by *PC Magazine.* We think you'll find our site indispensable before, during, and after your travels—with expert advice and tips; independent reviews of hotels, restaurants, attractions, and preferred shopping and nightlife venues; vacation giveaways; and an online booking tool. We publish the complete contents of over 135 travel guides in our **Destinations** section, covering over 4,000 places worldwide. Each weekday, we publish original articles that report on **Deals and News** via our free **Frommers.com Newsletters.** What's more, **Arthur Frommer** himself blogs 5 days a week, with cutting opinions about the state of travel in the modern world. We're betting you'll find our **Events** listings an invaluable resource: it's an up-to-the-minute roster of what's happening in cities everywhere—including concerts, festivals, lectures, and more. We've also added weekly **podcasts, interactive maps,** and hundreds of new images across the site. Finally, don't forget to visit our **Message Boards,** where you can join in conversations with thousands of fellow Frommer's travelers and post your trip report once you return.

SUGGESTED ITINERARIES IN HONDURAS

4

Planning your assault on Honduras—and I do not mean like American William Walker did when he attempted to invade the country in 1860—can be rather tricky. There is plenty to see, and the country is quite large and spread out. Careful planning is a must, especially if you are short on time. Few visitors have months to explore in Honduras, so below, we present both 1- and 2-week itineraries to help you make the most of your time.

Honduras has so many adventures on hand that 1 or 2 weeks won't get you everywhere, so relax and don't even try. Instead, we recommend you enjoy the nuggets—The North Coast, Gracias, and Copán—among other allures, saving the rest for another day. You may also review chapter 1, "The Best of Honduras," to find out what experiences or sights have special appeal to us, and then adjust the itineraries to suit your particular travel plans.

Like elsewhere in Central America, getting around can be slow, and you may be at the mercy of infrequent bus and plane schedules. While fine highways connect cities like San Pedro Sula and Tegucigalpa, traffic in rural areas moves a bit slower. Still, there is plenty to fit in certain pockets like the Bay Islands, North Coast, and the western side of the country. These destinations are relatively easy to reach, no more than a few hours by car or ferry from any major airport.

The itineraries that follow take you to some major attractions and some off-the-beaten-track ones. The pace may be a bit breathless for some visitors, so skip a town or sight occasionally to have some time to kick back—after all, you're on vacation. Of course, you can use any of these itineraries as a jumping-off point to develop your own custom-made trip.

THE REGIONS IN BRIEF

Covering 111,369 sq. km (43,000 sq. miles), Honduras is the second-largest country in Central America (Nicaragua is the largest) and the only one without volcanoes. It borders the Caribbean Sea, Pacific Ocean, Guatemala, Nicaragua, and El Salvador, and is only a short ferry ride from Belize. Like points on a compass, the country can be divided into four major geographical sections: the lush forests and coastline of the north; the impenetrable jungles of La Mosquitia of the east; the mountains and pine forests of the western and central parts of the country; and the dry, dusty south. Forty percent of Honduras is made up of rainforests, while the coasts comprise nearly 965km (600 miles) of beaches. Apart from the coasts and between San Pedro and the capital of Tegucigalpa, highways and paved roads are severely lacking, even to national parks and tourist attractions. In and around La Mosquitia and to/from the Bay Islands, transportation by water or air is your only option for getting around.

THE SOUTH The country's 100km (62-mile) Pacific Coast separates Honduras from El Salvador in the west and Nicaragua in the east, and marks the western boundary of the southern region, which extends up to the sprawling capital of Tegucigalpa (called Tegus by locals). Tegucigalpa is the cultural center of the country and home to several excellent museums, great restaurants and markets, and a smattering of luxury hotels. Just outside town, you will find small craft villages and one of the best national parks in the country, the La Tigra National Park.

THE WEST Mountains, cowboys, Maya ancestors, ancient ruins, cloud forests, Catholic festivals, and the largest lake in the country all join together to create western Honduras, one of the most diverse regions of the country. From the economic hub of the country, San Pedro Sula, you'll move southward across the fertile Sula valley to the Maya ruins of Copán; passing the bird-watching hotspot of Lago de Yojoa; the onetime capital of Central America, Gracias; the cigar and coffee center of Santa Rosa de Copán; and the colonial town of Comayagua.

THE NORTH COAST The North Coast is an eco-dream of lush tropical forests, 805km (500 miles) of empty white sand beaches, fruit farms, and enough adrenaline-pumping sports to keep you busy for months. Near La Ceiba, the country's official capital of ecotourism, you'll find the Cuero y Salado Wildlife Refuge, raging white water on the Río Cangrejal, the waterfalls and hiking trails of Pico Bonito National Park, and easy access to the Bay Islands and the Cayos Cochinos. Tela, with even more natural attractions, like the Lancetilla Botanical Garden and Los Micos Lagoon, is set to become the site of a major tourism project that could soon drastically change this laidback banana town. Elsewhere in the region, you'll find friendly Garífuna villages and the once-happening beachfront and Spanish fort in Trujillo.

THE BAY ISLANDS Stilted island houses, turquoise water, Garífuna settlements, and some of the best diving on Earth make the Bay Islands one of the leading attractions in the country. While you'll find a growing number of cruise ports and luxury resorts on Roatán and a number of hostels and cheap restaurants on the backpacker-paradise that is Utila, these two islands still retain their laidback charm. The least visited of the three Bay Islands, Guanaja, is practically untouched.

LA MOSQUITIA & OLANCHO La Mosquitia, the largest tract of wilderness in Central America, is often called a mini-Amazon. The region is as wild as they come and is made up of indigenous tribes, rarely visited biological reserves, and tiny coastal communities where electricity is a rare luxury. Tour groups are increasingly exploring the Río Plátano Biosphere Reserve via rafting trips, though they are facing competition from new community-based ecotourism projects to the reserve along the coast. Neighboring Olancho is packed to the rim with undisturbed national parks, cave systems, whitewater rivers, rural villages, and scenic vistas of every sort. However, bad roads and a history of highway robberies and drug trafficking have kept many away. Things appear to be on the upswing, with greater police control and the ongoing paving of several stretches of highway.

THE BEST OF HONDURAS IN 1 WEEK

This itinerary will take you to the major attractions in the country, from the Maya ruins of Copán to the mangroves and tropical forests of the North Coast. Alternatively, you may be content to spend your entire trip lying on the beach or diving in Roatán or Utila, rather than heading inland at all. (Though San Pedro Sula is the country's largest international airport, it's possible to take an international flight directly to Tegucigalpa, Roatán, or La Ceiba, too.)

Days 1 & 2: Arrive in San Pedro Sula and Head to Copán ★★★

Upon landing in San Pedro Sula, head directly to the town of **Copán Ruínas** and spend your first day exploring the town. The next morning, wake up early to tour the Maya ruins of Copán before the crowds arrive, along with visits to the **Museum of Mayan Sculpture** and **Las Sepulturas** (p. 122). Have lunch at **Hacienda San Lucas** (p. 125)—or save it for dinner—and then take the afternoon and evening to explore the markets, **Museo Regional de Arqueología Maya** (p. 123), or bars in town.

Days 3 & 4: Santa Rosa de Copán and Gracias ★★★ to Tela ★★

From Copán, travel away from the border and into the mountains to check out the **Flor de Copán cigar factory** (p. 132) in Santa Rosa de Copán, stopping at the Maya ruins of **El Puente** (p. 130) on the way. Then travel **La Ruta Lenca,** stopping in small villages and exploring colonial churches before settling into your hotel in **Gracias,** the capital of the department of Lempira.

Wake up early the next morning for your best chance at seeing the elusive resplendent quetzal and other wildlife during your hike through **Montaña de Celaque National Park** (p. 139). Afterwards, head to Tela on the coast to check into the **Hotel Telamar** (p. 158), once the home of United Fruit executives and now a four-star beach resort.

Days 5 & 6: Tela ★★

Wake up early to check out **Lancetilla** (p. 156), the world's second-largest botanical garden, or to take a boat tour in **Laguna de los Micos** (p. 156) in Parque Nacional Jeannette Kawas, or **Punta Sal** (p. 156), where you can spot howler monkeys, jaguars, and hundreds of species of birds. On the following day, take some time to lie on the beach and enjoy Tela's warm Caribbean seas and swaying palms. Take a long seafood-heavy lunch on the boardwalk, maybe followed by a few stiff drinks and more chilling out.

Days 7 & 8: La Ceiba ★★★

On your last full day, head a few hours up the coast to **La Ceiba,** perhaps to check into a rainforest-surrounded eco-lodge in **Pico Bonito National Park** (p. 174). You can easily spend 2 days here hiking, rafting, or on zip-line tours, so plan accordingly. Day-trip options abound, too, including snorkeling at **Cayos Cochinos** (p. 178), one of the most unspoiled coral reefs in the country, or visiting the Garífuna village of **Chachauate** (p. 179).

On Day 8, transfer to the San Pedro Sula airport to make your flight out of the country.

Honduras in 1 Week

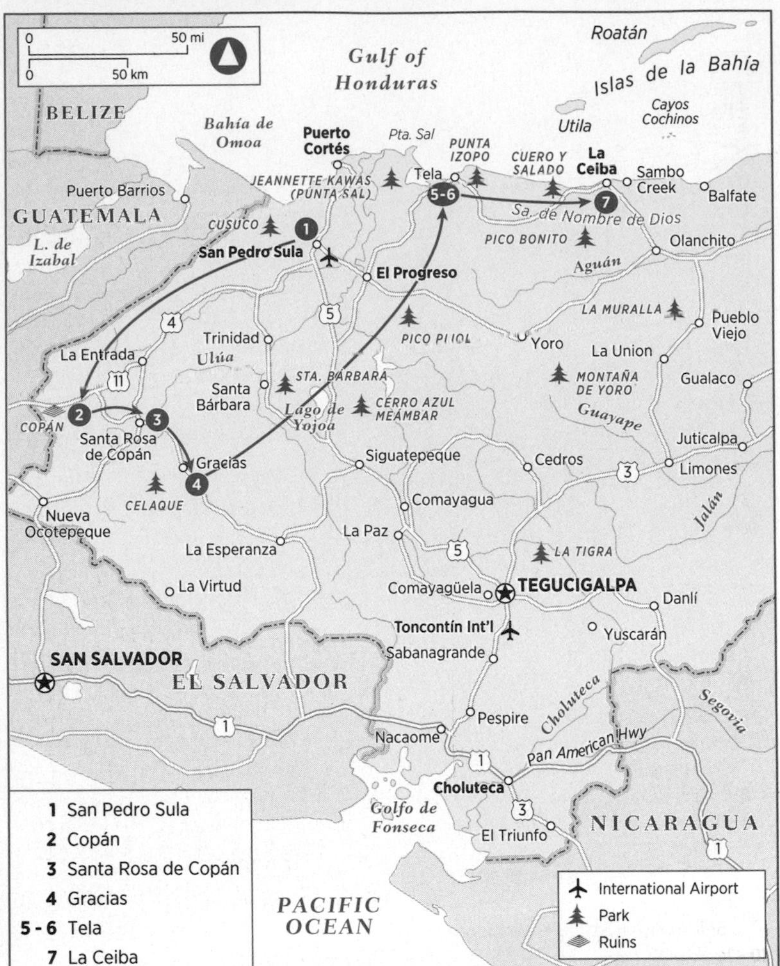

THE BEST OF HONDURAS IN 2 WEEKS

Two weeks in Honduras should give you plenty of time to hit many of the major sights, get you a little bit off the beaten track, and give you a few days to just relax. You'll have considerably more time so you can move at a slower pace—always a plus in Honduras. You'll be able to take in the beach, the rainforest, and even get your dive certification or have a traditional Caribbean island experience of sunbathing and rum drinks.

Day 1: Arrive in San Pedro Sula and Transfer to Copán ★★

Upon landing, transfer in San Pedro Sula, and head directly to the town of **Copán Ruínas.** Get settled in and just explore the town in the evening and listen to the adventure tales of other travelers over happy hour to prepare for the weeks ahead.

Days 2 & 3: Explore the Copán Valley ★★

Wake up early your first morning and get to the spectacular **Maya ruins** of Copán as soon as they open, well before the crowds begin to arrive. Have lunch at the park, and then check out the **Museum of Mayan Sculpture** and **Las Sepulturas** (p. 122). In the afternoon, take a leisurely stroll through the eco-trails of the jungle surrounding the ruins to look for coati, monkeys, blue morpho butterflies, motmots, and dozens of other rainforest creatures. Go back to the hotel, wash off the grime, change into a nice outfit, and head to **Hacienda San Lucas** (p. 125) for a five-course dinner accompanied by South American wines.

On day 2, head into the nearby mountains to visit one of the Chortí Maya communities. Watch as they show you their traditional ways of producing pottery and colorful cornhusk dolls.

In the afternoon, stop by the **Museo Regional de Arqueología Maya** (p. 123) and browse the handicraft markets for gifts or souvenirs.

Days 4, 5 & 6: Culture and Cloud Forest ★★

On day 4, head to the colonial town of **Gracias** (p. 134), once the capital of Central America. Drop off your bags and set out by private tour or your own vehicle to explore the small villages and centuries-old whitewashed churches along **La Ruta Lenca** (p. 140). On day 5, set off early to begin your guided ascent through the cloud forest of **Montaña de Celaque National Park** (p. 139). Camp at the summit and make your way back down to town the following day with open eyes to spot the elusive resplendent quetzal. Upon your return to town, eat a traditional Lenca meal at **Rinconcito Graciano,** and then retreat to the municipal hot springs to soothe those aching muscles.

Days 7, 8 & 9: Birds & Brew

On your return north, stop off for a day at **Lago de Yojoa** (p. 105), basing yourself at the wonderful **D&D Brewery,** the country's first microbrewery. The next day, take an early morning bird-watching trip on the lake or head up in the hills at **Cerro Azul Meámbar National Park** or **Santa Bárbara National Park** (p. 106 and p. 107).

Transfer from Lago de Yojoa to **La Ceiba** in time for a Garífuna lunch at **Chef Guity's.** Spend your afternoon kayaking at **Cacao lagoon** (p. 167) or hiking in **Pico Bonito National Park** (p. 174).

On your second day in La Ceiba, head out to **Cuero y Salado Wildlife Refuge** (p. 166), a massive estuary with almost 200 species of birds and other rare wildlife such as caimans, West Indian manatees, ocelots, monkeys, and sloths. You'll explore the canals and mangrove forest in what is without a doubt one of the most important natural reserves in Honduras by boat from the visitor center at Salado Barra.

Days 10–14: The Bay Islands ★★★

Now that you have hiked plenty and spent a good deal of time visiting national parks and major attractions, it's time to kick back and relax in the Caribbean sun and surf. From La Ceiba, catch a ferry or plane for a short trip to Roatán, the most developed of the **Bay Islands** (p. 187). Here, you can explore **West End Beach** (p. 199) and dive on the world's second largest barrier reef. In 3 or 4 days, you can attain a basic PADI dive certification or head to **Anthony's Key** (p. 194) for an introductory dolphin training course, and still have free afternoons to do leisurely beach activities. If you are looking for a little action, take part in zip-line canopy tours or look for pirate booty in the sea caves on the east end of the island.

THE BEST OF HONDURAS FOR FAMILIES

Parents and families that bring young or teenage children to Honduras are often surprised at the number of activities available to please everyone. Many of the activities are secretly educational, but kids won't care because most of them are downright cool. Wildlife and nature tends to always be a good bet, and this itinerary will take you both above and below the surface to appreciate it. Museums and touring ruins can be hit or miss, depending on the kids, so be careful not to overload them. The following itinerary encompasses several country highlights, such as the ruins, the rainforest, the big city, and the beach.

Day 1: Settling in the Capital

Arrive in **Tegucigalpa** (p. 60) and get settled into your hotel. Take it easy the first day by taking in **Chiminike,** an interactive science museum, which has a giant Operator game and a crawl through an intestinal tract (complete with fart noises). Next, take in the views of the capital and surrounding mountains from **Parque Naciones Unidas El Picacho.** There's a small on-site zoo with exotic rainforest animals from across the country—like monkeys, snakes, and macaws—that will be a primer on the creatures you'll soon be seeing in the wild.

Days 2, 3 & 4: Ruins & Museums

On your second day, transfer to the town of **Copán Ruínas** (p. 117) via the scenic highway past the villages and junco palm handicraft stands in the **Santa Bárbara** area. Get settled in after the long drive and spend the evening wandering around town and peeking in the markets. Eat some typical foods like *pupusas* at **Comedor y Pupuseria** Mary. Spend the next 2 days exploring the Maya ruins, visiting with the **Chortí Maya communities** outside of town on horseback, and soaking in the nearby hot springs. Don't forget a visit to **Casa K'inich,** the Maya children's museum where kids can learn about the Mayas' ancient ball courts.

Days 5–8: Adventure & Wildlife

At the start of day 5, transfer to the town of **La Ceiba** (p. 162), on the North Coast. Check into an eco-lodge in **Pico Bonito National Park** (p. 174), either the ritzy Pico Bonito Lodge, a yoga and raw-food retreat next door, or a waterfall-facing suite across the street. You'll spend the next several days in one of the most biologically diverse places on the planet—and a place with an array of adventurous activities that promises not to disappoint children of any age. You can whitewater raft down the Río Cangrejal, hike along rainforest trails, swim in waterfalls, go zip-lining, go bird-watching, and visit a serpentarium or a butterfly farm.

Days 9, 10 & 11: Snorkeling & Deserted Islands

From La Ceiba, transfer by boat to the **Cayos Cochinos** (p. 178), or Hog Islands. This pristine archipelago is home to numerous uninhabited islands and is a nature reserve. Base yourself at the one lodge here, **Plantation Beach Resort** (p. 180). Whether your kids want to dive or snorkel, they won't be disappointed with one of the most unspoiled sections of the world's second-largest barrier reef. Some might just be satisfied keeping lazy on the idyllic beaches or hiking around the trails on the island of **Cochino Grande.**

On day 11, transfer back to La Ceiba and then to San Pedro Sula to connect with an international flight home.

Honduras for Families

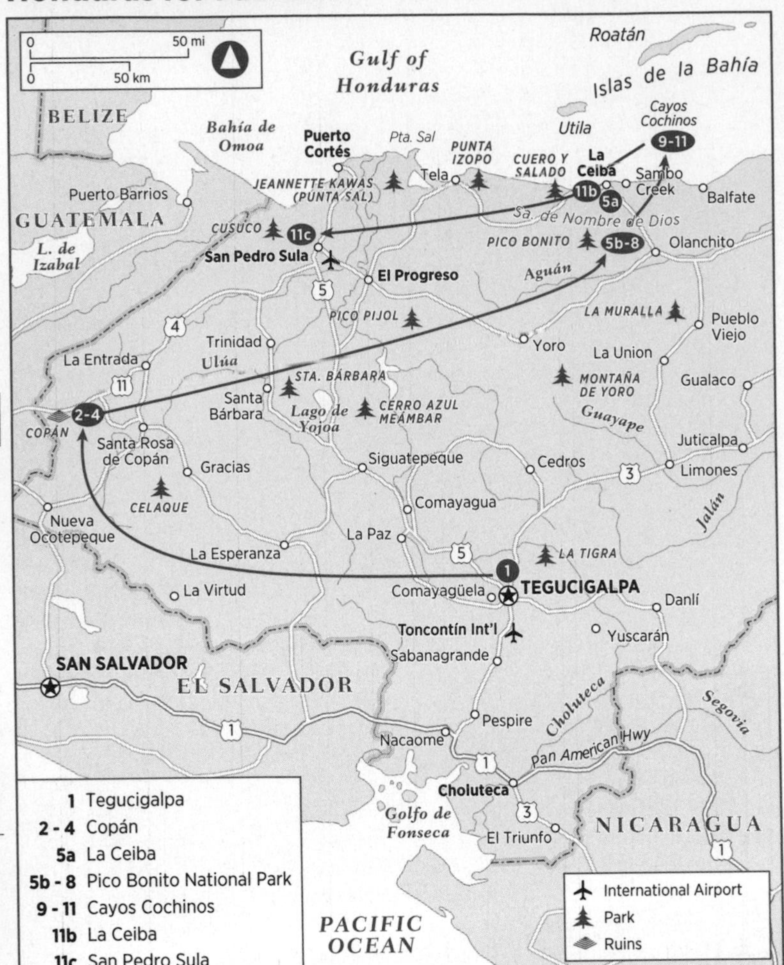

THE ULTIMATE BAY ISLANDS DIVE TRIP

The Bay Islands are much more than a dive destination now, but that doesn't mean you don't need to dive. Hardcore enthusiasts spend months at a time here checking out the reef at some of the lowest prices anywhere in the world. For many, this isn't their first trip, and they mix new dive spots with their favorites. New divers will rejoice in low fees and a wide range of dives for every skill level. This itinerary brings you to many of the top dive spots on Roatán and Utila, with ample time to take classes or side trips to other islands and still have time to take in some other island attractions.

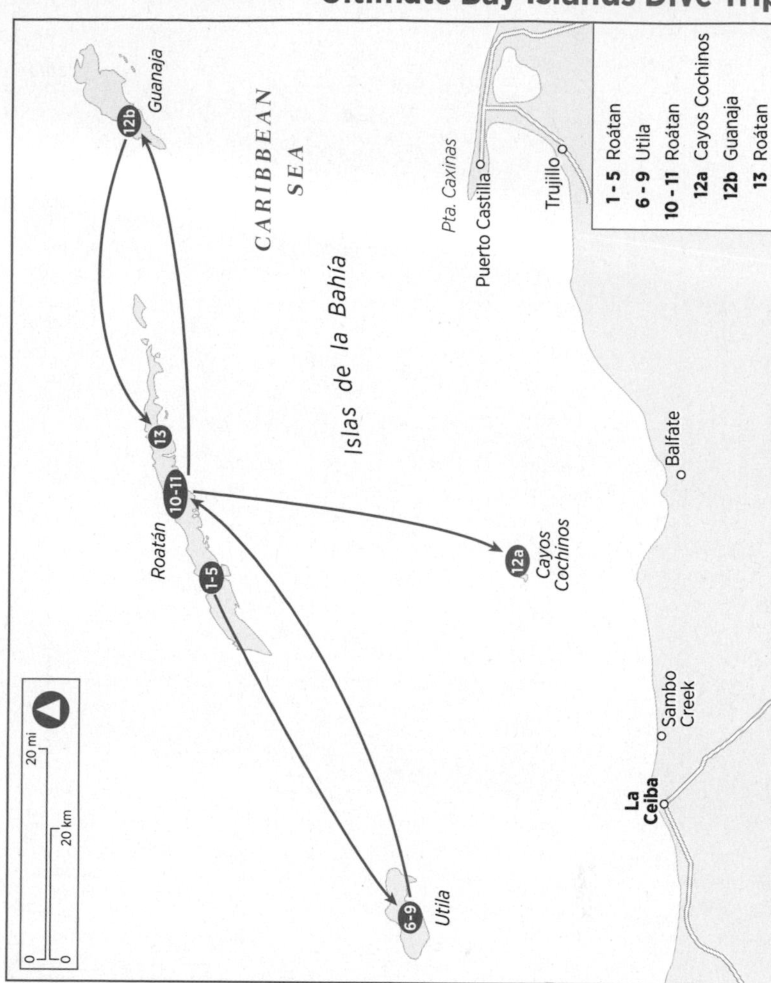

Day 1: Arriving Island Style

Arrive directly to **Roatán** (p. 187) or transfer from **La Ceiba** by either ferry or regional jet. Settle into your resort and get your first taste of the island life with a plate of seafood beside the water and a potent cocktail.

Days 2–5: Come on Baby, Don't Fear the Reef

If you have yet to dive or still consider yourself a beginner, don't hesitate to get your basic certification. In 3 or 4 days, you can attain your basic certification or, if it has been a while, just brush up your skills in the 80°F (27°C) water. The island is surrounded by more than 150 dive sites ranging from crevices and caves to wrecks and walls. Many are directly off shore and easily accessible to tourists. **Mary's Place** (p. 193), near Sarah Cay, is one of the most popular here and showcases a series of tunnels, walls, and canyons filled with black groupers, gorgonians, and large bearded fire worms. Don't miss **Spooky Channel** (p. 193) on the northwest shore for the abundant coral and sea whips. For wreck diving, try either the **Prince Albert** (p. 193) or **El Aguila** (p. 193), both of which are frequented by an array of rare marine life.

Days 6–9: A True Dive Village

Either by plane or by ferry, transfer over to **Utila** (p. 214) for a completely different dive-town vibe. Stay on the island's one town, East Harbour, or on one of the dive resorts on the desolate south coast, and take your pick of more than 130 or so buoyed dive sites, such as CJ's Drop Off, the Black Hills, or Pretty Bush. For a once-in-a-lifetime experience, sign up for a trip to spot and swim with whale sharks, which can be seen year-round in the Cayman channel off Utila.

Days 10, 11 & 12: More Sun & Sand

Head back to **Roatán** for a few more days. Maybe take a full-day dive trip to the **Cayos Cochinos** (p. 178) or **Guanaja** (p. 226), the other Bay Island. Maybe take an underwater photography or rescue diver course. If you are tired of diving at this point, you can spend a few days just hanging out on West Bay beach, swim with dolphins at Anthony's Key, take a canopy tour, or explore the mangroves over on the east end.

Day 13: Hasta Luego

When you are done with paradise—both below and above the surface—head back home.

LA MOSQUITIA & BEYOND

Much of Honduras remains relatively off the beaten track, but nowhere is more isolated and unexplored than La Mosquitia. The region has everything to tempt the adventurous spirit: several endangered indigenous groups, the three longest rivers in the country, biosphere reserves, empty beaches, rare wildlife, little-known archeological sites, and the lure of lost cities. Pair it with a short trip to an authentic part of the North Coast for an itinerary few have ever tackled.

Day 1: Settle In

Arrive at **La Ceiba** (p. 162) via road or regional jet from the international airport at San Pedro Sula. Take it easy for your first day and buy any last-minute supplies.

Days 2 & 3: *Bienvenidos* a la Mosquitia

The next morning, fly to the adjoined Miskito villages of **Raista** and **Belén** (p. 240), on the storied Mosquito Coast. If you're on a budget, make the full-day overland trip from La Ceiba via Tocoa and Palacios. Be welcomed properly to the region with a Miskito dance performance near a beachside bonfire with a traditional meal.

On day 3, take a boat trip across the **Laguna de Ibans** to **Parú** and **Banaka Creeks** (p. 240) to search for manatees, caimans, and an assortment of other wildlife. If you really want to get your hands dirty, an alternative is a half-day jungle survival course where you will learn the basics of medicinal plants and the lay of the land.

Days 4–7: Exploring the Unknown

By *pipante* canoe, head down the Río Plátano to the Pech and Miskito village of **Las Marías** (p. 242) in the heart of the UNESCO World Heritage **Río Plátano Biosphere Reserve** (p. 242). Base yourself at a small Pech *hospedaje,* and take day or multiday trips to different parts of one of the most incredible and least visited areas of wilderness in Central America. The most common trip is upriver to the mysterious **Walpaulban Sirpi petroglyphs** (p. 243), but there is much more to see. The 2-night/3-day round-trip guided hike to the top of the dramatic spire of **Pico Dama,** or the 2-day guided hike to **Pico Baltimore,** will give you unparalleled views of the surrounding jungle and provide ample opportunities to spot wildlife—though these are two moderately tough hikes that you won't soon forget.

Days 8 & 9: Bruuuuuuuuus!

Hire a boatman to take you to the frontier town of **Brus Laguna** (p. 245). Unless you want to fish for tarpon, you will set off to the Yamari Cabañas in the strangely placed savannah in the middle of the jungle. Here, you can kayak and inner tube across the swampland and canals in search of bird life. On your last day, before catching a flight to La Ceiba from the town airstrip, explore the British fort at Cannon Island.

Days 10 & 11: One Last Bit of Excitement

Upon your transfer back to La Ceiba, make your way to the blossoming Garífuna village of **Sambo Creek** (p. 172) for a few days of seafood stew and adventure excursions like canopy tours and beachside horseback riding. When you're ready, transfer back to San Pedro Sula for your flight home.

THE ADRENALINE-PUMPING ADVENTURE VACATION

Maybe it is the overflow from Costa Rica, but this Central American country is rapidly expanding the options for heart-pounding adventure sports. The North Coast, especially in the vicinity of La Ceiba, is the epicenter of activity, but intense hikes, canopy tours, and kayak trips can be found almost anywhere in the country. This itinerary takes you through some of the most popular excursions and one spectacular multiday trek that is rarely attempted.

Day 1: Next Stop, Wonderland

Arrive in La Ceiba via connecting flight or ground transfer from the international airport at San Pedro Sula. Settle in any of the small eco-lodges along the **Río Cangrejal** in the buffer zone of **Pico Bonito National Park** (p. 174) and simply soak in your first day of rainforest living.

Day 2: A Whitewater Paradise

The next morning, begin your assault on Honduras by undertaking the fastest whitewater in the country. The **Class III–V rapids on the Río Cangrejal** (p. 175) allow for some of the finest whitewater rafting in Central America and take you through one of the most biodiverse regions in the country. If you are inexperienced, you can opt for a lighter section of the river for a shorter run.

Day 3: Adrenaline Junkies Get Their Fix

Your next full day in the Pico Bonito area can be filled with a half-dozen or so different adventure excursions. Maybe in the morning you will take a guided hike to **El Bejuco,** a thundering 91m (299-ft.) waterfall, and after lunch add a

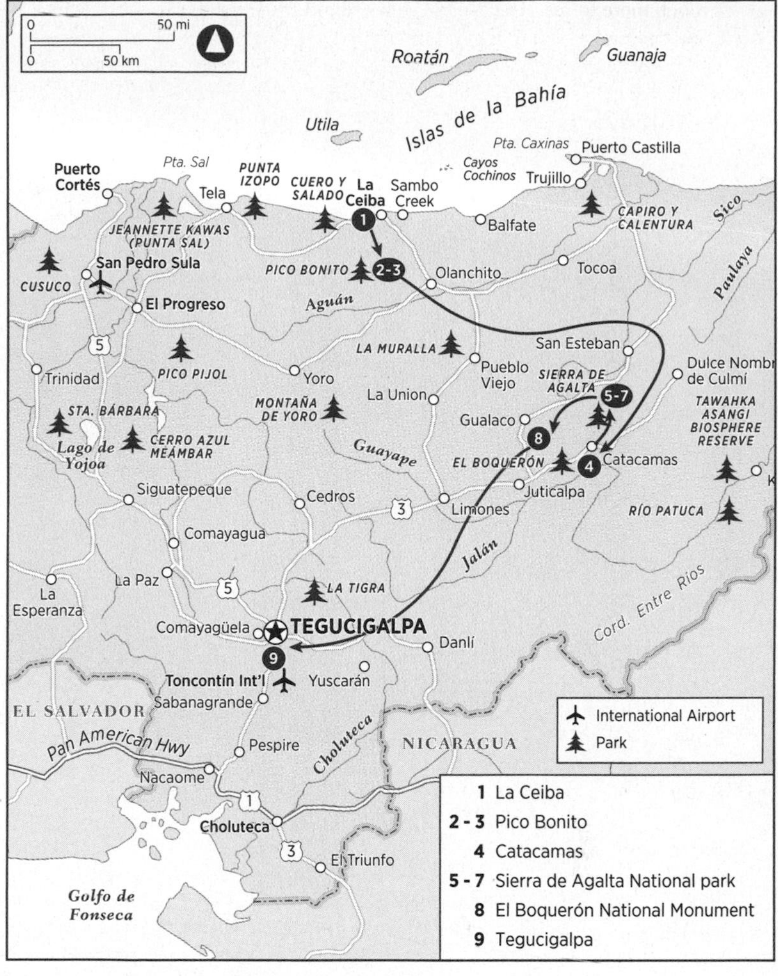

canopy tour, go climbing and rappelling, ride horseback, soak in a hot spring, or kayak in the nearby Cacao lagoon towards the coast.

Days 4–7: Reaching the Peak

Wake up early for the long drive through the mountains and forests of Olancho to the wild cowboy town of **Catacamas** (p. 257). Get your rest, because next morning, day 5, you'll be trekking into the depths of Sierra de Agalta National Park to the summit of the 2,354m (7,723-ft.) **Pico La Picucha** (p. 258); the trail begins at none other than the **Cave of the Glowing Skulls** (p. 259). You'll encounter toucans; a few monkeys; blue morpho butterflies; and if you're lucky, a tapir or a jaguar as you tramp your way across the tropical forests. You will camp 2 nights, giving you ample time to search out wildlife and still get down to the base in the afternoon on day 7.

Day 8: Exploring the Unexplored

While you are nearby, you might as well check out the 4,000 hectares (9,884 acres) of primary and secondary forests at **El Boquerón National Monument.** Follow the one large loop trail through the 1,433m (4,701-ft.) peak of Cerro Agua Buena and be back in town in time for dinner.

Day 9: Leaving on a Jet Plane

Catch a ride to either Tegucigalpa or San Pedro Sula for your flight home.

BEST OF TEGUCIGALPA & THE SOUTH

A business trip to the capital or a stopover as you drive along the Pan American highway can very easily be turned into a fine Honduras getaway. While the chaotic capital may not take much of your time on this itinerary, several quiet retreats and attractions are within a short drive.

Day 1: Land & Unload

Arrive in the capital of **Tegucigalpa** (p. 60) and settle in to your hotel.

Day 2: When in Rome

After breakfast, head straight for **Parque Morazán** (p. 64) downtown, the heart of the city. Check out the baroque **Cathedral** on the square, and then move to the more immaculate **Iglesia de Nuestra Señora de los Dolores.** If you have time, take in a museum such as the **National Identity Museum** or **National Art Gallery,** and then make your way up Paseo La Leona in **Barrio Buenos Aires** to watch the sunset over the sprawling city. Finish your day at the rustic El Patio restaurant, known for its Honduran cuisine.

Day 3: A Day Trip to the Jungle

Either camp in, stay in a rustic cabin near, or return to the city at night, but for the best experience, leave at the crack of dawn to reach **Parque Nacional La Tigra** (p. 76), a 238-sq.-km (92 sq.-mile) cloud forest park just 22km (14 miles) from Tegus. Hike around, and you might just spot a resplendent quetzal, puma, or agouti.

Day 4: Shopping in the Highlands

More laidback than a mountainous hike is a trip to the serene highland retreat of **Valle de Ángeles** and the 18th-century Spanish mining town of **Santa Lucía** (p. 80). These colonial villages are beloved by *capitalinos* for their cool climates, lazy cobblestone streets, and whitewashed houses with clay tile roofs. While you can hike to nearby waterfalls or go horseback riding, the main activity here is shopping. The streets are filled with small shops selling some of the best-quality handicrafts from around the country.

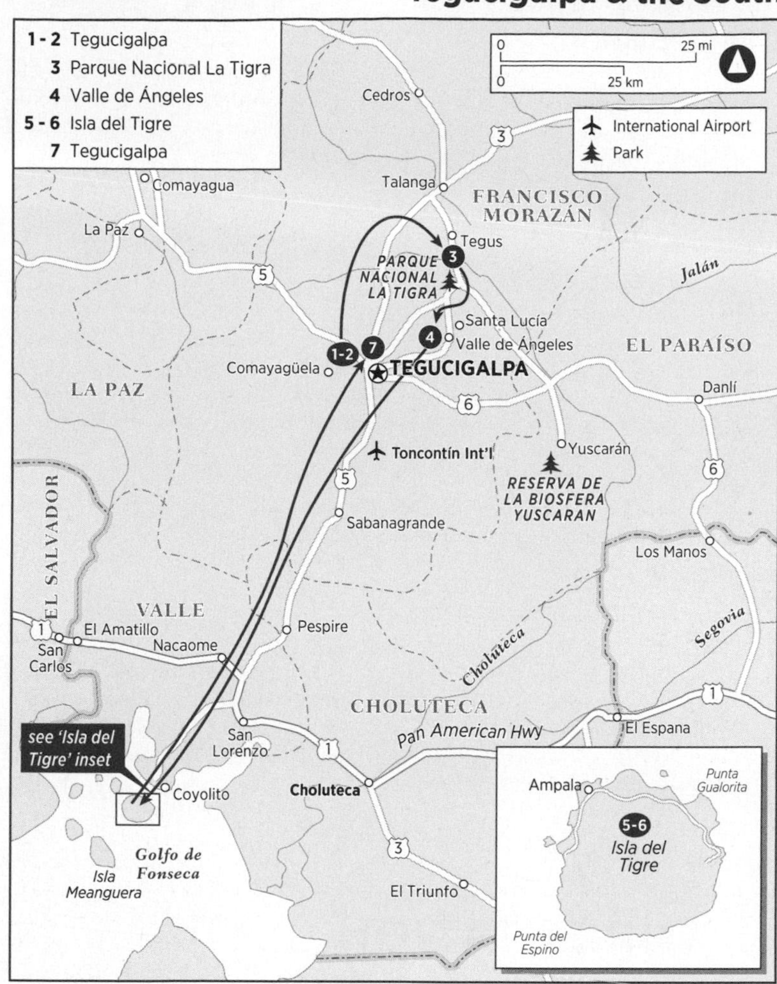

Days 5 & 6: An Island Breeze

For your last few days, head south to the Pacific coast to **Isla del Tigre** (p. 88). You'll feel like you stepped back in time as you walk past the colorful clapboard houses in the town of **Amapala.** Dine on fresh fish all you want and relax on several empty beaches—white or black sand—that see no more than a few visitors a week.

Day 7: Heading Home

Catch a skiff back to the mainland and back north to **Tocontín International** for your flight home.

TEGUCIGALPA

5

Many travelers would rather not try to pronounce the name of the capital of Honduras, let alone visit it. (By the way, it's pronounced "Te-goo-si-gal-pa".) Don't take whatever horror stories you have heard about Central American capitals too seriously, though. While it isn't a favorite tourist destination like Copán, the North Coast, or the Bay Islands, Tegus, as Hondurans call it, is actually a fairly pleasant place if you can get past the smog, shanty towns, and traffic. While it was long believed that the name was a Nahuatl word meaning "silver mountain," that is not likely the case. This was likely a ploy by developers hoping to lure miners and settlers to populate the city in the mid 1500s. The meaning of the name is more clearly defined as "place of colored stones."

The city sits snugly in a valley at about 1,000m (3,281 ft.), sheltering it from the sweltering heat that plagues San Pedro Sula and La Ceiba. There are several great museums and churches within the colonial center, a great clump of cloud forest nearby, and the largest cathedral in the country and a revered pilgrimage site only minutes from the center.

Tegucigalpa was founded on September 29, 1578, but it wasn't until 1880 that President Marco Aurelio Soto moved the capital here from Comayagua. In 1938, the city of Comayagüela was incorporated into Tegucigalpa and nearly doubled the size, which today stands at over 1 million inhabitants.

The city is no longer the economic center of the country (that honor now belongs to San Pedro Sula), and there is no major industry here now that the mines have closed, but as the capital and second-largest city in Honduras, it's still an important area for commerce and politics.

ORIENTATION

Getting There

BY AIR Although most international travelers fly into the larger San Pedro Sula Airport, Tegucigalpa's **Tocontín International Airport** (TGU; ✆ **504/2234-2402**) does have a few international routes. **American Airlines** (✆ **504/2220-7585**), **Continental Airlines** (✆ **504/2550-7124**), **Delta** (✆ **800/791-1000**), and **TACA** (✆ **504/2221-6495**) all land here from North American destinations.

Regional airlines serving the capital are **Taca Regional Airlines** (✆ **504/2281-8220;** www.flyislena.com), **Aerolíneas Sosa** (✆ **504/2443-2519;** www.aerolineasosahn.com), **Lanhsa Airlines** (✆ **504/9486-2145;** www.lanhsa.com), and **CM Airlines** (✆ **504/2234-1886;** www.cmairlines.com). There are direct flights to Roatán, La Ceiba, and San Pedro, while other destinations connect in La Ceiba.

Tegucigalpa

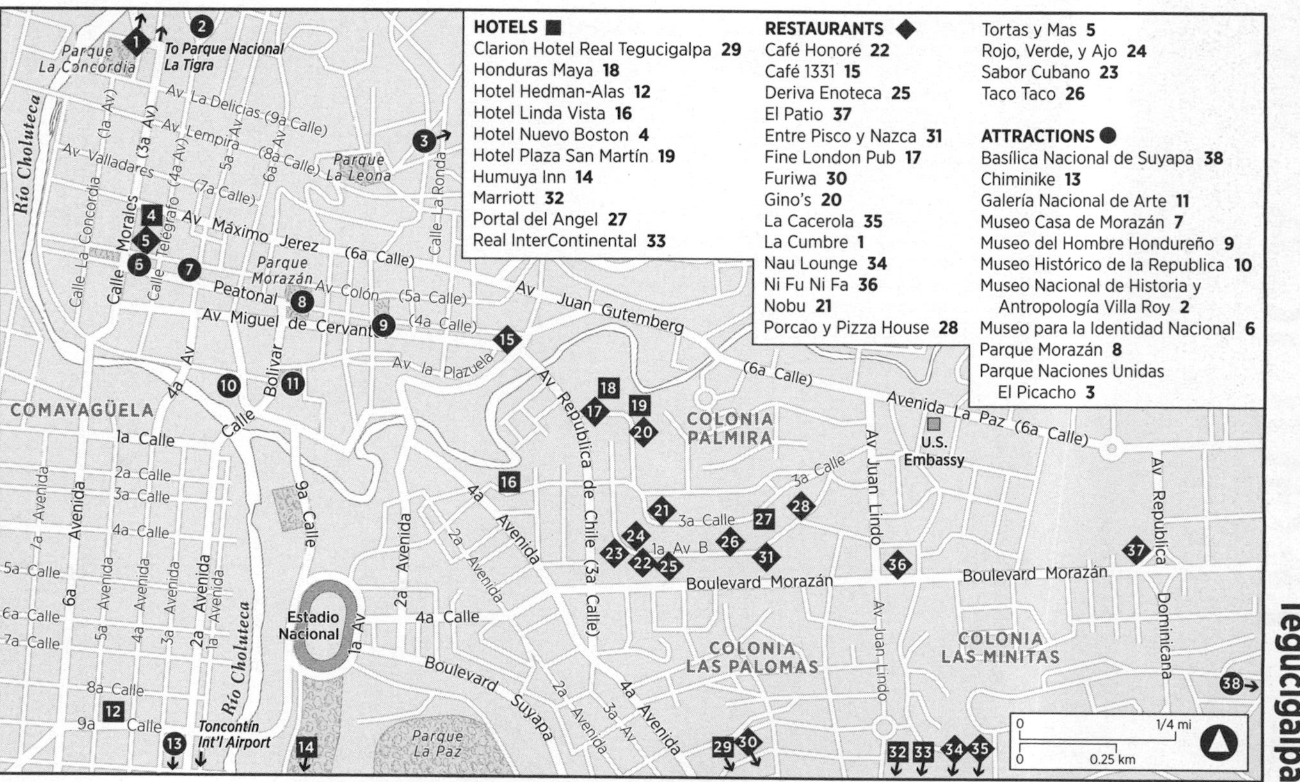

Tocontín Toils

After a TACA airlines jet carrying 124 passengers overshot the runway at Tegucigalpa's Tocontín International Airport and crashed in May 2008, killing five people, the airport was shut down for more than 6 weeks and was being considered for permanent closure. Many have long considered the airport one of the world's most dangerous because of the short runway and the proximity of nearby hills. While recent years have seen improvements to the terminal and general facilities, there is ongoing talk of building a new airport in a different location. Technology may just save Tocontín, though. In December 2008, new Delta B737-700 aircrafts—designed for short runways, extreme temperatures, and higher altitudes—began flying to the troubled airport 5 days a week from Atlanta.

Tocontín has just one ATM, a craft shop, a call center, and a small cafe—but little else. The airport is 6km (3¾ miles) south of the center on the highway to Choluteca. A taxi to downtown or Boulevard Morazán will be about L200 to L250. Alternatively, you can catch a northbound bus or collective taxi to the center of town for L20 right outside the main airport gates; just listen for the touts shouting "Te-goose."

BY CAR If you are exploring nearby regions or other parts of the country, renting a car can be a good and even economical idea. The highways leading to/from the city are generally in good condition, particularly the excellent CA 5 that runs to San Pedro Sula. You have to keep a close eye out for potholes and the occasional herd of cows, but compared to more rural parts of the country the roads are good.

Tegucigalpa is right on the CA 5, which ends 241km (150 miles) away in San Pedro Sula (3½–4 hr.), passing Lago de Yojoa, Siguatepe, and Comayagua en route. CA 5 also heads south to Choluteca, where you can connect with CA 1, or the Pan-American Highway that runs to El Salvador, Nicaragua, and beyond.

The CA 11-A road to Copán is a jaw-dropping route through the mountains, which is windy, mostly unpaved, and sometimes impassable due to rain. Many drivers prefer to head back toward San Pedro Sula and catch Hwy. 20 through Santa Barbara before hitting the lake.

If you're heading to the North Coast, you have two options: one is to go back to San Pedro Sula, and the other is an unpredictable route through the wild Olancho region that is prone to highway robberies and poor roads. Most choose the former.

Car-rental agencies are located both at the airport and in town. Companies include **Advance** (beside the Institute of Tourism, Col. San Carlos; ✆ **504/2235-9528;** www.advancerentacar.com), **Avis** (Edificio Marinakys at Blvd. Suyapa; ✆ **504/2239-5712;** www.avis.com), **Payless** (Edificio Saenz at Blvd. Europea; ✆ **504/2245-7054**), and **Hertz** (Centro Commercio Villa Real; ✆ **504/2235-8582;** www.hertz.com).

BY BUS Although Tegucigalpa doesn't have a main bus terminal, most of the bus companies have terminals within a few blocks of each other in the Comayagüela section of town. Because this neighborhood isn't safe, use caution getting there and do not leave your baggage unattended.

Hedman Alas (13a Calle and Av. 11; ✆ **504/2237-7143**), has luxury service four times a day to San Pedro Sula (3½–4 hr.; L505), where connections can then be made to Copán, Tela, or La Ceiba. **Viana Clase de Oro** (Blvd. FFAA, at the Esso station; (✆ **504/2225-6584**), runs five first- and economy-class buses daily to San Pedro Sula, between 6:30am and 6pm (L450–L780), that continue on to La Ceiba.

Other options for getting to San Pedro include the operator **Saenz** (Centro Comercial Perisur; ✆ **504/2233-4229**), which has regular and first-class, nonstop service six times a day to the capital (L456), along with **El Rey Express** (Banco Central; ✆ **504/2237-8561**), which stops in Comayagua, as well as San Pedro (L418). For La Ceiba (7 hr. away; L475), try the operator **Cristina** (✆ **504/2441-2028**), which departs five times a day between 5:30am and 3:30pm. **San Miguel Plus** (✆ **504/233-4851;** sanmiguelplus@gmail.com) has three daily trips from Tegucigalpa to Tela, which continue on to La Ceiba (L450).

Travelers crossing the El Salvador and Nicaragua borders have several options. To get to El Amatillo (3½ hr.; L140) on the El Salvador border, you have to catch one of the buses leaving from the Mercado Mayoreo, southwest of Comayagüela on the highway to Olancho. For the Nicaraguan border at El Paraíso (2 hr.; L120) via Danlí, try **Discua Litena** (Mercado Jacaleapa; ✆ **504/2230-0470**), which leaves every hour from 6:30am to 7:30pm.

If you're traveling elsewhere in Central America, your best choice is **Tica Bus** (16a Calle and Av. 5; ✆ **504/2220-0579;** www.ticabus.com), a company that has daily departures to San Salvador (6½ hr.; L950), Managua (7–8 hr.; L1,045), Guatemala City (14 hr.; L1,140), and journeys as far as Mexico and Panama. Also, for San Salvador, there's **King Quality** (6 hr.; L760; ✆ **504/2225-5415;** www.king-qualityca.com), at Boulevard Comunidad Economica Europea in Comayagüela, which has business class service twice a day with meals on board and free Wi-Fi (in Clase King). From San Salvador, they have connections throughout Central America, as well.

Visitor Information

The **Instituto Hondureño de Turismo** (Av. Cruz and Calle Mexico; ✆ **504/2220-1600;** www.letsgohonduras.com; Mon–Fri 7:30am–4:30pm) has friendly English-speaking staff who can provide general information and give you a copy of the excellent bilingual guide, *Honduras Tips.*

City Layout

Tegucigalpa is one of the few colonial cities in Central America that does not follow a typical Spanish layout with a grid of streets surrounding a central square, mostly because of the uneven surface of the city. The colonial center of the city is more of a narrow strip on a central grid of about 7 by 20 blocks, and there are several squares—the largest is Parque Morazán, or the Parque Central. The city's pedestrian-only street, **Calle Peatonal,** leads west from this square, and other main streets and avenues run into or parallel to it.

Most of the city's museums, churches, and artisan shops can be found within 6 blocks of Parque Central, too. From the center, the majority of the city branches out towards the south and the east. The commercial center and where you will find the best hotels, restaurants, and shops is Colonia Palmira, mostly on the north side of the fast food–lined Boulevard Morazán and in neighboring Colonia San Carlos. West of the Río Choluteca, a river that divides the city, and southwest of the center is the neighborhood of Comayagüela, where most of the city's bus terminals can be found; this is a poorer, less safe part of town.

Neighborhoods in Brief

The Colonial Center ★★ The colonial center (or downtown), while dirty, crowded, noisy, and dangerous at night, is hit or miss. Some can ignore the grime and chaos for the finer points and history, while others cannot. **Parque Morazán,** or Parque Central, is the epicenter of all activity in the city's colonial center, and nearly all important museums and churches can be found within a few blocks of it, as can the fast food chains and clothes shops for the fashion unconscious. There are hotels here, although few are worth staying in unless you are a backpacker with a non-existent budget.

Colonia Palmira and Colonia San Carlos East of downtown are these middle and upper class residential communities that are home to the majority of hotels, most popular restaurants, trendiest clubs, and a variety of shopping boutiques. This is the commercial heart and center of tourist facilities, such as embassies, airline offices, and travel agencies. Much of the action sits within a few blocks on either side of Boulevard Morazán.

Comayagüela This sprawling, slum-like neighborhood west of the Río Choluteca was once a city of its own, until it was absorbed into the Distrito Central in 1938. While home to numerous colonial buildings, most are falling apart and neglected. Apart from going to a bus terminal, there is really no need to visit here or stay here. It's quite a dangerous area, actually—so don't walk here alone, and take taxis to get in and out at night. The largest market in Tegucigalpa, the **San Isidro market,** which sprawls into the streets surrounding it, can be found here. Also, don't confuse Comayagüela with Comayagua. They are nothing alike. Comayagua is a colonial city off the highway to San Pedro Sula that is home to the country's largest Semana Santa festivities in Central America (see p. 114).

Boulevard Juan Pablo II and Southern Districts The area east of Parque La Paz and to the south of Boulevard Morazán holds numerous upscale residential districts that sit near the boulevards of Juan Pablo II and Suyapa. This is an area of some of the most recent development and where you can find the very best hotels, such as the Intercontinental, and the Multiplaza Mall complex, which is surrounded by massive international stores and restaurant chains, like any North American suburban shopping complex. It may lack Honduran character, but to businessmen in and out on quick trips who are only seeking comfort, it is the prime choice.

Suyapa Suyapa is a small city to the east of Tegucigalpa that has been eaten by the capital's urban sprawl. It is best known for the massive Santuario Nacional and Basílica de Suyapa, where the country's holiest Catholic shrine, the Virgin of Suyapa, is kept.

GETTING AROUND

ON FOOT Much of Tegucigalpa can be explored on foot. The colonial center and Colonia Palmira are all safe and secure during the day, though you should stick to taxi cabs during the night and never travel alone, just to be sure.

BY TAXI Taxis are cheap, plentiful, and far safer for getting between neighborhoods than walking or taking the public buses. Traveling within the center is usually less than L80.

BY CAR If you are just staying in Tegucigalpa for the duration of your trip, you likely do not need a rental car. Driving in Tegucigalpa is simply a mess. Most streets are one-way, and lanes are often nonexistent, particularly in the center. Traffic in Tegucigalpa tends to always be ferocious. Rarely are you alone on a street, and horns

Driving Tips

The most common problem that North American drivers in Honduras (and the rest of Latin America, for that matter) have is being a defensive driver. While in North America, you can drive in a lane and expect that a car won't try to push you out of your lane; that's not the case here. If you are not ready with your horn to maintain your lane, other cars will run you right off the road or into another vehicle. Do not be afraid to use your horn, and use your full concentration when driving.

are used at all times. It seems that some people even think that pounding the horn will get a stoplight to turn green. It won't. Sticking to taxis will avoid the frustrations of driving in the crowded city streets and finding places to park.

Most hotels in the capital have gated parking lots for visitors to use, usually free of charge, though you might need to get a stamp from the front desk. In upscale restaurants, usually there is either a valet attendant or a guy in front of the restaurant who will direct you to a spot. Parking elsewhere is where it gets tricky. Downtown, there are few parking lots or garages, so many end up parking on the streets, though this is usually illegal. It is not recommended to park downtown, especially at night, as break-ins are common. In malls, there are usually parking lots or garages, though they are so popular that you often need to wait around until a spot opens up. In some cases, you may park, and someone with a neon vest or reflector jacket will wave at you or possibly help you out of your car. He is there to watch your car and expects a small tip—just L10 to L20 will suffice—when you return.

[FastFACTS] TEGUCIGALPA

For additional practical information, see "Fast Facts: Honduras," p. 271.

Banks Most banks and ATMs are either downtown or along Boulevard Morazán, as well as in the malls and large hotels. **BAC** (Blvd. Morazán and Av. Cruz; Mon–Fri 9am–5pm, Sat 9am–noon) exchanges traveler's checks and has a 24-hour ATM, as does **Banco Atlántida** (Mon–Fri 9am–5pm; Sat 9am–noon) on Parque Central and **HSBC** (Mon–Fri 9am–5pm; Sat 9am–noon), with more than a dozen locations around town.

Currency Exchange There's an official currency exchange booth at the airport; less-official operations are on Calle Peatonal and in the Parque Morazán.

Drugstores Farma City (✆ **504/2232-7949**), with locations on Boulevard Morazán, downtown, and elsewhere in the city, is one of the most reputable in the country.

Emergencies For **police** or **medical** emergencies, dial ✆ **199.** For **fire** emergencies, dial ✆ **198.**

Hospitals **Honduras Medical Center** (Av. Juan Lindo; ✆ **504/2216-1201**), one of the country's top hospitals, is open 24 hours, as is **Clinica Viera** (across from the Alcadia; ✆ **504/2237-3156**).

Internet Almost every hotel in Tegucigalpa has either Wi-Fi or a computer station in the hotel. Outside of hotels, the best cybercafes with cheap prices and fast speeds can be found in malls, such as Computeck in the Multiplaza Mall. Elsewhere, your other best bet is downtown during the daylight hours, where you'll find dozens of **small cybercafes** to choose from. Most are within a block or two of Plaza Morazán.

Laundry & Dry Cleaning Most hotels have some sort of laundry service, though independent operators will do it for far cheaper. One to try is **Super Jet** (Av. Juan Gutenberg, before it turns into Av. La Paz), which has same-day service for L40 per kilo.

Police The main police office is at 5a Av. and Av. Lempira; police can be reached by dialing ✆ **504/2779-0476** or 199.

Post Office The downtown post office (Mon–Fri 7:30am–6pm; Sat 8am–1pm) is at Avenidas Barahona and Calle El Telégrafo. There is also a **DHL** (✆ **504/2220-1800**) and **Mailboxes, Etc.** (✆ **504/2232-3184**) on Boulevard Morazán.

Safety Tegucigalpa, as a whole, is not a safe city. Parts, such as the center of town and Boulevard Morazán, are fine for strolling during the day, but don't flash any valuables like jewelry, cameras, or iPods. In other areas, especially in Comayagüela and around the bus terminals, walk with extreme caution and try to avoid walking alone. At night, always take taxis wherever you go.

Telephone **Hondutel** (Mon–Sat 8am–8pm; Sun 10am–4pm), 1 block off the park at Avenidas Colón and Calle El Telégrafo, offers international calls, although you can find cheap call service at any of the cybercafes found all over the colonial center.

Water Unless you are a fan of Montezuma's Revenge, do not drink the water from the tap. Bottled water is cheap and plentiful, and most hotels will even leave complimentary bottles in your room.

5 WHERE TO STAY

Accommodations in Tegucigalpa run the gamut: there's a little bit of everything. The majority of visitors stay in the midrange to pricier digs in Colonia Palmira, close to the majority of restaurants and nightspots. While most hotels in the city are a part of chains, there are several excellent boutique hotels and B&Bs in restored houses scattered about. The cheapest rooms, sometimes running less than US$20 per night, are found in the downtown area and around the bus stations. There is not a high season for hotels in the capital, though the better hotels geared towards business travelers, like the Marriot and Real InterContinental, are more likely to be filled during the week.

Very Expensive

Marriott Tegucigalpa ☺ While it's a step down from the Real InterContinental next door, the Tegucigalpa Marriott—formerly the Crowne Plaza—is more or less exactly what you would expect from the international chain: it's big, with lots of facilities, a nice pool that will please any family, a few good restaurants, and a great breakfast buffet (complimentary); but otherwise, it's nothing you haven't seen before. Like the Real InterContinental, it is out of the way of the center and most attractions, unless chain restaurants and an air-conditioned mall are on your itinerary.

Av. Roble, beside Multiplaza Mall. www.marriott.com. ✆ **504/2232-0033.** 153 units. L2,774 double; L3,325 executive room. Rates include breakfast. AE, DC, MC, V. **Amenities:** Restaurant; bar; fitness center; pool; spa. *In room:* A/C, TV, hairdryer, minibar, Wi-Fi (fee).

Portal del Angel ★★ Some laughed when the idea of a luxurious boutique hotel in Tegucigalpa was being floated around, but Portal del Angel has been up and running for a decade now. Why? Because it has style. It's both hip and elegant at the same time. Marble pillars and wrought-iron balconies paired with tropical plants and floors say tropical opulence in every way. Rooms are better yet, with lots of space, good lighting from large windows, parquet and caoba floors, and locally made hand-carved chests and furniture. The bar closes at 10pm, but that's late enough for a fine Honduran cigar and glass from their decent wine list. It's in the Zona Viva neighborhood, within a block from a handful of the city's top restaurants and bars. Check their website for weekend and spa specials.

Av. República del Perú 2115, Colonia Palmira. www.portaldelangelhn.com. ✆ **504/2239-6538.** 23 units. L1,900 double. MC, V. **Amenities:** Restaurant; bar; pool. *In room:* A/C, TV, Wi-Fi (fee).

Real InterContinental ★★★ The guiding principle behind this hotel, the top hotel in the city, is to make guests feel like they aren't even in Tegucigalpa. Upon entering the property, you are transported to a world of marble floors and pillars, vaulted ceilings, Moorish arches, shaded lounges, tropical plants in all the right places, and trendy bars and restaurants that are destinations unto themselves. Rooms, remodeled in 2005, now have flat-screen TVs, clock radios with MP3 connections, and an earthy decor punctuated by some tasteful jungle-themed art. Executive suites have computers with flat-screen monitors, cordless phones, fax machines, and DVD players. The biggest downside to the hotel, especially if you are here to visit museums, is that you are isolated well away from the center, albeit in an up-and-coming area with chain restaurants and a mall.

Av. Roble, beside Multiplaza Mall. www.ichotelsgroup.com. ✆ **504/2290-2700.** 157 units. L2,679 double; L7,695 suite. AE, DC, MC, V. **Amenities:** Restaurant; bar; fitness center; pool. *In room:* A/C, TV, hair dryer, minibar, Wi-Fi (fee).

Expensive

Honduras Maya ★ Standing proudly on the top of the hill in what could be considered the best location in Colonia Palmira, the 10-story Honduras Maya hotel and convention center is a favorite of both business travelers and tourists. Much of the hotel has been renovated in the past few years, which has definitely helped revive it. Don't worry, though; the Mayan designs on the boxy facade are still there. The rooms, comparable to the Marriott and Real Intercontinental, have all been given a facelift, as well. Corner rooms have windows on two sides and thus the best views, which on clear days at sundown, show the city in a beautiful glow. There are several terraces with restaurants and bars, as well as a few shops and an attached casino, the best in the capital. On weekends, the hotel often hosts weddings and private parties, and may fill up with people milling about with cocktails.

3a Calle & Av. República de Chile, Colonia Palmira. www.hotelhondurasmaya.com. ✆ **504/2280-5000.** 163 units. L1,710 double; L4,750 suite. Rates include breakfast. AE, MC, V. **Amenities:** 2 restaurants; bar; gym; pool; tennis courts. *In room:* A/C, TV, minibar, Wi-Fi (fee).

Hotel Plaza San Martín The Plaza San Martín is the original and largest of the four hotels owned by the same company on the hill with the Honduras Maya. The focus here is on the standard business traveler, not so much the tourist. None of the hotels will knock your socks off, but they have everything you need, though not necessarily everything you want. Recent renovations have kept the San Martín up to date. All of the guest rooms have the same sort of bland flowered decor and clunky wooden furniture, though it varies quite a bit in size and shape from room to room. All have kitchenettes. The 20 junior suites are only slightly more in cost, yet significantly bigger, with an added living area. A small art gallery with mostly Honduran works is a nice touch to an otherwise boring business facility.

Calle Las Acacias 1438, Colonia Palmira. www.dhpsm.com. ✆ **504/2238-4500.** 110 units. L2,280 double; L2,660 suite. Rates include breakfast. MC, V. Free parking. **Amenities:** Restaurant; bar; free airport transfers; health center. *In room:* A/C, TV, kitchenette, minibar, Wi-Fi (free).

Clarion Hotel Real Tegucigalpa ★ This recently remodeled hotel, 2 blocks from the Multiplaza Mall, is one of the best values for high-end visitors. With prices quite a bit lower, on average, than the Marriott or InterContinental, this is a hotel you might want to check out. It succeeds on many levels, including the deep red, brown, and white decor that blankets the guest rooms to the shiny gray marble bathrooms. An oversized pool area with a decent-sized sun deck gives the hotel a resort feel that, frankly, I didn't expect the Clarion could pull off. A classy restaurant and bar, a few shops, and even a small casino give you little reason to leave.

Juan Manuel Galvez 1521, Col. Alameda. www.clarionhotel.com. ✆ **504/2286-6000.** 167 units. L1,500 double. Rates include breakfast. MC, V. **Amenities:** Restaurant; bar; free airport transfers; fitness center; pool; spa; Wi-Fi (fee). *In room:* A/C, TV, hair dryer.

Humuya Inn ★ 🎁 First-rate service and a well-maintained property are what make this surprisingly under-recognized hotel great. Rooms and common areas are painted brightly and have high wood-beam ceilings and tile floors. Indigenous art is sprinkled throughout, lending the hotel a personal touch that some of the larger and more expensive chain hotels in town lack. Rooms are clean, decently sized, and have the same amenities as hotels that charge twice the price. Some have balconies. The only potential drawback is that the hotel is in a residential area, about 10 minutes from the city center. In my opinion, this is actually a plus, since it helps keep your stay quiet.

Colonia Humuya 1150. www.humuyainn.com. ✆ **504/2239-2206.** 9 doubles; 3 suites. L1,615 double; L1,995 suite. MC, V. **Amenities:** Restaurant. *In room:* A/C, TV, fridge (suites only), hair dryer, Wi-Fi (free).

Moderate

Hotel Linda Vista This bed-and-breakfast, owned by two local lawyers, has just six rooms clustered in a small compound in Colonia Palmira, a few blocks from the Honduras Maya (see above) and the Peace Corps offices. The rooms and hallways are attractive, with ceramic floors, colonial-style furnishings, and framed artwork, but the best feature is their grassy patio and gardens with pretty views *(linda vistas)* of the city, as the name of the hotel suggests.

Calle Las Acacias 1438, Colonia Palmira. www.lindavistahotel.net. ✆ **504/2238-0188.** 6 units. L1,160 double. Rates include breakfast. MC, V. Free parking. *In room:* A/C, TV, Wi-Fi (free).

Inexpensive

Hotel Hedman-Alas While the location in the somewhat unsafe neighborhood of Comayagüela isn't great for a long-term stay, this hotel is a good choice if you just want a place to crash for a night or two, or you have an early bus to catch. The best bus line in Honduras runs it, and their Tegucigalpa terminal is just a few blocks away. Rooms are secure, clean, and have TVs. There are certainly better, more attractive rooms to be found in the city, but not at this price.

4a Av., btw. 8a & 9a Calles, Comayagüela. www.hedmanalas.com. ✆ **504/2237-9333.** 19 units. L380 double. Rates include breakfast. No credit cards. *In room:* A/C, TV.

Hotel Nuevo Boston One of the few acceptable budget places to stay in the city center, the American-owned Nuevo Boston is just a few steps from the Iglesia Los Dolores (see p. 73). The black-and-white checker tile floors give the place a classic feel. The rooms surround two small stone courtyards and are pretty basic; there aren't even TVs. Those facing the street are bigger and have balconies, while those that face inside are dingier. Reliable hot water and clean private bathrooms are available, though, which is about all you can hope for in this price range.

Máximo Jerez 321, Downtown. ✆ **504/2237-9411.** 7 units. L370 streetside double; L300 interior double. No credit cards. *In room:* Fan.

WHERE TO EAT

Honduran food does not standout to many first-time visitors. Rice, beans, and tortillas accompany almost every plate, and often, the quality differs little between a streetside stand and high-end restaurant. Tegucigalpa's dining scene is considerably more varied when compared to the rest of the country, though it lacks the quality and depth of other Latin American capitals. A growing number of mediocre international casual chains are popping up in the city, but there are a few strong independent standouts serving sushi, Italian, Mexican, Peruvian, and other cuisines.

Expensive

La Cumbre Restaurant GERMAN/INTERNATIONAL This one isn't easy to get to without a car—it's out of town on the road to El Hatillo—but for those with a local friend or a rental, you won't be disappointed. The food dabbles between German and general international dishes like their mouthwatering Jägerschnitzel or pork medallions with mango chutney. Standards like surf n' turf and pepper steak are spot on, as well. You can sit in their indoor dining room, but if you are making the trip out here, sit on their stone patio—the view won't get much better. You can see the lights of almost the entire Tegucigalpa metropolitan area twinkling below.

Km 7.5 Carretera al Hatillo. ✆ **504/2211-9000.** AE, MC, V. Main courses L250–L450. Daily noon–9pm.

Deriva Enoteca ★★ SOUTH AMERICAN This hip wine and tapas bar (*enoteca* means wine bar in Italian) from San Pedro Sula has expanded to Tegucigalpa. It has taken the space of the old Mangosteen location. Their menu, mostly Peruvian and other South American fare, focuses on dishes such as meats and seafood that go well with wine and *pisco,* as well as a selection of ceviches. The wine list, concentrating on bottles from Chile and Argentina, is the most sophisticated in the capital.

Av Republica de Argentina 2001, Colonia Palmira. ✆ **504/2235-4979.** Main courses L190–L380. AE, MC, V. Mon–Sat 10am–9:30pm.

El Patio ★★ HONDURAN In operation for 3 decades, El Patio is legendary in the capital for its Honduran cuisine. The rustic atmosphere, complete with a brick patio and open grill, seems to have struck a chord with the populace and has attracted everyone from priests, presidents, and famous Honduran musicians. Grilled meats and chicken are the specialty, and are all served with French fries, plantains, or onion rings. There's also *anafres* (refried bean and cheese fondue in a clay pot), surf n' turf, *chuleta de cerdo* (pork chops), and a large *pinchos* menu. The small meat plates with kebabed chicken, beef, pork, shrimp, or chorizo are all prepared in a dozen different ways.

Near the end of Blvd. Morazán, Colonia Palmira. ✆ **504/2221-4141.** Main courses L150–L265. MC, V. Daily 11am–11pm.

Entre Pisco y Nazca ★ PERUVIAN Filling the desperate need for Peruvian food in Tegucigalpa, this classy restaurant, first born in San Pedro Sula, arrived in late 2010. They serve a mostly standard set of national Peruvian *criolla* plates like *cebiches* (raw fish marinated in lime juice), *tiraditos* (thin-sliced raw fish in a spicy sauce), or *causas* (a layered potato casserole). The cocktail list is mostly *pisco*-based (Peru's national spirit), like the *pisco sour* (available as an ice cream, too) or the *chilcano* (with ginger ale and angostura bitters). The atmosphere is rather plain, though it serves as a sort of blank canvas for the food.

Av Republica de Argentina 1943, Colonia Palmira. ✆ **504/2510-2752.** www.entrepiscoynazca.com. Main courses L150–L320. AE, MC, V. Mon–Sat noon–9:30pm.

Nau Lounge ★ SUSHI I usually avoid adding hotel restaurants here, but this sushi bar and lounge in the Real InterContinental attracts a steady stream of hip 20-to-50-somethings every night of the week. Tables trickle out from a sleek bar and onto the inner patio of the hotel. The menu is simple, just a few dozen rolls and types of sashimi, though they'll also let you order food from Factory, the hotel's steak and lobster restaurant a few steps away, which shares the same courtyard.

Av. Roble, beside Multiplaza Mall. ✆ **504/2290-2726.** Main courses L140–L440. AE, MC, V. Sun–Thurs noon–midnight; Fri & Sat noon–1am.

Ni Fu Ni Fa ARGENTINEAN This Argentinean-style steakhouse is one of the current hotspots in Colonia Palmira. Thick slabs of beef—mostly high-quality imported cuts, including multi-person combination platters with chorizo, pork, ribs, and steak—are the modus operandi here. There's also a nice-sized salad bar and a full bar with a strong selection of Argentine wine. A second location recently opened in the Barrio Los Andes section of San Pedro.

Av. Republica de Chile, Colonia Palmira. ✆ **504/2221-2056.** Main courses L130–L340. AE, MC, V. Daily 11am–11pm.

Nobu JAPANESE Don't let the name mislead you. This Japanese restaurant isn't owned by famed chef Nobu Matsuhisa. It is, however, a fairly sophisticated and secluded spot, set in a Japanese garden. Sushi and sashimi—heavily relying on easy access to fresh seafood—make up almost the entire menu. There are also a handful of other dishes, including lettuce wraps, tempura, pad Thai, curries, and soups.

Av. República de Perú, Colonia Palmira. ✆ **504/2232-5348.** Main courses L190–L475. AE, MC, V. Mon–Sat noon–3pm & 6–11pm; Sun noon–7pm.

Moderate

Café Honoré ★★ DELI Café Honoré, a recently expanded, airy eatery with just a handful of tables scattered about an air-conditioned dining room and enclosed patio, is situated on a busy restaurant strip in Colonia Palmira and is best known for gourmet hot and cold sandwiches that most locals only dream of being able to eat daily. Only high-quality meats and cheeses (which are sold on the deli side of the restaurant) and freshly baked breads are used. Try the El Josefredo with Serrano ham and manchego cheese, or the turkey and cranberry. There's also a nice array of soups, including tasty corn chowder, Peruvian ceviche, carpaccio, a global wine list, Bloody Mary specials, and Putumayo music collections often playing.

Av. República de Argentina 1941, Colonia Palmira. ✆ **504/2235-7636.** Main courses L130–L250. AE, DC, MC, V. Mon–Fri 8:30am–9pm; Sat 8:30am–6pm.

Fine London Pub BRITISH/INTERNATIONAL While calling it a true English pub may be a bit of a stretch, this place works well enough. There's just one small front patio and one main dining room with a sports bar–like ambience. They serve a standard international menu with grilled meats, seafood, burgers, salads, and fried finger foods. The pub is a popular spot to meet for after-work drinks for both locals and visiting business travelers.

Av. República de Peru, across from Hotel Honduras Maya, Colonia Palmira. ✆ **504/2238-1446.** Main courses L171–L305. No credit cards. Mon–Thurs noon–midnight; Fri & Sat noon–2am.

Furiwa CHINESE This massive Chinese restaurant, reportedly the largest in all of Central America, is hidden among the American chains on Avenida Juan Pablo II. The first thing you notice is the sheer size of the place: a handful of dining rooms, six ballrooms, and a children's play area. It's big. And the portions match the architecture. The chef from Hong Kong dishes out heaping plates of Cantonese favorites like pan-fried noodles and spare ribs, not to mention the best dim sum in Honduras.

Blvd. Juan Pablo II. ✆ **504/2239-1349.** AE, MC, V. Main courses L100–L250. Mon–Sat 10am–10:30pm; Sun 7am–10:30pm.

Gino's ☺ ITALIAN Owned by the Honorary Consul General to Belize, Gino's is one of the few decent Italian eateries in Tegucigalpa. Expect nothing less than homemade sauces, pastas, and rosemary–and–sea salt–scented focaccia. Simple recipes and fresh ingredients are the key to first-rate Italian food, and Gino's has shown they can compete with the best of them. Finish your meal with a cappuccino and tiramisu, both of which alone are worth a trip to this casual and friendly little family place.

Av. República de Perú, beside Hotel San Martín, Colonia Palmira. ✆ **504/2238-1464.** Main courses L70–L140. MC, V. Mon–Fri 11am–6pm; Wed 11am–9pm; Sat 11am–3pm.

Porcao y Pizza House INTERNATIONAL While the food isn't great, Porcao has an inviting atmosphere that makes it worth a stop for at least a drink. Tables overlook one of the busiest corners of the Zona Viva, which means it's ideal for people-watching during weekend afternoons and evenings. Aside from some porcine items (in keeping with the restaurant's pig-themed decor), the menu features unmemorable wood-fired pizzas and steaks. I'd stick to the bar service, which has a nice selection of South American wines.

Av. República de Perú, Colonia Palmira. ✆ **504/2238-1686.** Main courses L90–L160. AE, MC, V. Mon–Sat noon–3pm & 6–11pm; Sun noon–7pm.

Rojo, Verde, y Ajo MEDITERRANEAN In the heart of the Colonia Palmira restaurant strip, this longtime standout continues to provide an eclectic range of international comfort foods, from Mediterranean to South Asian. Start off with one of their satays, then move to heavier fare like penne a la puttanesca or sea bass, shrimp, or salmon, which each feature a handful of preparations, such as pepper-crusted, and sauces, like honey, soy, and wasabi. Though the dining room feels a bit worn, the food is average on all fronts, and the crowd is on the older yuppie side, the restaurant is still one of the most reliable around.

Av. República de Argentina 1930, Colonia Palmira. ✆ **504/2232-3398.** www.rojoverdeyajo.com. Main courses L130–L350. MC, V. Mon–Wed noon–10pm; Thurs–Sat noon–11pm.

Sabor Cubano CUBAN This Cuban restaurant and bar beside Café Honoré draws a mixed crowd who come for both the food and the dancing. Typical Cuban dishes such as *Ropa Vieja,* shredded flank steak in a tomato sauce, and *Estofado de Cerdo,* braised garlic pork, are the norm in their simple pastel dining room. Cuban pastries such as flan and *Cascos de Guayaba* are served, though most with a sweet tooth come for Havana's favorite cocktails such as mojitos, daiquiris, and Presidentes.

On weekends, amid the twinkles of their back patio Christmas lights, you can hear live music and take in an occasional salsa lesson.

Av. República de Argentina 1933, Colonia Palmira. ✆ **504/2235-9947.** Main courses L100–L200. MC, V. Mon 11:30am–5pm; Tues–Thurs 11:30am–11pm; Fri & Sat 11:30am–2am.

Inexpensive

On the patio and inside the small market in front of **Iglesia Las Dolores** (p. 73), as well as in other locations around the city center, food stalls sell some of the tastiest dishes in the capital for the cheapest prices. You'll find Honduran *baleadas,* El Salvadoran *pupusas,* grilled chicken and beef kebabs, and the occasional intestine. As always with street food, try to stick to the cleaner stalls and the ones the locals are going to. Credit cards aren't accepted, and most meals cost between L10 and L60.

La Cacerola ★★★ HONDURAN This is my favorite restaurant in Tegucigalpa and the one I would recommend above all others. It's a pleasant, simple restaurant tucked away around the corner from the Mall Multiplaza. Their specialty is Honduran and Latin American soups, which are served in four sizes, from mini to Sopón. Each day, there is a choice of three soups, such as *tapado,* de res, or tortilla; mondongo; frijoles; and marinera. They also have a small sandwich selection (turkey cranberry, Cuban, chicken avocado) that pair well with a mini soup.

Av Republic de Costa Rica, Calle Copan 1642, Lomas del Mayab. ✆ **504/2202-3373.** Main courses L155–L150. MC, V. Mon–Sat 11am–8pm.

Café 1331 ★★ CAFE This is a true cafe in every sense of the word. Not only is it a perfect place for coffee, a glass of wine, and one of their salads or sandwiches, but it also serves as a hub of local art and culture. In addition to boasting free Wi-Fi, the cafe is attached to a small designer boutique and an art gallery attributed to an organization dedicated to women in the arts that is maybe the most sophisticated locale in the otherwise drab center of Tegucigalpa.

Av. Cervantes 1331, Downtown. ✆ **504/2237-9647.** http://muaartes.org.hn. Main courses L55–L110. No credit cards. Mon–Sat 10am–8pm.

Taco Taco MEXICAN Taco Taco is just a block from Boulevard Morazán, not far from many of the town's best dining choices. Yet it has maintained its backyard BBQ feel, with a handful of umbrella-covered plastic tables set upon the dirt front yard and the small interior dining room. The menu comprises authentic Mexican snack foods like tacos, *flautas,* and *chalupas,* all served with several homemade hot sauces. The beer and margaritas are all incredibly cheap, so many in for a long night start out here before moving to a more posh spot nearby. Don't confuse this restaurant with a similarly named Mexican restaurant, Taco Loco, on Boulevard Morazán.

Av. República de Perú, Colonia Palmira. ✆ **504/239-7131.** Main courses L75–L150. No credit cards. Daily noon–10pm.

Tortas y Mas MEXICAN If you want to find a meal between museum visits and prefer to avoid the fast food chains that dominate downtown, this small eatery with a maze of small, simple dining rooms is a good choice. Tortas, tacos, and chicken mole are all worth their weight in Aztec gold, while the cheap-as-chips margaritas are hard to avoid.

Av. Colón & Calle El Telégrafo, Downtown. ✆ **504/2222-8368.** Main courses L70–L140. AE, MC, V. Mon–Sat 10am–8pm.

WHAT TO SEE & DO

Attractions in Town

Parque Morazán downtown is usually the first stop on any tour of Tegucigalpa. This is the colonial heart of the city, and most museums can be found here. Few visitors who come to Tegucigalpa take the time to get to know the city. Usually, they land here or are just passing through, and stick around for no more than a day before hightailing it elsewhere in the country. Rightly so, as apart from museums, there is little to do here for the typical traveler. There are no formal tours of the city, and most of the sites are situated walking distance from each other in the colonial center and can be seen easily in a day.

The baroque **Cathedral,** on the eastern edge of Parque Morazán, was built between 1765 and 1782, and honors Saint Michael (San Miguel) the Archangel, Tegucigalpa's patron saint. **Iglesia de Nuestra Señora de los Dolores,** a few blocks northwest of the park, was built in 1732 and features an attractive selection of religious art, such as reliefs of the Stations of the Cross, along with a carved altar. The big plaza fronting the church is often packed with artisan stalls and food vendors. Other churches, such as **Parroquia San Francisco,** the oldest church in the city (it was built in 1592), and **Iglesia la Merced,** beside the Galería Nacional de Arte, are worth a look when they're open (hours vary).

Museo del Hombre Hondureño While few make the effort to visit this small museum, if you have an extra hour to spare, it isn't a bad option. The recently restored building, briefly the Supreme Court, hosts rotating exhibitions of Honduran art and artifacts, and holds a permanent collection of Republican-era paintings.

Av Cervantes y Calle Salvador Corleto. ✆ **504/2238-3198.** Free admission. Mon–Fri 8:30am–noon & 1:30–5pm.

Museo Casa de Morazán This museum opened in early 2010 and looks promising, even though the hours tend to be sporadic and there isn't much inside just yet. This is the restored birthplace of Francisco Morazán, a political visionary who was involved in various ideas of a Central American Republic. Apart from a few interesting artifacts and restored colonial era rooms, there isn't much here to see in the three rooms as of yet, and the space is primarily used for special events.

Av Colón y Av 5a, Archivo Nacional. No phone. Free admission. Hours vary.

Galería Nacional de Arte ★★ The most important art museum in the country, the Galería Nacional de Arte is housed beside Iglesia la Merced in a building that dates back to 1694, which in its past lives was a convent and home to the Universidad Nacional. The well-planned exhibits, labeled in both English and Spanish, are displayed chronologically according to when they were created. The exhibits begin with rock art and petroglyphs from pre-Mayan civilizations, and then move into stone and ceramic art from the Mayas and other indigenous groups. The colonial period is widely represented with oil paintings, gold and silver objects, sculptures, and religious art. The modern era has hundreds of excellent pieces from internationally known Honduran painters, like Pablo Zelaya Sierra and José Antonio Velásquez.

Plaza de la Merced. ✆ **504/2237-9884.** L50 adults. Mon–Sat 9am–4pm; Sun 9am–1pm.

Museo para la Identidad Nacional ★★ This brilliant museum opened in 2006 in the former Palace of Ministries. It features some surprisingly big-name art exhibitions from around Latin America and also displays the history of the country from its pre-Columbian beginnings to modern times via charts, photos, documents, scale models, art, and intriguing artifacts like the femur and tibia of a giant sloth. Their latest addition is *Virtual Copán,* an animated film showing four times a day, which takes you through a virtual tour of the Maya ruins and shows how they were built. It's a great introduction to the ruins if you haven't been there already.

Av. Barahona & Calle El Telégrafo. ✆ **504/2238-7412.** www.min.hn. L50 adults. Tues–Sat 9am–5pm; Sun 10am–4pm.

Chiminike ★★ ☺ This fun, funky children's museum is all about interactivity. Exhibits like a grocery store and construction site have been secretly designed to get kids to learn about the world without them knowing it. Shhh! Most fun is the room dedicated to El Cuerpo Humano, or the human body room, where there's a giant Operator game, a crawl through an intestinal tract, and the chance to make fart noises. Also in the museum is a giant volcano that produces "lava," a bubble room, a VW Beetle that encourages finger-paint graffiti, and a room tilted at a 22-degree angle.

Boulevard Fuerzas Armadas de Honduras, 7km (4¼ miles) S of the center. ✆ **504/2291-0339.** www.chiminike.com. L50 adults. Tues–Fri 9am–noon & 2–5pm; Sat & Sun 10am–1pm & 2–5pm.

Museo Histórico de la República If you have seen the other two museums that depict Honduran history, then this museum, which focuses on the Republican period, from when the country declared independence from Spain, probably isn't going to excite you. On display are portraits, furniture, documents, and photos of past presidents and other assorted historical paraphernalia. The colonial building it sits in, the old Presidential palace from 1920 to 1992, is the real attraction here and far more interesting.

Paseo Soto & Calle Mendieta. ✆ **504/2237-0268.** L55 adults. Wed–Sun 9am–noon & 1:30–4pm.

Museo Nacional de Historia y Antropología Villa Roy More historical than anthropological, this massive museum focuses on the history of the nation of Honduras from independence to modern times. Exhibits are long, highly detailed, very drawn out, and explained only in Spanish, yet they can be fascinating if the history of the country has ever piqued your interest. On display is everything from pre-Columbian archaeological finds, cars of ex-presidents, and everyday items from famous Hondurans to rooms dedicated to colonial times, ethnography, and natural history. The museum is set in a two-story colonial mansion that was once the home of President Julio Lozano, La Villa Roy.

Barrio Buenos Aires. ✆ **504/2222-3470.** L20 adults. Wed–Sun 8:30am–3:30pm.

Parque Naciones Unidas El Picacho ☺ This new park, about 6km (3¾ miles) from the center of town, is home to the huge concrete statue of Christ, Cristo del Picacho, that watches over the city. The main reason to come to this park is for the views of the capital and the surrounding mountains. But there's also a small zoo (L20 adults; Mon–Fri 10am–3pm, Sat and Sun 10am–4pm) with animals from around the country, like monkeys, snakes, macaws, and iguanas, as well as a taxidermy collection that, in my opinion, is located too close to the living creatures. Buses here leave from behind Iglesia de Nuestra Señora de los Dolores (see above).

Entrance 5km (3 miles) N of downtown. L20 adults. Daily 8am–5pm.

Attractions Outside Town

The **Basílica Nacional de Suyapa** ★ (www.virgendesuyapa.hn) is the largest cathedral in the country, but is perhaps better known for being the discovery site of a tiny cedar statue of the Virgin Mary. This statue, discovered in 1747, is famous throughout Honduras for its healing powers. The Virgin has long been the patron saint of the country and, in 1982, was even named by papal decree as the patron saint of all of Central America. The permanent home of the statue is actually the nearby Iglesia de Suyapa, but the statue is brought to this Gothic cathedral, which was built in 1954, for special events like the Feria de la Virgen de Suyapa. The cathedral's grounds are open to visitors every day, but the basilica itself is open only during Mass and holidays. To get here, take a taxi to Suyapa, 7km (4¼ miles) south of the center on Boulevard Suyapa, from Parque La Merced; a taxi should cost about L55 to L95.

Outdoor Activities

Tegucigalpa is far from a major golfing destination, but it does have a small, 9-hole course, considered one of the best in the country. The **Villa Elena Country Club** (✆ **504/2224-0400;** www.villaelena.synthasite.com) is 9km (5½ miles) north of the capital on the road to San Pedro Sula, and in a new residential and ecological reserve area. On the premises are a Mexican restaurant, a bar, and tennis courts.

For the best views of the city, hike up the steep twisting **Paseo La Leona** of Barrio Buenos Aires, which features a small, grassy park with benches, a playground, and a small cafe. There are a few interesting colonial mansions bordering the park, though all are private residences. If you want to save your strength, you can take a taxi there and walk back down to the center (just avoid doing so after dark).

For yoga classes and spa retreats, there's **Yoga's Garden Spa** (Carretera a Valle de Angeles Km. 5½; ✆ **504/2236-9139;** www.yogasgardenspa.com). The well-organized complex in a forested setting outside of the city holds regular yoga, Pilates, tai chi, and belly-dancing classes, as well as offering full spa services. Call ahead for hours and prices or to make a reservation.

Shopping

If you can't make it out to **Valle de Ángeles** or **Santa Lucía** (see p. 80), which sell myriad souvenirs for quite a bit cheaper than in the city, head to any of the artisan stalls by the Iglesia Los Dolores and the shops along Avenidas Miguel de Cervantes, just before the bridge to Colonia Palmira. Or check out **Multiplaza Mall,** on Avenida Juan Pablo II near the Marriott Hotel, which has all the chain shops and restaurants that you would expect in any big North American mall.

Tegucigalpa After Dark

The most elegant way to spend an evening in the capital is to head to a highbrow performance downtown at the spectacular Teatro Nacional Manuel Bonilla (Av. Barahona, at Parque Herrera; ✆ **504/2222-4366**), modeled after the Plaza Athenée in Paris. It has been restored every few decades, most recently in 2007. On select nights throughout the year, you will find opera, dance, and concerts featuring some of the best performers in the country. You can ask at the box office or check the local newspapers for dates and prices. If you walk in during the day, there's usually someone there to enthusiastically show you around and give you a bit of the history of the building.

A holy CELEBRATION

The Virgen de Suyapa, a cedar statue of the Virgin Mary, is one of the holiest Catholic relics in Honduras and Central America. Every February 3 and the week surrounding that date is **La Feria de la Virgen de Suyapa,** a time for celebration of the iconic statue throughout Tegucigalpa and the whole country. The processions and festivities in Tegucigalpa center around the Basílica de Suyapa.

There are several casinos in Tegucigalpa hotels, though the only one that's any good is the **Casino Royale** at the Honduras Maya (see p. 67). They have table games like blackjack, roulette, and baccarat, as well as a small section of slot machines. Bring an ID to get in and don't even think about wearing shorts—it's a dressy nightlife spot.

Most of the city's **bars and clubs** are located in **Colonia Palmira,** along Boulevard Morazán, and most have covers of about L100. **Bull Bar** (✆ **504/9781-0246**), on Avenidas República de Chile in Colonia Palmira, is a rock club that attracts a diverse, cool crowd. Long lines at the door can be a bit dissuading. On the third level of the Nova Centro mall in Barrio Pueblo Nuevo, there are several sleek nightspots and restaurants, like **Baretto's Lounge, Terrazza's Martini Bar,** and **Nox,** that stay open late and lure in all the young and pretty people. **Nau,** the sushi lounge in the Real InterContinental, also attracts a crowd on most nights. Most of the seating is outside on the patio surrounding the pool, so this is the spot for a laidback lounge experience with an attractive crowd.

Also, don't count out **Sabor Cubano** (Av. República de Argentina 1933; Mon 11:30am–5pm, Tues–Thurs 11:30am–11pm, Fri & Sat 11:30am–2am) for salsa dancing. Hipsters will want to check out **Café Paradiso** (Ave. Paz Barahona 1351, in Barrio la Plazuela; ✆ **504/2222-3066**), a cafe and cultural space with frequent film screenings, poetry readings, and live music.

If you'd like to catch a movie, the best theater is the **Cinemark** (✆ **504/231-2044;** www.cinemarkca.com) at the Multiplaza Mall on Avenida Juan Pablo II.

SIDE TRIPS FROM TEGUCIGALPA

Parque Nacional La Tigra ★

This 238-sq.-km (92-sq.-mile) cloud forest park, the first protected area in the country, is located, amazingly, only 22km (14 miles) away from Tegucigalpa. Named a national park in 1982, La Tigra had been nearly destroyed by loggers and the El Rosario Mining Company until the government stepped in, although much of what is left is secondary growth. Remnants of mine shafts and buildings can still be found in the park, although they should be avoided in most instances.

Most who visit the park are after one thing: birds. More than 350 species have been identified in the park, second in the country only to Lago de Yojoa, which has around 400. Rare species, such as the resplendent quetzal, the wine-throated hummingbird, and the rufous-browed wren, are seen by a lucky few, as are mammals such as pumas, agoutis, and armadillos. Plant life includes pine forests, bromeliads, orchids, ferns, lichens, and mushrooms.

There are eight good hiking trails through the park, as well as two entrances. At the first entrance, at Jutiapa, there's a small **visitor's center** (✆ **504/2238-6269;** www.amitigra.org) with a few cabins and a small new eco-lodge (L475 per person) with rooms for rent. Most hiking trails begin from here on the western edge, which are used by the majority of tourists and in good condition. The **Sendero Principal,** the main route through the park that extends 6km (3.7 miles) from one end to the other, follows what was once the main road for the miners, and has been allowed to deteriorate into a more natural state. Almost all other trails branch off from this one, including the **Sendero la Cascada,** a trail that reaches a small waterfall (it's best visited Oct–Feb) after 2km (1.2 miles). It connects to the **Sendero la Mina,** or the mine trail, several kilometers from the other end of the park. **Sendero las Plancitos,** an 8km (5-mile) loop from the Sendero Principal, is the longest, toughest, and least-used trail in the park and your best chance at spotting wildlife.

The second entrance, at the western end of the park, is located at the **El Rosario Mining Company headquarters,** 3km (1¾ miles) above the town of San Juancito. There's a small eco-lodge run by a German couple, **Cabaña Mirador El Rosario** (✆ **504/2987-5835;** L475 double), not far from the entrance. Camping is not allowed in the park; however, there is a small campground (L100 per person) near the Jutiapa entrance with fire pits and toilets.

GETTING THERE

Unless you are going with a tour company or have your own car, access to the park is not exactly easy. To get to Jutiapa by **bus,** you need to catch an El Hatillo–bound bus (the trip takes 1½ hr.; buses run daily every 45 min. beginning at 6am), from the Dippsa station at Avenidas Jerez and Avenidas Plazuela. Let the driver know you are going to the park, and he'll drop you about 2km (1¼ miles) from the entrance at Los Planes, the closest you can get. For the western entrance, take a San Juancito–bound bus (the trip takes 1½ hr.; buses leave daily at 3pm) from Mercado San Pablo. From San Juancito, you must walk the 3km (1¾ miles) uphill to El Rosario. **Amitigra** (✆ **504/2232-6771;** www.amitigra.org), a nonprofit ecological foundation in Tegucigalpa, controls access to the park and can make arrangements in the visitor's center for staying overnight.

The park is open daily from 8am to 5pm. Admission is L190 adults, L95 children.

Valle De Ángeles

The colonial mountain village of **Valle de Ángeles** ★ is 22km (14 miles) east of Tegucigalpa, just 8km (5 miles) past Santa Lucía. It is a route lined with the mansions of *capitalinos,* small country restaurants, plant nurseries, and artesania stands. Though it's nearly empty during the week, the town is packed full during the weekends with day-trippers from Tegucigalpa who come for the cool climate that an elevation of 1,310m (4,298 ft.) brings. It's more centralized and easier to get around than nearby Santa Lucía, and also a wee bit more touristy—but not necessarily in a bad way.

Renovations have virtually restored Valle de Ángeles to its 16th-century glory and helped preserve its tourist-friendly character. Several of the streets are pedestrian only and are lined with small shops selling handicrafts from all over the country—wood carvings, wicker baskets, hand-carved furniture, paintings, Lenca pottery, dolls, and even a leather factory and outlet. A few stores carry items from other Latin American destinations such as Guatemala, Mexico, and Peru. Items here cost quite a bit less than in Tegucigalpa or other parts of the country. Unlike in Santa Lucia, however, the colonial architecture of the church here has not been preserved and looks rather bland.

GETTING THERE

BY CAR You can drive to Valle de Ángeles from Tegucigalpa by heading east on Avenidas La Paz /Avenidas Los Próceres and following the numerous signs.

BY BUS From Tegucigalpa, you can catch a bus (L20) from the corner of Avenidas Los Próceres and Avenidas República Dominicana, 45 minutes from the park, which drops you off at the small lot a few blocks east of the central park. Buses run daily from 5:30am to 7pm. To Santa Lucía, minibuses (L10) run the 20-minute trip every 45 minutes from 5am to 5pm.

EXPLORING THE TOWN

The city centers around a small **central park** with a church, which is surrounded by a handful of small restaurants, and numerous roads that radiate out and are nearly all filled with shops. Most visitors are content to while away the days strolling through shops, staring at the inspiring mountain vistas, and dining in small country eateries.

The **Casa de la Cultura** on the park, beside Jalapeños restaurant, has contemporary art and craft exhibitions from local artists, though it won't take you more than a couple of minutes to walk through.

If you are looking to get some of that fresh mountain air in your lungs, the most popular hike from town is to the **Las Golondrinas Waterfall.** The trip begins about 1km (½ mile) outside of town, on the road to San Juancito, and runs through the pine forests and vegetation reminiscent of Parque Nacional La Tigra nearby. Ask anyone for directions to La Cascada or ask a taxi to drop you there. The trail is well marked, though not simple. The steep hike up will take roughly 2 hours.

Though there aren't any organized tours or good trails, La Florida restaurant outside of town on the road to Tegucigalpa offers **horseback riding** on short excursions (the rides are more popular with children than adults).

SHOPPING

An artisan school that was erected several decades ago in Valle de Ángeles has led to numerous handicraft shops in the surrounding streets, though most of the items sold here are produced in other parts of the country. The exception is the goods here are made of the assortment of precious metals, such as gold, silver, copper, tin, lead, and zinc, that were long extracted from area mines.

Locally made silver earrings and matching necklaces, gold rings, silver-plated mirrors, or picture frames are good buys and quite cheap compared to what you would spend in the U.S. or Europe. With the downturn of the mines, these items are not as plentiful or of as good quality as they once were.

Most of the shops sell more or less the same array of goods and none are particularly noteworthy. There are few specialty shops. Most sell some leather goods that come from mountain areas in the western part of the country, Lenca pottery from the Gracias area, junco straw mats from outside of Santa Bárbara, classic and contemporary paintings and prints from artists from Tegucigalpa and San Pedro Sula, and wood carvings from the North Coast.

WHERE TO STAY

Hotel Posada del Angel ★ The Posada is the best hotel in the center of town. Few will argue that. The two-level corner colonial-style building with stone courtyard set up with a decent pool and restaurant make it a favorite for both weekenders and the occasional foreign tourist. Rooms are simple brick-walled dwellings with TVs and private bathrooms. If you have a choice, opt for those on the upper level, which get better light and have small balconies looking out onto the pool. You get exactly what you pay for. Nothing more, nothing less.

2 blocks from the park. hotelposadadelangel@yahoo.com. ✆ **504/2766-2233.** 25 units. L600 double. MC, V. Free parking. **Amenities:** Restaurant; bar; pool. *In room:* A/C, TV, Wi-Fi (free).

Villas del Valle Owned by an American and his Honduran wife, this small hideaway amid the pine forests is popular with business retreats and weddings. Their brick cabins range in quality and price, though there is a rustic feel throughout. Each is isolated from the others and has a small porch with hammock, private hot-water bathrooms, and cable TV. Some have brick walls, some have drywall. A few of the top-tier rooms have mini-refrigerators and kitchenettes.

On the road to San Juancito, 1km (½ mile) from the center. www.villasdelvalle.com. ✆ **504/2766-2534.** 22 units. L700–L970 standard cabin; L1,311 family cabin. No credit cards. Free parking. **Amenities:** Playground; Internet (free in lobby); pool. *In room:* TV.

WHERE TO EAT

Café Del Valle ★ CAFE At the top of the hill on the road into town, this small cafe is one of the first you see and the last you will remember. The coffeehouse pumps out an array of breakfast items and light fare like homemade *pan de yema,* American breakfasts, pancakes, and *licuados.* Coffee is from artisanal growers from the area.

On the road out of town, .3km (¼ mile) from the center. No phone. Main courses L50–L150. No credit cards. Wed–Sun 10am–7pm.

La Casa de las Abuelas ★ HONDURAN A top spot for day trippers, this charming eatery in a 100-year-old adobe house serves a variety of oversized typical Honduran dishes, like *baleadas* and *anafres.* Their specialty, though, is their grilled steaks and pork chops.

Calle de Mineral, center. No phone. Main courses L50–L150. No credit cards. Thurs–Sun 9am–5pm.

El Anafre ITALIAN Across the park from Jalapeños, this small pizzeria is decorated with local themes and crafts. It gets lively on weekend nights with families coming for finger foods, pasta, *anafres,* brochettes, and the cheap wine and beer.

On the park. ✆ **504/2766-2942.** Main courses L80–L200. No credit cards. Wed–Sun 9am–8pm.

El Portal HONDURAN The first thing that piques your interest in this popular restaurant is the beautifully carved wooden doors and doorway. When you step inside, you realize that the intricate hand-carved woodwork is everywhere: rails, bar, chairs, and trim. On hand are mostly *típica* dishes, *chuletas de cerdo* (pork chops), steaks, and trout. The stone floors and knight armor give it a sort of medieval pub feel.

Just behind the church, on the left. ✆ **504/2766-3549.** Main courses L115–L230. MC, V. Wed–Sun 10am–7pm.

Jalapeños INTERNATIONAL Right on the park, this popular restaurant consistently lures diners with cheap comfort food and drinks. Burgers, sandwiches, salads, *típica* plates, and a mishmash of light appetizers draw the lunch and late-night crowds.

On the park. No phone. Main courses L80–L200. No credit cards. Wed–Sun 10am–7pm.

Santa Lucía

At more than 1,524m (5,000 ft.) above sea level, this serene, 18th-century Spanish mining town of Santa Lucía, about 30 minutes outside Tegucigalpa, is a favorite weekend retreat for the residents of Tegucigalpa. It was here that the most significant silver deposits in Honduras were found in the mid 1500s, bringing numerous settlers to the area and resulting in the founding of Tegucigalpa.

Narrow cobblestone streets and stone walls, surrounded in an array of multicolored flowers, gracefully wind their way up and down the hillsides past whitewashed houses with clay tile roofs, small artisan shops, outdoor cafes, an 18th-century church with Spanish oil paintings, and one decent mountain resort. The tourist herds don't put up the same numbers here as they do in nearby Valle de Ángeles, though they are here, and because of this, it feels more authentic and more like a living and breathing town.

GETTING THERE

The easiest way to get here from Tegucigalpa, a 20- to 30-minute ride, depending on traffic, is to take any San Juancito–bound **bus** and ask to be let off at the turnoff to town, a couple of kilometers from the actual center, where you can flag down any number of cars, *colectivo* taxis, or buses. Service runs in each direction about every 45 minutes from roughly 7:30am to 6pm.

You can **drive** to Santa Lucía from Tegucigalpa by heading east on Avenidas La Paz/Avenidas Los Próceres, following the numerous signs. The turnoff is about 14km (8¾ miles) from Tegucigalpa.

WHAT TO SEE & DO

Much like Valle de Ángeles, the favorite activities in Santa Lucía point towards taking it easy. You can loll around the shops or spend hours drinking and dining outdoors under the pines in country-style restaurants. The **central square** is pleasant enough, with a small fountain and flowering plants. You can feed fish in a small lagoon nearby. Flower and plant vendors, which supply Tegucigalpa, are found throughout the city and on the road in.

The most important site here is the 18th-century **church,** which features a crucifix—Christ of Las Mercedes, donated by King Phillip II of Spain in 1574—alongside some fine Spanish oil paintings. There is a brilliant, sweeping view of the clay tile roofs and valley below from the front of the church.

A site that you probably didn't expect to hear of in a colonial mining town is the **Santa Lucía Serpentarium** (free admission; daily 9am–4pm), a private serpent collection of native Honduran snakes. Many of the species can be found in nearby La Tigra National Park.

Spanish-language classes are often set in laidback destinations, as the human brain tends to adapt and memorize better when it is relaxed and focused. This is a big part of why the **Centro Hondureño de Español** (✆ **504/9964-1896;** L5,700 for 1 week of classes and accommodation) is based here, rather than Tegucigalpa. Group and private courses are paired with homestays with local families, an introduction to Honduran culture, and short tours and hikes to area sites. They also have a renowned program designed to assist international aid personnel in language preparation and understanding of the national culture.

WHERE TO STAY & EAT

Hotel Santa Lucía Resort ★ Hidden amongst the pines a little more than a kilometer outside of town is this snug little mountain resort. Rooms are both in the main lodge and in stand-alone cabins. The rooms in the main lodge have brick floors and slightly bigger bathrooms, while the cabins have hardwood floors, a space heater, and a small porch. Neither option is perfect, but their woodsy charm is touched up by accent rugs. They get the job done. Both are quiet and soak in the isolation. There is a sauna in the main lodge, as well as an on-site restaurant that has both indoor and outdoor seating, and serves Honduran and international staples.

1km (½ mile) from town. www.hotelsantaluciaresort.com. ✆ **504/2236-9179.** L760 double. No credit cards. Free parking. **Amenities:** Restaurant; sauna. *In room:* TV.

Don Quixote SPANISH At the entrance of town, up a pine-covered hill, this is considered one of the top restaurants in Santa Lucía. The theme of this Tegucigalpa spinoff is, as you may have guessed, Spanish cuisine—including but not limited to paella, of which nine varieties are offered. Many of the recipes are traditional from Galicia and have been passed down for generations, such as *Tortilla Española, Pulpo a la Gallega,* and *Zarzuela de Mariscos.* There are numerous international standards, like steaks, pasta, and salads, and a good wine list, too. A dining/conference room is available, though most choose to sit outdoors to commune with the trees and flowers.

Entrance to town, 1km (½ mile) from the center. ✆ **504/2779-0007.** Main courses L160–L300. MC, V. Daily 11am–5pm.

Portal La Leyenda Café Bar INTERNATIONAL While many come here on lunches from the capital, the ideal visit to this brick wall bohemian restaurant and art gallery is at night, when the bar is the central feature and the romantic glow of candlelight is the only way to see to the next table. Food here is light: sandwiches, *piqueos,* and small plates.

In town. No phone. Main courses L40–L150. No credit cards. Tues–Sun noon–9pm.

Restaurante Miluska ★ CZECH Owned by the Czech consul, this Eurocentric eatery is the most popular in town. Czech and German fare are dished out alongside Honduran *típica* plates in either their indoor dining room or shady outdoor patio. For a heaping, hearty meal, this is the right place.

In town. ✆ **504/2231-3905.** Main courses L80–L200. No credit cards. Tues–Sun 10am–8pm.

6 SOUTHERN HONDURAS

South of Tegucigalpa, the lush green mountains spread apart and valleys get wider until the entire landscape turns flat, grows blazing hot, and breaks apart into a multitude of small streams that twist their way through golden fields and mangrove forests until reaching the three-border area at the Golfo de Fonseca. It is the Pacific, so numerous beaches are strewn about the region, though they don't compare with those in neighboring El Salvador or Nicaragua. Cattle ranching, shrimp farming, cigar production, and mining are the major industries here, though some have taken their toll on the landscape and caused environmentalists to be up in arms—especially over shrimp farming.

Southern Honduras is a poor region, one of the poorest collections of departments in the country. It's also one of the least-visited parts of Honduras and mostly visited only by those passing through along the Pan-American Highway between El Salvador and Nicaragua—aid workers, volunteers, and weekenders from Tegucigalpa.

Still, all is not lost in Southern Honduras. If you have an adventurous spirit and enjoy the little-seen and almost-out-of-reach, you might be pleasantly surprised by what you will find here. Yuscarán, a charming colonial mining town with cobblestone streets sitting high enough to escape the heat, is for many visitors their favorite place in the country. Sierra de la Botija, a dry tropical forest in the highlands near the Nicaragua border, is home to white-faced monkeys, pumas, and all sorts of wildlife. Plus, while the Caribbean beaches in the north can get crowded, the Pacific beaches rarely see a footprint.

YUSCARAN

When silver ore was discovered in the mountains above Yuscarán at the end of the 17th century, a boom occurred in the little town that lasted nearly 100 years. While the days of wealth are long gone, the colonial core of the town, most notably the cobblestone square and whitewashed houses, remains intact and provides a quick getaway for a day or two from the chaos that is the capital.

Getting There

Yuscarán, just 66km (41 miles) from Tegucigalpa, is easily reached by **car** or **bus** by moving east from the capital on the road to Danlí for 47km (29 miles) and then hitting the turnoff for the last 17km (11 miles). There are half a dozen direct buses (L35; 2 hr.) daily.

0 25 mi
0 25 km
Siguatepeque
COMAYAGUA
Comayagua
La Paz
Cedros
Guayape
Limones
OLANCHO
Talanga
FRANCISCO MORAZÁN
PARQUE NACIONAL LA TIGRA
Jalán
Valle de Angeles
EL PARAÍSO
Comayagüela
TEGUCIGALPA
LA PAZ
Danlí
Toncontín Int'l
Yuscarán
RESERVA DE LA BIOSFERA YUSCARAN
Sabanagrande
Las Manos
EL SALVADOR
VALLE
El Amatillo
Nacaome
Pespire
Choluteca
Segovia
CHOLUTECA
San Lorenzo
Pan American Hwy
El Espana
San Marcos de Colon
Refugio de Vida Silvestre Ojochal
Isla del Tigre
Coyolito
Amapala
Isla Conchaguita
Choluteca
Golfo de Fonseca
Isla Meanguera
El Triunfo
NICARAGUA
International Airport
Park
Point of Interest
GUATEMALA
CARIBBEAN SEA
HONDURAS
Tegucigalpa
EL SALVADOR
NICARAGUA
Area of detail
PACIFIC OCEAN

Exploring the Town

There is plenty to do in Yuscarán to keep you busy for a few days. Get oriented by heading to the main square in the center of town, admiring the whitewashed colonial vibe and exploring the **Iglesia San Jose,** which finished construction in 1768. Numerous colonial houses can be found in the streets surrounding the square, but none are as important as **Casa Fortín** (free admission; daily 8am–noon and 2–4pm), a national monument that dates back to 1850. The building was once home to the wealthy Fortín family, which was involved in various business operations in the region and briefly in politics. The building now serves as the de facto town museum. The caretaker will gladly show you around, though the mediocre displays don't need much explaining.

An interesting side excursion is the **El Buen Gusto factory** (free admission; Mon–Sat 7am–noon, Mon–Fri 1–4pm), where they distill Honduras's favorite spirit, *Aguardiente,* which is sometimes called *guaro.* Just walk up to the plant and ask at the door for a tour, and someone will walk you through while explaining the distillation process (in Spanish).

If you are going to stick around for a while, check in at the **Fundación Yuscarán** beside the town hall on the square. Here, you can get maps and information on trips to the nearby hot springs and petroglyphs near the town of Oropolí, or arrange guided tours to the cloud forests in the Monserrat Biological Reserve.

During the first weekend in June, Yuscarán's annual **Mango Festival ★** is the best time of the year to hang around. Anything quasi-mango is celebrated in mango bobbing, parades, dancing, and the election of a mango queen. The favorite event, though, is "Donkey Polo."

Where to Stay

There are a few small guesthouses in town. All are quite simple, and the only one I can truly recommend is **Casa Colibri** (**© 504/793-7989;** L500 double), a restored colonial house right on the square with just two rooms with high ceilings, hot-water bathrooms, and TVs, and decorated in local handicrafts. The owners speak English, too.

DANLI

Although it was founded in 1667 by Spanish settlers—originally as San Buena Ventura—it took Danlí 3 centuries to rise to something more than a small shipping hub. Not far from the city, the 12km-by-25km (20-by-40-mile) Valle de Jamastrán provides conditions—rich soil and an average temperature of 75°F (24°C) and 75% humidity—comparable to the best tobacco-growing regions in Cuba. After the 1959 Communist Revolution, Cuban cigar makers flocked here with seeds in hand and quickly turned Honduras into one of the world's elite centers of cigar production; approximately 30% of the city's almost 70,000 residents work in the industry. The town itself retains its colonial air in the very center, though strip malls and fast food are inching their way closer every year. If you are not a smoker, there isn't much here apart from a few small festivals and an easygoing, small-town feel.

Getting There

Danlí is directly east of Tegucigalpa on CA 6, about 1½ hours away. Both minibuses and larger "chicken buses" run between Danlí and Tegucigalpa (L80–L100) throughout the day. Danlí's station is outside of town, so take a moto-taxi (L20) to get in and out.

Border Crossing: El Paraíso/Las Manos

To get to the Nicaraguan border from Danlí, you have to catch one of the minibuses that leave every 20 minutes or so from the station during daylight hours to El Paraíso (L20; 30 min.), and then transfer to Las Manos (L15; 30 min.) at the border, where connections to elsewhere in Nicaragua can be made.

What to See & Do

Apart from visiting the cigar factories, there is little to do in Danlí but soak in the small-town atmosphere of the shady square with a small fountain featuring sculptured stalks of corn growing out of it. There's a small **Museo Municipal** (L10 adults; Mon–Fri sporadically) in a colonial building, dating back to 1857, that adjoins the city building. It deserves only a quick look for the displays on tobacco and other regional industries, a small display of pre-Columbian artifacts, and colonial knick-knacks.

Festival Nacional del Maíz, or National Corn Festival, is held annually for an entire week at the end of August for a celebration of corn through pageants, parades, and feasting. **Domingo Gastronómico,** held the last Sunday of every month, showcases regional fare—think *mondongo* (tripe soup), grilled corn, and tamales—via tables set up around town by the city and sold at basement prices.

Where to Stay & Eat

Hotel La Esperanza Right at the entrance to town, La Esperanza is the only suitable option for most, though it is nothing to write home about. Many of the rooms have been renovated, though they still lack character. Facilities are clean, though. Some cheaper rooms are available without A/C.

At the entrance to town. ✆ **504/2763-3225.** 20 units. L600 double. No credit cards. Free parking. *In room:* A/C, fan, TV, no phone.

El Cafetal This restaurant and hotel just outside of town is the first you will see when traveling from Tegucigalpa. It is drive-up motel style, with basic amenities like A/C and cable, but hot water is spotty and the rooms are kind of run down.

½km (¼ mile) from town on the road to Tegucigalpa. ✆ **504/2763-2259.** 16 units. L600 double. No credit cards. Free parking. *In room:* A/C, fan, TV, no phone.

Rancho Mexicano MEXICAN Next door to Rincon Danlídense is this fun Mexican place, with decor straight out of Chiapas and a somehow fitting collection of antique farming equipment. The menu is more or less the same as every other Mexican restaurant in Honduras: tacos, *gringas,* and quesadillas served with rice and beans.

½ block from the park. ✆ **504/2763-3307.** Main courses L60–L140. No credit cards. Tues–Sun 11am–10pm.

Rincon Danlídense HONDURAN Inside a colonial-style building with a clay tile roof less than a block off the square, the Rincon Danlídense is the top spot in town for Honduran *típica,* regional plates, tacos, and hamburgers. The fare is a step up from almost anything else in town, which ranges from extremely simple to fast food. Come on the weekends for their beef soup.

½ block from the park. No phone. Main courses L50–L100. No credit cards. Tues–Sun 11am–10pm.

cigar factory TOURS IN DANLÍ

If cigars are what you had in mind when planning a trip to Honduras, look no further than Danlí. There are nearly a dozen factories scattered around town, several of which offer tours. Call ahead to arrange a tour. Most factories rarely see a visitor, though they do seem to enjoy showing visitors around when they pop up.

Camacho Cigars (© **305/592-0722;** www.camachocigars.com), acquired in 2008 by Swiss firm the Oettinger Davidoff Group, was the official cigar sponsor of the 2009 Grammy awards and has a cigar bar at Comerica Park in Detroit. They hold very in-depth, 3-day "seed to store" seminars at Camp Camacho in the valley for consumers and retailers throughout the year that includes all meals and accommodations, though you must reserve well in advance to attend.

Plasencia Tobacco (© **504/2763-2828**), on the road to the border, is one of the largest cigar factories in the world and employs more than 2,000 workers. It's owned by Cuban tobacco baron Don Nestor Plasencia, who also owns the nearby Paraíso Cigars.

Puros Aliados Cigar (© **504/2763-1486**), 1km (½ mile) east of town, will let visitors peek at their rolling plant for free, where you can watch the 150 or so rollers manufacturing the Puro Indio, Cuba Aliados, and Roly Cigars labels.

Gran Tabacaleras Unidas (© **504/2763-6072**), which makes the La Cubana label, has been operating in a small factory 5 minutes from town on the road to Las Manos since 1995. If you ask kindly, they will happily give you a brief, informal tour.

CHOLUTECA

Honduras's fourth-largest city and birthplace of Central American independence hero Jose Cecilio del Valle is the largest town in the south and a major stopping point for travelers cutting across the country between El Salvador and Nicaragua. Thus, the town is full of hotels, banks with ATMs, restaurants, and general facilities that are rare elsewhere in this region.

While there may be few tourist sites here, you won't be disappointed in Choluteca's colonial atmosphere that dominates the center of town. City officials have been slowly restoring some of the older buildings, tile roofs, and iron rails, and sprucing up the square. While the town is no tourist magnet like Gracias and can get hellishly hot, it can be a pleasant place to spend a day.

Getting There

Choluteca sits just off the Pan-American Highway. **Buses** depart from the main terminal on Boulevard Carranza and 3a Avenida NE, and several private terminals across the street. **Transportes Mi Esperanza** (© **504/2882-2712**) runs buses to and from Tegucigalpa (L65; 3½ hr.) from 4am to 6pm, including four *ejectivo* departures. For San Pedro Sula or the North Coast, transfer at Tegucigalpa.

What to See & Do

The colonial core of the city is the most interesting place to be in Choluteca. There are enough trees around the Parque Central to keep the sun from beating you into the ground and a few sights to hold your interest. The **Catedral Inmaculada**

Concepción dates back to the 17th century, though the facade was rebuilt in 1917. **Jose Cecilio del Valle's family home,** which features prominently on the back of the 100 lempira note, on the southwest corner of the square has been restored and turned into a small library and museum (free admission; hours vary) with old photos and colonial artifacts.

The small colonial town of **San Marcos de Colón,** 11km (6¾ miles) from the border, has a delightful square. It's in the hills (at an elevation of 960m/3,150 ft.) and catches a friendly breeze. The town is essentially a coffee-growing hub, but more importantly, it is an access point to the **Refugio de Vida Silvestre Ojochal** (Ojochal Wildlife Reserve; free admission), located between San Marcos de Colón and the Nicaraguan border. The park sees very few visitors, though, and that is not always a bad thing as far as national parks go. The mountainous terrain is blanketed with dry tropical forests—and spots of cloud forests—that hold many rare bird species and even larger mammals like white-faced monkeys. There are a few semi-maintained trails that run through the park. Ask around in San Marcos for guides and transportation to Duyusupo, a small town on the edge of the park.

If you are dying to see the Pacific and lounge on the beach, the only nearby option from Choluteca is at **Cedeño,** 33km (21 miles) away. The beach can get muddy and trash can be an issue, but more problematic are the extra-shady bars that make it an unsafe place to go on weekend nights.

Where to Stay & Eat

There are maybe a dozen hotels in Choluteca. While none of them are going to knock your socks off, all of them are comfortable and a decent value. **Hotel Gualiqueme ★** (✆ **504/2782-2750;** www.hotelgualiqueme.hn; L1,522 double), just across the suspension bridge right before you get into town, is the largest and has the most amenities. There are tile-floored rooms equipped with A/C, cable TV, and Wi-Fi. There's a nice pool on the grounds, plenty of trees and gardens, a bar, and a full-service restaurant. Hand-carved woodwork features prominently throughout the property.

The hotels in town are simpler, including the cozy **Hotel Bonsai** (1 block south of Parque Central; ✆ **504/2782-2648;** L350 double), which has a few air-conditioned rooms that surround a small courtyard.

Outside of fast food places and coffee at **Espresso Americano** (6a Av. NO), several small restaurants are worth a look for a decent *típica* plate or seafood. **Restaurante Acuarion** (corner of the square; no phone) serves steaks, *chuletas de cerdo,* grilled fish, and even *pupusas* in a quaint colonial building. **El Torito** (no phone), on the way out of town, is the most upscale restaurant in Choluteca and the only one

Border Crossings: El Triunfo/Guasaule

Direct buses serve the 45-minute ride (L30) to the border town of El Triunfo and its Nicaraguan counterpart, Guasaule, every half hour during daylight from the main terminal in Choluteca. Buses are waiting on the other side for connections to León and Grenada. This is one of the seedier border crossings in the country, so keep an eye on your belongings at all times and be on the lookout for pickpockets.

Border Crossing: El Amatillo/San Carlos

El Amatillo, on the border with El Salvador, can be reached either from Choluteca (L40; 2 hr.) or Tegucigalpa (L60; 3 hr.). Buses leave during the day every 30 minutes or so in both directions for both cities. The crossing is fairly straightforward; however, it tends to be dreadfully slow, and lines tend to be long. There is connecting transport on the other side to San Salvador and elsewhere in El Salvador.

that will accept credit cards. They serve steaks and all sorts of grilled animal products. For snacks and drinks on the weekend, look no further than **Tío Rico** (Calle Williams; no phone), which stays open until 2am and has live music.

ISLA DEL TIGRE

A 783m (2,569-ft.) conical volcano of Cerro Vejía, often enshrouded in clouds and fog, looms overhead and forms the center of this sleepy island. Once the major southern port in Honduras, Isla del Tigre is no more than a shade of its former glory, with fewer than 3,000 people living here. A visit here is like a walk back in time. Small communities of red, yellow, blue, and turquoise wooden houses are loosely strung along the one road that circles the island and survive mostly on fishing and subsistence farming. The scent of mangos and flowers sweetens every breeze. Dogs lie on the pavement and hardly twitch when cars pass a mere snail's length from their bodies. Traffic picks up during Semana Santa, but only mildly during summer weekends, with day-trippers from Tegucigalpa and elsewhere in the south. For the rest of the year, you might be the only tourists there.

The Golfo de Fonseca was discovered in 1522 by Andrés Niño, who named it after the Archbishop Juan Fonseca; however, the Spanish quickly moved on. Pirates, including Sir Francis Drake, frequently used Isla del Tigre as a base for raids on Spanish ships carrying gold and riches being exploited from South America. The first town was built in 1770 by El Salvador, but it wasn't until Honduras founded Amapala in 1833 that the island began to take off.

During the Republican era, the island became significant as the only official Pacific port. When the port moved to Henecan near San Lorenzo, though, it has been downhill ever since. Perhaps the last event of any interest occurred when the United States, which was assisting the Contras in their fight against the Sandinistas in Nicaragua, added a small radar and radio base on the top of the island to monitor troop movements, though it was deserted when the Sandinistas lost power.

There are rumblings of turning Isla del Tigre into a large-scale deepwater port, but for time being, the community has set its sights on tourism, giving the dock a facelift, organizing a homestay program, and encouraging building improvements and beautification projects around town.

Getting There

Without private transportation, getting to Isla del Tigre is a bit tricky. If traveling south from Tegucigalpa towards Choluteca by **bus,** you need to get off just before San Lorenzo for the turnoff to Coyolito. From here, you can catch frequent **minibuses**

> **Small Change**
>
> **With no banks on Isla del Tigre and little money coming in, there is always a shortage of small bills. Get change in Coyolito or elsewhere on the mainland, or you might be out of luck. If you are in a bind, try exchanging money at El Faro de Victoria.**

(L20) or hire a **taxi** (L200) for the 1-hour ride. If **driving,** you can park your car in any of the lots near the seafood shacks in Coyolito (L40 overnight, though you can bargain for longer stays).

To get to Amapala from Coyolito, you need to hire a **boatman.** Throughout the day, they leave from the pier frequently, and you can pay the per-passenger rate of L20. If you have a group or arrive in the late afternoon when no one else is making the trip, you can pay for a full boat (L140).

Exploring the Island

Isla del Tigre has just one town, **Amapala,** though there are smaller clusters of houses circling the island. At the main dock, you will find a small tourism office that can help you find a hotel, give you a map, or organize a tour. Upon leaving the dock, the town extends both ways along the coast and back toward the interior a few blocks to a small square with a church, market, and Hondutel call center.

If you want to explore elsewhere on the island, you can follow the one 17km (11-mile) road that follows the coast. You can walk, hire a moto-taxi, or wait along the road for the minibuses to pass. Both rides will charge you by the distance you travel. Prices are slightly higher than on the mainland. There are a few *miradors* set up with good views of the gulf, the islands, and El Salvador and Nicaragua.

Most tourists, both Honduran and international, who venture to Isla del Tigre are there for one thing: beaches and sun. There are approximately 20 white and black sand beaches here, some of them harder to reach than others and most of them deserted. From Amapala, the nearest stretch of sand is at **Playa El Burro** to the east of town, which faces Coyolito. The water is calm and clear, though some debris is strewn about and it can get rather muddy at low tide. You can hire a boatman right on the beach for fishing, tours, and transport to Coyolito. There are a few small *hospedajes* and restaurants here. You can walk here in about 25 minutes from town.

On the opposite side of the island is the largest beach, appropriately named **Playa Grande.** On the weekend, the beach fills up, and rickety little thatched-roof eateries set up shop and take up much of the sand. It's a hilly, 1-hour walk here or a 20-minute moto-taxi ride.

A bit farther on are the black sands of **Playa Negra,** though if you are not staying at the hotel, there is little reason to come here.

To explore the gulf and visit any of the islands, hire a **boatman** (L200–L400, depending on number of people and distance traveled) in either Coyolito or Amapala. One of the most common trips is to stop at Meanguera and check out its small town, have a nice lunch, and hang out on its pleasant black-sand beach. You can ask the boatman to circle Isla Meanguerita or Isla de los Pájaros (Bird Island). Apart from a few fisherman shacks, most of the other islands are uninhabited but can be worth your time if you are looking for an empty stretch of sand. Technically, you are required to head over to immigration in La Unión before crossing to the islands belonging to the El Salvador side, but for a short trip, there is very little chance you will have any problems.

The Tri-Border Gray Area

The rights to the Golfo de Fonseca have been frequently disputed among Honduras, Nicaragua, and El Salvador, the three countries that share the 261km (162-mile) shoreline. The chamber of the International Court of Justice (ICJ) settled the case in 1992 and awarded shared rights of the gulf among the three countries. Isla del Tigre, however, went to Honduras, and Meanguera and Meanguerita went to El Salvador.

Where to Stay

Homestays With activity at the port almost nonexistent now and jobs scarce, tourism is seen as Amapala's last hope. Various private homes in Amapala have cleaned up their extra rooms to be rented out for visitors. Renters and taxi drivers wait at the pier for passenger boats and sell the homestays to those without a room. Some are better than others, though you might not have much choice. Most are quite simple, though they will have modern private bathrooms with cold-water showers, fans, and locking doors. Prices (L300–L400) tend to be high compared to other parts of the country for what you get in terms of amenities, though the amount of character is priceless. You can contact the **Asociación de Casas de Huéspedes** (✆ **504/2795-8040**) to make a reservation.

Hotel Mirador de Amapala ★ The Mirador is the most complete and modern hotel on Isla del Tigre and a much better value than Hotel Playa Negra on the other side of the island. The property is set up on three levels on a jungle-clad hillside that's a 5-minute ride east of the pier, and it surrounds a large pool that looks out across the Golfo de Fonseca. There are quite a few terraces for lounging about and bringing a drink from the bar. Rooms are simple: tile floors, a fresh coat of peach paint, little to no decor, and back-straightening beds. The hotel can arrange jet-ski rental and boat tours.

Amapala. www.miradordeamapala.com. ✆ **504/2795-8407.** 30 units. L1,400 double. Rates include breakfast. MC, V. **Amenities:** Restaurant; bar; Internet (free in lobby); pool. *In room:* A/C, fan, TV.

Hotel Playa Negra After years of neglect, new owners took over this once-revered property in the hopes of returning it to its former glory. While Hotel Playa Negra isn't going to win any awards, so far, the new owners have done a good job of, at the very least, making the place habitable. The hotel has a clean pool, pool table, full meal plans, kayaks available to use, and their own boat service to islands in the gulf. Best of all, they have a lockdown on the best beach on the island, which is a 3-minute walk from the hotel. While the rooms are a bit worn and not exactly stunning, they are kept clean and are slowly being fixed up. The clay tile floors are well worn, and furniture is kind of a mishmash of what looks like anything they could possibly find on the island, with mismatching floral patterns and the occasional plastic chair with a glass table. Some rooms add a kitchen sink, minifridge, and microwave. The hotel is down an extremely dilapidated dirt path from the main island road, about a 20-minute taxi ride from the pier.

Playa Negra. hotelplayanegra@hotmail.com. ✆ **504/2795-8027,** or ✆ 504/2220-1183 in Tegucigalpa. 40 units. L1,500 double (can sleep up to 5 guests). L1,040 per person w/meals & transport to Coyolito. MC, V. **Amenities:** Restaurant; bar; pool. *In room:* A/C, fan, TV, minibar (some).

Where to Eat

El Faro de Victoria INTERNATIONAL Right on the waterfront, just to the right of the municipal pier, the open-air retreat is sometimes the only restaurant open during the week that is right in town. Hamburgers and basic island grub, like *pescado frito* and garlic shrimp, served with French fries, or rice and beans, is all you will find. There is a full bar, cold beer on hand, and an enticing little disco ball hanging from the tin roof—all the makings of a party, but even on the weekends, the floors stay clean.

To the right of the municipal pier. No phone. Main courses L60–L140. No credit cards. Daily 10am–10pm.

Veleros HONDURAN If you want a laidback place to hang out for the day, right in front of a calm beach, Veleros is your place. The thatched roof and wood-plank-floor patio is a traveler hangout, when there are travelers on the islands. You can also arrange boat trips to some of the islands and the mainland. They have a few simple rooms for rent. The menu is straight *típica* with a splash of seafood. You can get a decent *Catracho* breakfast with eggs, toast, plantains, cheese, and ham, while lunch and dinner brings lobster stuffed with shrimp, ceviche, and sandwiches to the table. To get here, take the bus or grab a taxi to Playa El Burro; the restaurant is just left of where the road ends.

Playa El Burro. No phone. Main courses L40–L140. No credit cards. Daily 11am–10pm.

WESTERN HONDURAS

7

The western part of Honduras is a land far removed from the country's beach mindset, yet it's still one of the most important regions for tourism. It's a place where cowboys share the streets with cars and where orchids grow amid plentiful pine forests. For many, this is the real Honduras, and it technically includes the must-see ruins of Copán; Santa Rosa de Copán, one of the centers of the country's cigar production; the breathtaking Lago de Yojoa; and Gracias, Central America's first capital and the gateway to the cloud forests of Parque Nacional Montaña de Celaque, all of which are covered separately below.

Your first foray into the west will most often be the pulsating capital of San Pedro Sula. While it lies in the corner of the region, you almost always have to come through this vibrant, cluttered city to get anywhere here. As you get farther away from San Pedro Sula, the population thins out substantially, the mountains grow taller, the pine forests become more dense, and the fog and mist thicken. Even deeper into the mountains are numerous Maya Chortí or Lenca villages such as La Campa, which have remained practically unchanged for centuries.

SAN PEDRO SULA

San Pedro Sula, the loud, brash, economic transportation hub of Honduras (241km/150 miles north of Tegucigalpa) often serves to introduce visitors to the western part of the country, if not the country as a whole, although many hightail it out of here almost immediately after arriving. This town holds little of interest to passing tourists, other than a few good hotels, westernized malls, North American chain restaurants, a few good markets, a couple of museums, and some upscale clubs. The chaotic, sometimes dangerous core—a true-to-form, unbearably hot concrete jungle within the Circunvalación that's full of rough-and-tumble residential neighborhoods—lacks much charm, and the city's wealthy cling to the suburbs on the outskirts and surrounding hillsides. The authentic Honduras jumped ship long ago, except for a few bright spots. The best way to make the most of your time here is not to expect to be awed, but to take it in stride. Check out the market and museum, catch a movie, find a nice restaurant or bar to dine and have a drink; better yet, make that a few drinks. Chances are your time here will be short.

The city was founded on June 27, 1536, by Don Pedro de Alvarado and was originally named Villa de San Pedro de Puerto Caballos, although it

International Airport
Park
Ruins
0 25 mi
0 25 km
BELIZE
Gulf of Honduras
Bahía de Omoa
Puerto Cortés
Omoa
Travesia
Baja Mar
Pta. Sal
Miami
Tornabe
La Ensenada
Triunfo de la Cruz
Tela
PUNTA IZOPO
JEANNETTE KAWAS (PUNTA SAL)
ATLÁNTIDA
Puerto Barrios
L. de Izabal
CUSUCO
CORTÉS
San Pedro Sula
El Progreso
GUATEMALA
SANTA BÁRBARA
PICO PIJOL
YORO
Yoro
Trinidad
Llama
Gualala
STA. BÁRBARA
COPÁN
La Entrada
Ulúa
Santa Bárbara
Lago de Yojoa
CERRO AZUL MEÁMBAR
COPÁN
Santa Rosa de Copán
COMAYAGUA
Siguatepeque
Gracias
CELAQUE
OCOTEPEQUE
La Campa
INTIBUCÁ
Belen Gaucho
San Manuel de Colohete
San Marcos de Caiquin
Nueva Ocotepeque
San Sebastian
Comayagua
Erandique
La Esperanza
La Paz
Yamaranguila
LEMPIRA
La Virtud
LA PAZ
Comayagüela
TEGUCIGALPA
Toncontín Int'l
Sabanagrande
SAN SALVADOR
EL SALVADOR
VALLE
Pespire
Nacaome
Choluteca
Golfo de Fonseca
CARIBBEAN SEA
GUATEMALA
HONDURAS
EL SALVADOR
Tegucigalpa
NICARAGUA
Area of detail

was quickly renamed San Pedro "Sula," from the Usula word that means "valley of birds." The town was intended to be a point of transfer of goods from Nicaragua, El Salvador, and Guatemala onto the coast at Puerto Cortes. However, persistent pirate attacks nearly destroyed that mission, and the town was practically deserted by the 19th century. It remained a rural backwater until the 1920s, when the United Fruit Company set up shop here to expand their banana plantations; the population subsequently exploded from about 10,000 to 100,000 in just a few years. Much of the country's industry and exportation still revolve around the city, which is the second-largest in the country, after Tegucigalpa. The population today is just over 500,000.

Essentials

GETTING THERE

BY PLANE Ramón Villeda Morales International Airport, sometimes just called **San Pedro Sula International Airport** (SAP), sits 15km (9¼ miles) east of the city on the road to La Ceiba. It is the country's busiest airport and offers the most international connections. **Continental, American Airlines, Delta, TACA,** and **Spirit** fly here directly from points in the U.S. such as Miami, Houston, Atlanta, New York, Los Angeles, and Fort Lauderdale. Regional airlines serving San Pedro include **Isleña Airlines** (✆ **504/5252-8322**), **Aerolíneas Sosa** (✆ **504/2550-6545;** www.aerolineasosahn.com), and **CM Airlines** (✆ **504/2668-0068;** www.cmairlines.com); these airlines fly to Tegucigalpa, La Ceiba, Roatán, Puerto Lempira, and other Central American destinations such as San Salvador, San José, Guatemala City, and Managua.

A taxi from the airport to the center of town should run about L260 to L300. There's also a **Hedman Alas** (✆ **504/2553-1361;** www.hedmanalas.com) bus terminal at the airport, with buses that run three times a day to Tela and La Ceiba or six times a day to their main hub in downtown San Pedro for connections to Copán or Tegucigalpa.

BY CAR All roads lead to San Pedro. It is the transportation hub of the country and almost always a necessary point of transfer between any two long-distance points. The best highway in the country and one of the best in all of Central America—CA 5—traverses the distance between San Pedro Sula and Tegucigalpa, and passes through Lago de Yojoa, Siguatepeque, and Comayagua along the way. It can be extremely crowded (semi trucks use this road to haul goods from one coast to the other), and accidents can sometimes drag traffic to a screeching halt; yet if things move smoothly, you can make the 241km (150-mile) trip between the coasts in under 4 hours on this road.

If you're coming to San Pedro Sula from Tela, La Ceiba, or elsewhere on the North Coast, take **CA 13.** If you're driving here from Copán, you have a pretty much straight shot on **CA 11** to the town of La Entrada, from where you will continue on **CA 4** to downtown.

Most major North American car rental agencies, such as **Avis** (✆ **504/2668-3164;** www.avis.com), **Budget** (✆ **504/2668-3179;** www.budget.hn), **Hertz** (✆ **504/2668-3156;** www.hertz.com), and **Thrifty** (✆ **504/2668-3154;** www.thrifty.com) have counters at the San Pedro airport, as well as offices in town.

BY BUS For years, there was only talk of a main bus terminal, but when that talk turned to action, few bus companies actually took initiative and moved their terminals there, scattering them across the city. In 2008, after much ado, all bus companies moved into the new terminal outside of town and closed their offices across San Pedro. The city's new station, the **Terminal Metropolitana de Autobuses,** is 5km (3 miles) south of town, on CA 5 towards Tegucigalpa, a L80 to L100 taxi ride from the center. It's full of restaurants, shops, and tour agencies.

Hedman Alas (7 and 8 Av., 3 Calle NO; ✆ **504/2553-1361**) is the best bus line in Honduras and the most useful for tourists who are sticking to the country's main destinations. It has mostly nonstop, first-class service several times per day to the San Pedro airport (L200; 20 min.), Tela (L325; 1½ hr.), La Ceiba (L418; 3 hr.), Copán Ruínas (L456; 3 hr.), Comayagua (L495; 3½ hr.), and Tegucigalpa (L535; 4½ hr.). The company also offers connecting service in Copán to Guatemala City (L1,140) and Antigua, Guatemala (L1,330).

Other companies that travel from San Pedro Sula to Tegucigalpa include **Saenz** (✆ **504/2553-4969;** L456), which has regular and *primera clase,* nonstop service six times a day to the capital; and **Viana** (Av. Circunvalación; ✆ **504/2556-9261**), which offers Clase Oro/Gold Class service to Tegucigalpa (L600), as well as La Ceiba (L342).

To reach Gracias, try **Gracianos** (✆ **504/2656-1403;** L100) at the main terminal, which has departures until 2pm for the 4½-hour ride that passes through Santa Rosa de Copán and La Entrada. To reach Tela, try **Tela Express** (9 Av. 9 and 10 Calle; ✆ **504/2550-8355;** L60), with five daily departures. If you're heading to La Ceiba and Trujillo, check out **Diana** (✆ **504/2441-6460;** L150) or **Cotuc** (✆ **504/2520-1597;** L150), which have nine and five daily trips, respectively, from the main terminal.

To reach Managua (L950) or Guatemala City (L1,330), your best choice is **TICA** (✆ **504/2556-5149**), which runs buses daily at 5am from the main terminal. Buses first stop in Tegucigalpa before heading out of the country. For San Salvador, **King Quality** (✆ **504/2553-4547;** www.king-qualityca.com; L874) has a daily service that departs San Pedro Sula at 7am and arrives around 2pm.

GETTING AROUND

Apart from a few of the major hotels, almost every site of interest to the typical traveler sits within the circular **Circunvalación** and can be reached on foot. Some areas can be dangerous, through, and robberies do occur, so it is best to take taxis, especially during the night.

While the confusing, crowded, and often dangerous public bus system here is of little use to travelers, **taxis** are cheap and plentiful. A ride anywhere in the center will rarely run over L60.

ORIENTATION

The dividing marker for San Pedro Sula is **Avenida Circunvalación,** a large boulevard that encircles the downtown area, with **Parque Central** at its center. Many amenities, like gas stations and restaurants, can be found radiating around the park. The center of town is laid out in a standard grid divided by four quadrants: northeast, southeast, northwest, and southwest. Avenues lead from north to south and streets from east to west. The area on the western side of the **Circunvalación,** including directly on the street, is where you will find the City Mall, Multiplaza Mall, several top hotels, and nearly all of the best restaurants and nightspots.

[FastFACTS] SAN PEDRO SULA

Banks & Currency Exchange **Banco Atlántida** (✆ **504/2558-1580**), on Parque Central, exchanges traveler's checks, gives cash advances on credit cards, and has an ATM. There are also ATMs in every mall, most of the large hotels, and some gas stations, and scattered about downtown in 24-hour booths. There's a black-market currency exchange at Parque Central, but rates are no different from the moneychangers in storefronts and at the airport.

Hospitals You can contact your embassy for a list of doctors in San Pedro or try **Centro Médico Betesda** (Av. 11a NO and Calle 11a NO; ✆ **504/2516-0900**), which is open daily 24 hours for emergencies and has consultations from 9 to 11am and from 3 to 6pm.

Internet and Call Centers Within a few blocks of Parque Central are literally a dozen small Internet cafes charging less than L20 per hour. These same cafes also have net phones for international calls and software for downloading digital photos. Alternatively, try the local telephone company **Hondutel,** at Av. 4a SO and 4a Calle SO, where you can make long-distance calls for a few lempiras a minute. There's also a cybercafe at the airport, but prices are four times as expensive.

Laundry & Dry Cleaning There are dozens of small *lavanderias* that will wash, dry, and fold your clothes in a day for less than L60 per kilo. For fast service, head to **Astroclean** (Av. 14a SO and Circunvalación), just across from the City Mall.

Newspapers The gift shop at **Gran Hotel Sula,** in Parque Central, stocks day-old (sometimes older) copies of North American newspapers.

Police The **Tourist Police** (Av. 12a NO and Calle 1a O; ✆ **504/2550-3472**) take calls daily, 24 hours.

Post Office The post office is at Av. 3a SO and Calle 9a SO Correos, and is open Monday to Friday 7:30am to 6pm and Saturday 8am to noon. You can send packages from here, but a safer and more efficient way is through **DHL** (Circunvalación at Brigada No. 105; ✆ **504/2550-1000**) or **FedEx** (Calle 17 and Av. 10 SO No. 56).

Visitor Information There is a small tourist information center in the tourist police booth beside the Museo Naturaleza.

Water While San Pedro Sula may seem like an American suburb at times, you should still stick to bottled water.

What to See & Do

Parque Central (Central Park) is the heart of San Pedro and located smack in the middle at 1 Calle and 3 Avenida. Most of the city's attractions, as well as restaurants and shops, are clustered around this park. Though the park lacks the charm of colonial centers in Tegucigalpa and Comayagua, it's still the most identifiable landmark (apart from the giant Coca Cola sign on one of the hillsides) and most popular meeting place in the city. Recent efforts have cleaned up this square and the pedestrian-only streets near it quite a bit. The **Cathedral** at the 3 Avenida side, built in 1949, doesn't have the history or elegance of some of the country's better-known churches, but nevertheless, it is worth a peek when it is open during Mass in this attraction-starved city.

Museo de Arqueología e Historia de San Pedro Sula (Museum of Anthropology and History of San Pedro Sula ★ Only a few blocks from Central Park, this must-see museum walks you through the history of the Sula Valley and Honduras from pre-Columbian times, during colonial rule, and into the modern era.

San Pedro Sula

ATTRACTIONS ●

Estadio Olímpico Metropolitano **30**
Guamilito Market **5**
Museo de Arquelogía e Historia de San Pedro Sula **18**
Museo de la Naturaleza **8**
Parque Central **14**

RESTAURANTS ◆

Arte Marianos **24**
Café Skandia **16**
Crepes **22**
Deriva Enoteca **20**
El Portal de las Carnes **26**
Entre Pisco y Nazca **21**
Hasta La Pasta **6**
Pizzeria Italia **12**
Restaurante Vicente **13**
Plaza Típica Coracts **17**
Restaurante Don Udo's **3**
Sushi Itto **2**
Wine & Tapas 188 **23**

HOTELS ■

Casa del Arbol Centro **11**
Clarion Los Proceres **7**
Crowne Plaza **10**
Gran Hotel Sula **15**
Guacamaya B&B **28**
Isabella Boutique Hotel **1**
Hilton Princess **25**
Hotel Copantl **29**
Los Jicaros **9**
Metrotel Express **19**
Real InterContinental **27**
Tamarindo Hostel **4**

parque NACIONAL EL CUSUCO ★

While it is difficult to reach and not nearly as majestic as Parque Nacional Celaque (see p. 139), El Cusuco is well worth the time and effort if you're in the San Pedro Sula area for a few days and have some time to spare. Set in the Merendón Mountain Range--45km (28 miles) away—the park is dominated by lush, unspoiled cloud forest and some of the most diverse avian life of any national park in the country. If you arrive early, you have the chance to spot quetzals (they're easiest to spot between Apr and June), toucans, parrots, and even a few mammals. There are two trails from the visitor center, Quetzal and Las Minas, which take no more than a few hours to explore. You can usually hire a guide from the visitor center for L90. Admission is L285, and the park is open daily from 8am to 4:30pm.

Jungle Expedition (✆ **504/9762-6620;** www.junglexpedition.org), based in San Pedro Sula, organizes various tours in and around the park, including night hikes, village visits, and waterfall rappelling that range from 6 hours to 3 days (beginning at L570 per person). Your best option for staying overnight here is in one of the cabins in Buenos Aires run by **Fundación Ecologista HR Pastor** (Av. 12a NO and Calle 1a, San Pedro Sula; ✆ **504/2557-6598**). Cabins run L230 per person and must be reserved in advance.

Most of the artifacts, which have labels in English and Spanish, were discovered in the area. There's a small bookstore and handicraft shop inside with a fine array of hard-to-find books on the Mayas, Honduran history, and handmade crafts from indigenous tribes.

3a Av. & 4a Calle NO. ✆ **504/2557-1496.** L50 adults. Mon–Sat 9am–4pm; Sun 9am–3pm.

Museo de la Naturaleza (The Nature Museum) The regional natural history museum details the plant and wildlife of the Sula Valley and the rest of the country through the art of taxidermy, bones, diagrams, and extensive charts and labels. It's worth a look if you have a particular interest in biology or have time to kill in San Pedro, but otherwise is skippable.

Calle 1 O & Av. 12a NO. ✆ **504/2557-6598.** L20 adults. Mon–Sat 8am–noon & 1–4pm.

Outdoor Activities

Soccer is undoubtedly the most popular pastime in Honduras, and San Pedro's **Estadio Olímpico Metropolitano** (5km/3 miles southeast of the center) is one of the top venues in the country for a match. Occasionally, national team games are held at the stadium, but you will most likely have to settle for one of the league games featuring either of the local teams: Motagua and Real España. You can buy tickets right at the doors, and games rarely sell out; tickets range from L100 to L500.

San Pedro Sula has two waterparks, Zizima and Wonderland, which provide welcome reprieve from the sweltering heat. **Zizima Eco Water Park** ☺ (Km 3 on the road to the airport; ✆ **504/2559-8600;** www.zizimawaterpark.com; L150 adults, L75 children under 12; Fri–Sun 9:30am–5:30pm) opened in 2007 to much applause. It is a huge, modern aquatic complex with a wave pool; dozens of slides, ranging from mildly intense to juvenile; pools and slides for inner tubes; Garífuna dance performances; and seven restaurants that are open every day of the week, even when the park is closed. The aim here is definitely at kids and families, and they flood the place, especially when school is out for the summer. **Wonderland** (in front of the Estadio Olímpico; ✆ **504/2559-9700;** L150 adults, L75 children under 12; Fri–Sun 10am–5:30pm) is the older and smaller of the two and has a lazy river, a wave pool, and a few slides. Unless there is some specific reason to come here, I would stick to Zizima.

Shopping

The sprawling **Guamilito Market ★**, between 8 and 9 Avenida and 6 and 7 Calles NO, sells products from around the country and from El Salvador and Guatemala, which fill up literally hundreds of small stalls. You'll find everything from hammocks, T-shirts, and pottery to cigars, Mayan figurines, jewelry, coffee, and Garífuna coconut carvings. Expect to bargain, and never accept your first price. Of special note is the small section of women who make tortillas not far from the food stalls—even if you don't buy anything, the market is worth a visit to see these women at work. The market is open daily from 10am to 5pm.

For high-quality hand-crafted leather handbags and purses, try **Danilo's** (Av. 18 SO and Calle 9, and also at the airport; ✆ **504/2552-0656**). **Maymo Art Gallery** (2 Calle SO and 7 Av. No. 24; ✆ **504/2553-0318**) exhibits and sells paintings from numerous Honduran artists, such as Benigno Gomez, Roque Zelaya, and Maury Flores.

The best malls in Honduras can be found in San Pedro. **City Mall** (Circunvalación and Carr), opened in late 2005, is home to more than 200 shops, a Cinemark movie theater, seven banks, and almost 30 restaurants.

Where to Stay

Like Tegucigalpa, San Pedro's hotel selection is geared mostly towards business travelers, who fill up the numerous international chain hotels on the Circunvalación throughout the work week. While most leisure travelers head from the airport to elsewhere and never actually set foot in the city, there are a few good budget and midrange options downtown.

VERY EXPENSIVE

Clarion Los Proceres Like the Hilton, the Clarion is close enough where you can walk to City Mall and the Zona Viva. This one is designed to suit mostly North American business travelers, with daily newspapers dropped in front of your door, free coffee, banquet facilities, computer hookups, multiple phone lines, and currency exchange. Still, though, the well-equipped rooms are somewhat bland. For slightly more, you can take the much more luxurious Hilton or, for slightly less, the still more stylish and modern Crowne Plaza.

17 Av. & 2 Calle, Bo Río de Piedras. www.clarionhotel.com. ✆ **504/2516-2727.** 37 units. L2,565 double. AE, MC, V. **Amenities:** Restaurant; bar; free airport transfers; fitness center. *In room:* A/C, TV, hair dryer, Wi-Fi (fee).

Crowne Plaza ★★ This former Holiday Inn was completely gutted before being reopened as a Crowne Plaza in late 2007. The result is well worth the effort. The hotel sits only a couple of blocks from the central park, right on one of the city's main thoroughfares, though the recent additions—with a sushi bar, sleek bar area, lounges for executive travelers, casino, and an outdoor pool—give you little need to leave. The rooms are quite nice and comparable to what you will find in the Hilton and Intercontinental. Deep red walls, beige carpet, iPod docking stations, and LCD TVs set a comfortable contemporary tone.

1 Calle & Av. 11 NO, Barrio Guamilito. www.crowneplaza.com/sanpedrosula. ✆ **504/2550-8080.** 125 units. L2,451 double. AE, MC, V. Free parking. **Amenities:** Restaurant; bar; fitness center; pool; Wi-Fi (free). *In room:* A/C, TV, iPod docking station.

Hilton Princess San Pedro Sula ★ Although the Hilton is 2km (1¼ miles) from the city center, it's just a banana's toss away from the Zona Viva and its nearby malls. The boxy yet elegant Republican-style building has all the amenities you would expect from a Hilton: a small sofa and seating area, Crabtree & Evelyn soaps, and HBO. There's also a decent but overpriced restaurant, an English pub, and a resort-like pool area that could easily fit in on any Caribbean beach. It's a small step down from the Real InterContinental in overall quality, but not by much.

10 Calle y Av. Circunvalación SO. www.sanpedrosula.hilton.com. ✆ **504/2556-9600.** 124 units. L1,786 double; L3,400 suite. AE, DC, MC, V. **Amenities:** Restaurant; bar; pool. *In room:* A/C, TV, hair dryer, minibar, Wi-Fi (fee).

Hotel Copantl ☺ The Hotel Copantl, the largest hotel in San Pedro Sula, is comparable to the Honduras Maya in Tegucigalpa in a number of ways. It's just outside the center and attracts loads of business travelers, and its large, upscale complex features restaurants, bars, a handful of tennis courts, and an Olympic-size swimming pool. Tile floors, floral bedspreads, and heavy wood furniture don't add much character to the rooms but are exactly what you would expect for this type of hotel. Additionally, the Copantl is home to the only major casino in the city, and its proximity to the Multiplaza Mall and Zona Viva is a big plus, especially for kids and teens.

Boulevard del Sur. www.copantl.com. ✆ **504/2556-7108.** 190 units. L1,710 double; L2,260 suite. AE, MC, V. **Amenities:** Restaurant; bar; fitness center; pool; tennis court. *In room:* A/C, TV, minibar, Wi-Fi (free).

Isabella Boutique Hotel ★★ Out of the several small boutique hotels that have opened outside of the Circunvalación, the Isabella is by far the best and one of the top accommodations in San Pedro Sula. Stylish and intimate, the little touches in this hotel—like accent rugs, contemporary art, LCD TVs, and iPod docking stations—are not the norm in Honduras by any means. Their Fussion restaurant is one of San Pedro's hippest and attracts a diverse crowd.

15th Ave. & 8th St. NO Barrio Los Andes. www.hotelisabellahn.com. ✆ **504/2550-9191.** 12 units. L2,185 double; L2,470 suite. Rates include breakfast. AE, DC, MC, V. **Amenities:** Restaurant; bar; pool. *In room:* A/C, TV, Wi-Fi (free).

Real InterContinental San Pedro Sula ★★ The best thing about this hotel is that it doesn't feel like it's in the city. The tropical plant–lined driveway and posh marble entryway give the impression of a resort atmosphere that is only further encouraged by the umbrellas, chaise lounges, turquoise pool, and waiters strolling around with rum-based drinks that have little umbrellas sticking out of them. The rooms and services are what you would expect from a Real Intercontinental: bright, luxurious, comfortable, clean, and modern. Most of the hotel was remodeled in 2007, so for the time being, it still has a leg up on the nearby Hilton Princess. They missed out on adding some local touches like local art, however, except in the beautiful Vertigo bar and Bambu restaurant.

Colonia Hernandez & Blvd. de Sur. www.ichotelsgroup.com/intercontinental. ✆ **504/2545-2500.** 149 units. L2,052 double; L7,695 suite. AE, DC, MC, V. **Amenities:** Restaurant; bar; pool. *In room:* A/C, TV, hair dryer, minibar, Wi-Fi (fee).

EXPENSIVE

Casa del Arbol Centro ★ From the moment you walk into this boutique hotel, you'll feel like you've set foot in a cozy hospital—the cleanliness is that noticeable. The rooms and bathrooms are practically spit-shine-clean, but otherwise standard with grayish walls, tile floors, and patterned bedspreads. There's also a small desk and a teensy weensy balcony that you can barely plant two feet on. The hotel is built around a big leafy tree, which gives it somewhat of a tropical vibe and adds some character that every other hotel in the city misses out on. It's not on the best street in town, so try to taxi in and out. They've added a newer, more modern and luxurious property, Casa del Arbol Galerias ★ northwest of the city in Colonia Jardines del Valle.

6 Av., between 2 & 3 Calle NO, Centro. www.hotelcasadelarbol.com. ✆ **504/2504-1616.** 13 units. L1,500 double. Rates include breakfast. AE, MC, V. **Amenities:** Restaurant; bar. *In room:* A/C, TV.

Gran Hotel Sula ★ Recent renovations have restored San Pedro's most classic accommodations to much of its kitschy glory. Rooms are decently sized and amenities are almost comparable to the Hilton or Real Intercontinental, including new flat-screen TVs that were added in 2008. Many of the rooms have balconies overlooking neighboring Parque Central; the lower levels can get a bit noisy, so opt for one of the higher levels or a room in the back, facing the pool. Their 24-hour Skandia coffee shop/diner and Granada restaurant (with an excellent Sunday brunch) make it hard to leave the hotel, but if you do, almost everything is just a few steps away.

Parque Central, Centro. www.hotelsula.hn. ✆ **504/2552-9999.** 117 units. L1,615 double. AE, MC, V. **Amenities:** Restaurant; bar; coffee shop; gym; pool. *In room:* TV, fridge (in suites); kitchenette (in suites); Wi-Fi (free).

MODERATE

Guacamaya B&B This pleasant little owner-operated B&B is in a large house near the Copantl. The tile floor rooms are brightly colored in red, blue, and other primary colors—almost like a Kindergarten class—and are clean and have lots of light. A business center and a plant-filled terrace are helpful if you are spending a couple of days here.

16 calle 19 y 21 ave S.O., Colonia Los Arcos. www.guacamayainn.com. ✆ **504/2556-8406.** 9 units. L1,325 double. Rates include American breakfast. AE, DC, MC, V. Free parking. *In room:* A/C, TV, fridge, hair dryer, Wi-Fi (free).

Los Jicaros Sitting directly behind the Crowne Plaza, this understated little hotel isn't the best choice in this price range, but if everything else is full—other hotels fill up frequently with business travelers on weekdays—it is cozy enough that you won't mind. Plus, being significantly smaller than some of the international chains, the service is much more personalized. Tile floors in the room and bathroom are shiny clean, and the rooms are decorated with clunky wooden furniture, 21-inch TVs, and walls painted in shades of orange and adorned by Honduran art (for sale). The hideous bedspreads need to go, though.

11 Av. & 2 Calle NO, Barrio Guamilito. www.usula.com. ✆ **504/2550-7003.** 10 units. L1,235 double. Rates include continental breakfast. Children under 12 stay free. AE, MC, V. Free parking. **Amenities:** Internet cafe. *In room:* A/C, TV.

Metrotel Express ★ Formerly the Microtel Inn and Suites, this hotel is all about location. If you plan to head out to the Bay Islands or elsewhere in the country and not spend much time in town, this is a mid-range oasis of calm and convenience by the airport. The rooms are reminiscent of a North American cookie-cutter chain hotel like a Days Inn, yet haven't been worn in. Larson's restaurant, their American diner, isn't half bad; it serves an all-day breakfast and is a much better option than the fast food over at the airport. Nice bonuses include a little pool area and helpful staff who can arrange trips to Lago de Yojoa or Tela.

Km 4 Blvd. al Aeropuerto. www.hotelhonduras.com. ✆ **504/2559-0300.** 60 units. L1,290 double. Rates include breakfast. AE, MC, V. **Amenities:** Restaurant; bar; pool. *In room:* TV, Wi-Fi (free).

INEXPENSIVE

Tamarindo Hostel The Tamarindo is the undeniable home of the San Pedro backpacker scene. Accommodations are divided between dorm-style rooms and simple yet spacious private rooms, all with their own bathroom and hot-water showers. Funky painted walls with Honduran art, graffiti, tapestries, and whatever else fits with Tamarindo's eclectic and cool vibe keep the decor interesting. The rooms and setting are not glamorous by any means. It's kind of like staying over at a group of college students' off-campus house. There are loads of extras, like a community room with TV and a DVD collection, two terraces with hammocks, free use of the kitchen, and even a small pool.

9 Calle NO & 11 Av. No. 1015, Barrio Los Andes. www.tamarindohostel.com. ✆ **504/2557-0123.** 6 units. L230 dorm bed; L600 double. MC, V. **Amenities:** Pool. *In room:* A/C, Wi-Fi (free).

Where to Eat

The dining scene in San Pedro Sula is the most cosmopolitan in Honduras. While there are plenty of soulless international and national chains every five steps, there are clusters of original bistros, wine bars, steakhouses, and sushi bars that concentrate mostly in the western half of the city or within a few blocks of the Circunvalación.

EXPENSIVE

Arte Marianos ★★ 🎁 HONDURAN/SEAFOOD On a gastronomic level, Arte Marianos is perhaps the most important restaurant in San Pedro. Their specialty is high-quality—with the prices to go with it—Honduran coastal and Garífuna specialties like conch ceviche; grilled and steamed fish platters; and *tapado,* a type of seafood stew made with coconut milk. There's a large wine list and a handful of grilled meat dishes. Every table is set with a side of delicious coconut bread. The often crowded restaurant is situated in a cheery converted nautical-themed house in the Zona Viva neighborhood with porthole-style windows.

9a Calle SO & 15a Av. SO, Zona Viva. ✆ **504/2552-5492.** Main courses L300–L600. AE, DC, MC, V. Daily 11am–10pm.

Deriva Enoteca ★★ SOUTH AMERICAN This hip wine and tapas bar, now in a new location in Colonia Rio de Piedras and a second location in Tegucigalpa, is one of the highlights of San Pedro's culinary scene. Chilean and Argentinean wines, available both as carry-out and from the restaurant, are the focus of the lounge-like setup, with a handful of sturdy wooden tables on the patio. Their menu, mostly Peruvian and other South American fare, focuses on dishes such as meats and seafood that go well with wine and *pisco,* as well as a selection of ceviches.

11 Ave. & 9 Calle, Col. Rio de Piedras. ✆ **504/2555-0535.** Main courses L190–L380. AE, MC, V. Mon–Sat 10am–9:30pm.

Entre Pisco y Nazca ★★ PERUVIAN Entre Pisco y Nazca has quickly become the go-to place in Honduras for Peruvian food and has even opened a second location in Tegucigalpa. Chef Yuri Larrea's food is pretty much what you would expect at a typical *cebicheria* in Lima. The atmosphere is simple, nothing too flashy, but the ingredients are fresh and of high quality. There are a mix of national plates and quite a few of their *cebiches* (raw fish marinated in lime juice) and *tiraditos* (thin sliced raw fish in a spicy sauce). Any of their *pisco*-based cocktails, like the *pisco* sour or *chilcano,* should do the trick to take your mind off the heat.

6 Calle, btw. 17 & 18 Av., Col. Rio de Piedras. ✆ **504/2510-2752.** www.entrepiscoynazca.com. Main courses L150–L320. AE, MC, V. Mon–Sat noon–9:30pm.

El Portal de las Carnes STEAK It is safe to say that El Portal de las Carnes is the best Uruguayan steakhouse in Honduras. That may sound like an understatement, but there are actually several of them spread around the country. Brochettes, ribs, sirloin, filet mignon, and national and imported beef of every other sort are paired with ceviches and seafood. The upscale rustic eatery is popular among the business crowd.

10 Calle & 15 Av., Barrio Suyapa. ✆ **504/2552-6137.** www.relportal.com. Main courses L152–L300. AE, MC, V. Mon–Sat 11:30am–2pm & 5–10pm.

Restaurante Don Udo's ★ INTERNATIONAL This often-crowded Dutch-owned restaurant has been a staple on San Pedro's restaurant scene for decades, though the original owners took off for Copán Ruínas to open a hotel. The colonial ambience at this first location attracts San Pedro's upper crust, who come for a decent variety of international dishes like pastas, steaks, seafood, and sandwiches. Their set lunch menus, usually three courses, are a great value. They have one of the more rounded wine lists in San Pedro, with bottles from Argentina, Chile, and Italy. Their outdoor patio occasionally has live music.

13 Av. NO & 7a Calle NO, Centro. ✆ **504/2553-3106.** Reservations recommended. Main courses L170–L420. AE, MC, V. Mon–Sat 11:30am–2pm & 6–11pm; Sun 10am–2pm.

Sushi Itto ★ JAPANESE This upscale sushi bar in Barrio Los Andes has one of the most complete Japanese menus around—loads of sushi and sashimi options, including boats for multiple eaters and dozens of specialty rolls such as the HondureñItto (shrimp, avocado, and banana) and the Narco Roll (crab, cheese, avocado, mushrooms, and chile). If sushi isn't your thing, Soba and Udon noodle dishes, teriyaki meats with fried rice, and Japanese-style brochettes with dipping sauces are served. Mondays are two-for-one rolls, while Tuesday and Wednesday abound with lunch combo specials. They will even deliver to your hotel.

16 Av. & 7a Calle NO, Barrio Los Andes. ✆ **504/516-1669.** www.sushi-ittohn.com. Reservations recommended. Main courses L120–L300. AE, MC, V. Mon–Sat noon–2pm & 6–11pm; Sun 10am–2pm.

Wine & Tapas 188 ★ SPANISH In the heart of San Pedro Sula's foodie hood, this cool little bistro that grew out of the more formal Bistro 188 next door has just a few tiny dining rooms with black leather seats and a leafy patio. The kitchen dishes out a range of small plates like fried plantains with chorizo, coconut curry shrimp, and steak in a jalapeño sauce. They have a stellar wine list, too.

8 Calle SO y 19 Av., Col. Rio de Piedras. ✆ **504/2516-3532.** Main courses L180–L260. AE, MC, V. Wed–Sat 6–11pm.

MODERATE

Crepes ★★ INTERNATIONAL/COLOMBIAN Modeled after a similar Colombian chain, Crepes serves sweet and savory crepes filled with anything you can imagine. The restaurant also serves *arepas* (a cornmeal patty stuffed with cheese or veggies), burgers, steaks, homemade soups, and even charcoal steaks that make for a sweet diversion from typical Honduran or North American fare. The vibe is fast and casual, but the space avoids feeling too much like a chain restaurant.

7 Calle, 19 Avenida SO, Col. Rio de Piedras. ✆ **504/2553-5797.** Main courses L75–L190. AE, MC, V. Daily 11:30am–10pm.

Hasta La Pasta ★ ITALIAN This popular Italian restaurant—it moved recently into a bigger location—soaks in the ambience with dim lighting and white tablecloths, though if I had my way, I would spread the tables out a bit more. The upscale southern Italian fare is some of the most reliable in San Pedro, with a concentration on fresh ingredients and homemade pastas and antipastos. A decent selection of both thin crust pizzas and wine complete the allure.

Av. 22 & Calle NO, Col. Moderna. ✆ **504/2550-5494.** Main courses L90–L275. MC, V. Daily 10am–10pm.

Pizzeria Italia PIZZA Adjacent to and run by the same owners of Restaurante Vicente (see below), Pizzeria Italia is the oldest pizzeria in town. Regardless of that claim, it's as classic a rustic pizzeria joint as they come, with just a few rickety tables. The pies beat those dished out at North American pizzeria chains that dominate the city, though, hands down.

Av. 7 & Calle 1 NO, Centro. ✆ **504/2550-7094.** Main courses L75–L200. MC, V. Daily 11am–10pm.

Restaurante Vicente ★ ITALIAN This restaurant has been open since 1962, and it's definitely an institution of sorts in town (as is the owners' other restaurant, Pizzeria Italia). It's more formal than the pizzeria and doles out standard Italian fare, such as pastas, risottos, calzones, and wine—it's a menu that has changed very little through the years, and it probably won't, since folks keep coming back.

Av. 7 & Calle 1 NO, Centro. ✆ **504/2552-1335.** Main courses L90–L275. MC, V. Daily 11am–10pm.

INEXPENSIVE

Café Skandia ★ ☺ INTERNATIONAL This 24-hour cafe and diner is the most dependable restaurant nearby Parque Central, and it's a gem of a '50s-style diner. It's like an authentic Johnny Rocket's; it would be hard to find a throwback this authentic in the U.S. Located in the Gran Hotel Sula (see p. 101) and branching out onto a small poolside patio, it serves hearty American and Honduran breakfasts, pancakes, French toast, *baleadas,* and roast chicken, as well as numerous other standards like burgers, onion rings, milkshakes, and even apple pie a la mode.

1a Calle O, at Parque Central, Centro. ✆ **504/2552-9999.** Main courses L55–L150. MC, V. Daily 24 hr.

Plaza Típica Coracts ★★★ HONDURAN A quick bite to eat in San Pedro doesn't necessarily have to be limited to Popeye's and Burger King. This large, covered, open-air food court just north of the plaza is the city's street-food mecca, with 20 or so stalls serving regional dishes from provinces such as Colón, Yoro, Cortés, and Atlántida, along with Guatemalan, Salvadorian, and Mexican fare. Standards are higher than for normal street fare, so the food, for the most part, is safe to eat.

Av. 3a NO & Calle 3a NO, Centro. No phone. Main courses L55–L100. No credit cards. Daily 8am–5pm.

San Pedro Sula After Dark

While the consensus has always been that La Ceiba has the best nightlife in Honduras, San Pedro isn't far behind, and it's catching up fast. Along the **Circunvalación** and in the **Zona Viva** (at Av. 15a and 16a SO, between Calles 7a and 11a SO in Barrio Suyapa) are the majority of the city's many bars, lounges, and clubs. The two-level lounge and dance club **B412** (9a Calle SO and Av. 16; Thurs–Sat 9pm–3am) is one of the favorite spots on the strip at the time of writing, particularly their open-air second level that overlooks the city. A block away, **The Cube** (8a Calle SO and Av. 16; Thurs–Sat 9pm–3am) attracts mostly young people intent on spending most of the night on a crowded dance floor.

The hottest late-night club in town is currently La Ceiba transplant **Hibou** (first floor of the City Mall; ✆ **504/9536-0035;** Thurs–Sat 9pm–4am). If you like DJs blasting loud house, techno, and salsa, crowds of hard-partying hip 20-somethings dressed to kill, and dancing until dawn, then this place is your best bet. Covers vary depending on the night, but usually range from L60 to L120.

If slinging back gin and tonics and playing roulette or blackjack are more your thing, check out **Casino Copán** in Hotel Copantl (p. 100).

LAGO DE YOJOA

Although it sits right off CA 5, between the major metropolises of San Pedro Sula and Tegucigalpa, far too few travelers do more than see this breathtaking lake out the bus window. Covering 89 sq. km (34 sq. miles), at 700m (2,297 ft.) above sea level and surrounded by misty pine-covered mountains that rise straight out of the water in places, coffee fincas, and two national parks, this is the largest natural lake in the country and is one of Central America's most overlooked natural attractions. The tranquil setting is home to several great hotels and guesthouses—not to mention dozens of fish restaurants with awe-inspiring views—so it's mind boggling that the place isn't swarming with busloads of tourists like Lake Atitlán in Guatemala.

Not that this is a bad thing, though. The serenity is the chief reason why most come. One group of travelers has long visited Yojoa: birders. These intense, dedicated enthusiasts come from around the world on very detailed tours in the hopes of spotting the rare and vast number of species that Yojoa is known for. Nearly 400 species have been identified on the lake and on its shores, making it one of the preeminent birding destinations in a country already known for birding. If you left your binoculars and avian identification charts at home, there are still plenty of ways to enjoy the setting, from renting a rowboat, to hiking in either of the two cloud forests, to touring a Lenca archeological site or just sampling beers in one of the country's only microbreweries.

Essentials

GETTING THERE & GETTING AROUND

You'll need to have your own **car** to explore the more remote corners of the lake, as there aren't taxis in town. The country's major highway, CA 5, which runs between San Pedro Sula and Tegucigalpa, passes right beside the eastern edge of the lake and the town of La Guama, from where you can easily take Hwy. 54 to the north and Peña Blanca. You can also get to/from San Pedro via Hwy. 54 (1½–2 hr.).

Any Tegucigalpa-bound **bus** that's coming from San Pedro will let you off at La Guama and vice versa; the ride from San Pedro Sula takes 3 hours (L150–L250). **Mini-buses** (L10) regularly ply the route between here and La Guama and Peña Blanca, as do **taxis** (L20).

ORIENTATION

CA 5 parallels the eastern edge of the lake, where most restaurants and hotels can be found, as well as the small town of La Guama and access points into Parque Nacional Cerro Azul Meámbar. On the north side of the lake, you will find the town of Peña Blanca, which is the largest town surrounding the lake and where small markets, a few banks, and cybercafes can be found. It is still a rather secluded place to base yourself, but the Parque Eco-Archeological de Los Naranjos is here, as well. On the western side of the lake, the roads are impassable except for four-wheel drive vehicles. This is also where you will find Parque Nacional Montaña de Santa Bárbara.

[FastFACTS] LAGO DE YOJOA

Bank **Banco Occidental** in Peña Blanca has a Visa ATM.

Hospital **Clinica Santa Cecelia** (✆ **504/2650-0010**) in Peña Blanca, at the turnoff to Los Naranjos, is open 24 hours.

Internet **Peña Blanca Net Café** (daily 8am–9pm) is one of the better options on the main strip and will also do international phone calls. Naturaleza restaurant on CA 5 has free Wi-Fi.

Tour Operators **D&D Brewery** (✆ **504/9994-9719;** www.dd-brewery.org) operates tours from Peña Blanca.

What to See & Do

Finca Paradise A few minutes past D&D Brewery, a visit to this 78-hectare (193-acre) eco-park makes for a pleasant way to spend a half day. Various trails dissect the property, passing clusters of citrus trees and coffee plants, a Lenca ball court, and cool streams. There is excellent bird watching within the park.

3km (1¾ miles) from the town of Peña Blanca, 1km (½ mile) past D&D Brewery, Los Naranjos. ✆ **504/9948-9766.** L100 adults. Mon–Fri 8am–7pm, Sat 8am–6pm, Sun 8am–3pm.

Parque Eco-Archeological de Los Naranjos ★ This small Lenca site on the northern edge of the lake is a far better eco-park than an archeological one. Just a few mounds and piles of stones can be found at the site, which dates back to approximately 700 B.C. More exciting are the 6km (3.7 miles) of stone paths and dirt trails that weave through much of the complex, including a hanging bridge. This is one of the best spots for bird-watching around the lake, and there's even a small tower for birders near the mounds. A small museum and visitor center with information on finds at the site and general background of the Lencas graces the entrance and parking area. To get here from La Guama or Peña Blanca, you can catch a minibus to El Jaral on Hwy. 54, which should drop you off on the main drag, if not right at the park. A second entrance has been added in Los Naranjos, though tickets must be bought at D&D Brewery before entering.

3km (1¾ miles) from the town of Peña Blanca, El Jaral. ✆ **504/2650-0004.** L114 adults. Daily 8am–4pm.

Parque Nacional Cerro Azul Meámbar ★★ The majestically misty mountains along the eastern side of the lake make up this 478-sq.-km (185-sq.-mile) park. The base of the park comprises coffee plantations and tropical forests, which turn to pine forests that then turn to cloud forests as the mountain climbs to a height of 2,047m (6,716 ft.). The park is a significant supplier of water to the surrounding

Volunteer Opportunities in Parque Nacional Cerro Azul Meámbar

The Christian NGO Proyecto Aldea Global/Project Global Village (© 504/ 2239-8400; www.paghonduras.org) has managed Parque Nacional Cerro Azul Meámbar since 1992. Conserving the natural environment, providing sustainable development for the rural communities that live in the buffer zone around Cerro Azul, and helping to jumpstart ecotourism projects is just part of the work they do in and around the park. Groups and individuals are encouraged to contact the nonprofit organization if interested in lending a helping hand to one of their numerous projects in the area.

communities and contributes more than 70% of the water to Lago de Yojoa. The isolation of the park means that wildlife here is flourishing. Several hundred bird species, including keel-billed toucans and resplendent quetzals, as well as more than 50 species of mammals, such as peccaries, tapirs, monkeys, pumas, and jaguars, can be found inside the park. Plus, there are loads of orchids, an elfin forest, and a handful of waterfalls.

From the visitor center near Los Pinos, there's access to three main hiking trails, ranging from 1.2km to 8km (.7 mile–5 miles) in length. There are several other trails into the park from surrounding communities, as well.

Like many of the cloud forests in Honduras, this one is nearly impossible to reach, even though it has six entrances. Public transportation to the park is nonexistent, and you definitely need a 4×4 to go on your own. The main entrance is at the town of Los Pinos. To get there, take the marked turnoff at La Guama from CA 5 and continue up the steep, bumpy road for about 15 minutes, until you reach Santa Elena, and then follow the signs until you reach Los Pinos and the visitor center. Trained guides are on hand for L200 per group.

Turnoff at La Guama for Los Pinos. © **504/2239-8392.** www.paghonduras.org. L20 adults. Daily 8am–6pm.

Parque Nacional Montaña de Santa Bárbara This cloud-forest park on the western side of Lago de Yojoa is dominated by the second-highest peak in the country, Santa Bárbara, which is sometimes called El Maroncho. The mountain is as pristine as they come, and visitors here are rewarded with some of the biggest biodiversity in the country. Orchids; more than 400 species of such birds as trogons, toucans, and woodpeckers; and butterflies, fungi, spider monkeys, anteaters, and jaguars can all be spotted. There is no infrastructure in the park whatsoever, but a few unmarked trails will take you to the 2,744m (9,003-ft.) summit, over about a 2- or 3-day walk. You can ask around for a guide in the villages of El Playón, Los Andes, or San Luis Planes, which border the park, for approximately L200 per day. You can get here by catching a bus from Peña Blanca to any of the towns that border the park, though it's most easily seen on a 2-night guided hike or bird-watching tour with Malcolm at D&D Brewery.

For information, try the Santa Bárbara tourist office at © **504/2643-2338.** Free admission.

Pulhapanzak Falls ★★ Pulhapanzak is the awe-inspiring waterfall that adorns the tourist brochures and posters you see when you land at pretty much every airport in Honduras. The 43m-high (141-ft.) waterfall on the Río Amapa crashes down to a rocky base and radiates a heavy mist from the moist tropical air. Occasionally, you can catch a glimpse of a scarlet macaw or toucan in the trees around the falls.

There's a pretty park with a cafeteria and picnic tables above the falls, as well as a few swimming holes. Guides, usually local kids who hang around the park, can take you in a small cave behind the waterfall for a small tip. It's a slippery and often muddy path down to the base, so be extra careful.

It's easiest to reach Pulhapanzak on a guided tour, since getting here by bus is time-consuming and complicated. (By public transportation, you must catch a San Pedro–headed bus from Peña Blanca, and then after about 10km/6¼ miles, get off at San Buenaventura. From here, you must catch a taxi westward, or walk 45 min. or so up a bumpy dirt road to the entrance.)

10 km NE of Peña Blanca, L20 adults. Daily 6am–6pm.

Cuevas del Taulabe When Hwy. CA 5 was being built, they discovered this underground passage. Explorers have traversed more than a dozen kilometers, and they still have yet to reach an end. Guides—they're free, but you should tip—at the entrance will lead you around the first few hundred meters into the cavern, a true show cave with electric lights, rails, and steps. It is possible to explore further in the cave, though you must make arrangements in advance with the mayor of Taulabe.

At the entrance are a few craft and food stands; of particular interest are the numbingly rich sweets hanging in plastic bags—they are famous in the region.

Km 140 on CA 5, just S of the S end of the lake. www.mitaulabe.com. L40 adults. Daily 8am–5pm.

Outdoor Activities

BOATING, KAYAKING & FISHING There are lots of opportunities to sail here. **Honduyate Marina** (right on CA 5; ✆ **504/2608-3726**) is the best operator to use for getting out on the water. They rent out sailboats, fishing boats, and jet skis, and even give tours on an old ferry. Another option is to head to the **D&D Brewery** (see below) and rent a rowboat there for about L55 for the day. Bass fishing, which once attracted fishermen here from around the world until the stocks were severely depleted, is slowly making a comeback in the lake.

BIRD-WATCHING ★★★ Hummingbirds, orioles, motmots, cuckoos, tanagers, toucans, woodpeckers, herons, and even the occasional quetzal are among the nearly 400 birds that have been recorded around the lake. Otters, bats, and iguanas are sometimes spotted, as well. Brit Malcolm Glasgow, D&D Brewery's on-site ornithologist (✆ **504/2994-9719**), is the best known guide in the area and has near-encyclopedic knowledge of the Yojoa's avian life. He leads half-day trips to the best birding spots on the lake via rowboat at a charge of L250 per person, as well as 2-day trips to Santa Bárbara National Park for L1,000 per person, including transport, food, and rustic accommodations in a family home. Minimum two people; prices drop for larger groups.

Where to Stay

EXPENSIVE

Finca Las Glorias Large groups of weekend vacationers from San Pedro and Tegus are the usual guests at this property on the north side of the lake. (If you come during the week, you'll probably have the place to yourself.) The stone walls, high-beam ceilings, and tile floors help lend a modern yet rustic feeling to the lodge and the cabins spread about the recently remodeled property. The lodge's ample porch seating enables you to enjoy the vast lake views. Active travelers will appreciate the access to horses, boats, and mountain bikes for exploring the area. There's even a small water park (L90 adults) on the property. On Sunday, the restaurant features live music and a seafood buffet.

2km (1¼ miles) from Peña Blanca. www.hotellasglorias.com. ✆ **504/2566-0461.** 35 units. L1,160 double; L2,320 cabin. AE, MC, V, DC. **Amenities:** Restaurant; bar; Internet (free, in business center); pool. *In room:* A/C, TV.

La Posada del Lago Right on CA 5, this upscale yacht club, which is also known as the Honduyate, is by far the fanciest place to sleep on the lake. All of the enormous rooms are bright, clean, and come with little extras like DVD players and sitting areas; most important, all rooms boast amazing lakeside views. The property also has a few small cabins nearby, which are older and far more rustic. The lodge and Chalet de Lago restaurant are a favorite of wealthy vacationing Hondurans and locals alike—this is very much the lake's social hub.

Km 161 of Hwy. CA 5. www.honduyatemarina.com. ✆ **504/2608-3726.** 9 units. L1,690 double; L2,090 suite; L285 cabin. Rates include breakfast. AE, MC, V. **Amenities:** Restaurant; bar; pool. *In room:* A/C, fan, TV/DVD player, Wi-Fi (free).

MODERATE

Brisas del Lago The largest hotel in the area is one of the classic stays on Lago de Yojoa, though Honduran families and business groups from San Pedro and Tegucigalpa are the only ones who visit. All rooms have a balcony and face the lake, along with little pluses like fine linens and clean tile floors, though they are otherwise quite plain and boring. The suites add an extra bedroom. They have a recreation center about a kilometer from the hotel with a large pool for adults, one for kids, a playground, paddleboats, a picnic area, and horses.

1km (½ mile) from La Guama on Hwy. 54. www.hotelbrisasdellago.com. ✆ **504/2238-5596.** 64 units. L750 double; L1,499 suite. AE, MC, V. **Amenities:** Restaurant; bar; recreation center (1km/½ mile away). *In room:* A/C, TV.

El Cortijo del Lago American John Chater, who has lived in Honduras for decades, and his wife Marta have built this small lodge on a beautiful strip of the lake between La Guama and Peña Blanca. It has been around for a few years, but recent expansions and renovations to the rooms have made it a viable option. There is not much going on in the way of decor, but the rooms are spacious and clean, and they have showers in the bathrooms. The rooms are on a hill, so the big windows, particularly in the rooms on the second floor, look down onto the lake and beyond to the mountains. They also have a few dormitory-style beds, a few small cabins, and a house for rent. The hotel has a couple of boats for excursions on the lake, and the Chaters work closely with Cerro Azul and Los Pinos, and can help arrange tours and transportation to the park.

2km (1¼ miles) from La Guama on Hwy. 54. www.elcortijodellago.com. ✆ **504/2608-5527.** 7 units. MC, V. L150 dorm bed; L300 cabin; L450 double; L1,400 house. **Amenities:** Restaurant; bar. *In room:* A/C, fan.

PANACAM Lodge ★★ These excellent cabins were completed in 2008 just beside the Los Pinos visitor center at Parque Nacional Cerro Azul Meámbar. Previously, there were a few rustic accommodations, but these new constructions have upped the game significantly. They are so close to the entrance of the park that you'll smell the pine, which is all around, and hear the squawks of toucans and hums of hummingbirds as soon as you step out the door. The cabins are quite simple, but well built and comfortable. They have nine cabins that sleep three, as well as two huge dorm-style mega habitations they rent out to groups of 20 or fewer. All have tile floors, electricity, private bathrooms, and small porches. There's a small restaurant that serves a full menu for breakfast, lunch, and dinner. This is one of those rare accommodations with prime access to a national park that is both cozy and economical. If you really want the best chance of seeing wildlife, spend the night in these cabins and wake up before dawn, when the birds and animals are most active. Don't forget to make reservations, as large groups occasionally take over the place.

Beside the Los Pinos Visitor Center, 8km (5 miles) from La Guama. www.paghonduras.org. ✆ **504/9865-9082.** 11 units. L850 cabins; L160 mega unit bed. No credit cards. Free parking. **Amenities:** Wi-Fi (free). *In room:* TV.

INEXPENSIVE

D&D Bed and Breakfast ★★★ Run by American expat and bluegrass musician Robert Dale, who also operates the attached D&D microbrewery, this quirky little compound is set on one of the most beautiful areas of the lake. The easygoing setup and service gives the impression that you're staying at a friend's house. Standard rooms in the lodge are quite plain and a bit cramped—they just barely fit a bed and bathroom—but the overall value and excellent atmosphere is good for the price. The cabins, one of which has a Jacuzzi, are much more spacious, newer, and have small porches with hammocks. As an added bonus, all water used at D&D—including the sinks and showers—is purified because of the leftovers used in the beer-making process. Also, Dale is about as knowledgeable on travel and the history of the region as anyone and is a good source of info for activities and planning the next stage of your trip. D&D can also arrange bird-watching excursions and trips to the national parks, and hook you up with a rowboat for exploring the lake. The place is incredibly popular, mostly with return visitors and Peace Corp workers, and booked full about 90% of the time, so be sure to reserve a room in advance. For this corner of the lake, it's best to take an El Mochito–bound bus from San Pedro Sula's main terminal. If you get lost, just ask around for "La Cerveceria."

3.7km (2¼ miles) past Peña Blanca, Las Naranjos. www.dd-brewery.org. ✆ **504/9994-9719.** 9 units. L50 camping; L100 dorm bed; L300 double; L600 cabin. Rates include breakfast. No credit cards. **Amenities:** Restaurant; bar; brewery; pool; Wi-Fi (free). *In room:* Fan.

Where to Eat

In addition to the below recommended restaurants, there's a string of maybe 30 or so seafood restaurants along CA 5 on the edge of the lake. All are open-air eateries serving more or less the exact same menu. You get to pick your fish, usually tilapia or bass, and the preparation such as *frito* (fried) or a la *plancha* (grilled). It comes whole with head, eyes, and tail, along with lime wedges and fried plantain chips. Main courses run L75 to L150, and the restaurants are generally open daily 10am to 8pm.

D&D Brewery ★★★ INTERNATIONAL When American expat Robert Dale discovered he couldn't get a decent pint in Honduras, he decided to brew his own. Thus, the D&D Brewery became the first and only microbrewery in the country. Using hops imported from Stowmarket in England, the tiny brewery pumps out porters, ales, lagers, and even mango beers, as well as their own sodas flavored with mango, apricot, and raspberry. Locally picked blueberries are used to make blueberry soda and the restaurant's famous blueberry pancakes. The rest of the menu is a mix of American and Honduran staples like omelets, fresh soups, burgers, burritos, pork chops, and *anafres* (black bean and cheese fondue, served with chips). Dale occasionally will bust out his guitar and supply bluegrass music to accompany your meal.

3.7km (2¼ miles) from Peña Blanca. ✆ **504/9994-9719.** www.dd-brewery.org. Main courses L76–L152; beers L30. No credit cards. Daily 10am–8pm.

Naturaleza Restaurant INTERNATIONAL This large complex contains not just the largest restaurant in the area, but also a peculiar collection of everything else that was once missing around the lake—like a natural history museum, butterfly farm (L50 adults; daily 8am–3pm), handicraft shop, pool, administrative offices for Parque Nacional Cerro Azul Meámbar, and conference facilities. There's even free Wi-Fi. The restaurant is still the main focus, however, and it's set in one big cafeteria-style, high-ceilinged dining room. The lengthy menu features international favorites like full American breakfasts, burgers, pasta, fried fish, and shrimp, all done up in a style that's comfortable but short on quality.

Km 160 of CA 5, La Guama. ✆ **504/2608-5505.** Main courses L100–L260. No credit cards. Daily 10am–8pm.

HIGHWAY CA 5 TO COPAN RUINAS

You can easily take a bus to Copán Ruínas, transferring in San Pedro Sula. But with your own wheels, you can take the well-maintained, paved Hwy. 20 that branches off CA 5 at the south end of Lago de Yojoa at Pito Solo, where the road winds its way through the mountains and valleys. The route's numerous ways to break up the journey make this one of the country's great drives. En route, you will pass pine forests, caves, hot springs, roadside fish restaurants, a lively *artesania* culture, and small, charming whitewashed colonial villages that you could almost fit in your pocket.

San Pedro Zacapa & Azacualpa

The first turnoff on Hwy. 20 from Pito Solo leads to these two sleepy, whitewashed villages on the rolling slopes of Santa Bárbara. Each cobblestoned town has a small square and a few cafes and restaurants. The main objective for most tourists, though, is not the small-town atmosphere, but the **Aguas Termales de Azacualpa** (L50 adults; daily 8am–5pm), tucked away in the hills nearby. These are true Central American hot springs with almost no infrastructure; just a parking lot, one concrete tub, and a makeshift sauna built of wood planks and plastic tarp. The springs are direct from the source in a few small sulfur-smelling, steamy streams that lead first through a fine-looking arch that has been naturally carved in the rock and then into the Río Jaitique. You have to be careful, as some of the places where the water first hits the surface are dangerously hot. You can walk through the arch down to the river where there are a few calm spots to cool off.

Minibuses (L10) make the trip to Zacapa and Azacualpa from Pito Solo (just wait at the turnoff) every 30 to 45 minutes or so during daylight hours. The hot springs are several kilometers past Azacualpa, on a very bumpy dirt road. This is a trip that's much easier with your own transportation.

Santa Bárbara

The largest town on the stretch of road between Copán and Lago Yojoa, right at the foot of the Santa Bárbara Mountain, makes a good base for exploring the surrounding villages or just a place to break up the journey. Plus, it's the only place with ATMs and cybercafes. The town was founded in 1761 by Jewish families from Gracias who have passed their blue-eyed features to the present generation, though the once colonial charm of this town is being paved over, and the 18th-century facades are turning to modern storefronts. The one part that modernization has not changed is the snowy white, 19th-century cathedral standing on the eastern side of the Parque Central.

GETTING THERE & GETTING AROUND

Junqueños (✆ **504/643-2113**) runs three daily buses to Tegucigalpa (L150; 4 hr.) from their terminal just north of the plaza. If headed to Lago de Yojoa, get off at Pito Solo (CA 5) and catch any of the buses headed north. For San Pedro Sula (L80; 1½–2 hr.), they have numerous buses from 5am to 5pm. To get to Copán, take any San Pedro bus, get off at La Ceibita, and transfer.

WHAT TO SEE & DO

The big attraction here is the junco handicrafts, though they are best found just outside of town. A few artisan shops and stands can be found on and near the square, such as **Artesania Lencon** (✆ **504/2643-2188**). About 3km (1¾ miles) on a hill-top southeast of town is a small fort, **Castillo Bográn,** with great views of the city and surrounding hills and forests. You can walk up in under 2 hours; otherwise, you can hire a cab (L30) to take you there.

WHERE TO STAY & EAT

Gran Hotel Colonial The Gran Colonial is the best place to stay in Santa Bárbara—there's no denying it. It's a big, mazelike place scattered about on three levels. The wide mix of rooms have all been updated at different times, so you might want to dig around to find one that's suitable. The decor is shabby, and the heavy wood furniture beyond tacky, though the bathrooms are modern and clean, and the hot water plentiful. On the entire route between Pito Solo and La Entrada, you have no better option.

Barrio El Centro. ✆ **504/2643-0808.** 52 units. L550 double. MC, V. Free parking. **Amenities:** Restaurant (across the street). *In room:* TV.

Mesón Casa Blanca HONDURAN A family home—more precisely, the large dining room—is the setting for what most agree is the best food in town. Meals are served in 2-hour time frames. Breakfast and dinner are a la carte, while lunch is buffet-style. Your options are limited to just a few *típica* plates—big plates—that rotate daily.

3 blocks SE of Parque Central. ✆ **504/2643-2839.** Main courses L50–L100. No credit cards. Daily 7–9am, noon–2pm & 6–8pm.

Restaurante La Casona HONDURAN Lots of shaky ceiling fans circle above one large white tile dining room that shows the steady erosion of decades of service. The food here is better than most. It's just *típica* and sandwiches, though that can be said for almost everywhere in town.

Just off Parque Central. No phone. Main courses L50–L150. No credit cards. Daily 8am–8pm.

Villages North of Santa Bárbara

The road weaves around north of Santa Bárbara and circles the mountain, passing countless small villages known for their easygoing nature and junco handicrafts. The wide-open vistas of pine forests and green hills assault you from every angle. It's a drive for the ages.

Gualala is the first village you see. The old-world, colonial atmosphere that Santa Bárbara is quickly losing hasn't been touched here. Apart from a quick drive through town and maybe snacking in a small country cafe, there is little to do but admire the cobblestone streets, whitewashed houses with tile roofs, flowering gardens in every yard, and the small square with its church.

On the highway between Gualala and the next town, **Llama,** lies a string of junco handicrafts stands selling every possible woven product in existence: chairs, dolls, baskets, and bags, as well as woven hammocks. **San Jose de los Colinas** is next. The town church dates back to the 16th century and is believed to be one of the oldest in the country.

If you are looking for a completely unspoiled town that has yet to pop on the tourist radar (at least, until this book is published), check out **Chinda,** just to the south of Trinidad. From the turnoff at the highway, head straight up the hill, and you will run into the small cobblestone square and its very traditional, rustic, white adobe church that dates to the mid-1900s. Apart from Sundays, the church is locked, but if you ask anyone nearby, they can point to the guy with the key—and he will even let you climb up into the tower, where a great view over the whitewashed houses and tile roofs unfolds.

Trinidad, set between the rivers Ulúa and the Chamelecón, is the last town of interest before getting on to CA 4, where you can head to Copán. Spanish settlers of Jewish backgrounds founded it in 1794. **Estancia El Pedregal** (**© 504/2552-6365;** www.estanciaelpedregal.com; L855 double), a small log cabin–like lodge with a few rooms, is a working farm set on 98 hectares (242 acres) of land in a beautiful spot among the mountains and forests, about 8km (5 miles) from Hwy. 20. Each room has A/C, a private bathroom with hot water, and a porch with a hammock. The land is used for cattle grazing, mango trees, and coffee plants. Their restaurant serves mostly regional dishes, as well as hand-kneaded bread baked in a clay oven and cheese made from the milk of their own cattle.

Any **bus** between Santa Bárbara and San Pedro Sula will stop on the highway turnoff to any of these villages.

COMAYAGUA

For more than 3 centuries Comayagua, which is 71km (44 miles) south of Lago de Yojoa, was the capital of Honduras, until it was moved to Tegucigalpa in 1880. The city was founded in 1537 by the Spanish explorer Alonso de Cáceres, and it has, without a doubt, the strongest colonial history in the country. Traces of the city's prominent past can still be seen in the architecture of the palaces, churches, and squares—all recently restored—in the city center. For much of the year, the town is empty, seeing only a trickling of tourists, but during Semana Santa (Holy Week) the city comes alive for the most passionate religious celebration in the country.

Essentials

GETTING THERE & GETTING AROUND

Comayagua is just a few blocks northeast of CA 5, which runs between Tegucigalpa (1½ hr. away) and San Pedro Sula (3½ hr. away). **El Rey Express** (**© 504/2237-8561**) runs hourly **buses** to both San Pedro (L200) and Tegucigalpa (L50). **Transportes Rivera** (1a Av. SO and 2a Calle SO; **© 504/2772-1208;** L200) runs to San Pedro hourly from 5am to 4pm. To get to Lago de Yojoa, get on any San Pedro–bound

Semana Santa ★★★

Semana Santa, or Holy Week, is a huge deal in Comayagua. From Palm Sunday to Easter Sunday, the city is flooded with tourists, pilgrims, day-trippers, and everyone else who wants to experience the most passionate religious celebration in Honduras. Processions and festivities occur every day in and around Comayagua's colonial churches and plazas. Good Friday is for many the most important day of this week; it's also when you will see *alfombras,* colorful sawdust carpets laid out to be trampled on during the solemn Via Crucis Procession, in which a volunteer carries a cross on his back through the streets beginning at 10:30am. If you plan on staying in the city during Semana Santa, be sure to book your hotel as much as 6 months in advance.

bus and ask to be let off at La Guama. Buses stop and can be boarded at the Texaco gas station towards the turnoff to the highway.

Anywhere in Comayagua can be reached on foot. The town follows a standard Spanish grid, surrounding the Parque Central. Nearly all churches, museums, and restaurants can be found within a few blocks of this square.

VISITOR INFORMATION

Banco Atlántida (1a Calle NO and 2a Calle NO; Mon–Fri 8:30am–3:30pm and Sat 8:30–11:30am) will exchange traveler's checks and has an ATM. In the Parque Central, there's a small **Tourist Center** (✆ **504/2772-2080**) with maps and brochures. To make long-distance calls, head to **Hondutel** (1a Av. NE and Calle 5a NO; daily 7am–noon and 12:30–9pm). Internet cafes are scattered all around the center.

What to See & Do

At the time of writing, the entire colonial center of town was undergoing a major renovation funded by the Spanish Cooperation Agency that was expected to last several years. In addition to the attractions reviewed in full below, you might stop to at least check out the exterior of the colonial churches **Nuestra Señora de la Caridad** (7a Calle NO and 3a Av. NO), a 16th-century building that became the de facto place of worship for native Indians of the area, and the **Iglesia y Convento de San Francisco** (Av. 1a NE and 7a Calle NO) by the Parque Central. Though the **Caxa Real** (1a Av. NE and 6a Calle NO), the country's first tax collection house and an important part of Honduran history, has been more or less completely destroyed by fires and earthquakes over the years, you can stop by to see its stone facade, which is sadly all that remains.

Catedral de Santa María ★★ The towering white cathedral on the north end of Parque Central, also known as La Iglesia de la Inmaculada Concepción, is considered by many to be the most beautiful cathedral in all of Honduras. Construction began on it in the late 17th century and was completed on December 8, 1711. Four of the original 16 hand-carved wood and gold-plated altars still survive. The clock in the church tower is one of the oldest in the world and the oldest in the Americas. Built around 1100 for the Alhambra in Granada, the clock was given to the town as a gift from King Phillip III and originally was placed in the Iglesia La Merced before being moved here. The church is undergoing an extensive renovation and is closed to the public for the next several years.

SE corner of Parque Central. Ask at the cathedral for admission prices & hours once it's reopened.

Iglesia La Merced Just 4 blocks south of Catedral de Santa María and fronting a small plaza of its own, Iglesia La Merced is the oldest church in Comayagua and one of the oldest in Central America. It was built in 1550, though an earthquake in 1774 destroyed one of the belfries and caused extensive damages. Inside are several paintings that date back to the 16th century.

1a Av. NE & 1 Calle NO. Free admission. Daily 7am–8pm.

Museo Colonial de Arte Religioso This museum, unfortunately destroyed by a fire in April of 2009, is located within a building that dates back to 1558 and was home to the first university in Central America. The collection, much of it now in ruins, derives from Comayagua's colonial churches, which were once virtual storehouses of valuable art. You'll see chalices, sculptures, paintings, and historical documents, such as Honduran general Francisco Morazán's marriage certificate. At last visit, the museum was still in ruins and a decision on the reopening was yet to be made.

Av. 2a de Julio & 3a Calle NO. ✆ **504/2772-0169.** Call for updates on the restoration.

Museo Regional de Arqueología Formerly a presidential mansion and the site of the National Congress of Honduras, this newly renovated museum surrounding a grassy courtyard is home to probably the most comprehensive collection of Lenca artifacts. Most pieces on display are from archeological sites within the valley and region surrounding Comayagua. Artifacts include textiles, pottery, stone carving, tools for grinding corn, and even petroglyphs; a few small rooms are also devoted to exhibits on national Honduran culture. There's a small craft store in the back of the museum.

6a Calle NO & Av. 20 de Julio. ✆ **504/2772-0386.** L20 adults. Tues–Sun 8am–4:30pm.

Where to Stay

Hotel America, Inc. This run-of-the-mill hotel in the center of the city, the largest in Comayagua, is the best that budget travelers have to make do with. It's not a terrible place, but the tacky, hospital-like rooms probably wouldn't be your first choice if there were a better option in this price range. On the plus side, the rooms are big, the bathrooms are clean, and there is even a decent-sized pool on the grounds. It could be worse.

Km 82 on CA 5. www.hotelamericainc.com. ✆ **504/2772-7672.** 61 units. L886 double w/AC; L800 double w/fan. MC, V. **Amenities:** Restaurant; Internet in lobby (free). *In room:* A/C (in some), fan, TV.

Hotel Casa Grande ★★ 🎁 This small bed-and-breakfast, hidden away on an unassuming street a few blocks from the square, is one of the most atmospheric places in Western Honduras. Chances are that when the city of Comayagua finishes its renovation and more tourists start arriving here, you'll hear much more about this colonial building–cum–bed-and-breakfast. Stone and *azulejo* tile walls and lots of tropical plants augment the lobby and halls, while wood floors and hand-carved wood furniture give the rooms a splash of personality.

7a NO Abajo, Comayagua. www.hotelcolonialcasagrande.com. ✆ **504/2772-0772.** 10 units. L952 double. Rates include breakfast. MC, V. **Amenities:** Internet in lobby (free). *In room:* A/C, fan, TV.

Hotel Santa Maria Right on the highway, this modern hotel lacks the charms of the cozy Hotel Casa Grande, but in regards to comfort and amenities, nothing compares to it in Comayagua. Rooms are clean and have the look and amenities of a

Holiday Inn. There are conference facilities and well-manicured gardens, but the best reason to stay here is the big, refreshing swimming pool.

Km 82 on CA 5. www.hotelsmc.com. ✆ **504/2772-7672.** 28 units. L1,360 double. MC, V. **Amenities:** Restaurant; bar; pool. *In room:* A/C, TV, Wi-Fi (free).

Where to Eat

Cactus Restaurant MEXICAN Right on a busy corner across from Iglesia La Merced, this Mexican restaurant is a welcome new addition to the Comayagua dining scene. Standard Mexican fare like tacos, *gringas,* quesadillas, and nachos, plus a few beef and shrimp plates, taste great and are all cheap. Tables are either indoors with A/C or on the outdoor patio, and both are graced by Mexican decor and music.

Parque La Merced. No phone. Main courses L55–L150. MC, V. Wed–Mon 11am–10pm.

Casa Castillo INTERNATIONAL Set in the renovated colonial Libertad Hotel on the south side of Parque Central, the atmosphere of this restaurant is a better reason to come here than the food, which is mediocre at best. Pastas, steaks, pork chops, sausage, and a few seafood dishes may come as a pleasant surprise if you are sick of Honduran foods, but otherwise, you should go elsewhere. The cheap, heaping breakfasts here are a better bet than lunch or dinner, though.

Parque Central. ✆ **504/2772-3528.** Main courses L130–L280. MC, V. Tues–Sun 9am–9pm.

Gota de Limon HONDURAN The food isn't bad at this spot, with its small dining room and a courtyard bar and grill, inside a spruced-up colonial building just behind the cathedral. It's mostly international comfort food with a few exceptions. Try the *bistec con salsa de champiñones* (steak in mushroom sauce), served with rice and salad, or the sandwiches. On weekend nights, it is a popular bar for 20-somethings, and a small dance floor appears out of nowhere. Occasionally, they have karaoke.

5a Calle NO, ½ block behind the cathedral. ✆ **504/2772-2378.** Main courses L50–L140. No credit cards. Daily 4pm–midnight.

Villa Real ★ HONDURAN/INTERNATIONAL Just behind the cathedral, this elegant restaurant makes good use of its colonial structure and flower-filled courtyard. Various rooms are filled with period furniture and art, which you are more than welcome to explore before or after your meal. Hearty Honduran *típica*—steak, rice, beans, tortillas, white cheese, and avocado—are standard fare here, as are *chuletas de cerdo* (pork chops) and grilled seafood.

Behind the cathedral, Parque Central. ✆ **504/2772-0101.** Main courses L100–L250. MC, V. Daily 11am–11pm.

Shopping

One shop on the northeast corner of Parque Central and a booth right on it sell handicrafts from around the region, such as hammocks, woven junco placemats, and hand-sewn dolls. Prices are reasonable.

Siguatepeque

Most know the name Siguatepeque from the shopping center and numerous large restaurants that line CA 5, which serves as the entrance to town. If you head in a couple of kilometers, you will find the center, which is not particularly attractive, apart from two small squares surrounded by bustling shops and cafes. The Spanish founded the city in 1689, though little in the way of colonial features remains.

There are a couple of good accommodations, though, if you are looking to break the journey between Tegus and San Pedro. There's **Hotel Plaza San Pablo** (✆ **504/2773-4020;** www.hotelplazasanpablo.com; L760 double), with 30 clean, modern rooms with private bathrooms and cable TV, just off the park. Also, the new seven-room B&B **Hotel Vuestra Casa** (✆ **504/2773-0885;** www.hotelvuestracasa.com; L800 double), on Boulevard Morazan, is promising.

COPAN RUINAS ★★ & COPAN ★★★

Not far from the Guatemalan border lies Copán, one of the most spectacular Maya ceremonial cities of Mesoamerica. The town of Copán Ruínas, 1km (½ mile) from the archeological site, is a small picturesque city with rough cobblestone streets and a buzzing central plaza that's the heart and soul of the place. It is reminiscent of a more compact version of Cuzco, Peru, although tourism is growing here at an equally impressive rate. For example, in the 1970s, there were just a couple of small hotels, mostly visited by archeologists. Now, there are more than 70. Copán is surrounded by beautiful forests with waterfalls, hot springs, and excellent bird-watching and adventure tourism possibilities.

Essentials

GETTING THERE

BY CAR If you're driving to Copán from San Pedro Sula, you have a pretty much straight shot on **CA 4** to La Entrada, where you can continue on **CA 11** to Copán; a 2½-hour drive in total.

Shameless Plug

If you're going on to Guatemala, be sure to pick up a copy of *Frommer's Guatemala.*

To get to and from Tegucigalpa is much trickier. From Copán, there is a beautiful route through the mountains to Gracias from La Esperanza on **CA 11-A,** but the road is windy, mostly unpaved, and sometimes impassable due to rain. Many drivers prefer to head back toward San Pedro Sula and catch **Hwy. 20** toward Santa Bárbara or head all of the way back and catch **CA 4.**

From the Guatemalan border at El Florido, it's just a 12km (7½-mile) drive to Copán Ruínas.

BY BUS **Hedman Alas** (✆ **504/2651-4037** in Copán Ruínas or 504/2651-4037 in San Pedro Sula; www.hedmanalas.com) offers five daily trips to San Pedro Sula, with connections to La Ceiba, Tela, and Tegucigalpa. They also run buses to Guatemala City daily at 1:30 and 6pm. The fare is L420 one-way, L800 round-trip. The one-way trip takes about 3 hours.

Copán Connections (✆ **504/651-4182**), below Twisted Tanya's, can arrange private buses and transportation to Antigua, Tikal, La Ceiba, Tegucigalpa, and the Bay Islands. Prices vary depending on the number of people.

Local buses also run from the dirt lot near the bridge at the entrance to town and head to La Entrada, 1 hour away, where riders can then transfer to a bus for Gracias, Santa Rosa de Copán, San Pedro Sula, or several other villages in the region.

GETTING AROUND

You can easily walk anywhere in Copán Ruínas, including from town to the archaeological site. However, if you need a **taxi,** they are plentiful and inexpensive. Most of

Border Crossing: El Florido

Crossing the border at El Florido on your way to Guatemala City or Antigua is relatively easy, and the crossing is now open 24 hours a day, so the long waits and crowds that the point was once known for have diminished significantly. Be prepared to pay the L20 departure tax (although some travelers have been asked for more) leaving Honduras and a L25 fee to enter Guatemala. Both sides accept lempira and quetzals, Guatemala's national currency, although moneychangers are everywhere. If you're driving a rental car, be sure to have all your papers in order and clear the trip with the rental-car agency in advance.

the taxis are small motor taxis or *tuk tuks,* which circulate around town and gather on the north and south sides of the central plaza. A taxi ride between town and the archaeological site should cost L20 per person.

ORIENTATION

It may be confusing, but the actual Maya ruins here are called Copán, while the little town is officially known as Copán Ruínas. Most folks refer to it generically as Copán or make the appropriate distinction when necessary. The town is very compact, and everything of importance is located within a 4-block radius of the central plaza. No official street names are actually used, and directions are given in relation to the central plaza or some other known landmark.

VISITOR INFORMATION

Banco Atlántida and **BAC** both front the central plaza and are fast and safe places to exchange money or use an **ATM.** To contact the local police, dial ✆ **504/2651-4060.** The post office (✆ **504/2651-4447;** Mon–Sat 8am–noon, Mon–Fri 2–5pm) is located just west of the Copán Museum.

There are a few **Internet cafes** around town; most charge around L20 to L40 per hour. For medical emergencies, ask your hotel or call Dr. Boqui at the **Clínica Handal** (✆ **504/2651-4408**). **Hondutel,** a half-block south of the central plaza, and **La Casa de Todo** (1 block from the park; ✆ **504/2651-4689**) are the best places for international phone calls. La Casa de Todo also has the best laundry service in town.

What to See & Do

Copán rivals La Ceiba and Roatán as one of the most tourist-friendly places in Honduras, and there are a growing number of ways to explore the city that go beyond the Maya ruins. You can now take a horseback ride into the hills, soak in a hot spring outside of town, or visit a coffee plantation and be back in town for happy hour. Just walk in to any tour operator or company office on or near the square to set up an excursion.

COPÁN ★★★

Copán is one of the grandest and most magnificently preserved of all Maya ceremonial cities. Surrounded by thick jungle and set beside the gentle Copán River, the ruins are famous for their raw stone-carved hieroglyphics, massive stelae, and the impressive Hieroglyphic Stairway. Your visit here should include the extensive archaeological ruins, recently excavated tunnels, and **Museum of Maya Sculpture.**

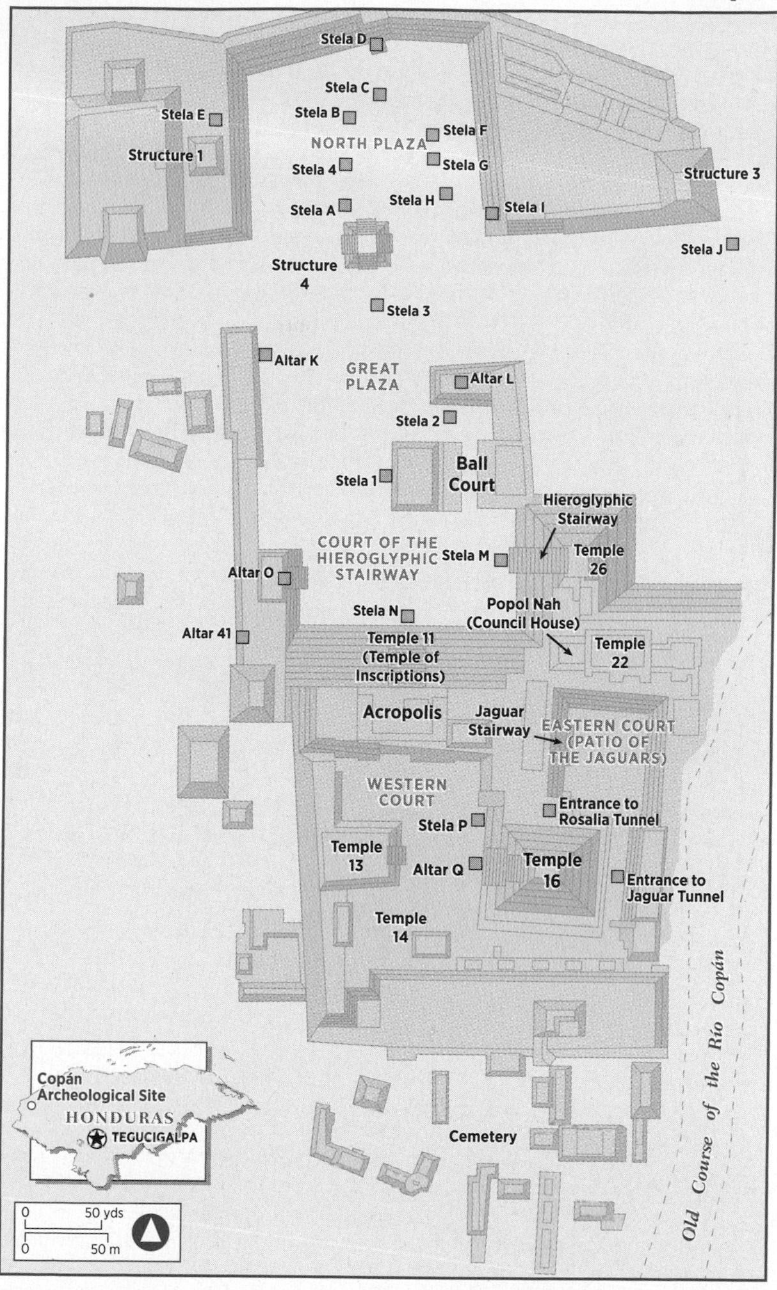

Stela D
Stela C
Stela B
Stela E
Structure 1
NORTH PLAZA
Stela F
Stela G
Stela 4
Stela H
Stela A
Stela I
Structure 3
Stela J
Structure 4
Stela 3
Altar K
GREAT PLAZA
Altar L
Stela 2
Stela 1
Ball Court
Hieroglyphic Stairway
COURT OF THE HIEROGLYPHIC STAIRWAY
Stela M
Temple 26
Altar O
Stela N
Popol Nah (Council House)
Altar 41
Temple 11 (Temple of Inscriptions)
Temple 22
Acropolis
Jaguar Stairway
EASTERN COURT (PATIO OF THE JAGUARS)
WESTERN COURT
Entrance to Rosalia Tunnel
Stela P
Temple 13
Altar Q
Temple 16
Entrance to Jaguar Tunnel
Temple 14
Old Course of the Río Copán
Copán Archeological Site
HONDURAS
TEGUCIGALPA
Cemetery
0 50 yds
0 50 m

The current area around Copán has been inhabited since at least 1400 B.C., and some of the earlier discoveries here show Olmec influences. The Great Sun Lord Quetzal Macaw, who ruled from A.D. 426 to 435, was the first of 16 consecutive kings who saw the rise and fall of this classic Maya city. Some of Copán's great kings included Smoke Jaguar, 18 Rabbit, and Smoke Shell. The history of these kings is meticulously carved into the stones at the ruins.

Copán was famously "discovered" in 1839 by the adventurer John L. Stephens, who documented the story in his wonderful book *Incidents of Travel in Central America, Chiapas and Yucatan* (1841). The book is beautifully illustrated by Stephens' companion Frederick Catherwood.

The entrance to the Copán archaeological site is located along a well-marked highway about a half-mile from the town of Copán Ruínas. The **visitor center** and ticket booth are at one end of the parking lot; the Museum of Maya Sculpture is at the other. The Copán Guides Association has a booth at the entrance to the parking area. Here, you can hire a bilingual guide for a 2-hour tour of the site, which includes the Sepulturas, for L950, no matter the size of your group. These guides are extremely knowledgeable and are highly recommended to hire for your first visit. They aren't necessary to tour the museum, as the signs are in English, or the tunnels, which are so short that the guide isn't necessarily of much value.

Admission to the Copán ruins and the Sepulturas (L285 adults) does not include a guide. Visits to the tunnels (L285) and Museum of Maya Sculpture (L135) are extra. Everything is open daily from 8am to 4pm.

Museum of Maya Sculpture ★★

Considering that the ruins get more and more crowded as the day goes on, I recommend that you visit the new Museum of Maya Sculpture (L135 adults; daily 8am–4pm) after seeing the ruins. The museum is located across from the entrance to the archeological park, a few hundred meters from the small visitor center where you pay your entrance fee. This large, two-story structure was built to protect some of Copán's more impressive pieces from the elements. Inside, you'll see beautifully displayed and well-documented examples of a broad range of stone carvings and hieroglyphics. At the center of the museum is a full-scale replica of the Rosalia Temple, which lies well preserved inside the core of Temple 16. The museum also contains the reconstructed original facade of one of the site's ball courts.

The Ruins ★★★

The ruins are at the end of a relatively short path from the museum exit. I recommend starting at the western plaza of Temple 16. As you face Temple 16, the Acropolis will be to your left. A trail and steps lead around the back, where you can enjoy a view over the Copán River to the surrounding mountains. Follow the path to the Patio of the Jaguars, where you'll find the entrances to the Rosalia and Jaguar tunnels. Continue on over the top of the Acropolis and the Temple of Inscriptions, and then down into the Great Plaza, where Copán's greatest hieroglyphic treasures were found.

The Temple of Inscriptions anchors the south end of the Great Plaza. To its east is the Hieroglyphic Stairway. This stairway, built by King Smoke Shell, rises up some 64 steps, each of which is carved or faced with hieroglyphs, telling the history of Copán's kings and their line of succession. To those literate in the language, the stairs once read as a giant book. Today, many of the carved stairs have fallen or faded, but enough remain to give a sense of the scale of this amazing achievement. The stairway is currently under cover, which makes it difficult to see. The lighting is poor, especially on cloudy days, but the trade-off in terms of preservation makes this necessary.

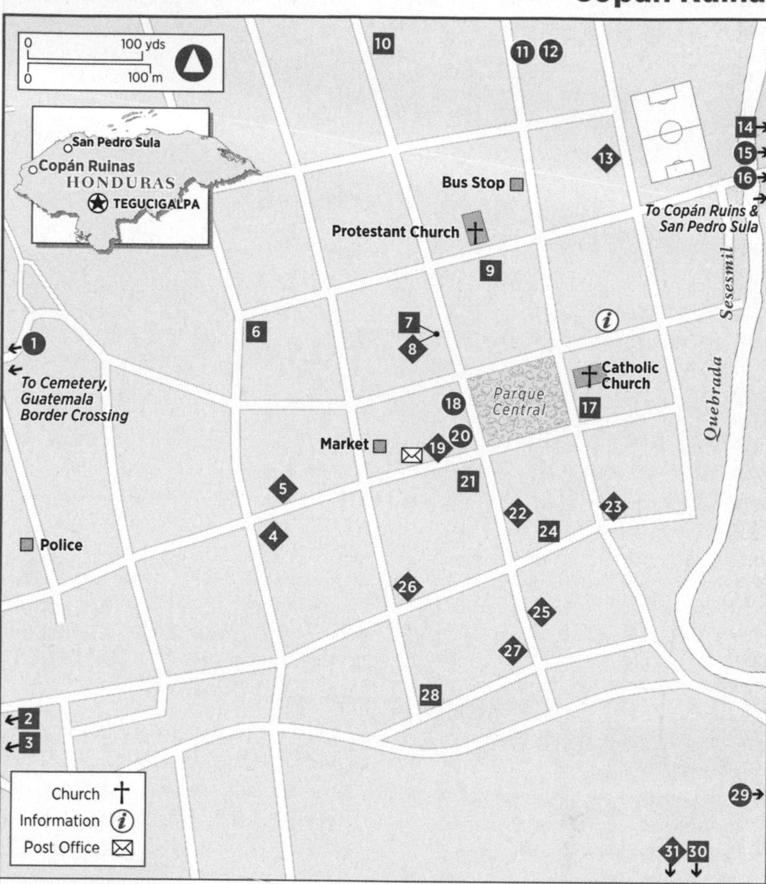

ATTRACTIONS ●

Alas Encantadas **1**
Café Welchez Coffee Plantation **15**
Fuerte Cabañas **11**
Los Sapos **29**
Macaw Mountain **12**
Museo Regional de Arquelogía **20**
Museum of Mayan Sculpture **16**
Photo Exhibition **18**

RESTAURANTS ◆

Baleada Stands **19**
Café San Rafael **25**
Café Welchez **8**
Carnitas N'ia Lola **27**
Churasqueria Momo's **23**
Comedor y Pupuseria Mary **13**
Hacienda San Lucas **31**
Jim's Pizza **22**
Llama del Bosque **5**
Twisted Tanya's **26**
ViaVia Copán **4**

HOTELS ■

Camino Maya **21**
Casa de Café **2**
Casa Rosada **6**
Don Udo's **28**
Hacienda San Lucas **30**
Hotel Plaza Copán **17**
Clarion Hotel Posada Real **14**
Iguana Azul **3**
La Posada de Belssy **9**
Marina Copán **7**
Terramaya **10**
Yat B'alam **24**

At the foot of the Hieroglyphic Stairway, and all around the Great Plaza, are examples of Copán's carved stelae. Many of these are carved on all four sides with detailed depictions of rulers, animals, and mythic beasts, as well as glyphs that tell their stories. Some of the stelae are originals, while others are replicas.

> **It Happened Here**
>
> **In 1839, American explorer John Lloyd Stephens bought the Copán ruins for $50 from a local landowner who felt that the land was just too rocky.**

Las Sepulturas ★

Located about 2km (1¼ miles) from the Great Plaza, Las Sepulturas is believed to have been a major residential neighborhood reserved for Copán's elite. The site gives you a sense of what the day-to-day living arrangements of an upper crust Maya may have been like. Las Sepulturas was once connected to the Great Plaza by a broad, well-worn causeway (which has been identified by NASA with digital satellite imaging), but today, it's reached via a gentle path through lush forests with excellent bird- and animal-watching opportunities.

The Rosalia & Jaguar Tunnels ★

Opened to the public in 1999, these two tunnels give visitors a firsthand look at the historical layering technique of the Maya builders, who would construct subsequent temples around and over existing ones, no matter how beautiful and intricate the original. Entrance to the two tunnels is an extra L285 above the general admission, though these are well-lit modern excavations and not tunnels left by the ancient Maya, so it's a tossup whether or not it's really worth the extra money. However, the tunnels are fascinating and do give you a further sense of the massive scale of the archaeological undertaking.

ATTRACTIONS IN & AROUND TOWN

Alas Encantadas This is a small butterfly garden and breeding project, owned by one of Honduras' premier naturalists Roberto Gallardo, with loads of winged creatures, exhibits illustrating the various stages of metamorphosis, and a botanical garden with more than 200 species of orchids. They've added a few nice cabins on the property, called La Chorcha Lodge (www.lachorchalodge.com; L1,292 double).

300m (984 ft.) outside of town on the road to the Guatemalan border. ✆ **504/2651-4133.** L100 adults, L35 children. Daily 8am–4:30pm.

Café Welchez Coffee Plantation ★ 🎁 Finca Santa Isabel is where the Café Welchez brand of shade-grown coffee is produced. The tour, which leaves by bus from Copán, begins in the mountain nursery and takes you through the entire processing method, with the occasional chance to spot birds and butterflies in the surrounding rainforest. Tours are given daily with **Yaragua Tours** (✆ **504/2651-4147;** www.yaragua.com).

Outside Copán. ✆ **504/2651-4200.** www.cafehonduras.com. Tours w/transportation $25 adults.

Casa K'inich ☺ The Casa K'inich, or the Maya Children's Museum, moved from its small spot on the north side of the square to a colonial fort on a hill overlooking the city of Copán Ruínas. It won't take much of your time, but it's worth a look for the interactive and educational exhibits that teach kids (and adults) how to count and add in different Mayan dialects and how to play the ancient ballgame of the Maya.

Fuerte Cabañas. ✆ **504/2651-4105.** www.asociacioncopan.org. L20 adults; children free admission. Mon–Sat 8am–noon & 1–4pm.

Los Sapos The small ceremonial site of Los Sapos, located across the river from Copán, is believed to be tied to ancient Maya birthing and fertility practices. This is a very small and minimally excavated site. You can see some stone carvings of *sapos*, or frogs, and the carved figure of a pregnant woman. In addition, the site features the exposed foundations of a few large structures. Several tour agencies in town offer horseback-riding tours that include a visit here.

5km (3 miles) from Copán Ruínas, on the grounds of Hacienda San Lucas. L40 adults. Daily 9am–5pm.

Macaw Mountain ★ ☺ Macaw Mountain is one of the newer attractions in Copán Ruínas and features an extensive collection of tropical birds, primarily parrots and macaws, and some local raptors. The way the birds are displayed makes this place special. (The enclosures are quite large and well done, and you can even walk through some of them.) This attraction is spread out over a lush setting of a tropical forest and coffee plantation, with a beautiful river and well-designed trails. There's an excellent riverside restaurant, the Jungle Bistro, run by Tanya from Twisted Tanya's in town, and a separate coffee shop with home-roasted beans.

4.8km (3 miles) west of the central plaza. ✆ **504/2651-4245.** www.macawmountain.com. L200 adults. Daily 9am–5pm.

Museo Regional de Arqueología Also known simply as the Copán Museum, this museum, under renovation at last visit (it should reopen in late 2011), holds a small collection of pottery and artifacts from the ruins, as well as a series of interpretive and explanatory displays. Perhaps the most interesting exhibit here is the complete burial niche of an ancient Copán scribe. If you're going to the ruins and the museum there, there's no need to visit this place. However, if you're hanging around town, it will take you only about 30 to 45 minutes to tour all the exhibits.

West side of Parque Central. L40 adults. Daily 9am–5pm.

Copan Photo Exhibition ★ This permanent photo exhibit, in conjunction with Harvard's Peabody museum, is a welcome addition to the main square. The collection of enlarged 19th-century black-and-white images detail the original excavation of the Copan ruins and shows what much of the town and archeological sites looked like when excavations began. You'll see the main square as a dusty lot and the pyramids as piles of stones.

West side of Parque Central. Free admission. Daily 9am–5pm.

Outdoor Activities

HIKING Base Camp Adventures (✆ **504/2651-4695**) has 2-, 4-, and 6- to 8-hour hikes (L150–L665 per person; minimum two people) that bring you to places tourists don't normally get to visit in the area, including to isolated Chortí villages and to waterfalls. Interaction with the local communities is the key feature of these trips.

HORSEBACK RIDING If you want to explore some of the nearby Chortí villages in the mountains, a horse is your best option. Contact any local tour agency such as **MC Tours** (✆ **504/2651-4453;** www.mctours-honduras.com), **Yaragua** (✆ **504/2651-4147**), or **Xukpi** (✆ **504/2651-4435**), which all have guides and horses on hand.

HOT SPRINGS & HEALTH RETREATS The **Luna Jaguar Spa Resort** (✆ **504/2651-4746**) was opened in January 2007 by an Italian company where a simple hot springs facility once stood. While they have a simple pool area you can

Spanish Schools

While it isn't as popular as Antigua, Guatemala, a few hours away, Copán has a decent offering for those seeking to improve their Spanish skills. Ixbalanque (✆ 504/2651-4432) has been running since 1990 and is one of the best-known language schools in Honduras. One week, with 20 hours of one-on-one classes, meals, accommodations with a local family, and a tour, costs L3,990. Guacamaya (www.guacamaya.com) has a similar program for L4,275 a week and also can arrange volunteer work.

enjoy for L60, the only real reason to make the trek all the way here (24km/15 miles) is to enter the Acropolis (L200 adults) just across a hanging suspension bridge over the river. It has a somewhat Disney-esque feel to it with statues and stelae, sort of like a small Xcaret, though there is nowhere else in Honduras like it. Once you cross the bridge into the Maya netherworld, you enter a place of lush rainforest intersected by stone paths and gurgling streams that cross in and around dozens of small steaming pools of varying temperatures with waterfalls trickling in and out of them. In comparison to most other hot springs in Honduras, this one has the most creative and intimate setup. The centerpiece of the Acropolis is a several-story thatched-roof building looking out over a series of waterfalls where a few massage tables sit (L400 for 25 min., L800 for 45 min.). *Colectivos* there cost L40, and the last one leaves at 4pm. From their office in their hotel (see above) in town, they offer packages that provide transportation to the spa.

Spa Ixchel (8km/5 miles south of Copán at Hacienda San Isidro; **✆ 504/2651-4114;** www.spaixchelhonduras.com), a coffee *finca,* offers mud baths, skin treatments, meditation sessions, massages, and Mayan Temescal treatments. Call ahead for reservations.

Shopping

The streets of Copán Ruínas are brimming with simple souvenir shops selling T-shirts, jade carvings, hammocks, masks, cigars, and Guatemalan crafts and textiles. Several good markets are scattered within a couple of blocks of the square, with independent vendors who haul their crafts in from the surrounding villages.

La Casa de Todo (**✆ 504/2651-4185**), 1 block downhill from the Banco de Occidente corner of the central plaza, is an excellent gift shop with unique local crafts, a coffee shop, an Internet cafe, and a simple restaurant serving Guatemalan fare; they even have a couple of rooms for overnight stays or can do your laundry. **Casa del Jade**, 1 block north of the plaza, is part of a Guatemalan chain that sells a wide variety of jewelry and collectibles that contain the Maya's preferred stone. The boutique gift shops beneath the hotel **Yat B'alam** (p. 127), on Calle la Independencia, have one of the most unique and upscale selections of Honduran-made crafts, accessories, and home furnishings.

Where to Stay

The best range of accommodations in Honduras can be found in Copán. At the top level, there is a rustic hacienda, large resort, and a few nice boutique hotels, while several fine B&Bs and hostels round out the mid- and lower-price ranges. The quality is quite good for every budget, so any traveler should be able to find a clean, comfortable place to stay.

EXPENSIVE

Casa Rosada ★★ Elegance and romance are two words that come to mind when trying to describe this charming Spanish colonial–style inn with just a few rooms. They don't overdo anything. Hand-carved wooden mirror frames and hand-woven accent rugs have been chosen with care. Rooms are appointed with brick floors and Honduran art on the walls—there's a small gallery downstairs—and big windows with views of the town and surrounding mountains. The bathrooms are the finest in Copán, with a shower featuring dual showerheads and speakers so you can listen to the radio while bathing. There's even a bidet. There are several great little nooks and patios amid gardens and plants where you can steal away with a good book. Casa Rosada is also one of the few hotels in the entire country that go out of their way to accommodate travelers with disabilities.

2 blocks NW of the park. www.lacasarosada.com. ✆ **504/2651-4321.** 5 units. L1,653 double. Rates include breakfast. MC, V. **Amenities:** Cafe. *In room:* A/C, TV/DVD player, hair dryer, Wi-Fi (free).

Clarion Hotel Posada Real What it lacks in proximity to the center it makes up for it with its isolated setting—the Posada Real, the largest hotel in the area, overlooks the hills and vegetation of the Copán valley. This hotel, which was recently taken over by the Clarion chain, more than any other in western Honduras, is a resort. The large spread, etched out of the dense jungle, surrounds a central courtyard that houses the pool. The rooms are a bit on the plain side, with reddish tile floors, gold or orange walls, wood furniture, and little else in the way of decor. The hotel is a hit with conferences, weddings, meetings, conventions, and most other large events.

1km (½ mile) from town, near the archeological site. www.posadarealdecopan.com. ✆ **504/2651-4480.** 80 units. L2,660 double. AE, MC, V. Free parking. **Amenities:** Restaurant; bar; pool. *In room:* A/C, fan, TV.

Finca El Cisne Agro-tourism is the name of the game here. In the lush hills 45 minutes away from Copán Ruínas, about 15 minutes beyond the Luna Jaguar Spa, Finca El Cisne is a working, 100-year-old coffee and cardamom *finca,* cattle ranch, and botanical garden full of tropical birds such as toucans and motmots. Lodging is in Casa Castejón, a five-room hacienda-style building with comfortable rooms and solar power. Most of the construction on the grounds uses native stones and wood, while meals use ingredients produced on the property. Transportation and meals are included in the price. You can take a day trip here for only L1,121.

26km (16 miles) from Copán. www.fincaelcisne.com. ✆ **504/2651-4695.** 5 units. L1,465 per person for 1 night, L2,500 per person for 2 nights. Rates include meals. MC, V. *In room:* Fan.

Hacienda San Lucas ★★★ 🎁 This is my favorite hotel in the area, set on a hillside across the river from and overlooking the Copán archaeological site. The rustic elegance of the rooms is a throwback to its former life as a farm and ranch, as are the high wood-beam and plank ceilings. The large rooms each are outfitted with two queen-size beds, a large shared veranda with hammocks, and a beautiful stone shower. However, TV and Internet are not available. The hotel restaurant serves excellent meals, and they have recently built a yoga platform overlooking the river and ruins. The hotel abuts the Los Sapos ruins and has several excellent hiking trails on its grounds. Sunsets are taken on a long lawn off the main lodge building.

5km (3 miles) S of Copán Ruínas on the road to Los Sapos ruins. www.haciendasanlucas.com. ✆ **504/2651-4495** or 504/2651-4495. 8 units. L1,615 double. Rates include full breakfast. AE, MC, V. **Amenities:** Restaurant; bar.

Marina Copán ★ One of the better hotels in Copán Ruínas proper spans an entire city block facing the central plaza. The rooms are all tastefully decorated and come with large TVs, while the suites have tons of space and other nice touches, such as a Jacuzzi, a kitchenette, and a view. My favorite is no. 331, a third-floor corner suite with a large balcony and a great view of town. Many of the standard rooms come with a balcony, so it's worth requesting one when you make a reservation. There's a pool in the center of the hotel and plenty of areas to relax among plants and fountains.

Parque Central. www.hotelmarinacopan.com. ✆ **877/893-9131** in the U.S. & Canada, or 504/2651-4070 in Copán Ruínas. 52 units. L1,615 double; L2,280–L4,750 suite. AE, MC, V. **Amenities:** Restaurant; bar; small gym; midsize pool; room service; sauna. *In room:* A/C, kitchenettes (in some), TV, Wi-Fi (free).

Terramaya ★★★ The first true boutique hotel in Copán Ruínas is operated by the same owners as Casa de Café. Mostly stark white walls, with a few colorful Mayan paintings to decorate, define the stylish property. It's a brand new building, but the architects did a good job of keeping to the colonial vibe of the rest of town with the clay tile roofs, white stucco walls, and stone patio. Really, the only downside is that it is up a steep hill, though the beautiful garden with a massage nook, and attractive lounge and library, make it worth the extra calories burned to get there. Opt for one of the two upper-level rooms with terraces, where you can sneak a nice view of the town center and surrounding valley. There is free breakfast (different every day) and all-day coffee, tea, and iced tea available for guests.

Av. Centro America, 2½ blocks N of Parque Central. www.terramayacopan.com. ✆ **504/2651-4623.** 6 units. L1,805 double. AE, DC, MC, V. Free parking. **Amenities:** Bar. *In room:* A/C, TV (in some), Wi-Fi (free).

MODERATE

Camino Maya ☺ The Camino Maya occupies prime corner space on the central plaza, and so it competes with the Hotel Plaza Copán for the title of best-located moderate hotel. The lower level is home to a small restaurant, while the second level holds the guest rooms. These rooms aren't terrible, but the floral bedspreads, tacky wallpaper and curtains, and mismatching wood and metal furniture could use a makeover. As space in the center of Copán is limited, the hotel's recreation area—especially popular with the younger crowd, with two pools, extensive gardens, hammocks strung from trees, two restaurants, and short trails—is 4 blocks from the main hotel. It has gone downhill in the past few years, however. Nonguests can use the facilities for L40 a day.

SE corner of Parque Central. www.caminomayahotel.com. ✆ **504/2651-4518.** 23 units. L1,350 double. Rates include breakfast. MC, V. **Amenities:** Restaurant; bar; pool. *In room:* A/C, fan, TV, fridge.

Casa de Café ★★★ This house–turned–bed-and-breakfast, located a few blocks outside the center of town, has a good view of the Copán valley and the mountains of neighboring Guatemala. The rooms are all cheery, bright, and comfortable. Those occupying the higher ground are a little older and smaller, but they have the aforementioned view from their shared veranda. The newer rooms have exposed-beam ceilings and beautiful mosaic tile sinks, with a veranda that lets out onto a small garden. The owners, one a sometimes guidebook writer, are extremely knowledgeable about the area, and they also rent out a few fully equipped apartments nearby. Breakfast is different each morning during your stay, and they provide free coffee, tea, iced tea, and purified water to guests free of charge. Nearly 2 decades old, this place just keeps getting better and better.

1 block S & 4 blocks W of the central plaza. www.casadecafecopan.com. ✆ **504/2651-4620.** 10 units. L1,045 double. Rates include full breakfast. AE, MC, V. **Amenities:** Wi-Fi (free). *In room:* No phone.

Don Udo's ★ It's small, but not too small. It's elegant, but still affordable. The decor features Guatemalan tapestries and rugs, but doesn't feel too rustic. The colonial building is older, but restorations have kept it up to date, lending a contemporary feel, and have added modern amenities like TVs and A/C. Don Udo's is an all-around decent pick. My favorite part of the hotel? The rooftop sauna and Jacuzzi; a nice place to relax at night after a day of touring the ruins. An excellent restaurant on the first level serves international and Honduran fare. If Casa de Café is filled, this hotel is probably the most similar alternative.

2 blocks SE of the park. www.donudos.com. ✆ **504/2651-4533.** 16 units. L1,045 double; L1,900 suite. MC, V. **Amenities:** Restaurant; bar; sauna; Wi-Fi (free). *In room:* A/C, fan, TV, hair dryer.

Hotel Plaza Copán This hotel has a good location on the corner of the central plaza, with a good deal to boot. All of the rooms are spacious and feature red tile floors and high ceilings. No. 213 comes with a king-size bed and a private corner balcony overlooking the central plaza. There's a small pool in the central courtyard and a simple restaurant.

Parque Central. www.plazacopanhotel.com. ✆ **504/2651-4508.** 20 units. L1,197 double. Rates lower in the off season, higher during holiday periods. AE, MC, V. **Amenities:** Restaurant; bar; small pool. *In room:* A/C, TV.

Yat B'alam ★★ Opened in late 2007, this absolutely charming independent hotel is one of the best values in western Honduras. I'm hesitant to call it a boutique hotel for fear that the price will go up; it's currently an absolute steal. If it were located in Antigua, just a few hours across the border, it would cost three times as much. The ground floor is laid out like a cobblestone colonial street lined with craft shops and a cafe. There are just a handful of rooms, all on the second level, with tiled floors, dark wood contemporary furniture, and deep red decor. The triples have particularly high ceilings, and rooms near the street have the best views. Common areas with couches are sprinkled throughout and boast good views, as well.

Calle la Independencia. www.yatbalam.com. ✆ **504/2651-4338.** 6 units. L1,235 double. MC, V. **Amenities:** Cafe. *In room:* A/C, fan, TV, fridge, Wi-Fi (free).

INEXPENSIVE

Iguana Azul ★ The best backpacker hostel in town, Iguana Azul has just three private rooms and two dorm-style rooms. All have shared baths. Everything is kept spotlessly clean—the bathrooms, sinks, tile floors—and the colonial building and common areas are loaded with extras that you are unlikely to find at other Copán hostels. Same owners as Casa de Café and Terramaya.

3 blocks SW of the park. www.iguanaazulcopan.com. ✆ **504/2651-4620.** 5 units. L100 dorm bed; L260 double. No credit cards. **Amenities:** Wi-Fi (free). *In room:* Fan.

La Posada de Belssy If you need a clean, no-frills room but have outgrown sleeping in backpacker dorms, cross your fingers that La Posada de Belssy isn't full. They have a small rooftop lounge that's always full of other travelers chatting about their Central American exploits, but few other amenities.

1 block N of the plaza. www.laposadadebelssy.com. ✆ **504/2651-4680.** 10 units. L300 double. No credit cards. *In room:* Fan, TV.

Where to Eat

Copán's dining scene seems to take more after Antigua, Guatemala, than anywhere in Honduras. Vibrant backpacker hangouts, vegetarian cafes, and pizza places are packed in the small cobblestone center. If you want standard international traveler fare, you'll find it, but if you are a little bit adventurous, you can discover regional dishes like authentic Mayan specialties and Salvadoran *pupusas*. Apart from the places listed below, try the *comedores* inside the small market, 1 block from the plaza behind the museum, which serve simple traditional foods.

EXPENSIVE

Hacienda San Lucas ★★★ INTERNATIONAL/HONDURAN The in-house restaurant at this lovely hotel is probably the best restaurant in Copán, and certainly the most atmospheric. Meals are served in an open-air patio in front of the old hacienda building. The five-course candlelit dinners are one of the finest culinary experiences in Honduras today, with the choice of main courses including the house specialty of fire-roasted chicken with adobo sauce, a mole based on the herbs, spices, and nuts used by the ancient Maya of this area. Lunches are a bit more casual and range from homemade tamales to a salad-and-sandwich combination. The dinner hours listed below are for seatings; you can then stay and enjoy the meal, which often takes around 2 hours. A taxi here from town should run you L50 to L75 each way.

5km (3 miles) S of Copán Ruínas on the rd. to Los Sapos ruins. ✆ **504/2651-4495.** www.haciendasanlucas.com. Reservations necessary. Main courses L135–L285; prix-fixe dinner L475. AE, MC, V. Daily 8:30am–3pm & 7–8:30pm.

Twisted Tanya's ★★ INTERNATIONAL Part upscale fusion restaurant and part itinerant party central, this place mixes together elegance and extravagance in equal doses. The lovely open-air, second-floor corner dining room has white muslin curtains and fancy table settings. Their theory is "if it is in the market, it's on the menu"; the white-board menu changes daily and may include anything from homemade curries with coconut rice to salmon in a Jack Daniel's glaze. There are always a couple of vegetarian items to choose from, as well. Twisted Tanya's offers a L418 prix-fixe menu of soup or salad, entree, and dessert. An early-bird backpacker special will get you soup, pasta, and dessert for just L114. The desserts here are all homemade, decadent, and deservedly renowned. Their popular two-for-one happy hour is from 4 to 6pm.

1 block S & 1 block W of the central plaza. ✆ **504/2651-4182.** www.twistedtanya.com. Reservations recommended. Main courses L300–L418. AE, MC, V. Mon–Sat 2–10pm.

MODERATE

Café San Rafael ★ INTERNATIONAL Wine and a dozen imported cheeses, from stinky blues to creamy camemberts, are the highlight of this delightful little garden cafe. Being from the producer of San Rafael coffee, they also have a full coffee bar, as well as small plates and sweets like their BBQ beef sandwich, sweet brie balls drizzled in honey, and bourbon chocolate cheese tart. There's free Wi-Fi for customers, too.

1 block from the park. No phone. Main courses L80–L200. MC, V. Daily 8am–10pm.

Carnitas N'ia Lola ☺ HONDURAN Grilled and barbecued meats are the specialty of this two-level restaurant literally on the edge of town. N'ia's is one of the most consistently popular restaurants in Copán, partly because of the decent grub and partly because of the waitresses who carry drinks and dishes from the kitchen on their heads. Brochettes, typical dishes, tacos, and steaks are all good. *Anafres,* a bean fondue eaten with tortilla chips, is served in place of bread. Happy hour is from 6:30 to 8:30pm.

2 blocks S of the central plaza. ✆ **504/2651-4196.** Main courses L120–L300. MC, V. Daily 7am–10pm.

Churasqueria Momo's ★ HONDURAN Beef is why most folks come to Momo's. Whether it's in kebab, *churrasco,* steak, or *pinchos* form, the charcoal-grilled beef here is hard to resist. (Unless, of course, you're a vegetarian.) The restaurant sits on a nice open-air patio overlooking the valley and farms below, and a small collection of birdcages, some housing macaws, hangs around the tables.

1 block SE of the plaza. ✆ **504/2651-3692.** Main courses L95–L190. MC, V. Daily 9am–10pm.

ViaVia Copán INTERNATIONAL/VEGETARIAN I find the food at this popular spot a bit disappointing, and the music tends to be a little bit too loud; but you can't beat it as a meeting place for locals and tourists alike. There are a few tables on a small, street-side porch and more in a lush open-air interior courtyard. While there are some chicken dishes on the menu, this place really caters to vegetarians. One of the best dishes here is the *capela,* a homemade carrot-and-pesto lasagna. There are a host of other options, including Thai curries, Indian *pakoras,* and hearty sandwiches, *baleadas,* and veggie burgers. This place is actually part of an extensive international chain that caters specifically to itinerant backpackers. Happy hour is from 5 to 7pm.

1½ blocks W of the central plaza. ✆ **504/2651-4652.** www.viaviacafe.com. Main courses L70–L90. MC, V. Daily 7am–midnight.

INEXPENSIVE

At night, in front of the Hondutel office just off the square, several *baleada, carne asada,* and taco carts stands set up. The *baleadas* are simple—just a corn tortilla with refried beans and fresh cream—and cheap (L10), while the *carne asada* generally is served on a plate with rice.

Café Welchez INTERNATIONAL Café Welchez's setting at the corner of the central plaza gives this small room cafe one of the best views in town. While it is a bit pricey compared with other restaurants in town, the food is decent, especially for a light meal, and it's a nice, quiet place to rest your feet and read a book. Try their *ticucos a la crema,* a corn tamale with red beans slathered in a creamy sauce. Quiche, sandwiches, locally grown coffees, iced coffees and drinks, and coconut flan round out the menu.

Central plaza. ✆ **504/2651-4070.** Main courses L60–L200. MC, V. Daily 7am–10pm.

Comedor y Pupuseria Mary ★★ SALVADORIAN/HONDURAN Sometimes good, simple, local, and regional foods become obscured by flashier international restaurants in Copán. This is one of the places that locals love and that you should not miss. The central focus of the cuisine here is the *pupusas,* a type of corn pancake filled with chicken, meat, beans, or cheese that comes from neighboring El Salvador. There are nearly a dozen variations that range from an unbelievable L10 to L15. Just a couple will get you full. The restaurant is open early and has typical breakfasts, set *típica* lunches, and nightly dinner specials. The restaurant moved in May of 2011 near the *futbol* pitch, where their small hotel can be found, as well.

Frente Campo de Futbol, Calle Sesesmiles. No phone. Main courses L10–L120. No credit cards. Daily 7am–10pm.

Jim's Pizza ★ ☺ INTERNATIONAL This expat and gringo hangout, sometimes called Pizza Copán, is the best place for a pie in Copán—period. You'll also find a small selection of subs, grilled chicken, and steaks. Their big-screen TV is usually fronted by sports fans who can't miss a game while on vacation.

1 block S of the plaza. No phone. Main courses L125–L225. MC, V. Daily 2–10pm.

Llama del Bosque HONDURAN This is the place to come for simple, local fare served fast and at reasonable prices. Start with black-bean soup and a hard-boiled egg, and then opt for any of the grilled meat plates. For lighter meals, there are sandwiches and burritos. This is also a great choice for breakfast.

1½ blocks W of the central plaza. ✆ **504/2651-4431.** Main courses L50–L150. MC, V. Daily 7am–10pm.

Copán Ruínas After Dark

Copán Ruínas is a relatively quiet town. Aside from the hotel and restaurant bars (of which Twisted Tanya's is always a good call), the most happening spot at last check seems to be **ViaVia Copán** (see p. 129). In addition, you might try the **Tun Club** (1½ blocks west of the central plaza; ✆ **504/2651-4410**) next door, which has a dance floor and occasionally hosts karaoke nights. **Barcito** (Calle Independencia, 1 block south of Parque Central), on a second-level corner, has light meals, cocktails, and a better-than-average wine selection.

Sol de Maya (✆ **504/2651-4758**), on Avenidas El Mirador, has a few German beers on tap that are brewed on the premises and serves a few German and Honduran dishes, including house-made sausages and spaetzel.

A noise ordinance in the center forces restaurants and bars in Copán to close by midnight.

Side Trips from Copán

LA ENTRADA & THE RUINS OF EL PUENTE ★

If you're planning on exploring western Honduras, you'll likely be stopping at La Entrada at one point. This town serves as a junction of CA 4 and CA 11, and so is lined with buses that lead to Copán (2 hr.), San Pedro Sula (1½ hr.), Santa Rosa (1½ hr.), and lesser-known villages in the region.

La Entrada is a dusty, uninteresting town that would serve as nothing more than a transport hub if it weren't for the **Maya ruins of El Puente,** which are just 10km (6¼ miles) away. The majority of the buildings on the site, opened in 1994, date back to the Late Classic Period, between the 6th and 9th centuries, and the site is the second most important archaeological park in all of Honduras after Copán—although you wouldn't know it by the number of visitors.

Unless your visit parallels that of a tour bus, you'll likely have the entire site to yourself. Of the more than 200 buildings found in the park, only 9 have been excavated. The centerpiece is a medium-sized pyramid set on a wide grassy plaza that's lined with a few other buildings that have been cleared from the encroaching jungle. There's a small visitor center and museum at the entrance, about a kilometer walk from the ruins.

To get to the El Puente archeological site, you will need to hire a taxi, which costs L230 round-trip from La Entrada. Admission is L55 adults, and the park is open daily from 8am to 4pm. Or you can go on a guided tour, through Hotel El San Carlos.

You can easily visit El Puente as a day trip, but if you'd like to stay overnight, **Hotel El San Carlos** (Junction of CA 4 and CA 11; ✆ **504/2661-2228;** www.hotelelsan-carlos.com; L600 double) is the most reliable place to stay in the area. Just a few meters from the junction, this 45-unit hotel actually isn't half bad. There's a pool (where you can listen to the squawks of their two macaws), clean rooms with cable TV, and a restaurant that happens to be the best in town.

SANTA ROSA DE COPAN

45km (28 miles) to Gracias; 110km (68 miles) to Copán

Santa Rosa is the commercial and administrative hub of western Honduras and, though it isn't overflowing with tourist sights, it makes a good base for exploring elsewhere in the department of Lempira. The town has long been known for growing high-quality tobacco—said to be the best in the country—and this crop has played an important part in the town's history. The Spanish established the La Real Factoría del Tabaco here in 1765, and it led to considerable wealth for the city. Today, the city still boasts a number of pretty, *azulejo*-covered colonial buildings that were built by the Spanish. And, while La Real Factoría is no more, tobacco remains an important part of the economy.

Essentials

GETTING THERE

BY BUS The city's bus terminal sits in a lot on the main road about 1.5km (1 mile) from the center. Direct buses make the 3-hour trip to San Pedro Sula about four times per day; tickets cost L80. To get to Copán Ruínas, you can take either a 2-hour direct bus (L40) or transfer midway in La Entrada (L20) for a Copán bus (L20). Buses also head to Gracias (L30; 1¼ hr.) and the Guatemalan border at Aguas Caliente (L75; 2½ hr.). All buses leave when they're full, not according to a set schedule.

BY CAR From San Pedro Sula, take CA 4 to La Entrada and head south on CA 11-A; the trip takes about 2½ hours. To drive to/from Copán, you must also go through La Entrada and transfer to Hwy. 11.

GETTING AROUND

Most of Santa Rosa can be seen on foot. The center radiates out only a few blocks in each direction from the square. It's easier to take a taxi, but you can also walk to the highway, bus terminal, and factories in about 20 minutes.

Taxis can shuttle you between the center and the highway for L15 to L20.

ORIENTATION

There are two sections of Santa Rosa. The first is the colonial core of the city, which centers on the top of a hill that includes Parque Central and the Centro Histórico. The other lines the highway about 1km (½ mile) from the center and is where you'll find the bus terminal, the cigar factory, and many poorly constructed residences.

VISITOR INFORMATION

Banco Atlántida (south side of Parque Central; ✆ **504/2662-0138**) and **HSBC** (1 block west of the plaza on Calle Centenario; ✆ **504/2662-0847**) have 24-hour **ATMs** and will exchange traveler's checks. The **tourist office** (✆ **504/2662-2234**)

An Easter Festival

While it isn't as large as the Semana Santa (Holy Week) celebrations in Comayagua, the 7 days before Easter are still quite a spectacle in Santa Rosa de Copán. Six traditional processions reenact the Easter story and begin on Holy Thursday. One highlight of the festivities is the colorful designs, created from dyed sawdust and street flowers, that are laid out in the street for the processions to march over.

is in a round building smack in the middle of Parque Central and doubles as a **cybercafe** (Mon–Sat 8am–noon and 1:30–6pm).

What to See & Do

In addition to seeing the following attractions, you can contact the tour company **Lenca Land Trails** (✆ **504/2662-1128**) to arrange tours into nearby Lenca villages and other destinations across the region.

Beneficio Maya One of Santa Rosa's main coffee producers is located in this small factory just down the street from the Flor de Copán Cigar Factory. The famous Café Copán brand of coffee, mostly exported to Europe, is processed here, while the beans are grown on the hills outside of town. Although it may say so on most tourist brochures and guidebooks, there is no official tour here, but if you ask nicely, they will show you around. Products can't be bought on-site, but can easily be purchased in shops in town.

6 blocks from the bus terminal, Barrio Miraflores. ✆ **504/2662-1665.** www.cafecopan.com. Free admission. Mon–Sat 10am–noon & 1–5pm.

Flor de Copán Cigar Factory ★★ Just entering this building is intoxicating—the scent of tobacco penetrates your skin as you enter the premises. During your tour, you'll get a fascinating look into a full-fledged, working Honduras factory. Highlights include peeks at warehouses full of drying tobacco leaves, as well as rooms of workers de-veining the leaves, shaping the tobacco, rolling the cigars, and finally packing the final product for export.

4 blocks E of the bus terminal, Barrio Miraflores. ✆ **504/2662-0111.** L40 adults. Daily 10am–2pm.

Shopping

Although you can't buy cigars at the Flor de Copán cigar factory, you can purchase them from the distributor, **Tabacos Hondureños S.A. ★★** (Centenario 73A; ✆ **504/2662-0111**), which has small shop right in town, 1 block from the park. Several large humidors stock a wide selection of cigar boxes from the Santa Rosa de Copán factory, which produces a variety of labels. Prices are significantly cheaper than they are outside of the country. A few handicrafts and regional products can also be found here and in the small shops around Parque Central.

Where to Stay

MODERATE

Casa Real ★ While it lacks the colonial style of Hotel Elvir and is a bit more out of the way from the center, the more modern Casa Real has by far the best setup in Santa Rosa. Their grassy courtyard is centered on a pleasant open-air restaurant, Casa

Romero, and a pool area that seems straight out of a Roatán resort. The rooms are, sadly, much plainer than the beautiful property, with clean tile floors and shoddy furnishings and decor. The price is good for what you get, but this hotel has the potential to be so much more—all it needs is an interior decorator.

Calle 2a & 3a NO. www.hotelcasarealsrc.com. ✆ **504/2662-0801.** 50 units. L980 double with A/C; L760 double without A/C. MC, V. **Amenities:** Restaurant; bar; fitness center; pool. *In room:* A/C (in some), fan, TV.

Hotel Elvir ★ This hotel has been open since 1955, but you wouldn't guess it, since it's undergone several renovations and remodels. The standard rooms are spacious but a bit boring and bland; the two suites are considerably nicer, larger, and have Jacuzzis. Still, the services are the best in the city, and the facilities—including a rooftop pool with great views and a delightful open-air colonial courtyard—are first rate. Best of all, the hotel is right in the heart of town, and hotel owner Max Elvir, one of the staunchest promoters of tourism in western Honduras (see "What to See & Do," above), is on hand to give you sightseeing tips and to arrange tours.

Centenario & Av. 3a NO. www.hotelelvir.com. ✆ **504/2662-0103.** 43 units. L750 double; L2,090 suite. Rates include breakfast. AE, MC, V. **Amenities:** Restaurant; bar; fitness center; pool; Internet in lobby (free). *In room:* A/C, TV.

INEXPENSIVE

Hotel VIP Copán Don't be fooled by the name—the VIP is in no way a place for VIPs. The hotel sits on a crowded and noisy street a block from the park, and a limo probably couldn't even get here if it tried. The standard rooms lack windows and A/C, and are a bit smaller than the suites and borderline dingy. The suites are much better. They are new, clean, and full of natural light, and some look out onto the small but nice pool area. Overall, the hotel isn't terrible, as long as you don't expect the royal facilities that the name implies. If the Elvir and the Casa Real are full or a bit out of your budget, you won't find a better hotel in town.

Calle 1a & 3a NE. hotelcopan@latinmail.com. ✆ **504/2662-0265.** 34 units. L475 double; L760 suite. MC, V. **Amenities:** Restaurant; bar; pool. *In room:* A/C (in some), fan, TV.

Where to Eat

EXPENSIVE

Flamingo's ★ INTERNATIONAL Newly remodeled, Flamingo's is the classiest restaurant in Santa Rosa and where the tobacco bigwigs dine when they're in town. The menu is mostly international, with a few coastal Honduran staples like conch soup and *pescado al ajillo* (fish in garlic sauce). Grilled meats, pastas, and salads are also served. There's a full bar and even a small wine list, perhaps the only wine list in the cowboy-friendly department of Lempira.

Av 1a SE. ✆ **504/2662-0654.** Main courses L95–L285. AE, MC, V. Wed–Mon 11am–11pm.

MODERATE

Lenca Maya Restaurant ★★ HONDURAN My favorite restaurant in Santa Rosa. The funky herb- and citrus-tree-filled garden with various nooks and levels is the setting for a restaurant that seeks to preserve Honduran recipes from around the country. There's Sopa de Caracol from the north coast and an Indian Chicken Soup from the highlands. Much of the grilled meat, their specialty, focuses on specific cuts and comes sided with *tostones,* refried beans, and a slab of *queso fresco.*

Calle Canales. ✆ **504/2662-6477.** Main courses L80–L200. MC, V. Daily 11am–9pm.

Pizza Pizza ★ ☺ PIZZA Owned by an American expat and his Honduran wife, Pizza Pizza is a favorite stop for everyone from budget travelers to expats to locals. It's in the courtyard of a small colonial building about 5 blocks south of Parque Central. Hand-tossed dough, homemade sauces, and a brick oven make this the best pizzeria in town—out of a total of three. The menu features a few pastas and sandwiches, too. Plus, it's a cybercafe, and there's a decent book exchange.

Centenario & 5a NE. ✆ **504/2662-1104.** Main courses L76–L152. No credit cards. Thurs–Tues noon–10pm.

Zotz INTERNATIONAL The best way to describe Zotz is to say it's like a T.G.I. Friday's that happens to incorporate the occasional Honduran twist. Along with the black-and-white photos and multiple TVs showing sports, you'll find the occasional Maya design on a tapestry or knick-knack. The food hews closely to American fare, with grilled standards like burgers, steaks, and chicken wings mixed in with fajitas, salads, and two dozen other options that have been battered and fried. Happy hours and drink specials keep the place busy with 20-somethings and office workers most of the week.

Centenario & Av. 3 NE. ✆ **504/2662-1950.** Main courses L95–L228. AE, MC, V. Daily noon–midnight.

INEXPENSIVE

Ten Nepel ★ CAFE This tiny cafe and coffee shop directly beside Hotel Elvir is good for java, juice, or a quick snack. There are just a couple of tables in an elegant setting, and highlights on the menu include the *granitas*, espresso, and bagels.

1 Calle NE & Av. 3 SO. ✆ **504/2662-3238.** Main courses L10–L40. No credit cards. Daily 8am–6pm.

GRACIAS

45km (28 miles) to Santa Rosa de Copán; 155km (96 miles) to Copán

You wouldn't know it just by looking at it, but this sleepy town was once the Spanish capital of Central America. After its founding in 1536, it was named Gracias a Dios, after founder Captain Juan de Chavez, a Spanish conquistador, spent many long days combing the mountains for a decent stretch of earth: *"Gracias a Dios que hemos hallado tierra llana"* ("Thank God that we found flat land") were reportedly the first words out of his mouth when he found the town. In 1544, Gracias became home to the Spanish Royal courthouse and was given jurisdiction over a territory that covered the vast area between Mexico and Panama, but that didn't last long. Four years later, the court moved to Antigua, Guatemala, and little else was heard about Gracias for many years.

Having been overshadowed by nearby Copán (and Antigua) for far too long, Gracias is now preparing to make a statement. Hotels are expanding, tours to nearby Lenca villages are drawing press, its hot springs are becoming more developed, and the number of visitors to the national park here, Parque Nacional Celaque, is growing every year. Major renovations have either recently finished or are ongoing in several colonial churches, the small fort above the city, several historical buildings, the Parque Central, and throughout the entire Ruta Lenca. When everything has been carefully restored, the town of Gracias will be nothing less than a major Central American attraction. For now, though, cowboy hats are still the favorite accessory, the dusty old square is the town hangout, and for many places in the region, the word "Gracias" still means "thank you."

NATIONAL hero: LEMPIRA

Honduras's currency, the lempira, was named after the Lenca warrior of the same name. In the early 1530s, as the Spanish conquistadors invaded Honduras for the first time, this warrior led an uprising that is remembered to this day and revered across the country. After the Spanish settled in Gracias a Dios and began to move freely across the region, Lenca attacks on small parties of conquistadors became common. The Spanish invited the native chiefs of the region to a meeting and, upon showing up, all were hung. However, one didn't show.

Lempira, which means "man of the mountain" in Lenca, gathered a large group of warriors at a fort at Peñol de Cerquín near Erandique, even convincing rival tribes to join them. They began raiding Spanish settlements, which prompted the Spanish to gather their own forces to retaliate. With all their might, they attacked Peñol de Cerquín for 6 months but could not take the fort. This resulted in Captain Alonso de Cáceres initiating a peace accord. From here, the details get murky, depending on whose history lesson you accept. Spanish historian Antonio de Herrera has described a scene where Lempira, upon calling for nothing less than a Spanish withdrawal from the region, was shot and killed by a Spanish soldier. Other accounts have a soldier, Rodrigo Ruíz, fighting Lempira to the death or Lempira escaping wounded, only to be later beheaded by the Spanish on his sickbed at Piedra Parada. Regardless of how Lempira died, the Lencas or other tribes never put forth significant resistance against the Spanish again.

Essentials

GETTING THERE

BY BUS The bus terminal is a dusty lot across the street from the market. Direct buses make the 5-hour drive from San Pedro Sula about five times per day; the ride costs L100. To get here from Copán Ruínas, you must first take a 2-hour bus ride to La Entrada (L40), and then transfer to a Copán bus (L30) for another 1-hour ride. Buses head to a few other nearby destinations, too.

BY CAR From San Pedro Sula (5 hr.) or Copán (3 hr.), take CA 4 to La Entrada, and then head south on CA 11-A until you hit Gracias.

ORIENTATION & GETTING AROUND

Gracias comprises a small grid of streets that sits on a dash of flat land in the most mountainous part of Honduras, at the foot of the pine-covered Montaña de Celaque. Roads leading to the city are only partially paved, which is why getting there often requires going through San Pedro Sula, even if you're coming from Tegucigalpa.

Apart from its surrounding sites, most of the attractions in Gracias can be seen on foot. The colonial core of the city is concentrated around a small grid of streets less than 10 blocks long.

To get to Celaque or to the hot springs, you will need to take a **taxi,** which can be found near the market or the park. Alternatively, you can visit on a guided tour.

VISITOR INFORMATION

Gracias itself lacks an ATM, but **Banco de Occidente** at the Parque Central will exchange currency and traveler's checks. There are a few small cybercafes around the park, but most are quite slow. For international phone calls, head to **Hondutel** (daily 7am–9pm), 1 block from the park, beside the post office. The **tourist office** is in a small kiosk in the middle of the park (Mon–Fri 8am–noon and 2–5pm, Sat 8–11:30am).

What to See & Do

The **Parque Central,** a small tree-filled square surrounded by colonial buildings, is the most active spot in town, which isn't saying much. **La Iglesia de San Marcos,** on the southern side of the park, was built in the late 1800s. Beside it, you can find the remnants of the **Audiencia de los Confines,** now the home of the parish priest. One block to the north is **Las Mercedes,** the most attractive of the three colonial churches in the city. The facade dates back to 1610. The park underwent a major renovation in 2008 and 2009, and is looking better than ever.

Balneario Aguas Termales ★ ☺ After a day of hiking the steep hills of Celaque, there's nowhere better to turn than this naturally steamy pool of thermal water. The Balneario hot springs complex sits hidden on a hill submerged in pine forests outside of town. Several pools ranging from 92° to 96°F (33°–36°C) attract a steady stream of tourists and locals. It's most crowded on nights and weekends, and particularly family-friendly (there are even changing rooms here, a rarity in the country). There are a small cafe and bar near the pools, or you can buy some oranges, which are believed to help give your skin a healthy glow, from any of the vendors working the site.

6.5km (4 miles) S of Gracias. L40 adults. Daily 8am–8pm.

Casa Galeano & Jardín Botánico ★ Once the home of a wealthy colonial family, this restored colonial house from the 1840s has quickly become one of the best museums in western Honduras outside of Copán. Colonial artifacts, models of villages, old photographs, murals, and pre-Columbian tools are paired with a brilliant folk art collection of masks and other items created by the region's indigenous cultures. There are rotating art exhibitions, as well, mostly from unknown regional artists. In the rear of the building is a botanical garden. The collection of plants here, originally began by the Galeanos, is one of the oldest botanical gardens in Central America. It's quite small, but the assortment of native species is good.

In front of Iglesia San Marcos. L30 adults. Daily 9am–6pm.

El Fuerte de San Cristóbal This small fort, perched atop a hill just a short walk from the Parque Central above Hotel Guancascos, affords the visitor the best views of Gracias. Apart from the tomb of one time Honduras (1841–42) and El Salvador (1847–52) President Juan Lindo and a few Spanish cannons, there is little of cultural interest here. The fort was renovated in late 2007.

4 blocks W of Parque Central, above Hotel Guancascos. Free admission. Daily 8am–4pm.

Termas del Rio This hot springs facility owned and operated by the Posada de Don Juan is at Km 7 on the road to Santa Rosa. There are two elegant-looking pools of different temperatures, one of which is quite large, as well as changing facilities and a small restaurant. If you are turned off by the number of people using the public facilities, these more modern and private springs are probably for you. Reservations are needed to visit.

Km 7 on the road to Santa Rosa. ✆ **504/656-1480.** josearmando_morales@yahoo.com. L100 adults. Daily 7am–9pm.

Shopping

Try the gift shops at Guancascos, Rinconcito Graciano, and Posada de Don Juan. Authentic Lenca crafts, mostly ceramics, can be found in small shops in the nearby towns along the Ruta Lenca.

Where to Stay

Guancascos ★ What sets this hotel apart from others in Gracias is the view. Since it's located on an old coffee farm on the hillside below San Cristóbal Fort, guests can see the city's entire grid of streets, colonial churches, and terracotta roof tiles from the porch chairs of the top-level rooms. All rooms have wood floors, simple furniture, and regional accents like handicrafts and paintings. The friendly Dutch owner works tirelessly to promote ecotourism and community projects, and also runs a bilingual school. She also makes sure the gardens are full of flowering shrubs and trees, which attract a loyal following of hummingbirds and butterflies, and is a wealth of information on the area—the owner can easily set up guided tours of Parque Nacional Celaque. The open-air restaurant here (also with great views of the city) doubles as a common area.

Below Fuerte de San Cristóbal. www.guancascos.com. ✆ **504/2656-1219.** 11 units. L475 double. MC, V. **Amenities:** Restaurant; Wi-Fi (free). *In room:* TV.

Hotel Finca El Capitan While it doesn't have the colonial vibe that the places in the center of town have, Finca El Capitan does take advantage of its surrounding lush foliage. The rustic ranch-style buildings here, topped with clay tile roofs, all have porches with hammocks and rocking chairs that face the central gardens, gazebos, stone paths, and swimming pool. No two rooms are the same here, and the sizes of each differ slightly—though the quality is uniform throughout. The bedspreads are worn and the furniture is basic. The hotel has a similar feel to—and attracts a similar crowd as—the Villas del Agua Caliente; consisting of Hondurans on family reunions or business retreats.

Beside Iglesia Santa Lucia. www.hotelfincaelcapitan.galeon.com. ✆ **504/2656-1659.** 14 units. L650 double. No credit cards. **Amenities:** Restaurant; bar; Internet in business center (free); pool. *In room:* A/C, fan, TV, fridge (in some).

Hotel Real Camino Lenca This new hotel in a renovated colonial building isn't nearly as nice as its main competition, Posada de Don Juan, though their deluxe rooms do have excellent spa-quality showers. Otherwise, the rooms face an inner courtyard and don't get much natural light, and the decor is rather plain.

3 Av. & Calle Cisneros. www.hotelrealcaminolenca.com. ✆ **504/2656-1932.** 14 units. L723 standard double; L820 deluxe double. AE, MC, V**. Amenities:** Restaurant. *In room:* A/C, fan, TV, Wi-Fi (free).

Posada de Don Juan ★★★ No hotel in Gracias is better prepared to handle the onslaught of tourists expected to descend on Gracias in the not-too-distant future. Major renovations have more than doubled its size, adding a full restaurant and bar, a beautiful courtyard pool, an array of luxury rooms, and a conference room. Even the smaller older rooms have gotten a facelift with fresh new decor, though the prices have stayed the same. If the older rooms are nice, the new rooms are a thing of beauty. With earthy tones fitting for Gracias, dark hardwood furniture, high-beamed ceilings, and everything from the light fixtures to the door handles being expertly picked, these are by far the best in town.

In addition, the hotel has built its own private hot-spring facilities on the road to Santa Rosa, Termas del Rio, which are open to the public and can be included in package stays at the hotel.

1 block from the park. www.posadadedonjuanhotel.com. ✆ **504/2656-1020.** 42 units. L855 standard double; L1,235 deluxe double. AE, MC, V. **Amenities:** Restaurant; bar; Jacuzzi; pool. *In room:* A/C, fan, TV, Wi-Fi (free).

Villas del Agua Caliente ☺ This series of rustic cabins is strewn on a hillside a few hundred meters from Balneario Aguas Termales (see above), which makes it a big plus for families. It's a bit isolated, so if you don't have a car, getting in and out can be problematic. Some of the bungalows have several bedrooms and could sleep a decent-sized family, while others are smaller yet still spacious. Simple handmade wood furniture, Lenca decor, and wall hangings define the otherwise bland rooms. Oddly, the bathrooms feature electric showers, even though the hotel has access to the nearby natural hot spring water. While the restaurant is cheap (and their Sunday brunch is highly recommended) and the gardens are nice, the main reason to stay here is the access to those hot springs.

At hot springs. ✆ **504/2608-5370.** 16 units. L300 double. Rates include breakfast. No credit cards. **Amenities:** Restaurant; bar. *In room:* Fan, TV.

Where to Eat

El Portal HONDURAN Adjoining the Hotel San Francisco, El Portal is a one-room bar and restaurant with some of the best *comida típica* and international dishes in the city. *Anafres,* a bean and cheese fondue that's occasionally made with sausage, is great here, especially accompanied by one of their cheap drinks. Fajitas, tacos, steaks, and burgers round out the menu.

Calle del Comercio, half block from Bancafe. ✆ **504/2656-1559.** Main courses L76–L228. MC, V. Daily noon–10pm.

Guancascos ★★ INTERNATIONAL/HONDURAN The food is only part of the allure of this restaurant in the Guancascos hotel (see above)—the elevated view is the main attraction. The small on-site gift shop and availability of information on sights and activities in the area means that the restaurant serves as something of a visitor's center, too. The quite-good food ranges from local staples like *baleadas* and Honduran breakfasts to German-style artisan breads and fresh juices.

Below Fuerte de San Cristóbal. ✆ **504/2656-1219.** www.guancascos.com. Main courses L57–L190. MC, V. Daily 7am–10pm.

Meson de Don Juan ★ HONDURAN This restaurant in Posada de Don Juan hotel expanded drastically in 2008 to become the largest, most sophisticated restaurant in town. It's very modern, with a mix of contemporary and rustic furniture, and features a flat-screen TV near the bar. They make a mean *chuleta de cerdo* (pork chop) with plantains, but the seafood dishes (tilapia, especially), steaks, burgers and sandwiches, pastas, and full Honduran breakfasts are also quite good. There are even a few vegetarian entrees.

Inside Posada de Don Juan. ✆ **504/2656-1020.** www.posadadedonjuanhotel.com. Main courses L76–L228. AE, MC, V. Daily 6am–10pm.

Rinconcito Graciano ★★★ HONDURAN "We dreamers are in a world of our own," said Lizeth Perdomo, owner and chef of Rinconcito Graciano, who is actively involved in tourism and historic preservation in the area. Her approach is nothing less than extraordinary: rescue traditional Lenca recipes—some of them passed down from her mother and grandmother—and use mostly organic produce from local farmers. Many of the herbs are grown right in her kitchen garden. Few of the dishes can be found in restaurants elsewhere in the country, such as *ticucos* (a tamale with legumes, beans, and *loroco*), *chorocos* (a tamale recipe from San Manuel de Colohete), and *lengua de res* (tongue). There is a wide variety of vegetarian dishes, as well. The walls of the dining room are painted with the deep red of an indigenous plant, the wooden tables and chairs are handmade and cushions are old coffee sacks, and even the menu is made of recycled material and handwritten. A one-of-a-kind place that should not be missed.

2 blocks S of the municipal market on Av. San Sebastion. ✆ **504/2656-1171.** Main courses L75–L150. No credit cards. Daily 11am–9pm.

Side Trips from Gracias

PARQUE NACIONAL MONTAÑA DE CELAQUE ★★★

Meaning "box of water" in the Lenca dialect, Celaque is one of the largest tracts of cloud forest remaining in Central America and one of the most unspoiled national parks in the country. Its 11 rivers supply villages as far away as El Salvador with fresh water. Nearly 50 species of mammals, several hundred species of birds, and a few dozen reptiles have been identified in the park. Celaque's pine forests hide rare wildlife, such as resplendent quetzals, ocelots, jaguars, monkeys, and pumas, but consider yourself lucky to catch a glimpse of just one of these, as the dense mist and fog often obscure views.

The only way to see the park is by hiking a pretty steep ascent, and the often wet and muddy trails along the way make it difficult for older travelers and those who aren't physically fit. From the visitor center on the Gracias side, one main trail leading uphill branches off into several other trails. (A few well-marked signs and ribbons mark where the trails break off.) The shortest trail takes about 2 to 3 hours and lets you off at a small outlook where the Santa Lucia waterfall can be seen from afar. A more difficult hike is the 2,383m (7,818-ft.) climb up Cerro El Gallo, which winds for about 3 or 4 hours through spider-monkey stomping grounds before reaching the top. Hardest of all is a hike to the top of Cerro de las Minas, the tallest peak in Honduras at 2,849m (9,347 ft.); it requires at least 2 days.

There are a few small campsites on the El Gallo and Las Minas trails, and you can also bunk at the **visitor center** for L50.

The park is easily reached by car from Gracias, which is 9km (5½ miles) away, although tours often leave from Santa Rosa and other towns that surround the park. From Gracias, you can also take a moto-taxi for about L100 to the end of the road, which is a 30-minute walk or so to the visitor center.

Guides are not required, but recommended. Walter Murcia, who runs **Puma Trail Tours** (✆ **504/2656-1113;** waltermurcia@hotmail.com), is the most respected guide in the area. Other guides can be arranged in Gracias at **Hotel Guancascos** (✆ **504/2656-1219;** www.guancascos.com) or through **Colosuca-Celaque** (✆ **504/2656-0627**). It's best to arrange a guide a few days in advance. Expect to pay anywhere between L200 and L400 per day for a guide per group, depending on the quality of the service and training of the guide. Admission to the park is L50 adults.

LA RUTA LENCA ★★

La Ruta Lenca, or the Lenca Route, is a grassroots tourism initiative to help bring tourism revenue to the small villages south of Gracias and give tourists insight into a little known indigenous group, the Lencas. The cultural group was derived from Chibcha-speaking Indians who came from Colombia and Venezuela more than 3,000 years ago. They number around 100,000 in Honduras and 40,000 or so in El Salvador and are known throughout the country for their earthenware pottery; several towns also have small craft cooperatives. The best times to visit any Lenca villages are during Sunday markets and *guancascos,* annual gatherings between two villages to celebrate peace. La Ruta Lenca, the circuit, passes through the mountain villages of La Campa, Belén Gualcho, San Manuel de Colohete, San Sebastián, Corquín, and Mohaga, among others that surround Gracias. This string of rural towns that dots this part of the country features adobe houses, corn and bean fields, the occasional museum and colonial church, and beautiful mountain views. During the rainy season (Apr–Nov), the hills and trees are a vibrant green, and the scent of flowering plants wafts though the air.

The association of guides **Colosuca-Celaque Tours** (✆ **504/2656-0627** or 504/2222-2124 ext. 502; www.colosuca.com), based in Gracias and Santa Rosa, give tours for L200 to L300 per group of one to five to Lenca villages and provides the opportunity to combine trips with activities such as studying colonial architecture, mountain biking, hiking, bird-watching, and horseback-riding tours. The guides are all locally trained, and many are actively involved in cultural preservation.

La Campa ★★

La Campa is the first town you reach when leaving Gracias, just 16km (10 miles) away on a well-paved road. The village is quite small, just a few hundred residents who live in a cluster of adobe houses with tile roofs scattered on a few hills. The centerpiece of town is Iglesia de San Matías, built in 1690 and restored in 1938, which sits at the lowest point in the village with the houses sort of hovering around it. The sheer white facade backed by the rocky cliffs is a sight to behold. The church is only officially opened for Mass, though you can usually find someone to open it for a small tip. The interior is quite plain, apart from one faded oil painting and a beautiful carved wood altar. The price for photos inside the church is L30 each—yikes!

Ceramics are a big part of life in Lenca villages. La Campa is best known for massive handmade urns—perfectly cylindrical—called *cántaros.* You can see a few examples in front of the municipal building. Several artisan workshops in town, such as **Alfarería Lenca** and the home of **Doña Desideria Pérez,** are open to visitors and have small shops where you can buy the signature Lenca bowls, plates, wind chimes, and vases. The workshops love visitors and are eager to explain their work process. High on the hill near the road in is the **Centro de Interpretación de Alfarería Lenca** or **La Escuelona** (L30 adults; daily 8am–4:30pm), set in a colonial building with many examples of Lenca pottery with explanations and details on historical significance.

As far as any sort of facilities go on La Ruta Lenca, La Campa is the most advanced, with a municipal building across from the church that contains a small tourist office and several small hotels such as **Hostal J.B.** (✆ **504/551-3772;** hostal_jb@yahoo.com; L200 double) and the new **Hotel Bellavista** (✆ **504/625-4770;** similar prices). You can inquire at either Hostal J.B. or the tourist office regarding guided hikes and rides on horseback in the area that visit caves, canyons, a coffee plantation, and nearby villages such as **Cruz Alta,** famous for its *tejado de pino,* a type of basketry made with pine needles. Also try hiking guide Carlos David Perez (www.visitlacampa.blogspot.com), who leads walks in the area, including to Cueva Taistado, a cave in a nearby village.

If you don't have time to push farther into the hills, a stop here can be done rather quickly from Gracias. To get to La Campa, there's one daily **bus** from Gracias (L20) at noon that continues to San Marcos de Caiquín and San Manuel de Colohete; the return stops in La Campa between 6:15 and 6:45am.

San Marcos de Caiquín

Continuing from La Campa, the road gets a little less smooth, and it winds up about 6km (3¾ miles) over the hills to a fork. If you stick to the right, you will reach San Manuel de Colohete, while to the left is this small adobe village amidst the pines. There are just a few simple *comedores* and *pulperias* in the quiet village, as well as a small church, built in 1750, that was renovated in recent years. Several family homes will rent out rooms to visitors for a small price.

San Manuel de Colohete

A bumpy 14km (8¾ miles) from La Campa, 1½ hours from Gracias, sits San Manuel de Colohete, one of the favorite stops on any tour of La Ruta Lenca. The town itself is the largest in the area, though that isn't saying much. There are just a few narrow, twisting streets on a flat piece of land with a small grassy square on the far end. The locals don't see many visitors and are still surprised when one shows up, though they are quite friendly, and if you need any help, they will point you in the right direction.

Of all the **colonial churches** along La Ruta Lenca, San Manuel de Colohete's is the one you should not miss. The intricately carved white facade that dates back to 1721 was recently renovated, and at last check, they were still working on the roof and back end of the church on the outside. To get inside, though, you must be here on Sunday—otherwise no one can open up the doors. Inside are several frescos that date back 400 years and an ornate wooden altar.

The southern end of **Parque Nacional Celaque** (see p. 139) butts right up against the town and provides a misty cloud cover that sometimes engulfs it. A little-used trail to the summit can be attempted from the town of **El Naranjo,** a 30-minute walk away. Numerous other hikes can be had into the park or to various unspoiled Lenca villages, like the 6-hour walk to Belén Gualcho.

The best time to visit is on the 1st and 15th of every month, when San Manuel hosts a lively outdoor market (6am–noon), where people from the surrounding villages come to sell their produce and general knick-knacks.

San Sebastián

The road gets even worse past San Manuel de Colohete and ends in San Sebastián, except for an almost impenetrable road to Belén Gualcho. There is talk of paving the road in the near future, which would complete a full circuit around Parque Nacional Celaque. For now, though, the few who make it here will find another charming colonial village, much like the others, with an impressive church and small square, but with far fewer visitors. In town, you can rent rooms from a few basic *comedores* and simple *hospedajes.*

Belén Gualcho

Better reached from Santa Rosa de Copán than Gracias, Belén Gualcho is best known for its Sunday-morning market. Get here early, as the market tends to dissipate by 11am. This one is set high—1,600m (5,249 ft.)—on the mountain and features one of the most ornate cathedrals of anywhere along La Ruta Lenca. Some argue that the three domes and mountain setting rank it above the church in San Manuel de Colohete.

There are a couple of basic hotels and *comedores* that fill up on weekends with market goers, as well as a Hondutel and cybercafe. There is access into Celaque just outside of town, and the route to the summit is quite common. You can even return via the Gracias Trail. The route tends to be confusing, so you will need a guide (contact **Colosuca-Celaque Tours,** see above; or ask around in town), but the full hike up can be done in about a half day. Other hikes can lead you to San Sebastian (5–8 hr. one way) or to the Santa Maria de Gualcho waterfall (5–6 hr. round-trip), past the village of El Paraiso.

There are two daily buses (L50) here from Santa Rosa de Copán at around 3am and 8am for the 2- to 3-hour ride, with service doubling on Sundays.

San Juan

In between Gracias and La Esperanza awaits this quickly developing coffee town with an expanding list of tourist services. A **visitor's center** (✆ **504/2754-7150**), aka La Casa de Gladis Nolasco, on the principal road near the Hondutel office, can arrange a number of activities, such as hikes through the cloud forest and to visit waterfalls, coffee tastings, tours of small-time coffee roasting and processing operations, 4×4 trips, horseback rides, and visits to hot springs and a petrified forest. There are a few simple guesthouses here, but it is advisable to continue on to Gracias or La Esperanza unless you have a good reason to stay the night. There are four morning **buses** (L40; 6–9:30am) to La Esperanza daily and less frequently to Gracias (L40; usually once per morning).

Erandique

The colonial village of Erandique, 24km (15 miles) south of San Juan and the highway, is quite difficult to reach without your own transportation and still difficult with it due to the poor road. If you can complete the trip, you'll find an attractive cobblestone town with three small colonial churches. Erandique is quite remote where it stands so isolated from the rest of the world. It isn't lonely, though; cloud forests, opal mines, waterfalls, and historical sites dot the area. The mines—or rather, the effects of the mines—are one of the first things you will encounter here. Any outsider who sets foot here will surely be approached by visitors selling opals, such as black, white, and rainbow.

Lenca warrior Lempira, who led a guerilla assault on the Spanish and became a national hero, led his attacks from a small fort in the mountains near Erandique. The Peñol de Perquín, as well as the Piedra Parada—the rock where Lempira was assassinated—can be visited on a 1- or 2-day hike from Erandique. You will have to first walk to the village of San Antonio Montaña and continue on the light trail. Ask locals for directions. Buses (L80) to either La Esperanza (2½ hr.) or Gracias (2 hr.) leave at 5am from the Parque Central, with return service at noon from either town.

The Road from Gracias to La Esperanza

The road from Gracias winds over coffee plantations and through lush green valleys. This is the heart of Honduras's coffee country, with shops in every town buying coffee direct from farmers for export. While the road is slowly being improved, at present, it is still mostly unpaved and bumpy. Four-wheel drive is a must in the rainy season.

La Esperanza

The capital of the department of Intibucá, La Esperanza is large enough that it has a few modern shopping centers and fast food restaurants, yet still small and rural enough that Lencas still come down from the surrounding hills in traditional dress and feature prominently in the landscape of the city. The Intibucá department is one of the poorest in all of Honduras, which has led numerous NGOs, Peace Corps workers, and missionary groups to base themselves here. The town itself is somewhat noisy, chaotic, and ramshackle. The colonial past is apparent on only a few streets. At 1,600m (5,249 ft.), La Esperanza is one of the highest cities in Honduras—and the cool climate here is a point of pride.

GETTING THERE

There's a dusty square where the old market used to be that serves as a bus terminal, though some **buses** also leave from the stadium near the highway to Siguatepeque. Destinations include San Pedro Sula (L100; 3½–4 hr.), Gracias (L100; 4 hr.), Siguatepeque (L60; 1 hr.), Tegucigalpa (L90; 3 hr.), and Marcala (L40; 1½ hr.), as well as numerous small towns in the region. Apart from Gracias, which leaves only once per day, buses depart for most destinations throughout the daylight hours.

VISITOR INFORMATION

La Esperanza is a center for facilities for people who live within a few hours' radius. There are several **banks** and standalone **ATMs** on the road outside of town, near the gas stations. **Cybercafes** are everywhere in the center. The best is Explored, which also offers international phone calls at rates cheaper than Hondutel on Parque Central.

WHAT TO SEE & DO

The tree-filled **Parque Central** and the two colonial churches in the center are worth a quick look, but they won't keep you interested for long. The town's main attraction, **La Ermita,** is a small shrine and chapel on the hillside that's home to the statue of the Virgin of Fatima on the west end, where you can get a good view of town. The Casa de Cultura, in the municipal building on the western side of town, has a few displays on Lenca culture and old photographs of the city alongside a small artesania shop.

The NGOs based here have actively tried to set up tourism initiatives in the villages outside of town. A trip about 11km (6¾ miles) outside of town through the Valle de Azacualpa takes you to **Chiligatoro,** a small lagoon with rowboats for rent. Several rural Lenca villages are here, spread out along the farmland, where the residents still sport traditional dress.

One of the more interesting attractions is **Cerro Los Hoyos,** 6km (3¾ miles) northeast of La Esperanza, a 1½-hour hike up to a forest-covered plateau that overlooks the farms of the Valle de Azacualpa. Cylindrical holes found here of various sizes are believed to be pre-Columbian obsidian mines, though outlandish theories claim that the holes are left by extraterrestrials.

WHERE TO STAY

Hotel Cabañas Los Pinos ★★ ☺ This funky mountain resort set amid the dense pine forests outside of town, originally called Hotel Doors and Windows, features an array of unique cabins designed of either wood or stone. An Iranian artist and photographer, who spent several decades in the U.S. before buying the hotel, owns the resort, and his touches can be found throughout. All cabins are different sizes and shapes, and each features interesting wooden furniture hewn from branches and logs. The walls are painted in soothing yellows and oranges, while a few have wacky, multicolor designs. The feel here is woodsy, though rooms and facilities are quite comfortable, and the upkeep is tremendous. The pool is top notch and the center of most activity here, which makes it easy for kids to keep busy. If you want to get a real sense of your surroundings, I recommend staying at Los Pinos rather than in town. Also, don't get it confused with the Los Pinos cabins near Lago de Yojoa.

2km (1¼ miles) from La Esperanza on the rd. to Siguatepeque. www.lospinosresort.com. ✆ **504/2783-2034.** 33 units. L580/person. MC, V. **Amenities:** Restaurant; bar; pool. *In room:* TV.

Hotel Mina This motel-style building with two levels of rooms surrounding a central parking area is the most modern in La Esperanza. Rooms have been recently remodeled, and new rooms were being added at last check. They vary in size, but all feature modern private bathrooms with steady hot water, tile floors, and a mix of exposed brick and yellow-painted walls. Clean, simple, and reliable.

2 blocks from the stadium. ✆ **504/2783-1071.** 31 units. L600 double. MC, V. Free parking. **Amenities:** Restaurant. *In room:* TV.

Hotel Molina Real Set in a residential neighborhood not far from the Texaco station, this new hotel has some hits and misses. The hits: It's quiet and easy to get in and out; the rooms are big; the walls are nicely painted; and there are clean tile floors, high wood-beamed ceilings, and comfy beds. The misses: The walls are a sad concrete brick, the bathrooms seem unfinished and are comparable to a rest stop, and if you aren't driving, getting there and away means a 5-minute walk to the highway to catch a cab.

3 blocks from the highway. ✆ **504/2783-4067.** 12 units. L350 double. No credit cards. Free parking. *In room:* A/C, TV.

Posada Mi Antigua Casa ★ This large colonial home has been passed down through a single family since it was built in 1846 and makes for a fine place to stay. The open-air cobblestone courtyard filled with plants and flowers, combined with stone archways, colorfully painted walls, wood-beam ceilings, iron chandeliers, and a smattering of antiques, adds tons of character—as does the friendly owner, a character herself. The rooms are quite cozy, with big, soft beds, but the carved wooden furniture and brick floors set with oriental carpets maintain the authenticity of the building.

SE corner of the park. may_aguero@yahoo.com. ✆ **504/2783-0415.** 3 units. L400/person. Rates include breakfast. No credit cards. *In room:* TV.

WHERE TO EAT

El Fogon ★ HONDURAN This popular bar and grill is a lively place. Set on two levels, the restaurant's back patio is full of color and character, with its jungle-painted walls and red-and-yellow checkered tile floors. There's a surprisingly large collection of archeological artifacts on display in glass cases, such as jade pieces, arrowheads, pottery shards, hand axes, and other Lenca finds. The menu is quite lengthy but focuses on meats and regional dishes such as *típicas, chuletas de cerdo* (pork chops), BBQ ribs, chorizo, and quite a few preparations of pork and chicken. For the daring, try *El Destazo:* 3 bull testicles, a 1.7kg (60-oz.) steak, and sides such as salad, refried beans, tortillas, fries, and veggies. The bar area in back is a popular place with 20- and 30-somethings on nights and weekends.

2 blocks W & 1 block N of Parque Central. ✆ **504/2783-0111.** Main courses L100–L180. MC, V. Sun–Thurs 9am–10pm; Fri 9am–11pm; Sat 9am–midnight.

La Hacienda Lenca STEAKHOUSE This steakhouse has the food that you would think Opalaca should have and is set in a colonial atmosphere that's almost as nice. Meats are the specialty, particularly steaks and mixed grilled plates designed for sharing, with thick cuts of chorizo, pork, and beef. If meat isn't your forte, you probably won't find much solace here.

1 block S of Parque Central. ✆ **504/2783-0111.** Main courses L100–L300. MC, V. Daily 8:30am–10:30pm.

Opalaca's INTERNATIONAL Without a doubt, Opalaca's is the most elegant joint in town. It's in a colonial building—one of the oldest in La Esperanza—a few blocks from the church on the road to the La Gruta. The graceful dining areas are in several rooms with touches of Spanish style like wood-beamed ceilings and antique knick-knacks. The food is not overly adventurous and is somewhat mediocre. National and international comfort foods like pork chops, steaks, and sandwiches are served in decent-sized portions.

2 blocks W of the church. ✆ **504/2783-0503.** Main courses L80–L200. MC, V. Daily 8am–10pm.

Yamaranguila

A pleasant side excursion is to the predominantly Lenca village of Yamaranguila, just a few kilometers outside of La Esperanza. An antiquated Lenca form of traditional government, where the Vara Alta (sort of like a mayor) oversees the preparations and planning of *guancascos* ceremonies and general governance, is still in place. The colonial village has its charm, particularly around the small stone square that's encircled by whitewashed houses with tile roofs. If you are around in early December, be sure to come for their small festival, which gets particularly lively. La Chorrera, a small waterfall about 2km (1¼ miles) from town, is an easy hike from the center. Just ask anyone for *"la cascada,"* to show you the way. **Buses** (L10; 20 min.) run every hour or so to/from La Esperanza.

THE NORTH COAST

8

Everywhere you look in the North Coast region of Honduras, the tourism infrastructure is thriving and playing off the region's healthy cultural and environmental diversity. Garífuna villages and mestizo cities live alongside a growing number of North American retiree communities, and ecotourism is on the verge of a major eruption—swanky new jungle lodges and yoga centers are being erected on former chocolate plantations, and hiking trails are carving their way through national parks like Pico Bonito.

Zip-line tours are now as common as pan de coco, kayaking and canoe tours can be had in every mangrove-forested lagoon, and serious birders are descending upon the region like migrating herons. Up and down the coast, major beach projects are being talked about, and some are already in the works; the most significant, at Los Micos Lagoon, could possibly turn Tela Bay into the next Cancun.

Though it seems like the North Coast is finally getting its moment in the spotlight, this part of the country is steeped in history. Spanish explorers and conquistadors first entered the country here, and colonial-era forts still guard the coast from would-be pirate attacks. The Garífuna, an ethnic group descended from Carib Indians and West African slaves, arrived along this coast at the end of the 18th century. And the remaining presence of the businesses Dole and Chiquita means that lingering remnants of Honduras's role as a banana republic are still woven into the social fabric of this region, even with tourism now evolving into the primary economic force.

PUERTO CORTES

Puerto Cortés, located 64km (40 miles) north of San Pedro Sula, isn't nearly as drab as the name "largest container port in Central America" makes it sound. It is set on a small peninsula surrounded by the Caribbean Sea, with a few decent beach hotels on the outskirts. The occasional cruise ship has even started to appear. Because it's the closest beach destination to San Pedro Sula, city dwellers flock here in droves on the weekends—though most prefer Omoa, not much farther away. The port—the most important in Honduras—dominates the center, and massive cranes and container ships guard against any views of the ocean. The city itself is not particularly attractive, with uneven sidewalks, potholes in the streets, and rundown neighborhoods.

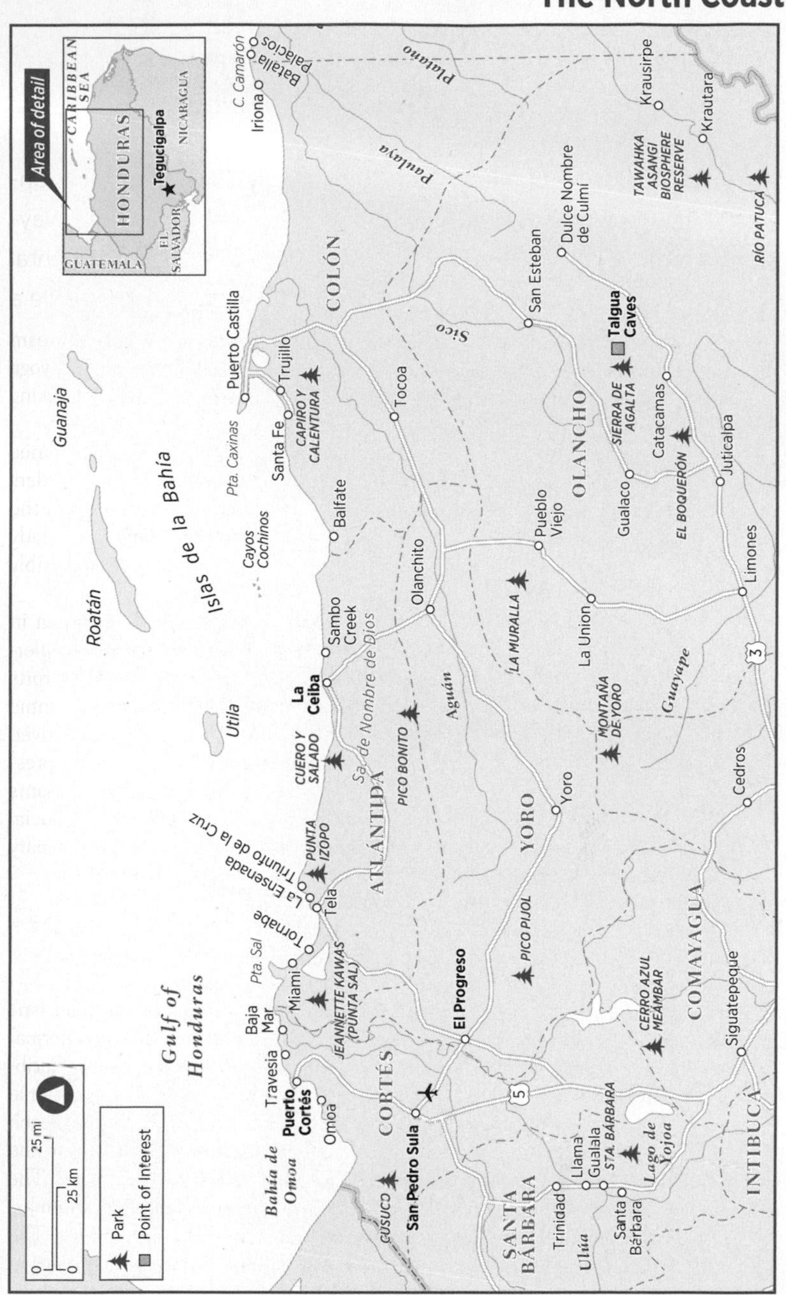
Area of detail
HONDURAS
CARIBBEAN SEA
Tegucigalpa
NICARAGUA
GUATEMALA
EL SALVADOR
Gulf of Honduras
Bahía de Omoa
Islas de la Bahía
Roatán
Guanaja
Utila
Cayos Cochinos
Pta. Caxinas
Pta. Sal
C. Camarón
Puerto Cortés
Omoa
Travesia
Baja Mar
Miami
Tornabe
La Ensenada
Triunfo de la Cruz
Tela
La Ceiba
Sambo Creek
Balfate
Santa Fe
Trujillo
Puerto Castilla
Iriona
Batalla
Palacios
San Pedro Sula
El Progreso
Olanchito
Tocoa
San Esteban
Dulce Nombre de Culmí
Pueblo Viejo
La Union
Yoro
Gualaco
Catacamas
Juticalpa
Limones
Cedros
Siguatepeque
Trinidad
Llama
Gualala
Santa Bárbara
Krausirpe
Krautara
CORTÉS
ATLÁNTIDA
COLÓN
YORO
OLANCHO
COMAYAGUA
SANTA BÁRBARA
INTIBUCÁ
Platano
Paulaya
Sico
Aguán
Guayape
Ulúa
Sa. de Nombre de Dios
Lago de Yojoa
CUSUCO
JEANNETTE KAWAS (PUNTA SAL)
PUNTA IZOPO
CUERO Y SALADO
PICO BONITO
CAPIRO Y CALENTURA
PICO PIJOL
CERRO AZUL MEÁMBAR
STA. BÁRBARA
MONTAÑA DE YORO
LA MURALLA
SIERRA DE AGALTA
EL BOQUERÓN
TAWAHKA ASANGI BIOSPHERE RESERVE
RÍO PATUCA
Talgua Caves
Park
Point of Interest
0 25 mi
0 25 km
5
3

The Spanish conquistador Hernán Cortés first founded the city in 1524 as La Natividad, though in a few years, it was ransacked by natives and burnt to the ground. In 1536, Pedro de Alvarado founded Villa de Puerto Caballos (Port of Horses) as an intended deepwater port. Theories run rampant, but the name is believed to derive from an incident with horses falling from a ship and drowning during an unloading process. The name stuck until 1869, when it was changed to Puerto Cortés in honor of the famous conquistador.

Essentials

GETTING THERE

BY CAR An excellent paved highway, CA-5, runs from Puerto Cortés to San Pedro Sula that can bring you between the two cities within 45 minutes.

BY BUS For San Pedro Sula (L80), you will need to visit the terminal at Av 4a and Calle 4a, which has frequent service from 5am to 5pm for the 1- to 1½-hour ride. For Omoa, buses depart every 20 to 30 minutes from the Citral Costenos terminal (Calle 3a; L20). Some buses continue on to Corinto and the Guatemalan border.

BY FERRY From Puerto Cortés, there is ferry service to Big Creek/Mango Creek and Placencia, Belize (and adjoining bus transfers to Belize City) with the **D-Express** (✆ **504/2665-0726;** www.belizeferry.com) on Mondays at 11:30am, returning Fridays at 9:30am. The trip takes 4 hours and costs L1,045. It departs from the dock next to La Laguna Bridge and Delfin restaurant.

VISITOR INFORMATION

Banco Atlántida (Av. 2a and Calle 4 este) and **HSBC** (Av 2a and Cale 2 este) have Visa **ATMs** and will exchange currency. **Cybercafes** are found all over town. International phone calls can be made at **Hondutel** (Calle 1a and Av. 3a). If you are entering or departing the country by sea, you should stamp in and out at **Migración** (Av. 5 and Calle 3; ✆ **504/2665-0582;** Mon–Fri 8am–12:30pm and 1–5pm, Sat 8am–noon).

What to See & Do

While no beaches exist in the port area, a 5- to 10-minute drive or cab ride to the outskirts of town will bring you to numerous beaches, some of which are better than others. The municipal beach, **Playa Coca Cola,** was named after a Coca Cola depot that once sat there. On weekends, this is where you will find the most vibrant beach crowds, as well as seafood shacks selling cheap meals. The beach is mediocre at best, though, and during weekdays, it is empty; however, a few new hotels and restaurants have managed to set up shop. If you can't handle the vicious sand flies and the heavy accumulation of driftwood and other debris that wash up on shore, head to **Playas El Faro** and **Cieneguita,** to the south of town, which are significantly cleaner and home to the area's best hotels.

Where to Stay

Hotel Centro The best of several mediocre hotels in the center—1 block from the park—is not much more than a drive-in motel with rooms surrounding the parking lot. Clean tile floors and private bathrooms that you don't have to squirm at with hot water are the highlights. The hotel has cheaper rooms without A/C, as well. The other options nearby, like the Hotel Buenos Aires, are less clean and the rooms dingier.

Av. 3a & Calle 2a. ✆ **504/665-1160.** 26 units. L600 double. No credit cards. Free parking. *In room:* A/C (in some), fan, TV.

Hotel Costa Azul Costa Azul isn't marketed as a retro-style hotel, but it should be. The '70s are beautifully preserved here in the modish egg chairs made of sea grass and other furniture, the layout, colors fit for shag carpeting, and the diner-like restaurant. Rooms are outfitted in a similar style with tile floors and green accents. Bedding, bathrooms, and furniture are somewhat worn, but nevertheless clean. Their spread—which includes a gym, disco, two restaurants, soccer pitch, and horses—is on Playa El Faro, with a big empty stretch of sand, except for sand flies and driftwood. The waves are quite strong offshore, so the in-ground pool surrounded by loungers and flowers, just a bit back from the beach, is preferable to most. They've added a second hotel at Playa Coco Cola, as well.

Playa el Faro. www.hotelcostazul.net. ✆ **504/665-2260.** 60 units. L800 double. MC, V. Free parking. **Amenities:** 2 restaurants; bar; gym; pool; Wi-Fi (free). *In room:* A/C, TV.

Villas del Sol ★ The cleanest and most modern hotel on Playa Coca Cola is right in the center of the weekend beach action, but during the rest of the week, it is quiet. The small resort is clean and modern, with contemporary art adorning the rooms and hallways. The decor of the rooms is a mish-mash of colors and patterns, and it doesn't always work but manages to at least be interesting.

Playa Coca Cola. www.villadelsolhn.com. ✆ **504/2665-4939.** 17 units. L1,350 double. MC, V. Free parking. **Amenities:** Restaurant; bar; pool. *In room:* A/C, TV, Wi-Fi (free).

Where to Eat

Albert's Café HONDURAN This clean, air-conditioned cafe in the center has about 25 tables, tile floors, and a TV showing *telenovelas* or a game. This place is open early for their hearty Honduran breakfasts, and the rest of the day has a wide range of comfort foods like burgers, sandwiches, tacos, burritos, *baleadas,* grilled meats, shrimp, and grilled or fried fish. Execution is consistent, but you won't be overwhelmed with flavor.

Av. 2 & Calle 2. No phone. Main courses L40–L100. No credit cards. Daily 7am–7pm.

Bohio Bar INTERNATIONAL On weekends, this open-air spot near the stadium is a popular place for 20- and 30-somethings to drink and eat appetizers before trucking off to nearby discos. During the days and the rest of the week, the crowd is light. The food is pretty basic, all in all: grilled fish and shrimp, ceviche, grilled meats, burgers, and a long drink menu that includes cheap beer.

Av. 4 & Calle 5. No phone. Main courses L60–L200. No credit cards. Tues–Sun noon–10pm.

Espresso Americano CAFE The Honduran answer to Starbucks has even set up in Puerto Cortés. The food is light, just pastries and snacks. While they do serve cappuccinos, mochas, and every other standard trendy hot coffee drink, my main reason for including a mention of the little cafe is for their iced drinks—iced chai, iced lattes, and juices that do wonders in the unrelenting coastal heat. Plus, they have A/C, one of the only restaurants in town with it that isn't a North American fast food chain.

Av. 2, btw. Calles 1 & 2. No phone. Drinks L20–L60. No credit cards. Daily 8am–8pm.

Tapadero's ★ SEAFOOD The most gentrified place in Cortés proper, in my opinion, Tapadero's serves seafood and Garífuna specialties from their plant-filled open-air dining area. Standouts include snails in butter sauce, crabmeat with rice and beans, and fresh fish served in garlic sauce, steamed, grilled, or fried. If you are not in the mood for seafood, they also serve tacos and fried chicken.

Calle 5, btw. Avs. 3 & 4. No phone. Main courses L60–L240. AE, MC, V. Tues–Sun noon–10pm.

Side Trips from Puerto Cortés

The seaside Garífuna villages of **Travesia** and **Bajamar** are some of the most lively and traditional in the country. Bajamar is home to the most important Garífuna festival in Honduras, which is held between July 9 and 24—July 16 is the peak of festivities. During this period, Garífuna from across the country visit, as do many others, for the dance and drum performances and heavy eating and drinking. During the rest of the year, the towns are quiet. In Travesia, the beaches tend to see a few visitors who drive up and rent small thatched *champas* for a few lempira or come to dine in some of the beachfront seafood restaurants.

Fronteras del Caribe (✆ **504/2665-5001;** L300), a hotel and restaurant, is the best spot both to eat and stay. It's right on the beach, surrounded by coconut trees, at the entrance to Travesia. All rooms are clean and have private bathrooms and ceiling fans. It's actually far better than anywhere in the center of Cortés.

The road there runs east of the center, though it is quite bumpy, and after rains, huge puddles can prevent passage to all but the most powerful of cars. A taxi ride to Travesia will cost about L80 to L100. Infrequent **buses** depart from Calle 5a este and Avenidas 4a a few times a day.

OMOA

Omoa is about as laidback a place as you will find. Gentle breezes from the Merendón mountain range, the backdrop of the town, swoop down across the jungle-clad coastline and leave the hustle and bustle of Puerto Cortés far behind. This sleepy beach community takes more of an easygoing, Belizean vibe, and the atmosphere has much more of a beach and tourist scene than in neighboring Puerto Cortés. While San Pedro residents and foreigners are increasingly flocking here to build vacation homes, mostly outside of town, the crowds are minimal, and on most days, you will have the town almost to yourself. While tourism here could one day take off, the municipality hasn't helped their cause much. They've allowed a line of giant oil processing towers to be placed right in the center of town, and they've let the beach erode almost completely. Three significant earthquakes in 2009 caused considerable damage to a few buildings, as well. History buffs take note: Omoa is also home to one of the most important colonial-era forts in the Caribbean: Fortaleza de San Fernando, which recently finished an extensive renovation.

Essentials

GETTING THERE

Omoa is 18km (11 miles) west of Puerto Cortés and 35km (22 miles) from the Guatemalan border at Tegucigalpa. **Buses** for Cortés (L20), from where you can transfer to San Pedro Sula, depart from a small terminal on Calle 3a every 20 to 30 minutes during daylight hours. If you're headed to the border, go to the highway and flag down any passing bus to Corinto, where you can stamp out of the country and then continue on. Chances are others will be waiting, too. If you have a group together, **Roli's Place** (✆ **504/2658-9082**) can organize transfers to Puerto Barrios in Guatemala or to La Ceiba to connect to the ferries for the Bay Islands.

VISITOR INFORMATION

Nearly everything in Omoa is compact and sits on a 2km (1¼-mile) stretch of road between the highway and the beach, with the fort about at the halfway point. There is no ATM here, though **Banco de Occidente** on the highway exchanges traveler's checks and will exchange currency. Two **cybercafes** have the ability to make international phone calls: One is at the entrance to town on the highway, and the other is a few hundred meters in.

What to See & Do

Omoa's main attraction is undoubtedly the **Fortaleza de San Fernando de Omoa,** set right in the center of the town. It is one of the architectural highlights of Honduras and a gem of a colonial fort, the largest in Central America. Slaves—both Indians and Africans—supplied the labor for much of the construction of the fort, which began in 1759 and never technically finished. It was designed to ward off pirate attacks from such legendary buccaneers as Peg Leg and Black Diego, who were after the silver shipments from the Tegucigalpa mines that were headed to Spain.

A visit won't take much time. Most of the rooms in the fort are gated off, though you can climb the stone stairs and walk around the top of the fort to admire the dozens of cannons and lookout towers. A 2-year reconstruction was completed at the end of 2008 and the national monument is looking better than ever, though it still gets just a few visitors a day. There is a small **museum** (L40 adults; Mon–Fri 8am–4pm, Sat and Sun 9am–5pm) set in one of the outer buildings, with a collection of artifacts from the fort such as cannons, guns, scale models, and photos. Guides are available at the entrance for a negotiable fee, usually L40 to L60 for a short tour.

Off the highway just outside of Omoa, at El Paraiso towards Cortés on a privately owned Paraíso Rainforest Reserve, **Rawacala Eco Park** (**© 504/2556-9466;** www.bttours.net; Tues–Sun 8am–6pm) has set up a 2-hour combination hiking trip and canopy tour (L665 per person). The canopy tour, or zip-line, consists of seven cables and a Tibetan bridge that total 1,100m (3,609 ft.) in length. Once your adrenaline eases, you walk to a small waterfall and swimming hole to cool off. There is a fairly wide range of elevation on the property, sea level to 1,200m (3,937 ft.), which has resulted in astounding biodiversity; the British Institution Operation Wallacea frequently brings students and researchers here. More than 350 species of birds have been recorded on the property.

There used to be a dive operator here leading trips to the Cayos Zapatillos, wrecks, and other sites in the area, but at the moment, Omoa is without a dive shop. It's a shame, too, because there are a lot of great dive spots extremely close to Omoa.

For beachgoers, the public beach beside the pier right in town is so-so. The water is clear and shallow; however, debris from the rivers on both sides of it can be an issue. The community has done a good job of keeping the beach and water clean in recent years, though, so expect improvements. A few kilometers down the highway from the entrance to town (about a 45-min. walk), you can hike to a river with a nice swimming hole and waterfall. The trail is a bit difficult to spot, so just ask anyone for directions to *"la cascada."*

Where to Stay

Bahía de Omoa Across the beach from the pier, near Aqui Pancha restaurant, is this two-level home owned by a friendly Dutch/German couple, who rent out a few comfortable rooms. The second-level units all have high-beamed ceilings, clean tile floors, and private hot-water bathrooms. Mayan decor gives some excitement to the otherwise lifeless walls. If you just want a room and don't need the extra facilities, look no further.

Across from Flamingo's. ✆ **504/2658-9076.** 4 units. L500 double. No credit cards. Free parking. *In room:* A/C, fan, TV.

Coco Bay One of the newer hotels in town, a 5-minute walk to the beach, this isn't terrible, but it's not great either. The property is surrounded by dense jungle and set up in halves: one half is a single level of rooms, while the other half holds the parking lot (parking spots face the rooms), flower gardens, a good-sized pool and lounge area, and restaurant. The rooms are quite simple and designed to sleep families. Most of the rooms have four single beds, and some have two showers. Floors are white tile, and walls are pastel colors. A few badly framed prints appoint each room, and a lot of work is still needed on decor, which is almost nonexistent.

Btw. the fort & the beach. ✆ **504/2658-9007.** 12 units. L1,150 double. MC, V. Free parking. **Amenities:** Restaurant; bar; pool. *In room:* A/C, fan, TV.

Flamingo's Right on the beach beside the pier, hidden among the coconut trees, Flamingo's is the top "beach" hotel in Omoa. The location is great, and ample windows help the cause. The building is fairly new, and all rooms still have that air of newness: clean tile floors, walls with fresh orange paint, and bathrooms that still shine. While it lacks a pool, I would still choose Flamingo's over Coco Bay.

On the beachfront. ✆ **504/2658-9199.** flamingosomoa@yahoo.com. 10 units. L1,200 double. MC, V. Free parking. **Amenities:** Restaurant; bar. *In room:* A/C, fan, TV.

Roli's Place For years, Roli's has been the backpacker hangout of Omoa and the unofficial tourist center. Here, you can find out what to do in town, find a bus transfer, pick up a map, and surf the Web. Oh, let's not forget to mention sleep. The Swiss hosts have built air-conditioned cabins, though the budget crowd sticks to the dorm rooms, hammocks, and campsites, which are significantly cheaper. Roli's is a good place to chat with other travelers and make friends to hit the town.

Btw. the fort & the beach. www.omoa.net/roli.html. ✆ **504/6258-9082.** 8 units. L100 dorm bed; L240 double. No credit cards. **Amenities:** Cybercafe; bikes; kayaks. *In room:* A/C, fan, TV.

Sueños de Mar B&B ★ At the end of the beach, which gets lively with the neighboring discos on the weekends, this small Canadian inn is one of the best new additions to the Omoa waterfront. The simple tile-floored rooms surround a small courtyard. Bathrooms are clean and modern with electric showers. The hotel has a restaurant popular with tourists (see below) and beach goers, as they serve more than just rice and beans.

NW end of the beach, Barrio El Playa. www.suenosdemar.com. ✆ **504/2630-5605.** 6 units. L665 double. No credit cards. Free parking. **Amenities:** Restaurant. *In room:* A/C, fan, TV, Wi-Fi (free).

Where to Eat

Aqui Pancha HONDURAN Across the street from Flamingo's, this simple *comedor* has everything you need to satisfy your seafood fix. The longtime owner, Pancha, knows her way around the kitchen. Prices are average for the beachfront strip—it's actually just off the beach, though the fish is just as fresh as anywhere else. It's an authentic local place that most foreigners bypass. Before setting off, buy a bag of coconut bars from the kitchen—they are the best in town.

On the beachfront, across from Flamingo's. No phone. Main courses L80–L140. No credit cards. Daily 8am–10pm.

Punto Italia ITALIAN Away from the beach, on the road to the highway, this trendy restaurant and gourmet grocer is the most upscale option in Omoa. Apart from selling liquor, wine, olives, and hard-to-find foodstuffs, they put out a decent wood-fired pizza and pasta selection, along with steaks and seafood. Their second-floor dining area/lounge is open-air but blocked from the elements with a funky white wind stopper, a fashionable accent that shows lots of San Pedro Sula influence.

Btw. the fort & the highway. © **504/2658-9125.** Main courses L100–L200. MC, V. Wed–Sun noon–10pm.

Restaurante Fisherman's ★★ SEAFOOD Huge plates—as in the "if you can finish one, call me and I will be your manager for eating competitions" kind of big—are the specialty of this simple eatery. Two, maybe three, could split a plate easily. Their menu is similar to the others along the beachfront, with a mix of Honduran staples and seafood dishes like *sopa marinera* or fresh fish either breaded or grilled. The entrees come with a pile of plantain chips, salad, and beans that can barely fit on the plate. They also have iguana in coconut sauce.

On the beachfront. No phone. Main courses L100–L250. MC, V. Daily 8am–10pm.

Scapate HONDURAN Right beside the pier and attached to Flamingo's, this restaurant serves a little bit of everything. Dining is in the big open-air, two-level *champa*. Shrimp or fish—grilled, fried, steamed, or in garlic sauce—is the most popular choice. Their ceviche lacks sufficient chunks of fish or shrimp, so it is more soupy and full of tomatoes than most. Their breakfasts—Honduran, American, and various a la carte options—are above average for Omoa.

On the beachfront. © **504/2658-9199.** Main courses L60–L140. MC, V. Daily 8am–10pm.

Sueños de Mar ★ INTERNATIONAL This newish restaurant in the hotel of the same name prides itself on its Canadian breakfasts, like bacon, eggs, and hash browns, or pancakes. They have a decent beach menu, too, ranging from tuna salad sandwiches to *flautas* and tacos, burritos, and quesadillas. Even popcorn. You can use the hotel's Wi-Fi signal from indoors in the large dining area, on their patio, or in their beachfront seating.

The very end of the beach. © **504/2630-5605.** www.suenosdemar.com. Main courses L60–L135. MC, V. Daily 8am–4:30pm.

TELA

At Tela, a beachside town 87km (54 miles) east of San Pedro Sula, a major resort project has attracted big names such as Westin and Hilton, though so far, little has gotten off the ground. The major government tourism initiative, with help from the World Bank, was all set to turn Tela Bay into one of the most important beach destinations in Central America. Chances are it still will happen, though not as soon as developers had hoped. The hopes are that there will be two four- and five-star mega-resorts, an 18-hole designer golf course from Gary Player, and a marina operating in the area. Controversy has been swirling around the project, though, as opposition groups are claiming that a Cancun-like resort would completely wipe out the already fragile ecosystem at the city's Laguna de los Micos and do little for the Garífuna communities there. These groups may have run out of luck, though. Ground has already been broken, roads are being expanded, and 20 new bilingual tourist police officers have been trained and hired.

The conquistador Cristóbal de Olid founded this city on May 3, 1524, the day of the Holy Cross, and gave it the name Triunfo de la Cruz. The abbreviation of the name would eventually lead to the shortened name of Tela. In the early 1800s, the Garinagu began to arrive here from Roatán and set up communities all over Tela Bay, many of which are still around to this day. Towards the end of the century, the municipality began to form around the banana plantations of the Tela Railroad Company, a subsidiary of the United Fruit Company, which owned the Chiquita brand. The company monopolized city politics, until moving its offices to La Lima in 1976.

Today, as tourism grows, its days as a banana republic are in the past. While the skeletal remains of the Tela Railroad and United Fruit offices are gathering dust, the employee homes have been turned into one of the country's finest resorts, the Hotel Telamar.

Essentials

GETTING THERE

BY CAR Tela sits directly on CA 13, halfway between San Pedro Sula and La Ceiba, each a little more than an hour away, depending on traffic.

BY BUS Any bus headed between La Ceiba and San Pedro Sula will make a stop at Tela. For San Pedro, try Tela Express (2a Av. NE, just past the train tracks; **© 504/2550-8355;** L60; 1½ hr.) with five daily departures. If heading to La Ceiba (L40; 1½ hr.) or Trujillo (L120; 5 hr.), catch a Cotuc bus (at the Dippsa gas station on the highway) or head to the mini-bus terminal at 9a Calle NE.

GETTING AROUND

ON FOOT Anywhere in the actual city of Tela can be reached on foot; however, for most of the surrounding big attractions, you will need some form of motorized transport.

BY CAR Your own car is the best method of transport if you wish to explore the national parks and coast on your own. There are no car-rental agencies in Tela, so you'll have to head to the airports in La Ceiba (p. 162) or San Pedro Sula (p. 92).

BY TAXI Taxis are best for getting to Lancetilla, the surrounding beaches, and Garífuna villages along the coast, but most drivers won't make the long trips to the national parks. A ride in town should cost no more than L20.

BY BUS Minibuses and pickups ply the highway and coastal roads, though they are infrequent.

ORIENTATION

The city of Tela sits on the southernmost point of Tela Bay; Parque Nacional Punta Izopo and Parque Nacional Jeannette Kawas/Punta Sal flank each side of the city and are connected by unpaved roads that are sometimes impassable when it rains. The city center, Tela Vieja, is quite compact, with a small grid of streets hugging the coast. The Río Tela splits the town into two, with Tela Vieja on the east and Tela Nueva—home of the Villas Telamar and the old Tela Railroad buildings—on the west bank.

VISITOR INFORMATION

All amenities can be found in Tela Vieja. The most convenient bank, **Banco Atlántida** (4a Av. NE and 9a Calle NE), has an **ATM** and exchanges traveler's checks. You

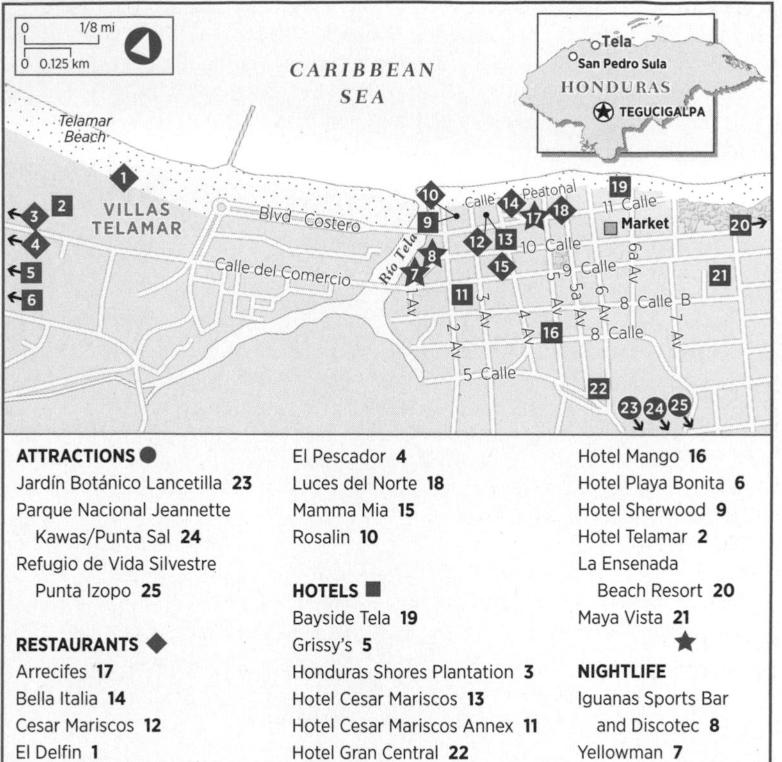

can make international calls at **Hondutel** (4a Av. NE and 7a Calle NE; daily 7:30am–9pm) or at most of the **cybercafes** near Parque Central. The **Tourist Police** (✆ **504/448-0253;** daily 24 hr.) can be found at 11a Calle NE and 4a Avenidas NE.

For tourist information, try the **Tela Chamber of Commerce** (www.telahonduras.com) or **PROLANSATE** (Edificio Kawas, at Calle del Commercio; ✆ **504/2448-2042**), which has brochures, maps, and information regarding the national parks in the area.

What to See & Do

Moving west from Tela along the coast, you will encounter the Garífuna communities of Triunfo de la Cruz, Tornabé, San Juan, La Ensenada, Río Tinto, and lastly Miami. The farther you get from Tela, the more traditional the villages become.

Miami ★★★, which sits on a small sandbar between the ocean and the Los Micos lagoon in Parque Nacional Jeannette Kawas/Punta Sal, is the most interesting to visit. Literally unchanged for 200 years, the village is completely comprised of thatched huts without electricity or running water. Local boatmen can paddle you out on dugout canoes or take you out on motorized boats into the lagoon. Once you reach the town, you can lounge on the empty white sand beach there or munch on fresh seafood from the informal restaurants the locals set up for tourists.

You can get to Miami with your own car, but the village is more commonly visited on tours to the national park with **Garífuna Tours** (✆ **504/2448-2904;** www.garifuna tours.com). The standard L55 park admission fee applies to entering the village.

Jardín Botánico Lancetilla ★★ Lancetilla, the second largest tropical botanical garden in the world, was established in 1926 by American botanist William Popenoe, who was hired by United Fruit to research varieties of bananas and figure out how to best treat diseases found in the plantations. Popenoe was a curious fellow, though, and quickly began to import plants and fruits from around the world to Lancetilla, including the African palm, which has long been one of the most important cash crops in the country. United Fruit continued Popenoe's work for years after he left. The Honduran government, which took control in 1974, continues the research today at the garden.

The 1,680-hectare (4,151-acre) park has more than 1,200 species of plants, such as palms, fruit trees, and hardwoods, along with poisonous and medicinal varieties that are superbly labeled and organized. From the visitor center, which is about 2km (1¼ miles) from the highway, you walk through a large bamboo forest to the arboretum, which makes up the most visited section of the park. Here, you will find Popenoe's house and a small graveyard where his wife Dorothy is buried. Guides lead groups on hour-long tours of the arboretum (L95). Trails delve deeper into the biological reserve, which includes significant tracts of primary and secondary tropical and subtropical humid forests.

Botany is not the only science of interest in the park. Ornithology is a big deal here, too. Nearly 400 species of birds have been recorded in Lancetilla, as well as numerous butterflies and reptiles. Bird tours (arranged at the garden, call a few days ahead of time; L300 per group) leave at dawn in the hopes of spotting trogons, tanagers, orioles, motmots, and toucans, among others.

There's a small cafeteria and a few basic cabins with A/C and private bathrooms (L380) near the visitor center, but they're occasionally filled with researchers.

5km (3 miles) N of Tela. ✆ **504/2448-1740.** L115 adults. Daily 7:30am–3pm.

Parque Nacional Jeannette Kawas/Punta Sal ★★★ Parque Nacional Punta Sal was renamed after the Honduran activist and President of PROLANSATE, Jeannette Kawas Fernández, who was killed after establishing the park amid controversy from business groups who claimed the land. Few will argue, though, about the amazing biodiversity in the 782 sq. km (302 sq. mile) park. Wildlife found here includes marine turtles, dolphins, manatees, caimans, migratory birds (especially Nov–Feb), ocelots, peccaries, monkeys, and many others.

Located on the western end of the Bay of Tela, the park is divided into two parts: the lagoon and the peninsula. Acting as a barrier for Tela Bay from the *nortes,* strong winds that blow in the winter months, the peninsula is made up of a triple threat of postcard-perfect beaches, pristine coral reefs, and lush green jungle—dolphins and howler monkeys are regularly seen during the snorkel tours here. Los Micos Lagoon is separated by a small sandbar from the ocean, and surrounding it are numerous canals that weave through mangrove forests where hundreds of bird and animal species can be seen.

Nearly every tour operator in Tela, including **Garífuna Tours** (✆ **504/2448-2904**), leads almost daily tours to either the peninsula or the lagoon. You can also hire a boat in Miami, though prices are similar and will not include transportation from Tela. Touts with boats on the municipal beach in Tela also sell tours to Punta Sal, though

Yo Quiero Hablar Español

The M@ngo Café (✆ 504/2448-0338; www.mangocafe.net) has the only Spanish school in town, with 20 hours of one-on-one introductory classes per week for L2,166. Intermediate and advanced classes, as well as discounts at the affiliated Hotel Mango (see below), are also available.

they lack information on the wildlife and culture, and the boats are less comfortable. You can haggle down for the cheapest prices, especially if you have a large group.

15km (9¼ miles) NE of Tela. L55 adults; tours L475–L570 per person, depending on group size. Daily 8am–6pm.

Refugio de Vida Silvestre Punta Izopo ★ Twelve kilometers (7½ miles) from Tela on the eastern end of Tela Bay, Punta Izopo has a similar ecosystem to Jeannette Kawas, yet is far less visited. Here, the Lean and Hicaque rivers empty into the ocean in a maze of canals and lagoons sheltered by mangroves. The diverse bionetwork harbors caimans, manatees, turtles, monkeys, and a long list of avian life. The reserve is best explored by kayak. **Garífuna Tours** (✆ **504/2448-2904;** www.garifunatours.com; L475–L570) and most other Tela tour operators regularly lead trips here using top kayaks. You can also recruit boatmen in Triunfo de la Cruz (just west of the park), though you will need to get a group together to make it worthwhile.

12km (7½ miles) SE of Tela. Free admission; tours L475–L570 per person, depending on group size. Daily 8am–6pm

Outdoor Activities

A dozen kilometers or so of white sand **beaches** backed by lazy palm trees stretch around Tela Bay. The best beach in the city proper is in front of the Hotel Telamar (p. 158) west of the Río Tela, which is open to the public and has beach chairs and umbrellas for rent (L25). In Tela Vieja, the beachside boardwalk has a few restaurants, bars, and craft vendors, though the beach is often dirty and unsafe to leave your valuables. About a 20- to 30-minute walk from the city along the beach, on the eastern end of the bay, the La Ensenada Beach Villas and Resort is fronted by the clearest water and calmest ocean anywhere on the bay. The feel is much more Caribbean here. Outside of town, decent beaches can be found in the Garífuna villages like Tornabé and Miami.

Shopping

A few souvenir shops are scattered around Tela Vieja. The best is **Casa del Sol,** a chain that is right in the Hotel Cesar Mariscos (see below). For jewelry and crafts, try the vendors that line up on the boardwalk and also near the El Delfin restaurant and the beach at the Villas Telamar. A special buy are the coconut bars and *pan de coco,* or coconut bread, that roving Garífuna women sell from baskets that they carry on their heads.

Where to Stay

EXPENSIVE

La Ensenada Beach Villas and Resort ★ Appearing literally out of nowhere in 2008, this midsize condo resort has transformed the far eastern end of Tela Bay. Set on a stretch of beach with clear turquoise water, the hotel is practically by itself, sans palm trees, private pier, and passing boats. There is a massive pool area just off the beach that is the hub of all activity, with several bars and restaurants branching off it, sort of like the Villas Telamar, as well as a thatched-roof swim-up or walk-in bar in the middle of the water. The rooms are back from the beach and lack ocean views, although they do front another pool that lacks all the bells and whistles of the other. The rooms are true condos, with separate bedrooms with private bathrooms, kitchens, and living areas.

3km (1¾ miles) E of Tela center. www.laensenadatela.com. ✆ **504/2557-9562.** 94 units. L2,480 double. AE, MC, V. Free parking. **Amenities:** Restaurants; bars; pool. *In room:* A/C, TV, hair dryer, kitchen, Wi-Fi (free).

Honduras Shores Plantation The Honduras Shores Plantation is billed as an eco-lodge, but it is really nothing more than a condo complex. It's set on 32 hectares (79 acres), amid 240 residential lots, and is fronted by a decent stretch of beach. The one- and two-bedroom cabanas are rented by the day, week, or month and give discounts to returning customers, thus attracting lots of snowbirds from up north. Think of the layout and decor of a typical Florida condo, but make it new, add a kitchen, and drop it a few kilometers from any crowd, and you pretty much get an idea of the rooms here.

6km (3¾ miles) W of Tela, San Juan. www.hsphonduras.com. ✆ **504/2448-0342.** 12 units. L1,730 1-bdrm; L2,470 2-bdrm. MC, V. **Amenities:** Restaurant; bar; children's splash area; gym; pool. *In room:* A/C, TV, kitchen.

Hotel Telamar ★★ ☺ The Telamar is easily one of the best, most unique accommodations in the country today and exactly the kind of place that will set Tela apart from places like Cancun, Mexico, and Costa Rica in the years to come. This one-time gated community for Tela Railroad Company executives has been renovated to become a full-scale village-style resort. Guest accommodations are in either the neighborhood of pastel-colored, 1- to 4-bedroom stilted villas or the new main buildings. Rooms in the more modern hotel section face the ocean or the pool, while the remodeled villas face either the ocean or the gardens. They have a corner of the property dedicated to family-friendly aquatics, and kids will delight in their 91m-long (300-ft.) swimming pool with a slide, along with the bridges, children's play area, and a second, smaller pool. Even if mega-resorts do open in this region soon, it will be hard to match the history and character here.

1km (½ mile) W of town, Tela Nueva. www.hoteltelamar.com. ✆ **504/2269-4414.** 210 units. From L2,660 double; from L5,930 villa. AE, MC, V. **Amenities:** Restaurants; bars; golf course; pool; tennis court. *In room:* A/C, TV, hair dryer, kitchens (in villas), Wi-Fi (free).

MODERATE

Bayside Tela At the other end of the Calle Peatonal from Hotel Sherwood, this hotel opened in 2008. Unlike the others down the beach, this one has a somewhat younger vibe that's evident right from the lobby bar and restaurant that spills onto the sidewalk. The rooms, half of which overlook the beach, are fresh and new with crisp white linens, a shiny white bathroom, new TVs, beige walls, and a black dresser. They'll also arrange tours to Punta Sal for guests.

Calle Peatonal. ✆ **504/2448-1210.** 8 units. L1,045 double. MC, V. **Amenities:** Restaurant; bar. *In room:* A/C, TV.

Cesar Mariscos Annex ★ This renovated century-old building, not far from the Puente Vieja in downtown Tela, is one of the best deals in the city. Fine-looking exposed brick walls give the singles, doubles, and triples here a refined look and feel. Handmade wood furniture and decor comprised of local art and handicrafts lend the hotel a uniquely Tela-ized feel, as do the open-air wraparound hallways surrounding the three-level building that afford decent views of a grungy part of the old city. The hotel was bought out by the Cesar Mariscos hotel on the beach and, arguably, has more style than their beachfront property.

½ block from the Puente Viejo on Calle del Commercio, Tela Vieja. www.hotelcesarmariscos.com. ✆ **504/2448-0303.** 14 units. L1,064 double. Additional beds L220. MC, V. *In room:* A/C, fan, TV, no phone.

Grissy's Just meters from an empty beach a few kilometers west of town, Grissy's is a locally owned hotel with all-inclusive packages (accommodations, meals, drinks, and airport transfers). Only some rooms have small kitchens and sitting areas, but all are large, new, and kept immaculately clean (but with drab whitish-gray tile floors). The thatched-roof terrace and thatched umbrellas at their beach and poolside restaurant create a resort-like ambience whose only match is at the Telamar. The friendly English-speaking staff rent jet skis and other sports equipment and will lead personal tours of the national parks.

2km (1¼ miles) W of Tela, Barrio El Paraiso. www.grissys.com. ✆ **504/2415-3064.** 9 units. L1,330 double; L1,995 suite. AE, MC, V. **Amenities:** Restaurant; bar; gym; pool; jet ski rental. *In room:* A/C, TV, kitchen (in suites), Wi-Fi (free).

Hotel Cesar Mariscos A small step up from the Sherwood, this hotel is right next door on the Tela beachfront. It's owned by Caribe Expeditions, a tour operator that runs trips to Punta Sal, and was built in 1996 above the well-known restaurant of the same name. Cheery rooms with tile floors and lots of light look out onto their small infinity pool and the beach. Opt for the rooms with private balconies. The property also has one five-person apartment with a small kitchen.

Calle Peatonal & Av. Uruguay, around town. www.hotelcesarmariscos.com. ✆ **504/2448-2083.** 20 units. L1,330 double; L2,090 apt. Rates include continental breakfast. MC, V. **Amenities:** Restaurant; bar; pool. *In room:* A/C, TV.

Hotel Playa Bonita They self-promote this hotel as budget smart, which I think is as good a term as any. Each room features two beds with orthopedic mattresses and fun red-and-white-striped comforters. Throughout the hotel, you will find walls painted cheery oranges and light green, and handmade Honduran wood furniture is scattered in hallways and patios. The decor is light; just a few framed pictures on each wall and little accents like flowers and handicrafts show plenty of the hand-picked, personal touches of the owners. They have an oversized terrace overlooking the beach and a patio with a very small pool that's good for a quick soak. Their beach is the same stretch of sand as the much more expensive Telamar, which is the best in Tela center.

Just W of Hotel Telamar. www.hotelplayabonitatela.com. ✆ **504/2448-3450.** 11 units. L1,200 double. Rates include breakfast. MC, V. Free parking. **Amenities:** Bar; cafe; pool. *In room:* A/C, TV, Wi-Fi (free).

Hotel Sherwood The Sherwood, right on the end of the liveliest section of the beachside boardwalk in Tela Vieja, was Tela's top hotel long before tourism was a cause to celebrate here. While the new resorts outside of the city are a much better value, the Sherwood still has its quirky charms. Some of the rooms are outdated, depending on when renovations took place, because none of them were done at the same time. Color schemes, floors, walls, bedspreads, and furniture are all different, so it is impossible to sum them up here—look at a few before deciding on one. The

Presidential Suite, appointed with rattan furniture and only slightly more expensive than the standard rooms, is the best room in the house. All rooms have ocean views—the best are from the third floor—and, apart from the singles, have a private balcony facing the beach.

Calle Peatonal & Av. 3a NE. www.hotelsherwood.com. ✆ **504/2448-1065.** 34 units. L1,525 double; L1,843 presidential suite. MC, V. **Amenities:** Restaurant; bar; pool. *In room:* A/C, TV.

INEXPENSIVE

Hotel Gran Central ★★ 🎁 This completely restored building 2 blocks from Parque Central is easily one of the best architectural transformations on the North Coast. What was once a dilapidated building now has a decidedly tropical urban feel, with high ceilings, a few exposed-brick walls, black-and-white tiled floors, and potted plants sitting everywhere. Rooms have wood shutters, palm trees painted on the walls, high ceilings, and private terraces. If they replaced the worn furniture—especially the couches—with more modern pieces, they could charge quadruple the rate. It reminds me of some of the chic boutique hotels in renovated colonial buildings that are all the rage up in Cartagena, Colombia.

Av. Honduras. www.hotelgrancentral.com. ✆ **504/2448-1099**. 8 units. L950 double; L1,520 suite. AE, DC, MC, V. **Amenities:** Restaurant; bar. *In room:* A/C, fan, TV.

Hotel Mango This hotel, overlooking the Río Tela on the Tela Vieja side of the city, is owned by Garífuna Tours. Mostly *gringos* who are studying at their Spanish school (see "Yo Quiero Hablar Español," above) or taking a tour stay here, so the mostly uninspiring, simple yet clean rooms get filled. They have a nice little bar and restaurant on a terrace overlooking the river that doubles as the common area for the place. Discounts are available for longer stays.

Av. Panama & the Río Tela. www.mangocafe.net. ✆ **504/4248-0338.** 10 units. L304 single; L420 double. No credit cards. **Amenities:** Restaurant; bar. *In room:* A/C (additional L100), TV.

Maya Vista ★★ Maya Vista's French-Canadian owners have created a tiny paradise of sorts in the city proper, just a block from the Río Hiland, where it meets with the Caribbean. Quiet and relaxing, with tall leafy trees that are woven through the design of the whole building, the property is suggestive of a tree house. A rooftop lookout tower and several thatched-roof terraces with hammocks allow for expansive views all the way to Punta Izopo. Rooms with one to three beds are decorated with murals of Maya designs and beach themes; I recommend opting for one of the slightly more expensive rooms with balconies. The owners will create meal and accommodation packages on request.

8a Calle NE & 9a Av. NE. www.mayavista.com. ✆ **504/2448-1497**. 9 units. L855–L1,140 double. AE, MC, V. **Amenities:** Restaurant; bar. *In room:* A/C, TV, fridge (in some).

Where to Eat

EXPENSIVE

El Delfin ★ INTERNATIONAL This thatched-roof beach *palapa* in front of the Telamar supplies the beach chairs and sometimes the music for the cleanest and most prime piece of sand in Tela. During the day, it's mostly filled with hungry beachgoers who come for sandwiches, burgers, grilled seafood, and shrimp every which way. Towards sundown, the bar heats up, and margaritas, mojitos, and *Cuba libres* can be spotted at every table. There's occasionally live music.

1km (½ mile) W of town, Tela Nueva. ✆ **504/2269-4414.** Main courses L115–L270. MC, V. Daily 7am–11pm.

MODERATE

Arrecifes ★ SEAFOOD This bar/restaurant on the *malécon* has a smaller menu than Cesar Mariscos and Rosalin, which are a few doors down, though prices are about 10% less. Service tends to be slow, though the drinks are quite cheap. While there isn't much in the way of chef's specialties, standard seafood dishes like ceviche, grilled shrimp in garlic sauce, snapper prepared in a number of ways, and conch are just as tasty as at the neighbors.

Calle Peatonal & Av. 5a NE. ✆ **504/2448-1065.** Main courses L75–L200. No credit cards. Daily 10am–midnight.

Cesar Mariscos ★ SEAFOOD/INTERNATIONAL All activity on Tela's small beachfront boardwalk, including children selling *pan de coco,* revolves around this restaurant, which is widely considered the best in town. Tables are set in the indoor dining room, under the boardwalk canopy, or under the umbrellas on the sidewalk. While they have beef on the menu, seafood is the specialty here. The shrimp in garlic sauce is one of the best on the North Coast, while the grilled fish, lobster, and seafood stew all taste equally as sweet.

Calle Peatonal & Av. Uruguay. ✆ **504/2448-2083.** Main courses L95–L305. MC, V. Daily 7am–10pm.

El Pescador ★★ HONDURAN This lively Garífuna restaurant in the village of San Juan, just up the coast from the city, relies on the catches of neighborhood fishermen. It's just a small shack on a beautiful stretch of clean beach with plastic chairs and tables and a sandy concrete floor. Seafood specialties like grilled shrimp, fish, lobster, and *tapado,* a Garífuna seafood stew with fish, coconut, and cassava, are all on the menu. Their piña coladas are as refreshing as they come.

2km (1¼ miles) W of town, San Juan. ✆ **504/2448-1073.** Main courses L95–L190. No credit cards. Wed–Mon 9am–7pm.

Luces del Norte ★ SEAFOOD Between the park and the beach, this concrete-floor seafood restaurant, livened up with plants, is a local favorite. Red snapper is one of their many specialties, and it's served up fried, grilled, steamed, or in a number of sauces. The menu is large and branches out beyond Honduran seafood into Chinese rice dishes, pastas, and breakfast. The kitchen is small, so the food tends to take a while if there is a crowd. They have a small book exchange in the dining room. Bring bug spray; the mosquitoes tend to be nasty in this part of town.

1 block N of the park. No phone. Main courses L120–L200. MC, V. Daily 8am–9pm.

Rosalin ★ SEAFOOD/INTERNATIONAL The restaurant at the Hotel Sherwood has a similar menu and similar prices to Cesar Mariscos next door, and the food is prepared more or less the same way. The people-watching is better next door, but other than that, you can expect the same service, good grilled seafood specialties, stews, and a few beef dishes. The dining borders the hotel's swimming pool, which adds a bit of ambience and occasionally some noise when kids are playing there.

Calle Peatonal & Av. 3a NE. ✆ **504/2448-1065.** www.hotelsherwood.com. Main courses L95–L305. MC, V. Daily 7am–10pm.

INEXPENSIVE

Bella Italia ☺ ITALIAN Run by Italian expats who spent many years in Santa Rosa de Copán managing a similar restaurant, this is one of the best of several pizzerias in town. With tables right on the sidewalk facing the beach, the restaurant serves a full range of pastas, pizzas, and calzones that any homesick North American child will appreciate.

4a Av. NE & Calle Peatonal. © **504/2448-1055.** Main courses L75–L190. No credit cards. Daily noon–8pm.

Mamma Mia ★ ITALIAN A favorite expat hangout for the sports and music videos on the TV, cheap meals, and the Internet cafe and call center across their little courtyard. Pizza and southern Italian fare, and a few Garífuna dishes, are quite good, and the prices are among the lowest in town. Occasionally, they will hold Garífuna cultural performances.

1 block W of the park. © **504/2448-4301.** Main courses L60–L140. No credit cards. Daily noon–9pm.

Tela After Dark

The sidewalk tables at **Arrecifes** on the boardwalk, just past Cesar Mariscos, attract an upscale young crowd who come for cheap mixed drinks, beer, and a kitchen that stays open late. The bar at El Delfin restaurant (see above) gets busy on the weekends, when there is occasionally live music. The **Hotel Telamar** property also boasts a small bar and disco that is usually filled with upper-crust locals and hotel guests. There is a smattering of discos in town, but all are a bit seedy. The most popular are **Iguanas Sports Bar and Discotec** (10a Calle NE and 2a Av. NE; no phone) and **Yellowman** (10a Calle NE and 2a Av. NE), next door to each other in the Zona Viva. Covers on Fridays and Saturdays are L100.

LA CEIBA

La Ceiba, the third-largest city in Honduras and the capital of the department of Atlántida, is named after a huge Ceiba tree on the coast that was once a community-meeting place. Recently, the city (97km/60 miles east of Tela) has become known as the country's ecotourism headquarters. The city itself, established only a little more than a hundred years ago, is sort of thrown together and dirty, its beaches are polluted, and it doesn't hold much of interest to passing tourists. It works best as a base to explore the countless remarkable attractions that are within a short drive, such as Class IV whitewater rapids, hiking trails through several stunning national parks, a wildlife refuge with caimans and manatees, vast empty beaches, sprawling pineapple plantations, and much more. Let's not leave out that the city is the jumping-off point for the Bay Islands, by both ferry and plane, and the Cayos Cochinos. Whether you like the gritty town or not, you must come through La Ceiba if you want to experience the finest natural wonders in Honduras.

Essentials

GETTING THERE

BY AIR **La Ceiba's Golosón International Airport (LCE)** (© **504/2443-3925**) is 12km (7½ miles) west of the city on the road to Tela. The only international airlines that land at the airport are **TACA** (© **504/2441-3191**) and **Skyservice** (© **800/701-9448**), which makes seasonal flights to Toronto.

If you are flying to/from the Bay Islands or anywhere else in Honduras, you can try domestic airlines, such as **Isleña** (© **504/2441-3354;** www.flyislena.com), **Aerolineas Sosa** (© **504/443-1399**), or **Lanhsa Airlines** (© **504/2442-1283**), as all offer daily flights. Honduras-based **Rollins Air** (© **504/2440-2696;** www.rollinsair.

La Ceiba

ATTRACTIONS ●
Museo de Mariposas **25**
Parque Nacional Pico Bonito **22**
Refugio Nacional de Vida Silvestre Cuero y Salado **21**

RESTAURANTS ◆
Chef Guity's **3**
Costa Azul **7**
D'Var **10**
Expatriates Bar & Grill **18**
Espresso Americano **17**
La Palapa **8**
Laura's Bakery **20**
Pupuseria Universitaria **2**

HOTELS ■
Coco Pando Resort **14**
Banana Republic Guest House **19**
Gran Hotel Paris **16**
Hotel Olas del Mar **1**
La Aurora **23**
La Quinta **24**
Palma Real **15**
Quinta Real **6**

NIGHTLIFE ★
El Guapo **5**
Hibou **13**
La Palapa **9**
Le Pacha **12**
Mango Tango **11**
Snake Bar **4**

Celebrating San Isidro

More than 200,000 visitors from around Honduras and Central America descend upon La Ceiba during **La Feria San Isidro,** or Carnaval week, which takes place every May and culminates on the third Saturday of the month. While the celebration of the city's patron saint, San Isidro, is the motive, the festival has far less of a religious theme than that in Comayagua. Here, it's more of a big party, where live music, dancing, parades, an endless lineup of food and T-shirt vendors, and endless intoxication takes place each night in a different part of town. The last night of the festival is the most intense, with horses, floats, and costumed dancers parading down Avenida San Isidro. It's not as organized as carnival in Rio or Mardi Gras, but a spectacle to behold nevertheless. Reserve hotel rooms months in advance during this time of year.

com), a charter jet, also began flying from La Ceiba to Grand Cayman in March 2009 and also has service to Costa Rica, Panama, Jamaica, and Cuba upon government approval.

A 10- to 15-minute taxi ride from Golosón International to anywhere in the center should cost about L115.

BY BOAT From La Ceiba, two high-speed ferries run twice a day to Roatán and Utila from the Muelle de Cabotaje, 5km (3 miles) east of La Ceiba. For Roatán, the **Galaxy Wave** (✆ **504/2443-463**) departs La Ceiba at 9:30am and 4:30pm, returning at 7am and 2pm from the terminal at Dixon's Cove. The one-way price is L524, and the ferry has room for 360 people; it offers A/C, a sun deck, and a small snack shop. The open sea can get choppy at times, particularly in the afternoon, and vomit bags are passed out and frequently used.

The **Utila Princess II** (✆ **504/2425-3390**) makes the hour-long trip back and forth between the Municipal Pier Utila. The Princess, which is about one-third the size of the Galaxy Wave, departs La Ceiba at 9:30am and 4pm, returning at 6:20am and 2pm. The price is L425 each way.

Yachts from around the Caribbean commonly stop in La Ceiba and occasionally will take on passengers for a fee or in exchange for work. If you are looking for a ride or need a place to anchor, the **Lagoon Marina** (✆ **504/2440-0614;** www.lagoonmarina laceiba.com) is your best bet. There are 25 slips for boats up to 37m (120 ft.) in length, as well as a nice pool area, bar, and apartments for rent by 2-week period (US$750).

BY BUS Two luxury bus companies, Hedman Alas and Viana Express, have their own terminals in town. **Hedman Alas's terminal** (✆ **504/2441-2199;** www.hedmanalas.com) is on the main highway east of town towards Trujillo, beside the Supermercado Ceibeño #4. Their four daily buses (5:15am–5:30pm) make the trip to Tela (L260; 1½–2 hr.) before heading to San Pedro Sula (L300; a total of 3–3½ hr.), where connections can be made to Copán and Tegucigalpa. **Viana** (✆ **504/2441-2330**), whose terminal is just west of the main bus terminal, near the Esso gas station, has similar service.

All other bus companies operate out of the main terminal (Mercado San Jose, Blvd. 15 de Septiembre) about 2km (1¼ miles) west of the center. **Diana** (✆ **504/2441-6460;** L90) has nine daily departures for San Pedro Sula between 6am and 5:30pm. For the 7-hour ride to Tegucigalpa, **Cristina** (✆ **504/2441-2028;**

L275) departs five times daily between 5:30am and 3:30pm. For the 3-hour trip to Trujillo, try **Cotuc** (✆ **504/2441-2199;** L100), which runs throughout the day from 8am to 6pm.

BY CAR La Ceiba straddles CA 13 on the North Coast about halfway between San Pedro Sula and Trujillo. There aren't as many big car-rental companies in the city as there are in San Pedro or Tegucigalpa, but there are a few. Apart from **Avis** (CA 13 at La Ceiba; ✆ **504/2441-2802;** www.avis.com), most rental companies have counters at the airport, including **Advance** (✆ **504/2441-1105;** www.advancerentacar.com) and **Ace** (✆ **504/2441-2929**).

GETTING AROUND

Almost everything of interest within the city sits within a 10-block radius of the Parque Central, so getting around on two legs is easy. But **buses** are a cheap and useful way to get around to outlying areas. You can easily flag down any of the frequent buses on the main highway going in the direction you are headed, either towards Tela or Trujillo (less than L20 for short distances).

A **taxi** anywhere in the center should run no more than L40, while trips to the airport or the ferry terminal are about three or four times more.

ORIENTATION

The city of La Ceiba is sandwiched between the imposing green mountains of Pico Bonito National Park and the Caribbean Sea. Much of the town straddles the highway, CA 13, although urban sprawl is heading in every direction. A handful of estuaries split the town into several sections, with the center surrounding the wide, shady Parque Central. Two main avenues, San Isidro and 14 de Julio, run parallel to the beach. The mostly Garífuna neighborhood, Barrio La Isla, to the northeast of the park along the beach, is where you will find the Zona Viva, quite a few hotels, restaurants, and tour operators.

[FastFACTS] LA CEIBA

Banks **Banco Atlántida** (Av. San Isidro and 6a Calle) and **BAC** (Av. San Isidro and 5a Calle) in the center of town have 24-hour ATMs and will exchange traveler's checks. Both have second locations at the Megaplaza Mall.

Hospitals **Eurohonduras** (1a Calle and the beach; ✆ **504/2443-0244**) is open 24 hours.

Internet There are four or five cybercafes within 2 blocks of the park with high-speed service for less than L30 per hour. They also provide cheap international calls. The best operation in town, however, is **Planet Cyber** at the Megaplaza Mall.

Laundry **Lavamatic Ceibeño** in Barrio La Isla, at Av. Pedro Nufio and Calle 6, has coin-operated machines and drop-off service for L55 per 4.5kg (10 lb.). It's open daily from 7:30am to 9pm.

Post Office The post office is at Av. Morazán and 14a Calle, and is open Monday to Friday 8am to 4pm, Saturday 8am to noon.

Telephone **Hondutel** (Av. Rosa and 6a Calle) offers local and international calls.

Tourist Information There's a **visitor center** on the first floor of the Banco de Occidente building on Parque Central (✆ **504/2440-1562;** Mon–Fri 8am–4pm). There's another office (✆ **504/2440-3044**) at Av. San Isidro and 8a Calle with more brochures and maps.

Tourist Police To reach the police, call ✆ **504/2441-0860,** daily 24 hours.

What to See & Do

While there is little to do in the city, apart from visiting the Butterfly Museum, La Ceiba's coastal location and proximity to several national parks gives you plenty of options on how to spend your day. Besides the listings below, refer to activities in Sambo Creek, Pico Bonito, and the Cayos Cochinos, which are all accessible on day trips.

Museo de Mariposas ☺ This private 92-sq.-m (990-sq.-ft.) museum exhibits more than 14,000 butterflies, moths, and insects from more than 100 countries, although more than 9,000 are from Honduras. Highlights include blue-tipped damselflies, flying cockroaches, walking sticks, and black tarantula wasps. Specimens are displayed in glass cases that cover the walls, and guided tours point out the largest, smallest, most colorful, heaviest, and most unusual. Other exhibits include butterfly traps, information posters, night-collecting setups, and a 25-minute video on insects (available in English or Spanish).

Casa G-12, 3 blocks S of Hotel La Quinta, Colonia El Sauce. ✆ **504/2442-2874.** www.hondurasbutterfly.com. L75 adults; L35 children. Mon–Sat 8am–5pm.

Refugio Nacional de Vida Silvestre Cuero y Salado ★★★ Three rivers—the Cuero, Salado, and San Juan—feed this massive estuary that is one of the most important natural reserves in Honduras. Since wildlife is abundant, with just a little luck, you will see a decent selection of birds and mammals. There are almost 200 species of birds on record in the reserve, as well as sloths, ocelots, jaguars, otters, howler and white-face monkeys, iguanas, caimans, and the elusive West Indian manatee.

The reserve is nearly impossible to find on your own, even if you're a seasoned guidebook writer. (It *can* be done with lots of stopping and asking the locals, though.) The best way to explore the canals and mangrove forests is by boat from the visitor center in Salado Barra. Two-hour motorboat tours are standard and explore the canals nearest the visitor center, although some longer tours are available and have a much better chance of encountering manatees. Going with a tour operator (L760–L950) such as **Garífuna Tours** (**✆504/2440-3252;** www.garifunatours.com) or **Omega Tours** (**✆ 504/2440-0334;** www.omegatours.info) is a much easier way to see the park (they provide transportation) and far cheaper, in most instances. If you are going on your own, you will have to fork over money for admission, plus the entire cost for the boat and guide, rather than splitting it.

Considering wildlife-watching is best done at dawn, you might want to stay the night at the visitor center's dorm lodging, which runs from L135 per person, or pitch a tent (L55) on the premises of the park. There's a small cafeteria by the visitor center.

30km (19 miles) W of La Ceiba. ✆ **504/2443-0329.** L189 adults. Rail journey L190; guide L125; 2-hr. boat tour L275. Daily 6:30am–6pm.

Outdoor Activities

BEACHES/SWIMMING The beaches in La Ceiba city are polluted and possibly even dangerous to your health and physical well being. If you must, the beach in front of the Quinta Real (see below) is the most manicured, although the water is still putrid. A much better beach is Playa de Peru, a couple of kilometers east of the Muelle de Cabotaje, or at Sambo Creek, 21km (13 miles) east of the center.

Studying Spanish

La Ceiba is home to a handful of language schools, most offering 20 hours of classroom work a week, homestays with local families (optional), workbooks, some organized activities, and three daily meals. Two recommended schools are AmeriSpan (✆ 215/2751-1100; www.amerispan.com; $270 per week) and the Central American School (✆ 504/2440-1707; www.ca-spanish.com; $150 per week).

There is also a popular swimming hole at Río María, between Playa de Peru and Sambo Creek—look for the signs that say "Ecological Area." Getting there is a bit more of an adventure. You must hike about 45 minutes through the wilderness along the river, where you will catch stunning glimpses of the Cayos Cochinos far off in the distance and the occasional toucan. Your reward: an eco-paradise with a series of cool, clear water pools.

HORSEBACK RIDING ★ While horseback riding is more common in the mountains of the western half of Honduras, tours are increasingly popular along the North Coast. **Omega Tours** (✆ **504/2440-0334**) has several different rides. Day trips include a ride along the beach (6 hr.) near the Río Bonito and another ride (4–8 hr.) near Pico Bonito National Park. All trips (L760–L1,425) include a free night in their lodge. They also offer multiple day trips on the Río Sico (6 days) and the Río Blanca Valley (3 days).

KAYAKING ★ At Cacao Lagoon, east of La Ceiba past the village of Roma, **La Moskitia Ecoaventuras** (✆ **504/2550-2124**) offers kayaking trips. The lagoon is a twisting maze of mangroves, where sightings of howler monkeys, bats, kingfishers, herons, and other wildlife are frequent. The 5- to 6-hour trip includes a relaxing visit to a sheltered beach.

Shopping

The best place for a wide selection of handicrafts, including Garífuna dolls, Lenca pottery, tribal textiles and jewelry, and other assorted items from around the region and country, is the **Rain Forest Souvenir shop** (Av. La Bastilla; ✆ **504/2443-2917**). Alternatively, **Souvenir El Buen Amigo** (✆ **504/2414-5504**) sells a variety of handicrafts and regional items at their two locations, beside Expatriates Restaurant in Barrio El Iman and on Av. 14 de Julio, downtown. **PiQ' Art Gallery** (Av. Morazán, beside Farmacia Kielsa; ✆ **504/2440-4041**) sells paintings from Honduran artists, as well as assorted crafts and furniture. They just opened a small cafe and plan on turning it into a bed-and-breakfast, too.

The **Mall Megaplaza,** at Avenidas Morazán and 22a Calle, is home to North American chain stores, fast food restaurants, a movie theater, an Internet cafe, and a few banks. Visiting this mall makes for a completely un-Honduran experience, but there is air conditioning. It's open daily from 10am to 9pm.

Even if you don't buy anything, it's worth the effort to walk through La Ceiba's main rambling **street market ★**, where you'll find plenty of mouthwatering fruits and vegetables on display. Be sure to wash any in purified water before eating them, though. If you look hard enough, you'll find a *baleada* stand or two. For stuff like CDs, DVDs, shoes, sunglasses, beach towels, or crafts, look no further. The market is on

6a Calle and Avenidas 14 de Julio, and is open Monday to Saturday 6am to 5pm, Sunday 6am to noon. It costs L10 to L50 to enter the market grounds.

Where to Stay

The accommodations found within the center of La Ceiba mostly fall in the budget and mid-range categories. While none are spectacular, most are suitable for short stays and have all the standard amenities you will find anywhere else. Apart from the Quinta Real on the waterfront, most hotels are strewn about the city center and along the highway. Increasingly, travelers are turning towards the more interesting mid-range to pricier accommodations in the Rio Cangrejal section of Pico Bonito National Park and in Sambo Creek.

EXPENSIVE

Quinta Real ★★ ☺ Quinta Real is a resort in the heart of the city fronting the beach. If you're looking for a true beach resort, forget it. The beach here is polluted and filthy, although they at least try to give the impression of cleanliness. Best for you and the kids to stick by their glitzy pool area, where you can still look out onto the ocean. Don't get this hotel confused with the Palma Real, which is 22km (14 miles) to the east. Unlike that quiet oasis, this hotel is carved out of the otherwise rough-and-tumble Zona Viva, and surrounded by raucous bars and restaurants. It manages to be an oasis of sorts, however, by keeping clean, modern, and exclusive. Tiled floors, light wood furniture, and your average beach decor fill out the clean, modern rooms. Suites feature an extra sitting room. It's not the Ritz, but it's the classiest thing in La Ceiba proper.

Av. 15 de Sept. y Av. Victor Hugo, Zona Viva. www.quintarealhotel.com. ✆ **504/2**440-3311. 81 units. L1,660 double; L3,420 suite. AE, MC, V. **Amenities:** Restaurant; bar; pool. *In room:* TV, hair dryer, Wi-Fi (free).

MODERATE

Coco Pando Resort ★ A few kilometers west of La Ceiba and halfway to the airport, this small hotel, which attracts a mostly international crowd, feels more out of the way than it actually is. If you don't have a car or intend to be moving around a lot, staying here might be an issue, though they do offer free pick-ups and drop-offs. Pine-wood walls and tile floors make the large rooms lean towards the rustic; however, they do have everything you could ask for, like a minifridge, A/C, and purified water dispensers. Their Iguana Bar and Restaurant in a beachfront *champa* is one of the better dining options in the area. All-inclusive packages are available, as well.

5km (3 miles) W of La Ceiba, on the road to the airport. www.cocopando.com. ✆ **504/9969-9663.** 7 units. L1,045 double (high season); L665 double (low season). MC, V. **Amenities:** Restaurant; bar; Internet in lobby (free). *In room:* A/C, fan, TV, fridge.

Gran Hotel Paris While most hotels located on a town's main square can boast a good location, that's not necessarily the case for the Gran Hotel Paris, which is located on Parque Central. While it does have its charm, La Ceiba's main square is noisy, crowded, dirty, and hard to get around because of the steady traffic circling it. You may want to opt for one of the better hotels along the beach or outside of town if you're looking for quiet. If you want to be right in the action, though (a big plus during the Feria de San Isidro), look no further than the Gran Hotel Paris. Plain, uninteresting rooms with standard amenities, like a 27-inch TV, call to mind those at chains like the Motel 6. All rooms have been remodeled recently, so they could be worse. Rooms in the front overlook the square, while the ones in back look onto the leafy courtyard and the surprisingly pleasant pool.

Parque Central. ✆ **504/2440-1414.** hotelparis@psinet.hn. 63 units. L940 double. MC, V. **Amenities:** Restaurant; bar; pool. *In room:* A/C, TV.

INEXPENSIVE

La Aurora The big square glass La Aurora is right on the highway, not far from hordes of fast food chains and gas stations, which makes it especially convenient if you intend on exploring destinations outside the city. Little differentiates the hotel from a standard Days Inn just off a highway exit in the United States. It even smells the same, with chlorine from the pool wafting through the halls. Rooms are bland, but the beds are comfortable, the floors are clean, and there's even a small couch in most.

Carretera La Ceiba-Tela. ✆ **504/2440-2060.** 45 units. L880 double. MC, V. **Amenities:** Jacuzzi; pool. *In room:* A/C, TV, minibar, Wi-Fi (free).

Banana Republic Guest House This small guesthouse is owned and operated by Jungle River Tours and set in a restored house on a downtown La Ceiba side street. There's a mix of rooms, with private and shared bath, and two dorms that sleep 5 or 6. All have high ceilings, wood floors, and are clean but otherwise simple. There are lots of common areas with hammocks and gardens where you can chat with other travelers who probably just got back from one of the day tours run out of this spot.

Av. La República & Calle 12, Barrio Solares Nuevo. www.jungleriverlodge.com. ✆ **504/2440-1268.** 6 units. L150 dorm bed; L285 double without bath; L342 double w/bathroom. AE, MC, V. **Amenities:** Restaurant; bar; Internet in lobby (free). *In room:* Fan.

Hotel Olas del Mar This beachfront hotel in the center, just across the bridge to the Zona Viva, is good if you just want something cheap and simple. The rooms are basic but clean, the outside hallways have a few nice lounge areas, and the view is the same as from the Quinta Real. The beds are a bit stiff, and the rooms are bare-bones plain—but compared to similar-priced hotels in the area, it's a steal. Did I mention they have a big sun deck facing the beach that's a nice place to kick off your sandals and relax?

Av. 14 de Julio & 1 Calle, Zona Viva. www.hotelolasdelmar.com. ✆ **504/2440-1857.** 19 units. L600 double. MC, V. **Amenities:** Restaurant; karaoke bar. *In room:* A/C, TV, Wi-Fi (free).

La Quinta This property is not to be confused with the Quinta Real on the beach, which you might call its evil twin. La Quinta Hotel is right on a busy street well away from the beach and had long been the best hotel in town until the Quinta Real arrived. The 113 rooms surround shady patios and a nice-sized pool that's the center of action during the day. The night belongs to their restaurant and piano bar, however. The rooms vary in size and quality, depending on the wing of the hotel, but all have the same worn '90s flair.

Av. San Isidro. www.hotellaquinta.net. ✆ **504/2443-0223.** 113 units. L1,310 double. AE, MC, V. **Amenities:** Restaurant; bar; pool. *In room:* A/C, TV, Wi-Fi (free).

HOTELS OUTSIDE LA CEIBA

Palma Real Beach Resort ★ The Palma Real, the only true beach resort on La Ceiba's Caribbean coast, is 22km (14 miles) east of the city on the road to Trujillo, just past Sambo Creek. This sprawling residential and entertainment complex is on a beautiful stretch of sand, seemingly in the middle of nowhere, and has a massive pool that stretches across almost the entire property. The facilities, which are also used by the residents of the 150 villas in the complex, include a small water park (the Water

Jungle, with a wave pool, lazy river, and a few slides), Hola Ola Theater (with nightly shows and live music), the Caña Brava Restaurant (with buffet meals), several a la carte restaurants, and the Guiffitti Disco. The rooms at the resort are exactly what you would expect, nothing more and nothing less: clean tile floors, clunky wood furniture, and unadventurous bedspreads and decor. Packaged deals attract plenty of Canadians, Hondurans, and El Salvadorans.

Km 20 Carretera La Ceiba-Trujillo. www.grupopalmareal.com. ✆ **504/2429-0501.** 160 units. L2,280 double. AE, MC, V. **Amenities:** Restaurant; bar; disco; pool; tennis courts. *In room:* A/C, TV, hair dryer, Wi-Fi (free).

Where to Eat

The mix of Garífuna cooking, fresh and affordable seafood, and a lively atmosphere make La Ceiba one of the country's best places to grab a bite to eat. The traveler will find plenty of international dishes being offered at almost every restaurant, though they'll be more impressed if they stick to regional specialties such as garlic shrimp, grilled kingfish, or ceviche.

MODERATE

Costa Azul SEAFOOD This popular beachfront *champa* in the Zona Viva dishes up an array of seafood fishes and standard international grub. It's not nearly as good as Playa Taty's that held the space before, but straightforward, somewhat uninteresting shrimp and grilled fish dishes, seafood stews, and sandwiches are at least reasonably priced.

Beachfront, 1 block E of Hotel Quinta Real, Zona Viva. ✆ **504/2440-1314.** Main courses L165–L300. MC, V. Wed–Sat 11am–11pm; Sun 11am–8pm.

D'Var Resta & Playa ★ CONTINENTAL Just behind Costa Azul, this laidback lounge with Miami Beach–style white curtains is a popular pre-clubbing spot for La Ceiba's well-to-do 20- and 30-somethings. The menu is classier than most nearby, with filet mignon and garlic shrimp alongside a few pastas. The cocktail and wine list is better than most on the strip. On weekends, D'Var is extremely busy after 10pm.

Behind Costa Azul, 1 block E of Hotel Quinta Real, Zona Viva. No phone. Main courses L165–L300. MC, V. Wed–Sat 6pm–2am.

Expatriates Bar & Grill ★★ INTERNATIONAL As you can probably guess by the name, Expatriates is a big-time hangout for the English-speaking crowd in La Ceiba. Their charcoal grill pumps out goodies similar to those at any respectable North American grill, like steaks, fish, shrimp, and chicken breasts. Spicy chicken wings, nachos, and even vegetarian dishes are a welcome retreat for homesick snowbirds. The *chuletas* (pork chops) are served with beans and rice and are mouthwatering. Flat-screen TVs provide the best access in La Ceiba to any North American sporting event. A decent selection of Honduran cigars, a full bar, plenty of tropical cocktails, and free Wi-Fi are added bonuses. A *champa*-style thatched roof is the ceiling of the second-level restaurant, and they have an uncovered section great for stargazing.

Calle 12, Colonia El Naranjal. ✆ **504/2440-1131.** Main courses L95–L265. MC, V. Mon–Fri 3:30–11:30pm; Sat & Sun 11am–late.

La Palapa INTERNATIONAL This rambunctious *palapa* directly behind the Quinta Real (p. 168) is one of the most happening spots in town for food and drinks. It's better known for drinking than eating, though they have a fairly large menu, and the place isn't nearly as grimy as some other restaurants in town. The food is modeled after a Mexican grill and is heavy on lots of finger foods, as well as platters of chorizo and grilled meat, steaks, tacos, nachos, fish, and pasta. Service tends to be slow. There's a DJ or live music on the weekends.

Beside Hotel Quinta Real, Zona Viva. ✆ **504/2443-3844.** Main courses L95–L300. MC, V. Daily 11am–late.

INEXPENSIVE

Chef Guity's ★ HONDURAN Hidden away on a shady piece of beach in the Zona Viva, sandwiched between the bridge and the Quinta Real, this simple eatery is renowned for its Garífuna seafood specialties. Views and breezes from the ocean add to the pleasure of dining at this rustic restaurant, though it is the food that sets it apart. The ceviche (raw seafood marinated in lime juice) makes for a good choice of appetizer. Grilled kingfish, seafood stews, *caracoles* (snails), steaks, and chicken round out the entree options, all of which attract a loyal following of mostly locals.

Beachfront, Zona Viva. No phone. Main courses L75–L190. No credit cards. Mon–Sat 11am–10pm.

Espresso Americano CAFE While the world domination of Starbucks has yet to hit Honduras, this clean and stylish chain is the closest thing the country has to the American coffee shop for now. All sorts of frothy coffee drinks, like mochachinos, iced chai, and *granitas,* as well as your standard cappuccino, coffee, and espresso, can be ordered.

Av. San Isidro, near 7a Calle. No phone. Main courses L40–L100. No credit cards. Daily 8am–8pm.

Laura's Bakery ☺ CAFE/BAKERY The always-fresh selection of preservative-free baked goods at Laura's easily makes it tops in a long line of La Ceiba bake shops. Their subs and sandwiches, both on fresh French baguettes, are good for a meal, while other sugary snacks like pies, pastries, muffins, biscotti, and cookies make for good pick-me-ups any time of the day. The sweet cinnamon rolls are great with a mug of java.

Calle 13a; also at the Megaplaza Mall. ✆ **504/2443-1494.** Main courses L40–L100. No credit cards. Mon–Fri 6am–7:30pm; Sun 7am–5pm.

Pupuseria Universitaria ★ EL SALVADORAN *Pupusas* are the El Salvadoran equivalent to the Honduras *baleada.* Both are simple snack foods that use more or less the same ingredients. The bigger-than-normal *pupusas* here are filled with either *chicharrón* (fried pork) and cheese, or just plain cheese, wrapped in a doughy corn tortilla and served with hot sauce. Other classic El Salvadoran items are on the menu, as well. On weekends, the tables fill up with a pre-club crowd who come here to snack and drink.

1a Calle & Av. 14 de Julio, Zona Viva. No phone. Main courses L50–L150. No credit cards. Daily 11am–9pm.

La Ceiba After Dark

La Ceiba is known for its nightlife, though standards rise and fall. Most clubs are open from Wednesday or Thursday through Saturday from the afternoon until the early morning, and covers are generally L100 to L200. Several new clubs, almost all side-by-side on 1 Calle in the Zona Viva, have upped the quality of La Ceiba's nightlife considerably. At last check, the places to be were at **Le Pacha ★★** (no phone), a large tented lounge and disco with beach frontage, as well as **Hibou ★** (✆ **504/2440-1700**), a multi-part club on the beach at Avenidas Bonilla, with a

Volunteer Opportunities in Northern Honduras

The North Coast of Honduras, centering on La Ceiba, is one of the most active volunteering centers in Central America. Dozens of organizations have offices in the city and help arrange projects for anyone willing to lend a helping hand. Two standouts are **Guaruma** (✆ **504/2406-6782**), a Honduras-based non-profit organization that helps promote environmental awareness and conservation in the Río Cangrejal watershed on the eastern edge of Pico Bonito National Park, and **Children of the Light** (✆ **504/3304-1414**; www.thechildrenofthelight.org), a Christian organization that has built a school and organized other community outreach projects for street children in the region.

full-on disco and raised dance floor, several bars, and DJs blasting the latest Top 40 reggaeton and rock tracks. **La Palapa** (✆ **504/2443-3844**), behind the Quinta Real, is popular with visitors and upscale Hondurans who want to eat and drink with a group of friends but don't want to stand in a crowded disco. There's occasionally live music. On the other side of the Quinta Real are a few, somewhat seedier, bars on the beachfront such as **El Guapo** and **Snake Bar.**

There is a cluster of discos and grungy multi-level bars in the Zona Viva on Calle 1a, like **Mango Tango** (no phone), that can be good for a drink or two, though the crowd varies, depending on the night.

SAMBO CREEK

While only 21km (13 miles) east of La Ceiba, the laidback Garífuna community of Sambo Creek seems like a world away. Several tourism initiatives spurred by NGOs and Peace Corps workers have increased tourism significantly. Some travelers even prefer to base themselves here, as there are decent tourist facilities, as well as a clean beach and several excellent traditional Garífuna seafood restaurants. Boatmen can even arrange trips to the Cayos Cochinos if you get a group together. Several residential communities popular with expats and several good hotels that are a far better value than anything in La Ceiba fringe the town. The pollution and debris that plagues La Ceiba's city beaches are rare here, and the community is active in keeping the sand clean—which is why many Ceibeños come here for a swim.

Getting There

Any eastbound **bus** from La Ceiba will drop you off at the entrance to Sambo Creek (L20). *Colectivo* **taxis** also run back and forth every 20 to 30 minutes from Barrio Potreritos (Calle 6, between Av. 4 and 5 behind Hondutel).

What to See & Do

Apart from the beaches at Sambo Creek or a trip to the Cayos Cochinos (see p. 178), there is a burgeoning assortment of activities to partake in. **Glenda's Paradise Hot Springs Resort** (L150 adults; daily 10am–6pm), just past Sambo Creek on the road to Trujillo, is the most popular thermal spring facility in the La Ceiba area, though facilities are basic. The water is a constant 105°F (41°C) in the stone-lined natural pool, partly covered by a small *champa* to stop the sun. A more modern cold-water pool for cooling off is here, too, along with a picnic area and a small stand selling food and drinks.

Turaser (✆ **504/2429-0509**), out of the Palma Real Resort, operates a canopy tour, just outside of Sambo Creek on the road to Trujillo (look for signs along the highway). The zip-lines are a 30-minute horseback ride through thick rainforest from the tour office. The 13 different cables end at a small waterfall and swimming hole fed by thermal springs. Departures are at 9am and 2pm. The tour costs L855.

Where to Stay

Hotel Canadien The Hotel Canadien is just past the very similar yet much smaller Villa Helen's. Their spread is horseshoe-shaped, with a pool and garden in the middle and the guest rooms and other buildings surrounding it, except for the open end that faces the beach. There's a fine restaurant, El Mirador, on the rooftop with Honduran and international dishes. They might lack TVs, but all rooms are considered suites with a separate living room that has a fold-out futon, minibar, and private balcony with hammock. There aren't many bells and whistles, and the decor and wooden furniture are quite plain—but the price is very reasonable and would be at least 25% higher in La Ceiba.

Turnoff 200m (656 ft.) past the main Sambo Creek entrance. www.hotelcanadien.com. ✆ **504/2440-2099.** 40 units. L950 double. MC, V. Free parking. **Amenities:** Restaurant; free airport transfers; pool. *In room:* A/C, fan, minibar.

Villa Helen's The white, two-level Villa Helen's is the first hotel you come to after the Mango Tree Villas residential complex at this turnoff, just east of the main entrance to Sambo Creek. The first thing you see—and where you will spend most of your time—is the nice open, airy lower level with lots of tropical plants and flowers.

Guifiti

Among Garífuna communities on the Bay Islands or along the North Coast, the drink of choice is *Guifiti,* a traditional drink that combines alcohol with medicinal plants. Most families have their own, closely guarded recipe that is passed down through generations. Many people who do labor-intensive work that causes back strains and whose water supply is often tainted with parasites use *Guifiti* as a preventive cure for many of these ailments.

Garífuna sometimes alter recipes to provide different results. The most common recipes use around 7 different plants and roots, though some may contain as many as 40. The plant parts are chopped up and stuffed in a bottle, which is then filled with rum. Many of the plants added have sexual effects. They add certain seaweeds for more semen, a tree bark to cure menstrual cramps, and a certain herb to give more stamina in the bedroom. Other plants will reduce fevers and stress. It is quite common for many medicinal plants to be added for a sort of cure-all elixir. Many Garífuna believe that it is necessary to treat all body parts at once, so the entire body is strengthened and the weak parts can be healed faster.

If you want to try *Guifiti,* just show up to any Garífuna festival, and you'll see it being passed around. Occasionally, in small villages, you can find jugs with homemade *Guifiti* for sale. Some non-Garífuna restaurants and bars on the Bay Islands will even sell shots of *Guifiti.*

The hotel has both a large dining space for their excellent restaurant and bar with North American and Honduran food that sits underneath the stilted building, and a garden area with hammocks, a small pool, and fountain. The standard rooms and suites range in size and decor, with different styles of tile floors and worn beds. The suites add a balcony. The best rooms are in the stand-alone cabins that add a kitchen, living room, and small patio. There's private beach access directly from the pool area.

Turnoff 200m (656 ft.) past the main Sambo Creek entrance. www.villahelens.com. ✆ **504/408-1137.** 14 units. L665 double; L912 suite; L1,400 cabin. MC, V. Free parking. **Amenities:** Restaurant; bar; pool. *In room:* A/C, TV, kitchens (in cabins).

Where to Eat

Champa Kabasa ★ HONDURAN In Sambo Creek, you have the option of the hotel restaurants and the shacks to the east of the center, all of which are decent, but this beachfront *champa* stands out head and shoulders above them all. They serve seafood and Garífuna specialties like seafood stew, *sopa de caracol* (snail soup), fried and grilled snapper, and numerous other traditional dishes. On weekends, it's a lively place with a mix of beachgoers and locals, and later in the evening, becomes the prime night spot.

The beach & Calle Principal. No phone. Main courses L60–L200. No credit cards. Sun–Thurs noon–10pm; Fri & Sat noon–midnight or later.

PICO BONITO NATIONAL PARK ★★★

Named after a jagged green 2,436m (7,992-ft.) mountain just south of La Ceiba, Pico Bonito National Park is central to La Ceiba's eco-future. Outside of boasting one of the top nature lodges in the world, the more than 100,000-hectare (247,105-acre) park ranges in altitude from sea level to more than 2,000m (6,562 ft.), which results in seven different ecosystems and an extremely high level of biodiversity. While much of the park is off-limits and remains unexplored, large tracts exist of nearly virgin rainforest, cloud forest, waterfalls, rivers, and crystalline pools to explore. Bird life includes more than 400 species, such as toucans, trogons, motmots, and hummingbirds, while mammals spotted here include jaguars, ocelots, tapirs, pumas, deer, and white-faced and spider monkeys, as well as hundreds of species of reptiles, amphibians, and butterflies.

Because the area is quickly becoming the center of ecotourism in Honduras, the road that runs up into Pico Bonito National Park along the whitewater of the Río Cangrejal has seen the construction of several new eco-lodges in recent years and several more on the way. Nearly every adventure-tour operator runs rapids tours, hiking trips, mountain biking runs, and canopy tours in the area, and has built or is building an inexpensive eco-lodge. Previously, the only access to the park was through the Lodge at Pico Bonito.

Getting There & Getting Around

While public transportation can get you to different points of the park, if you are visiting, you will most likely be coming in the hands of one tour operator or another, which will provide transportation. To get to the Río Cangrejal side, you will need to go to Km 8.8 on the La Ceiba–Yaruca highway, near the town of **Las Mangas.** A Yaruca-bound **bus** from La Ceiba will let you off here, or a taxi should be about L250 to L285 from the center (half that from the ferry dock). This entrance is increasingly being used by independent hikers. For the side of the Lodge at Pico Bonito (for which entrance must be arranged in advance), you can catch any Tela- or San Pedro–bound bus and get off at the town of **El Pino,** 10km (6¼ miles) west of the airport, where you can hop in a **taxi** (L40) for the few kilometers to the lodge.

What to See & Do

HIKING ★★ There are several entrances into Pico Bonito and a few different ways to see the park; fortunately, access is getting easier. The most common entry point and closest to La Ceiba is through the Lodge at Pico Bonito. In the past, you had to be a guest to access their trails; however, guided tours (L570 per person) are available for non-guests and include lunch at the lodge. Their private trails have the best infrastructure and contain several bird-watching towers, well-marked stone paths, and a swimming hole on the Coloradito River. You must make reservations in advance with the lodge.

In the town of El Pino, 19km (12 miles) west of La Ceiba, next door to the lodge and just past the Quebrada Seca Bridge, there is another entrance, which most tour operators in La Ceiba use. Here, you will find the 2.4km (1.5-mile) Zacate River Trail, which passes a few nice swimming holes and ends at the Cascada Zacate. The **El Pino Tourist Committee** (✆ **504/3386-9878**) arranges guided hikes on the trail for L500 per person, including the L120 park admission fee. Alternatively, just hop on any Tela- or San Pedro Sula–bound bus and ask to be let off at El Pino.

On the Río Cangrejal side of the park, a trail entrance is near the town of **Las Mangas.** There is just one main trail that shouldn't take more than 2 to 3 hours each way. It begins with a hanging bridge over the river and extends to the 60m (197-ft.) Cascada El Bejuco, as well as a couple of smaller waterfalls.

The nonprofit community organization **Guaruma** (✆ **504/2406-6782;** www.guaruma.org) gives two different guided hikes in the park, led by trained young locals: the 2-hour (L60 per person) **Guaruma trail** and the 4-hour (L120 per person) **La Muralla trail.** Reservations should be made a few days in advance. **Jungle River Tours** (✆ **504/2440-1268**) and **Omega Tours** (✆ **504/2440-0334**) also run guided hikes here that include a free night at their lodges.

WHITEWATER RAFTING ★★★ The Río Cangrejal, cutting its way right through Pico Bonito National Park, offers some of the best whitewater rafting and kayaking anywhere in Central America. Plus, it is only 45 minutes from La Ceiba. The river is populated by Class II–V rapids, which pass through lush green forests, beside waterfalls, and over—sometimes into—massive granite boulders. Trips begin with a short hike to the drop-in site and last 2½ to 7 hours, depending on the sections of the river you sign up for.

Nearly every tour operator in La Ceiba does some kind of rafting or kayaking trip on the Río Cangrejal. Prices are significantly cheaper than a rafting trip in North America or Europe, ranging from L665 to L1,140. **Jungle River Tours** (✆ **504/2440-1268;** www.jungleriverlodge.com) and **Omega Tours** (✆ **504/2440-0334**) throw in free nights in their lodges (see "Where to Stay," below) with their tour, while **Garífuna Tours** (✆ **504/2440-3252;** www.garifunatours.com) offers package deals that combine rafting trips with other activities around La Ceiba. All trips with these operators include lunch, transport to/from La Ceiba, experienced guides, and quality safety equipment.

CANOPY TOURS There are now two zip-line canopy tours near La Ceiba, in which participants are strapped to a long metal line and propelled by gravity at high speeds from platform to platform over the jungle. The tours are the closest the average person can get to swinging on a vine like Tarzan through the jungle. **Jungle River Tours** (✆ **504/2440-1268;** www.jungleriverlodge.com) offers a tour that runs over the Río Cangrejal in Pico Bonito National Park. The exhilarating 2½- to 3-hour excursion unfolds over a total of eight high wires, the longest being 201m (659 ft.). The trip costs L665 and includes a free night at the Jungle River Lodge, but not transport (that runs an additional L40–L150).

HORSEBACK RIDING ★ Omega Tours (✆ **504/2440-0334**) has several different horseback-riding trips that explore trails and villages in the buffer zone of the National Park. One leads to the village of La Colorada, a petroglyph rock, and/or the small Maya ruins of Chibcha. All trips (L760–L1,425) include a free night in their lodge.

YOGA A yoga teacher for almost 40 years, New Jersey native Wendy Green has Ashtanga yoga classes open to the public at her riverside studio, Casa Verde (no phone; www.wendygreenyoga.com) beside Villas Pico Bonito on Mondays, Wednesdays, and Fridays at 7am (L200 suggested donation).

Where to Stay

Apart from the Lodge at Pico Bonito that sits within the park, the following properties are all located in the buffer zone of the national park along the Rio Cangrejal south of La Ceiba.

VERY EXPENSIVE

The Lodge at Pico Bonito ★★★ When you first arrive at Pico Bonito, you'll be greeted by a tuxedoed staff member who'll hand you a tropical drink with a little umbrella. It only gets better from there. The Lodge at Pico Bonito is the only luxury eco-lodge in all of Honduras, and the luxury shows: The 21 posh cabins here are adorned with Hemingway-esque rattan furniture and wood floors, small porches dissected by lazy hammocks, and chic modern bathrooms decorated with Mexican tiles. The cabins are connected to the main lodge via a raised wooden walkway that runs through cacao and coffee trees. Pico Bonito purposely lacks cable TV and Wi-Fi, but does have quieter amenities rarely found in eco-lodges, such as warm showers, in-room massage services, gourmet dining in its insanely overpriced yet still amazing Mesoamerican-themed restaurant, and a full bar.

The lodge is set at the foot of 2,438m (8,000-ft.) Pico Bonito, which has 99,957 hectares (247,000 acres) of pristine cloud forest and rainforest, home to crocodiles, spider monkeys, tapirs, and jaguars; 81 hectares (200 acres) of the property are the buffer area of Pico Bonito National Park. They have a private butterfly sanctuary and serpentarium on the grounds and run a number of guided hiking and other adventure tours.

La Ceiba, Atlántida, CP 31101. www.picobonito.com. ✆ **888/428-0221** or 504/2440-0388. 21 units. L4,560 standard cabin; L6,175 superior cabin. AE, MC, V. **Amenities:** Restaurant; bar; Internet in lobby (free); pool. *In room:* A/C, fan.

Las Cascadas ★★ Las Cascadas is far more chic and luxurious than the Lodge at Pico Bonito, yet it doesn't feel pretentious at all. Located beside a waterfall and several small creeks that run into the Río Cangrejal, it would be hard to imagine a more dramatic setting. The two suites and two cabins are all constructed of polished river stone, wood, and thatched roofs, and all include screened-in porches overlooking the waterfall, stone showers, queen-size mahogany canopy beds, and one or two single beds. The suites are attached to the lodge, while the cabins are separate. The Bejuco cabin adds a Bali-style outdoor shower, while the River House adds a kitchen. All rooms are all-inclusive, which includes beer and wine. ***Note:*** This lodge does not allow young children as guests.

Km 8.8 on the La Ceiba–Yaruca Hwy. www.lascascadaslodge.com. ✆ **877/271-6407** in U.S. or ✆ 504/9805-2200. 4 units. L3,135 per person, based on double occupancy. Rates include meals, drinks & airport transfers. AE, DC, MC, V. **Amenities:** Restaurant; bar; free airport transfers; Internet in lobby (free); Jacuzzi; pool. *In room:* A/C, fan, hair dryer.

EXPENSIVE

Casa Verde ★★ This yoga–and–raw-food retreat is the first of its kind in Honduras. Owned by Americans Wendy Green and Garth Kelly, the wellness program attracts people from all over the world (usually in 1-, 2-, or 4-week periods), who come for a change in their lifestyle and food choices. The property is a model of green living: there is an outdoor shower under a mango tree and a composting toilet, all buildings were constructed without machines, and no chemicals are used anywhere on the grounds. Wendy serves guests raw food, much of it grown right on the property. Nightly documentaries focus on eating right and the principles of yoga. When there isn't a retreat, Casa Verde's two rooms—one stylish large bungalow (sleeps three) and a smaller room in the main house—can be rented by the night. Yoga is also open to the public on Monday, Wednesday, and Friday (see above).

Río Cangrejal Road. www.wendygreenyoga.com. No phone. 2 units. L21,375 per person per week. Rates include raw food, yoga & consultation. No credit cards. *In room:* kitchen.

Villas Pico Bonito ★★ Across the river from Cascada El Bejuco, this series of villas on the Río Cangrejal side of the park are geared more toward older, more independent travelers and families. Each of the eight accommodations is quite different, though they range from a small *casita* to two-level two-bedroom villas with a pool. Except for the oversized studio, all rooms have decks, patios, or screened-in porches with great views over the river, wooden blinds, living rooms, and full kitchens with modern appliances. Their best villa is El Disco, set in a massive thatched-roof *champa* that contains two bedrooms with en-suite bathrooms and sits beside the hotel's beautiful riverfront infinity pool. If you don't want to cook your own food in your kitchen or on the nearby barbecue grills, you'll appreciate the full-service restaurant, Hidden Paradise. The owner, who is continually at work improving the facility, has a friendly kinkajou (a rainforest mammal that looks like a cross between a ferret and a monkey) that roams the property.

Río Cangrejal Rd. www.villaspicobonito.com. ✆ **504/2449-0045.** 8 units. MC, V. From L950 standard lodge; L1,650 studio; L3,705 Cangrejal River Lodge. MC, V. Free parking. **Amenities:** Restaurant; free airport transfers. *In room:* Kitchen, Wi-Fi (free).

MODERATE

Casa Cangrejal ★ This small, Canadian-owned B&B is beautifully constructed of river stones and wood, giving it the feel of a medieval castle. Numerous artful touches grace the building, such as bright orange or green walls and blue bedspreads, a crab design in a common room floor, a manmade pond, and a few stone patios with funky wooden chairs that are great for bird watching. The amenities are basic, and you won't find a TV here, though they do have Wi-Fi. If you're looking for a real retreat that takes you away from the norm in both setting and architecture, Casa Cangrejal is a gem. While children are allowed, the hotel is oriented to adults. At last visit, they were building a private cabin just up the hill from the main lodge.

Río Cangrejal Rd. www.casacangrejal.com. ✆ **504/2408-2760.** 4 units. L1,710 double. Rates include breakfast. *In room:* Wi-Fi (free).

Omega Lodge ★★ High on the hills, the big mosquito-screened windows ensure great views of the forest below at this small lodge, one of the oldest in the area. There is a mix of rooms, several of them brand new. Every budget has a place: backpackers in the dorms (free when you book a trip), couples in the private rooms (they have shared bathrooms, though), and small groups or families can take the split-level cabins with hardwood floors, ceilings, and hand carved furniture that add a Zen-like quality to the lodge. Extras include a small pool, views of the waterfall from behind the lodge, and a better-than-usual restaurant *champa* with German food, along with a lively bar that attracts visitors from all of the nearby hotels.

Río Cangrejal Rd., just before El Naranjo. www.omegatours.info. ✆ **504/2440-0334.** www.omegatours.info. 20 units. L400 double; L950 cabin. MC, V. **Amenities:** Restaurant; pool.

INEXPENSIVE

Jungle River Lodge This small lodge beside the Río Cangrejal in Pico Bonito National Park is owned by Jungle River Tours and is most often used in conjunction with one of their tours, usually for free. The lodge itself is constructed of all-natural materials and completely submerged in the jungle. Rooms, which are a mix of dark, dingy dorms and some doubles with and without bathrooms, are smallish and basic, but for the price and the convenience, they can't be beat. A pool table, bar, and restaurant overlook the river. A backpacker favorite.

Km 8.8 on the La Ceiba-Yaruca Hwy. www.jungleriverlodge.com. ✆ **504/2440-1268.** 7 units. L228 dorm bed; L570 double without bathroom; L760 double w/bathroom. AE, MC, V. **Amenities:** Restaurant; bar. *In room:* Fan.

CAYOS COCHINOS ★★★

When skies are clear, you can see the Cayos Cochinos, or Hog Islands, off the north coast of Honduras—that's how close to the mainland they are. Thirty kilometers (19 miles) northeast of La Ceiba, these two small islands, 13 coral cays, and a few tiny sandbars—almost all privately owned—are as close to paradise as one could imagine. The two main islands, Cayo Menor and Cayo Mayor/Grande, are home to just one luxury eco-resort, a few private homes, a research station, and one small Garífuna community. That's it. If isolation is what you want, then look no further. The vibe here is highly similar to the laidback San Blas Islands off the coast of Panama.

The coral reefs surrounding the islands are some of the most undisturbed on the Mesoamerican Barrier Reef System and were designated as a Marine Protected Area in 1993 and a Marine Natural Monument in 2003. No commercial fishing is allowed in the 489-sq.-km (189-sq.-mile) reserve, and rules are strictly enforced, which has allowed the reefs and the fish that live on them to flourish. Wildlife on the land—which is also protected—includes pink boa constrictors, iguanas, sea turtles, and tropical birds, among other amphibians and reptiles. The islands were actually named, at least as legends go, because pirates planted hogs there for a convenient food supply during their travels.

Volunteer Opportunities in the Cayos Cochinos

Research and volunteering opportunities in the Cayos Cochinos are run in conjunction with the **Honduras Coral Reef Fund (© 504/2442-2670; www.cayoscochinos.org)**. The organization leads all scientific research on the islands, which includes surveying the reef, protecting sea turtle nesting sites, collecting data on the pink boas, and establishing ecotourism projects on Chachauate, among other tasks. There are basic accommodations at the HCRF Marine Research Center on Cayo Menor. Bookings and 12-day scheduled programs are run through Biosphere Expeditions (www.biosphere-expeditions.org); you must have a PADI open-water certification for some programs.

Getting There & Getting Around

The Cayos Cochinos can be reached only by **boat,** most often via a day trip from La Ceiba. The trip takes approximately 1 to 1½ hours, depending on the tide. The easiest way to get there is either by staying at the Plantation Beach Resort, which provides transportation, or by visiting on a tour with **Garífuna Tours** (© **504/2440-3252**) in La Ceiba, which runs almost-daily snorkel tours to the cays, including a stop for lunch at Chachauate. This tour runs L650 adults.

It is also possible to reach the cays from the towns of Sambo Creek and Nueva Armenia by hiring a local **boatman** or fisherman, but sometimes you must get a small group together to make it affordable. One such boatman who runs trips is **Omar Acosta** (© **504/2408-1666;** L665 per person). Dive boats frequently come on day trips from Roatán, while yachts from around the Caribbean moor here, as well.

To enter the Cayos Cochinos, you must pay a L190 fee (L100 when you come with a tour operator) at the Fundación Cayos Cochinos research station on Cayo Menor.

What to See & Do

Tiny **Chachauate Cay ★** is home to the only permanent settlement in the Cayos Cochinos. The Garífuna village has no running water or electricity, and the only bathrooms are in communal outhouses. The thatched houses are home to just a few dozen families who eke out a living from fishing and tourism. There are a couple of small eateries serving fried fish and plantains, plus a few craft stands set up informally when a tour boat arrives. Locals rent out their homes to visitors for around L100 per night.

The mountainous **Cayo Grande** is home to several good **hiking trails** through the lush jungle, beginning right at Plantation Beach resort and running to the highest points of the island—from where, on a clear day, you can see 30km (19 miles) in every direction. At the highest point, at 140m (459 ft.), there is a small lighthouse.

The turquoise waters and unspoiled coral reef around the Cayos Cochinos are an ideal spot for underwater exploring, so much so that many prefer **diving and snorkeling** here to the Bay Islands. There are more than 60 dive sites scattered around the reserve, and many others that have yet to be named. Within the walls, drifts, small wrecks, and sea mounds, you'll find sponges, grunts, sea fans, sea whips, grouper, lobsters, sea urchins, and parrotfish. Less common are manta rays, bottlenose dolphins, whale sharks, and hawksbill turtles. Most dive resorts in the Bay Islands will lead day trips here, but the only dive operation based in the Cayos Cochinos is at the Plantation Beach Resort (see below).

Where to Stay

Plantation Beach Resort ★★ Located on Cochino Menor, this upscale resort is as removed from the modern world as a beach resort can get while still managing to be comfortable. Electricity is the biggest amenity, and that's a good thing—there's nothing to distract you from soaking in the beautiful surroundings. The lodge—set on 4 hectares (10 acres) of virgin forest—was built of stone and mahogany native to the tiny island. Rooms vary in size, but the quality is roughly the same throughout, with tile or wood floors punctuating a rustic yet cozy setup. Plantation has one of the better dive operations in the country and offers PADI certification courses. Transportation to the resort is not included with a stay, but the hotel will arrange pickup from San Pedro Sula or La Ceiba. Their small restaurant is *the* hangout in town for visiting yachties who moor near the hotel.

Cochino Menor, Cayos Cochinos. www.plantationbeachresort.com. ✆ **504/3371-7556.** 12 units. L1,900 double. All-inclusive weekly fee w/diving L18,981; all-inclusive weekly fee without diving L13,205. V. **Amenities:** Restaurant; bar. *In room:* Fan.

TRUJILLO

The coastal city of Trujillo, long a beach retreat for the people of San Pedro Sula and Tegucigalpa, has yet to fully recover from the 1998 devastation of Hurricane Mitch. It's not that the place is a mess, but rather that tourists haven't been flocking here. The beaches are now in good shape and the airport has been repaired—there just aren't any flights. Trujillo seems to have completely missed the rampant progress going on in places like La Ceiba, 165km (103 miles) east, but that might change: The first rumbles of development have begun west of the city, and there's even talk of adding a cruise terminal here—yet at the rate things are going, any significant change is still a ways off.

Trujillo has borne witness to many of the most significant events in Central American history. On August 14, 1502, Christopher Columbus set foot on the American mainland here for the first time on his fourth and final voyage. The first Catholic Mass on the continent soon followed. In 1860 the North American William Walker, after having previously taken over Nicaragua with a small army and a failed attempt to invade Costa Rica, took the fort of Trujillo. After 5 days of fighting with British and Honduran forces, however, Walker surrendered and was executed by Honduran authorities. In the early 1800s, Trujillo was one of the first places on the mainland where Garífuna settlers—after they were dumped on Roatán by the British—began to build communities. Their influence is strong along the coast of Trujillo Bay to this day.

Essentials

GETTING THERE

BY CAR CA 13, which begins at El Progresso outside of San Pedro Sula, runs parallel to the coast all the way to Trujillo, first stopping in Tela and La Ceiba. Two more scenic roads run through the interior of the country through Olancho, Hwys. 39 and 23; but neither are well paved, and both are often impassable during heavy rain.

BY BUS The terminal for **Cotuc** (✆ **504/2444-2181**) buses is in Barrio Cristales, although they also stop at the Texaco gas station towards the entrance to town, about a kilometer from the center. Cotuc buses travel daily to La Ceiba (L100; 3 hr.), Tela (L150; 4½ hr.), and San Pedro Sula (L200; 6 hr.). **Cotraipbal** also runs buses to these destinations, which depart from the terminal next to the Texaco station, almost every other hour for the same price.

BY BOAT While it isn't one of the high-speed super ferries that operate between Roatán, Utila, and La Ceiba, the **Bimini Breeze** (✆ **504/2987-0875**) gets you back and forth between Trujillo and Guanaja, eventually. At last check, the ferry wasn't running on a regular basis, so be sure to call ahead for times. You can buy tickets directly on the boat for L650 or call for reservations.

Trujillo is also the jumping-off point for **cargo boats** down the Mosquito Coast that will take on passengers, which leave only sporadically from the Muelle de Cabotaje. Boats run to Brus Laguna at least once a week, usually leaving in the afternoon and arriving in the morning. The fee is L250.

GETTING AROUND

Trujillo's center is easily navigable by foot, even when you factor in having to walk up and down the hill to the beach below. The bus terminal and many of the town's hotels will need to be reached by taxi, however. Local buses run sporadically to Santa Fe to the west, leaving from the old cemetery. More frequent buses head east to Puerto Castillo from the Texaco terminal.

ORIENTATION

The colonial center of Trujillo is built on a hill beside the town's fort, high up from the bay and surrounded by green mountains. A few roads lead down to the beach below the center, where there is a string of seafood shacks and the Garífuna neighborhood of Cristales. A single dirt road runs west along the coastline to the Garífuna communities of Santa Fe and Guadalupe. The airport, 1km (½ mile) away from Trujillo's center, is on the eastbound road outside of town. Puerto Castillo, Trujillo's deepwater port, is 8km (5 miles) east across the bay.

VISITOR INFORMATION

Banco Atlántida, on the Parque Central, has a 24-hour **ATM** and will exchange traveler's checks. Internet access can be found at a number of small shops near the park or at Casa Kiwi (see "Where to Stay," below). You can make long-distance phone calls at **Hondutel,** 1 block south of the park. For tourist information, see the **Trujillo Pages** (www.trujillohonduras.com).

What to See & Do

Cementerio Viejo ★ Now that the weeds have been pulled and the site is renovated, the gates of this old cemetery in the center of town have officially been unlocked and opened to the public. Many of the graves date back more than 300 years, the most significant being that of William Walker, the American adventurer who launched several invasions of Central American nations and was shot by firing squad in Trujillo in 1860. His grim end is noted on his epitaph with the word *"fusilado."*

5 blocks SE of Parque Central. No phone. Free admission. Daily dawn–dusk.

Fortaleza de Santa Bárbara ★ Imposing its iron fist from its elevated point in the center of town is the Fortaleza de Santa Bárbara, a Spanish colonial fortress that was erected to help defend Trujillo Bay from pirate attacks. The 17th-century fort, which was renovated in 2005, was reportedly much bigger centuries ago and extended all the way down to the beachfront. Today, you will find a vast outline of stone walls with moss growing through the cracks and a couple of small buildings. A row of iron cannons point out towards the water below and, if you've drunk plenty of *Guifiti* (a Garífuna moonshine), incoming buccaneers. There is a small museum within the fortress with a collection of colonial items, muskets, pirate relics, naval memorabilia, and Garífuna masks.

NE corner of Parque Central. No phone. L100 adults. Daily 8am–noon & 1–4pm.

Museo Rufino Galán This idiosyncratic little museum is closer to a junk heap than an official museum. The barely standing wood building, a few blocks from the square, is filled with piles of pre-Columbian artifacts, alleged pirate relics, books, chests, farm equipment, old tools, and anything else that is good at collecting dust. There's even a pet spider monkey tied up outside. You may have to ask around for the owner, as the museum doesn't follow any set hours.

Calle 18 de Mayo & the Río Cristales. No phone. L50 adults. Hours vary.

Parque Nacional Capiro y Calentura The 1,235m (4,052-ft.) mountain that stands proudly behind the center of Trujillo is the setting for this 4,500-hectare (11,120-acre) national park. There is very little infrastructure to the park, and hikers rarely come this way. Those who do come are rewarded with vibrant bird life, including macaws, the occasional howler monkey, and several distinct zones of tropical forest. The entrance to the park is via a dirt path south of town, and the park office is staffed only on rare occasions. It takes about 3 hours to reach the top of the peak, where there is a small radar station. For the best bird-watching, it's best to set out before dawn.

3km (1¾ miles) S of Parque Central. L60 adults. Daily 8am–4pm.

Refugio de Vida Silvestre Guaimoreto Similar to Cuero y Salado and the Laguna de los Micos near La Ceiba, Guaimoreto, 5km (3 miles) east of Trujillo, is a large lagoon surrounded in mangrove forest, intersected with canals, and home to abundant wildlife. Migratory birds flock here from November to February. Due to the lack of tourists in Trujillo, there aren't any tour operators that arrange trips here anymore—you must go to the lagoon and negotiate with a local fisherman for a canoe or boat ride (roughly L285 per 2 hr.). **Casa Kiwi** (✆ **504/2434-3050;** www.casakiwi.com) sometimes will arrange trips here, as well.

5km (3 miles) E of Trujillo. ✆ **504/434-4294.** Free admission.

Outdoor Activities

The main reason why most visitors trek all the way out to Trujillo is for its **beaches.** Wide golden sands, gentle breezes, very few waves, and even fewer beachgoers make the beaches here seem like deserted islands. The best places to enjoy the sun are in front of the *champas* below the fort, where you can borrow a beach chair, or near the airport and the Christopher Columbus Resort (see "Where to Stay," below). Emptier beaches can be found hidden below the road in the small coves that stretch for several kilometers to the west of town.

To the west of Trujillo, down a potholed dirt road, is a string of Garífuna fishing villages. All are home to a few thatched seafood shacks, a basic *hospedaje* or two, *punta* music flowing through the air, and serene beaches with rarely a soul in sight. **Santa Fe,** 12km (7½ miles) from Trujillo, is my favorite stop because of its legendary **Comedor Caballero ★★**, aka Pete's Place, a traditional Garífuna restaurant on the beach with some of the best seafood on the North Coast. A bit farther out—and even more difficult to reach—are the villages and beaches of **San Antonio** and

Guadeloupe. Buses leave from the Cementerio Viejo in the center of town to these villages several times per day.

Shopping

You can find small artisan shops around Parque Central and towards the beach. The best is **Artesma Garífuna** (✆ **504/2434-3583**) in Barrio Cristales, which sells beach gear, coconut carvings, drums, and an array of little knick-knacks. The gift shop **Made in Honduras** (✆ **504/2839-2768;** www.hondurastreasures.com) opened in 2008 across the road from the airport in a purple and turquoise wooden house. The 100% fair-trade handicrafts, from a co-op of 80 craftspeople, include tree-bark paintings, coffee, jewelry, and nativity scenes from La Mosquitia, Olancho, and the North Coast. Displays in the store describe how most items were made, by which family, and where.

Where to Stay

MODERATE

Casa Alemania ★★ Friendly owners German Gunter and his Honduran wife Paula, both trained massage therapists, run this beachfront Trujillo inn between town and the airport, which has somehow managed to stay under the radar, though it has been open since 2004 and is a tremendous value. My vote goes here for the best accommodations in town. Gunter's theory is that he will get you anything you need to make your stay worthwhile, which includes German food and beer. Polished hardwood floors and trim are matched with soft white linens and big windows that face the beach (take any of the three rooms on the second level for the best views). The larger rooms add a small kitchenette with sink and minifridge. If you are on a budget, they will do their best to accommodate you with their dorm-style beds or camping space that has shower access and electricity.

Beachfront, btw. the center & airport. ✆ **504/2434-4466.** 10 units. L580 double; L750 larger room. MC, V. Free parking. **Amenities:** Restaurant; bar; massage/spa services. *In room:* A/C, fan, TV/DVD player, kitchenette (some).

Hotel Christopher Columbus ★ ☺ The Hotel Christopher Columbus surely has seen better days. It was once billed as one of the top hotels on the North Coast, but then Hurricane Mitch scared off all the customers. Now, it is simply starving for guests. They keep the lime green paint fresh, but the place is practically always empty, and it's beginning to show its age. Rooms are very outdated, almost to the point of being cool again—they call to mind a '50s-style roadside motel, with retro furniture and even spots of Astroturf on the terrace. Still, the full-scale resort, located on one of the best stretches of beach in town, is a decent stay, and the surprisingly friendly and upbeat staff helps you overlook any failings. Added family favorite bonuses are that the lobby is nice and well kept, the pool area isn't bad, and they have a small dock, kayaks, and snorkel equipment for guests to use.

1km (½ mile) E of Parque Central, beside the airport. ✆ **504/2434-4966.** 71 units. L1,330 double. AE, MC, V. **Amenities:** Restaurant; bar; pool; tennis courts; kayaks; snorkel equipment. *In room:* A/C, TV.

Tranquility Bay ★ Tranquility Bay's five small seaside cabins are tucked away down a forested hill near the beach, a few kilometers west of town. Each cabin has a terra cotta roof, a small porch with a couple of chairs, walls decked out in cheery yellow paint, and a few splashes of Honduran decor. Though the cabins aren't luxurious, they are clean and a decent overall value. The new Canadian owners have done a good job of maintaining and improving the property. There's a nice big, inviting pool close to the beach, and they have a small creek that runs through the property. If you don't have your own transport, access to town can be an issue.

3km (1¾ miles) W of town. www.tranquilitybayhonduras.com. ✆ **504/2928-2095.** 5 units. L1,140 double. No credit cards. **Amenities:** Restaurant; bar. *In room:* Fan.

INEXPENSIVE

Casa Kiwi ★ Six kilometers (3¾ miles) east of Trujillo on the road to Puerto Castilla, a New Zealand woman has set up Casa Kiwi, Trujillo's best backpacker hangout. The quickly expanding compound is right on a quiet stretch of beach with little other civilization around. The rooms, all available at bargain prices, are in your choice of dorms, private rooms, or cabins. While the dorms are clean and the cabins are more private, the middle rooms are the best overall value. Apart from Casa Kiwi's standalone bar and restaurant, there are loads of little extras—like a pool table, and bike and snorkeling rentals. This place also hosts the occasional weekend bonfire party and arranges tours.

6km (3¾ miles) from Trujillo, on the rd. to Puerto Castilla. www.casakiwi.com. ✆ **504/4234-3050.** L150 dorm bed; L630 double; L650 cabin. No credit cards. **Amenities:** Restaurant; bar; Internet cafe. *In room:* A/C (in cabins), fan.

Hotel O'Glynn As far as inexpensive hotels in the center of town go, this rickety old place is still the best option. It is partly in an old wood building and partly in concrete additions that have been made over the years. Stick to the more charming older rooms with balconies. Overall, the rooms are clean, and they have a generator for when the power goes out, which is uncommon in town.

4a Calle. ✆ **504/2434-4592.** 25 units. L500 double. No credit cards. **Amenities:** Restaurant; bar; pool. *In room:* A/C, fan, TV.

La Quinta Bay Hotel If you tried to get any closer to the airport, you'd be on the runway. The La Quinta, which has no relation to the U.S. chain of the same name, is right on the side of the airport, across from Hotel Christopher Columbus and the beach. If planes were still running, staying here might be a rather noisy endeavor, but for now, it's quite convenient and quiet. The rooms are simple yet clean and more modern than those at the Columbus. There is no restaurant on-site, so you're stuck with the facilities on the beach or will have to catch a cab into the center.

1km (½ mile) E of Parque Central, beside the airport. ✆ **504/2434-4732.** 25 units. L600 double. MC, V. *In room:* A/C, TV.

Where to Eat

Los Coco's Bar & Grill INTERNATIONAL On the beach beside hotel Christopher Columbus, this *champa* has been recently renovated to become the most stylish restaurant in Trujillo. Thin white curtains hanging from the thatched roof and white leather lounge chairs give a South Beach element to a city not normally known for its panache. The food varies from tasty Honduran seafood to so-so international comfort food: four types of ceviche, shrimp scampi, fried fish, nachos, and hamburgers.

Beachfront, beside Hotel Christopher Columbus. No phone. Main courses L100–L160. MC, V. Daily noon–9pm; open later on weekends.

Merendero del Centro HONDURAN This bustling little *típica* restaurant is good for quick and simple, but filling, Honduran breakfasts of beans, corn tortillas,

eggs, and ham. They're best known for their *baleadas* and dirt-cheap lunch specials, though. Plastic tables and kids running around add some authenticity, if nothing else.
3a Calle. No phone. Main courses L55–L110. No credit cards. Daily 6am–8pm.

The Mystic ★ INTERNATIONAL A great new addition to Trujillo's dining scene is this beachside shack with a pool table at the Banana Beach hotel. There's Tex-Mex, a buffalo chicken sandwich, grilled fish, and even surf-and-turf. Everything is made daily by German chef Juergen. There are a few decent cabins on the property for rent, as well (L1,140 cabin).
Sante Fe. ✆ **504/9986-9247.** Main courses L70–L390. No credit cards. Wed–Sun 11am–10pm.

Playa Dorado ★★ ☺ SEAFOOD Of the several *champas* on the beach below the fort (any of which are the most atmospheric places to eat in town), Playa Dorado is the best. The owners will let you pick your fish, priced by size, and how you want it prepared. Their shrimp in garlic sauce, *camarones al ajillo,* sautéed with garlic and lime, and served with a big plate of French fries, has my mouth watering even as I type. There are a few beef items on the menu, but considering that you are on the beach, I'd stick with seafood.
Beachfront, below the fort. No phone. Main courses L75–L225. No credit cards. Daily 11am–9pm.

Trujillo After Dark

Rogue's Gallery, sometimes called Jerry's, in the concrete, tin-roofed building near the beach *champas,* is good for a sunset cocktail or beer. There are a couple of decent beachfront bars beside the Hotel Christopher Columbus that change owners and names with every passing tide. **Truxillo Disco,** at the edge of a bluff facing the sea, is the most popular disco in town for locals. It's a little bit sketchy. Don't show up before 10pm or you'll be alone. There's no cover.

THE BAY ISLANDS

9

Las Islas de la Bahía, or the Bay Islands, are best known for their clear Caribbean waters and their pristine coral reef—the second-largest in the world. The three main islands of Roatán, Utila, and Guanaja, along with Barbareta and 60 or so other tiny cays, have long been one of the major dive destinations in the world. Although they are no longer the cheapest places in the world to get dive certification, prices remain considerably cheaper than anywhere else in the Caribbean, and package deals for divers are vast. All-inclusive tours that include lodging, food, dives, airfare, and anything else you can throw in can be had for any visitor seeking a deal.

The cultural makeup of the islands has been a tumultuous one. The first pre-Columbian settlers were likely related to the Pech Indians on the mainland, and a few small archeological sites are still scattered among the surrounding hills. Christopher Columbus is believed to be the first European to find the islands, when he anchored in Guanaja in July of 1502. In the following decades, Spanish ships came to take native slaves and set up encomiendas, where, in exchange for Christianization, the indigenous people were forced to pay tribute and labor to the Spanish Crown.

As the Spanish began to loot the New World of its gold and transport the riches across the Caribbean back to Spain, the islands became a hideout for French and English raiding boats. Pirates such as Henry Morgan and John Coxen began to frequent the islands for the next 2 centuries, although they left little trace. War broke out between England and Spain in 1739, and the British took control of the islands and set up forts at Port Royal in Roatán. They were returned to Spain in the treaty of Aix-la-Chapelle in 1748, taken back by the British during another war in 1779, and then left uninhabited after Spanish attacks in 1782. In 1797, the British dumped a few thousand Garífuna, descendents of Carib Indians and African slaves from the Cayman Islands, at Punta Gorda in Roatán; many settled there while others headed for the mainland.

In the 1830s, a new wave of white and black settlers came from the Caymans and set up the main towns that remain population centers today. The British government claimed control over the islands during this time, and although Honduran sovereignty of the islands was recognized in 1859, many of the islanders continued to see themselves as a part of the British Empire.

Today, the Bay Islands are at a major turning point in their history. Fishing, which has been the lifeblood of the islanders for several centuries, is quickly being replaced by tourism as the most important trade. Luxury home developments targeting North Americans are creeping onto every island, and slews of Latino workers from the mainland are attracted by the high standards of living and available work, while the native Afro-Caribbean population is getting pushed to the fringes of the islands. Developers are snapping up entire chunks of land, such as the West End in Roátan, and hotels and resorts are replacing the islands' once traditional stilted wood houses. The influx of cruise ships on Roatán has already added adventure parks and tour buses, and there's talk of more ports and bigger ships.

For the time being, however, the Bay Islands are still serene Caribbean hideouts, where English just happens to be the mother tongue and the American dollar is the main currency.

CLIMATE The average annual temperature of the Bay Islands is about 85°F (29°C) and fluctuates from the upper 80s in the summer, when the humidity becomes especially high, to the low 80s during the winter (Nov–Feb). Cold fronts at any time of the year can drop the temperature into the high 60s, though they usually disappear after a few days.

Water temperatures here are ideal for much of the year, ranging from 81° to 88°F (27°–31°C). When diving, 3.5mm shorty wetsuits are recommended, though for much of the year, they are not even necessary. High season is almost year-round in the Bay Islands, and it can be especially difficult to find rooms during holiday weeks. Things get a bit slower from January to February and during the hurricane season between September and November, and prices will drop significantly.

ROATÁN

Roatán, 29km (18 miles) east of Utila, is the largest, most developed, and most visited of the Bay Islands. The real estate market has been hot in recent years, but is now closer to spewing lava as once-quiet beach communities become full-scale resorts or second homes for North Americans, who are flocking here like barracudas and snapping up every inch of available land. The cruise season is also expanding rapidly—Royal Caribbean and Carnival cruises alone have invested a combined $80 million in two new cruise terminals, Mahogany Bay and Town Center at the Port of Roatán, which are expected to bring nearly a million cruise passengers each year. When a cruise ship (or three!) docks, look out: the island teems with craft markets and tour buses, and the best beaches like West Bay become crowded with families of sun worshippers.

Much of the new development is on the west side of the island, where tourism and a growing condo scene is concentrated, while Garífuna communities dominate the much more rural and raw eastern half. But if you look in the right places, you can still see the Bay Islands of yesteryear. Many of the island's hills remain undeveloped enough to be covered in tropical oak, evergreen palms, and gumbo limbo trees, and just one road (partly paved, partly potholed) runs the length of the island.

Diving and snorkeling remain the most popular activity on the island, but other options are expanding rapidly. Now, you can also zip-line across the jungle-clad hills, take a submarine hundreds of meters into the ocean, search for pirate booty in little-explored sea caves, or take an aerial real estate tour.

A Tale of Two Currencies

The U.S. dollar is sometimes thought of as the official currency of the Bay Islands as it is accepted almost everywhere. Many resorts, restaurants, and tour operators, especially on Roatán, list prices only in dollars, and most ATMs will dispense both currencies. For your convenience, we have listed prices in the Bay Islands in both U.S. dollars and Honduran lempira.

Essentials

GETTING THERE

BY PLANE While most tourists come from La Ceiba via ferry or flight, an increasing number of international travelers are flying directly into Roatán's Juan Manuel Gálvez International Airport, sometimes called simply **Roatán International Airport** (**RTB; ✆ 504/2445-1088**). It's 3km (1¾ miles) from Coxen Hole on the highway to French Harbour. Continental, Delta, American Airlines, and TACA fly here directly between points in the U.S. such as Houston, Newark, Atlanta, and Miami, as well as from San Salvador, El Salvador. If you are flying out of Roatán to an international destination, don't forget you will have to pay the US$34 departure tax at the airport.

If you are flying to or from La Ceiba, Tegucigalpa, Utila, or San Pedro Sula, you are limited to domestic airlines. **Isleña** (**✆ 504/2445-1918;** www.flyislena.com), **Aerolineas Sosa** (**✆ 504/2445-1154**), **Lanhsa** (**✆ 504/2445-0397;** www.lanhsa.com), and **CM Airlines** (**✆ 504/234-1886;** www.cmairlines.com) all offer daily flights.

Bay Island Airways (**✆ 504/2946-5665** or ✆ 504/933-6077; www.bayislandairways.com) offers inter-island transport via small seaplanes from the West End, as well as real estate and 15-minute flyover tours. Prices range from L4,180 (US$220) for two people to the Cayos Cochinos to L7,220 (US$380) for two people to Guanaja. **Roatán Air Services** (**✆ 504/2455-6879;** www.roatanair.com), based in Coxen Hole, also runs charter flights to Guanaja, Utila, and the Cayos Cochinos in their 3-passenger Cessna 172 and a 6-passenger Aero Commander 560. Similarly, they'll run aerial photography and real estate tours (L3,040/US$160 for 30 min. in the Cessna).

Most tourists will take a taxi from the airport, which should run under L290 (US$25) to anywhere on the island. If you walk out of the airport to the highway, you can also catch one of the frequent microbuses or shared taxis (L20–L40/US$1–$2 per person) that run during the day.

BY FERRY Roatán's super ferry, the **Galaxy Wave** (**✆ 504/2445-1798** or 504/2443-4630; www.safewaymaritime.com), zooms passengers from the ferry terminal at Dixon's Cove in Roatán to La Ceiba at 7am and 2pm, and returns at 9:30am and 4:30pm. The price is L524 (US$28) each way, and the ferry has room for 360 people and offers A/C rooms, a sun deck, and a small snack shop. It looks like a monster compared to Utila's small ferry and is much more stable; however, folks with weak stomachs might end up feeling sick by the time they step off the ship, particularly during the choppier afternoon trips. From the ferry terminal, you can catch a taxi, rent a car, or catch a bus simply by walking out to the main road.

The Bay Islands

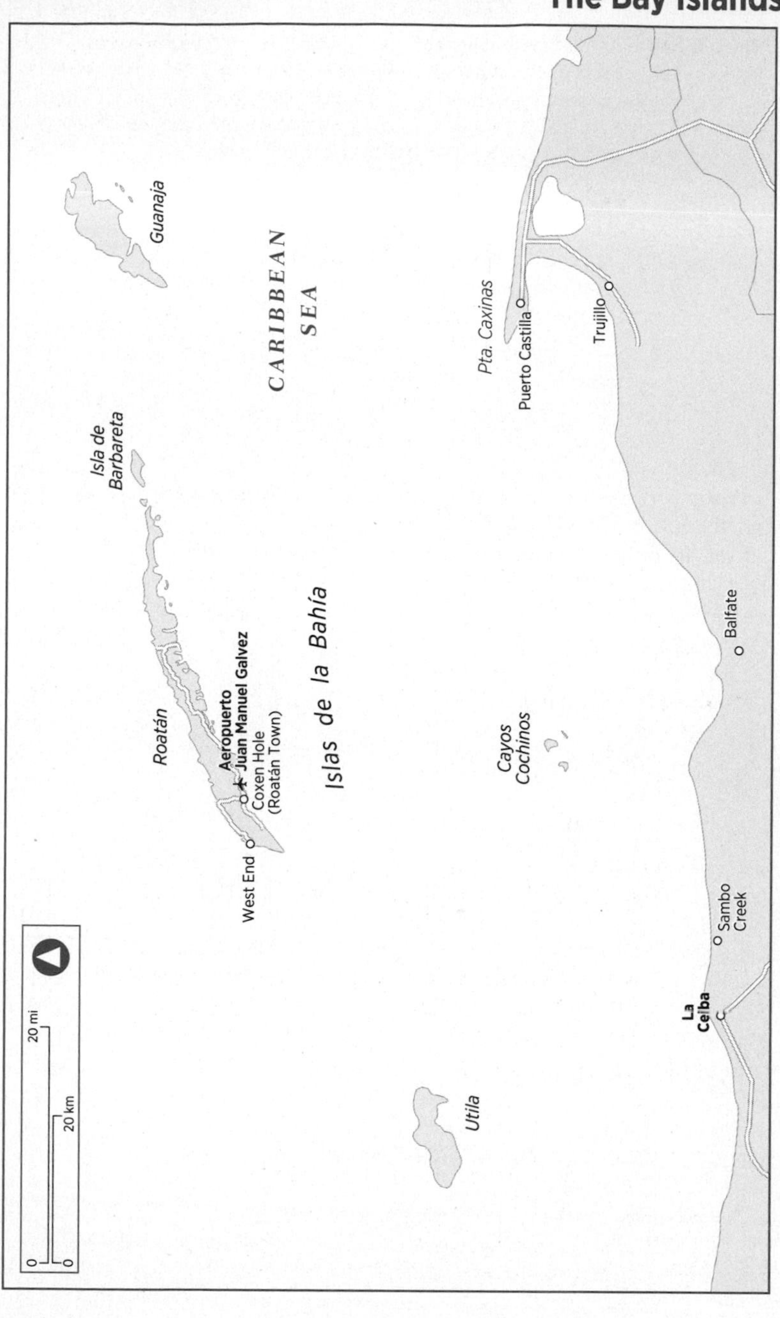

A **catamaran** service (✆ **504/3346-2600;** vfine@hotmail.com; L1,100/US$55) now operates daily for the 3½-hour ride between Roatán and Utila. The 12m (39-ft.) *Nina Elisabeth II* departs East Harbour in Utila at 6:30am and returns from Roatán's West End at 1pm. Reservations are encouraged.

BY CRUISE SHIP At last check, Royal Caribbean, Costa, Voyager, and Norwegian/NCL make port calls at Coxen Hole's Port of Roatán, while Carnival, Ryndam, Spirit, and Princess make port calls at Mahogany Bay.

GETTING AROUND

BY BUS During daylight hours, minibuses ply back and forth from one end of the island to the other on Roatán's one main road for a fare of L20 to L40 (US$1–$2) per person, depending on how far you travel. Most buses will travel only east or west, from Coxen Hole to one end of the island.

BY CAR Several car-rental agencies have stands at the airport, including **Caribbean Rent a Car** (✆ **504/2455-6950;** www.caribbeanroatan.com) and **Avis** (✆ **504/3374-8964;** www.avis.com). Prices range from L855 to L1,520 (US$45–$80) per day.

BY TAXI Taxi stands are located in every major tourist center, and waiting taxis sit outside most of the island's largest resorts. Prices are relatively high, compared with the mainland. A ride from the airport or Coxen Hole to the West End will run about L300 to L400 (US$15–$20). After 6pm, when the buses stop running, fares go up. *Colectivo* taxis, which pick up other passengers, are a cheaper option and run set routes much like a bus.

BY WATER TAXI Water taxi service runs daily from 9am to 9pm and is a convenient way to get between West End and West Bay. Just flag down a passing boat at any dock and one should stop. The fare is L50 (US$3).

BY SCOOTER You can rent motorized scooters at stands across the island. **Captain Van's Rentals** (✆ **504/2403-8751;** www.captainvans.com; L740 (US$39) per day) on the West End and in West Bay is the most popular and accessible operator for visitors. They'll also rent by the week at a discounted rate.

ORIENTATION

Roatán sits 56km (35 miles) from La Ceiba on the North Coast of Honduras and smack dab in between Utila and Guanaja. The 64km-long (40-mile) island, no more than 4km wide (2½ miles), has a mountainous center that is covered in lush, green jungle. One main highway zigzags from one end of the island to the other, hitting every major settlement along the way. Coxen Hole, in the center of the island, is home to the majority of the population and is the transportation hub of Roatán.

VISITOR INFORMATION

Most of the large hotels, such as the Mayan Princess (p. 206), have **ATMs,** and there are a few standalones scattered about in the West End and elsewhere. All other **banks** can be found in Coxen Hole or French Harbour. You can exchange traveler's checks at BANFAA, located in the airport.

You can find **cybercafes** and calling centers scattered about the major tourist centers, but these computers tend to be slow. Most hotels now have Wi-Fi or a computer with Internet access for guests to use.

The majority of hospitals can be found in Coxen Hole, although many travelers prefer the small **Anthony's Key Medical Clinic** (✆ **504/2445-1003**) in Sandy Bay.

Roatán

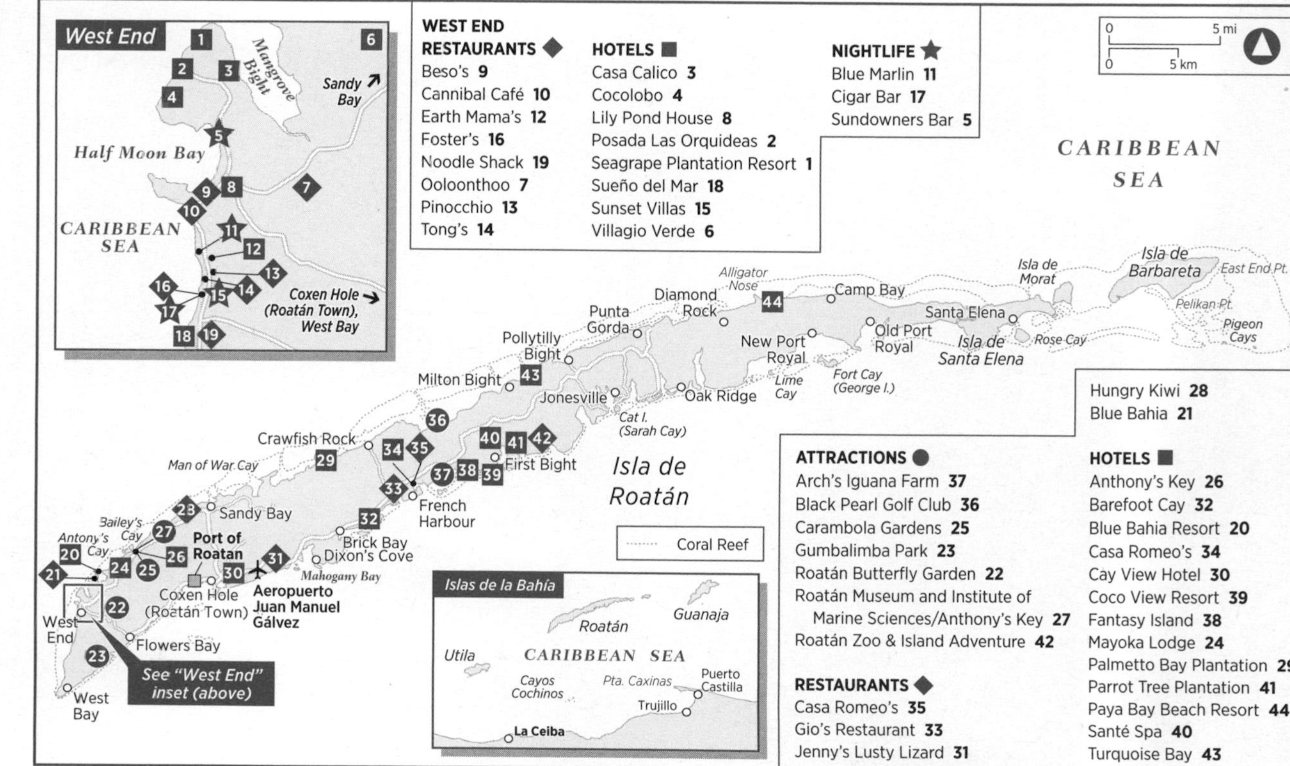

West End
Mangrove Bight
Sandy Bay
Half Moon Bay
CARIBBEAN SEA
Coxen Hole (Roatán Town), West Bay
WEST END RESTAURANTS
Beso's 9
Cannibal Café 10
Earth Mama's 12
Foster's 16
Noodle Shack 19
Ooloonthoo 7
Pinocchio 13
Tong's 14
HOTELS
Casa Calico 3
Cocolobo 4
Lily Pond House 8
Posada Las Orquideas 2
Seagrape Plantation Resort 1
Sueño del Mar 18
Sunset Villas 15
Villagio Verde 6
NIGHTLIFE
Blue Marlin 11
Cigar Bar 17
Sundowners Bar 5
0 5 mi
0 5 km
CARIBBEAN SEA
Isla de Barbareta
East End Pt.
Isla de Morat
Pelikan Pt.
Pigeon Cays
Rose Cay
Isla de Santa Elena
Santa Elena
Camp Bay
Old Port Royal
Alligator Nose
Diamond Rock
Punta Gorda
New Port Royal
Lime Cay
Fort Cay (George I.)
Pollytilly Bight
Milton Bight
Jonesville
Oak Ridge
Cat I. (Sarah Cay)
Crawfish Rock
First Bight
Isla de Roatán
Man of War Cay
French Harbour
Sandy Bay
Bailey's Cay
Antony's Cay
Port of Roatan
Brick Bay
Dixon's Cove
Mahogany Bay
Aeropuerto Juan Manuel Gálvez
Coxen Hole (Roatán Town)
West End
Flowers Bay
West Bay
See "West End" inset (above)
Coral Reef
Islas de la Bahía
Roatán
Guanaja
Utila
CARIBBEAN SEA
Cayos Cochinos
Pta. Caxinas
Puerto Castilla
Trujillo
La Ceiba
Hungry Kiwi 28
Blue Bahia 21
ATTRACTIONS
Arch's Iguana Farm 37
Black Pearl Golf Club 36
Carambola Gardens 25
Gumbalimba Park 23
Roatán Butterfly Garden 22
Roatán Museum and Institute of Marine Sciences/Anthony's Key 27
Roatán Zoo & Island Adventure 42
RESTAURANTS
Casa Romeo's 35
Gio's Restaurant 33
Jenny's Lusty Lizard 31
HOTELS
Anthony's Key 26
Barefoot Cay 32
Blue Bahia Resort 20
Casa Romeo's 34
Cay View Hotel 30
Coco View Resort 39
Fantasy Island 38
Mayoka Lodge 24
Palmetto Bay Plantation 29
Parrot Tree Plantation 41
Paya Bay Beach Resort 44
Santé Spa 40
Turquoise Bay 43

Coxen Hole

Coxen Hole, the largest city and capital of the department of the Bay Islands, isn't the idyllic beach paradise that you might expect to find in Roatán. It's more of, well, a hole. Like it or not, though, chances are you are going to pass through the city, which is home to the airport and functions as a transportation hub for buses and taxis, as well as the setting for the new Port of Roatán cruise terminal and shopping center, which is only functional when a cruise ship is in town. Apart from a few small hotels and restaurants, there isn't much in the way of tourist amenities—you're probably better off basing yourself in another part of Roatán.

SHOPPING

Named after the local slang for pre-Columbian artifacts, **Yaba Ding Ding** (Bonilla Building, near the waterfront; no phone; www.yabadingding.com) is one of the best craft shops in all of Honduras. The store stocks one of the most complete collections of Honduran crafts, including Lenca pottery, straw baskets and weavings from the highlands, Garífuna art, and more. It's open Monday to Saturday from 9am to 5pm. In town, just beside Yaba Ding Ding, is **HB Warren,** one of the best supermarkets and general stores in town.

WHERE TO STAY & EAT

Cay View Hotel Of the handful of small, budget, crumbling hotels that sit on the water near the ferry dock at Coxen Hole, the Cay View is probably the best. With 19 rooms, it's certainly the largest. Rooms aren't pretty and are quite worn, but there are A/C, cable TV, and a decent Honduran restaurant and bar overlooking the water. It's a handy spot to keep in mind only if you arrive to the island too late to drive to a different part of Roatán and just want a cheap place to stay for 1 night.

Oceanfront, Coxen Hole. ✆ **504/2445-0269**. 19 units. L760 ($40) double. No credit cards. **Amenities:** Restaurant; bar. *In room:* A/C, TV.

Jenny's Lusty Lizard CARIBBEAN Outside of Coxen Hole, on the road to French Harbour and the airport, is this small restaurant, popular with expats. Lobster and shrimp gumbo, burgers, sandwiches, and a range of tasty island grub and cold drinks are on hand. Before leaving, pick up one of their homemade salsas, like their Roatán Rectal Fire.

On the rd. to French Harbour, Coxen Hole. ✆ **504/9935-8136.** www.lustylizards.com. Main courses L75–L228 ($4–$12). No credit cards. Mon–Sat 11am–9pm.

Dixon's Cove

This newly redeveloped seaside community is where a large percentage of visitors to Honduras first set foot. While there was a ferry terminal here already, the town became home to a brand-new cruise ship terminal in 2009, in which Carnival Cruise Lines has invested heavily. Most passengers will hightail it to other parts of the island upon arrival, though new developments make it harder to leave Mahogany Bay (the newly minted name for what was formerly known as Dixon's Cove), including 8 hectares (20 acres) of white sandy beachfront, a giant chairlift that runs between the pier and the beach, and a large shopping and entertainment complex with the same cruise ship shops and restaurants that are found at every port (and are open only when a ship is at port).

OUTDOOR ACTIVITIES

SHARK DIVING For about a decade, two Italians have been operating **Waihuka Adventure Diving** (Dixon Cove, Las Palmas; ✆ **504/2445-1283;**

SCUBA DIVING IN roatán ★★★

Roatán is nothing less than a diving paradise. There are more than 130 dive sites scattered around the island, and in just one day of diving, you can experience the full range of dives from coral reefs, canyons, and walls to wrecks and tunnels. The waters are crystal clear, and the reef, part of the second-largest barrier reef in the world, runs just offshore. Many of the best dive sites are literally right off the dock or within a 5-minute boat ride. Following is a list of the best dive sites:

- **Mary's Place ★★★**: Mary's Place, near Sarah Cay, is one of the most legendary dive sites around the island. Here, you crawl through volcanic tunnels, crevices, and canyons around a reef plateau that has vertical walls that drop as much as 36m (118 ft.). You'll encounter black groupers, feather black coral, gorgonians, large bearded fireworms, and barrel sponges.
- **Four Sponges ★**: This dive site in Sandy Bay is one of the most complete and is the best for beginning divers. The site is defined by its different levels of reef that range from 3m to 36m (9¾ ft.–118 ft.), allowing for the opportunity to encounter a wide range of sea life like electric blue chromis, barracuda, toadfish, yellow jawfish, scorpionfish, and sponges.
- **Prince Albert Wreck:** Since it sank back in 1985 near Coco View Resort, the 50m (165-ft.) ship *Prince Albert* has attracted more soft coral growth than any other wreck on the island. There's also a sunken DC-3 plane that you can explore nearby.
- **Calvin's Crack:** This Jonesville dive site is defined by the huge crevice that runs through the reef, ranging from 9m to 24m (30 ft.–79 ft.) in depth—Calvin must have been a big guy. Brain, leaf, and black coral; sponges; gorgonians; rainbow parrotfish; fan leaf algae; and the occasional seahorse can often be sighted along the walls of the crevice.
- **Spooky Channel ★★**: The Spooky Channel (sometimes called Wayne's Place), on the northwest shore near Sandy Bay, is, well, spooky. The floor, ranging from 6m to 27m (20 ft.–89 ft.), is lined with sea whips and crabs, and cleaner shrimp crawl about on the abundant coral formations.
- **El Aguila Wreck:** *El Aguila* is a 61m (200-ft.) cargo ship that sank in 1997 by Anthony's Key Resort and was later split in three by Hurricane Mitch. It sits 30m (98 ft.) below the surface of Sandy Bay. You can find green moray and garden eels in varying spots around the wreck, as well as large grouper, blue parrotfish, glassy sweepers, nudibranchs, and anemones.

www.sharkdiveroatan.com) at Dixon's Cove. They offer guided dives with Caribbean reef sharks that are not chummed. Most dives go about 21m (69 ft.) below the surface and encounter as many as 15 sharks at a time. They offer dives Monday to Saturday at 9am, 11:30am, and 2pm (L2,850/$150 per person; 2 person minimum). Equipment rental is available at the center for an additional cost. Cruise passengers who wish to dive are expected to have been diving in the previous 6 months.

TRANSPORTATION

While many activities provide transportation, reaching a location on your own by private taxi is quite easy. Here are average prices from the port:

Location	Distance from the Cruise Dock	One-Way Taxi Fare
Dixon's Cove	15 min.	L200 ($10)
Sandy Bay	15 min.	L200 ($10)
Gumbalimba Park	20 min.	L300 ($15)
West Bay Beach	25 min.	L400 ($20)
West End Beach	20 min.	L300 ($15)

Flower's Bay

While this Afro-Antillean community lacks beach, it does have large unobstructed stretches of rocky-bottom clear waters, though there is quite a bit of trash. For the foreign tourist, Flower's Bay is perhaps best known when driving at night for the literally thousands of crabs that move across the coastal road by the dozens, many of which are seen plastered to the cement the next day. A fascinating ride on a scooter.

Sandy Bay

Sandy Bay is a tranquil town on the North Coast that has become a popular stop on many cruise ship tours, which come to experience the cultural highlights of the islands. Standout attractions here include the Roatán Museum and Institute of Marine Sciences, and a dolphin encounter. Sandy Bay is also home to one of the island's most popular resorts, Anthony's Key Resort (see below). Note that while the beaches in the reserve are stunning and surrounded by some of the most dramatic coral formations in Roatán, the beaches in town are murky and scruffy.

WHAT TO SEE & DO

Carambola Gardens These tropical gardens, across from Anthony's Key Resort, have a nice collection of native plants of the Bay Islands, and are a good spot on Roatán to check out rare iguanas and parrots. You can spend a couple of hours here easy, just taking in the views of reefs below, strolling around the trails, and hiking to the top of "Carambola Mountain." Kids might not enjoy this as much as some of the older visitors. On cruise ship days, the serenity can be lost.

Sandy Bay. ✆ **504/2445-3117.** www.carambolagardens.com. L200 ($10) adults. Daily 8am–5pm.

Dolphin Encounter ★★★ ☺ On Bailey's Key, which is part of Anthony's Key Resort, the famous bottlenose dolphin encounter program gives visitors the rare chance to interact with these wonderful creatures. Open-water dives, snorkel programs, and beach encounters are the most common option, and allow for physical interaction with dolphins. More involved are the training programs, where you can work with the training staff at the Roatán Institute for Marine Sciences in 1-day, 2-day, or weeklong sessions. There's also a dolphin show Thursday to Tuesday at 4pm.

Kids can get in on the dolphin action, too: Every summer, Anthony's Key Resort and the Institute of Marine Sciences offer **dolphin scuba camps** (L16,150/$850 per camper), where children can learn about dolphins and even swim and interact

VISITING ROATÁN BY cruise ship

Visiting Roatán by cruise ship is becoming an increasingly attractive option for travelers, as more and more cruise lines send ships here and prices drop by the season. In 2008, the port at Coxen Hole took in approximately 200 ship calls and over 430,000 passengers, and in 2011, that number is projected to hit nearly a million. Passenger numbers have risen dramatically as both Royal Caribbean and Carnival Cruise Lines opened their own terminals. There is talk of adding terminals on Utila, Trujillo, and near Tela Bay when the Los Micos Resort project is completed, so passengers can see more of the country and stay longer, but so far, it is just talk.

While plans for new terminals have not been finalized elsewhere in Honduras, new terminals are coming to fruition on Roatán. The Roatán Town Center at the Port of Roatán (www.portofroatan.com), funded by Royal Caribbean, was inaugurated in the final days of 2008 and opened a bright new retail complex at the port with such stores as TOUS Jewelry and Espresso Americano coffee.

At Dixon's Cove, Carnival Cruise Lines constructed an entire new terminal called Mahogany Bay with 8 hectares (20 acres) of waterfront, and even more retail and entertainment space, as well as a giant chair lift that takes passengers from the port to Carnival's own private beach.

I have mixed feelings on both. It is good that the cruise ships bring jobs and a little bit more money into the pockets of islanders, but for travelers wanting an authentic Roatán experience, the cruise ships aren't the way to get it. Especially at Mahogany Bay, you are completely sheltered from nearly all island life if you don't go on an excursion to another part of the island. It's basically a fenced off part of the island filled with Carnival's own shops and restaurants, the same ones you'll find at every other port. If you just want a nice day in the sun and sand, you'll find it, and maybe that is enough.

For most cruise passengers, the biggest question is how to spend their day at port. When you step off your boat at Coxen Hole, you will find a seemingly bustling street filled with a few simple restaurants, bars, cybercafes, Caribbean straw markets, and various gift shops—the typical spread for a Caribbean cruise port—but this is all you will find in Coxen Hole. When there isn't a cruise ship in town, this street is empty, and few shops open their doors. This is one of the least attractive places on the entire island of Roatán, and most passengers take excursions elsewhere on the island.

with them. They get to practice their scuba diving and snorkeling, as well as learn about the ecosystem and cultures of Roatán. Think of it as an exotic summer camp.

Bailey's Key, Roatán Institute for Marine Sciences, Sandy Bay. ✆ **504/2445-3008.** www.anthonyskey.com. L1,180 ($62) for dolphin encounter; L2,600 ($137) for dolphin dive.

Roatán Museum and Institute of Marine Sciences ★★ The Institute of Marine Sciences is the island's main scientific research center and is host to technical lectures and serious research, but it's also a place where tourists can learn about the ecology of the Bay Islands through captivating exhibits. Displays feature fish, reptiles, birds, plants, and other examples of island life, and exhibits focus on the history and culture of the area. The facility is part of the 13-sq.-km (5-sq.-mile) Sandy Bay marine reserve.

Roatán Institute for Marine Sciences, Sandy Bay. ✆ **504/2445-3008.** L100 ($5) adults. Daily 8am–5pm.

CRUISE SHIP SHORE excursions

Most tours can be booked through the property, the local agencies, or through the cruise ships. Most ships and itineraries have a similar range of options available. Here are some of the most common:

BEACHES

Few will argue that **West Bay Beach** ★★★, sometimes called Tabyana, is not the best on Roatán. Turquoise water, excellent snorkeling, clean white sand, swaying palm trees, tropical drinks served in coconuts—every cliché you can think of about a Caribbean beach can be found here. From Coxen Hole, there are a few ways to get to West Bay. First, you can take a set excursion with nearly any company that serves cruise ships; however, the price may be inflated for the service they provide. Most excursions to West Bay Beach are simply bus transport and maybe snorkel gear. If you want to save money, just hire a taxi for the 20- to 30-minute ride to West Bay. You can rent snorkel gear right from the beach, eat lunch from one of a dozen restaurants, and then hire a taxi to get back, even having time to stop off in the West End. Elsewhere on the island, fine sands can be found at West End, Paya Bay, and Camp Bay, though the parks listed below have nice beaches, as well.

ROATÁN-IN-A-BOTTLE PARKS

Two parks on the island try to offer a range of activities that can please an entire family and provide transportation directly from the cruise terminals. If you decide to stay in or near Coxen Hole, I recommend **Maya Key** ★ (✆ **504/ 9995-9589;** www.mayakeyroatan.com; must be booked directly from your cruise ship), a private cay owned by Anthony's Key Resort. It has a small pier just east of the cruise terminal, where a pontoon boat takes cruise passengers to and from the property. While it is no more than a half-kilometer off shore, the cay seems like an entirely different part of the Bay Islands. The tropical paradise vibe isn't lost. There's a nice clean beach, a pier jutting out over clear waters, and unspoiled reef that's great for snorkeling. After the buffet BBQ lunch, a group of Garífuna in traditional dress does a series of dances that are as good as any cultural performances on the island. There's a nice pool, a gift shop, and a small zoo on the property, as well.

Gumbalimba Park ★ ☺ (✆ **504/ 2445-1033;** www.gumbalimbapark.com) has the greatest range of activities of any of the parks, though it is also the farthest away, sitting near West Bay. The park has a small zoo on a small island surrounded by a moat with a handful of monkeys and parrots, a cheesy pirate cave, a pool, a private beach, all sorts of water sports, and a canopy tour. At last visit, they were building an insectarium and a pirate fort.

CANOPY TOURS

Zip-lining or canopy tours are wildly popular in Honduras, and this is especially true for Roatán. There are four companies with zip-line courses on the island: **Gumbalimba Park** (✆ **504/ 2445-1033;** www.gumbalimbapark.com), **South Shore Canopy Tour** (no phone; www.southshorecanopy.com), **Pirates of the Caribbean Canopy** (✆ **504/2455-7576;** www.roatanpiratescanopy.com), and **Palmetto Ridge Canopy** (✆ **504/ 2445-7853;** www.tropicalrez.com). All are quite similar and run between L1,140 and L1,425 ($60–$75) per person.

NATURE AND CULTURAL TOURS

For those who are looking to learn a little about the island's history, culture, or wildlife, there is a large lineup to choose from. One of the most popular excursions on the island, the **Dolphin Encounter at Anthony's Key** ★★ (✆ **504/ 2445-3008;** www.anthonyskey.com), near Sandy Bay, enables guests to dive or snorkel with the resort's resident bottlenose dolphins. There will be plenty of chances to pet, kiss, and get your photo taken with these mammals as trainers make them perform and detail their learning process. The dolphin encounter area is at Bailey's Key, a private cay owned by Anthony's Key and operated by the Roatán Institute for Marine Sciences. Prices range from L1,178 ($62) for the dolphin encounter to L2,603 ($137) for a dolphin dive when booked directly through the resort.

Also in Sandy Bay, **Carambola Gardens** (✆ **504/2445-3117;** www.carambolagardens.com; L200/$10 adults) is a nice way to explore the plant life of the islands. A few light trails will take you through their vast collection; you might even spot an iguana or two. While the **Roatán Butterfly Garden** (✆ **504/2445-4481;** www.roatanbutterfly.com; L140/$7 adults) in the West End is nice, I don't recommended it for cruise passengers unless they are extremely interested in butterflies, as a visit here will take more time in transport than in seeing the butterflies and exhibits.

At the **Roatan Zoo & Island Adventure** (no phone; www.roatanzoo.com; L475/$25 adults, L285/$15 children), located at Blue Ocean Reef, is an 4.5-hectare (11-acre) sanctuary for Honduran flora and fauna. Animals are brought to the park after being confiscated from the illegal animal trade, orphaned, injured, or donated by private individuals, and the goal is to rehabilitate the animals enough to return them to the wild. Open daily 8am to 4pm.

For those who are less active, or who dislike diving or snorkeling but still want to witness the magic that is the world's second-largest barrier reef, you have several options. Two companies offer **glass-bottom boat rides ★**: **Und**erwater Paradise (✆ 504/2445-6465; L380/$20 adults, L190/$10 children) from West End and Coral Explorer (✆ 504/4255-5379; www.roatancoralreefexplorer.com; L380/$20 adults, L190/$10 children) from West Bay.

The Roatán Institute of Deep Sea Exploration ★ (no phone; www.stanleysubmarines.com; L7,600–L22,800/$400–$1,200 per person) is an experience you won't find in many other places in the world. Inside a small two-passenger submarine, you will descend anywhere from 305m to 610m (1,000 ft.–2,000 ft.) and see marine life that few divers could ever imagine, including the rare Lophelia Reef.

East of Coxen Hole is one unusual excursion, though I am not crazy about it. Near French Harbour, you can visit Arch's **Iguana Farm** (✆ **504/2975-7442;** www.archiguanafarm.com; L160/$8 adults). While seeing hundreds of iguanas climb over each other in stinky passion to eat handfuls of lettuce is fine, the monkeys and coati in tiny cages with little access to food and water are beyond sad. I do not recommend a visit here for this reason alone.

ROATÁN-BASED COMPANIES FOR SHORE EXCURSIONS

While every cruise line sells excursions and activities to points all over the island, locally based companies offer many of the same tours, sometimes even a greater variety, for much less. Just like your cruise ship–arranged excursions, they'll be waiting outside the ship for you when you touch land, with transport ready to go. Here are the most popular operators:

- **Tabyana Tours** (✆ 504/2445-1115)
- **MC Tours** (✆ 504/2445-2431; www.mctours-honduras.com)
- **Tropical Rez** (✆ 504/2445-7853; www.tropicalrez.com)
- **Roatán Shore Tours** (✆ 504/9959-1140; www.roatanshoretours.com)

OUTDOOR ACTIVITIES

WINDSURFING The steady winds and lack of waves make Sandy Bay a fine place to take up windsurfing. **Wind Surf Honduras** (✆ **504/2445-3292;** www.windsurfhonduras.com; Tues–Sun 10am–6pm) has 60 boards on hand for all skill levels, which they rent for L380 ($20) per hour, including the use of a harness and sail. Lessons range from L950 ($50) for 1½ hours to L2,300 ($120) for 6 hours.

WHERE TO STAY

Anthony's Key Resort ★★★ For 4 decades, Anthony's Key Resort has been one of the leading dive and leisure destinations in the Bay Islands. If you are looking for a hotel that will completely transport you to another world, this is it. The vast complex is submerged in mangrove and palm forests, and is reminiscent of an island village where frequent water taxis shuffle you back and forth from place to place. The property is set partly on two small cays and partly on the north shore of the island near Sandy Bay. There are 56 single-unit wooden bungalows, 10 of them on the hill on the main island, with the rest on the key. Bailey's Key, just west of the main key, is home to the best beach on the property and their dolphin encounter lagoon. Also on the grounds are the Institute of Marine Sciences and Roatán Museum, which guests can enjoy for free.

Anthony's Key Resort, Sandy Bay. www.anthonyskey.com. ✆ **504/2445-3049.** 56 units. From L11,761 ($619) per person for a 4-night dive package w/3meals per day & activities. MC, V. **Amenities:** Restaurant; bar; pool; Wi-Fi (fee). *In room:* A/C (in some), fan.

Blue Bahia Resort ★★ Owned by American Kent, this mish-mash of large comfortable cabins comes with a kitschy island decor that ranges from seagrass furniture and wood carvings to brightly colored tiles and tapestries. I like the Penthouse, a large room above the restaurant with a small sitting area and great views. There's a small Infinity Pool and a nice stretch of beach where you can just spot the dolphins jumping over at Anthony's Key nearby. The Octopus Dive School is on-site, as is the best BBQ on the island (see below). They offer deals for longer stays and dive packages.

Blue Bahia, Sandy Bay. www.bluebahiaresort.com. ✆ **504/2445-3385.** 9 units. From L1,900 ($100) studio to L3,400 ($179) 2 bedroom loft. MC, V. **Amenities:** Restaurant; bar; pool. *In room:* A/C, fan, TV, kitchen, Wi-Fi (free).

Mayoka Lodge ★ Mayoka is the most luxurious place to stay, not just in Roatán, but in the whole of Honduras—and it has the price tag to go with it. The beachfront property in Sandy Bay is laid out with one main house and five pods, 23 sq. m to 27 sq. m (248 sq. ft.–291 sq. ft.) hexagon-shaped buildings detached from the main complex. Upon your chauffeured arrival to Mayoka, you are treated to a Champagne reception before settling in. Extras include a fully equipped wet room with all sorts of water toys (kayaks, snorkel gear, and beach gear), a media room with a 45-inch LCD TV, bar and billiards room, private dock, wine cellar, private chef, tennis courts, and infinity pool. Keep in mind there are six rooms here, enough room for 12 people, so creative groups can indulge in the same amenities as the filthy rich.

Sandy Bay. www.mayokalodge.com. ✆ 504/2445-3043. 1 unit. L12,825 ($675) per night (low season). Rates are all inclusive. MC, V. **Amenities:** Pool; Wi-Fi (free). *In room:* A/C, fan, TV/DVD player, hair dryer.

WHERE TO EAT

Blue Bahia Beach Grill ★★★ BBQ One of the best restaurants on the entire island, the BBQ centric beach grill in the Blue Bahia hotel revolves around the use of their own smokehouse and USDA certified meats. Smoked wahoo salad, pulled pork, and beef brisket, served in a sandwich or on their own, are all worth making the trip to Sandy Bay for. There's also seared ahi tuna, ceviche, juicy steaks, and lots of other goodies to choose from. Even the breakfast menu—eggs any style, succulent coconut pancakes, thick-cut bacon—deserves mention. I just drooled.

Sandy Bay. ✆ **504/2445-3123.** www.bluebahiaresort.com. Main courses L133–L380 ($7–$20). MC, V. Tues–Sun 7am–late.

Hungry Kiwi ★ CONTINENTAL In the old Que Tal Café space (and using some of the same menu), this pleasant New Zealander–operated cafe serves a general international menu all day long, ranging from prime rib and lamb chops to soups and wraps. There's a full coffee bar and a decent wine list. Dining is in their air-conditioned dining room or on a sunny terrace.

Lawson's Rock Beach Club, Sandy Bay. ✆ **504/2445-3295.** www.hungrykiwi.com. Main courses L133–L418 ($7–$22). MC, V. Mon–Sat 8am–10pm.

West End

West End, so-called because it is on the west end of Roatán, is the tourist center of the island and is home to the most hotels, restaurants, bars, dive shops, tour operators, and general tourist amenities. From the highway, the town hugs the road and the beach in both directions for just a kilometer or so. The town itself is quite small and has a sort of thrown-together feel to it, since buildings are scattered about with no apparent order. Prices tend to be cheaper here than in the West Bay, thus attracting plenty of backpackers and diehard divers, although it is still more upscale than anywhere on Utila.

GETTING THERE

The West End can be reached by **bus** from Coxen Hole (L40/$2), a **water taxi** (L50/$3) from West Bay, or a regular **taxi** from anywhere on the island. There is a taxi stand near the entrance to the highway where a few cabs (L200/$10 to Coxen Hole) are usually waiting, though if you stick to the *colectivo* cabs, the ones with other people in them, the prices are 75% less.

WHAT TO SEE & DO

If you want to explore the island for a day or two, a great option is to rent a mountain bike, scooter, or motorcycle. **Captain Van's** (✆ **504/2403-8751;** www.captainvans.com) has locations in both the West End, on Main Street near the Baptist Church, and the West Bay Mall. Prices begin at L170 ($9) per day for a bike and L740 ($39) per day for a scooter.

Central America Spanish School Mainland Institute, the Central America Spanish School, has two locations on Roatán, at Posada Arco Iris in the West End and at Bananarama Resort in West Bay. Weeklong courses include 20 hours of one-on-one course work and classroom materials. You can add accommodation and even pair your studies with PADI certification at Bananarama's dive school.

West End & West Bay. ✆ **504/9815-8650.** www.ca-spanish.com. L3,800 ($200) adults.

Gumbalimba Park ★ ☺ Gumbalimba is a good place to come if you have just a day in Roatán and want to experience as much as you can—which is why the place is often packed when a cruise ship is in town. It's kind of a one-stop adventure shop. There's a zip-line section, a large stretch of beach with clear kayaks, Snuba (a combination of snorkeling and scuba diving), snorkel gear, a pool, and even a small cave

diving OPERATORS IN ROATÁN

Almost every hotel on the island has a dive center or can give you special rates with one. Dive packages and certification courses attract a majority of travelers to Roatán, where rates are some of the lowest in the world, at less than $40 per dive. Prices are not as cheap as Utila or Guanaja, though they are not far off. Here are a few recommended dive schools, listed according to their location:

FRENCH HARBOUR

Coco View Resort (✆ **504/2911-7371;** www.cocoviewresort.com)

Fantasy Island Resort (✆ **504/2455-7499;** www.fantasyislandresort.com)

SANDY BAY

Anthony's Key Resort ★ (✆ **504/2445-3049;** www.anthonyskey.com)

Octopus Dive School ★ (✆ **504/2403-8071;** www.roatan-octopusdiveschool.com)

WEST END

Coconut Tree Divers (✆ **504/2445-4081;** www.coconuttreedivers.com)

Native Sons (✆ **504/2445-4003;** www.nativesonsroatan.com)

Reef Gliders (✆ **504/2403-8243;** www.reefgliders.com)

Sueno del Mar Dive Center (✆ **800/298-9009;** www.suenodelmar.com)

WEST BAY

Bananarama Dive Resort (✆ **504/2445-5005;** www.bananaramadive.com)

with cheesy replica pirates and exhibits that describe their historical relationship with the Bay Islands. The main attraction, though, is the nature trail that runs through an area of very dense jungle and is filled with rare tropical plants and flowers native to the region, as well as a hanging rope bridge over a small lake, cages of macaws and other parrots, and a small island that's home to a few monkeys. A new insectarium and a replica pirate fort you can walk through should be ready by late 2011.

On West Bay Rd., btw. West End & West Bay. ✆ **504/2445-1033.** www.gumbalimbapark.com. Park L320 ($17) adults; park & zip-line L1,045 ($55) adults. Daily 9am–4pm.

Roatán Butterfly Garden Try to spare a few hours for a visit to Roatán's butterfly garden. Tours are self-guided through the 278-sq.-m (2,992-sq.-ft.) walk-through enclosure, and they give you a small chart to identify the 30 or so rare butterfly species and tropical plants. Separate from the butterflies are a few cages of birds native to Honduras, such as aracaris and toucans.

Near the entrance to the hwy., West End. ✆ **504/2445-4481.** www.roatanbutterfly.com. L140 ($7) adults. Sun–Fri 9am–5pm.

OUTDOOR ACTIVITIES

BEACHES West End beaches are smallish and not nearly as nice as those in the West Bay (just a quick water ferry ride away), but there are a few spots where the water is just as clear as anywhere on the island. Half Moon Beach is probably the best option.

SUBMARINES/GLASS-BOTTOM BOATS If you don't dive, snorkel, or even swim, but still want to experience the undersea world of the Bay Islands, you have a few options. The **Roatán Institute of Deep Sea Exploration** (no phone; www.stanleysubmarines.com; L7,600–L22,800/$400–$1,200 per person) offers 305m to

610m (1,000 ft.–2,000 ft.) dives and shark dives inside the safety of a submarine. The small vehicles have room for just one pilot and two passengers. **Underwater Paradise** (✆ **504/2445-6465**) has semi-submarine glass-bottom boat tours three times daily from the Half Moon Bay Resort for L380 ($20) adults and L190 ($10) children, and the **Coral Explorer** (✆ **504/2455-5379**; www.roatancoralreefexplorer.com) has a similar tour from West Bay.

AERIAL TOURS For another unique perspective on the island, **Bay Island Airways** (✆ **504/2946-5665** in the U.S. or 504/2933-6077; www.bayislandairways.com) offers a variety of ways to view the island from the air. They have aerial real estate tours (L6,840/$360 per hr. for two), trips to the Pigeon Keys (L10,000/$520 for a 3-hr. tour for two), and simple sightseeing and photography tours (L2,470/$130 for a 15-min. flight for two).

FISHING The waters surrounding Roatán are full of Pelagic species like tuna, wahoo, mahi-mahi, blue and white marlin, shark, and king mackerel. **Early Bird Fishing Charters** (✆ **504/2445-3019;** www.earlybirdfishingcharters.com), a member of the conservation-minded Fishermen's Association of Roatán, leads frequent excursions from the West End to waters all around the island. Prices begin at L7,600 ($400) for a half-day tour with one to four people. **Pescado Roatán** (✆ **504/9930-6139;** www.pescadoroatan.com) specializes in fly, flats, and remote deep-sea trips, all using new boats and top-of-the-line equipment. Pricing ranges from L950/$50 to L2,850/$150 per hour.

SHOPPING

All shops are on Main Street in the West End, but most are little stores selling a mishmash of things. One standout store is **Wave Gallery** (✆ **504/2445-4303**), a bright yellow house on the beach that's worth a browse for its paintings, jewelry, and crafts made by Honduran artists.

The **Roatán Marine Park Office** (Half Moon Bay, West End; ✆ **504/2445-4206;** www.roatanmarinepark.com) has an eco-store selling dive maps and some equipment, and offers information on saving the reef and natural sites in the Bay Islands. You can also buy a L190 ($10) Roatán dive tag/bracelet here.

WHERE TO STAY

Casa Calico Clean and cheery rooms, a good value, and a location away from the noise of Main Street (it's set back from Half Moon Bay) about sum up this little hotel's assets. Either single or deluxe suites, which sleep four and have full kitchens, are available. Rooms are spacious and clean, but a bit rustic—if you don't need luxury, they won't be bad at all. Apart from the backpacker dorms in the dive hotels, this is really your only option in this price on the West End, and it's the only inexpensive spot with amenities. They also have one-bedroom apartments and a beach house, used for the TV show *Temptation Island,* available for rent by the week or month.

Mangrove Bight, West End. www.casacalico.com. ✆ **504/2445-4231.** 9 units. L760 ($40) double. Rates include breakfast. MC, V. **Amenities:** Restaurant; kayaks. *In room:* A/C, fan, fridge, Wi-Fi (free).

Cocolobo ★★ This lovely little property in Mangrove Bight, built in 2005, gets rave reviews from everyone who visits. Stylish rooms, all identical with white walls and honey-colored Honduran pine floors, front the Caribbean. There's no beach here, but an attractive pool area that fronts the ocean is almost as nice. The friendly owners will give you a small guide of their personal recommendations for what to see, do, eat, and drink on the island. Two two-bedroom cottages with full kitchens are also available for rent.

Mangrove Bight, West End. www.cocolobo.com. ✆ **504/9898-4510.** 12 units. L2,375 ($125) double; L12,350/$650 cottages. MC, V. Free parking. **Amenities:** Pool; bar; Wi-Fi (free). *In room:* A/C (in some), fan, minifridge.

The Lily Pond House ★★ This charming little house, just off the main road near Half Moon Bay, is inundated in lush garden and trees, making it just as attractive for the birds and butterflies as those who are looking for something completely different from the typical dive resorts that make up much of the accommodations in Roatán. The honeymoon suite is the largest of the four rooms, although they don't really differ all that much in size or amenities. All are quite spacious, with wood floors and canopy beds. Plus, they have private entrances, en-suite bathrooms, and porches, so you can keep your privacy. It's a quiet, relaxing place surrounded by green. They also hold yoga classes on the rooftop garden three times a week.

Half Moon Bay, West End. www.thelilypondhouse.com. ✆ **504/2403-8204.** 4 units. L1,800 ($95) double. No credit cards. **Amenities:** Restaurant; free airport transfers. *In room:* A/C, TV/DVD player, fridge, Wi-Fi (free).

Posada Las Orquideas Posada Las Orquideas sits in front of Mangrove Bight, where there isn't a beach—but there is a dock and a wharf with beach chairs, and the town beaches are just a 10-minute walk away. The three-level building opened in April 2006, and the rooms still seem new with their shiny wood floors and wicker furniture. There's a nice balcony in every room, with a table and hammock where you can watch the boats pass by in the water below. The Posada is an overall good value.

Right from the hwy., West End. www.posadalasorquideas.com. ✆ **504/2445-4387.** 18 units. From L1,330 ($70) double (low season); from L1,520 ($80) double (high season; July–Sept; Dec–April). AE, MC, V. Free parking. **Amenities:** Internet (free, in lobby); kayaks. *In room:* A/C (L285/$15), fridge, kitchen (in some).

Seagrape Plantation Resort Seagrape mostly attracts divers who come to take advantage of the dive packages run through the resort's own dive shop. They have five roomy pastel-colored Caribbean-style bungalows with pine-wood floors and hammock-laden decks. Everything is modern, and the bathrooms are clean. The decor is fairly boring and simple throughout, but that seems to be the standard theme all over West End. The shore in front of the property is rocky, and there's no beach; but they do have an oceanfront pool and patio that make up for it. The main town and beaches are just a short walk away.

Right from the hwy., West End. www.seagraperoatan.com. ✆ **504/2445-4428.** 22 units. From L1,140 ($60) double. 4-night dive package L5,415 ($285) based on double occupancy. AE, MC, V. **Amenities:** Free airport transfers; Internet (free, in lobby); pool; dive shop. *In room:* A/C, fan, TV (in some), fridge.

Sueño del Mar ★ Voted the best dive shop on Roatán by *Scuba Diving* magazine, this sort of charming, imitation colonial-style white building is one of the nicer options right in the heart of West End, though it does cater mainly to divers. The bright, clean rooms have tile floors, and most have small balconies that look out onto the Caribbean. There's a nice chunk of beach fronting the property, with a volleyball court and lively little bar.

West End. www.suenodelmar.com. ✆ **504/2445-4343.** 16 units. L1,330 ($70) double. Package w/2 daily dives L9,500 ($499) per person per week. MC, V. **Amenities:** Bar, Wi-Fi (free). *In room:* A/C, fan, minifridge.

Sunset Villas ★ Sunset is the most luxurious place to stay by West End standards and has the most beautiful pool area in town. Rooms are rented from the hotel or the 1- or 2-bedroom condos in the villas that make up the property. The large condos are the better value, particularly if you are sharing a 2-bedroom. The living rooms are appointed with a typical Floridian-like decor, with tiled floors and wicker furniture, while the bedrooms are a bit more elegant. Flat-screen TVs and large patios or balconies are added bonuses. The biggest downside of the property is that the rooms lack any decent views of the ocean, but all villas do look out on the large pool area. Their restaurant is in the Buccaneer, which sits towards the beach directly in front of the property, just a couple of minutes' walk away.

Left from the hwy., West End. ✆ **504/2445-4100.** 29 units. From L1,710 ($90) double; L3,000 ($158) villa. MC, V. **Amenities:** Restaurant; bar; Internet (free, in lobby); pool. *In room:* A/C, fan, TV, kitchen (in condos).

Villagio Verde ★ If you prefer the peace and tranquility of the jungle and don't mind being a 20-minute walk from the ocean and town, this small Dutch-owned property on the way to Sandy Bay is for you. The wood cabins are pretty standard, although they have nice patios with hammocks. There's a lovely little pool and lots and lots of plants, as well as a few friendly dogs that will follow you around the property.

West End, on the rd. to Sandy Bay. www.roatanvillagioverde.com. ✆ **504/2445-4046.** 4 units. L1,615 ($85) double. Rates include breakfast. MC, V. **Amenities:** Airport pickup; pool, Wi-Fi (free). *In room:* A/C (in some), fan, minifridge.

WHERE TO EAT

Besos ★★ INTERNATIONAL While the name is a bit corny, this new martini lounge and upscale restaurant fills a much needed gap on West End's higher end. Dark woods, white curtains, and the occasional piece of bamboo or carved wood create an ambiance rare in these parts. Dishes are more creative than most from the neighborhood: Neapolitan-style pizzas, lobster gnocchi, mojito chicken, lobster sliders, and ahi tuna ceviche. Free Wi-Fi for customers.

Main St., West End. ✆ **504/3302-6093.** www.besosroatan.com. Main courses L150–L475 ($8–$25). AE, MC, V. Mon–Sat 11am–10pm, Sun 5–9pm.

Cannibal Café ★ ☺ MEXICAN This wildly popular restaurant and bar in front of the Sea Breeze Inn is always a great choice for a snack or drink. It's set in a rustic wooden shack and serves the sorts of standard Americanized Mexican fare, like burritos and nachos, that appeal to hungry divers. Get a margarita to wash your meal down, and you'll fit right in at this lively little spot.

Main St., West End. ✆ **504/2445-4026.** Main courses L75–L150 ($4–$8). No credit cards. Mon–Sat 10:30am–10pm.

Earth Mama's ★★ CAFE A pleasant garden cafe adjoining the yoga center of the same name serves a variety of light, healthy meals that are a nice change of pace from the carb-heavy burgers that dominate the West End. There are salads (Thai chicken), wraps (seafood salad), and a few random appetizers like chicken skewers and summer rolls. I usually stick to their smoothies, which are a little bit pricey, but quite good—and they'll add energy and antioxidant boosts to most and let you choose from five types of milk (such as soy, vanilla almond, and rice).

Main St., West End. ✆ **504/9607-0704.** www.earthmamasroatan.com. Main courses L105–L170 ($5.50–$9). No credit cards. Tues–Sun 7am–3pm.

Foster's ★ INTERNATIONAL Foster's is in a stilted house in the middle of the ocean, connected to the shore by a hundred or so meters of dock. You literally can't get a better sea view from here, which is why this is the spot in town for a sunset meal or drink. Burgers, chicken wings, coconut shrimp, seafood, and steaks make up most of the menu. It can get boisterous on weekend nights, when there is either a DJ or live band.

On dock off Main St., West End. ✆ **503/2403-8005.** www.fostersroatan.com. Main courses L130–L380 ($7–$20). AE, MC, V. Mon–Sat 10:30am–midnight.

Noodle Shack ★ JAPANESE This tiny noodle spot—there are just a couple of stools—definitely helps to add a bit of diversity to the dining scene here. You choose your noodle (udon, sticky rice, vermicelli, lo mein) and then choose your sauce (sesame ginger, red curry, miso ginger), and meat (veggie, shrimp, chicken) or lack thereof. Simple. Delicious. Filling, but not gut busting. They offer a few rolls and soups, too.

Main St., West End. No phone. Main courses L75–L150 ($4–$8). No credit cards. Tues–Sat noon–8pm.

Ooloonthoo ★★ INDIAN Ooloonthoo is probably the best restaurant in Roatán. Canadian chef Paul James and his Indian wife have done such a good job of giving this restaurant an authentic Indian coastal feel, you might just think you're in Goa while dining here. The decor of the hilltop house is simple, with little touches like background Indian music, silk saris draped across the ceiling, and banana leaves strewn on the tables all adding to the am-I-still-in-Honduras ambience. Curries made from scratch dominate the menu, such as the *Goan* Pork *Vindaloo* or *Rajasthani* Red Lamb, while other highlights include *Pappadums* (fried lentil wafers) and Bengali Fish *Johl.* Recently, chef James began offering Indian cooking classes ($10 per person; half-day).

Right from hwy. to Sandy Bay, West End. ✆ **504/2403-8866.** www.ooloonthoo.com. 2-course menu L712 ($38). MC, V. May–Nov Mon–Fri 6–9pm; Dec–Apr Sun–Fri 6–9pm.

Pinocchio INTERNATIONAL This restaurant boasts an eclectic menu that lets you combine your choice of sauce with your choice of fish or meat, so that you end up with some interesting combinations, like a somewhat strange peanut butter shrimp or, my favorite, Thai ginger lobster. Sweet and savory crepes are available, too. It's in a small house up an inclined dirt alley off Main Street. On my last visit, this place was open sporadically, so be sure to call ahead.

Main St., West End. ✆ **504/2445-4466.** Main courses L95–L230 ($5–$12). No credit cards. Thurs–Tues 6–9pm.

Tong's ★ THAI One of the more romantic settings on the West End, Tong's offers both an indoor dining room and an intimate outdoor patio and pier with tables that sit right out over the water. Thai staples are all worth trying: Pad Thai, Tom Yam, or any of their three curries (Panang, green, or red).

Main St., West End. ✆ **504/9682-4288.** Main courses L230–L340 ($12–$18). MC, V. Tues–Sun noon–2:30pm & 5:30–9:30pm.

WEST END AFTER DARK

Apart from the listings below, there's a booze cruise that departs from the water taxi dock on Tuesdays and Fridays at 3pm ($50 open bar; $20 cash bar).

Cigar Bar ★ Under new management, this elegant wooden bar in the Palm's complex is the spot for puffing on a stogie (mostly Hondurans and Cubans) and sipping on a scotch. Occasionally, they'll have specials like a cigar and a mojito for $6.

Main St., West End. No phone. Daily 11am–late.

Sundowners Bar ★ This thatched-roof beach bar and their recently expanded patio is one of the West End's main hangouts. Its prime spot on one of the best sections of beach in town draws lots of walk-ups, as do the specials on beer, mixed drinks, and the 4-to-7pm happy hour. Try the Monkey La-La, a frozen blend of Kahlúa, ice cream, coconut, and vodka.

Main St., West End. ✆ **504/2445-4158.** Daily noon–late.

Blue Marlin This bar—basically a wooden patio that runs between the street and the water—is beloved for the cheap drinks. On weekend nights, the crowd spills out into the street. Formerly the Purple Turtle.

Main St., West End. No phone. Daily noon–late.

West Bay

About 2km (1¼ miles) southwest of the West End sits a 1.5km (1-mile) stretch of powdery white sand, set against the mellow tides of a perfectly turquoise sea. This is West Bay, the finest beach in all of Honduras and one of the top beaches in all of the Caribbean. If your ideal vacation is to lounge around in the sand and sun with a continuous rotation of tropical drinks being brought your way, look no further. The focus here is less on diving—although diving is still a big deal—than general beach-going activity. When you decide to move from your palm-fringed slumber, you can ride jet skis, take a boat tour, or browse the souvenir stands sprinkled across the beach. If you want to snorkel, you can rent gear almost anywhere and walk a couple meters into the water where all sorts of colorful fish are swimming around a good tract of coral reef.

Almost the entire beach is chock-a-block full of hotels and condos, the majority of which have no more than a few dozen rooms. West Bay has so many new hotel and condo projects in the works that it sometimes feels more like a construction site than a resort area. The town used to be sorely lacking in restaurants and other tourist amenities, but the kinks are slowly being worked out. Come when a cruise ship is in town, and the place can be downright crowded, but for much of the week, West Bay is still an idyllic beach resort.

WHAT TO SEE & DO

The 1.5km (1 mile) **West Bay Beach ★★★** is the main attraction here and one of the region's best beaches. The water resembles an aquarium of sorts, since you can see right down to the bottom and watch brightly colored marine life pass you by. Many of the resorts have beach chairs and umbrellas set up in the sand, although you may need to pay a fee and get a wristband to use them. Apart from snorkeling, you can rent wave runners or go parasailing, ride a paddle boat, or water-ski.

WHERE TO STAY

Bananarama Apart from the 2-bedroom beachfront King House that's available for rent and includes a full kitchen, none of the rooms at Bananarama are what you would call luxurious, but more along the lines of simple and rustic. They all vary in size and quality, but are brightly colored and have a decent selection of amenities. At this price, you probably won't find anything this comfortable in West Bay. Bananarama doesn't have a pool, but it does sit on a nice stretch of beach with chairs for guests. Stays also include breakfast at their restaurant, the Thirsty Turtle Bar and Grill, and use of kayaks. Their PADI 5-star Gold Palm dive center, which offers a full range of certification courses and packages, is one of the best known on the island, and many guests here make use of it. On Sundays, they host a beach party with Garífuna fire dancers and crab races.

West Bay, Roatán. www.bananaramadive.com. ✆ **504/2445-5005.** 21 units. From L1,824 ($96) double; L4,200($221) villa. Rates include breakfast. No credit cards. **Amenities:** Restaurant; bar. *In room:* A/C, fan, TV, fridge, Wi-Fi (free).

Cabana Lana This little building sits right on West Bay beach and is nearly swallowed up by surrounding resorts. Your choice is between the upper and the lower unit, though they are equal in size and shape. Both have full modern kitchens, one bedroom, a living room with a pullout bed, and large patios with excellent views of the turquoise water that is just 15m (49 ft.) away. The decor is the same, tired island style in every Floribbean condo.

West Bay, Roatán. www.islandhouseroatan.com. No phone. 2 units. L23,750 ($1,250) per week. MC, V. **Amenities:** Wi-Fi (free). *In room:* A/C, TV/DVD player, hair dryer, kitchen.

Infinity Bay Spa & Resort ★★★ Similar to the Mayan Princess, though it intends to become more luxurious when it is finished, Infinity Bay is another new condo/resort complex that opened in late 2007. Here, studios and 1-, 2-, and 3-bedroom condos are set in three-level villas facing the pool or West Bay beach. All rooms are very modern, with stainless steel appliances, flat-screen TVs, tiled floors, and contemporary furniture and decor. At last visit, the main restaurant and spa were still under construction, though all of the condos were finished. Highlights are their long dock that extends far into the water, poolside bar, and beachfront restaurant.

West Bay, Roatán. www.infinitybay.com. ✆ **504/2445-5016.** 145 units. L2,850 ($150) studio (low season), L3,610 ($190) studio (the rest of the year); from L7,315 ($385) 2-bdrm. condo; from L9,595 ($505) 3-bdrm. condo. MC, V. **Amenities:** Restaurant; bar; free airport transfers. *In room:* A/C, fan, TV, kitchen (in condos), Wi-Fi (free).

Mayan Princess ★★ ☺ The Mayan Princess is the most luxurious resort in Roatán and one of the top accommodations in all of Honduras. The posh units are privately owned and rented out through the hotel management. The 1-bedroom and 2-bedroom condos still feel like the tile has just been laid and the wicker furniture never sat in. They have full kitchens, a dining area, living rooms, and a patio or balcony that faces the ocean or sprawling pool area that runs almost the length of the complex and is bordered by tropical gardens interwoven with waterfalls and walkways. The oceanfront side of the property is the best in the West Bay because of the primo beach chairs and umbrellas, and the good bit of shade that covers their beach bar and restaurant, one of the best all-around dining options in the West Bay. Kids' programs and the extra-large pool make this the most family-friendly hotel on the beach.

West Bay, Roatán. www.mayanprincess.com. ✆ **504/2445-5050.** 60 units. From L2,451 ($129) double (weekdays); from L3,021 ($159) double (weekends). MC, V. **Amenities:** Restaurant; bar; pool; Wi-Fi (free). *In room:* A/C, fan, TV, kitchen.

West Bay B&B ★ Considering that the back end of the much more expensive Infinity Bay is just as far from the beach as this small, owner-run bed-and-breakfast, this might be the best deal anywhere on the Bay Islands. There are five rooms with a varying number of beds and one 2-room condo. Some rooms can sleep up to six. The rooms feel a bit bare but are nicely decorated, and the common room is quite comfortable, with a big couch, Internet cafe, and DVD collection you are free to use.

West Bay, Roatán. www.westbaybedandbreakfast.com. ✆ **504/2445-5080.** 6 units. L1,121–L1,880 ($59–$99) double; L1,880 ($99) condo. Rates include breakfast. MC, V. **Amenities:** Restaurant; Wi-Fi (free). *In room:* A/C, TV, minifridge.

West Bay Lodge These Oregonian-owned and -operated bungalows are 5 minutes from the beach. Facilities are a bit rustic, but the service is personable and amenities are there: a fine pool, well maintained gardens, a breakfast *palapa,* lender cellphones, and a welcome drink. Two of the bungalows add small kitchens, though all have decent-sized porches with hammocks. Inside, the TVs are a little small and the decor a bit more Polynesian than Caribbean, but all in all, most are satisfied.

West Bay, Roatán. www.westbaylodge.com. ✆ **504/2445-5069.** 4 units. L1,805 ($95) double (3-night min.). MC, V. **Amenities:** Restaurant; bar; pool; Wi-Fi (free). *In room:* A/C, TV/DVD player, hair dryer, minifridge, kitchen (in some).

WHERE TO EAT

Beach Club San Simon ★ CONTINENTAL San Simon isn't just a restaurant, but a place to enjoy the beach. Many come from other parts of the island and spend the day here, renting out their beachside cabanas or lounge chairs. The main dining area is under their elegant beachfront *palapa.* They're known for their rotisserie chicken, which is prepared using an old Venetian recipe. The rest of the menu jumps around quite a bit and doesn't always work: pastas, filet mignon, grilled fish and lobster enchiladas, or fish tacos. It fills up on cruise-ship days and is occasionally closed for private parties.

West Bay Mall, West Bay. ✆ **504/2445-5035.** www.thebeachclubroatan.com. Main courses L75–L230 ($4–$12). AE, MC, V. Daily 10am–10pm.

Bite on the Beach ★ CONTINENTAL Spread out on a deck at one end of West Bay Beach, this restaurant has been in operation for more than a decade, though it has changed hands a few times. It boasts one of the better menus around, with tasty fare that combines a choice of lobster, shrimp, chicken, beef, or pork with a choice of flavors like coconut, Thai curry, olive pesto, or pineapple.

West Bay. ✆ **504/2403-8064.** Main courses L160–L418 ($8–$22). AE, MC, V. Mon–Sat noon–8pm.

Celeste's Island Cuisine CONTINENTAL The specialty of this thatched-roof grill attached to West Bay Lodge are their gourmet *baleadas,* which are stuffed with almost any sort of protein: lobster, shrimp, grouper, chicken, pulled pork, beef, and more. They serve lobster dinners for two and a full international menu, including breakfast. They have some mean looking jars of homemade *Guifiti*, a Garifuna libation, behind the bar.

West Bay Lodge, West Bay. ✆ **504/2445-5069.** Main courses L119–L418 ($6–$22). AE, MC, V. Tues–Sat 8am–9pm; Sun & Mon 8am–3:30pm.

Mangiamo ★★ DELI This small deli and gourmet food market in the West Bay Mall is a place where you can grab a quick fresh-ground coffee from Olancho or a fancy sandwich—from hot pastrami to basil cashew chicken. Their breakfast menu is my favorite on the island: Eggs Benedict, breakfast burritos, stacks of pancakes, and egg sandwiches with pancake buns. Wine and beer to stock your fridge with can be purchased here, too.

West Bay Mall, West Bay. ✆ **504/2445-5035.** www.roatandeli.com. Main courses L75–L230 ($4–$12). AE, MC, V. Mon–Sat 8:30am–5pm.

French Harbour

French Harbour was once better known as the home of one of the largest fishing fleets in the western Caribbean, but is quickly becoming engulfed by the onslaught of tourism and residential developments aimed at foreigners. While the compact town and port hold most of the town's population, the area as a whole is more spread out and less self-contained than West End and West Bay. Most of the hotels are fairly isolated and have their own private beaches, dive centers, and restaurants, so most visitors find little reason to leave their individual compounds or venture into town. A Megaplaza Mall, the first on the islands, with many chain restaurants and stores, opened in late 2009 on the highway.

VISITOR INFORMATION

Banco Atlántida (✆ **504/2455-7484;** Mon–Fri 9am–4pm and Sat 8:30–11:30am), on the highway at the turnoff to the center, has an **ATM** and will exchange travelers' checks. The Megaplaza Mall has a few ATMs, as well as lots of international chain stores and restaurants. Also at the turnoff are several gas stations and a cybercafe.

WHAT TO SEE & DO

Arch's Iguana Farm Several thousand iguanas inhabit this property in French Key, just east of French Harbour, towards Fantasy Island. There are four different species on the farm, all native to the Bay Islands, and they are absolutely everywhere. Watch when you walk—these things are literally falling out of the trees and out of the bushes. There's also a small pool with sea turtles and tropical fish. The place is overall pretty basic and an interesting excursion; however, the treatment of the coati, white-faced monkey, and spider monkey make it a place for those with any sort of a conscience to avoid.

French Key, just E of French Harbour. ✆ **504/2975-7442.** L160 ($8) adults. Daily 8am–3:30pm.

OUTDOOR ACTIVITIES

Golf The Pete Dye–designed **Black Pearl Golf Club ★★**, Roatán's first golf course, is an 18-hole, par-72 resort course measuring 7,057 yards. Set at the Pristina Bay, the course opened in 2010 and frequently hosts tournaments and special events. The Sky Lounge and 19th Hole restaurants are open during playing hours. Call ahead for tee times and prices.

Pristine Bay, Big Bight. ✆ **504/3318-2146.** www.blackpearlgolf.com.

WHERE TO STAY

Casa Romeo's In the actual town of French Harbour—there is a greater range of options outside of town—the most reliable accommodations are at Casa Romeo's, overlooking the harbor and attached to the best-known Italian restaurant on the island. Amenities aren't great, and the feel is a bit worn; but there is little other option if you need to stay in town.

Main St., French Harbour. www.casaromeos.com. ✆ 504/4255-5854. 7 units. L1,425 ($75) double. MC, V. **Amenities:** Restaurant. *In room:* A/C, TV.

WHERE TO EAT

Casa Romeo's ITALIAN Romeo's, set in the hotel of the same name, has been a Honduras institution since 1976, and many of the recipes have been passed down since the 1940s from Romeo's father, Don Di, who owned the famous Maxim's in La Ceiba and later the Buccaneer Inn on Roatán. The menu ranges from

Italian standards like penne *alla* carbonara to thick cuts of beef and seafood that are prepared every which way—from *fra diavolo* (in spicy tomato sauce) to breaded and grilled. My favorite item is the conch chowder. The restaurant is on the edge of the harbor and makes good use of the view.

Main St., French Harbour. ✆ **504/2455-5854.** Main courses L150–L285 ($8–$15). AE, MC, V. Mon–Sat 10am–2:30pm & 5–10pm.

Gio's Restaurant ★ SEAFOOD Few dare to utter the name Gio's without mentioning king crab, and for good reason: People have been flocking to this restaurant since it opened several decades ago for its special king crab *al ajillo* (in garlic sauce). Other seafood dishes and even steaks are finely executed and cater to finicky international tourists. There are two separate dining rooms: one is open-air on the dock, while the other sits inside with the A/C blasting. All seats have inviting views of the harbor and make ideal spots for relaxing with a drink in your hand for the rest of the day.

Main St., under El Faro Inn, French Harbour. ✆ **504/2455-5214.** Main courses L190–L380 ($10–$20). MC, V. Mon–Sat 10am–2pm & 5–10pm.

WHERE TO STAY OUTSIDE OF FRENCH HARBOUR

Barefoot Cay ★ ☺ A small walk-on barge regularly travels the 30m (98 ft.) back and forth from the main island and the 1.6-hectare (4-acre) island of Barefoot Cay, a newish resort area on the south shore of Roatán. Apart from the marina, which attracts yachties from around the Caribbean, and diver lofts, the property has just a few bungalows, two with two bedrooms and two with one bedroom. The spacious buildings have full kitchens and patios, as well as Balinese showers, which are partially open-air. The pool area—with its adjacent two-level cabana—is the social center of the property and a decent place to grab a meal or drink, or to soak in a 360-degree view of the cay. On the waterfront, there's a 79m-long (259-ft.) dock and a thatched-roof *palapa* with a lowered platform, which grants easy access for kayakers who want to circle the cay or snorkelers who want to explore the reef that's just offshore.

Btw. French Harbour & Brick Bay. www.barefootcay.com. ✆ **504/2455-6235.** 11 units. L4,275 ($225) loft; L4,750 ($250) partial villa; L6,175 ($325) bungalow. MC, V. **Amenities:** Restaurant; bar; pool; spa services; kayak & snorkel equipment. *In room:* A/C, fan, TV/DVD player, fridge, kitchen, Wi-Fi (free).

Coco View Resort Coco View is one of the oldest resorts on the island and a specialist in dive packages, which the majority of visitors here take advantage of in some form. The rooms comprise water bungalows, cabanas, and ocean-front rooms divided among two-level buildings on the shore. Each structure has a similar wood design with tiled bathrooms and waterfront porches, although amenities and size vary from room to room. The whole property boasts a rustic appeal and communal atmosphere, which many divers have fallen in love with and keep coming back to, often in large groups. If you're not a diver, you may feel out of place. One downside is that the hotel is a bit isolated, so catching transportation elsewhere can be difficult or expensive; you might want to rent a car if you stay here.

Coco View Resort. www.cocoviewresort.com. ✆ **504/2911-7371.** 26 units. L4,465 ($235) w/dives. Packages from L23,700 ($1,249) 5–14 nights. MC, V. **Amenities:** Restaurant; bar; fitness center; Internet. *In room:* A/C, fan, fridge (in some).

Fantasy Island This 8.5-hectare (21-acre) island is one of Roatán's original megaresort complexes and is still one of the largest hotels on the island. Even without Mr.

Roarke and Tattoo there to oversee operations, the complex has grown to include an impressive array of attractions like a pool, several bars and restaurants, numerous lounges, a private dock, a major dive operation with a handful of boats and certification courses, and a huge crescent-shaped beach that sits right in front of the hotel. The rooms, which are set back from the beach in two-level structures, have basic beach decor, wood floors, wicker furniture, and plain bedspreads. Each room has a beachfront balcony. They are nothing fancy, but casual and friendly, which could describe the general feel of the entire property.

Fantasy Island Resort, French Harbour. www.fantasyislandresort.com. © **504/2455-7499.** 115 units. L2,375 ($125) per person. Rates include 3 meals per day & diving. MC, V. **Amenities:** Restaurant; bar; pool; tennis courts. *In room:* A/C, fan, TV, fridge.

Palmetto Bay Plantation ★★★ Isolated on a stretch of Roatán's loneliest shore, this hotel has given the island one of its first tastes of the worldly exotic, with the Balinese-style eco-friendly beach houses. This notion was pushed further with the filming of *Temptation Island International*. Their collection of villas varies slightly, but all can sleep at least four. Some have two bedrooms, while others have three. A few lack A/C (there's a decent breeze here, so you don't necessarily need it), while a few lack an ocean view. Their best room, the Coconut Grove Cottage, has a private plunge pool and sits right on the beach. Each of the bungalows has high ceilings, hardwood floors, and a full kitchen. The property is spectacular, through and through. The infinity pool fronts a glass-and-wood pyramid that holds the restaurant and bar. The whole place feels—and is—rather isolated, so you have the entire beautiful beach all to yourself and the others at the resort. The atmosphere is polished, but it doesn't lack charm.

N of French Harbour. www.palmettobayplantation.com. © 504/9991-0811. 27 units. L4,560 ($240) villa. Packages for additional L1,045 ($55) adults, L665 ($35) children per day available. Weekly rates available. MC, V. **Amenities:** Restaurant; bar; free airport transfers; Jacuzzi; pool; kayaks; Wi-Fi (free). *In room:* A/C, kitchen.

Parrot Tree Plantation ★ This sprawling, 68-hectare (168-acre) gated community is already turning heads all over the Caribbean, although it is far from complete. Right now, visitors can stay in rooms, villas, or condos, and visit the Santé Spa. More houses and a 150-room luxury hotel are in the works, though it could be a few years before it's completed. The rooms available differ drastically in size and style, although all are bright, new, and clean, and can be rented by the day, week, or month. The turquoise waters are home to a small marina with moorings for up to 20 berths; beachside, there is a vast collection of constructions, including a pool, a few shops, a popular *palapa* restaurant, and eventually a steakhouse. Plans include adding up to five restaurants, a fitness center, a yacht club, and numerous other goodies that should give you little reason to leave the resort.

Parrot Tree Plantation, E of French Harbour. www.parrottreeplantation.com. © 504/3320-7177. 66 units. L4,389 ($231) 2-bdrm. villa. MC, V. **Amenities:** Restaurant; pool; spa. *In room:* A/C, fan, kitchen (in some) Wi-Fi (free).

Santé Spa ★ This wellness facility and B&B on a cay near Parrot Tree Plantation is one of the best little accommodations on the island. Without road access, there's little noise, apart from the wind in the palms and crashing surf. Accommodations are in either two rooms in the main building or a small cottage near the lagoon. Decor and amenities are simple, yet cozy and charming. Prices include use of the spa facilities, a morning yoga session, and continental breakfast.

E of French Harbour. www.santewellnesscenter.com. ✆ **504/2408-5156.** 3 units. L2,375 ($125) double or cottage. MC, V. **Amenities:** Pool; spa. *In room:* A/C ($10 per day), fan, minibar Wi-Fi (free).

Turquoise Bay ★ Quietly, Turquoise Bay has grown a loyal following of returning customers. The resort is quite secluded on the north side of the island, about 15 minutes east of French Harbour. It's not flashy or overly luxurious, and it isn't going to really "wow" you like Palmetto Bay; but overall, the ambience is pleasant, and the price is good. The spacious contemporary rooms—set in four-unit bungalows—are decorated with splashes of African flair. Each has a different bright color scheme, but all are done up quite nicely, the tile floors and bathrooms are clean, and the balconies have an ocean view. There's a pool and a National Geographic dive center on the property.

Milton Bight. www.turquoisebayresort.com. ✆ 504/2**413-2229.** 26 units. L17,290 ($910) per week (all-inclusive). MC, V. **Amenities:** Restaurant; bar; free airport transfers; pool. *In room:* A/C, TV.

Oakridge & Jonesville

The last communities reachable by a paved road on the south side of the island, Oakridge and Jonesville are connected to each other along the coast through canals in the mangroves. The people are mostly of Afro-Antillean descent, and many of the houses are built on stilts in a traditional style. Investment here is lacking, compared with the western end of the island, though tourist visits here are not unheard of, and many prefer this atmosphere that is considerably more authentic than the West End. While you won't find luxury here, there are a few good places to stay and eat.

WHAT TO SEE & DO

Boatmen line the road into Oakridge, flagging down cars and taxis with tourists for informal **tours of the mangroves** and seaside villages. A narrow channel has been cut through the thick web of mangrove forests for access to some residential areas. Parts are dirty, though lately, the locals have been adamant about trying to keep the mangroves clean. There is fine bird life in the mangroves, even the occasional boat-billed heron. Alligators once lived in these parts, too, though sightings are rare these days. Just watch out for duppies! (Duppies are a sort of island ghost—for more info, see p. 215.) Sometimes, you have to bargain hard to get a good price. Prices are based on distance traveled. Most will combine a trip to the mangroves (L285–L475/$15–$25) with a stop at the Hole in the Wall restaurant (L475–L760/$25–$40 combined). Ask for Eric for an honest and reliable driver and guide.

OUTDOOR ACTIVITIES

KITE SURFING With deep water just off shore past the reef, the south shore and east end of Roatán is one of the best spots in the Bay Islands for kite surfing, sometimes called kite boarding. The wind is ideal during the months of January to April and July to September, though the sport can be done any time of the year. **Kite Honduras** (✆ **504/3312-8439;** www.kitehonduras.com), based at Marble Hill Farms, offers beginner to advanced lessons using IKO instruction methods, with board rentals and repairs, as well as customized trips for advanced riders. Lessons start at L3,325 ($175) for 3 hours and include equipment rental, instruction, and boat support.

WHERE TO STAY & EAT

Marble Hill Farms There are just three *casitas* on this 10-hectare (25-acre) plot outside of Oakridge. Only a few acres of the land are used as an actual farm (more of a garden), the rest is left wild and untamed. Two of the units have two rooms, while the other is a suite. Those with two rooms have a screened-in patio and kitchenette. The suite adds a small plunge pool. The units are fairly rustic, with shiny wood floors and cheery, brightly painted bare walls. Kayak and dive packages are available, which the property is increasingly focusing their attention on.

2.4km (1½ miles) E of the Oakridge turnoff. www.marblehillfarms.com. ✆ **970/688-4120** in the U.S. 3 units. L2,565 ($135) per person w/3 meals per day & use of snorkels & kayaks. No credit cards. **Amenities:** Restaurant; Wi-Fi (free). *In room:* A/C, fan, kitchenette.

Reef House Resort ★ This small, intimate resort has live-in owners who take meals with the guests and even run the dive operation. The tile-floor rooms are plantation style, with a large porch running the length of the building. The property sits right against the ocean, with concrete steps that drop off right into the water. All buildings are wood and painted pastel colors. The resort is extremely popular with divers, and they offer a full line-up of certification and specialty courses. There is excellent diving right in front of the property.

Oakridge. www.reefhouseresort.com. ✆ **866/478-4888** in the U.S. 12 units. L2,755 ($145) per person per night; L17,000 ($895) per week, based on double occupancy. Rates include 3 dives per day, 3 meals per day, transport, equipment & unlimited shore dives. No credit cards. **Amenities:** Restaurant; bar; Wi-Fi (free). *In room:* A/C, TV.

B.J.'s Backyard ★ SEAFOOD This fish shack and Internet cafe, right on the Oakridge waterfront, has been a favorite of fishing-industry employees for 3 decades. The fish and shrimp, grilled or fried, are usually pulled out of the water that day and are some of the freshest on the island. Their bread pudding with rum sauce is a must-try. Boatmen hang around their dock to take passengers through the mangroves.

Waterfront, Oakridge. No phone. Main courses L100–L210 ($5–$11). No credit cards. Wed–Mon noon–9pm.

Hole in the Wall Restaurant ★★ INTERNATIONAL Although it was destroyed by fire a few years back, the loyal customers pitched in to save it. Maybe the isolation is why I am so fascinated by this place: It can be reached only by boat from Oak Ridge or Jonesville. This means the restaurant doesn't attract the typical tourist, but rather an interesting and sometimes eccentric mix of locals and expats that live nearby. On a jetty of sorts over the water, the walls of the open-air restaurant and bar are plastered with the graffiti of good times past. Their $15 all-you-can-eat Sunday shrimp and/or lobster BBQ is a culinary highlight of the area, though their burgers, lobster rolls, and other pub food aren't bad, either. Most tourists will combine a boat trip here with a ride through the mangroves (see above).

Jonesville. No phone. holeinthewallroatan@yahoo.com. Main courses L80–L200 ($4–$10). No credit cards. Daily noon–9pm.

Punta Gorda

The village of Punta Gorda stands where the paved road ends on the north side of the island. It was here in 1797 that the British dropped approximately 5,000 Garífuna ashore, after they began to rebel against colonial rule in St. Vincent, about 1,600km (994 miles) to the southeast, off the coast of Venezuela. While many Garífuna went to the mainland and settled on the coasts of Honduras and Belize, some stayed around and settled here. The village is the only almost entirely Garífuna settlement still on the island. There is little in the way of tourist amenities here, and the town is quite poor. Houses are built on stilts over the water, and those on the shore are made of cement blocks with tin roofs and are painted in bright pink or turquoise. Each year,

pirates OF THE BAY ISLANDS

As much as the Garífuna or the Spanish, pirates have played an important role in the history of Roatán. Since the early days of the Spanish conquest of Latin America, buccaneers have hid out on the island to raid the gold and other treasures that were loaded on the ships and passing through the Bay of Honduras en route to Spain.

For much of the 17th century, the island was used to gather wood and make ship repairs and to trade slaves. The English Fort at Old Port Royal was taken over and became a safe harbor for all sorts of riffraff. In the late 1600s, Henry Morgan hid out here with several ships and untold amounts of booty. Other famous names, such as Captain John Coxen or the Dutchman Van Home, also frequented Roatán. As many as 5,000 pirates were believed to have settled here; many towns are named after these sea dogs, and thousands of locals are descended from them. For the most part, the pirate reign ended in 1650, when Spain, under the command of Francisco Villanueva Toledo, attacked Port Royal with four warships and forced the pirates to flee.

The island's pirate history has brought treasure hunters in recent years. Countless tales abound of buried treasure hidden in the sea caves surrounding Santa Helena and the eastern reaches of Roatán. Some claim that lost artifacts such as the chain of Huayna Capac, taken from the Inca ruler by the Spanish, and a golden life-size virgin created by priests in Panama that was loaded on a ship in Colón and never made it to Europe, are hidden somewhere on the island. Archaeologist Mitchell-Hedges, famous for his crystal skull, lived on the island for almost a decade in the 1920s and '30s, and did considerable exploring on the eastern end. He was one of the first adventurers to explore Old Port Royal, and legend has it he even found several chests filled with gold and silver, which he snuck off the island and sold off in England but never reported. In the 1960s, adventurer Howard Jennings followed an old naval survey map a friend, Robin Moore, had found at the British Museum and passed along. Rumors swirl that he eventually discovered a treasure chest filled with gold nuggets and 29kg (65 lb.) of pure silver in a secret compartment. Like Mitchell-Hedges, Jennings had to immediately leave the island, though he did return a few years later with his wife in the hunt for more.

a festival is celebrated on April 12, the day the original Garífuna settlers arrived on the island, and features lots of dancing, drumming, and drinking.

WHERE TO STAY

While there are no quality hotels near Punta Gorda, several spectacular villas, all with the same owner, are available for rent near Pollytilly Bight. **Brisa del Mar** (© **843/682-3814;** www.villasdelmarroatan.com; $1,800 per week) is a 2-bedroom Balinese-style villa with an infinity pool and tropical chic decor. The larger **Fuego del Mar** ($2,700 per week) and **Mariposa del Mar** ($2,700 per week) have similar amenities and sit on bluffs with incredible views of several acres of waterfront. All properties share an on-site spa with a full range of services.

The East End

Past Oak Ridge on the south shore and Punta Gorda on the north shore, the main paved road ends and becomes a bumpy dirt path. Small cars make their way here in only the best conditions; large trucks and 4×4s are the preferred vehicle of choice, after boats. Some villages lack road access and hug the coastline. These are some of the poorest communities on the island, and some even lack electricity and plumbing. It is like a step back in time.

Two of the best beaches on Roatán, **Paya Bay** and **Camp Bay** ★★ (the largest beach still undeveloped on the island), are known only by locals and visitors at the one small resort on this end of the island, **Paya Bay Beach Resort** (see below). Here, just to the east of Punta Gorda, the hills grow larger, and the small coves become more dramatic. Getting around and to these beaches isn't easy unless you have four-wheel drive, but the payoff is worth it: Clean white sand and clear waters are backed by lush jungle. They are the hidden paradises that everyone thinks were bulldozed off the island decades ago.

Little more than an historical footnote, in the 17th century Port Royal was a base for pirates, as well as the British military. The remains of two British forts at the edges of the harbor, Fort Frederick and Fort George, can still be seen, though a house has mostly covered Fort Frederick. Fort George, on the cay, is slightly more visible, though only the foundation remains. The area has seen an increase in recent years of private development, mostly houses of expats and wealthy Hondurans, who prefer the isolation, wild surroundings, and cheap property to the more commercialized West End.

Past Port Royal is Old Port Royal, the site of a failed Providence Company settlement in the 1630s, though little remains. Heading east, Roatán breaks apart into three small islands: **Santa Helena, Barbareta,** and **Morat.** The islands lack any infrastructure and are populated only by a few small fishing communities. Pristine reefs that are often visited on dive excursions surround all. There are a few rarely visited beaches here, as well as loads of sea caves in the limestone cliffs that are believed to hold artifacts from the Payas and possibly pirate booty. Beyond these islands sit the Pigeon Cays, tiny spits of land much like those in the Cayos Cochinos. All three islands and the cays are reachable by boat from Oak Ridge.

WHERE TO STAY

Paya Bay Beach Resort ★ One of the most overlooked properties on the entire island, Paya Bay doesn't get much respect because it is far away—well past the end of the paved road—from the rest of the island. Yet the setting is the isolated, tropical paradise that many hope for when planning their vacation. The 9-hectare (22-acre) property has several private beaches, a hammock station beside an excellent snorkeling cove, and several patios. They can arrange bird-watching and hiking trips, visits to Pigeon Cay, and diving on the reef. The resort hosts monthly naturists' weeks, when an isolated section of the resort, including a small beach and cove, become clothing optional. The rooms here have both ocean- and beach-view balconies and 4.5m (15-ft.) ceilings. They have a refined, wooden setup with bright walls and motifs from the Paya culture.

Paya Bay, Roatán. ✆ **504/2435-1498.** www.payabay.com. 12 units. L3,496 ($184) double. All-inclusive packages L22,781 ($1,199) per person w/transport, 3 meals per day & 2 snorkeling excursions per day. MC, V. **Amenities:** Restaurant; bar; transport. *In room:* A/C, TV/DVD player, minifridge.

UTILA

Utila has only one main settlement, called East Harbour, or simply Utila Town. Although it is the smallest of the three main Bay Islands and the nearest to the mainland (29km/18 miles west of Roatán), Utila is still the wildest and most untouched.

ISLAND slang

Roatán's English creole is saturated with an endless number of phrases and words that aren't typical of the English language. Here are a few of my favorites:

- **Monkey La-La:** One of Roatán's favorite creamy cocktails is named after the Monkey La-La, but this creature is no monkey. The Monkey La-La is the name locals have given the basilisk lizard, which lives on the island. The creature is sometimes called the "Jesus Christ lizard" because it can seemingly run across the water.
- **Yaba Ding Ding:** Pottery and clay beads are occasionally pulled out of the ground when constructing a new house or digging a sewer on the island. This is the name the islanders have given to pre-Columbian artifacts.
- **Duppies:** Antillean folklore is richer than most think. Duppies are ghosts or evil spirits that live in the mangroves and may guard hidden treasure, although they are unable to turn corners.

Islanders, many of them the descendents of pirates and Garinagu from the Caymans, are eager to casually chat with anyone about the weather or local news. Some may even tell you that Captain Morgan's lost booty from his raid on Panama in 1671 is still hidden in the surrounding hills.

Apart from a few chic dive resorts, almost the entire population of Utila is clustered together along one stretch of coast, while the other nearly 80% or so of the island is made up of mangroves and wetlands. Many have called this island a backpacker paradise because of the cheap accommodations and restaurants, the bar scene that rages well into the night almost every night, and the sandy bottom rates for dive certification—once considered the lowest in the world. It is far less polished than, say, Roatán, but beach resorts are slowly starting to carve their way out of the mangroves outside of town. Even the certification costs are roughly on par with Roatán these days. Chances are that it is going to be a good while before a dirt-cheap dorm bed in a rickety old wooden house goes out of style in Utila, though.

Essentials

GETTING THERE

BY PLANE Just one airline, **Lanhsa** (✆ **504/9935-8832;** www.lanhsa.com), currently make the 20-minute trip between Utila and La Ceiba or Roatán, with connections to Tegucigalpa and San Pedro Sula. Check with the airline for the latest schedules. Taxis, which cost L40 to L60 ($2–$3), await flights for the 10-minute trip to town.

BY FERRY The **Utila Princess II** (✆ **504/2425-3390**) makes the hour-long trip back and forth between the municipal pier Utila and the Muelle de Cabotaje dock in La Ceiba. The ferry departs Utila daily at 6:20am and 2pm, and returns to La Ceiba at 9:30am and 4pm. Ticket booths are located on both piers. The price is L425 ($23) each way. In 2009, a **catamaran service** (✆ **504/3346-2600;** vfine@hotmail.com; L1,040/$55) began operating the 3½-hour ride between Roatán's West

Sun Jam Festival

For 1 weekend night every August for the past decade, partygoers from around Honduras have descended upon the tiny 1.2-hectare (3-acre) island of Water Cay off Utila for this raucous festival. Local fishermen wait at Utila's pier to transport attendees to the festival, where top DJs from around the region pump electronic music to a lively and often intoxicated crowd. The crowd is limited to 1,500, so buy your tickets (L760/$40) a few weeks in advance. For info, visit www.sunjamutila.com.

End (departing at 1pm) and Utila's East Harbour (departing at 6:30am) on the 12m (39-ft.) *Nina Elisabeth II.*

GETTING AROUND

There are just a few cars on Utila, let alone taxis. Considering almost everywhere is within walking distance or reached over water, the only time you will really need a taxi or a car is to get back and forth from the airport. Rented golf carts, scooters, and bicycles are the most common vehicle-assisted ways to get around the island. Visit **Lance Bodden Rentals** (✆ **504/2425-3245**), behind BGA bank, to make arrangements. Discounts are given for long-term rentals.

ORIENTATION

The crescent-shaped East Harbour on the eastern end of Utila is where 90% of the population of the island lives. The municipal pier marks the center of town, and Main Street, the main road on the island, runs perpendicular about a kilometer in each direction. To the left is Sandy Bay, and to the right is a small peninsula that ends at the bridge that connects to Bando Beach. With a few exceptions, almost all hotels and tourist amenities can be found within a kilometer of the pier. Another road, Cola de Mico/Monkey Tail Road, branches off Main Street up over Pumpkin Hill, eventually leading to the airport and the north side of the island.

VISITOR INFORMATION

There are two banks in East Harbour, both conveniently within a hummingbird's flight of the pier. Both **Banco BGA** (✆ **504/2425-4117**) and **Banco Atlántida** (✆ **504/2425-3374**) exchange traveler's checks and have an **ATM.** They are open Monday to Friday from 8:30am to 3:30pm and Saturday from 8:30 to 11:30am. **Mango Tree House,** on Main Street just to the left from the pier, is the island's most reliable Internet cafe and can also make international phone calls. **Hondutel,** beside the Bay Island College of Diving, also has phones for international calls.

What to See & Do

Central America Spanish School Giving the only formal Spanish lessons on Utila, the Central America Spanish school is a mainland institute that takes advantage of the island's sun and laidback learning environment. They also offer weeklong packages that are paired with PADI certification. So, you can learn to speak Spanish and dive all in the same week for probably the lowest price you might ever find (L7,600/$400). Housing is available for an extra L2,280/$120 per week.

Main St. ✆ **504/2425-3788.** www.ca-spanish.com. L3,800 ($200) 20 hr. of lessons.

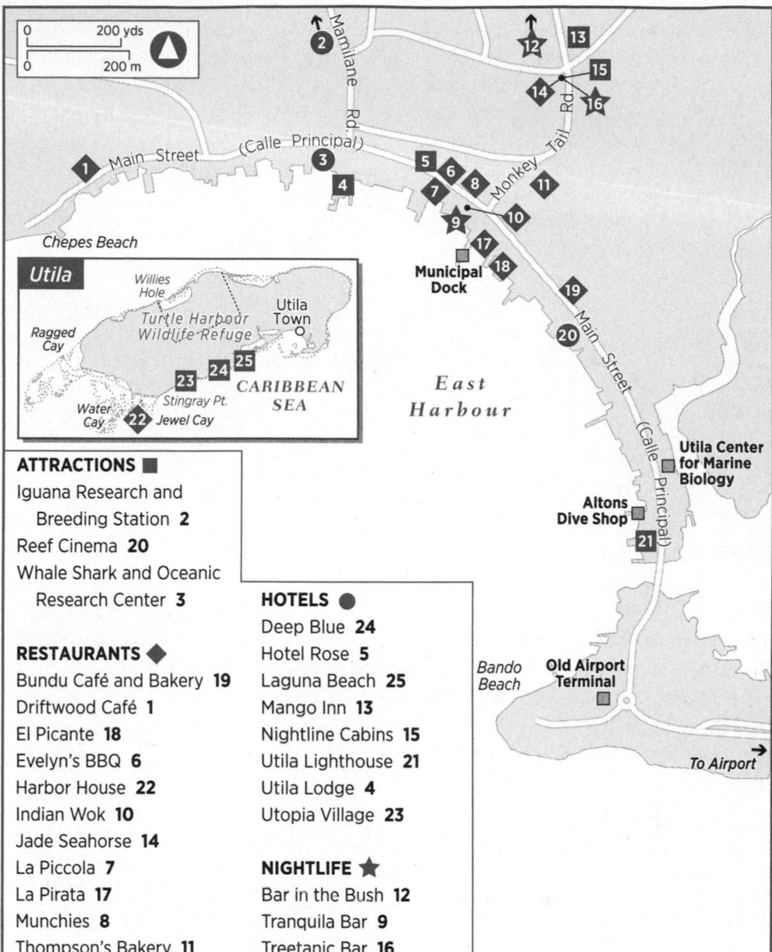

Iguana Research and Breeding Station ☺ The small, nonprofit German-run station is a learning center for those interested in not only iguanas, but also the tortoises, snakes, frogs, spiders, fish, and other animal life found on the Bay Islands. Many live species can be found in aquariums, terrariums, and outdoor breeding cages, and your admission includes a brief tour where kids can walk into—if they dare—some of the enclosures. This is one of the few places in the world you can catch a glimpse of the spiny tail or swamp iguana, a species endemic to Utila and in danger of extinction because of the islanders' love of eating them and the destruction of the mangroves. Longer tours to the Bat Caves, Pumpkin Hill, and the mangrove forests are also available, as well as volunteering opportunities.

Follow Mamilane Rd. until you see the signs for the turnoff. © **504/2425-3946.** www.utila-iguana.de. L40 ($2.20) adults. Mon, Wed & Fri 2–5pm.

Reef Cinema Apart from the guys from La Ceiba that sell pirated DVDs near the pier, Reef Cinema is the only other place to catch a semi-new flick. The small theater has nightly showings, including two on Saturdays, of the latest North American blockbusters via a small projector. They also have an attached video store that rents DVDs.

Main St., just past Cola de Mico Rd. © **504/2425-3254.** Sun–Fri 7:30pm; Sat 6:30 & 8:30pm.

Whale Shark and Oceanic Research Center ★★★ The whale shark, the largest fish in the world, is seen year-round in Utilian waters, and the island is a hotspot for whale shark research. This small organization is focused on protecting these creatures and the coral reefs by collecting data with the help of divers and operators, educating the public, and hosting and participating in major studies. The good news for visitors to Utila is that they have a full line of courses and tours. Their 4-hour whale shark encounter and research trips include a short background lecture on whale shark ecology, the use of snorkel gear, and the possibility of seeing whale sharks up close in the water. They also offer PADI specialty courses such as AWARE fish ID, Coral Reef Conservation courses, and underwater photography. Volunteers are often needed to help with whale shark research and development of the program.

Main St., in front of the Bay Islands College of Diving. © **504/2425-3760.** www.wsorc.com. Free admission. Daily 8am–7pm.

Outdoor Activities

SWIMMING While Utila isn't known for its beaches like other places in Honduras, it does have a few decent options for sunbathers and swimmers. There are several good beaches within walking distance of town. **Bando Beach** (© **504/2425-3137**), just past the bridge from the Point, is privately owned, and you must pay a small admission (L40/$2) to get in. Occasionally, they host Full Moon parties that attract top DJs from the region. There's a small beach bar that also rents snorkel gear and kayaks. **Chepes Beach,** to the west of Sandy Bay, is the main public beach. They are constantly at work there at improving the infrastructure by adding sand and facilities.

The small, uninhabited **Water Cay** is similar to many of the beaches you'll find in the Cayos Cochinos: It's made of a cluster of palm trees circled by a white sandy beach and turquoise water. Charters and dive trips often stop here for lunch or weekend barbecues and parties. The first weekend of August, it is host to the largest party in Utila, the Sun Jam festival (see above).

FLOAT UTILA What was once a trend in the '80s has been brought back to Utila. **Float Utila** (© **504/2424-3827;** www.floatutila.com; $30 for 60-min.) gives patrons the experience of euphoria while floating in their flotation tank, believed to be the world's largest. The tank is filled to a depth of 304mm (12 in.) with a sterile water solution saturated with 907kg (2,000 lb.) of Epsom salt. Some say it is as rejuvenating as a massage, that it relieves depression, and will even reduce the symptoms of jet lag.

KAYAKING A few hotels and several shops in town, including **Utila Water Sports** (© **504/2425-3264;** www.utilawatersports.com), **Kayak Utila** (no phone; www.kayakutila.com), and the bar at Bando Beach (see above), rent sit-on-top kayaks to explore the channels, lagoons, and the mangroves around the island.

THE WORLD'S whale shark HEADQUARTERS

The waters off Utila are one of the top places on planet Earth to spot the elusive whale shark during the months of February to April, when it is most prevalent, though it can be seen here year-round. The island has become known as the whale shark capital of the Caribbean, as it is home to two research programs: the **Whale Shark and Oceanic Research Center** (www.wsorc.com) and **Utila Whale Shark Research** (www.whaleshark.org). It is the largest fish in the Earth's oceans, weighing as much as 20 tons and reaching as much as 20m (66 ft.) in length, though it is known as being extraordinarily gentle and does not prey on humans.

The fish is highly endangered due to over-fishing, particularly in China and Southeast Asia, where a single whale shark fin, considered a delicacy, can be sold for as much as $10,000. Significant scientific research didn't even occur on the creatures until the 1990s; however, long-term photo and satellite tracking projects are ongoing right from Utila. They live in the open ocean, usually in tropical and temperate waters from 70° to 82°F (21°–28°C), eat mostly plankton, and are highly migratory. One tagged whale shark was tracked across more than 12,800km (7,954 miles) in less than a 3-year period. Utila's 4-hour whale shark encounter trips ★★★ are one of the island's most incredible attractions. On these excursions, you'll search the waters of the eastern and northern coast for birds and giant boils of frenzied fish, and with a little luck, you'll find a whale shark feeding there. Your captain will circle around so you are right in the fish's trajectory, and you can jump right in the water with mask and snorkel and wait as the massive creature passes beneath you. ***Remember:*** They can come to you, but you cannot approach them. Contact either institute if you would like to volunteer to help with research, snorkel with a whale shark, or even adopt one of the creatures by sponsoring their satellite tagging.

HORSEBACK RIDING Located on the road to the airport, **Red Ridge Stables** (✆ **504/2390-4812**) leads horseback-riding treks to the inner jungle, Pumpkin Hill Beach, the freshwater caves, and to other destinations on the island that aren't submerged completely in swamp and mangroves. Trips run L665 ($35) for a 2-hour ride.

SNORKELING & SCUBA DIVING With prices hovering around L4,750 ($250) for a PADI 4-day open-water certification, it is no wonder that scuba divers from around the world descend on this small island. Almost any certification or course can be taken on the island from a number of dive shops. There are roughly 90 permanent mooring buoys around the island, giving access to the reefs, wrecks, walls, and tunnels that frequently line the pages of top diving magazines. The most frequent whale shark sightings tend to be in March and April.

The dive shops on Utila are second to none in Honduras. On Main Street in East Harbour, dive instructors seem to outnumber people five to one. Competition is high, and the operators can be catty at times; but standards tend to be relatively high. Prices, although they have risen slightly with increased development on the island, are still among the cheapest in the world. Some operators to try include: **Alton's Dive Center** (✆ **504/2425-3704;** www.diveinutila.com), **Bay Islands College of Diving** ★ (✆ **504/2425-3291;** www.dive-utila.com), **Captain Morgan's Dive**

TOP FIVE dive sites IN UTILA

- **CJ's Drop Off:** Near Turtle Harbour, on the north side of the island, these dramatic coral cliffs sink about 5m (16 ft.) to 300m (984 ft.)—one of the biggest vertical drops in the entire Caribbean. The walls are teeming with sea life. There's a chance to see stingrays, moray eels, and hawksbill turtles.
- **Halliburton:** Sunk by divers, for divers. This large wreck, submerged in 30m (98 ft.) of water, is covered in brightly colored sponges and coral, including fireworms found on the deck. Moray eels are often seen around the hull of the ship, while groupers and barracudas can be seen all around it.
- **Stingray Point ★**: Two reef walls sprinkled with canyons and topped by a coral garden come together at this site on the western end of the island. Spotted eagle rays and stingrays can often be found in the sandy channels here. Large sea fans and soft coral plumes are particularly copious in the area.
- **The Maze:** This north-side site is defined by the wide canyon and a significant wall drop (40m/131 ft.). Elkhorn coral and star coral are matched in beauty by the variety of plant life, such as sea fans and rope sponges. The famous Willy's Hole, filled with glassy sweepers, is also found here.
- **Black Hills ★★**: Black Hills, a large seamount with steep drop offs, is about 1.5km (1 mile) off the south shore of Utila and home to a vibrant array of sea life such as hawksbill turtles, queen angelfish, thousands of blue and yellowtail wrasse, horse-eye jacks, sea horses, and spadefish. Sea fans, whips, gorgonians, and other sea plants litter the site.

Shop (✆ **504/2425-3349;** www.divingutila.com), **Deep Blue Divers** (✆ **504/2425-3211;** www.deepblueutila.com), **Utila Dive Center ★** (✆ **504/2425-3350;** www.utiladivecenter.com), and **Utopia Dive Village** (✆ **504/3344-9387;** www.utopiadivevillage.com).

Where to Stay

EXPENSIVE

Deep Blue ★ This award-winning PADI resort is, like all other upscale accommodations in Utila, west of Sandy Bay and can be reached only by boat. The 10 deluxe rooms, all in one main building, are clean and contemporary without being overly posh. They have hardwood floors, handmade wood furniture, and pleasant blue bedspreads and curtains, and feature art provided by Gunter Kordovsky, who runs Gunter's Driftwood gallery (see "Shopping," below) in town. Deep Blue, which has three great dive sites just off its shores, has long been one of the most respected dive operators on the island, and many of the guests here take advantage of all-inclusive dive packages. The resort is also heavily involved in the study of whale sharks, through its Whale Shark Research Project (see above for info).

W of Sandy Bay. **www.deepblueutila.com.** ✆ **504/2425-2015.** 10 units. 1-week dive packages from L22,800 ($1,200) per person based on double occupancy (high season); 1-week non-diver L20,900

($1,100). Rates include 3 meals per day & dives. MC, V. **Amenities:** Restaurant; bar. *In room:* A/C, fan, fridge, Wi-Fi (free).

Laguna Beach ★★ This 5.6-hectare (14-acre) luxury property, one of the few on the island, is just across the lagoon from Sandy Bay and is reached only by boat. Apart from one two-bedroom beach cabin, accommodations are in single- or double-room bungalows that sit on stilts on the mangrove-shrouded waterfront. The medium-sized bungalows were constructed using pine native to the island and have small porches over the water. The rooms are quite rustic, with simple furniture and no TVs, but there are other surprising extras, like a weekly beach BBQ and a whale shark–shaped pool. The property has a very communal atmosphere, and contact with other guests is common. Plus, there are an astounding nine boats, including a luxury yacht (the *Utila Aggressor*) that is available for excursions and cocktail parties. Their diving equipment is among the best on the island, and most who visit the resort come here on some sort of dive package.

W of Sandy Bay. www.utila.com. ✆ **504/2425-3239.** 20 units. L2,760 ($145) double (high season). 7-night all-inclusive dive packages start at L28,405 ($1,495) per person. MC, V. **Amenities:** Restaurant; bar; bicycles; Internet (free, in lobby); pool; kayaks. *In room:* A/C, fan.

Utopia Village ★★★ Utopia Village is a type of accommodation that's somewhat new to Utila: a stylish, boutique resort. It was created by a group of seven ex-pat friends who have combined their individual talents to create the first truly upscale boutique hotel on the island. Rooms are in one of two buildings and adorned with hardwood floors, contemporary furniture, and a decor that swings between Caribbean and Balinese. The overall feel of the beachfront property is hip and a tad New Age; but they don't go overboard, and the result is more than pleasant. They have quite a few extras that can keep you busy when you aren't underwater: kayaks, a pool table, sand volleyball court, corn hole (a bean bag game popular in the U.S.), and a TV room with a large DVD collection. One downside, or upside, is that the resort is a couple kilometers from town, and you can only get back and forth by a 20-minute boat ride.

W end of the island. www.utopiautila.com. ✆ **504/3344-9387.** 19 units. Diving, fishing & spa packages available. 7-night dive package (shoulder season) L22,952 ($1,208). $291 per person double (high season), minimum 4-night stay. MC, V. **Amenities:** Bar; spa. *In room:* A/C, fan, fridge, Wi-Fi (free).

MODERATE

Nightline Cabins (Jade Seahorse) ★★ 🎁 If Peter Pan came to Utila, this is where he would stay. The Nightline cabins at the Jade Seahorse are one of the most unique accommodations in all of Honduras—or Central America, for that matter. It's a wonderland of brightly colored mosaic tiles, leafy trees, plants, sculpture, and design. Every inch of the property is covered in some sort of whimsical decor or piece of art, mostly from flea market purchases in LA and markets in Central America. Each room is unique, utilizing bright colors and uncharacteristic layouts. All bathrooms have unique details, like curved glass walls and seashell soap trays. At night, the trees and walkways are lit up quite prettily for visitors to the restaurant and Treetanic bar.

Cola de Mico Rd. www.jadeseahorse.com. ✆ **504/2425-3270.** 6 units. L1,425 ($75) double. MC, V. **Amenities:** Restaurant; bar. *In room:* A/C, Wi-Fi (free).

Utila Lodge ★★ ☺ Sometimes just called the Lodge, this small hotel spread out on stilts over East Harbour has been a staple on the Utila dive scene for a few decades. The worn cabins, built entirely of island pine, are situated completely over the water, and all have screened-in porches where you can relax in a hammock and watch the sun sink into the harbor. Kids will appreciate the charts of underwater life and abundance of reference books everywhere *(or at least they should!)*. Accommodations are not luxurious, but it's clean, comfortable, and has all the modern amenities the high-end resorts on the west end of the island do. At the end of their huge dock, there's a Jacuzzi, a perfect way to end the day after a few dives. Many who stay here come in conjunction with the associated Bay Islands College of Diving, which sits next door. As a result, the lodge offers facilities to the entire dive community of Utila, including a 24-hour trauma center equipped with the island's only hyperbaric recompression chamber.

W of the municipal pier. www.utilalodge.com. ✆ **504/2425-3143.** 8 units. L3,021 ($159) non-diver double (Aug–Jan); L3,971 ($209) diver double (Feb–May). 7-night dive packages start at L18,981 ($999) per person, including 3 meals a day, dives & equipment, airport transfers & a bottle of wine. MC, V. **Amenities:** Restaurant; bar; Jacuzzi; fishing equipment; kayaks. *In room:* A/C, fan, TV, Wi-Fi (free).

INEXPENSIVE

Hotel Rose Let's face it: Hotel Rose isn't spectacular. The hallways and rooms feel like a small dentist's office in the bad part of town, and the furnishings leave something to be desired. However, for those on a budget—and to save cash for diving—it does the job. It's definitely rough around the edges, but compared to what else is out there at the same price, it is a good choice.

Main St., Utila. ✆ **504/2425-3127.** 11 units. L600 ($30) double. No credit cards. *In room:* A/C, fan, TV.

Mango Inn ★ In the budget to midrange category, the Mango Inn, tucked away on a busy corner on Cola de Mico Road, is without question the best option on the island. There are a variety of rooms spread around the leafy property, many of them facing the large pool area. The deluxe cabins were built in 2003 and have high ceilings, huge tiled showers, a small sitting room, and porch, while the less expensive rooms all have similar amenities but are slightly smaller and older. Last but far from least, the huge Mango Cottage, next door to the hotel, comes with a full kitchen and family room, screened veranda, two bedrooms, and fresh modern decor. Dive packages with two daily dives begin at L12,331 ($649) and are available via the Utila Dive Center, which has the same owners. They have a decent restaurant serving brick-oven pizza that shows nightly movies.

Cola de Mico Rd. www.mango-inn.com. ✆ **504/2425-3335.** 16 units. L950 ($50) double (June–Dec), L1,045 ($55) double (Jan–May); L1,710–L2,845 ($90–$150) deluxe cabins; L2,470–L2,945 ($130–$155) Mango Cottage. MC, V. **Amenities:** Restaurant; bar; pool; Wi-Fi (free). *In room:* A/C, fan, TV, fridge (in some).

Utila Lighthouse Utila Lighthouse is a traditional-style two-level Bay Island stilted house set over the water, on a quiet corner of town near the bridge to Bando Beach. Built in 2006 by a local family, the hotel still feels untouched, and the shiny wood floors and the flowered bed linens haven't seen much wear. The Lighthouse has a very simple, clean island style. A wraparound patio with ample seating and great views of the harbor and lagoon surrounds the entire building. There is little in the way of resort amenities, but all the dive centers, restaurants, and shops of East Harbour are within a short walk of the property.

About 10 min. to the R from the municipal pier, just before the bridge. www.utilalighthouse.com. ✆ **504/2425-3164.** 12 units. L950 ($50) double per night; L5,605 ($295) double per week. No credit cards. *In room:* A/C, fan, TV, fridge, kitchenette, Wi-Fi (free).

HOUSE OR CONDO rental ON UTILA

The increasing number of cabins and beach houses being built on Utila has led to a glut of properties that sit empty for much of the year. Some business-savvy individuals have turned to renting out their vacation homes while they are away. Most have cleaning services, full kitchens, and space for entire families. They may lack restaurants and a concierge, but make up for it with personal touches and great value. There are dozens of properties to choose from. Here are three that are recommended:

- **Island Life Tours** (✆ **504/9937-5437;** www.islandlifetours.com; L950–L2,280/$50–$120 per night, with discounts for week-long stays) rents out several properties on the cays and on the south shore of the island that are unbelievably inexpensive and quite charming. One sits underneath the Harbour House restaurant, while another on Rocks Cay sits on its own private little islet—with a walkway to the cay, a private dock, and BBQ area—and can sleep up to 10.
- **Laguna Vista** (✆ **504/3344-9545;** www.vrbo.com/229936; L2,850/$150 per night, with a 3-night minimum) is perhaps the most luxurious rental option on Utila, though it isn't right on the beach. The two-bedroom spread has a beautiful pool area with a Jacuzzi and your own thatched-roof party *champa.* Compared to a rental in, say, Florida or the Bahamas with these amenities, it's a steal.
- **Life's a Beach Villa** (✆ **504/2333-4139;** www.destinationutila.com; L4,750/$250 per day, L28,500/$1,500 per week) is a three-bedroom beachfront villa with 2½ baths. The contemporary house is Wi-Fi ready and pimped out with modern amenities like flat-screen LCD TVs, a speaker system, a Weber gas grill, and a wine refrigerator.

Shopping

Unlike Roatán, Utila offers next to nothing in the way of shopping outside of the basic necessities. **Dive Shack Utila** (✆ **504/2337-3252**), at Broussard's Plaza beside the municipal pier, has the largest selection of dive equipment on the island, both used and new. **Gunter's Driftwood Gallery** (✆ **504/2425-3113;** daily with sporadic hr.), 50m (164 ft.) west of Mango Inn, is more of a workshop than store, yet sells an impressive collection of wooden carvings designed mostly from found driftwood. **Bay Islands Originals** (no phone; daily 9am–noon, Mon–Fri 1–6pm), across from the Reef Cinema, seems like it got lost from the cruise ship terminal on Roatán. Still, it is the only decent gift shop on the island and the only place that sells beach items like towels, sunglasses, and bathing suits.

Where to Eat

Perhaps better than anywhere else in Honduras, Utila's selection of restaurants pulls off the party-friendly, international backpacker vibe. Full breakfasts of vegan food and fresh fish are on almost every menu, while happy hours often lead one into the next. Apart from the restaurants listed below, on the main drag, there are a few mainland women who sell *baleadas* ★ (L10/50¢), Honduras's favorite snack (a corn tortilla slathered with bean and cheese), and a taco stand.

MODERATE

El Picante ★★ MEXICAN This eye-catching yellow restaurant is the first thing you'll see when you arrive at the municipal pier. Because of its elevated position sticking out onto the harbor, there's probably not a better view of the water than from here, nor a better breeze. The menu is standard Mexican fare in heaping portions: quesadillas, enchiladas, fajitas, tacos. Sadly, no fish tacos, though.

Right from the municipal pier. ✆ **504/2424-3244.** www.elpicanteutila.com. Main courses L95–L190 ($5–$10). No credit cards. Wed–Sat 5–10pm; Sun 9am–noon.

Evelyn's BBQ ★ INTERNATIONAL From the slow, chatty waiters to the almost excessive Bob Marley and Jamaica memorabilia on the walls, this place exudes a definite island vibe. The BBQ dishes, mostly made on the streetside charcoal grill—blackened mahi-mahi, grilled shrimp, jerk chicken, and steaks—are well worth the price. When it rains, this creaky wooden building's streetside porch is the best place to watch the parade of tourists running through the mud, trying not to get wet.

Left from the municipal pier. No phone. Main courses L95–L230 ($5–$12). MC, V. Daily noon–10pm.

Harbour House ★★ INTERNATIONAL This multilevel pirate-themed bar on the Cay has become one of the best reasons to get out of East Harbour and is just a good place to break up the day if you're hanging out on Water Cay. The proprietor pieced together a recipe book from the Cay, dishes that may have been forgotten otherwise, and uses a few on the menu. There are fish burgers, beef burgers, grilled fish, and fish dishes of all sorts, as well as a full bar. For L150/$8, they'll give you a ride to the Cays at 11am, time for a quick tour, a delicious meal, and return you to Utila at 2pm.

Main pier, the Cay. ✆ **504/9937-5437.** www.harborhouseutila.com. Main courses L95–L230 ($5–$12). MC, V. Daily noon–10pm.

Jade Seahorse ★ CARIBBEAN/INTERNATIONAL This restaurant, set on the ground floor of the Nightline Cabins (see above), looks like your grandfather's tool shed after eating peyote. In keeping with the whimsical theme of the hotel, the restaurant is cluttered with woodcarvings, mosaics, ship wreckage, and whatever else can be hung on a wood beam. Thankfully, the food is not as off the wall, but dishes like their West Indian vegetarian chili or any of the seafood entrees slathered in coconut, citrus, or other creative sauces *are* delicious.

Cola de Mico Rd. ✆ **504/2425-3270.** www.jadeseahorse.com. Main courses L95–L180 ($5–$9). No credit cards. Daily 6–10pm.

La Piccola ITALIAN Sometimes called Kate's Italian Restaurant, La Piccola is an Italian restaurant that's actually run by Italians—and without question, it is the most elegant restaurant offering on Utila. Dining rooms are set around a candlelight patio and a leafy garden. Impressively, this restaurant suits any budget. They offer cheaper dishes aimed at budget travelers—a must on this island—like spaghetti with meat sauce, along with less backpacker-ish dishes like filet mignon, and red snapper in a pesto sauce. There's even a decent wine list, with bottles from South America and Europe.

Left from the municipal pier. ✆ **504/2425-3746.** Main courses L95–L290 ($5–$15). No credit cards. Wed–Sun 5–10pm.

INEXPENSIVE

Bundu Café and Bakery INTERNATIONAL/BREAKFAST Open for breakfast, lunch, and dinner, the Bundu is a top choice for hungry divers looking for a carbo-licious meal. Crepes, banana pancakes, and omelets are top breakfast items, while half-pound burgers, chicken salad and avocado wraps, and pizzas make up the lunch and dinner menus. A big plus is the huge book exchange here, the largest on the island, as well as the free Wi-Fi and full bar.

Left from the municipal pier. ✆ **504/2425-3557.** Main courses L60–L120 ($3–$6). No credit cards. Thurs–Mon 6am–10pm.

Driftwood Café ★ ☺ INTERNATIONAL This restaurant, reaching over the water in Sandy Bay, claims home-style Texas cooking as its line of attack, but the menu is actually more eclectic and well rounded. Beer-battered fish and chips, BBQ ribs and chicken, T-bone steaks, and one hell of a fish stick are all on offer. Sundays mean smoked brisket, along with a daylong happy hour. To start the night off right, try their Chilled Monkey Balls, a potent shot featuring house-made Kahlúa.

Left from the municipal pier, Sandy Bay. No phone. Main courses L75–L190 ($4–$10). No credit cards. Daily 8am–9:30pm.

Indian Wok ★ INDIAN/JAPANESE This little Canadian-run spot opened up in the alleyway between the main drag and Tranquila's. They serve up a little bit of everything from around Asia: curries, stir-fries, sushi, noodles, satay, and tandoori chicken. It's mostly made from scratch, but the wait isn't too long.

Left from the municipal pier, behind Tranquila's. ✆ **504/3320-6909.** Main courses L100–L200 ($5–$10). No credit cards. Daily noon–3pm & 6–10pm.

Munchies INTERNATIONAL Set in the Island House, which was built in 1864 and is the oldest building on Utila, this one's a crowd favorite for breakfast—they have several dozen options like breakfast burritos, granola, eggs, and bacon that are served all day long. Their ice cream and fruit shakes are a fine way to beat off the heat while watching passersby from the rickety wood porch.

Main St., Utila. ✆ **504/2425-3168.** Main courses L60–L120 ($3–$6). MC, V. Daily 7:30am–10pm.

La Pirata INTERNATIONAL This rooftop bar and grill just beside the municipal pier is on the third floor—one of the best lookout points in Utila. The menu is typical Utila: grilled snapper, garlic shrimp, ceviche, sandwiches, and chicken wings. The atmosphere is straight out of an American sports bar, with whatever game showing on the flat-screen TV. There are loads of large tables to hold any dive group, and the open sides allow the breeze to roll in. For a sunset drink or a nightcap after a big diving day, it's a good choice and worth the hike up the stairs.

Broussard Plaza. ✆ **504/4225-3114.** Main courses L80–L200 ($4–$10). No credit cards. Daily 8am–2pm & 5pm–3am.

Thompson's Bakery ★ BAKERY The best bakery in town with some of the cheapest snacks around, which are good to go. The most talked-about items are on the breakfast menu. You'll find pancakes, full Honduran breakfasts, coconut and banana bread, and their famous biscuit sandwiches with ham, egg, and cheese. While there is plenty of seating inside, the concrete floors and fans are unable to relieve the intoxicating heat of the ovens and sun.

Cola de Mico Rd. No phone. Main courses L20–L60 ($1–$3). No credit cards. Daily 6am–noon.

Ouch! Watch Out for Sand Flies

One thing the Bay Islands do not lack is sand flies, sometimes called no-see-ums. These pesky little gnat-like creatures, ⅓ the size of mosquitoes, bite and leave annoying little red bumps that you cannot help but itch. While some of the major resorts send their staff out to rake the sand, which kills sand fly eggs, much of the islands just have to deal with them, especially on Utila, where they are particularly fierce. There is no best repellent for these nasty buggers. Some recommend Cactus Juice Sun Cream or coconut oil, while others feel just regular bug spray works best.

Utila After Dark

On any given night of the week, East Harbour in Utila is one of the most happening spots in Honduras. Fueled by the dive crowd that often hits the bottle after stepping off the boat, you have a dozen happy hours to choose from. The night starts early and ends late. Apart from the spots listed below, most restaurants and a smattering of smaller watering holes make for lively places to grab a Monkey La-La or frosty beer.

Bar in the Bush On Wednesdays and Fridays, when everywhere else in town closes, the party moves up Cola de Mico road to this late-night bar. It's the closest thing to a discotheque on Utila. On any given night, you'll see DJs spinning the latest reggaeton and dance tracks to an already toasted crowd.

W of Cola de Mico Rd. No phone. Wed–Fri 9pm–late.

Treetanic Bar ★ This bar, fashioned after a shipwreck and set high in a cluster of mango trees at the Jade Seahorse (see above), easily makes for the most surreal setting in town. The nightly happy hour, from 5 to 6pm, has a loyal following of dive instructors and expats.

Cola de Mico Rd. ✆ **504/2425-3270.** www.jadeseahorse.com. Daily noon–3pm & 6–10pm.

Tranquila Bar ★ Tranquila is where the party usually starts for the night. Set on a wooden dock over the water just west of the pier on Main Street, the dive boats often pull right beside the bar when they are done for the day to pull off their flippers and replenish everyone's fluids. Happy hour is from 3 to 7pm. They serve a basic island menu here, as well.

Main St., Utila. No phone. Sun–Thurs 3pm–midnight; Fri & Sat 3pm–3am.

GUANAJA

It's a funny little place, Guanaja. In many ways, it's the forgotten Bay Island. Christopher Columbus landed here on July 30, 1502, during his fourth and final voyage to the Americas, but he didn't stay long. Over the next few centuries, the island became a favorite pirate hideout and was visited by everyone from Henry Morgan and Blackbeard to the Barbarossa brothers. Today, most locals base themselves around the small key Bonacca Cay, while the main island remains practically untouched apart from a few scattered settlements. The islanders, an amalgamation of culture if there ever was one, jump back and forth between Caribbean English and Spanish, and everyone seems to be related in some way.

Time is told in hurricanes by the roughly 10,000 or so residents here. In 1998, Hurricane Mitch's 483kmph (300-mph) winds blew over the island's once-dominant pine trees and knocked many of the stilted houses right off their stilts. Especially hard hit was Mangrove Bight, on the eastern end of the island, which was virtually wiped off the map. A decade later, while nearby Roatán and Utila are experiencing rampant development, Guanaja has seen very little. Hotels and restaurants close on a frequent basis, but then are bought by someone else and reopened. It's a constant cycle. There is frequent talk of large luxury resorts opening here, but so far, little action. Some development is occurring on the west end, mostly because North Americans and wealthy Hondurans are building vacation homes and a marina there, but for now, Guanaja remains one of the most unspoiled places in the Caribbean.

Essentials

GETTING THERE

BY AIR Guanaja's airstrip sits in the middle of the main island, across from Bonacca, beside a mangrove-lined canal. This is one of the most no-frills airports you will ever see, down to the baggage claim area, which is on the docks—bags are unloaded via rolling carts that come right from the plane. Once you have your luggage, you will need a boat transfer to your hotel (which should be able to arrange a boat for you) or a water taxi to Bonacca (which wait for arriving planes).

Just one airline makes the 30-minute trip on an almost daily basis between Guanaja and La Ceiba, with connections to Tegucigalpa and San Pedro Sula. **Aerolineas Sosa** (© **504/2453-4359**) makes the trip daily at 10am and 4pm. Air-taxi service **Lanhsa Airlines** (© **504/2442-1283;** www.lanhsa.com) also makes trips to and from La Ceiba and Roatán. Passengers can buy tickets at any of the airline offices on Bonacca, right near the taxi dock (you can't buy a ticket at Guanaja's airport). Keep in mind that all planes that land in Guanaja are small, averaging just 15 to 20 seats, so luggage restrictions often apply.

Charter flights are also available to/from Roatán and Utila, although these are quite expensive, and you will need to make arrangements well in advance. Try **Roatán Air Services** (© **504/2455-6879;** www.roatanair.com), based in Roatán, which operates two planes: a three-seat Cessna 172 and a six-seat Aero Commander 560. They'll take you to any of the other islands or even just take you in the air for aerial photography or sightseeing. Prices begin at L3,040 ($160) for 30 minutes in the Cessna. **Guanaja Air** (© **901/507-5297;** www.guanajaair.com) is another charter option and is the only operation based on Guanaja. They charge L3,705 ($195) per person each way (two-person min.).

BY FERRY Unlike Roatán and Utila, Guanaja lacks regular ferry service from the mainland. In 2007, a very slow, no-frills ferry service called the ***Bimini Breeze*** (© **504/2987-0875** for reservations) began between Trujillo and Guanaja, though it rarely runs. You can buy tickets directly on the boat for L650 ($34).

Occasionally, you can ask around on the docks of La Ceiba, Trujillo, and ports along the Mosquito Coast for transport to Guanaja via freighters, although expect to wait around for up to a few weeks.

GETTING AROUND

BY WATER TAXI Even though regular water-taxi service prices are quite high, because of the cost of fuel here, water taxis are one of the best ways to get around the island. Standard prices are listed at the airport and on the ferry dock at Bonacca town. You can generally flag down a taxi while waiting on any dock.

BY FERRY There is one regular ferry service from Bonacca to Savannah Bight on the Sava, which runs back and forth several times a day. This is by far the cheapest way to get around the island at about L20 ($1) each way.

ORIENTATION

Guanaja lies approximately 70km (43 miles) from the North Coast of Honduras and just 12km (7½ miles) east of Roatán. It is the tallest of the Bay Islands and is almost completely covered by hills. The western tip is cut off from the rest of the island by a small canal, "the Cut," running just beside the airport. Bonacca town, the center of nearly all services and the most populated part of the island, isn't actually on the main island, but is off a small cay hanging just off the south coast. There are no roads on the island except one small stretch that runs for just a few kilometers between the settlements of Savannah and Mangrove Bights, on the eastern end of the island.

VISITOR INFORMATION

Apart from the occasional shop that sells basic supplies, almost all facilities of any kind can be found in Bonacca town. The town's only cybercafe is on the main street turning left from the ferry dock, as is the bank **Banco Atlántida** (© **504/2453-4262**), which exchanges currency and traveler's checks, and several small pharmacies. For phone service, make a right from the docks to the **Hondutel** office (© **504/2455-1389**).

What to See & Do

Bonacca town ★★★, a short ride from the main island, is the most populous part of Guanaja and one of the most unique communities in the Bay Islands and the entire Caribbean. It's also known as Bonacca Cay, and by locals as simply the Cay. Though the vibe here remains refreshingly laidback, there's a desire to clean up and begin attracting more tourists to what many jokingly call the "Venice of Honduras." (In late 2007, Bonacca was completing one of its first municipal projects in years—adding plumbing.)

The population in Bonacca primarily comprises immigrants from the Cayman Islands who settled here in the 1830s, with a growing number of Latinos from the mainland and a scattering of expats. Apart from the many stilted pastel houses that branch out all across the water and line the canals, there are three small guesthouses, a couple of churches, and a handful of shops and tiny restaurants. The town is divided into small clusters with silly nicknames, like Firetown, Honkytown, Funkytown, and Vietnam. But perhaps because of its overall small size, Bonacca is an extremely tightly knit—and gossipy—place. If you're walking from one end to the other, someone on the other end will likely have already heard about you by the time you arrive.

Most hotels will give tours of Bonacca, but you can just as easily visit on your own. Locals, including New York–raised Hundo Sanders, give informal tours of the town for a small fee. You'll have to ask around town for info, as Hundo doesn't work out of a formal tour center.

Outdoor Activities

HIKING Being the most mountainous of the Bay Islands does have its advantages. Several kilometers of hiking trails can be found crisscrossing the tiny island, mostly

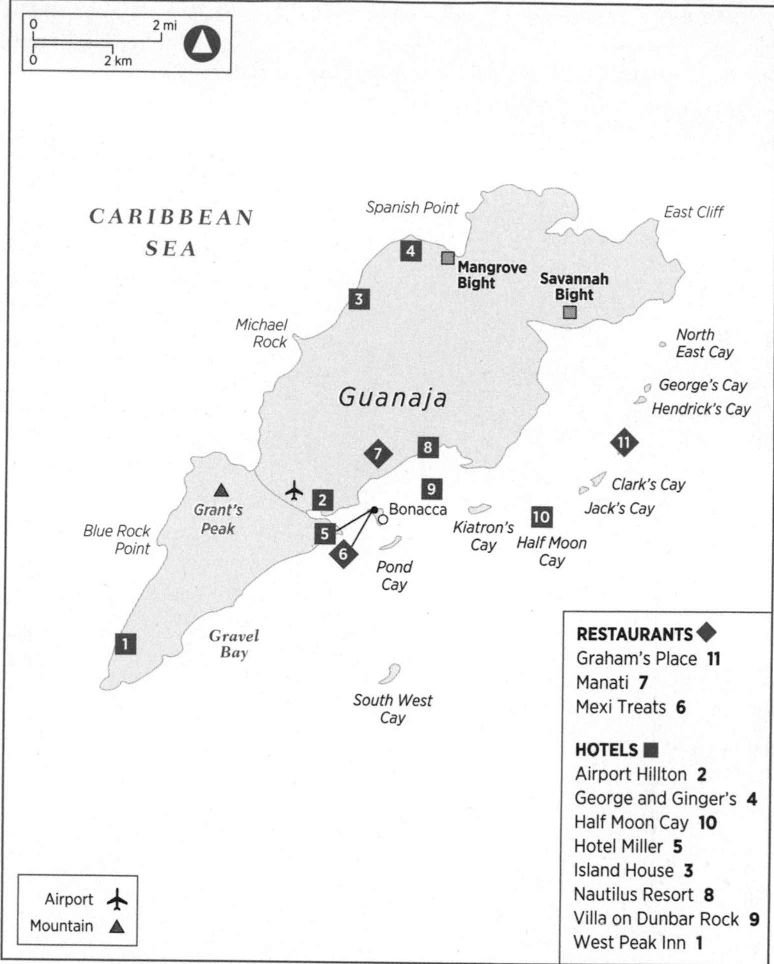

from the northern side. The **Big Gully Waterfall** is a short hike from Michael's Rock on the north side of the island, through fields of avocado, coco plums, and banana trees. The falls have a small pool at the bottom, but it isn't very deep unless there's a good rain the day before. From the falls, you can continue to the highest point on the island at 408m (1,339 ft.). Between the settlements of Mangrove and Savannah Bights, on the eastern end of the island, there's a small pre-Columbian ruin, one of the very few on the Bay Islands. Signs pointing it out are nonexistent, though, so you'll have to simply keep a look out for it or ask a local where it is.

SWIMMING If Caribbean crowds turn you off, but you still want crystal clear water and coral reefs, Guanaja is the place for you. Miles of sandy white beaches backdropped by untouched lush green hills are the island's specialty. The best beaches are at the northern side of the island near **Michael's Rock** or at the **West End** near the West Peak resort. Smaller strips of sand can be found elsewhere, including on the cays that are sprinkled about off the southern coast out from Savannah Bight.

SCUBA DIVING ★★ As with everywhere else in the Bay Islands, tourism in Guanaja is oriented towards diving. Every resort on Guanaja has dive masters and boats, and offers packages for divers by the week and sometimes month. The reef here isn't affected by the island runoff like in Utila and Roatán, but some damage has occurred from pollution from Bonacca and Savannah Bight. Still, Guanaja's reef is in pretty good shape and sees very few divers compared with the other islands. Every resort on the island has its own dive outfit and offers accommodation and dive packages. Diving without a room is generally more expensive and will cost about L760 to L950 ($40–$50) per tank. **Nautilus** (**© 952/2953-4124;** www.usdivetravel.com) offers dive packages and dives without accommodations.

FISHING Bone fishing is a popular activity in Guanaja and can be done just off shore all around the island. A world record for largest bonefish was set here not long ago. Every hotel can offer a trip. Deep-sea charters frequently troll for marlin, tuna, wahoo, mahi-mahi, mackerel, and barracuda. **Fly Fish Guanaja** (**© 970/708-0626;** www.flyfishguanaja.com) has all-inclusive 7-day saltwater fly-fishing trips from Roatán, including round-trip airfare, for L57,000 ($3,000).

KAYAKING California-based operator **Half Moon Bay Kayak Co.** (**© 650/773-6101**; www.hmbkayak.com) runs 8-day sea kayaking trips in Guanaja based at Graham's Place for L32,300 (from $1,700) per person, not including airfare. Trips are led by Doug Connor, who has operated Caribbean Kayak Adventures in Guanaja since 1998, and use a motorized support boat so kayakers can return to the lodge each night and start from a new location the following day. **West Peak Inn** (see below) also runs trips that begin and end at their cabins and camp on beaches the rest of the week.

Where to Stay

EXPENSIVE

Half Moon Cay ★★ It's not every day that you can rent out your own private island. Approximately 1.5km (1 mile) of paradisiacal white sandy beach and crystalline water surround the one elevated 160-sq.-m (1,722-sq.-ft.) main house, two smaller guest houses, more than 185 sq. m (1,991 sq. ft.) of wooden walkways and patios, and oodles of palm and pine trees that fill out the cay. Each building is made entirely of mahogany and features 3.5m (11-ft.) vaulted ceilings, full kitchens, dining rooms, and several bedrooms. The ambience is sort of a cross between *Lord of the Flies* and an elegant Old World explorer's club. The service staff do not live on the property but are at hand when needed. Rates do not include food and drink.

Half Moon Cay, Guanaja. www.halfmoonisland.com. No phone. 1 unit. L114,000 ($6,000) per night w/10-night min. (sleeps 8–10). MC, V. **Amenities:** Jacuzzi. *In room:* A/C.

Villa on Dunbar Rock ★★ Few hotels can lay claim to a setting so dramatic—this chic white house literally sits on Dunbar's Rock, a picturesque location off Sandy Bay that also happens to have caused much controversy—city officials sold this rock, a local landmark, to a hotel developer and were literally chased off Bonacca Cay as a result. The property itself resembles something better suited for the island of Capri or a Dalí painting than the Caribbean backwater. The four guest rooms are clean but fairly sparse and basic, with wood furniture, tile floors, and fans. Apart from the small

dive sites IN GUANAJA

- **Mestizo Reef:** The life-sized statue of Christopher Columbus at this site was erected in 2006 in honor of the 500-year anniversary of Columbus discovering Guanaja. There's also a statue of Lenca hero Lempira, Spanish canons, vases, and 16th-century relics.
- **Vertigo:** The drastic drop off—from 11m (36 ft.) to almost 48m (157 ft.)—on this section of the barrier wall is teeming with life. Black and white crinoids can be spotted here, along with deep-water gorgonians, barrel sponges, grouper, and trumpetfish.
- **Don Enrique Wreck:** This classic Guanaja dive centers on a sunken shrimp boat at about 27m (89 ft.) of water, although the mast stands upward to about 15m (49 ft.) below the surface. Lots of colorful fish circle the site, and spotted eagle rays are frequently seen.
- **Jado Trader Wreck:** This is one of Guanaja's most visited sites and one of the most talked-about wrecks in the Caribbean. The sunken freighter sits in 33m (108 ft.) of water on a sandy shelf beside a barrier wall. It's a deep descent, even for advanced divers, but the rewards—morays, grouper, yellowtail, and the occasional hammerhead shark—are well worth it.
- **Pinnacle:** Near the canal, the Pinnacle is a favorite among locals. The site, dominated by black coral, has a range between the sand bottom at 41m (135 ft.) to within 16m (52 ft.) of the surface and is frequently visited by schools of jacks and blue chromis.

deck that leads to the dock and a small garden, you are mostly limited to the inside of the hotel (which boasts an honor bar and dining room) and a few balconies.

Sandy Bay, Guanaja. www.villaondunbarrock.com. ✆ **504/9918-8855**. 4 units. L22,743 ($1,197) per person per week, which includes transport, meals, diving & fishing. No credit cards. **Amenities:** Dining room. *In room:* Fan, no phone.

MODERATE

George & Ginger's Clearwater Paradise ★ The latest small hotel to open on Guanaja is also one of the best. The three-level building on the north side is spotlessly clean, and the rooms are simple and sparse, with tile floors and unexciting decor. The friendly owners go out of their way to make you feel at home. Their three daily meals come highly recommended and use fruits and vegetables from their own garden.

N side of the main island. www.clearwaterparadise.com. ✆ **504/3303-7444.** 8 units. L17,100 ($900) per person per week. Rates include 3 meals per day & dives. MC, V. **Amenities:** Restaurant; bar; free airport transfers. *In room:* Fan, satellite TV, minifridge.

Island House This small wooden hotel on the northwestern side of the island is owned and operated by Bo Bush, a local islander descended from English pirates, and his family. Bush is a wealth of knowledge about the island and even gives informal bar hops and tours of Bonacca. The property has one main house and two small guesthouses, all set into the pine-covered hillside. Rooms have Spanish tile floors, simple wooden furniture, and balconies, as well as fans and satellite TV. There's good snorkeling and diving right off the beach, and you're free to use the hotel's kayaks to paddle around nearby Michael's Rock. The dock bar is a good gathering place for the few locals who live on this side of the island.

Michael's Rock, Guanaja. www.bosislandhouse.com. ✆ **504/2991-0913.** 5 units. 7-day dive packages L13,300 ($700). Rates include 3 meals per day & welcome cocktail. MC, V. **Amenities:** Restaurant; bar; free airport transfers; Internet (free, in lobby). *In room:* Fan, satellite TV.

Nautilus Resort There are seven rooms with A/C at Nautilus, which sits in Sandy Bay just across from Dunbar Rock on a wide stretch of white sandy beach. The resort has simple cabins and amenities, and is run by the same managers as the Villa at Dunbar Rock. Few who are not die-hard divers make it here, unless they are accompanying those who are.

Sandy Bay, Guanaja. www.guanajaproperties.com/hotel. ✆ **504/2453-4389.** 8 units. L18,905 ($995) per person per week w/diving. Rates include 3 meals per day & dives. MC, V. **Amenities:** Dining room. *In room:* A/C, no phone.

West Peak Inn On the very northwestern tip of Guanaja sits West Peak Inn, on 4.8km (3 miles) of pristine turquoise water and white sands. The property itself is quite small and laidback—if you like lots of noise and people, this isn't the place. The handful of wood buildings forms a small compound with a dock, restaurant, and storage rooms, along with the four solar-powered cabins. All have private bathrooms—the water doesn't get warm until the afternoon, though—and screened-in patios. They're all just off the beach, one of the best in all of Guanaja. There are a few trails through the banana, mango, and pineapple plantations that run up the hillsides for you to explore—plus, you can use their sit-on-top kayaks, snorkels, and fishing gear, if diving isn't your thing. They'll also run weeklong kayaking trips that begin and end at the hotel—you'll camp on beaches the rest of the time.

Closed for the Season

With most hotels being owned by expats who live on the property for only part of the year, sometimes business operations can be somewhat sporadic and often pass from one hand to the other year after year. Even many of the hotels in operation on Guanaja are listed as for sale by island realtors.

West End, Guanaja. www.vena.com/wpi. ✆ **504/3377-6114** or 831/786-0406 in the U.S. 4 units. L3,420 ($180) double w/3 meals per day & dock fishing. Children's discount available. **Amenities:** Restaurant; bar; free airport transfers; kayaks; snorkel gear. *In room:* Fan.

INEXPENSIVE

Airport Hillton No, not that Hilton: You won't find Paris and Nicky here, but the Airport Hillton does have the sort of charm that you could only find in Guanaja. The small three-room hotel, constructed in classic Bay Island style, sits in the isolated bay fronting the island's airport. The rooms aren't posh by any means but have private bathrooms, hot water, fans, and satellite TV. It's run by American Captain Al, who has lived on the islands for decades, and his son Andy. The Hillton also has an oceanfront bar and restaurant, and Captain Al operates the Thirst and Last Stop Bar/snack stand at the airport. If you need to charter a boat, he can help you out with that, as well.

Guanaja Airport. ✆ **504/2453-4469.** 3 units. L950 ($50) double. No credit cards. **Amenities:** Restaurant; bar. *In room:* Fan, satellite TV, no phone.

Hotel Miller There are three small guesthouses on Guanaja and other informal rooms for rent, but Hotel Miller is by far the best and the only one that actually attempts to appear like a working hotel. The two-story house sits smack dab in the middle of Bonacca town, a few minutes from the taxi dock. For the Bay Islands, the place is far from idyllic—it resembles grandma's house with its lace curtains and collection of beat-up Victorian furniture, rooms are dingy and worn, there's no ocean view, and not much light comes in from the small windows. Still, the place is clean, and the price is the best you will find anywhere in Guanaja. For those on extremely tight budgets, ask about the even cheaper rooms without TV or A/C.

Bonacca town, Guanaja. ✆ **504/2453-4527.** 29 units. L610 ($32) double. No credit cards. **Amenities:** Dining room; Internet in lobby (free). *In room:* A/C (in some), satellite TV (in some), no phone.

Where to Eat

Graham's Place ★ SEAFOOD On a small cay a short taxi ride away from Bonacca or Savannah Bight, Graham's Place is by far the most attractive restaurant in Guanaja, primarily because of its sweeping views of the main island, and it's also a major party location. The menu at the thatched-roof, open-air restaurant is defined by whatever's fresh in the cooler, mostly recently caught fish. It also features sandwiches, chicken, and meat dishes, along with a long list of tropical drinks and beers. The dock area where the restaurant resides functions as an aquarium of sorts, since there's a small pen keeping the tropical fish, stingrays, and sea turtles—bought so they wouldn't be eaten by the locals—from swimming away. The owner, Graham, who hails from the Cayman Islands, also has a few apartments for rent.

Graham's Cay, Guanaja. ✆ **305/2407-1568.** www.grahamsplacehonduras.com. Main courses L135-L300 ($7-$15). No credit cards. Daily 7am-10pm.

Manati GERMAN This German-run eatery in Sandy Bay is one of the best all-around restaurants anywhere on the island. They serve mostly German specialties like weiner schnitzel and even German beer, as well as grilled fish and typical island plates based on the latest catch. The place fills up on the weekends.

Sandy Bay, Guanaja. ✆ **504/2408-9830.** www.manati-hn.com. Main courses L115-L350 ($6-$18). No credit cards. Tues-Sun noon-10pm (hours may vary).

Mexi Treats MEXICAN The only Mexican or remotely Latin place on Guanaja is this favorite of hungry divers, who often stop here to refuel with lunch, and other tourists staying on the island. It's the only true fast food joint in the area, with a menu of *chilaquiles, baleadas,* nachos, burritos, and burgers. It's a bit of a dive, but for a cheap, hearty meal (and for fast food that doesn't seem mass produced) it's your best choice.

Bonacca. ✆ **504/2453-4170.** Main courses L55-L110 ($3-$6). No credit cards. Mon-Fri 8am-1:30pm & 6-9:30pm; Sat & Sun 6am-10pm.

LA MOSQUITIA

10

La Mosquitia is the largest tract of virgin tropical rainforest in Central America and the Northern Hemisphere; it's nothing less than a mini-Amazon. While it covers the entire northeastern part of the country, the region is only sparsely populated with villages of indigenous groups like the Pech, Tawahka, Garífuna, and Miskitos, as well as an increasing number of mainland mestizos. The region has five distinct natural zones: the Río Plátano Biosphere Reserve, the Tawahka Anthropological Reserve, the Patuca National Park, the Laguna de Caratasca Wildlife Refuge, and the Rus Rus Biological Reserve. Many of the zones are practically untouched and packed with rare wildlife of every imaginable sort. Yet there is not a luxury eco-lodge in sight. Apart from a few ingenious tour companies, the region is almost unexplored and just waiting for a tourist boom. If you are looking for an adventure or a place well off the beaten path, you've got it.

This region was inhabited as far back as 1000 B.C. by Chibcha-speaking Indians who migrated here from South America, which over time, split up into separate indigenous groups, such as the Pech and Tawahka. Christopher Columbus, the first European to visit, stopped briefly on his fourth voyage in 1502. Spanish missionaries were the first to explore the region, though it took them nearly a century of rebellion from the tribes to establish any sort of permanent settlement. (It didn't help that pirates frequently raided Spanish ships laden with riches from South America, which deterred further settlements.) Government control over the region has been loose, at best; it wasn't until the 1950s that any sort of formal governance began to take shape here, but at times, lawlessness still reigns supreme, as the region is too big and sparse to properly control.

While the tourist infrastructure is slowly improving in La Mosquitia, it is still relatively small and, in many cases, practically nonexistent. Phones are rare, which makes hotel reservations almost impossible, though there is always a room somewhere, even if it means a hammock in a family's hut. Transportation between each village, while the distances are relatively short, can take a day of waiting until a boat or plane fills up. Not all is bad, though; most of the towns are within the confines of the Río Plátano Biosphere Reserve or a short distance from it, so tours—either set up in advance with La Ruta Moskitia (www.larutamoskitia.com) or arranging a less formal one in the spur of the moment—are quite easy. Most visitors, unless on a multiday tour, will base themselves in Las Marías, Raista/Belén, or Brus Laguna, and take day tours from there.

Apart from Puerto Lempira, which is on the far corner of La Mosquitia and reached by plane, all towns are within a 30-minute to 6-hour boat ride from one another. When entering the region by land, nearly all visitors make the trip from west to east, so the villages are listed as such.

ESSENTIALS

Getting There

BY AIR All commercial flights to La Mosquitia originate in La Ceiba. **Aerolineas Sosa** (✆ **504/2433-6432;** www.aerolineasosahn.com) flies to Brus Laguna three times per week, leaving at 10am and returning at 11am, as well as to Puerto Lempira. **Lanhsa Airlines** (✆ **504/2442-1283;** www.lanhsa.com) also flies to Puerto Lempira on a semi-regular basis from La Ceiba. Flights are often canceled due to weather and lack of passengers. **Sami Airlines** (✆ **504/2442-2565** in La Ceiba or 504/2433-8031 in Brus Laguna) occasionally flies from La Ceiba to Brus Laguna or Belén. The runway at Palacios, which was once the main access point in the region, is currently closed due to lack of repair and most likely won't open anytime soon.

BY BOAT Along the North Coast of Honduras, irregular boat service links the coast of La Mosquitia to the rest of the country. The docks at **Puerto Castilla** just beyond Trujillo are the best place to get word of the next boat, which generally leave at least once per week. Don't expect a luxury cruise, though; these are cargo ships with absolutely no facilities for travelers. You are pretty much stuck with sleeping on the deck in the open air and having to provide your own food.

BY BUS It is possible to make it to La Mosquitia by bus, although if your plan is to go during the rainy season (Oct–Jan), don't expect this to always work. From **Tocoa,** just south of Trujillo, you can catch a pickup truck, or *paila,* to Batalla leaving from the municipal market daily between 7 and 11am. The ride is 4 to 5 hours and costs L400. In Batalla, there will be boats waiting to take you the additional 1- to 2-hour journey to Palacios, Raista, and Belén for roughly L200.

Getting Around

BY BOAT Traveling independently in La Mosquitia isn't cheap or easy—it's much easier to get around here with a tour operator. Though options are still extremely limited and you should always expect to wait around a few days here and there, your best method of independent transport is by water. Along the coast, you can almost always find a boat to take you from one community to the next. Often, the locals expect tourists to hire a local boatman for a private boat and will stay mum on information on when the next boat leaves.

Since regular schedules aren't posted, you just have to cross your fingers and hope you speak to the right person. There is sporadic yet direct boat service, priced per boat, between most major destinations, such as Palacios to Raista and Raista to Brus Laguna. If your Spanish is good, you can also ask around at the docks for *colectivo* boats, which are considerably cheaper but leave sometimes on a weekly basis.

BY AIR **Sami Airlines** (✆ **504/2442-2565** in La Ceiba or 504/2433-8031 in Brus Laguna) can get you from one town to the next via four-person planes. They have offices in Ahuas, Palacios, Belén, Brus Laguna, and Puerto Lempira. Keep in mind there are no scheduled flights here. When they fill up, a plane comes and leaves. Sometimes, a group will come together, and a flight can be set up in a matter of hours. Other times, you will have to wait for several days or even a week of maybes.

Tour Operators

If you have a limited amount of time or a set schedule for traveling in La Mosquitia, a trip with a tour operator is your only choice. Most have several tours available that

> **Small Bills**
>
> With not a bank between Trujillo and Puerto Lempira, it is best to bring all the lempira you will need—and then some—into La Mosquitia with you. Get rid of your big bills and come with as many small ones as you can. It will save you considerable trouble.

will combine multiday rafting trips down the Río Plátano or Río Patuca, visits to indigenous villages, wildlife watching, hiking, and stays at private campgrounds and lodges. They make use of planes and have arrangements with local transportation organizations to make sure your trip moves smoothly. Trips can last anywhere from 3 days to several weeks. Some operators to try include:

- **La Ruta Moskitia ★★★** (© **504/2443-1276;** www.larutamoskitia.com), a 100% community-owned and -operated tourism initiative, offers both day trips and tours from Raista, Belén, Plaplaya, Batalla, and Brus Laguna, as well as multiday tours through the region that have been applauded by the international media. Both land- and air-based tours are available. They list on their website upcoming tours that you can join (thus reducing the price by being in a group) and offer tips to help plan an independent adventure. Check their website for the latest news and updates in the region.
- **La Moskitia Ecoaventuras ★** (© **504/2440-2124;** www.lamoskitiaecoaventuras.com) has 8- to 12-day rafting expeditions on the Tawahka Asangni Biosphere Reserve and custom bird-watching tours throughout La Mosquitia. Owned by naturalist Jorge Salaverri, they run the most frequent rafting trips, roughly one per month, down the Río Plátano.
- **Omega Tours** (© **504/2440-0334;** www.omegatours.info) has a wide variety of tours from La Ceiba to La Mosquitia, including 8- to 12-day trips on the Río Patuca, a 13-day trip on the Río Plátano, and many shorter trips to see petroglyphs and isolated villages.
- **Mesoamerican Ecotourism Alliance/MEA** (© **800/682-0584**; www.travelwithmea.org) offers a handful of very specific, all-inclusive, multiday tours in La Moskitia, including bird-watching and rafting the Río Plátano, which can be paired with excursions in other parts of the country or Central America.

BATALLA

While it has always played second fiddle to nearby Palacios on the other side of Bacalar Lagoon, safety concerns and lack of tour opportunities there have finally given this lively Garífuna village a chance to be on the radar. They have been developing their own tourism programs with the help of La Ruta Moskitia and given a much-needed infusion of culture to this frontier area of La Mosquitia. Apart from hammocks strung in rustic family huts, there are no accommodations in Batalla. Most opt to stay in Palacios or head deeper into the region, while hanging out here for the day. The town is quite small. Just a cluster of small houses and huts scattered out on a sandy bank.

Getting There & Getting Around

BY TRUCK & BOAT By road, you can reach Batalla from the town of Tocoa by *paila,* or pickup truck (L500). Trucks leave from the municipal market in Tocoa (not far from Trujillo), at around 7am to noon for the 5-hour ride, though if you want to continue on to Raista/Belén, you will want to get on the first truck. There is usually one stop along the way at a simple *comedor.*

From Batalla, you can catch the *colectivo* boat for the 1- or 2-hour ride—depending on water levels and if rafts are needed—to Palacios (L250), where boat service to other parts of La Mosquitia can be found.

What to See & Do

Outside of watching the local women make casaba bread, there are two tours the community has set up for travelers; these can be arranged on arrival, though it is better to set them up ahead with La Ruta Moskitia. The first is a 2-hour cultural activity that takes place in the evening, where the 20-odd-member village folkloric dance and drum group perform **Garífuna songs and dances,** followed by a traditional Garífuna meal (generally seafood soup, and coconut and ginger bread).

The second, a **boat tour** in Laguna Bacalar, has long been the most popular tour out of Palacios, where it can be arranged, as well, though the guides tend to be more enthusiastic from Batalla. You'll travel by motorized canoe through canals through the mangrove forests that line the edges of the lagoon while looking for birds, monkeys (howler and white-face), and the highly endangered Caribbean manatee.

Prices for both activities are dependent on how many people will attend, though they are usually between L180 and L300 per person.

PALACIOS

The mixed mestizo and Miskito town of Palacios, the second largest settlement in La Mosquitia, sits on the opposite side of the Bacalar Lagoon from Batalla and is no longer the access point for travel in La Mosquitia. That honor has shifted to Brus Laguna and, more recently, Raista/Belén. This is partly because the town no longer has a landing strip, partly because regular flights to other parts of the region are now common, and partly because of safety concerns. Drug runners coming from South America often hang out here, thus the city is becoming increasingly known for lawlessness. Still, for travelers entering La Mosquitia overland, it is often a necessary stop.

Getting There & Getting Around

Now that the airstrip has fallen into ruin and regularly scheduled flights go to Brus Laguna and Raista/Belén from La Ceiba, Palacios has been cut out of the picture for many travelers. However, for those on a budget, a trip here is still the cheapest way to get into La Mosquitia. With better connections to other points, you no longer need to hang around. You can arrive in the morning and be on your way out by the afternoon.

Most arrive here from Tocoa via Batalla (see above) in the morning and catch the connecting ***colectivo* boat** to Raista/Belén (L200; 2½ hr.). It is also possible to hire an *expreso* boat—ask around for Dona Anna Marmol to set something up—to take you to Raista/Belén (L800; 1½ hr.).

A new service between Palacios and Brus Laguna began in late 2008 and, at press time, was still up and running, and hopefully will continue service. The boat, the ***Miss Liseth*** (© **504/9762-5846;** L400), owned and operated by Miguel Guzman, departs Brus Laguna at 2:30am on Monday, Wednesday, and Friday and arrives at 5am. The boat departs for the return to Brus Laguna at 4pm and arrives at 7pm.

What to See & Do

As tourism efforts shift to Batalla, there is even less to do in Palacios than in years past. As long as you have low expectations, you will survive. The town's one attraction, the Río Plátano **Biosphere Museum** on the main drag, has basic displays with facts on the reserve, but was shuttered at last check.

Where to Stay & Eat

There are a few basic hotels in Palacios, such as **Hotel Moskitia** (**© 504/2978-7397;** L400 double) that has a small restaurant and 10 rooms with private bathrooms, fans, and TVs. Slightly larger and more rustic, the **Hotel Río Tinto** (**© 504/2966-6465;** L150) on the waterfront has 15 rooms with private bathrooms and a simple *comedor.*

LAGUNA DE IBANS

Surrounding Laguna de Ibans are a collection of Miskito and Garífuna villages that are increasingly becoming the focus of tourism in La Mosquitia and the main access point for trips to Las Marías and beyond.

> **Quote**
>
> **"Now I'm hiding in Honduras. I'm a desperate man. Send lawyers, guns, and money. The s*#! has hit the fan."**
>
> **—Warren Zevon, "Lawyers, Guns and Money"**

Plaplaya

This Garífuna village at the western edge of the Laguna de Ibans and the Caribbean is best known for creating the Sea Turtle Conservation Project, which protects the green, loggerhead, and leatherback turtles that nest on the nearby beaches every year. Tours for the beaches depart during the evenings from February to September to help spot egg-laying turtles and nests. There are just a few very basic accommodations and *comedores,* all in family homes, in Plaplaya.

GETTING THERE & GETTING AROUND

The boat between Raista/Belén and Palacios will stop in Plaplaya, though be sure to tell the boat driver ahead of time. Pickup trucks also drive to Raista/Belén on occasion.

WHAT TO SEE & DO

Like in Batalla (see above), if you have a group together, you can arrange a Garífuna cultural night with a traditional meal. More unique to Plaplaya, though, is a seasonal grassroots conservation project. From April to July, the village becomes involved with the **Sea Turtle Conservation Project ★★**. With the help of volunteers, everyone joins together to help protect the loggerhead and leatherback turtles that nest on Plaplaya's beaches annually. Duties involve collecting the eggs, which hatch 3 months later, and reburying them in a protected sanctuary before poachers and animals get to them. Ask in town for Dona Patrocinia for more information.

Cocobila

This mostly Garífuna community of Cocobila, a sort of extension of Raista/Belén to the west, is a quiet village full of shady trees, friendly faces, and wooden houses painted in bright pastel colors. While there are no tours here to speak of, the people rarely see any visitors and love to chat with them when they come.

Pickup trucks running between Plaplaya and Belén will stop here along the one road that runs through the center of the land strip, though you can easily walk here in about 45 minutes.

Raista/Belén ★★

These two connected Miskito towns sit on a thin strip of land between the Laguna de Ibas and the Caribbean. If it weren't for the grassy airstrip, often used for soccer games or grazing horses, you wouldn't realize you had left one town and entered the next. Both places are extremely laidback and undeniably pleasant. Flowering bushes and fruit trees decorate the colored little plank-board houses with neat little yards. They are carved out of the fields, mangroves, and forests, and connected by a web of footpaths and one sandy road that runs parallel to the beach. Raista is slightly more compact and has a greater concentration of trees and shade than Belén. A growing number of tour options, proximity to Las Marías, a steady number of incoming flights, and better boat traffic have recently made these tiny villages the center of tourism in La Mosquitia.

Facilities here are still quite rustic. Electricity runs only part of the day and via personal generators at some houses at other times. There are just a few basic *comedores* and little shops with basic supplies, all of which are run out of family homes.

GETTING THERE & GETTING AROUND

BY BOAT To hire a boatman to take you elsewhere in La Mosquitia, ask the Bodden family in Raista at **Raista Ecolodge** or Mario Miller in Belén at **Pawanka Beach Cabins.** Prices—while they fluctuate, often depending on gas prices—at last check were: Raista/Belén to Palacios (L800; 1½ hr.), to Las Marías (L4,000 roundtrip with a 3-day wait; 5 hr.), and to Brus Laguna (L1,500 for 1–4 people; 2 hr.).

There is also a ***colectivo* boat** (L250; 2 hr.) that leaves almost daily from Río Plátano, a small town where the river meets the ocean, to Brus Laguna. You'll have to catch an early-morning pickup from the main road in Raista/Belén or walk for 2 hours to get to Río Plátano for the departure. Speak with Melissa Bodden at Raista Ecolodge for details.

BY AIR **Sami Airlines** (✆ **504/2433-8031**) has sporadic flights to/from Belén to Brus Laguna, La Ceiba, and elsewhere in La Mosquitia. When there are enough passengers, a plane comes. It's as simple as that. Sometimes, you can wait a week, other times, just a day or two. The Sami Airline office sits right off the runway in Belén.

WHAT TO SEE & DO

While they are rarely used, apart from walking by the locals, the seemingly endless, sand-dollar-rich, wide white-sand **beaches** that run nearly the entire length of the coast of La Mosquitia are one of the country's overlooked gems. There is practically no garbage here, apart from bits of driftwood and other rubbish that has washed up from other parts of the Caribbean. The water is warm, and you can spot the occasional dolphin passing by. Nowhere else in the entire Caribbean will you see this much unused beachfront. Sand flies and mosquitoes are a slight concern, though they are not nearly as bad as in the Bay Islands.

The most popular tour, especially for those not going to Las Marías, is to hire a boatman to take you to explore the wildlife-infested **creeks of Parú, Ilbila,** and **Banaka** (L1,500 for 1–3 people), where there are good opportunities to spot birds, deer, paca, and monkeys. There are even occasional reports of jaguar sightings, though don't hold your breath. There will be some leisure time to float on inner tubes, as well.

During the nighttime, a favorite excursion is to go **crocodile spotting** (L600 for 1–3 people) in the small canals and mangroves near Belén. In the early evening, you'll venture by boat armed with flashlights to search out the red-eye reflections of crocodiles and caimans. You'll likely spot plenty of bird life, too, during the 1- to 2-hour trip.

Like in nearby Garífuna villages, Raista/Belén loves to put on a show for visitors who set up the cultural activity ahead of time. During the night, a local women's group performs a series of **traditional Miskito songs and dances** (L850 per group), passed down from generation to generation. A traditional dinner is also served.

A very basic, 4- to 5-hour **jungle survival course** (L600 for 1–3 people) can be taken from Raista, as well. A local guide will teach how to find food and water, identify medicinal plants and teach you their uses, and explain how to find your way in the jungle.

Previously, there was the **Raista Butterfly Farm** at the Raista Ecolodge, though at last visit, it was not operating.

For all activities, contact Melissa Bodden at **Raista Ecolodge** and Mario Miller at **Pawanka Beach Cabanas** before arrival. Prices are dependent on the number of participants.

WHERE TO STAY & EAT

On the very, extremely, utterly, remarkably rare occasion that the following two hotels are booked, there are a number of other small guesthouses or rooms in family homes that will not be. I recommend avoiding the small guesthouse beside the airstrip, however.

Raista Ecolodge ★★ Built in 2006 and run by the friendly Bodden family, who spearhead tourism in Raista, these eight cabins are the number-one choice for tour groups passing through, though few groups are large enough to fill the place. Built in a traditional style on stilts, with wood plank floors and walls, and a thatched roof, the spacious rooms have been covered in screen in the open spaces to keep the bugs out, though every bed (a single and a double in every room) is still topped with a mosquito net. Each room has a decent-sized private porch with a couple of hammocks. From all rooms, you are quite close to the lagoon, so the sounds of the birds and water should be more than enough to lull you away to sleep. There is no electricity in the cabins (there is in the family house for part of the day, along with a phone where you can make international calls), but they do provide candles and purified water. The cold-water bathrooms are shared, but the toilets are modern and kept clean. The excellent kitchen will prepare all meals for you (L50–L65). Melissa, who speaks some English, can arrange tours and help arrange transportation to anywhere in La Mosquitia.

Raista, lagoon side. www.larutamoskitia.com. ✆ **504/2408-4986.** 8 units. L200 single; L360 double. No credit cards. **Amenities:** Restaurant.

Pawanka Beach Cabañas A 10-minute walk past the airstrip bordering the beach, owner Mario Miller's three stilted *cabañas,* a stone's throw from the Caribbean, are the best accommodations in Belén. The property is isolated outside the central part of town near a small wetland area—you need to cross a creaky wooden bridge to get on the property. The rooms are of similar quality to those at the Raista Ecolodge, with beds with comfortable mattresses and mosquito nets, and shared modern bathrooms. There is no electricity on the property. Basic meals (L50–L65) are served out of the kitchen.

Belén, Caribbean side. www.larutamoskitia.com. ✆ **504/2433-8150.** 3 units. L200 single; L360 double. No credit cards. **Amenities:** Restaurant.

The Miskito

The origins of the Miskito culture are not entirely clear. Most have come to agree that the dark-skinned group is a mix of escaped slaves, pirates, and an unidentified indigenous group. Today, they inhabit much of the Mosquito Coast, as well as parts of Olancho and Nicaragua. They survive on subsistence farming, lobster diving, fishing, and sailing. Although some may claim otherwise, the Miskito culture was not named after the abundance of mosquitoes in the region, but rather from the word musket, which the British trained the group to use to help push the Spanish out of the region. The British influence is undeniable. About a quarter of their language derives from English, such as the word "kitchen," the days of the week, and the charming phrase "think you," as well as surnames such as Bodden, Wood, and Denson.

RESERVA DE LA BIOSFERA DEL RIO PLATANO ★★★

This is simply one of the most astounding natural reserves in the entire world. The Río Plátano Biosphere Reserve, named a UNESCO World Heritage site in 1980, is home to more than 525,000 hectares (1.3 million acres) of wetlands, beaches, pine savannahs, tropical forests, and rivers. Here, indigenous communities of the Pech and Miskito live much the way they have for hundreds of years. The reserve is home to some of the highest levels of biodiversity anywhere in the world, and nearly 400 species of birds have been recorded here, including great green and scarlet macaws, harpy eagles, jabirus, toucans, kingfishers, aplomado falcons, and numerous migratory species. The lagoons and rivers are home to manatees, southern river otters, caimans, and several rare species of sea turtle. On land, you'll find Baird's tapirs, jaguars, giant anteaters, spider monkeys, white-tailed deer, and white-lipped peccaries, among others. While extensive tourism infrastructure is lacking here, and there isn't even a visitor's center or park admission fee, community-based ecotourism programs are steadily growing in Las Marías and Raista/Belén.

It's easiest to visit the reserve via a guided tour, though coming on your own is not unrealistic. The easiest way is to make your way to Las Marías or Brus Laguna, both inside the northern end of the park, where you can find lodging and arrange for tours deeper into the wilderness. To get the most out of the reserve and increase your chances to see wildlife, a rafting trip down the Río Plátano (see "Rafting Down the Río Plátano," below) is a must. The best time to visit is during the dry seasons, which run from February to May and from August to November. The rainy season, from November to January, can sometimes make travel here difficult. Regardless of when you come, there is little chance you will not encounter a short downpour.

Las Marías ★★

Las Marías is, traditionally, a Pech community on the Río Plátano, near the highlands of the rainforest. It is the village farthest into the biosphere reserve from the coast and the base for most to explore the reserve. Community-based tourism programs, with the help of international NGOs, have created more than 150 trained workers in tourism (124 secondary guides, 24 primary guides, and 7 naturalists) out of 106 Pech and Miskito—roughly 50/50—families. A variety of tours exploring the wilderness, hikes to several nearby peaks, wildlife watching, and community-based programs and basic tourist facilities have helped make Las Marías one of the most successful cultural and natural conservation projects in all of Latin America.

One boat landing near several guesthouses, a couple of churches, a small *pulperia,* and a school clustered together in a general area mixed with patches of wilderness is often considered the village of Las Marías. That is half true. The term village is applied quite loosely here. There is not exactly a center of town, but rather clusters of thatched-roof wooden houses scattered along both sides of the sloping banks of the Río Plátano for several kilometers.

GETTING THERE

Las Marías is easiest reached by motorboat from Raista/Belén or Brus Laguna, though it can also be reached by rafting downriver from Olancho. The price isn't cheap: L4,000 round-trip per boat for the 5- or 6-hour ride from Raista, with a 3-day wait. The price is fixed, so there is no use bargaining.

WHAT TO SEE & DO

Since taking the path of tourism, Las Marías has not let a moment go to waste. Over the past few years, the community has been developing numerous new tours and hiking routes, all the while training guides and naturalists. They have become highly organized, as you will come to find out. Upon your arrival you will be approached by the *sacaguia,* a head guide elected every 6 months to be the go-to person for visiting groups and assigning guides to them. He will handle the money, arrange your tours and walk you through them, and answer any questions you might have. For every tour you book, the *sacaguia* will get a small coordination fee (L100) from the group. He'll also ask for a small donation for repairs and trail maintenance. It is not obligatory, but L50 to L100 is a nice gesture and definitely appreciated. Prices per tour depend on the number of guides required—which get a per-day fee multiplied by the number of guides. Primary guides receive L250 per day, while secondary guides receive L150 per day. At the end, a small tip (10% or so) is suggested. Keep in mind that these prices are per group and going towards a community that has chosen to preserve the wilderness around them, rather than tear it down.

The most popular tour is without a doubt the ***pipante* canoe ride to the Walpaulban Sirpi petroglyphs** (2–3 guides). The 1-day excursion involves traveling upriver from Las Marías for 1 to 2 hours to the famous ancient petroglyphs (see "The Lost Cities of the Rainforest," below) found carved into rocks right in the Río Plátano. Before arrival, you will stop at the entrance to the Cuyusca trail, and then hike for 1 to 2 hours to search for wildlife such as monkeys and toucans while walking and from a small observation tower. After lunch by the petroglyphs and a soak in the river to cool off, you'll return back to Las Marías.

A second set of petroglyphs, **Walpaulban Tara,** can also be visited on a 2-day trip (3 guides) that has a similar itinerary to Walpaulban Sirpi, which you will also see, but spends the night in a small *hospedaje* at the start of the trail and heads farther upriver the following day.

The most difficult hike, which is gaining in popularity, is to the jungle-clad, jagged point of **Pico Dama.** The 3-day round-trip hike (3 guides, plus canoe) begins 2 hours upriver at Quebrada Sulawala, where you will make your way across farmland and into unspoiled primary and secondary forests that climb the mountain. The path is often slick and muddy, so proper footwear is a must. You reach a simple cabin the first

rafting DOWN THE RÍO PLÁTANO ★★★

One of the most—if not *the* most—incredible journeys in all of Central America is a 10- to 14-day rafting trip down the most remote parts of the Río Plátano, sure to suit your adventure lust. You begin in the mountains of Olancho, just east of Catacamas, where you will likely camp the first night. Early the next morning, you'll load up all the gear on mules and trek over steep, often muddy hills and through mestizo farms for about 8 hours before reaching the headwaters of the river, where you will make camp. For the next 5 or 6 days, you will travel down the Plátano as it makes its way towards the Caribbean. Each night, you will stop at beaches and small clearings, and set up camp, and your guides will cook dinner over an open fire. At some campsites you can trek into the forests to see waterfalls, explore caves, and visit little-known archeological sites.

You'll paddle anywhere from 5 to 8 hours every day, at times through Class III–IV rapids. Massive, 2m-long (6½-ft.) green iguanas will drop from the trees and cannonball into the water as you go by because they are frightened of the raft—they rarely, if ever, come into contact with humans. Most who make this trip will not have another chance to get this close to rare wildlife in their lifetime, outside of a visit to a zoo. On one particularly rainy trip, I have seen with my own eyes: two enormous tapirs, several river otters, several snakes, an anteater, spider monkeys, howler monkeys, white-faced monkeys, a harpy eagle, dozens of macaws and toucans, kingfishers, herons, hummingbirds, toads, butterflies, and hundreds of other tropical creatures. This is on one trip! The isolation of the park has kept general human traffic at a minimum, thus retaining the abundance of wildlife. While the majority of visitors make it only as far as Las Marías, from where going upriver is impossible outside of a short distance, only a group or two come this way every month.

Likely on the seventh day, depending on the speed of the river and how hard you paddle, you will come to the **Walpaulban Sirpi** petroglyphs (and several other petroglyphs), a few hours above the Pech community of Las Marías, where you will spend the night. Some will stay here and hike to Pico Dama or do another excursion, while others will continue the next day by *pipante* to the coast and then transfer back to La Ceiba.

The price for a 10-day trip isn't cheap ($1,300–$1,500 per person), but you must consider it includes all food, guides, transportation in and out of La Mosquitia, and the *pipante* ride from Las Marías. If you head to Las Marías on your own on a shorter trip, there's a good chance you will spend half that price. Regardless, this is an adventure you are always going to remember, and you will feel satisfied knowing that few have ever gone the same path. The trip was named as one of *National Geographic*'s Top 50 Adventures of a Lifetime in 2006.

For those who have any fears on making the journey, I have seen a mother from New Jersey and her five kids, one just 5 years old, do the trip with ease.

Tours can be arranged in Las Marías or Brus Laguna.

evening, which you will make your base for the next 2 nights. On the second day, you will ascend through the lush jungle for 2 hours to the base of the peak. You'll have excellent prospects for spotting birds and mammals the entire time. You will be rewarded with a view of the treetops that will extend as far as the Caribbean. You'll return to camp that day and hike out to the river the next and back to Las Marías.

The 2-day hike (2 guides) to **Pico Baltimore** is another crowd favorite. It is slightly less difficult than the trip to Pico Dama, yet will give ample chances to spot wildlife while hiking to an impressive tract of primary and secondary forests. You'll leave right from Las Marías and sleep in a simple cabin at the base of the mountain. On the second day, you will wake up early to hike to the summit and return to Las Marías that afternoon.

Even easier is the 1-day hike (1 guide) to **Pico el Zapote.** For the best chance to see wildlife, leave as early as you are willing. You'll start from Las Marías and walk over relatively flat terrain, apart from the short but steep hike up the mountain. You'll be back in town by the afternoon.

The 2-day hike (3 guides, plus canoe) to Cerro Mico doesn't face any steep inclines, though it does cover a mix of flat and rolling terrain and is set mostly in thick jungle. After a *pipante* ride to the mouth of Quebrada Sulawala, you will follow the creek for a few hours, set up camp, and reach the top of the small Monkey Hill. As you suspect, there are good chances of spotting monkeys. You'll return to the Río Plátano by following another creek and be back to Las Marías by the early evening.

While you can arrange for a guided walk along the **Village Trail loop** (L250), this is one you can easily do on your own if you just want to walk and have no desire to learn about medicinal plants. From the boat landing, just follow the dirt footpath, passing Pulperia Yehimy, to the small airstrip that's overgrown with grass and weeds. Here, you'll find another guesthouse, school, and a small medical center. Continue across a little bridge, past two churches, and you will come back to the river. The entire walk should take only a couple of hours.

WHERE TO STAY

There are a half-dozen simple guesthouses in Las Marías, though the majority of visitors stay at the two on the river next to the boat landing. **Doña Rutilla** is the only place in town with a generator and a public telephone, and can accommodate the greatest number of visitors—20—in its six stilted, thatched-roof cabins. Each room has several beds, with a comfortable mattress and mosquito net. The toilet, like all others in town, is an outhouse with bucket flush. Meals can be prepared for a small fee. **Doña Justa** next door is quite similar, though the rooms are a bit bigger, have porches with hammocks, and overlook a nice flower garden. If either of these is full, you can follow the village trail to reach another three small guesthouses with similar facilities. Rooms run from L80 to L120 per person.

BRUS LAGUNA

Brus Laguna is a genuine frontier town, mostly Miskito, where horses outnumber cars in the small grid of dirt streets and it's surrounded by a sea of swamp, mangroves, and savannah. The town clusters around a few blocks close to the covered main pier, but urban sprawl has added a smattering of houses and cattle ranches as far as 5km (3 miles) out into the wilderness. Electricity runs only from 9am to noon and 6 to 9pm, though several shops and hotels have generators. With the most frequent air service from La Mosquitia to the rest of Honduras, Brus Laguna has become the most modern settlement in the region after Puerto Lempira, though let's not forget that it's still the back of beyond.

The inland town's namesake lagoon is the second largest lagoon in La Mosquitia. It was originally named Brewer's Lagoon, after the pirate "Bloody Brewer," who used the inlet as his hideout. The lagoon is quite unique in that during the rainy season, it

THE lost cities OF THE RAINFOREST

A few years after conquering the Aztecs, conquistador Hernán Cortés arrived in Trujillo and began searching for a lost city of gold called Hueitapalan. He heard tales of a city of white stones hidden deep in the jungle, though he never found it. Decades later, in 1544, the Bishop of Honduras Cristóbal de Pedraza wrote the King of Spain describing a white city in unexplored territory where, as his guides explained to him, the people ate on plates of gold.

The site is mentioned in ancient Toltec and Mayan texts as the origin of the deity Quetzalcoatl, who was said to have come from a race of white-skinned people and likely stood in northeastern Honduras, in what is now La Mosquitia. So far, no one has given any defining evidence or proof of the city existing, though dozens of pilots, Ewan McGregor, and other adventurers have gone searching. Some have even claimed to have found it—without proof—in the past century.

While Ciudad Blanca has remained elusive, hundreds of stone ruins have been uncovered across what is now the Río Plátano Biosphere Reserve. Most of the sites have been only glanced over by archeologists, and most agree there are hundreds if not thousands more sites yet to be discovered. The Walpaulban Sirpi petroglyphs, carved in rocks in the middle of the Río Plátano and dating back more than 1,000 years, are the most famous attraction thus far. Meaning "small written stone" in Pech, the carving shows what appears to be a monkey or figure moving across a bridge from left to right. It was believed to have been created by the ancestors of the Pech tribe, though no one has been able to say for sure.

Other petroglyphs, such as at Piedra Floreada and Walpaulban Tara, also reveal a mix of geometric shapes and figures, while some locations are made up of small mounds or cave dwellings. While archeologists are becoming increasingly aware of the importance of some of the tribes and civilizations that inhabited the jungles of La Mosquitia, the inaccessibility of the region has resulted in few significant studies and great stretches of the imagination.

is filled with fresh water as the Sigre, Twas, and Patuca rivers flow into it, but is filled with salt water the rest of the year.

Getting There

BY AIR **Aerolineas Sosa** (✆ **504/2433-6432;** www.aerolineasosa.com) flies to Brus Laguna three times per week from La Ceiba, leaving at 10am and returning at 11am. **Sami Airlines** (✆ **504/2433-8031**) has several flights a week to Raista/Belén and La Ceiba, as well as on occasion to Puerto Lempira and Ahuas.

Brus Laguna's small airstrip sits a few kilometers from the town center. Just follow the main drag straight through the fields and ranches. You can buy tickets for either airline at the general store just up from the pier, on the right. The owner will also give you a lift to the airstrip for L50, and he has radio contact with the pilots—who are never on time—for when they will land, so you won't have to wait around in the field.

BY BOAT Brus Laguna is the central point for boats to anywhere in La Mosquitia, though times and prices can still be sporadic. *Expreso* boats can be hired to go to Raista/Belén (L1,500 for 1–4 people; 2 hr.) and Las Marías (L5,000; 5–6 hr.; includes a 3-day wait). There is also a ***colectivo* boat** (L250; 2 hr.) that leaves almost daily from Brus Laguna to Barra Plátano, a small town where the river meets the ocean, and where you can walk for 2 hours to Raista/Belén.

Thanks to an increase—ever so slightly—in passenger traffic, two new boat services to/from Brus Laguna started in 2008, though let's cross our fingers that they stick around for awhile. The first is between Palacios and Brus Laguna on the ***Miss Liseth*** (© **504/9762-5846;** L400), owned and operated by Miguel Guzman. The boat departs from Brus Laguna at 2:30am on Monday, Wednesday, and Friday and arrives at 5am. It starts its return to Brus Laguna at 4pm and arrives at 7pm.

The second service was set to go to Ahuas—where connections to Puerto Lempira can be made—on a semi-regular basis at last visit, but prices and schedule were yet to be determined at press time. Ask at the General Store in Brus Laguna, or Dorkas or **Macoy Wood** (© **504/2433-8009**) for more information.

Visitor Information

The small **general store,** at the corner just up from the pier, is your one-stop shop for almost anything. Basic supplies, airline tickets, hotel information, simple meds, snacks, fishing tackle, money exchange, and transportation information are all found here.

There is a **Hondutel** on the main street where you can make international phone calls. A small shop beside Hotel Ciudad Blanca is the best **cybercafe** in town, and they can do international phone calls, as well.

What to See & Do

History buffs will appreciate a visit to the English fort on **Cannon Island.** In the 18th century, the island was used as a base to launch naval raids and to help defend the lagoon against the Spanish. The iron cannons, which give the island its name, still remain. In 1822, the island was occupied by several hundred Scottish settlers who were lured by a fellow Scot, Gregor Macgregor, to the promises of a new nation called the Territory of Poyais. When they arrived and discovered they had been misled and were expected to head into unconquered indigenous lands, they stayed put. After three-quarters of the settlers died of disease and other complications, they fled to British Belize. Macgregor escaped to Venezuela to set up other schemes. Ask any boatman in town or contact La Ruta Moskitia to arrange a trip (L250–L300) here.

Outdoor Activities

FISHING While cultural and wildlife tours are on the rise, **fishing** has always been the game in Brus Laguna. The abundance of snook, tarpon (sometimes as large as 90kg/198 lb.), and grouper has attracted elite anglers from all over the world to Brus Laguna, though the lack of proper facilities has led to a downturn. There was a proper lodge set up at Cannon Island for several years, and there was even talk of renovating; but so far, anglers will just have to stay in town. **Team Marin Fishing** (© **504/9987-0875;** www.teammarinhondurasfishing.com) runs the most frequent and serious tours (all-inclusive) in the lagoon, which includes fishing, all meals, round-trip airline tickets from La Ceiba, a local guide in La Ceiba, a local English-speaking fishing guide for all fishing excursions, boat transport, and airport transfers. Tours start at $889 per person, based on double occupancy, for a 3-night/4-day excursion. Team Marin also runs a unique 4-day jungle trip to the rarely visited Lalla Sanni ruins, at $517 per person.

KAYAKING, INNER TUBING, HORSEBACK RIDING Nearly every other tour in Brus Laguna can be set up with **La Ruta Moskitia** (www.laruta moskitia.com) or with Dorkas Wood (✆ **504/2443-8009**) at the **Yamari Savannah Cabañas.** One of the more relaxed options is to explore the creeks and lagoons deep in the pine savannah by **kayak or rubber inner tube.** Guides will point out the birds and other wildlife you pass by—which, unless you set out quite early, will be few. You can also ride through the savannah on **horseback,** even riding to and from the Yamari Cabañas.

Where to Stay & Eat

Hotel Ciudad Blanca ★ This new hotel, sometimes called Tawan Pihni (the Pech name), a few blocks from the center, finished construction in late 2008 and is by far the most modern and impressive hotel in Brus Laguna, which isn't saying much. It may lack character, but these kinds of amenities here in the middle of nowhere make up for it. Tile floors and white walls keep the cool feeling amid that god-awful heat, though if they ever get that pool in like they are planning, it would help considerably. All rooms have private bathrooms with reliable hot-water showers, A/C, and TVs. There are a couple of cheaper rooms that lack A/C.

R at the 2nd st. from the pier. ✆ **504/2433-8029**. 20 units. L350 single; L500 double. No credit cards. **Amenities:** Restaurant; Internet (30 min. free per day, in lobby). *In room:* A/C (in some), fan, TV.

Hotel La Estancia Still one of the better accommodations in Brus Laguna, the Hotel La Estancia, just left of the pier, is a step down from the new Ciudad Blanca, but still does the job if all you are looking for is a place to rest your head and keep cool. Bedspreads and decor, as well as the entire front facade, could use a facelift; but the property is kept clean, and a generator will keep that A/C pumping all day long. You'll catch more light and a bigger breeze from the rooms on the second level. Cheaper rooms can be had with shared bathrooms.

Waterfront, Brus Laguna. ✆ **504/2433-8043**. 12 units. L350 double. No credit cards. **Amenities:** Restaurant. *In room:* A/C, fan, TV.

They Were Probably Great Listeners

When Christopher Columbus reached La Mosquitia, the first European to do so just after stopping in Trujillo and Guanaja, he called the Mosquito Coast "La Costa de las Orejas," or the Coast of the Ears, because of a few Indians he encountered with long ears. Thankfully, this name never stuck.

Hotel Villa Bíosfera This is the place to go if, for some reason, everything else is full, which probably won't happen. The tin-roof hotel with a wraparound porch sits on stilts over the waterfront directly beside the main pier. Rooms are small and fit just the bed and small desk. They don't get much light—try to get #5, the Río Plátano room, which has two windows—and there is no generator to work the fan and lights, apart from regular electricity hours. For a midday nap, you can lie out on the hammocks and catch the best breeze in town off the canal.

Main St. ✆ **504/9919-9925**. 8 units. L200 single; L350 double. No credit cards. *In room:* Fan.

Yamari Savannah Cabañas ★★ If you dropped this place in the Amazon, the price would be 10 times as much, and there would be 30 rooms. This is a helluva deal for an authentic jungle experience. The Yamari cabins sit about an hour from town in an isolated setting in the heart of the pine savannah on the bank of a small canal. There are just three rooms, designed exactly like those at Pawanka in Belén. Each has four beds with mosquito netting and solar lighting. The small site restaurant dishes out local meals for reasonable rates (L80–L100). Friendly owners Dorkas and Macoy Wood can set up nighttime crocodile excursions, horseback riding, fishing, and other activities. Transportation to the property is not included in the price and runs, depending on the price of gas, about L200 to L250 per group each way. Be sure to reserve a room ahead of time, as the hotel generally is closed when there are no guests.

1 hr. from Brus Laguna. www.larutamoskitia.com. ✆ **504/2443-8009.** 3 units. L200 per person. No credit cards. **Amenities:** Restaurant.

Mapak Almuk ★ HONDURAN This small, tin-roof restaurant has the most regular operating hours in town, which still are not set in stone. Seating is scattered about on a half-dozen wooden tables and a small patio that looks over the main road. There is no menu; the woman who cooks and serves gives you the options for the day based on what they have fresh or frozen. Breakfast is a straightforward Catracho breakfast with rice, beans, plantains, cheese, and tortillas. The other meals are similar, but add fried chicken, fried fish, or beef. There's a full bar, too, the only one in town, and the place will stay open late if there is a customer.

Main St. No phone. Main courses L50–L100. No credit cards. Daily 8am–2pm & 6–9pm.

Merendero Emilia HONDURAN This small eatery, right in a family home, serves simple lunches and dinners. It's almost right across the street from Mapak Almuk and slightly cheaper, though you get what you pay for. Fried chicken is sometimes all they have.

Main St. No phone. Main courses L50. No credit cards. Daily noon–2pm & 6–9pm.

LAGUNA DE CARATASCA & EASTERN LA MOSQUITIA

The largest lagoon in La Mosquitia, Laguna de Caratasca, is on the far eastern edge of the country near the border with Nicaragua. The shallow lagoon is rich in fish, birds, and other wildlife, including manatees, and much of it, especially the adjoining lagoons and canals, has been only lightly explored.

The rest of the eastern region of Honduras's wildest territory is one of the most isolated and raw places in Central America. Rafting trips down the two longest rivers in the country, Río Coco and Río Patuca, which only a handful of people take every year, are one of the only ways to see much of the terrain. The last remaining Tawahka people are almost entirely contained in the region, mostly in the remote Reserva de la Bíosfera del Tawahka Asangni.

Puerto Lempira

Puerto Lempira, with a population hovering around 6,000, is the largest town in La Mosquitia and the capital of the Gracias a Dios department. A Parque Central and a decent range of facilities—including 24-hour electricity—give the feel of a town elsewhere in Honduras. From a tourism perspective, little is going on in Puerto Lempira at the moment, though the potential is there. In the 1980s, the CIA made Puerto Lempira, which is on the far eastern border, the base for their insurgency against the

Border Crossing: Leimus

While this border crossing into Nicaragua was once quite complicated, new roads have made it considerably easier. Every day at 7:30am, a single bus (L250) will depart from Parque Central in Puerto Lempira for the 4- to 5-hour ride to Leimus on the Río Coco, which doubles as the border. Buses return from Leimus at 7am and 4pm. After paying your L150 entry fee to get into Nicaragua, direct buses *should* be waiting for the 5-hour ride to Puerto Cabezas.

Sandinistas in nearby Nicaragua, though the latest influx of characters has been caused by cocaine smuggling from South America to the States.

GETTING THERE

BY AIR **Aerolineas Sosa** (© **504/2433-6432;** www.aerolineasosa.com) flies to Puerto Lempira Monday to Saturday from La Ceiba, leaving at 8am and returning at 11am. **Sami Airlines** (© **504/2433-6016**) has sporadic service—they'll go if there are enough passengers—to La Ceiba, Raista/Belén, Wampusirpi, and Ahuas. Both airlines have offices in town and at the airstrip, which is located about 20 minutes from the center walking. A taxi should run no more than L60.

VISITOR INFORMATION

The only bank in all of La Mosquitia, **Banco Atlántida** (next to Hotel Flores; Mon–Fri 8am–4:30pm and Sat 8:30–11:30am), may lack an ATM but will exchange traveler's checks and give cash advances on Visa cards. The **Hondutel,** just off the park, has the cheapest international phone calls. Several **cybercafes** can be found in town, though they tend to be slow and expensive (L20 per 15 min.).

There is a small **hospital** and **pharmacy** (© **504/2433-6978**) about 2km (1¼ miles) southwest from the center. Both are open 24 hours.

The **MOPAWI headquarters** (© **504/4233-6022;** www.mopawi.org) south of the dock has a small general store with maps and basic supplies. The organization heads development in nearby national parks and works closely with indigenous groups. They will also occasionally accept volunteers.

WHAT TO SEE & DO

While there is little to do in town—La Ruta Moskitia has yet to set up a local affiliation, though they are looking into it—there are several small, pleasant Miskito towns on different parts of the lagoon that can be visited for a day or two.

Mistruk, 18km (11 miles) south of Puerto Lempira, on the side of a sparkling clear freshwater lagoon, is the easiest option. A series of thatched-roof wooden bungalows (L400–L450) with private bathrooms and solar power, and fronting a relaxed beach, is a favorite of weekenders. You can get here by road from Puerto Lempira, turning right at the fork toward Mistruk, rather than Leimus and the border. A round-trip taxi here for the day will run you about L650, but you can easily rent a bike in town near the pier (L100–L150 per day) to get here in a few hours.

More isolated is **Kaukira,** which is reached only by boat from Puerto Lempira. There is a simple cabin there for visitors to rent (L100). There is excellent bird-watching, including frequent sightings of macaws. You can also walk to a nice beach in 20 minutes or so from the pier. A few villagers actually speak English here and can even set up hikes and multiday tours into the surrounding jungle. *Colectivo* boats (L100; 1½ hr.) leave Kaukira at 6am and return from Puerto Lempira's main pier around 10am, which make day trips all but impossible. You can hire an *expreso* boat for around L1,100, though few do.

WHERE TO STAY & EAT

Puerto Lempira hotels are focused toward the Honduran business traveler, not necessarily tourists. The best hotel in town, usually full, is **Los Pinares** (✆ **504/2433-6679;** L880 double), with A/C and TV in the rooms, a pool, and a generator for electricity. **Hotel Yu Baiwan** (✆ **504/2898-7653;** L500 double), a half-block from the pier, is the top choice in town, though not by much. It has nine clean rooms with private modern bathrooms, A/C, TVs, and the best restaurant in Puerto Lempira, Lakou Payaska. **El Gran Samaritino** (✆ **504/2433-6482;** L450 double), 1½ blocks to the west of the main street, is similar and has the same amenities, but the rooms are a bit dingy.

Ahuas

The Miskito village of Ahuas can be reached by boat from Brus Laguna and Puerto Lempira—although you could wait weeks for a transfer—and by Sami Airlines flights from Puerto Lempira. With around 1,500 people, it is the largest town on the Río Patuca and a center of missionary work in the region. The town is set back a kilometer from the river and is made up of a decent medical center, a few churches, and a small guesthouse. Previously, tourists would come here to explore the nearby Tawahka Asangni Reserve, but an airstrip farther upriver in Wampusirpi has mostly put an end to that.

Wampusirpi

Further upriver from Ahuas, Wampusirpi is the center of a few dozen small communities that pride themselves on their handicraft skills, particularly *tuno,* a type of craft designed from tree bark. While originally Tawahka, Miskitos escaping violence along the border near Puerto Lempira in the 1980s pushed the majority of them out. Apart from the airstrip, one extra rustic guesthouse, a Catholic mission, and a small health clinic, there are absolutely no facilities here. Most arrive by flights and boats from Puerto Lempira and other parts of the region in the hopes of heading farther upriver—ask in town when the next cargo boat will head to Krausirpi.

Reserva de la Bíosfera del Tawahka Asangni ★★

This isolated 230,000-hectare (568,342-acre) reserve, which borders Nicaragua, Olancho, and the Río Plátano Biosphere Reserve, was created in 1999 in the hopes of saving the last remaining home of the highly threatened Tawahka indigenous group who number under 1,000 and live in only a handful of communities here along the Patuca and Wampú rivers. They are the last of Honduras's indigenous groups to be contacted by the outside world and still live a life based on subsistence farming,

No Sumo Here

Miskito and Ladino tour guides often call the Tawahka people the *Sumo,* and the term is sometimes listed as such when identifying the indigenous group in guidebooks and other publications. The term is actually derogatory and was invented by the Miskitos for a group they considered to be inferior.

Drug Trade on the Rise in La Mosquitia

As the drug war in Mexico and South America spreads throughout Central America, La Mosquitia, in particular, has been affected greatly. The lack of police presence in the region has allowed shipments of drugs to pass freely. You'll occasionally see men with decked-out SUVs in otherwise poor communities and occasionally hear the sounds of small planes in the night. It is rare that the drug trade affects a passing tourist in the region. The dealers pretty much stick to themselves, and they aren't trying to peddle their goods to the local communities. Still, these types are best avoided, so stay away from the seedy discos and pubs that tend to attract them.

foraging, and hunting. The Tawahka are renowned throughout the country for their long dugout canoes—hollowed out of single pieces of mahogany—that can reach as much as 10m (33 ft.) in length. Few people here can read and write; most do speak Twank, their ancestral language, though Miskito terms are becoming more common.

There are a number of 100%-Tawahka communities nearby, including Krautara, Yapuwás, and Kamakasna. Krausirpi, although it has an increasing number of Miskito settlers, is the center of the reserve, and there is a distant hope that ecotourism initiatives, like the Pech have done in Las Marías, will take hold here.

Rafting trips from Catacamas down the Río Patuca will stop here and are the timeliest way of visiting the reserve. The trips may hang around for a few days and take brief tours to caves and archeological sites, and go on hikes in the rainforest. While you cannot reach Krausirpi by air, you can fly into Wampusirpi and cross your fingers there is a cargo boat heading upriver, as they sometimes do.

OLANCHO

11

Perhaps no region holds as much potential as Olancho, the wild, sometimes lawless cowboy country of Honduras that occupies nearly one-fifth of its total territory. Some of the best attractions in the entire country can be found here. Near Catacamas, you will find the increasingly popular Talgua Caves, a place where a few amateur spelunkers discovered a chamber filled with the remains of several hundred skeletons glowing with calcite that date back thousands of years.

In Sierra de Agalta National Park, whose mountains separate the country from the jungles of La Mosquitia, you can climb to the top of Pico La Picucha, one of the most difficult and untrodden treks in all of Honduras. The region is a place that the rest of the population has seemingly forgotten—even the largest city, Juticalpa, doesn't surpass 35,000 people, though little-known indigenous groups such as the Tolupan continue to make their home here. Raw and unspoiled, you'll find an abundance of unexplored mountains, bio-rich forests, and ecological reserves all within access of every major airport on the mainland.

In fact, the area has every reason to be hopeful. However, for the time being, Olancho is almost entirely ignored by most travelers and left out of many guidebooks because of a plethora of safety concerns and a poor series of roadways. While there is help on the horizon—a gradual paving of the highways and an increasing police presence—it is going to be a long time before you will see a Hilton here.

Like in La Mosquitia, scientists are discovering that history extends much further in Olancho than anyone had previously thought. The discoveries at Talgua have set off an investigation into the pre-Columbian cultures that date back more than 3,000 years and inhabited the plains of the region, which were important meeting points between indigenous ideas moving in both directions between the Americas. Dozens of small ruins have been found throughout the region, and Stone Age tools are frequently pulled up from building sites in the Belén neighborhood of Juticalpa.

Weather varies drastically here, as the region is the country's largest. The dry season runs from approximately February to April, but in the mountains and forests in the north of the region, a heavy downpour can occur at any time of year. The changing altitudes keep the temperature from getting out of control like on the coast. At night, especially if you are hiking in the mountains, be sure to bring a light jacket. During the month of April, fields are burned throughout Olancho, and the air quality tends to decrease drastically.

Keeping Safe in the Wild East

All is not roses in Olancho. There are dangers here that are slowly being addressed, or at the very least, acknowledged. While police presence can be seen throughout the region—expect to be stopped at roadblocks several times and asked for ID and registration—the region is not exactly under full government control. The road between La Unión and Olanchito has even become known as "El Camino de la Muerte," or Road of Death, because of the number of highway robberies that have occurred here.

That's not to say everyone who drives here will experience some sort of trouble. Most do not. I have driven the road myself and lived to write this book. However, you should take extreme caution when driving in this region. **Do not drive alone, do not stop to talk to anyone, and absolutely do not drive at night.** Most of the roads, including the highways, are unpaved, full of potholes, and prone to causing flat tires. A truck with four-wheel drive is a must in most parts of the region, especially when it rains, which is almost always. Drug traffic coming up through La Mosquitia from South America has been another issue in recent years, and corruption within the police force has even helped to enable it. I have heard unconfirmed reports of everything from small planes landing right on the highway to roadblocks only being held on the opposite side of the road during days a shipment might come through. As long as you stay away from any drug activity here, this shouldn't be a concern to travelers. Olanchanos are actually quite hospitable to foreign visitors and proud to show them around.

JUTICALPA

Juticalpa, the birthplace of former President Manuel Zelaya, was founded in the early to mid-16th century by Spanish settlers on the site of an unidentified Indian village and not far from another Spanish settlement of San Jorge de Olancho. It is the largest town in the region—the only one of any significant size, with about 34,000 residents—and is an unattractive collection of concrete buildings and uneven sidewalks. Juticalpa has one excellent restaurant; however, a much better selection of hotels exists in Catacamas a few kilometers up the road. If you are coming here and are not a Peace Corps worker, it is likely you've come for the assortment of natural sights just outside of town, such as Monumento Natural El Boquerón or Parque Nacional Sierra de Agalta.

Juticalpa is famous throughout the country for two culinary products: *Cuajada* and *Coyol* wine. *Cuajada* is a hard, salty cheese produced at area dairy farms; *Coyol* wine is the fermented sap of the Coyol palm, and is harvested in March and April and sold in plastic soda bottles.

Getting There

BY CAR & BUS Juticalpa, 170km (106 miles) northeast of Tegucigalpa, can be reached via the paved Hwy. 15 from the capital. Just east of the city is Hwy. 39, which connects with Corocito and Tocoa in the north, where you can transfer to CA 13 that runs along the North Coast to either Trujillo or La Ceiba.

Transportes Discovery/Aurora (© **504/2885-2237**) sends regular buses to Tegucigalpa (L100; 3 hr.) and Catacamas (L20; 45 min.) from 6am to 4pm at their terminal on the highway at the entrance to town, about 1km (½ mile) from the center. The main terminal, across the street, has local bus service to the North Coast and destinations throughout Olancho.

Visitor Information

Banco Atlántida, on the Parque Central, has the town's lone **ATM.** There are pharmacies and Internet cafes found all over town, while you can make long-distance calls at the **Hondutel** at 5a Avenidas and Calle 1a.

Where to Stay & Eat

Hotel Boquerón A few blocks outside of the center, on the outskirts of town, the Boquerón is the largest and most expensive hotel in Juticalpa, though it's not great. The pool is so-so, the bar tends to be loud until late, and the decor is beyond outdated. The rooms are rather large, though, and there's a pleasant garden area with a few places to sit, which at least make it an option.

Calle Guatemala, 5 blocks NW of Banco Occidental. ✆ **504/2785-3933.** 38 units. L900 double. Rates include breakfast. No credit cards. Free parking **Amenities:** Restaurant; bar; gym; pool. *In room:* A/C, TV Wi-Fi (free).

Hotel Honduras Hotel Honduras, 1 block from the park, is the next best option if the Posada del Centro is booked. The rooms are clean, have A/C, and aren't cramped like the remaining third-rate dives in Juticalpa. The biggest downside, apart from the decor or lack thereof, is that most of the rooms face the inner hallway and don't get much natural light.

4a Av. SE & Calle 4a. ✆ **504/2785-1331.** 12 units. L320 double. Rates include breakfast. No credit cards. **Amenities:** Internet in lobby (free). *In room:* A/C, TV.

Hotel Posada del Centro ★ The top dog in Juticalpa, the Posada del Centro is an exceptional value. Apart from having a full range of amenities, the entire facility is bright, clean, and modern. Rooms are big and have matching gray bedspreads and shiny tile floors. The decor is simple yet balanced. While from the price, you might not suspect it, the Posada feels like a real hotel and has a complete array of services. If you need a comfortable base for exploring nearby mountains and forests, you won't be disappointed.

Calle Perulapán & 8a Av. SO. ✆ **504/2785-3413.** 25 units. L765 double. Rates include breakfast. MC, V. **Amenities:** Restaurant; Internet in lobby (free). *In room:* A/C, TV.

Oregano ★★ ITALIAN Juticalpa is perhaps the last possible place you would expect one of the most creative kitchens in the country. Just a handful of chairs along a long bar fit in this shockingly narrow—1.8m (6 ft.) across—restaurant in the town center. Decor consists of soft white clouds painted on the blue ceiling like a Las Vegas casino and a collection of random foodie art framed on the wall. The menu, made up of an array of mostly eclectic Italian dishes, does not disappoint. The Caribbean chicken curry, which dumps a coconutty sauce over a breaded chicken breast, is my personal favorite, though their 8-oz. filets and *Gambery a la Parmesana* are also tempting. Thin-crust pizzas are made here, too, with an interesting selection of toppings like shrimp, anchovies, chorizo, ham, and olives.

2a Calle & Av. 8a NO. No phone. Main courses L120–L190. MC, V. Mon–Sat noon–3pm & 5–9pm.

Monumento Nacional El Boquerón ★

The 4,000 hectares (9,884 acres) of primary and secondary forests in this fine protected area hide within them two river canyons, one mountain, and several small farming communities. The park is the site of Olancho's original Spanish settlement, San Jorge de Olancho, until what locals claim was a volcanic eruption—though it was more likely a mudslide, as a volcano is nowhere in sight. This a great place to come for day hikes from either Catacamas or Juticalpa.

The entrance to El Boquerón is on the highway between Juticalpa and Catacamas, where the road crosses the Río Olancho at a small farming community also named El Boquerón. From here, trails follow one large loop, beginning by following the river north through the forest, past a few lush swimming holes, and into the canyon. The farther into the canyon you get, you will notice the trees and plants begin to become more tropical and the air more moist. The path crosses the river and moves uphill to the community of La Avispa. Total time so far is 3 hours.

From here, you can ask around for directions to the Caves of Tepezcuintle, about 30 minutes away, turn back to the highway, or continue the loop uphill to the beautiful and rarely visited cloud forest that surrounds the 1,433m (4,701-ft.) peak of Cerro

Agua Buena. More rewarding is to camp on this trail in order to be there in the early morning, when the toucans and quetzals are more likely to be seen. The trail continues downhill to the tiny village of El Bambú, from where it is a 45-minute hike along a dirt path back to the highway.

You can arrange for **guided hikes** (L120–L150 per day) here by visiting the **Turisol office** (✆ **504/2988-4666**) at the Hotel Honduras in Juticalpa or by asking around in the town of El Boquerón for informal guides.

CATACAMAS

Catacamas is what could be considered the cultural home of Olancho. Here, the roughhewn ways of the buckaroo and vast natural beauty of the region seem to intertwine. Here, the gun still rules, and during late-night revelry, bullets are sometimes fired into the air. Even the best bar in town, smack in front of the park, is called Vaqueros, aka Cowboys. This is literally where the paved road ends and where the wild frontier that stretches across the wide expanse of practically lawless jungle begins. While not firmly on the tourist trail, Catacamas is catching on.

There is little, scratch that, nothing to do in town, but Catacamas makes a good base for sights nearby. The mix of paved and dirt roads that run through the town hold several decent hotels, restaurants, gas stations, and banks that, if heading into the jungle, you won't see again for hundreds of kilometers. If you're feeling adventurous, Catacamas is also a jumping-off point for rafting trips through La Mosquitia (see p. 244).

Getting There

BY CAR & BUS Catacamas, the end of the road, is 40km (25 miles) past Juticalpa on the paved Hwy. 15. **Transportes Discovery/Aurora** (✆ **504/2899-4393**) has service every half-hour to Tegucigalpa (L120; 3½ hr.) and Juticalpa (L20; 45 min.) between 6am and 4pm at their terminal on the highway. To get anywhere else it is best to transfer in Juticalpa.

Visitor Information

The only **ATM** in town is at BGA bank, 2 blocks from Parque Central. There is a **Hondutel** a half-block east of the park, and several **cybercafes** are scattered around town.

What to See & Do

PARQUE NACIONAL SIERRA DE AGALTA ★★

The vast, untrammeled mountain range of Sierra de Agalta National Park contains one of the largest tracts of virgin cloud forests in all of Central America and forms the mountainous backbone of the country that separates most of the population from the jungles of La Mosquitia. The 27,000-hectare (66,718-acre) protected area is most often visited on short day hikes from Gualaco and Catacamas, or to see the Talgua caves, though a steady number of travelers make the 2- to 5-day trek to the heart of the reserve at Pico La Picucha, one of the most difficult and most rewarding hikes in the country.

Began in 1987, the park covers a range of climates and microclimates that hold a goldmine of biodiversity. Above 2,000m (6,562 ft.), you will find cloud forests pulsating with rare birdlife (400-plus species) and 61 species of mammals, such as monkeys, jaguars, and tapirs, that have yet to be frightened off by human traffic. Rare

> **Disappearing Waterfalls**
>
> **If you read in an old guidebook about the Chorros de Babilonia, a series of eight beautiful waterfalls that drop a collective 150m (492 ft.), you won't find them. A controversial dam project has slowed the falls to nothing more than a trickle.**

plant life, including a dwarf forest, waits at every turn. Trails are not well marked here, however, so hiring a guide for hikes is a must.

There are two main entrances to the park: one at the Cuevas de Talgua near Catacamas and the other on the complete other side of the mountains near Gualaco. The Catacamas entrance (see "La Cueva de Talgua," below) is newer, shorter, and quickly becoming the more visited of the two. Improvements to the trails here are ongoing. From the Gualaco side, the trail starts about 16km (10 miles) north of town near the town of El Pacayal—look for a small sign that reads "Sendero La Picucha."

PICO LA PICUCHA

One of the most challenging and fascinating treks in Honduras, the climb to 2,354m (7,723-ft.) **Pico La Picucha ★★★**, brings you face to face with one of the most unspoiled cloud forests anywhere. You'll likely spot many brightly colored hummingbirds, toucans, a few monkeys—howler, spider, or white-face—and with luck, even a tapir or jaguar. There are only a few simple shelters but no villages to stop and buy food, so carrying sufficient supplies and equipment is a necessity. There are clean streams throughout the trip to fill up water bottles, though.

The route can be climbed from either the Catacamas or Gualaco entrances. From Catacamas, the hike is steeper, yet you can reach the summit and back in 2 days. The Gualaco route takes 3 to 5 days but gives you more time to enjoy the forest and search for wildlife. Plus, it is a bit easier. As mentioned above, hiring a guide is essential. Tour agencies in La Ceiba, including **La Moskitia Ecoaventuras** (**✆ 504/2550-2124;** www.lamoskitiaecoaventuras.com) can arrange multiple-day hikes here with food and transportation, including to La Picucha. For lower fees (L200–L250 per day), you can ask around at La Comedor Sharon in Gualaco for local guides who are no less knowledgeable on the trails and wildlife.

LA CUEVA DE TALGUA

This might be a big disappointment to some—it was to me—but I think it is best to get it out of the way immediately: you can't see the skulls in the so-called "Cave of the Glowing Skulls." The part of the cave where the skulls are stuck in calcite is blocked off behind a locked gate, so there is no getting by it. You can't even bribe the guides. Forget I said that.

Anyway, the 30-minute guided walk through the cave—which is intersected by metal walkways, rails, electric lighting, and geological formations—is average compared with other caves in the country and often is filled with noisy school kids. Still, you cannot deny the link to history this cave has and the allure of the sheer mystery that surrounds it. The trained guides give a detailed account of the discovery and the latest in the archeological research on the site, along with pointing out the more interesting stalactites and stalagmites.

The Cave of the Glowing Skulls

George Lucas couldn't have written up a story like this. Err, wait. Tales of crystal skulls of Mesoamerican origin have long been a common theme in adventure folklore. There have even been actual skulls found—including in Honduras—though most, if not all, of them have been proven frauds, depending on whom you speak to.

In April of 1994, a group of amateur spelunkers from the U.S. and Honduras inspected a small chamber while exploring an unmarked cave in Olancho. No one was prepared for what they would find. When they turned their flashlights into the chamber, dozens of glowing skeletons were staring back at them. Through radiocarbon dating the site has been traced to the Early to Middle Pre-Classic period, or, in human terms, about 850 to 1000 B.C. More than 20 skeletal deposits have been found in the cave, nearly all of them containing more than one skeleton and numbering more than 200 in total. The bones were painted in red pigment and later research determined that they had been carried to the cave in bundles.

Technically, the skulls are not glowing. Years of water dripping from the limestone roof have cemented them onto the cave in a thick layer of calcite, which has made the bones difficult to remove and study. When a light is shone on the bones, the calcite reflects it. The discovery alerted archeologists who had previously focused all their attention in the Copán Valley and never suspected that an advanced society could have developed here. Further studies have revealed a village, not far from the cave entrance on the west bank of the Río Talgua, with the remains of more than 100 small structures that resemble others in southeastern Mesoamerica. It was likely that the people had formed a trade network with the Mayas, as jade and other objects have been discovered with the skeletons and at the village site.

Maybe even more appealing to the cave is the short walk through Sierra de Agalta National Park along the river and through the forest. There is a small site museum near the bathrooms with photos of the skulls, artifacts found in the caves, and information on the biodiversity found within the park.

To get to the caves you must drive about 4km (2½ miles) from town, continuing on the road from Juticalpa, which becomes a bit rougher, though was being paved at last visit. Look for signs for the turnoff that will take you on a very bumpy grass and mud road—if it rains, you will need four-wheel drive—towards the village of Guanaja. The site is just beyond the village. You can hire a **taxi** for about L300 round-trip or catch the 6, 11am, or 3pm **bus**—returning at 7am, noon, and 4pm—from Catacamas at Colonia Palmira (ask around in town). Cave admission is L120, which includes a guide. The caves are open Tuesday through Sunday, from 9am to 4pm.

LAS CUEVAS DE SUSMAY

Although they are less developed and have no significant historical appeal like caves at Talgua, the Susmay caves are much more interesting to spelunkers. Prior spelunking experience and proper equipment are a must. The three main caves are best known as sand, dry, and water. The **water cave** ★ is the favorite. You'll need snorkel equipment to make your way through the deep underground river, filled with tiny black fish. Not far inside, you come to a large cavern with thousands of spooky black bats overhead. The other caves are connected, and all are unmarked. It is best to hire a guide in Gualaco or nearby villages to be safe. To reach the caves, you will need your own transportation. Head from Gualaco to the village of Las Joyas de Zacate and follow the trail across the creek and into the forests until coming to the cave.

Where to Stay & Eat

Hotel Juan Carlos If you have your own transportation and want to get an early start at the caves or Sierra de Agalta National Park, the Juan Carlos is a good choice. As these rooms are quite simple—clean tile floors, empty white walls, and a bed with a thin mattress—you'll find more comforting amenities at Papabeto.

Barrio San Jose, on the rd. to the Talgua Caves. ✆ **504/2899-4212.** hoteljuanc@yahoo.com. 30 units. L400 double. MC, V. Free parking. **Amenities:** Restaurant; bar. *In room:* A/C, fan, TV, Wi-Fi (free).

Hotel Meylling For the price, this is one of the best budget hotels in the country. There are few places where you will get this kind of value for less than an Andrew Jackson (that's a $20 bill for non-U.S. readers): spacious, clean rooms with cable TV, fans, A/C, and electric showers. It opened in 2003, but the two-level building still feels brand new thanks to the freshly painted walls and sparkling tile bathrooms. Decor is lacking, and the general plainness of everything isn't exactly a charm-fest—but for the price, what could you expect? This is as reliable a cheap hotel as you will find in Honduras.

2 blocks S of the park. ✆ **504/2899-1716.** 27 units. L400 double. No credit cards. Free parking. *In room:* A/C, fan, TV.

Hotel Papabeto ★ You might not suspect it from the name, but Papabeto looks like a small Ramada hotel in a U.S. suburb. It's not flashy, but it's sparkling clean, amenity-rich, and a great value. A walled courtyard features an inviting indoor pool with manicured gardens and a bar that's an especially nice retreat after a long hike. Rooms are cozy, a little boring, and modern, with bathrooms that are beyond clean. There's a full-service international restaurant, one of the most reliable options in town.

2 blocks E of the park. hotel_papabeto@yahoo.com. ✆ **504/2899-5006.** 10 units. L830 double. MC, V. Free parking. **Amenities:** Restaurant; bar; Internet (in lobby); pool. *In room:* A/C, TV, Wi-Fi (free).

GUALACO

The tiny blip of a town of Gualaco sits at the base of Sierra de Agalta National Park, right on the rough, unpaved Hwy. 39, about 2 hours from Juticalpa. The population survives on ranching and logging. Unless you are making an excursion into the park or just need a stop on the long, lonely highway, there is little reason to come here. Facilities are basic but comfortable enough after a 4-day hike until catching the next bus out.

Getting There

The easiest way in and out of Gualaco is through Juticalpa, from where you can catch transfer to Tegucigalpa and beyond. **Buses** (L50) depart from the traffic triangle from 6:30am to 4:30pm every day. To get to the North Coast, you can catch the afternoon bus to Trujillo (L100; sporadic times). If you want to get to La Ceiba or Tela, get off at Tocoa and transfer.

Horse Rage

While passing through Olancho, you might see an unusually high number of dead horses on the sides of the road. This isn't due to some tropical outbreak, but rather retaliation by drivers against ranchers who do not control their livestock. Horses on the road put drivers in danger, especially at night on the unlighted highway, so the armed drivers take action and kill the creatures. Sadly, this happens on a regular basis.

Where to Stay & Eat

There is a small selection of hotels and restaurants in town, all quite simple. **Hotel Mi Palacio** (**© 504/2989-9130;** L180 double), right at the triangle, was built in 2005 and still has that new feeling. They offer a dozen basic rooms with hot showers, TVs, and fans. To eat, try **Restaurante El Muelle** (no phone), also at the triangle, which dishes out set lunch and dinner plates—usually a choice of chicken or beef. **Comedor Sharon** (no phone), serves *típica* plates and can help you find guides to hike La Picucha.

EL CARBON

This Pech Indian village, one of just a few remaining in the entire country, sits on the Juticalpa–Tocoa Highway. There is a mix of thatched-roof adobe houses and newer constructions made out of concrete. There are no facilities to speak of, though travelers in the past have been able to rent rooms here. There are several excellent hikes through tropical and cloud forests, to several small peaks, pre-Columbian ruins, and various waterfalls and swimming holes not far from town that make for an interesting excursion. There are several guides in the village you can hire for multiday trips (there's often a Peace Corp volunteer in the village that can help with this); otherwise, inquire at **La Moskitia Ecoaventuras** (**© 504/2550-2124;** www.lamoskitiaecoaventuras.com) in La Ceiba.

LA UNION

La Unión is best known as a launching point for trips in Parque Nacional La Muralla (see below), but highway robberies on the roads into town have practically cut off the tourist trade completely. The village of 3,000 is quite safe on its own, and there are a few small guesthouses and *comedores,* none of them worth mentioning, to keep you with a roof over your head and a full belly.

Unless you're driving, getting here and away requires several transfers. From Tegucigalpa, go first to Juticalpa, and then catch either of the two daily **buses** (L80; 3½ hr.). From La Unión, you may be able to catch passing Tegus-bound buses from Sonaguera if you wait by the highway. For the North Coast, a 6:30am bus leaves for Olanchito (L80; 3½ hr.), where you can transfer to Trujillo (for La Ceiba, transfer at Mamé).

The Last of Los Tolupanes

Farther afield in the mountains, deep within the wilds of the Yoro and Olancho departments, you can find the Tolupan people. They have all but disappeared from the Honduran landscape, and the group numbers not much more than 1,000 people. They are believed to have descended from the Sioux tribe in the southwestern United States, though many argue that theory. They had once occupied a large portion of northern and eastern Honduras, though when they refused to convert to Catholicism during the arrival of the Spanish they were brutally enslaved and pushed to the fringes of the country, where they have remained to this day.

Parque Nacional La Muralla

La Muralla National Park ★, 14km (8¾ miles) from La Unión, was once the favorite park in all of Honduras, superbly maintained and frequently visited by foreign travelers. Now, with the visitor center closed and a history of highway robberies and deadly clashes between environmentalists and loggers, few make it here. It's a sad, sad story, and it seems all funds have now shifted north towards La Ceiba and Pico Bonito National Park. Travelers do still make it here on a regular basis, though—mostly hardcore birders for the quetzals, toucanets, and other species that inhabit the pine and cloud forests. While there are four trails that run through the park, none have been maintained in years; if you plan to hike, you'll need to bring a machete to chop your way through the overgrowth. When the park was up and running, there was a simple cabin at the visitor center, but it was locked at last check and showed no signs of being opened anytime soon. To reach the park from La Unión, hire a **taxi** (L400) for the uphill ride.

YORO

The Yoro department, bordering Olancho, centers on just one town, the unappealing village of Yoro. The few that do make it this way do have a good variety of facilities to choose from: a bank with an ATM, Hondutel, and a few hotels and restaurants. There are several interesting hikes to a nearby cloud forest, and Yoro is also the home of the famous *Lluvia de Peces,* or rain of fish (see below).

Yoro lays on the east-west Hwy. 23 that stretches across the center of Olancho. On the main road in town, buses go to and from San Pedro Sula (L90; 3½ hr.) every couple hours.

If you make it to Yoro during the middle of June, the annual shindig, the **Festival de la Lluvia de Peces,** is in full swing with parades, feasts, and dancing. ***Note:*** This is not the actual rain of fish. This occurs in late June/early July and is a bit difficult to predict.

What to See & Do

The 11,206-hectare (27,691-acre) reserve, **Parque Nacional Pico Pijol,** is yet another large tract of cloud forest with few to no facilities but an abundance of wildlife. The only way to visit the park is with a guide, which you can hire in Yoro (check with the tour office on Parque Central). Bird life, including plenty of quetzals, is the

THE RAIN OF fish

"Donde hay lluvia de peces cual milagro celestial," or, "Where there is rain of fish, like a heavenly miracle," goes the popular folk song *Conozca Honduras.* For more than a century, a strange phenomenon has been occurring in the El Pántano neighborhood of Yoro in late June and early July that has continually baffled scientists, has been quoted in a *CSI* episode, and was the subject of a National Geographic special. Once a year, after a period of heavy rain, villagers go outside to find hundreds of living fish flopping on the ground. The silver fish are about 13cm (5 in.) in length, and on report of their arrival, everyone rushes out with baskets to collect the creatures for the next meal. While there are many theories behind this phenomenon, no one has been able to come up with a definitive answer. The most common claim is that the fish swim up the Río Aguán from the Caribbean and, following a quick flood during a heavy storm, swim into the fields. When a sudden drop in pressure causes the fields to dry up, the fish are left to the dirt. Still, many tell a much different account that has been one of the staples of Honduran folklore. When Spanish Catholic missionary Manuel Subirana visited Honduras in the mid-19th century and encountered countless impoverished people, he prayed for 3 days and 3 nights. He asked God for a miracle and to help provide food for all. The next day, the fish appeared.

main lure to the park, so be sure to get there early in the morning. A machete is a must here, as you literally must chop your way through the forests, though you can occasionally find a hunting trail. To get there, you will need to first head to the village of Morazán near Santa Rita, where you can catch a bus or taxi to any of the small villages that sit within the boundaries of the park.

Where to Stay & Eat

Lodging and food in Yoro is quite basic, but it is sufficient for a night or two. Try **Hotel Palace Inn** (✆ **504/2671-2229;** www.hotelpalaceinn.blogspot.com; L250 double) on the main road for a clean room with private hot-water bathroom and free Wi-Fi. For lunch and dinner, I hope you like *típica,* because that is all there is in the few restaurants surrounding the Parque Central.

12 PLANNING YOUR TRIP TO HONDURAS

Sometimes, planning your trip can be almost as fun as the trip itself. You can read up on all the things you can do. You can read magazines and explore the blogosphere. You can read the literature of the place and hear stories from others who have been there. You can look at photos and brochures. You can even read the entire guidebook from cover to cover. Now, all that's left is to experience the place in the flesh—to see, smell, hear, and feel your destination.

There are many things to consider when planning your trip, especially to Honduras. The landscape is quite diverse, with mountains, rivers, beaches, islands, and several types of forests. If you like more off-the-beaten-track locations, Honduras sure has plenty of those—or if you prefer the more manicured resorts, it has those, too. Do you like cities (San Pedro Sula, La Ceiba, Tegucigalpa)? Do you want to see wildlife (Pico Bonito National Park, Río Plátano Biosphere Reserve)? Do you want to loll around on the beach (Roatán, Omoa, Isla del Tigre)? Or do you want to experience history (Copán, Gracias, Trujillo)? Do you want to volunteer, learn to dive, or learn a new language? The country offers a little bit of everything. It's fun for the whole family, or even a solo traveler.

Though there are some concerns, most parts of Honduras are safe and secure. Women travelers won't encounter the Latino machismo as much here as in Mexico or South America. It's tamer here for most—a bit more tranquilo. Gay and lesbian travelers might not feel as welcome here as in North America or Europe, but in major tourist areas, they'll be fine. A little discretion can go a long way in cities and rural areas, where archaic attitudes still run deep.

Apart from how to get there and where to go, your biggest choice to make will likely be when to go. While Honduras sits entirely in the tropics and the weather is warm—often blazing hot—all year round, torrential rain (even hurricanes, though they are not frequent) may make you want to rethink some of your plans, especially if you want to do lots of outdoor excursions. Rain can happen anytime of the year—sometimes just a squirt, other times a deluge—and this can affect many of the poorly paved roads in the country. It doesn't mean you can't get around; it might just mean you'll need four-wheel drive instead of a VW Beetle.

The following section will help in finding out how to arrange your trip. You'll discover what preparations and precautions you need to take, the types of tours you will find, safety precautions, whether you need any shots, and any Customs-related information so you can get your suitcase full of rum and cigars back into your home country. For additional help in planning your trip and for more on-the-ground resources in Honduras, please turn to "Fast Facts" on p. 271.

GETTING THERE

By Plane

Honduras has four international airports, in San Pedro Sula (p. 94), Tegucigalpa (p. 60), Roatán (p. 188), and La Ceiba (p. 162). While Tegucigalpa tends to be far from most major tourist attractions, more and more flights are shifting to San Pedro Sula, which isn't much of a tourist destination in itself. From San Pedro, you will generally find the cheapest and most frequent flights, plus it is a hub of bus travel and is within a few hours drive of almost anywhere in the country. La Ceiba is the point of transfer between the Bay Islands and the mainland, and is near many major attractions on the North Coast; however, few international flights outside of charters land here. If your trip centers on the Bay Islands, flying into Roatán tends to be easiest; however, you will generally find considerably less-expensive deals by flying to the mainland and transferring by bus and ferry to the islands.

There is an international departure tax of approximately US$34, payable in cash only in U.S. dollars or Honduran lempiras, from any of these airports. The departure tax on all domestic flights is approximately US$1.50 and is also payable only in U.S. dollars or Honduran lempiras.

To find out which airlines travel to Honduras, please see "Airline Websites," p. 279.

FROM NORTH AMERICA

There are nonstop flights and connections from the United States and Canada to every international airport, although the most frequent flights land in San Pedro Sula's Ramón Villeda Morales International Airport (SAP) and Tegucigalpa's Tocontín International Airport (TGU). The major carriers are **American** (**© 800/433-7300;** www.aa.com), **Continental** (**© 800/231-0856;** www.continental.com), **Delta** (**© 800/221-1212;** www.delta.com), **TACA** (**© 800/400-8222;** www.taca.com), and **Spirit** (**© 800/772-7117;** www.spiritair.com). There are daily nonstop flights from Miami, Atlanta, Houston, Ft. Lauderdale, and Newark (seasonally) to San Pedro Sula and/or Tegucigalpa. There are also nonstop flights to Roatán (Bay Islands) on Thursdays, Saturdays, and/or Sundays with Continental (Houston), Delta (Atlanta), and TACA (Miami and Houston).

FROM EUROPE

Apart from a seasonal weekly charter between Milan and Roatán, there are no other direct flights from the U.K. and Europe to Honduras. Delta, Continental, and American Airlines fly between Europe and Honduras through transfer points in the United States.

FROM AUSTRALIA & NEW ZEALAND

From Australia and New Zealand, your best bet for getting to Honduras is by connecting in a North American gateway such as Los Angeles or Houston, and then taking any of the airlines listed under "From North America," above.

By Bus

Bus travel to and from other Central American countries is quite common with long-term travelers, but it might be too slow-going if you're visiting a region for a short period of time.

The most common long-distance bus operator in the region is **Tica Bus** (16a Calle and Av. 5; © **504/220-0579;** www.ticabus.com), which has daily departures from Tegucigalpa to San Salvador (6½ hr.), Managua (7–8 hr.), and Guatemala City (14 hr.) that continue as far as Mexico and Panama.

Hedman Alas (13a Calle and Av. 11; © **504/237-7143**), which offers daily service from Copán to Antigua and Guatemala City, is a better way to get around in Honduras and has more frequent departures. **King Quality** (© **504/2553-4547;** www.king-qualityca.com) has daily service between San Salvador, El Salvador, and Tegucigalpa or San Pedro Sula.

There are many less-direct routes to the El Salvador, Guatemala, and Nicaragua borders via slow, crowded chicken buses that make as many stops as physically possible, can fit an infinite number of passengers, and rarely cost more than a dollar or two. Most will stop at the border where buses are waiting on the other side. If you are on a budget or just traveling a short distance, they aren't a bad choice, but if you have money or less time, stick to a reputable company—prices anywhere in the region rarely top L100 per hour of travel, and they will help you move through immigration smoothly and help you bypass much of the crime that takes place in border areas.

By Car

The major entry point by road into Honduras is along the Pan-American Highway, which cuts across a tiny southern corner of the country between the borders of El Salvador and Nicaragua, covering just 105km (65 miles). This is the most common point of road access into the country and connects to Tegucigalpa and San Pedro Sula via CA-4. While mountains and jungle isolate much of the rest of the border territory, there are smaller border crossings into El Salvador, Guatemala, and Nicaragua.

For information on car rentals and gasoline (petrol) in Honduras, see "Getting Around by Car," later.

By Boat

Cruise-ship visits to Honduras have exploded in recent years as both Royal Caribbean and Carnival Cruise Lines have opened new terminals on Roatán, attracting more than a dozen different cruise lines. So far, the only other cruise port is at Puerto Cortés, though stops here are rare. There is talk of adding terminals on Utila, Trujillo, and near Tela Bay, though so far, no concrete plans have been launched.

There is also one regular international ferry route in Honduras. From Puerto Cortés, 64km (40 miles) north of San Pedro Sula, **D-Express** (© **504/991-0778;** www.belizeferry.com) runs a ferry service to Big Creek/Mango Creek and Placencia, Belize, on Mondays at 11:30am, returning Fridays at 9:30am. The trip takes 4 hours and costs L1,000. Along the coast of La Mosquitia and from Puerto Castilla near Trujillo, cargo boats headed along the coast to Nicaragua and beyond will occasionally take on passengers.

GETTING AROUND

By Plane

While regional air carriers are more expensive than transportation by road or ferry, they are still relatively reasonably priced and can shave a day or two off your total travel times within Honduras. The country has several domestic airlines: Taca's regional airline **Isleña** (✆ **504/2445-1918;** www.flyislena.com), **Aerolineas Sosa** (✆ **504/2445-1154**), **Lanhsa** (✆ **504/2445-0397;** www.lanhsa.com) and **CM Airlines** (✆ **504/234-1886;** www.cmairlines.com), all offering daily flights on select routes to and from major destinations in the country, including San Pedro Sula, Tegucigalpa, La Ceiba, Roátan, Guanaja, Utila, Puerto Lempira, and Brus Laguna. Schedules tend to be erratic and change frequently, depending on demand.

Sami Airlines (✆ **504/2442-2565**) offers service when there is demand and has charter flights in four- to six-person planes to La Ceiba and destinations in La Mosquitia such as Ahuas, Palacios, Belen, Brus Laguna, and Puerto Lempira. **Bay Island Airways** (✆ **504/2933-6077;** www.bayislandairways.com) offers transport around the Bay Islands via small seaplanes.

By Car

Car rentals are readily available at most major airports from multinational companies such as Avis, Payless, Hertz, and Budget, as well as local companies.

The highways along the North Coast, between San Pedro Sula and Tegucigalpa, and between San Pedro Sula and Copán, are the best in the country and are comparable to highways in North America—even lined with many of the same gas stations and fast food restaurants.

Elsewhere, things aren't so good. In some places, roadwork is finally beginning, and paved routes are, in general, becoming more common—though in a significant part of Honduras, the roads are downright nasty. Most are either partially paved or unpaved, with massive uneven surfaces and bumps. Flat tires are incredibly common; therefore, there are mechanics along every highway and major route who can fix your tire in a matter of minutes for just a few lempiras.

Roads are also frequently flooded or impassable during the rainy season, and communities can at times be completely cut off from the country.

Apart from driving on the major highways, you will need to rent a car or truck with four-wheel drive to even consider driving in other parts of Honduras, particularly rural areas.

Gasoline is sold as "plus" and "premium." Both are unleaded; premium is just higher octane. Diesel is available at almost every gas station, as well. When going off to remote places, try to leave with a full tank of gas because gas stations can be hard to find. If you need to gas up in a small town, you can sometimes get gasoline from enterprising families who sell it by the liter from their houses. Look for hand-lettered signs that say GASOLINA. At the time of writing, a gallon of premium cost 100 lempira, or roughly $5 per gallon.

By Bus

There are literally hundreds of bus companies in Honduras, most operating out of dirt lots and offering travel only to nearby destinations.

Routes between major cities often have the best buses and the fastest service, and are a cheap and easy way to get from place to place. To more off-the-beaten-path destinations, the buses are usually slow and crowded, but full of local color.

While most bus companies offer only one route between two major destinations, two luxury bus companies popular with foreign travelers travel to major cities: **Hedman Alas** (✆ **504/2237-7143;** www.hedmanalas.com) has frequent service between San Pedro Sula, Tegucigalpa, Tela, La Ceiba, and Copán; **Viana Clase de Oro** (✆ **504/2225-6584**) has five first-class buses journeying daily between Tegucigalpa and San Pedro Sula that continue on to La Ceiba. You can expect to pay roughly L25 to L100 per hour of bus travel on a luxury service. For local buses, you might pay a 10th of that.

Robberies of tourist buses, while infrequent, have occurred. Riding in buses at night, apart from major routes, is not advised.

TIPS ON ACCOMMODATIONS

Accommodations in Honduras range from full-scale resort complexes and luxury hotels aimed at business travelers to small guesthouses, bed-and-breakfasts, and rooms rented out of someone's house.

In general, accommodation rates in Honduras are significantly cheaper than those in Europe or North America. High tourist season in Honduras is during national holidays and the dry season, running roughly from January to June, depending on what part of the country you're visiting. Hotels may charge higher rates, or they may not. Apart from the Bay Islands, most hotels do not have high-season rates. The prices listed in this book are rack rates, but many hotels offer cheaper rates and promotional deals through their websites.

Apart from a few major international chain hotels and beach resorts that allow kids to stay free, most hotels don't offer discounts for children—though it never hurts to ask. If you're visiting an eco-lodge or hotel in any area near the jungle, most accommodations have either screened-in windows or provide mosquito nets. The exceptions are the bare-bones beach shacks along the coast and rustic huts in La Mosquitia.

Don't be shy about negotiating a discount during the off season, as some hotel owners are willing to pass a travel agent's 10% to 20% commission on to you in the form of a discount.

Prices shown reflect double occupancy; ask for details about a "single" rate, as single rooms are often small and come with a twin-size bed.

HEALTH

Staying Healthy

GENERAL AVAILABILITY OF HEALTH CARE

Contact the **International Association for Medical Assistance to Travelers** (**IAMAT;** ✆ **716/754-4883,** or 416/652-0137 in Canada; www.iamat.org) for tips on travel and health concerns, and for lists of local English-speaking doctors. The U.S. Embassy in Tegucigalpa (✆ **504/2236-9320;** http://honduras.usembassy.gov) also has a list of English-speaking doctors that you can download from their website. The United States **Centers for Disease Control and Prevention** (✆ **800/311-3435;** www.cdc.gov) provides up-to-date information on health hazards by region or country, and offers tips on food safety. The website **www.tripprep.com,** sponsored by a consortium of travel medicine practitioners, may also offer helpful advice on traveling abroad. You can find listings of reliable clinics overseas at the **International Society of Travel Medicine** (www.istm.org).

BEFORE YOU GO

Hepatitis A, polio, tetanus, smallpox, and **typhoid** shots are recommended (but not required) for visitors planning to be in contact with local residents on an extended basis. **Hepatitis B** is suggested, as well, but not required. **Malaria** and **yellow fever** are extremely rare, yet if you intend on visiting extremely remote areas in La Mosquitia, you may want to discuss with your doctor your options for prevention. A short case of diarrhea or a 24-hour stomach bug is usually the most serious medical issue a traveler will face. It can occur even if you avoid unwashed vegetables and drink only bottled water, so bring antibiotics such as ciprofloxacin or levofloxacin to help. In most cases, you just have to drink lots of water and sweat it out.

Common Ailments

TRAVELER'S DIARRHEA Few visitors to Honduras experience anything other than run-of-the-mill **traveler's diarrhea** in reaction to unfamiliar foods and any microorganisms in them, although outbreaks of cholera and hepatitis have occurred in recent years. Honduras's tap water should be avoided. Bottled water is widely available throughout the country and cheap. You can eat fruits and vegetables, just be sure that they are washed in purified water before you eat them; that concern applies mostly to street vendors, as any upscale or tourist restaurant knows to use purified water. If your stool is bloody or diarrhea persists for more than 72 hours, you should seek medical attention.

CHOLERA Outbreaks of cholera do still occur in Honduras on a somewhat regular basis, usually in the rainy season. To avoid the disease, always wash your hands before eating, drink only bottled water, and be careful with what you eat.

TROPICAL ILLNESSES Mosquito-borne illnesses such as **malaria** and **dengue fever** do occur in Honduras, especially during the rainy season, when mosquitoes are most prevalent. Malaria can best be treated with chloroquine, a once-weekly pill found in most drugstores in the country, while dengue fever usually lasts for just a few days and is untreatable. The best prevention for either disease is fending off mosquito bites by wearing long-sleeve clothing, spraying insect repellent, and using mosquito nets. Repellent with 25% to 35% DEET, which should be applied to skin and clothing—but never on open wounds, eyes, or children under 2 years of age—will last up to 3 hours and is widely considered to be the most effective. **Typhoid fever** is caused by ingesting contaminated food or water. Symptoms, which resemble those of malaria, include fever, headaches, muscle aches, dizziness, nausea, and abdominal pain. It usually goes away on its own, but the use of ciprofloxacin or levofloxacin will help alleviate symptoms. **Yellow fever** no longer occurs in Honduras, or elsewhere in Central America, for that matter.

BUGS, BITES, & OTHER WILDLIFE CONCERNS While Honduras is a relatively untamed country with all sorts of wildlife, most animal injuries are related to someone's attempt to touch or feed an animal. This is a big no-no. Even dogs and cats in the streets should be avoided. Any animal bite should be immediately washed with soap, and then add an antiseptic such as alcohol or iodine. Visit a doctor immediately to see if rabies shots will be needed. It is wise to begin taking antibiotics, as many wounds tend to become infected.

Snake and **scorpion** bites, while rare, do occasionally affect the passing traveler. Poisonous snakes found in Honduras include the fer-de-lance, bushmaster, coral snake, and several rattlesnakes. Snakes rarely attack humans except when they get too close or accidentally step near them. If a venomous snake bites someone, keep the victim at rest and immobilized and take them to the nearest medical center. A digital photo of a snake or remembering the markings and color of the skin can be extremely helpful to a doctor.

Scorpions can be found all over the country. They are not life threatening, but their stings do hurt. If bitten, pack the wound with ice and go to the nearest medical facility. To prevent scorpion bites, be sure to inspect your bed before getting in, and your shoes and clothes before putting them on.

LEISHMANIASIS Sand flies, sometimes called no-see-ums, are far more annoying than mosquitoes in Honduras, in most cases. On the Bay Islands (more so on Utila and Guanaja than Roatán) and along the North Coast, they can be extra pesky, and traditional mosquito repellents don't always seem to work. Usually, their bites only cause small red, itchy bumps, but they can also cause **leishmaniasis,** an infection that causes ulcers to appear over exposed parts of the body. To prevent against sand fly bites, sleep with a finely netted mosquito net and wear long sleeves and pants when these critters are near.

CHAGAS' DISEASE **Chagas'** is one of those rare diseases that everyone talks about but always thinks is an urban legend. In the walls and roofs of houses, mostly substandard buildings made of mud or adobe brick, in lowland and coastal areas throughout Latin America, blood-sucking triatomine insects bite and lay their feces on human skin, usually the face. When itching, the human rubs the feces into the bite or on an open sore. The infection leads to swollen glands and fever, usually 1 to 2 weeks after the bite, and then goes into remission for periods of years and sometimes never returns. Young children are especially susceptible to this disease.

HIV/AIDS HIV is a very serious danger in Honduras, and numbers have spiraled out of control in recent years. The relaxed attitudes toward prostitution by men are the likely cause, and a large percentage of sex workers in the country are infected. Many continue working. San Pedro Sula and the North Coast are areas that have been hit especially hard by HIV/AIDS. Use of a condom is a wise move on many levels.

What to Do If You Get Sick Away from Home

Medical care in Honduras is a mixed bag. In rural communities, proper medical facilities may be nonexistent. Doctors and hospitals tend to be considerably better in larger cities, such as San Pedro Sula or Tegucigalpa, where many doctors are English-speaking. In smaller towns, always visit a private clinic instead of a public hospital. Some rural areas have only a basic clinic, and you'll need to travel to the nearest large town for more complicated procedures. We list **hospitals** and **emergency numbers** under "Fast Facts" throughout this guide.

If you suffer from a chronic illness, consult your doctor before your departure—especially if planning to visit high altitudes. Pack **prescription medications** in your carry-on luggage, and carry them in their original containers, with pharmacy labels—otherwise, they won't make it through airport security. Carry the generic name of prescription medicines, in case a local pharmacist is unfamiliar with the brand name.

For travel abroad, you may have to pay all medical costs upfront and be reimbursed later. We list additional **emergency numbers** in "Fast Facts," p. 272.

[FastFACTS] HONDURAS

Area Codes The international area code in Honduras is 504. All local phone numbers are eight digits, plus the area code. Numbers either start with a 2 (landline) or a 9 (cellular).

Business Hours Banks are open Monday to Friday from 8:30am to 4:30pm, and on Saturday from 9am to noon. General business hours are Monday through Friday from 9am to 5pm, although most restaurants and shops stay open to at least 8pm and are open Monday through Sunday.

Car Rental See "Getting There by Car," earlier in this chapter.

Cellphones See "Mobile Phones," below.

Crime See "Safety," below.

Customs

What You Can Bring into Honduras

Any travel-related merchandise brought into Honduras, such as personal effects or clothing, is not taxed. Visitors entering Honduras may also bring in no more than 400 cigarettes, 500g (18 oz.) of pipe tobacco, or 50 cigars, and 2.5L (2¾ qt.) of alcoholic beverages per adult.

What You Can Take Home from Honduras

For information on what you're allowed to bring home, contact one of the following agencies:

U.S. Citizens: U.S. Customs & Border Protection (CBP), 1300 Pennsylvania Ave. NW, Washington, DC 20229 (✆ **877/287-8667;** www.cbp.gov).

Canadian Citizens: Canada Border Services Agency (✆ **800/461-9999** in Canada, or 204/983-3500; www.cbsa-asfc.gc.ca).

U.K. Citizens: HM Customs & Excise at ✆ **0845/010-9000** (020/8929-0152 from outside the U.K.), or consult their website at www.hmce.gov.uk.

Australian Citizens: Australian Customs Service at ✆ **1300/363-263** or log on to www.customs.gov.au.

New Zealand Citizens: New Zealand Customs, The Customhouse, 17–21 Whitmore St., Box 2218, Wellington (✆ **04/473-6099** or 0800/428-786; www.customs.govt.nz).

Disabled Travelers There are more options and resources out there than ever before for travelers with disabilities, and even in Honduras, it is increasingly common to see hotels and restaurants that are wheelchair-accessible, though for the moment, this is limited mostly to large resorts and hotels in major cities. It's best to call ahead (especially with restaurants) to inquire about an establishment's facilities.

Many travel agencies offer customized tours and itineraries for travelers with disabilities. Among them are **Flying Wheels Travel** (✆ **507/451-5005;** www.flyingwheelstravel.com); **Access-Able Travel Source** (✆ **303/232-2979;** www.access-able.com); and **Accessible Journeys** (✆ **800/846-4537** or 610/521-0339; www.disabilitytravel.com). **Avis Rent a Car** has an "Avis Access" program that offers such services as a dedicated 24-hour toll-free number (✆ **888/879-4273**) for customers with special travel needs; special car features such as swivel seats, spinner knobs, and hand controls; and accessible bus service.

Organizations that offer assistance to disabled travelers include **MossRehab** (www.mossresourcenet.org), the **American Foundation for the Blind** (✆ **800/232-5463;** www.afb.org), and **SATH** (Society for Accessible Travel & Hospitality; ✆ **212/447-7284;** www.sath.org). **AirAmbulanceCard.com** is now partnered with SATH and allows you to pre-select top-notch hospitals in case of an emergency. Also check out the quarterly magazine ***Emerging Horizons*** (www.emerginghorizons.com) and ***Open World*** magazine, published by SATH.

Doctors Many doctors in Honduras, especially in San Pedro Sula and Tegucigalpa, speak basic English; for a list of English-speaking doctors, call your embassy.

Drinking Laws Possession and use of drugs and narcotics are subject to heavy fines and jail terms. The legal drinking age in Honduras is 21. Alcohol is sold every day of the year, except during elections, and can be bought from almost any grocery store or bodega. Proof of age is sometimes required at bars and nightclubs, so it's always a good idea to bring ID when you go out.

Driving Rules See "Getting Around," earlier in this chapter.

Electricity Most electrical outlets in Honduras are wired as in the U.S., with 110 volts, 60 cycles, although there is some 220-volt electricity, as well.

Embassies & Consulates The **U.S. Embassy** is in Tegucigalpa, at Avenida La Paz (✆ **504/2236-9320;** http://honduras.usembassy.gov).

The **Canadian Embassy** in Tegucigalpa is at Edificio Finaciero Banexpo Local #3, Col Payaqui, Blvd. San Juan Bosco (✆ **504/2232-4551;** www.embassyhonduras.ca).

The **British Consulate** can be found in Tegucigalpa at Colonia Reforms 2402 (✆ **504/2237-6577;** reforma@cascomark.com).

There are no Australian or New Zealand embassies or consulates in Honduras.

Emergencies For a police emergency, call ✆ **199.** For fire, call ✆ **198.** To call an ambulance, dial ✆ **195.**

Family Travel Hondurans and families go together like peanut butter and jelly. Most hotels in the country that cater to national tourists have playgrounds, children's swimming pools, family-style accommodations, and other extras that both kids and adults will appreciate. Adult-only hotels do exist, though they are relatively few. In the Bay Islands and the resorts along the North Coast, condo-style rooms are quite common. Most have kitchens, which can do wonders for saving money and keeping homesick kids from misery.

When choosing lodging, check to see if a suite is cheaper than booking two connecting rooms. Most suites have a sofa bed, or at the very least, the hotel can add an extra cot-style bed. A good bet for families spending several days in a destination is an *apart-hotel* or a *cabaña,* which are self-catering units with living areas and kitchens—these options are frequently less expensive than a hotel room. Hotel chains such as the Hilton and the Clarion occasionally offer specials for families with kids, but as a general rule, kids are either free when sharing a room with their parents or are charged a minimal fee for an extra bed.

Recommended family travel websites include **Family Travel Forum** (www.familytravelforum.com); **Family Travel Network** (www.familytravelnetwork.com); and **Family Travel Files** (www.thefamilytravelfiles.com).

To locate accommodations, restaurants, and attractions that are particularly kid-friendly, look for the "Kids" icon throughout this guide.

Gasoline Please see "Getting Around By Car," earlier in this chapter.

Insurance The cost of travel insurance varies widely, depending on the cost and length of your trip, your age and health, and the type of trip you're taking, but expect to pay between 5% and 8% of the vacation itself. You can get estimates from various providers through **InsureMyTrip.com.** Enter your trip cost and dates, your age, and other information for prices from more than a dozen companies.

For information on traveler's insurance, trip cancelation insurance, and medical insurance while traveling, please visit www.frommers.com/planning.

Internet & Wi-Fi No matter where you are in Honduras, you should find Internet access, either in a cafe, mall, or cybercafe. Most hotels, even hostels, have their own Internet service, and more and more are beginning to have Wi-Fi service. Roughly 90% of these hotels offer Wi-Fi for free, yet some international chain hotels in Tegucigalpa and San Pedro Sula, as well as a few resorts on Roatán, charge a fee that ranges between US$6 and US$15 per day. If the hotel does not have Internet service, the hotel staff can usually point out where to find it. Expect to pay approximately 20 lempira per hour.

Language Spanish is the main language in Honduras, but most people on the Bay Islands speak English. The Native languages of Lenca, Miskito, and Garífuna are also spoken in some regions. See also "Useful Terms & Phrases," on p. 281.

Legal Aid If you need legal help, your best bet is to first contact your local embassy or consulate.

LGBT Travelers In general, Honduras is not a gay-friendly country, even in larger cities; however, few gay travelers will encounter any issues of discrimination. Several organizations have formed in the past decade in response to discrimination in Honduras against gays and lesbians in the country such as **Grupo Prisma** (✆ **504/2232-8342**) and **Comunidad Gay Sampedrana** (✆ **504/2550-6868**). Both lack websites, but you can call either one for updated information on the LGBT community in Honduras. **Toto Tours, Inc.** (✆ **800/565-1241;** www.tototours.com) occasionally offers trips to Honduras. **The International Gay and Lesbian Travel Association** (**IGLTA;** ✆ **800/448-8550** or 954/776-2626; www.iglta.com) is the trade association for the gay and lesbian travel industry and offers an online directory of gay- and lesbian-friendly travel businesses; go to their website and click on "Members."

Mail At the time of writing, it costs L80/L120 to mail a postcard/letter to the United States, and L120/L180 to Europe. You can get stamps at a post office and at some gift shops in large hotels. The Honduran postal service is renowned for being considerably more reliable than in other Central American nations, though if you are sending anything of value, it is still recommended to use an international courier service or wait until you get home to post it. **DHL, EMS Courier,** and **FedEx** have offices in major cities around the country, such as San Pedro Sula and Tegucigalpa. Refer to the "Fast Facts" listings of any major city. ***Note:*** Despite what you may be told, packages sent overnight to U.S. addresses tend to take 3 to 4 days.

If you're sending mail *to* Honduras, it generally takes between 10 and 14 days to reach Tegucigalpa or San Pedro Sula, although it can take as much as a month to get to the more remote corners of the country. Plan ahead. Also note that many hotels and eco-lodges have mailing addresses in the United States. Always use these addresses when writing from North America or Europe.

Medical Requirements Hepatitis A, polio, tetanus, smallpox, and typhoid shots are recommended (but not required) for visitors planning to be in contact with local residents on an extended basis. Hepatitis B is suggested, as well, but not required. Malaria and yellow fever are extremely rare, yet if you intend to visit extremely remote areas in La Mosquitia, you may want to discuss with your doctor your options for prevention.

Mobile Phones Honduras's largest phone companies, such as Telefonica, operate on a GSM 850 or 1900 MHZ frequency, which several large North American carriers also use, though these frequencies are rare in other parts of the world. Any dual or multiband GSM cellphone will work in Honduras, but you might pay expensive roaming rates; check with your cellphone company before leaving. (In the U.S., T-Mobile and AT&T uses this quasi-universal system; in Canada, Rogers customers are GSM.)

If your cellphone does not have this capability, you can rent a phone, either before you leave home or upon arrival in Honduras. Pre-departure, North Americans can rent a phone from **InTouch USA** (✆ **800/872-7626;** www.intouchglobal.com) or **RoadPost** (✆ **888/290-1606** or 905/272-5665; www.roadpost.com).

In Honduras, you can rent a phone at **kiosks** located on the arrival level at the San Pedro Sula or Tegucigalpa airport; they are open daily from 6am to 9pm. Depending on your service, you may be able to insert your own SIM card, though you'll likely still pay regular roaming rates. Some cellphone companies in Honduras will rent phones with prepaid calling cards. Local calls have similar rates and plans as they do in North America or Europe. Using calling cards and receiving calls is free; however, this option does not allow you to dial internationally.

Money & Costs The unit of currency in Honduras is the **lempira** (L). The value of the lempira has held steady around the current exchange rate of about 19 lempira to the U.S. dollar, which is the rate used for prices listed in this book. Bills come in denominations of 1, 2, 5, 10, 20, 50, 100, 200, and 500. There are no lempira coins. American dollars are commonly accepted in the Bay Islands and in major tourist destinations, particularly at hotels—as a result, some hotel reviews in the Bay Islands also list rates using U.S. dollars.

Honduras levies a steep 12% **sales tax,** called ISV (Impuesto de Servicios), on all goods and services except medicine. There is a 4% tourism tax added to all hotel rates, tours, and car rentals, additional to the 12% ISV, although small hotels and community-based tour operators may not add the tax, especially if you can pay in cash. Many high-end hotels and restaurants also add a 10% service charge, which is meant to take care of tipping.

Frommer's Honduras lists exact prices in the local currency. The currency conversions quoted above were correct at press time. However, rates fluctuate, so before departing, consult a currency exchange website such as **www.oanda.com/convert/classic** to check up-to-the-minute rates.

ATMs ATMs are the most common way for travelers to exchange money in Honduras, and most cities have multiple banks with ATMs, many of them operating 24 hours. **BAC, Unibanc,** and **Banco Atlántida** are the most reliable and are compatible with a variety of networks, including Cirrus, PLUS, Visa, and MasterCard. Honduran banks do not usually charge a fee to use their ATMs, but your own institution might charge you for foreign purchases or withdrawals, so check before you go. You'll find ATMs in banks, grocery stores, gas stations, airports, malls, and pharmacies.

Traveler's Checks Traveler's checks are becoming less and less common, yet are still used occasionally and can be exchanged at most banks in the country, though a 2% fee is often charged. Visa and MasterCard are widely accepted throughout Honduras, and American Express and Diner's Club are becoming increasingly common, although 12% surcharges are normal. Dollars, pounds, and euros can be exchanged in banks and many hotels, as well as with unofficial street moneychangers found in parks, airports, and border crossings.

Beware of hidden credit-card fees while traveling. Check with your credit or debit card issuer to see what fees, if any, will be charged for overseas transactions. Recent reform legislation in the U.S., for example, has curbed some exploitative lending practices. But many banks have responded by increasing fees in other areas, including fees for customers who use credit and debit cards while out of the country—even if those charges were made in U.S. dollars. Fees can amount to 3% or more of the purchase price. Check with your bank before departing to avoid any surprise charges on your statement.

For help with currency conversions, tip calculations, and more, download Frommer's convenient Travel Tools app for your mobile device. Go to www.

THE VALUE OF THE LEMPIRA VS. OTHER POPULAR CURRENCIES

L	A$	C$	Euro (€)	NZ$	UK£	US$
L1	$.05	C$.05	€.04	NZ$.09	£.03	$.05

frommers.com/go/mobile and click on the Travel Tools icon.

Newspapers & Magazines The weekly *Honduras This Week* is the major English-language newspaper in the country and can be found in most major tourist areas, though at last visit, the paper was not being published.

The Bay Islands have two monthly English-language magazines, the *Bay Islands Voice* and *Utila East Wind.*

There are five main daily Spanish newspapers—all owned by politicians and leaning one way or the other. These include *El Heraldo, La Prensa, La Tribuna, El Tiempo,* and *El Nuevo Día.*

Packing Except for a few mountainous areas, weather in Honduras tends to be uniformly hot and sticky with some rain, so you will need to pack accordingly. Think lightweight and fast-drying shirts and shorts, or pants and a light rain jacket. Apart from a few top restaurants, discos, and churches, a dress code in Honduras is pretty much non-existent. When required, it usually just means no shorts and no tennis shoes. Nights in the mountains can get somewhat brisk, so it's probably a good idea to bring a light sweater and pants along, though that's not to say that anyone has ever gotten frostbite here. Considering jungle covers much of the country, long shirts and pants are a good idea to keep insects away from your skin, though again, lightweight is recommended. For more helpful information on packing for your trip, download our convenient Travel Tools app for your mobile device. Go to www.frommers.com/go/mobile and click on the Travel Tools icon.

Passports Citizens of the United States, Canada, Great Britain, South Africa, New Zealand, and Australia require valid passports to enter Honduras as tourists. Citizens of any of these countries conducting business or enrolled in formal

Honduras is a relatively inexpensive destination, especially if you're coming from a place like London or San Francisco. You'll find some of the world's cheapest diving here, even though average prices on the Bay Islands are even higher than on the mainland. Even compared to other Central American destinations like Costa Rica or Mexico, prices for food and accommodations are, on average, quite a bit lower. Here is a brief list of prices to expect:

WHAT THINGS COST IN HONDURAN	LEMPIRAS
Baleada	10
Bottle of Salva Vida beer	30
Típico plate	80
Four-day dive certification	4,750
1 night in a moderately priced hotel	1,100
3-hour bus ride	100
1 Gallon (3.8L) of premium gas	100
Admission to most museums	20–40
Admission to most national parks	200

educational programs in Honduras also require visas. Tourist cards, distributed on arriving international flights or at border crossings, are good for stays of up to 90 days. Keep a copy of your tourist card for presentation upon departure from Honduras. (If you lose it, you'll have to pay a small fine.) You can extend your visa once, for another 90 days, at any immigration office for US$20. See www.frommers.com/planning for information on how to obtain a passport.

Honduran Embassy Locations

In the U.S.: 3007 Tilden St. NW, Suite 4M, Washington, DC 20008 (✆ **202/966-7702;** www.hondurasemb.org).

In Canada: 151 Slater St., Suite 805, Ottawa, ON K1P 5H3 (✆ **613/233-8900;** www.embassyhonduras.ca).

In the U.K.: 115 Gloucester Pl., London, W1U 6JT (✆ **020/7486-4880;** www.fco.gov.uk).

In Australia: Level 7, 19-31 Pitt St., Sydney NSW 2000 PO Box H6 Australia Square NSW 2000 (✆ **02/9247-1730**).

Petrol Please see "Getting Around by Car," earlier in this chapter.

Police Honduras's police force can be a hit or miss for travelers. In places such as Tela, Copán Ruínas, San Pedro Sula, and a few other destinations, tourist police have been established to protect travelers and assist them if an issue arises. If you've been robbed, your insurance company will most likely ask for a police report, called a *constancia,* which you can get at any police station. It is rare that police officers in Honduras will speak English.

In other parts of the country, the police are generally helpful; however, when you are in a car they tend to be more corrupt. Road stops are common throughout the country and generally police will ask for your vehicle's registration and let you go on your way. Some officers will go to great lengths to find some minor reason to ticket you. This goes double for *gringos.* Usually, they want a small bribe. Don't pay it. Say you don't speak Spanish. They will give up. If you are pulled over for a driving infraction, most officers will give you the option of a bribe, as well. Just deny all and threaten to call your embassy. They'll usually back off.

Safety Like most other Latin American countries, Honduras has its good parts and bad parts concerning safety. Violent crimes do occur in the country, and foreign visitors have on rare occasions been murdered, raped, assaulted, or kidnapped. While it is mostly contained to major cities, violent crime is a serious issue and contributes to the country's frightening murder rate, which is one of the highest in the world. While tourist areas are considerably safer than other parts of the country, common-sense safety methods should be used.

A traveler's principal concerns are pickpockets and break-ins, which do occur in large cities, especially Tegucigalpa, San Pedro Sula, and La Ceiba. The downtown areas of each of these cities tend to be the most dangerous, and gang violence was a serious issue in Tegus for a number of years, though this is no longer the issue it once was.

In Olancho and La Mosquitia, drug smugglers coming up through Central America from South America do exist, though it is rare that a foreign tourist will encounter anything of the sort. Drug use and possession in general is not taken lightly in any Latin American country, and numerous tourists have been given long sentences in Honduran jails. Do not buy, transport, or carry drugs in Honduras. If you are caught with drugs, your embassy will not help you. Police presence on highways in Olancho tends to be minimal; therefore, cars are often the targets of armed robbers. You should use extreme caution when traveling in this region and never drive at night.

Chances are you won't see or have any problems, though with some very simple precautions, you will considerably decrease your chances of being the victim of a crime.

In downtown areas, do not walk alone, especially at night, and use taxi cabs called from a trusted source, such as your hotel manager, to get from place to place. Note a cab driver's name and license number, and do not allow him to pick up other passengers, agree on the fare before you depart, and have small bills available for payment. When driving, do so with your doors locked and windows up, especially in downtown areas, where carjacking is more common. For bus travel, stick to daylight hours and, when possible, go with first-class operators. Never leave valuables in your rental car, and always keep a close eye on your belongings when in public. Don't flash gold or silver jewelry, large amounts of cash, iPods, or digital cameras. Even slick new US$300 backpacks are an attractive item for local thieves and the occasional sleazy backpacker. While you may not always be able to just blend in, you do not have to act like an easy target. If you are the victim of a crime, contact a police officer immediately, either in person or by dialing **✆ 199.**

Senior Travel Seniors will find plenty of discounts at museums and attractions, but not much else in Honduras. Members of **AARP** (601 E St. NW, Washington, DC 20049; (**✆ 888/687-2277;** www.aarp.org) get discounts on hotels, airfares, and car rentals. AARP offers members a wide range of benefits, including *AARP: The Magazine* and a monthly newsletter. Anyone over age 50 can join.

Many reliable agencies and organizations target the 50-plus market. **Elderhostel** (**✆ 877/426-8056;** www.elderhostel.org) arranges outstanding study programs in Honduras for those aged 55 and over. Cruise companies that visit the Bay Islands, such as **Carnival** (**✆ 888/CARNIVAL;** www.carnival.com) and **Royal Caribbean** (**✆ 866/562-7625;** www.royalcaribbean.com), offer discounts to senior cruise passengers. **INTRAV** (**✆ 800/456-8100;** www.intrav.com) is a high-end tour operator that caters to the mature, discerning traveler (not specifically seniors), with trips around the world that include guided safaris, polar expeditions, private-jet adventures, and small-boat cruises down jungle rivers.

Recommended publications offering travel resources for seniors include the quarterly magazine ***Travel 50 & Beyond*** (www.travel50andbeyond.com) and ***Travel Unlimited: Uncommon Adventures for the Mature Traveler*** (Avalon).

Single Travel On package vacations, single travelers are often hit with a dreaded "single supplement" to the base price. To avoid it, you can agree to room with other single travelers or find a compatible roommate before you go from one of the many roommate-locator agencies. **Travel Buddies Singles Travel Club** (**✆ 800/998-9099;** www.travelbuddiesworldwide.com), based in Canada, runs small, intimate, singles-friendly group trips and will match you with a roommate free of charge. **TravelChums** (**✆ 212/787-2621;** www.travelchums.com) is an Internet-only travel-companion matching service with elements of an online personals–type site, hosted by the respected New York–based Shaw Guides travel service. **Backroads** (**✆ 800/462-2848;** www.backroads.com) offers more than 40 active-travel solo trips to destinations worldwide.

For more information, check out Eleanor Berman's latest edition of ***Traveling Solo: Advice and Ideas for More Than 250 Great Vacations*** (Globe Pequot), a guide with advice on traveling alone, either solo or as part of a group tour.

For more information on traveling single, go to www.frommers.com/planning.

Smoking In early 2011, a new smoking law went into effect banning smoking from many public and private places, though at press time, there were still questions regarding how the law would be enforced.

Student Travel While student discounts will not save you significant amounts of cash while in Honduras, you'd be wise to arm yourself with an **International Student Identity Card (ISIC),** which offers substantial savings on plane tickets and the occasional entrance fee. It also provides you with basic health and life insurance and a 24-hour help line. The card is available from **STA Travel** (✆ **800/781-4040** in North America; www.statravel.com, or www.statravel.co.uk in the U.K.), the biggest student travel agency in the world. If you're no longer a student but are still under 26, you can get an **International Youth Travel Card (IYTC)** from the same people, which entitles you to some discounts (but not on museum admissions). **Travel CUTS** (✆ **800/667-2887** or 416/614-2887; www.travelcuts.com) offers similar services for both Canadians and U.S. residents. Irish students may prefer to turn to **USIT** (✆ **01/602-1600;** www.usit.ie), an Ireland-based specialist in student, youth, and independent travel.

Telephones Kiosks and convenience stores throughout Honduras sell phone cards with individual instructions on long-distance dialing, and phone booths at telephone centers will provide instructions on dialing.

To place a call from your home country to Honduras, dial the international access code (011 in the U.S. and Canada, 0011 in Australia, 0170 in New Zealand, 00 in the U.K.) plus the country code (504), followed by the number in Honduras. For example, a call from the United States to Tegucigalpa would be 011+504+2 (or 9)+000+0000. ***Note:*** Recently, all phone numbers in Honduras changed from seven to eight numbers. An extra 2 (land line) or 9 (cellphone) have been added at the beginning of each number.

To place a call within Honduras, all you have to do is dial the number, as area codes are non-existent (dial 193 for an international operator).

To place a direct international call from Honduras, dial the country code of the destination you are calling, plus the area code and the local number.

Time Honduras is on Standard Time year-round and is in the Central Time Zone. It is 6 hours behind GMT.

Tipping Diners should leave a 10% to 15% tip in restaurants, although some high-end restaurants automatically include gratuity. In hotels, tipping is left to the guest's discretion. There's no need to tip taxi drivers. For help with tip calculations, currency conversions, and more, download our convenient Travel Tools app for your mobile device. Go to www.frommers.com/go/mobile and click on the Travel Tools icon.

Toilets You won't find public toilets or "restrooms" on the streets in most Honduran cities, but they can be found in hotel lobbies, bars, restaurants, museums, and bus stations. Large hotels and fast food restaurants are often the best bet for clean facilities. Restaurants and bars in resorts or heavily visited areas may reserve their restrooms for patrons. Most toilets in the country are the western kind with a typical flush handle. There is one big difference though: toilet paper isn't flushed. It goes in a small trashcan beside the toilet. In extremely rural areas, a simple latrine is standard. Usually, there will be a bucket of water nearby that you use to rinse everything down.

Visitor Information You'll find a municipal or regional tourism office in nearly every city throughout the country, often in small booths in central parks and squares, that are generally open Monday to Friday 8am to 4pm, often with a 1-hour break at noon. The Instituto Hondureño de Turismo (IHT), or the National Tourism Institute, does not have offices abroad but promotes the country through its website: www.letsgohonduras.com. Additional websites of interest include:

- **www.bayislandsvoice.com:** A monthly news magazine covering the history, art, culture, dining, development, and social issues of Roatán, Utila, and Guanaja.

- **www.hondurasweekly.com:** This English-language news site with weekly features, videos, weather reports, and news.
- **www.honduras.com:** An excellent full online and print bilingual guidebook to the major tourism destinations in Honduras, with information and maps that are updated seasonally by the Institute of Tourism.
- **www.larutamoskitia.com:** The definitive site for exploring La Mosquitia. Questions about when to go, how to get there, what to do, and what you will see are all answered in detail. The site is run by a nonprofit, community-based tour agency that leads multiday tours throughout the region and arranges day tours from individual communities.
- **www.sidewalkmystic.com:** An independent online self-planning guide to Honduras, with descriptions of highlights, travelogues, hotel and restaurant listings, and other how-to information.
- **www.lagringasblogicito.blogspot.com:** One American woman, an avid gardener who moved to La Ceiba in 2001, has been blogging about her experiences here ever since and has become one of the most followed English-language blogs in Honduras.
- **www.guanajaguide.com:** A basic online guide to living, visiting, and buying property on Guanaja with links to hotels, tour operators, the latest news on the island, and transportation.
- **www.birdsofhonduras.com:** Avian specialist Robert Gallardo, an American who has lived in Honduras for more than a decade, reveals a very detailed look into the habitats and scientific research regarding bird life in the country. There are hundreds of photos, trip reports, and dozens of other resources that will be helpful to any birder.
- **www.sarahlagringa.wordpress.com:** A Peace Corps volunteer details her day-to-day life from a village in Olancho.

You can also find a list of Frommer's travel apps at www.frommers.com/go/mobile.

Water See "Health," earlier in this chapter.

Wi-Fi See "Internet & Wi-Fi," earlier in this chapter.

AIRLINE WEBSITES

MAJOR AIRLINES

Aeroméxico
www.aeromexico.com

Air France
www.airfrance.com

American Airlines
www.aa.com

British Airways
www.british-airways.com

Continental Airlines
www.continental.com

Delta Air Lines
www.delta.com

Iberia Airlines
www.iberia.com

TACA
www.taca.com

United Airlines
www.united.com

US Airways
www.usairways.com

BUDGET AIRLINES

Bay Island Airways
www.bayislandairways.com

CM Airlines
www.cmairlines.com

Isleña Airlines
www.flyislena.com

Lanhsa
www.lanhsa.com

Rollins Air
www.rollinsair.com

Spirit Airlines
www.spiritair.com

USEFUL TERMS & PHRASES

13

GLOSSARY OF SPANISH-LANGUAGE TERMS

The official language of Honduras is Spanish. Honduran Spanish is similar to that of other Central American countries, though it varies considerably from that of Spain or South America. You do not hear the "tú" pronoun frequently here; the term "vos" is used instead. Vos derives from the term "vosotros," which is not used often in Latin America outside of Argentina. Most Hondurans speak at a relatively relaxed pace, tend to annunciate rather clearly, and do not often drop final consonants.

While it is widely spoken, Spanish is a second language for many in the country. Indigenous languages such as Garífuna, Miskito, Pech, and Ch'ortí are spoken in isolated parts of the country, but generally used alongside Spanish. On the Bay Islands and some parts of La Mosquitia, English is more common; however, due to the increasing number of mainlanders settling on the islands, Spanish is becoming more widely spoken.

GREETINGS & FORMALITIES

English	Spanish	Pronunciation
Hello	**Buenos días**	*bweh*-nohss *dee*-ahss
How are you?	**¿Cómo está usted?**	koh-moh ehss-tah oo-stehd
Very well	**Muy bien**	mwee byehn
Thank you	**Gracias**	grah-syahss
Good-bye	**Adiós**	ad-dyohss
Please	**Por favor**	pohr fah-vohr
Yes	**Sí**	see
No	**No**	noh
My name is . . .	**Me llamo . . .**	meh *yah*-mo
And yours?	**¿Y usted?**	ee oos-*tehd*
It's a pleasure to meet you.	**Es un placer conocerle.**	ehs oon plah-*sehr* koh-noh-*sehr*-leh
No problem.	**No hay problema.**	noh aye proh-*bleh*-mah

GETTING AROUND/STREET SMARTS

English	Spanish	Pronunciation
Excuse me. (to get by someone)	**Perdóneme.**	pehr-*doh*-neh-meh
Excuse me (to begin a question)	**Disculpe**	dees-*kool*-peh
I'm sorry, I don't understand.	**Lo siento, no entiendo**	loh *syehn*-toh no ehn-*tyehn*-doh
Would you speak slower please?	**Puede hablar un poco más lento?**	*pweh*-deh ah-*blahr* oon *poh*-koh mahs *lehn*-to
Do you speak English?	**¿Habla usted inglés?**	*ah*-blah oo-*stehd* een-*glehss*
I don't understand Spanish very well.	**No (lo) entiendo muy bien el español.**	noh (loh) ehn-*tyehn*-do mwee byehn el ehss-pah-*nyohl*
Would you spell that?	**¿Puede deletrear eso?**	*pweh*-deh deh-leh-treh-*ahr eh*-so
Would you please repeat that?	**¿Puede repetir, por favor?**	*pweh*-deh rreh-peh-*teer* pohr fah-*vohr*
What does ___ mean?	**¿Que significa ___?**	Keh seeg-*nee*-fee-ka
Where is . . . ?	**¿Dónde está . . . ?**	dohn-deh ehss-tah
the station	**la estación**	la ehss-*tah*-syohn
the bus stop	**la parada**	la pah-*rah*-dah
a hotel	**un hotel**	oon oh-*tehl*
a restaurant	**un restaurante**	oon res-tow-*rahn*-teh
the toilet	**el baño**	el *bah*-nyo
To the right	**A la derecha**	ah lah deh-*reh*-chah
To the left	**A la izquierda**	ah lah ees-*kyehr*-dah
Straight ahead	**Adelante**	ah-deh-*lahn*-teh
How do I get to . . . ?	**Cómo llego a . . . ?**	*koh*-mo *ye*-go a
Is it far?	**Está lejos?**	es-*ta le*-hos
What time does	**¿A qué hora**	ah keh *o*-ra
leave/arrive	**sale/llega**	*sa*-le/*ye*-ga
the flight	**el vuelo**	el *vweh*-loh
the train	**el tren**	el tren

KEY QUESTIONS

English	Spanish	Pronunciation
Who?	**¿Quién? ¿Quiénes?**	*kyehn kyeh*-nehs
What?	**¿Qué?**	keh
When?	**¿Cuándo?**	*kwahn*-doh
Where?	**¿Dónde?**	*dohn*-deh
Why?	**¿Por qué?**	pohr-*keh*
How?	**¿Como?**	*koh*-moh
Which?	**¿Cuál?**	*kwahl*
How many? / How much?	**¿Cuánto? ¿Cuántos?**	*kwahn*-toh, *kwahn*-tohs

SHOPPING & DINING

English	Spanish	Pronunciation
I would like	**Quiero**	kyeh-roh
to eat	**comer**	ko-mehr
a room	**una habitación**	oo-nah ah-bee-tah-*syohn*
the check	**la cuenta**	la *kwen*-tah
the laundromat	**la lavanderia**	la-ven-da-*re*-ah
the pharmacy	**la farmacia**	la far-ma-*cee*-ah
the ATM	**Ee cajero automático**	el ka-jhe-ro ow-to-*mah*-tee-ko
I'm looking for a size . . .	**Busco una talla . . .**	boos-koh *oo*-nah *tah*-yah
small	**pequeño**	peh-keh-nyoh
medium	**mediano**	meh-dyah-noh
large	**grande**	grahn-deh
How much is it?	**¿Cuánto cuesta?**	*kwahn*-toh
Can I see it?	**Puedo verlo/a?**	*pweh*-doh *ver*-lo
I'll take it	**Lo llevo**	lo *ye*-voh
Breakfast	**Desayuno**	deh-sah-*yoo*-noh
Lunch	**Comida**	coh-*mee*-dah
Dinner	**Cena**	seh-nah
A menu please?	**¿Una carta por favor?**	*oo*-nah *kahr*-ta pohr fah-vohr
What do you recommend?	**¿Qué recomienda usted?**	*keh* reh-koh-*myehn*-dah oos-tehd

WHO

English	Spanish	Pronunciation
I	**yo**	yoh
you	**usted/tú**	oos-*tehd*/too
him	**él**	ehl
her	**ella**	*eh*-yah
us	**nosotros**	noh-*soh*-trohs
them	**ellos/ellas**	*eh*-yohs, *eh*-yahs

WHEN

English	Spanish	Pronunciation
now	**ahora**	ah-*oh*-rah
later	**después**	dehs-*pwehs*
in a minute	**en un mInuto**	ehn oon mee-*noo*-toh
today	**hoy**	oy
tomorrow	**mañana**	mah-*nyah*-nah
yesterday	**ayer**	ah-*yehr*
in a week	**en una semana**	ehn *oo*-nah seh-*mah*-nah
at	**a las**	ah lahs

NUMBERS

English	Spanish	Pronunciation
1	**uno**	(*oo*-noh)
2	**dos**	(dohss)
3	**tres**	(trehss)
4	**cuatro**	(*kwah*-troh)
5	**cinco**	(*seen*-koh)
6	**seis**	(sayss)
7	**siete**	(*syeh*-teh)
8	**ocho**	(*oh*-choh)
9	**nueve**	(*nweh*-beh)
10	**diez**	(dyehss)
11	**once**	(*ohn*-seh)
12	**doce**	(*doh*-seh)
13	**trece**	(treh-seh)
14	**catorce**	(kah-*tohr*-seh)
15	**quince**	(*keen*-seh)
16	**dieciséis**	(dyeh-see-*seh*-ees)
17	**diecisiete**	(dyeh-see-*syeh*-teh)
18	**dieciocho**	(dyeh-*syoh*-choh)
19	**diecinueve**	(dyeh-see-*nweh*-veh)
20	**veinte**	(*beh*-een-teh)
21	**veintiuno**	(beh-een-*tyoo*-noh)
30	**treinta**	(*treh*-een-tah)
40	**cuarenta**	(kwah-*ren*-tah)
50	**cincuenta**	(seen-*kwehn*-tah)
60	**sesenta**	(seh-*sehn*-tah)
70	**setenta**	(seh-*tehn*-tah)
80	**ochenta**	(o-*chehn*-tah)
90	**noventa**	(noh-*behn*-tah)
100	**cien**	(syehn)
200	**doscientos**	(doh-*syehn*-tohs)
500	**quinientos**	(ken-ee-*en*-tos)
1,000	**mil**	(meel)
5,000	**cinco mil**	(*seen*-koh meel)

DAYS OF THE WEEK

English	Spanish	Pronunciation
Monday	**lunes**	(*loo*-nehss)
Tuesday	**martes**	(*mahr*-tehss)
Wednesday	**miércoles**	(*myehr*-koh-lehs)
Thursday	**jueves**	(*wheh*-behss)

English	Spanish	Pronunciation
Friday	**viernes**	(*byehr*-nehss)
Saturday	**sábado**	(*sah*-bah-doh)
Sunday	**domingo**	(doh-*meen*-goh)

COMMON HONDURAN WORDS & PHRASES

Spanish	Pronunciation	English Meaning
Boca	(boh-ka)	Appetizer
Bola	(boh-la)	Slang for lempira (like "buck" for the dollar)
Campos	(cahm-pose)	Banana plantation workers on the North Coast
Caracol	(cah-ra-col)	A conch, which is a slang term for Bay Islanders from people on the mainland
Catracho	(cah-*trah*-cho)	Honduran
Chacalín	(chah-kah-*leen*)	River shrimp
Champa	(*cham*-pah)	A thatched roof, open-air hut
Finca	(*feen*-cah)	Agricultural complex
Guaro	(goo-*ah*-ro)	Aguardiente
Ladino	(lah-dee-no)	Person of mixed Spanish and indigenous blood
Machangai	(mah-*chawn*-guy)	Slang for the trucks that transport the lower classes
Palapa	(pah-lah-pah)	A stilted thatched hut, often on the beach
¡Que Leche!	(kay *lay*-chay)	How lucky!
Pipante	(pee-*pawn*-tay)	A dugout canoe propelled by poles
Pisto	(*pees*-to)	Noun meaning bread or dough (money)
Tegus	(tay-goose)	Tegucigalpa
¡Vaya Pues, que le vaya bien!	(*vah*-yah poo-es kay lay *vah*-yah *be*-en)	Alright then, have a good trip!
Zona Viva	(tho-nah *vee*-vah)	A part of town with a high concentration of bars or night spots

HONDURAN WILDLIFE

14

Honduras is one of the most biodiverse countries in Latin America. With more than 45% of the country covered in forest, by far the highest amount in all of Central America, much of the flora and fauna of the country remain pristine and untrammeled. The range of species here is breathtaking—especially birds. Species rarely seen elsewhere in Latin America, like the resplendent quetzal and toucan, are a dime a dozen in Honduras and in relatively easily accessible locations. Tourists have explored few of the national parks, and if you visit one there's a good chance you will be the only one there.

FAUNA

Mammals

Many consider Honduras the best place in Central America to see mammals. While threats from hunters, poachers, and shrinking habitat increase, in places such as Sierra de Agalta and Pico Bonito national parks, and the Río Plátano Biosphere Reserve, mammal sightings are relatively common. While catching a glimpse of a jaguar or ocelot is unlikely, seeing a monkey or one of almost 100 species of bats is a safe bet.

Jaguar *(Panthera onca)* This cat measures from 1 to 1.8m (3¼–6 ft.) plus tail and is distinguished by its tan/yellowish fur with black spots. Often called simply *tigre* (tiger) in Honduras. **Prime Viewing:** Jaguars exist in all major tracts of primary and secondary forest in Honduras, as well as some open savannahs. However, jaguars are endangered and extremely hard to see in the wild. The largest concentrations of jaguars can be found in the Río Plátano Biosphere Reserve in La Mosquitia and Pico Bonito National Park near La Ceiba.

Ocelot *(Leopardus pardalis)* Known as *tigrillo* in Honduras (as is the similar-sized margay), the tail of this small cat is longer than its rear leg, which makes for easy identification. Ocelots are mostly nocturnal, and they sleep in trees. **Prime Viewing:** The ocelot inhabits all regions of Honduras, with the greatest concentration found in La Mosquitia.

Jaguarundi *(Herpailurus yaguarondi)* This smallish to midsize cat, with a solid black, brown, or rust colored coat, can occasionally be spotted in a clearing or climbing trees. The jaguarundi has a unique look for a wild cat, with a face often compared to that of a weasel or otter. Jaguarundis are diurnal hunters. **Prime Viewing:** Jaguarundis are most frequently spotted in the middle elevation moist forests in Olancho or Western Honduras. They are sometimes mistaken for a tayra.

Paca *(Agouti paca)* The paca, a nocturnal rodent, inhabits the forest floor, feeding on fallen fruit, leaves, and some tubers dug from the ground. **Prime Viewing:** The paca is most often found near water throughout many habitats of Honduras, from river valleys to swamps to dense tropical forest. However, since they're nocturnal, you're much more likely to see their smaller cousin, the diurnal agouti *(guatusa)*.

Tayra *(Eira barbara)* This midsize rodent is part of the weasel family. Tayras run from dark brown to black, with a brown-to-tan head and neck. Long and low to the ground, they have a long bushy tail. **Prime Viewing:** Often called *tolumuco* in Honduras, tayras are found across the country, in forests as well as plain areas, and in trees as well as on the ground.

Baird's Tapir *(Tapirus bairdii)* Known as the *danta* in Honduras, Baird's tapir is the largest land mammal in Honduras and a relative of the rhinoceros. Tapirs are active both day and night, foraging along riverbanks, streams, and forest clearings. **Prime Viewing:** An endangered species, tapirs can be found in wet forested areas, particularly on the North Coast and throughout La Mosquitia. The Río Plátano Biosphere Reserve has a particularly high concentration of this mammal.

Coatimundi *(Nasua narica)* Known as *pizote* or *pezote* in Honduras, the raccoon-like coatimundi is active both day and night; it is equally comfortable on the ground and in trees. **Prime Viewing:** The coati is not as frequently seen in Honduras as it is in Costa Rica or places farther south, though sightings do occur on occasion in a variety of habitats across Honduras. Social animals, they are often found in groups of 10 to 20.

Collared Peccary *(Tayassu tajacu)* Sometimes called *jagüilla* in Honduras, the collared peccary is a black or brown pig-like animal that travels in small groups of 5 to 15 members (larger where populations are still numerous) and has a strong musk odor. **Prime Viewing:** You can find them in low- and middle-elevation forests throughout Honduras.

Northern Tamandua *(Tamandua mexicana)* Better known as the collared anteater (*oso hormiguero* in Spanish), the northern tamandua grows up to 77cm (30 in.) long, not counting its thick tail, which can be as long its body. It is active diurnally and nocturnally. **Prime Viewing:** Look in low- and middle-elevation forests in most of Honduras, especially in the Río Plátano Biosphere Reserve.

Three-Toed Sloth *(Bradypus variegatus)* The larger and more commonly sighted of Honduras's two sloth species, the three-toed sloth has long, coarse brown-to-gray fur and a distinctive eye band. They have three long and sharp claws on each foreleg. These slow-moving creatures are entirely arboreal. **Prime Viewing:** Sloths live in low- and middle-elevation forests in most of Honduras, though overhunting has made them move to extremely remote locations. While sloths can be found in a wide variety of trees, they are most commonly spotted in the relatively sparsely leaved cecropia.

Mantled Howler Monkey *(Alouatta palliata)* Sometimes called *mono congo,* the highly social mantled howler monkey grows to 56cm (22 in.) in size and often travels in groups of 10 to 30. The loud roar of the male can be heard as far as 1.6km (1 mile) away. **Prime Viewing:** Look in wet and dry forests across Honduras, especially La Mosquitia and along the North Coast. Almost entirely arboreal, they tend to favor the higher reaches of the canopy.

White-Faced Monkey *(Cebus capucinus)* Known as both *mono carablanca* and *mono capuchin* in Honduras, the white-faced or capuchin monkey is a midsize species (46cm/18 in.) with distinct white fur around its face, head, and forearms. It can be found in forests all around the country and often travels in large troops or family groups. **Prime Viewing:** You can see them in wet and dry forests across Honduras.

Central American Spider Monkey *(Ateles geoffroyi)* Known as *mono araña* in Honduras, the spider monkey is one of the more acrobatic monkey species. A large monkey (64cm/25 in.) with brown or silvery fur, it has long thin limbs and a long prehensile tail. It is active both day and night, and travels in small to midsize bands or family groups. **Prime Viewing:** They live in wet and dry forests across Honduras.

Nine-Banded Armadillo *(Dasypus novemcinctus)* This is the most common armadillo species. Armadillo is Spanish for "little armored one," and that's an accurate description of this hard-carapace-carrying mammal. The nine-banded armadillo can reach 65cm (26 in.) in length and weigh up to 4.5kg (10 lb.). The female gives birth to identical quadruplets from one single egg. **Prime Viewing:** You'll find them in low- and middle-elevation forests, as well as farmland, in most of Honduras. These prehistoric-looking animals are nocturnal and terrestrial.

Birds

The array of habitats and microclimates are host to an impressive count of resident and migrant birds. The number of species is fast approaching 800, and the area has long been beloved by ornithologists. In other words, Honduras is one of the world's great bird-watching spots.

Jabiru Stork *(Jabiru mycteria)* One of the largest birds in the world, the jabiru stork stands 1.5m (5 ft.) tall, with a wingspan of 2.4m (7¾ ft.) and a .3m (1-ft.) bill. An endangered species, the jabiru is very rare. **Prime Viewing:** The wetlands of southern Honduras and in La Mosquitia are the best places to try to spot the jabiru stork.

Keel-Billed Toucan *(Ramphastos sulfuratus)* The rainbow-colored canoe-shaped bill and brightly colored feathers make the keel-billed toucan a favorite of bird-watching tours. The toucan can grow to about 51cm (20 in.) in length. It's similar in size and shape to the chestnut mandibled toucan. Honduras is also home to several smaller toucanet and aracari species. **Prime Viewing:** Lowland and middle elevation forests, including Lancetilla near Tela, Pico Bonito National Park, and Lago de Yojoa, are the best places to see them.

Scarlet Macaw *(Ara macao)* Known as *guara roja* in Honduras, the scarlet macaw is a long-tailed member of the parrot family. It can reach 89cm (35 in.) in length. The bird is endangered over most of its range, particularly because it is so coveted as a pet. Its loud squawk and rainbow-colored feathers are quite distinctive. **Prime Viewing:** Look for them in low-lying tropical forest, especially La Mosquitia.

Resplendent Quetzal *(Pharomachrus mocinno)* Perhaps the most distinctive and spectacular bird in Central America, the resplendent quetzal, of the trogon family, can grow to 37cm (15 in.). The males are distinctive, with bright red chests, iridescent blue-green coats, yellow bills, and tail feathers that can reach another 76cm (30 in.) in length. The females lack the long tail feathers and have a duller beak and less pronounced red chest. **Prime Viewing:** High-elevation wet and cloud forests, particularly in La Tigra, Montaña de Celaque, Sierra de Agalta, or La Muralla National Parks, are the best places to see them.

Magnificent Frigate Bird *(Fregata magnificens)* The magnificent frigate bird is a naturally agile flier, and it swoops (unlike other seabirds, it doesn't dive or swim) to pluck food from the water's surface—or, more commonly, it steals catch from the mouths of other birds. **Prime Viewing:** Look along the shores and coastal islands of both coasts; they are often seen soaring high overhead.

Montezuma's Oropendola *(Psarocolius montezuma)* Montezuma's oropendola has a black head, a brown body, a yellow-edged tail, a large black bill with an orange tip, and a blue patch under the eye. These birds build long, teardrop-shaped hanging nests, and are often found in large groups. They have several distinct loud calls, including one that they make while briefly hanging upside down. **Prime Viewing:** You can spot the birds in low and middle elevations in La Mosquitia and along the North Coast.

Roseate Spoonbill *(Ajaia ajaja)* The roseate spoonbill is a large water bird, pink or light red in color and with a large spoon-shaped bill. Also known as *garza rosada* (pink heron). They were almost made extinct in the United States because their pink wings were sought for feather fans. **Prime Viewing:** Low-lying wetlands, both fresh and salt water, along both coasts are the best places to see them.

Cattle Egret *(Bubulcus ibis)* The cattle egret changes color during breeding: A yellowish buff color appears on the head, chest, and back, and a reddish hue emerges on the bill and legs. **Prime Viewing:** They are usually seen anywhere there are cattle, hence the name, but can also often be found following behind tractors.

Boat-Billed Heron *(Cochlearius cochlearius)* The midsize boat-billed heron (about 51cm/20 in.) has a large black head, a large broad bill, and a rusty brown color. **Prime Viewing:** They are seen throughout the country, near marshes, swamps, rivers, and mangroves. The best spots are in La Mosquitia, Cuero y Salado, and elsewhere along the North Coast.

Laughing Falcon *(Herpetotheres cachinnans)* The laughing falcon gets its name from its loud, piercing call. This largish (56cm/22-in.) bird of prey's wingspan reaches an impressive 94cm (37 in.). It specializes in eating both venomous and non-venomous snakes, but will also hunt lizards and small rodents. **Prime Viewing:** They are most commonly found in lowland areas, near forest edges, grasslands, and farmlands.

Mealy Parrot *(Amazona farinosa)* Called *loro* or *loro verde,* this large, vocal parrot is almost entirely green, apart from a touch of blue on the top of its head and small red and blue accents on its wings. *Loro* means parrot, and *verde* means green, so you and locals alike may confuse this parrot with any number of other local species. **Prime Viewing:** It's most common in lowland tropical rainforests on the North Coast and La Mosquitia.

Scarlet-Rumped Tanager *(Ramphocelus costaricensis)* With a striking scarlet red patch on its backside, this is one of the most commonly sighted tanagers in Honduras. **Prime Viewing:** The best places to spot them are in lowland and mid-elevation areas.

Osprey *(Pandion haliaetus)* These large (.6m/2-ft., with a 1.8m/6-ft. wingspan) brownish birds with white heads are also known as *gavilán pescador* or "fishing eagle." In flight, the osprey's wings "bend" backward. **Prime Viewing:** They can be seen flying or perched in trees near water in lowland coastal areas and wetlands across Honduras.

Pygmy Owl *(Glaucidium brasilianum)* Unlike most owls, this small (about 38cm/15-in.) grayish brown or reddish brown owl is most active during the day. **Prime Viewing:** They inhabit low and middle elevations along the north Pacific slope, in wooded areas, as well as forest edges and farmlands.

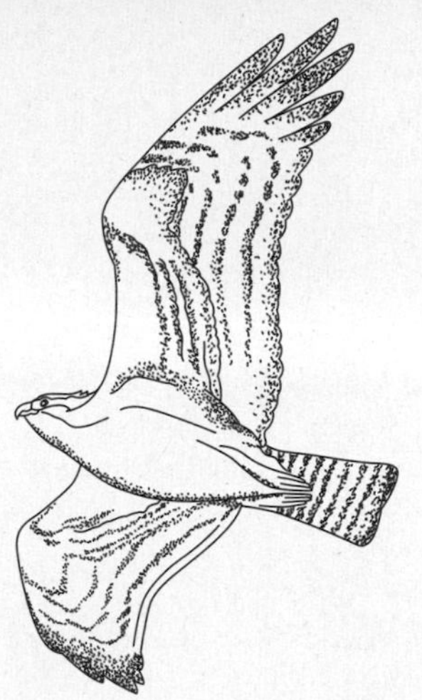

Violet Sabrewing *(Campylopterus hemileucurus)* The largest hummingbird found in Honduras, the violet sabrewing shines a deep purple when the sun strikes it right. Its beak is long, thick, and gently curving. **Prime Viewing:** Spot them in mid- and higher-elevation rain and cloud forests countrywide.

Amphibians

Frogs, toads, and salamanders are found throughout Honduras, and because of their bright and bold colors, you can easily spot them, even in dense tropical foliage.

Marine Toad *(Bufo marinus)* The largest toad in the Americas, the 20cm (7¾-in.) wart-covered marine toad is also known as *sapo grande* (giant toad). The females are mottled in color, while the males are uniformly brown. These voracious toads have been known to eat small mammals, along with other toads, lizards, and just about any insect within range. They also have a very strong toxic chemical defense mechanism. **Prime Viewing:** They live in forests and open areas throughout Honduras.

Mexican Burrowing Toad *(Rhinophrynus dorsalis)* The blob-like, 7.6cm (3-in.) Mexican burrowing toad will inflate like a blowfish when frightened. It often has a single red, orange, or yellow line down the center of its brown or black back. **Prime Viewing:** Look for them in lower-elevation forests, and moist grasslands and farmlands.

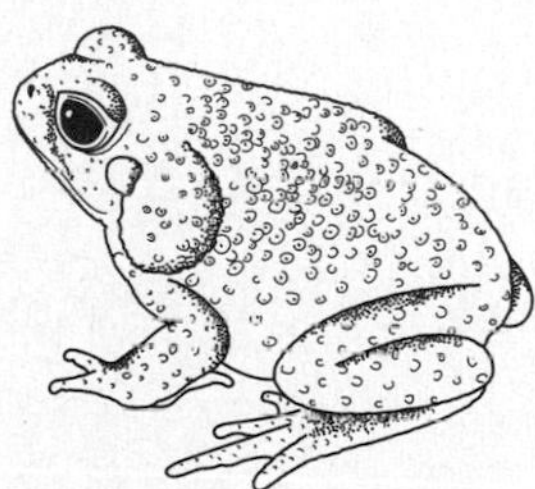

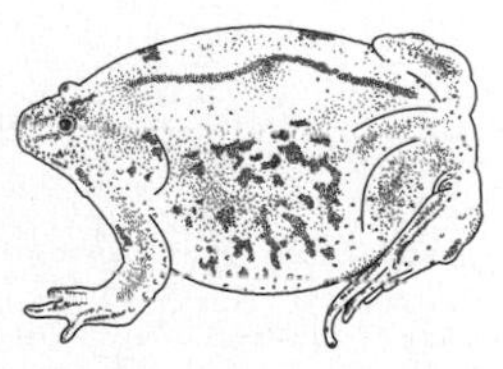

Red-Eyed Tree Frog *(Agalychnis callidryas)* The colorful 7.6cm (3-in.) red-eyed tree frog usually has a pale or dark green back, sometimes with white or yellow spots, with blue-purple patches and vertical bars on the body, orange hands and feet, and deep red eyes. This nocturnal amphibian is also known as the gaudy leaf frog or red-eyed tree frog. **Prime Viewing:** Low- and middle-elevation wet forests throughout Honduras are their territory. This is a very beautiful and distinctive-looking frog that you will certainly see on T-shirts and postcards, if not in the wild.

Reptiles

Honduras is home to slews of reptile species, ranging from cute little geckos to fearsome fer-de-lance pit vipers. The country is home to more than 100 species of snakes and several dozen lizards, as well as crocodiles and several species of sea turtles.

Boa Constrictor *(Boa constrictor)* Adult boa constrictors average about 1.8 to 3m (6–9¾ ft.) in length and weigh over 27kg (60 lb.). Their coloration camouflages them, but look for patterns of cream, brown, gray, and black ovals and diamonds. **Prime Viewing:** You can spot them in low- and middle-elevation wet and dry forests; they often live in rafters and eaves of homes in rural areas.

Fer-de-Lance *(Bothrops atrox)* Often called *barba amarilla* in Honduras, the aggressive fer-de-lance can grow to 2.4m (7¾ ft.) in length. Beige, brown, or black triangles flank either side of the head, while the area under the head is a vivid yellow. These snakes begin life as arboreal but become increasingly terrestrial as they grow older and larger. **Prime Viewing:** They are found throughout the country.

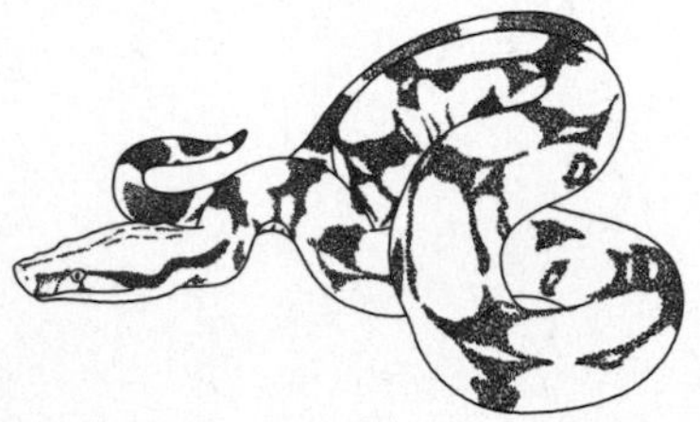

Mussurana *(Clelia clelia)* This bluish-black, brown, or grayish snake grows to 2.4m (7¾ ft.) in length. While slightly venomous, this snake has rear fangs and is of little danger to humans. In fact, it is prized and protected by locals, since its primary prey happens to be much more venomous pit vipers, like the fer-de-lance. **Prime Viewing:** You can see them in open forests, pastures, and farmlands across Honduras.

Tropical Rattlesnake *(Crotalus durissus)* This pit viper has a triangular head, a pronounced ridge running along the middle of its back, and (of course) a rattling tail. It can reach 1.8m (6 ft.) in length. **Prime Viewing:** They are mostly found in low-elevation dry forests and rural areas.

Leaf-Toed Gecko *(Phyllodactylus xanti)* Spotting the 6.8cm (2¾-in.) leaf-toed gecko is easy—it loves to be around buildings and other areas of human activity. **Prime Viewing:** They are common on the ground and in the leaf litter of low- and middle-elevation forests.

Smooth Gecko *(Thecadactylus rapicauda)* The smooth gecko's autonomous tail detaches from its body and acts as a diversion to a potential predator; it grows back later in a lighter shade. **Prime Viewing:** Find them in low-elevation wet forests on the North Coast and Bay Islands, as well as in urban and rural residential environments.

Green Iguana *(Iguana iguana)* Green iguanas can vary in shades ranging from bright green to a dull grayish-green, with quite a bit of orange mixed in. The iguana will often perch on a branch overhanging a river and plunge into the water when threatened. **Prime Viewing:** You can spot them in all lowland regions of the country, living near rivers and streams, along both coasts.

Basilisk *(Basiliscus vittatus)* The basilisk can run across the surface of water for short distances by using its hind legs and holding its body almost upright; thus, the reptile is also known as the "Jesus Christ lizard" or "Monkey La-La." **Prime Viewing:** They are found in trees and on rocks located near water in wet forests throughout the country.

American Crocodile *(Crocodylus acutus)* Although an endangered species, environmental awareness and protection policies have allowed the massive American crocodile to mount an impressive comeback in recent years. While these reptiles can reach lengths of 6.4m (21 ft.), most are much smaller, usually less than 4m (13 ft.). **Prime Viewing:** They live near swamps, mangrove swamps, estuaries, large rivers, and coastal lowlands on the North Coast.

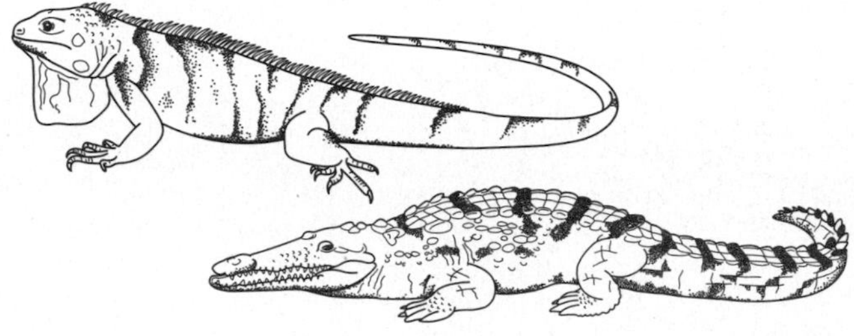

Sea Life

With a 735km (457-mile) Caribbean coastline in the north and a 153km (95-mile) Pacific coastline in the south, on top of a good chunk of the world's second-largest barrier reef along the Bay Islands, Honduras attracts its fair share of marine species.

Whale Shark *(Rhincodon typus)* Although the whale shark grows to lengths of 14m (46 ft.) or more, its gentle nature makes swimming with them a special treat for divers and snorkelers. **Prime Viewing:** They can frequently be spotted off Utila, as well as occasionally off the other Bay Islands.

Leatherback Sea Turtle *(Dermochelys coriacea)* The world's largest sea turtle (reaching nearly 2.4m/7¾ ft. in length and weighing more than 544kg/1,199 lb.), the leatherback sea turtle is now an endangered species. **Prime Viewing:** The best places to spot these massive reptiles are on the north side of Utila and along the Mosquito Coast.

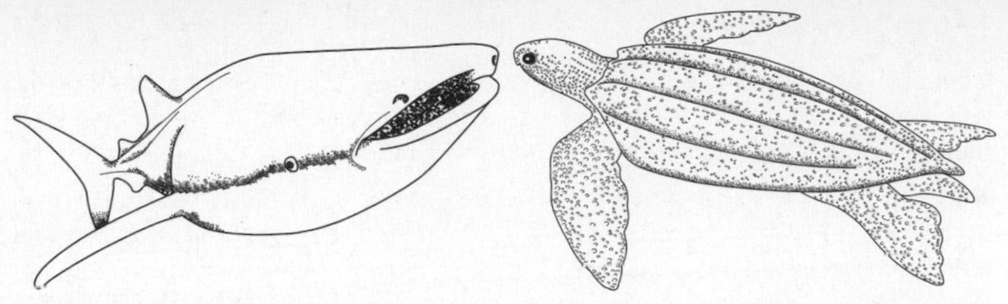

Olive Ridley Sea Turtle *(Lepidochelys olivacea)* Also known as *tortuga lora,* the Olive Ridley sea turtle is famous for its massive group nestings, or *arribadas.* **Prime Viewing:** Olive ridleys can be seen nesting on beaches or inhabiting the waters in the south of the country in the Golfo de Fonseca.

Moray Eel *(Gymnothorax mordax)* Distinguished by a swaying serpent-head and teeth-filled jaw that continually opens and closes, the moray eel is most commonly seen with only its head appearing from behind rocks. At night, however, it leaves its home along the reef to hunt for small fish, crustaceans, shrimp, and octopus. **Prime Viewing:** Spot them along rocky areas and reefs off the Bay Islands and North Coast.

Humpbacked Whale *(Megaptera novaeangliae)* The migratory humpbacked whale spends the winters in warm southern waters and has been spotted close to Honduran shores. These mammals have black backs and whitish throat and chest areas. Females have been known to calve here. **Prime Viewing:** They are most common in the waters off Utila.

Bottle-Nosed Dolphin *(Tursiops truncates)* Their wide tail fin, dark gray back, and light gray sides identify bottle-nosed dolphins. Dolphins grow to lengths of 3.7m (12 ft.) and weigh up to 635kg (1,400 lb.). **Prime Viewing:** They swim along both coasts and the Bay Islands.

Manta Ray *(Manta birostris)* Manta rays are the largest type of rays, with a wingspan that can reach 6m (20 ft.) and a body weight known to exceed 1,361kg (3,000 lb.). Despite their daunting appearance, manta rays are quite gentle. If you are snorkeling or diving, watch for one of these extraordinary and graceful creatures. **Prime Viewing:** They thrive along the north coast and around the Bay Islands.

Brain Coral *(Diploria strigosa)* The distinctive brain coral is named for its striking physical similarity to a human brain. **Prime Viewing:** See them off the Bay Islands and Cayos Cochinos.

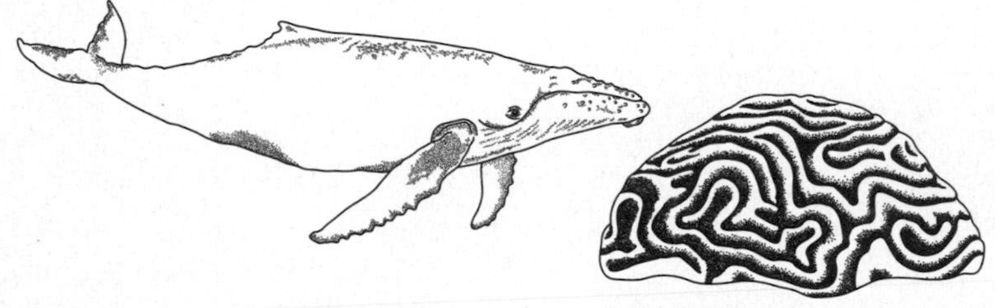

Invertebrates

Creatures that give schoolgirls the willies are some of the most abundant, fascinating, and easily viewed fauna in Honduras. Hundreds of thousands of invertebrates are found in the country, including moths, butterflies, ants, beetles, bees, and even crabs.

Blue Morpho *(Morpho peleides)* The large blue morpho butterfly, with a wingspan of up to 15cm (6 in.), has brilliantly iridescent blue wings when opened. Fast and erratic fliers, they are often glimpsed flitting across your peripheral vision in dense forest. **Prime Viewing:** You can see them throughout the country, particularly in moist environments.

Leafcutter Ants *(Atta cephalotes)* You can't miss the miniature rainforest highways formed by these industrious little red leafcutter ants, as they carry their freshly cut payload. The ants do not actually eat the leaves, but instead feed off a fungus that grows on the decomposing leaves in their massive underground nests. **Prime Viewing:** The ants can be found in most forests.

Golden Silk Spider *(Nephila clavipes)* The common neo-tropical golden silk spider weaves meticulous webs that can be as much as .5m (1¾ ft.) across. The adult female of this species can reach 7.6cm (3 in.) in length, including the legs, although the males are tiny. The silk of this spider is extremely strong and is being studied for industrial purposes. **Prime Viewing:** Look for them in lowland forests on the North Coast.

Mouthless Crab *(Gecarcinus quadratus)* The nocturnal mouthless crab is a distinctively colored land crab with bright orange legs, purple claws, and a deep black shell or carapace. **Prime Viewing:** They are found on Golfo de Fonseca.

FLORA

Trees

As you may have guessed, the huge swaths of rainforests and cloud forests found in Honduras hold an awesome array of trees. Indigenous groups throughout the country still can identify trees and their medicinal uses, though with the quickening encroachment of western civilization, that knowledge is slowly fading away. Don't be afraid to learn the names of trees. Love them. Be a tree hugger and be proud of it.

Ceiba *(Ceiba pentandra)* Also known as the kapok tree, ceiba trees are typically emergent (their large umbrella-shape canopies emerge above the forest canopy), making the species among the tallest trees in the tropical forest. Reaching as high as 60m (197 ft.), their thick columnar trunks often have large buttresses. Ceiba trees may flower as little as once every 5 years, especially in wetter forests. **Prime Viewing:** See them throughout the country.

Guanacaste *(Enterolobium cyclocarpum)* The guanacaste tree is one of the largest trees found in Central America. It can reach a total elevation of over 39m (128 ft.); its straight trunk composes 9 to 12m (30–39 ft.) of the height (the trunk's diameter measures more than 1.8m/6 ft.). **Prime Viewing:** See them throughout the country.

Strangler Fig *(Ficus aurea)* This parasitic tree gets its name from the fact that it envelops and eventually strangles its host tree. The *matapalo,* or strangler fig, begins as an epiphyte, whose seeds are deposited high in a tree's canopy by bats, birds, or monkeys. The young strangler then sends long roots down to the earth. The sap is used to relieve burns. **Prime Viewing:** They are found in primary and secondary forests countrywide.

Cecropia *(Cecropia obtusifolia)* Several cecropia (trumpet tree) species are found in Honduras. Large, hand-like clusters of broad leaves, and a hollow, bamboo-like trunk characterize most. They are "gap specialists," fast-growing opportunists that can fill in a gap caused by a tree fall or landslide. Their trunks are usually home to Aztec ants. **Prime Viewing:** See them in primary and secondary forests, rivers, and roadsides countrywide.

Gumbo Limbo *(Bursera simaruba)* Called the *indio desnudo* in Honduras. The bark of the gumbo limbo is its most distinguishing feature: A paper-thin red outer layer, when peeled off the tree, reveals a bright green bark. Both names refer to reddish skin. The bark is used as a remedy for gum disease; gumbo limbo–bark tea allegedly alleviates hypertension. Another remarkable property is the tree's ability to root from its cut branches, which, when planted right end–up, develop roots and leaves, forming a new tree within a few years. **Prime Viewing:** You can see them in primary and secondary forests countrywide.

Flowers & Other Plants

Honduras has an amazing wealth of tropical flora in its 5,000 hectares (12,355 acres) of forest cover, which includes more than 10,000 vascular plants and 600 or so species of orchids. The 36 protected cloud forests here blossom with a web of bromeliads, mosses, vines, and ferns, as well as vast tracts of pine forests, low-lying primary and secondary tropical forests, dry forests, savannahs, wetlands, and dozens of other categories only a hardcore plant nerd could identify.

Guaria Morada *(Cattleya skinneri)* Showing off a purple-and-white flower, this plant is also called the "Easter orchid," as it tends to flower between March and April each year. **Prime Viewing:** You can see them throughout the country from sea level to 1,220m (4,003 ft.).

Heliconia *(Heliconia collinsiana)* There are more than 250 species of tropical heliconia, several dozen of which are found in Honduras. The flowers of this species are darkish pink in color, and the underside of its large leaves is coated in white wax. **Prime Viewing:** See them in low to middle elevations countrywide, particularly in moist environments.

Hotlips *(Psychotria poeppigiana)* Related to coffee, hotlips is a forest flower that has thick red "lips" that resemble the Rolling Stones logo. The small white flowers (found inside the red lips) attract a variety of butterflies and hummingbirds. **Prime Viewing:** You'll find them in the undergrowth of dense forests.

Red Torch Ginger *(Nicolaia elatior)* The tall red torch ginger plant has an impressive bulbous red bract, often mistaken for the flower. The numerous, small white flowers actually emerge out of this bract. Originally a native to Indonesia, it is now quite common in Honduras. **Prime Viewing:** The best places to see them are in moist environments and gardens.

Poor Man's Umbrella *(Gunnera insignis)* The poor man's umbrella, a broad-leaved rainforest ground plant, is a member of the rhubarb family. The massive leaves are often used, as the colloquial name suggests, for protection during rainstorms. **Prime Viewing:** They are found throughout the country, in low- to middle-elevation moist forests.

Index

See also Accommodations and Restaurant indexes, below.

General Index

A

AARP, 277
Access-Able Travel Source, 271
Accessible Journeys, 271
Accommodations, 268. *See also* Accommodations Index
- best, 9–10
- Brus Laguna, 248
- Catacamas, 260
- Cayos Cochinos, 180
- Choluteca, 87
- Comayagua, 115–116
- Copán Ruínas, 124–128
- Danlí, 85
- Gracias, 137–138
- Gualaco, 261
- Guanaja, 230–233
- Isla del Tigre, 90
- Juticalpa, 255–256
- La Ceiba, 168–170
- La Esperanza, 144
- Lago de Yojoa, 108–110
- La Mosquitia, 241, 245, 248, 251
- Las Marías, 245
- Omoa, 151–152
- Palacios, 239
- Pico Bonito National Park, 176–178
- Puerto Cortés, 148–149
- Puerto Lempira, 251
- Roatán
  - Coxen Hole, 192
  - East End, 214
  - French Harbour, 208
  - Oakridge and Jonesville, 211–212
  - Punta Gorda, 213
  - Sandy Bay, 198
  - West Bay, 205–207
  - West End, 201–203
- Sambo Creek, 173–174
- San Pedro Sula, 99–102
- Santa Bárbara, 112
- Santa Lucía, 81
- Santa Rosa de Copán, 132–133
- Tegucigalpa, 66–69
- Tela, 157–160
- Trujillo, 183–184
- Utila, 220–223
- Valle de Angeles, 78–79
- Yoro, 263
- Yuscarán, 84

Acosta, Omar, 179
Active vacations, 31–44
- best adventure activities, 7
- organized adventure trips, 42–44
- suggested itinerary, 56–58

Aerial tours, Roatán, 201
Aerolíneas Sosa, 60, 94, 162, 188, 227, 235, 246, 250, 267
Aguas Termales de Azacualpa, 111
Ahuas, 251
AirAmbulanceCard.com, 271
Airline websites, 279–280
Air travel, 265, 267. *See also specific destinations and airlines*
- La Ceiba, 162
- La Mosquitia, 235
- San Pedro Sula, 94
- Tegucigalpa, 60

Alas Encantadas (Copán Ruínas), 122
Alfarería Lenca (La Campa), 140
Alton's Dive Center (Utila), 219
Amapala, 4, 89
American Airlines, 60, 265
American crocodile, 293
American Foundation for the Blind, 271
American spider monkey, 288
AmeriSpan (La Ceiba), 167
Amitigra, 77
Anthony's Key Medical Clinic (Roatán), 190
Anthony's Key Resort, 38, 198
Archaeological sites and ruins
- Copán, 118–123
- El Puente, 130–131

Archeological digs and research, 35
Archeological Institute of America, 35
Arch's Iguana Farm (Roatán), 208
Area codes, 271
Arrecife Tours, 42
Art, 22
Artesania Lencon (Santa Bárbara), 112
Artesma Garífuna (Trujillo), 183
Art galleries
- La Ceiba, 167
- Roatán, 201
- San Pedro Sula, 99

ATMs (automated-teller machines)
- Comayagua, 114
- Copán Ruinas, 118
- Gracias, 135
- La Ceiba, 165
- La Esperanza, 143
- Lago de Yojoa, 106
- Puerto Cortés, 148
- San Pedro Sula, 96
- Santa Rosa de Copán, 131
- Tegucigalpa, 65
- Tela, 154
- Trujillo, 181

Audiencia de los Confines (Gracias), 136
Australia
- customs regulations, 271
- passports, 276

Avenida Circunvalación (San Pedro Sula), 95
Avis Rent a Car, 271
Azacualpa, 111

B

Backroads, 277
Baird's tapir, 287
Bajamar, 150
***Baleadas*, 23**
Balneario Aguas Termales (near Gracias), 136
Banco Atlántida, 65, 274
- Brus Laguna, 250
- Comayagua, 114
- Copán Ruinas, 118
- Guanaja, 228
- Juticalpa, 255
- La Ceiba, 165
- Puerto Cortés, 148
- Roatán, 208
- San Pedro Sula, 96
- Santa Rosa de Copán, 131
- Tela, 154
- Trujillo, 181
- Utila, 216

Banco BGA (Utila), 216
Banco de Occidente, 135, 151
Bando Beach (Utila), 218
Banks and ATMs. *See also specific banks*
- Comayagua, 114
- Copán Ruinas, 118
- Gracias, 135
- La Ceiba, 165
- La Esperanza, 143
- Lago de Yojoa, 106
- Puerto Cortés, 148
- San Pedro Sula, 96
- Santa Rosa de Copán, 131
- Tegucigalpa, 65
- Tela, 154
- Trujillo, 181

Barbareta, 214
Barcito (Copán Ruínas), 130
Bar in the Bush (Utila), 226
Base Camp Adventures (Copán Ruínas), 40, 123
Basílica Nacional de Suyapa, 75
Basilisk, 293
Batalla, 236–238
Bay Island Airways, 188, 201, 267, 280
Bay Islands, 12, 46, 186–233
- climate, 187
- dive itinerary, 52–54

Bay Islands College of Diving (Utila), 219
Bay Islands Originals (Utila), 223
Beaches. *See also specific beaches*
- best, 6
- Guanaja, 229–230
- La Ceiba, 166–167
- La Mosquitia, 240
- Roatán, 196, 200, 214
- Tela Bay, 157

Trujillo, 182
Utila, 218
Beer, 24
Belén Gualcho, 142
Beneficio Maya (Santa Rosa de Copán), 132
Beverages, 24–25
B412 (San Pedro Sula), 105
Big Gully Waterfall, 229
Biking, 35
Billed heron, 290
***Bimini Breeze* (ferry), 181, 227**
Biosphere Museum (Palacios), 238
Bird-watching, 35–36, 288–291
Jardín Botánico Lancetilla, 156
Lago de Yojoa, 108
La Muralla National Park, 262
Macaw Mountain (Copán Ruínas), 123
Parque Nacional Capiro y Calentura, 182
Parque Nacional La Tigra, 76
Pico Pijol National Park, 262–263
Refugio de Vida Silvestre Guaimoreto, 182
Río Plátano Biosphere Reserve, 242
Black Hills (dive site), 220
Black Pearl Golf Club (Roatán), 208
Blue Marlin (Roatán), 205
Boating (boat rentals)
Chiligatoro, 143
Lago de Yojoa, 108
Boats, ferries, and cruises, 215, 266
Batalla, 238
Brus Laguna, 246–247
Cayos Cochinos, 179
Guanaja, 227
Isla del Tigre, 89
La Ceiba, 164
La Mosquitia, 235
Las Marías, 243
Palacios, 238
Puerto Cortés, 148
Roatán, 188, 190, 197
Trujillo, 181
Bonacca town (Guanaja), 228
Books, recommended, 20–22
Bottle-nosed dolphin, 294
Boulevard Juan Pablo II (Tegucigalpa), 64
Brain coral, 294
Brus Laguna, 245–249
Bugs and bug bites, 39, 269
Bull Bar (Tegucigalpa), 76
Business hours, 271
Bus travel, 266–268
Catacamas, 257
Choluteca, 86
Comayagua, 113–114
Copán, 117
Danlí, 84
Gracias, 135
Gualaco, 260
Isla del Tigre, 88–89
Juticalpa, 254–255
La Ceiba, 164–165
La Esperanza, 143
Lago de Yojoa, 105
La Mosquitia, 235
Omoa, 150
Parque Nacional La Tigra, 77
Puerto Cortés, 148
Roatán, 190
Sambo Creek, 172
San Juan, 142
San Pedro Sula, 94–95
Santa Lucía, 80
Santa Rosa de Copán, 131
Tegucigalpa, 62–63
Tela, 154
Trujillo, 180
Valle de Angeles, 78
Yuscarán, 82
Butterflies
Museo de Mariposas (La Ceiba), 166
Raista Butterfly Farm, 241
Roatán Butterfly Garden, 197, 200
By water taxi, Roatán, 190

C

Cabs
Copán, 117
Isla del Tigre, 89
Lago de Yojoa, 105
Roatán, 190
Sambo Creek, 172
San Pedro Sula, 95
Tegucigalpa, 64
Tela, 154
Cacao Lagoon, 167
Café Paradiso (Tegucigalpa), 76
Café Welchez Coffee Plantation (near Copán Ruínas), 122
Calendar of events, 25–26
Calvin's Crack (dive site), 193
Camacho Cigars, 37, 86
Camp Bay (Roatán), 214
Camping, near Parque Nacional La Tigra, 77
Canada
customs regulations, 271
passports, 276
Cannon Island, 247
Canopy tours (ziplining), 36
Pico Bonito National Park, 176
Roatán, 196
Sambo Creek, 173
Captain Morgan's Dive Shop (Utila), 219
Captain Van's Rentals (Roatán), 190, 199
Carambola Gardens (Roatán), 194, 197
Carnival Cruise Lines, 192, 195, 266, 277
Car rentals
La Ceiba, 165
San Pedro Sula, 94
Tegucigalpa, 62
Car travel, 266, 267
Catacamas, 257
Copán, 117
driving tips, 65
Gracias, 135
La Ceiba, 165
Lago de Yojoa, 105
Puerto Cortés, 148
Roatán, 190
San Pedro Sula, 94
Santa Lucía, 80
Santa Rosa de Copán, 131
Tegucigalpa, 62, 64
Tela, 154
Trujillo, 180
Valle de Angeles, 78
Casa de la Cultura (Valle de Angeles), 78
Casa del Jade (Copán Ruínas), 124
Casa del Sol (Tela), 157
Casa Fortín (Yuscarán), 84
Casa Galeano (Gracias), 136
Casa K'inich (Copán Ruínas), 122
Casa Kiwi (Trujillo), 182
Casa Verde (near La Ceiba), 41
Casino Copán (San Pedro Sula), 105
Casino Royale (Tegucigalpa), 76
Castillo Bográn (Santa Bárbara), 112
Catacamas, 257–260
Cathedral (Catedral)
Choluteca (Catedral Inmaculada Concepción), 86
Comayagua (Catedral de Santa María), 114
San Pedro Sula, 96
Suyapa (Basílica Nacional de Suyapa), 75
Tegucigalpa, 73
Cattle egret, 290
Cave of the Glowing Skulls, 258–259
Caves of Tepezcuintle, 256
Caxa Real (Comayagua), 114
Cayo Grande, 179
Cayos Cochinos, 178–180
Ceiba trees, 295
Cellphones, 273–274
Cementerio Viejo (Trujillo), 181
Centers for Disease Control and Prevention, 268
Central American School (La Ceiba), 167
Central America Spanish School, 41, 199, 216
Centro de Interpretación de Alfarería Lenca (La Campa), 140
Centro Hondureño de Español (Santa Lucía), 80

Centro Médico Betesda (San Pedro Sula), 96
Cerro Los Hoyos, 144
Chachauate Cay, 179
Chagas' disease, 270
Chepes Beach (Utila), 218
Children, families with, 272
best activities for, 8–9
suggested itinerary, 51
Children of the Light, 42, 172
Chiligatoro, 143
Chiminike (Tegucigalpa), 74
Chinda, 113
Cholera, 269
Choluteca, 86–88
Chorros de Babilonia, 258
Chortí-Maya, 12
Cigar Bar (Roatán), 204–205
Cigars
Danlí, 86
factory tours, 36–37
Flor de Copán Cigar Factory (Santa Rosa de Copán), 132
Cinemark (Tegucigalpa), 76
Circunvalación (San Pedro Sula), 95
City Mall (San Pedro Sula), 99
Ciudad Blanca, 246
CJ's Drop Off (dive site), 220
Climate, 25
Clínica Handal (Copán Ruinas), 118
Clínica Viera (Tegucigalpa), 65
CM Airlines, 60, 94, 188, 267, 280
Coatimundi, 287
Cocobila, 239
Coffee, Beneficio Maya (Santa Rosa de Copán), 132
Collared peccary, 287
Colonial Center (Tegucigalpa), 64
Colonia Palmira (Tegucigalpa), 64, 76
Colonia San Carlos (Tegucigalpa), 64
Colosuca-Celaque Tours, 40, 139, 140, 142
Columbus, Christopher, 14, 248
Comayagua, 113–117
Comayagüela (Tegucigalpa), 64
Comunidad Gay Sampedrana, 273
Conservation, 27
Consulates, 272
Continental, 265
Continental Airlines, 60
Copán, 117–122
Copán Connections, 117
Copán Museum (Copán Ruínas), 123
Copán Photo Exhibition, 123
Copán Ruínas, 117–131
accommodations, 124–128
getting there, 117
Highway CA 5 to, 111–113
nightlife, 130
outdoor activities, 123–124
restaurants, 128–130
shopping, 124
side trips from, 130–131
Coral Explorer (Roatán), 201
Cortés, Hernán, 246
Cotuc, 95, 165, 180
Courier services, 273
Coxen Hole, 192
Cristina buses, 63, 164
Crocodiles, 241, 293
Cruise lines and ships, 277
Roatán, 190, 195
shore excursions, 196–197
Cruz Alta, 141
The Cube (San Pedro Sula), 105
Cueva de Talgua, 258–259
Cuevas del Taulabe, 108
Cuevas de Susmay, 259–260
Currency exchange, Tegucigalpa, 65
Customs regulations, 271

D

D&D Brewery, 106, 108
Danilo's (San Pedro Sula), 99
Danlí, 84–86
Deep Blue Divers (Utila), 220
Delta Airlines, 60, 265
Dengue fever, 269
D-Express, 148, 266
Diana
La Ceiba, 164
San Pedro Sula, 95
Dining. *See also* Restaurants Index
Choluteca, 87
Comayagua, 116
Copán Ruínas, 128–130
Gracias, 138–139
Gualaco, 261
Guanaja, 233
Isla del Tigre, 91
Juticalpa, 256
La Ceiba, 170–171
La Esperanza, 145
Lago de Yojoa, 110–111
Omoa, 152–153
Puerto Cortés, 149–150
Roatán, 192, 198–199, 203–204
French Harbour, 208–209
West Bay, 207
Sambo Creek, 174
San Pedro Sula, 102–104
Santa Bárbara, 112
Santa Lucía, 81
Santa Rosa de Copán, 133–134
Tegucigalpa, 69–72
Tela, 160–162
Trujillo, 184–185
Utila, 223–225
Valle de Angeles, 79
Disabled travelers, 271–272
Discua Litena (Tegucigalpa), 63
Dive Shack Utila, 223
Diving, 37–38
Cayos Cochinos, 179
Guanaja, 230, 231
Roatán, 193, 200
Utila, 219–220
Dixon's Cove (Roatán), 192, 195
Doctors, 272
Dolphin Encounter (Roatán), 194–197
Dolphins, 294
training, 38
Domingo Gastronómico (Danlí), 85
***Don Enrique* (wreck), 231**
Drinking laws, 272
Driving tips, 65
Drugstores, Tegucigalpa, 65
Drug trade in La Mosquitia, 252

E

Early Bird Fishing Charters (Roatán), 201
Earth Mama's (Roatán), 41
Earthwatch, 44
East End (Roatán), 213–214
Eating and drinking, 22–25. *See also* Restaurants
Domingo Gastronómico (Danlí), 85
Ecologically oriented volunteer and study programs, 44
Economy, 19–20
***El Aguila* (wreck), 193**
El Amatillo, 88
El Bambú, 257
El Boquerón, 256–257
El Buen Gusto factory (Yuscarán), 84
El Carbón, 261
El Cusuco National Park, 32, 98
Elderhostel, 277
Electricity, 272
El Florido, 118
El Fuerte de San Cristóbal (Gracias), 136
El Naranjo, 141
El Pino, 175
El Pino Tourist Committee, 175
El Puente, 130–131
El Rey Express
Comayagua, 113
Tegucigalpa, 63
El Rosario Mining Company headquarters (near San Juancito), 77
El Triunfo, 87
Embassies and consulates, 272
Emergencies, Tegucigalpa, 65
Erandique, 142
Estadio Olímpico Metropolitano (San Pedro Sula), 98
Etiquette, in the wilderness, 39

F

Families with children, 272
best activities for, 8–9
suggested itinerary, 51
Fast food chains, 23
Feria de la Virgen de Suyapa, 26, 76
Feria de San Isidro (La Ceiba), 26
Feria Juniana (San Pedro Sula), 26
Feria San Isidro (La Ceiba), 164
Ferries and boats, 215, 266
Batalla, 238
Brus Laguna, 246–247
Cayos Cochinos, 179
Guanaja, 227
Isla del Tigre, 89
La Ceiba, 164
La Mosquitia, 235
Las Marías, 243
Palacios, 238
Puerto Cortés, 148
Roatán, 188, 190, 197
Trujillo, 181
Festival de la Lluvia de Peces (Yoro), 262
Festival Nacional del Maíz (Danlí), 85
Finca Paradise (Lago de Yojoa), 106
Fishing, 38
Brus Laguna, 247
Guanaja, 230
Lago de Yojoa, 108
Roatán, 201
Float Utila, 218
Flor de Copán Cigar Factory (Santa Rosa de Copán), 132
Flowers, 296–297
Flower's Bay (Roatán), 194
Fly Fish Guanaja, 38, 230
Flying Wheels Travel, 271
Fortaleza de San Fernando de Omoa, 151
Fortaleza de Santa Bárbara (Trujillo), 181–182
Four Sponges (dive site), 193
French Harbour (Roatán), 208–211
The Friends of El Hogar, 42
Frogs, 292
Frommers.com, 44
Fuerte de San Cristóbal (Gracias), 136
Fundación Yuscarán, 84

G

Galaxy Wave, 164, 188
Galería Nacional de Arte (Tegucigalpa), 73
Gallardo, Roberto, 36
Gap Adventures, 43
Garífuna Day, 26
Garífuna Festival (Bajamar), 26
Garífuna people and culture, 12, 15–16
Batalla, 238
cuisine, 23
Garífuna Tours, 42, 43, 156, 157
Cayos Cochinos, 179
La Ceiba, 166
Pico Bonito National Park, 175
Gays and lesbians, 273
Geckos, 292–293
Geography and geology, 26–27
Glasgow, Malcolm, 35–36
Glass-bottom boat rides, Roatán, 197, 200, 201
Glenda's Paradise Hot Springs Resort (near Sambo Creek), 172–173
Golf, 38
Roatán, 208
Golfo de Fonseca, 88, 90
Golosón International Airport (La Ceiba), 162
Gracianos (San Pedro Sula), 95
Gracias, 4, 134–139
road to La Esperanza, 143
Gran Tabacaleras Unidas (near Danlí), 86
Green iguanas, 293
Grupo Prisma, 273
Guacamaya (Copán Ruínas), 41, 124
Guadeloupe, 182–183
Gualaco, 260–261
Gualala, 113
Guamilito Market (San Pedro Sula), 99
Guanacaste tree, 296
Guanaja, 226–233
Guanaja Air, 227
Guaruma, 44, 172, 175
Guaruma trail, 175
Guasaule (Nicaragua), 87
***Guifiti*, 173**
Gumbalimba Park, 36, 196, 199–200
Gunter's Driftwood Gallery (Utila), 223

H

Haab Calendar, 18
Half Moon Bay Kayak Co., 40, 230
Halliburton (dive site), 220
HB Warren (Roatán), 192
Health and spa retreats, best, 4–5
Health concerns, 39, 268–271
Hedman Alas, 266, 268
Copán, 117
La Ceiba, 164
San Pedro Sula, 94, 95
Tegucigalpa, 62–63
Hibou (La Ceiba), 171–172
Hibou (San Pedro Sula), 105
Hiking, 38–40
Cayo Grande, 179
Cerro Los Hoyos, 144
Copán Ruínas, 123
El Boquerón, 256–257
Guanaja, 228–229
Las Golondrinas Waterfall, 78
Parque Nacional La Tigra, 77
Pico Bonito National Park, 175
Historical sites, most intriguing, 8
History of Honduras, 11–20
HIV/AIDS, 270
Homestays, Isla del Tigre, 90
Honduras Coral Reef Fund, 44, 179
Honduras Medical Center (Tegucigalpa), 65
Hondutel
Brus Laguna, 247
Catacamas, 257
Comayagua, 114
Copán Ruinas, 118
Gracias, 136
Juticalpa, 255
La Ceiba, 165
Puerto Cortés, 148
Puerto Lempira, 250
San Pedro Sula, 96
Tegucigalpa, 66
Tela, 155
Trujillo, 181
Utila, 216
Honduyate Marina (Lago de Yojoa), 108
Horseback riding, 40
Brus Laguna, 248
Copán Ruínas, 123
La Ceiba, 167
Pico Bonito National Park, 176
Utila, 219
Valle de Angeles, 78
Hospitals
La Ceiba, 165
Lago de Yojoa, 106
San Pedro Sula, 96
Tegucigalpa, 65
Hotel Guancascos (Gracias), 139
Hotels, 268. *See also* Accommodations Index
best, 9–10
Brus Laguna, 248
Catacamas, 260
Cayos Cochinos, 180
Choluteca, 87
Comayagua, 115–116
Copán Ruínas, 124–128
Danlí, 85
Gracias, 137–138
Gualaco, 261
Guanaja, 230–233
Isla del Tigre, 90
Juticalpa, 255–256

Hotels *(cont.)*
La Ceiba, 168–170
La Esperanza, 144
Lago de Yojoa, 108–110
La Mosquitia, 241, 245, 248, 251
Las Marías, 245
Omoa, 151–152
Palacios, 239
Pico Bonito National Park, 176–178
Puerto Cortés, 148–149
Puerto Lempira, 251
Roatán
Coxen Hole, 192
East End, 214
French Harbour, 208
Oakridge and Jonesville, 211–212
Punta Gorda, 213
Sandy Bay, 198
West Bay, 205–207
West End, 201–203
Sambo Creek, 173–174
San Pedro Sula, 99–102
Santa Bárbara, 112
Santa Lucía, 81
Santa Rosa de Copán, 132–133
Tegucigalpa, 66–69
Tela, 157–160
Trujillo, 183–184
Utila, 220–223
Valle de Angeles, 78–79
Yoro, 263
Yusçarán, 84
Hot springs (thermal baths)
Aguas Termales de Azacualpa, 111
Balneario Aguas Termales (near Gracias), 136
Glenda's Paradise Hot Springs Resort (near Sambo Creek), 172–173
Termas del Rio (near Gracias), 136
HSBC
Puerto Cortés, 148
Santa Rosa de Copán, 131
Humpbacked whale, 294
Hurricane Mitch, 13

I

Iglesia de Nuestra Señora de los Dolores (Tegucigalpa), 73
Iglesia de San Marcos (Gracias), 136
Iglesia La Merced
Comayagua, 115
Tegucigalpa, 73
Iglesia San Jose (Yuscarán), 84
Iglesia y Convento de San Francisco (Comayagua), 114
Iguana Farm (Roatán), 197
Iguana Research and Breeding Station (Utila), 217–218
Iguanas, 293
Iguanas Sports Bar and Discotec (Tela), 162
Independence, 16
Independence Day, 26
Inner tubing, Brus Laguna, 248
Insects, 295
Instituto Hondureño de Turismo, 63
Insurance, 272
International Association for Medical Assistance to Travelers (IAMAT), 268
International Gay and Lesbian Travel Association (IGLTA), 273
International Student Identity Card (ISIC), 278
International Youth Travel Card (IYTC), 278
Internet access, 272–273
Copán Ruinas, 118
La Ceiba, 165
Lago de Yojoa, 106
Tegucigalpa, 65
Invertebrates, 295
Isla del Tigre, 88–91
Isleña Airlines, 94, 162, 188, 267, 280
Itineraries, suggested, 47–59
Ixbalanque (Copán Ruínas), 41, 124

J

Jabiru stork, 289
***Jado Trader* (wreck), 231**
Jaguar, 286
Jaguar Tunnels (Copán), 122
Jaguarundi, 287
Jardín Botánico (Gracias), 136
Jardín Botánico Lancetilla (near Tela), 32, 156
Jonesville (Roatán), 211–212
Jose Cecilio del Valle's family home (Choluteca), 87
Journey Latin America, 43
Jungle Expedition, 40, 98
Jungle River Tours, 35, 36, 42, 43, 169, 175, 176
Jungle survival course (Raista), 241
Junqueños (Santa Bárbara), 112
Juticalpa, 254–257

K

Kaukira, 250–251
Kayaking, 40
Brus Laguna, 248
Guanaja, 230
La Ceiba, 167
Lago de Yojoa, 108
Utila, 218
Kayak Utila, 40, 218
Keel-billed toucan, 289
King Quality, 63, 95, 266
Kite Honduras (Roatán), 42, 211
Kite surfing, 42
Roatán, 211

L

La Campa, 140–141
La Casa de Todo (Copán Ruínas), 118, 124
La Ceiba, 162–172
accommodations, 168–170
banks and ATMs, 165
getting around, 165
getting there, 162, 164–165
hospitals, 165
nightlife, 171–172
orientation, 165
outdoor activities, 166–167
restaurants, 170–171
shopping, 167–168
sights and attractions, 166
visitor information, 165
La Chorrera (near Yamaranguila), 145
Ladinos (mestizos), 12
La Entrada, 130
La Ermita (La Esperanza), 143
La Escuelona (La Campa), 140
La Esperanza, 143–145
Lago de Yojoa, 105–111
Lagoon Marina (La Ceiba), 164
Laguna Bacalar, 238
Laguna de Caratasca, 249–252
Laguna de Ibans, 239–241
La Moskitia Ecoaventuras, 40, 42, 43, 167, 236, 258, 261
La Mosquitia, 46, 234–252
getting around, 235
getting there, 235
suggested itinerary, 54–56
tour operators, 235–236
La Muralla trail, 175
Lance Bodden Rentals (Utila), 216
Language, 273
Language immersion, 41
Lanhsa Airlines, 162, 188, 215, 227, 235, 267
La Palapa (La Ceiba), 172
La Ruta Lenca, 140–145
La Ruta Moskitia, 40, 43, 236, 248
Las Golondrinas Waterfall, 78
Las Mangas, 174, 175
Las Marías, 242–245
Las Mercedes (Gracias), 136
Las Sepulturas (Copán), 122
La Tigra National Park, 31–32, 76–77
Laughing falcon, 290
Laundry and dry cleaning
La Ceiba, 165
San Pedro Sula, 96
Tegucigalpa, 66
La Unión, 261

Lavamatic Ceibeño (La Ceiba), 165
Legal aid, 273
Leimus, 250
Leishmaniasis, 270
Lempira, 135, 142
Lenca Land Trails (Santa Rosa de Copán), 132
Lenca Route, 140
Lencas, 12
  cooking, 24
Le Pacha (La Ceiba), 171
LGBT travelers, 273
Llama, 113
Lodging, 268. *See also* Accommodations Index
  best, 9–10
  Brus Laguna, 248
  Catacamas, 260
  Cayos Cochinos, 180
  Choluteca, 87
  Comayagua, 115–116
  Copán Ruínas, 124–128
  Danlí, 85
  Gracias, 137–138
  Gualaco, 261
  Guanaja, 230–233
  Isla del Tigre, 90
  Juticalpa, 255–256
  La Ceiba, 168–170
  La Esperanza, 144
  Lago de Yojoa, 108–110
  La Mosquitia, 241, 245, 248, 251
  Las Marías, 245
  Omoa, 151–152
  Palacios, 239
  Pico Bonito National Park, 176–178
  Puerto Cortés, 148–149
  Puerto Lempira, 251
  Roatán
    Coxen Hole, 192
    East End, 214
    French Harbour, 208
    Oakridge and Jonesville, 211–212
    Punta Gorda, 213
    Sandy Bay, 198
    West Bay, 205–207
    West End, 201–203
  Sambo Creek, 173–174
  San Pedro Sula, 99–102
  Santa Bárbara, 112
  Santa Lucía, 81
  Santa Rosa de Copán, 132–133
  Tegucigalpa, 66–69
  Tela, 157–160
  Trujillo, 183–184
  Utila, 220–223
  Valle de Angeles, 78–79
  Yoro, 263
  Yuscarán, 84
Long Count Calendar, 18
Los Micos Lagoon, 156
Los Sapos (near Copán Ruínas), 123
Luna Jaguar Spa Resort (near Copán Ruínas), 123–124

M

Macaw Mountain (Copán Ruínas), 123
Made in Honduras (Trujillo), 183
Maduro Dive, 38
Magnificent frigate bird, 289
Mail, 273
Malaria, 269
Mall Megaplaza (La Ceiba), 167
Mango Festival (Yuscarán), 84
M@ngo Café (Tela), 157
Mango Tango (La Ceiba), 172
Mango Tree House (Utila), 216
Mangrove tours, Roatán, 211
Manta ray, 294
Mantled howler monkey, 288
Markets and shopping, best, 5–6
  La Ceiba, 167–168
Mary's Place (dive site), 193
Maya Calendar, 18
Maya Children's Museum (Copán Ruínas), 122
Maya Research Program, 35
Maymo Art Gallery (San Pedro Sula), 99
The Maze (dive site), 220
MC Tours, 40, 43, 123, 197
Medical requirements for entry, 273
Mesoamerican Ecotourism Alliance/MEA, 43, 236
Mestizo Reef, 231
Mestizos (Ladinos), 12
Miami, 3, 155–156
Michael's Rock (Guanaja), 230
Migración (Puerto Cortés), 148
Military rule, 16, 18–19
Miskito culture, 242
Miskito songs and dances, 241
Mistruk, 250
Mobile phones, 273–274
Money and costs, 274–275
Montezuma's oropendola, 289
Monumento Nacional El Boquerón, 34, 256–257
MOPAWI headquarters (Puerto Lempira), 250
Morat, 214
Moray eel, 294
MossRehab, 271
Mountain Travel Sobek, 43
Multiplaza Mall (Tegucigalpa), 75
Museo Casa de Morazán (Tegucigalpa), 73
Museo Colonial de Arte Religioso (Comayagua), 115
Museo de Arqueología e Historia de San Pedro Sula, 96, 98
Museo de la Naturaleza (San Pedro Sula), 98
Museo del Hombre Hondureño (Tegucigalpa), 73
Museo de Mariposas (La Ceiba), 166
Museo Histórico de la República (Tegucigalpa), 74
Museo Municipal (Danlí), 85
Museo Nacional de Historia y Antropología Villa Roy (Tegucigalpa), 74
Museo para la Identidad Nacional (Tegucigalpa), 73–74
Museo Regional de Arqueología (Comayagua), 115
Museo Regional de Arqueología (Copán Ruínas), 123
Museo Rufino Galán (Trujillo), 182
Museum of Anthropology and History of San Pedro Sula, 96, 98
Museum of Maya Sculpture (Copán), 118, 120
Music, 22

N

National Audubon Society, 36
National parks and bio-reserves, 31–35
Natural resources, 27
Nature Museum (San Pedro Sula), 98
Nau (Tegucigalpa), 76
Nautilus, 230
Newspapers and magazines, 275
New Zealand, customs regulations, 271
Nicaragua, border crossings into
  El Amatillo/San Carlos, 88
  El Florido, 118
  El Triunfo/Guasaule, 87
  Leimus, 250
Nightlife
  Copán Ruínas, 130
  La Ceiba, 171–172
  Roatán, 204–205
  San Pedro Sula, 104–105
  Tegucigalpa, 75–76
  Tela, 162
  Trujillo, 185
  Utila, 226
Nine-banded armadillo, 288
North coast, 146–185
The North Coast, 46
Northern tamandua, 287
NPH International, 42
Nuestra Señora de la Caridad (Comayagua), 114

O

Oakridge (Roatán), 211–212
Ocelot, 286

Ojochal Wildlife Reserve, 87
Olancho, 46, 253–263
Omega Tours, 35, 40, 42, 43, 166, 167, 175, 176, 236
Omoa, 150–153
Osprey, 290
Outdoor activities. *See also* Active vacations
  Brus Laguna, 247–248
  Copán Ruínas, 123–124
  Guanaja, 228–230
  La Ceiba, 166–167
  Roatán, 192–193, 200–201
  San Pedro Sula, 98–99
  Tegucigalpa, 75
  Trujillo, 182–183
  Utila, 218–220
Overseas Adventure Travel, 44

P

Paca, 287
Packing tips, 275
Palacios, 238–239
Palmetto Ridge Canopy, 36, 196
Parque Central
  Gracias, 136
  La Esperanza, 143
  San Pedro Sula, 95, 96
Parque Eco-Archeological de Los Naranjos (Lago de Yojoa), 106
Parque Morazán (Tegucigalpa), 64, 73
Parque Nacional Capiro y Calentura, 33, 182
Parque Nacional Celaque, 141
Parque Nacional Cerro Azul Meámbar, 32, 106
Parque Nacional El Cusuco, 32, 98
Parque Nacional Jeannette Kawas/Punta Sal, 32–33, 156–157
Parque Nacional La Muralla, 34, 262
Parque Nacional La Tigra, 31–32, 76–77
Parque Nacional Marino Cayos Cochinos, 33
Parque Nacional Montaña de Celaque, 32, 139
Parque Nacional Montaña de Santa Bárbara, 32, 107
Parque Nacional Pico Pijol, 34, 262–263
Parque Nacional Sierra de Agalta, 34, 257–258
Parque Naciones Unidas El Picacho (Tegucigalpa), 74
Parroquia San Francisco (Tegucigalpa), 73
Parrots, 290
Paseo La Leona (Tegucigalpa), 75
Paya Bay (Roatán), 214
Peñol de Perquín (near Erandique), 142
Pérez, Doña Desideria, 140
Pescado Roatán, 201
Petroglyphs, 243, 244
Pico Baltimore, 245
Pico Bonito National Park, 33, 174–178
Pico Dama, 243
Pico el Zapote, 245
Pico La Picucha, 258
Piedra Parada (near Erandique), 142
Pinnacle (dive site), 231
PiQ' Art Gallery (La Ceiba), 167
Pirates, 15
  Bay Islands, 213
Pirates of the Caribbean Canopy, 36, 196
Planning your trip, 264–280
  accommodations, 268
  customs regulations, 271
  disabled travelers, 271–272
  electricity, 272
  embassies and consulates, 272
  family travel, 272
  getting around, 267–268
  getting there, 265–266
  health concerns, 268–271
  insurance, 272
  Internet and Wi-Fi, 272–273
  LGBT travelers, 273
  mail, 273
  medical requirements for entry, 273
  mobile phones, 273–274
  money and costs, 274–275
  newspapers and magazines, 275
  packing tips, 275
  passports, 275–276
  police, 276
  safety, 276–277
  single travel, 277
  student travel, 277–278
Plaplaya, 239
Plasencia Tobacco (near Danlí), 86
Playa Cieneguita (near Puerto Cortés), 148
Playa Coca Cola (near Puerto Cortés), 148
Playa de Peru (near La Ceiba), 166
Playa El Burro (Isla del Tigre), 89
Playa El Faro (near Puerto Cortés), 148
Playa Negra (Isla del Tigre), 89
Police, 276
  Tegucigalpa, 66
Popol Vuh, 18
Post office
  La Ceiba, 165
  Tegucigalpa, 66
Post offices, San Pedro Sula, 96
Prescription medications, 270
Prince Albert (wreck), 193
PROLANSATE (Tela), 155
Proyecto Aldea Global/Project Global Village, 107
Puerto Castilla, 235
Puerto Cortés, 146–150
Puerto Lempira, 249–251
Pulhapanzak Falls, 107–108
Puma Trail Tours, 139
Punta Gorda (Roatán), 212–213
Puros Aliados Cigar (near Danlí), 86
Pygmy owl, 290

R

Rafting, Río Plátano, 244
Rain Forest Souvenir shop (La Ceiba), 167
Raista/Belén, 3–4, 240–241
Raista Butterfly Farm, 241
Rawacala Eco Park, 36, 151
Red Ridge Stables (Utila), 40, 219
Reef Cinema (Utila), 218
Refugio de Vida Silvestre Guaimoreto, 33, 182
Refugio de Vida Silvestre Ojochal, 32, 87
Refugio de Vida Silvestre Punta Izopo, 33, 157
Refugio Nacional de Vida Silvestre Cuero y Salado, 33, 166
Regions in brief, 45–46
Religion, 13
Reptiles, 292
Reserva de la Bíosfera del Río Plátano, 34, 242
Reserva de la Bíosfera del Tawahka Asangni, 34, 251–252
Reserva Marina Turtle Harbour, 33
Responsible travel, 28–30
Restaurants. *See also* Restaurants Index
  Choluteca, 87
  Comayagua, 116
  Copán Ruínas, 128–130
  Gracias, 138–139
  Gualaco, 261
  Guanaja, 233
  Isla del Tigre, 91
  Juticalpa, 256
  La Ceiba, 170–171
  La Esperanza, 145
  Lago de Yojoa, 110–111
  Omoa, 152–153
  Puerto Cortés, 149–150
  Roatán, 192, 198–199, 203–204
    French Harbour, 208–209
    West Bay, 207
  Sambo Creek, 174
  San Pedro Sula, 102–104

Santa Bárbara, 112
Santa Lucía, 81
Santa Rosa de Copán, 133–134
Tegucigalpa, 69–72
Tela, 160–162
Trujillo, 184–185
Utila, 223–225
Valle de Angeles, 79
Río Plátano Biosphere Museum (Palacios), 238
Río Plátano Biosphere Reserve, 242, 246
Roatán, 187–214
accommodations, 192, 198, 201–203
beaches, 196
Coxen Hole, 192
cruise ships and shore excursions, 195–197
currency, 188
Dixon's Cove, 192–194
East End, 213–214
Flower's Bay, 194
French Harbour, 208–211
getting around, 190
getting there, 188, 190
nightlife, 204–205
Oakridge and Jonesville, 211–212
orientation, 190
outdoor activities, 192–193, 200–201
Punta Gorda, 212–213
restaurants, 203–204
Sandy Bay, 194–199
shopping, 192
shore excursions, 196–197
sights and attractions, 194–197
visitor information, 190
West Bay, 205–207
West End, 199–205
Roatán Air Services, 188, 227
Roatán Butterfly Garden, 197, 200
Roatán Charters, 43
Roatán-in-a-Bottle Parks, 196
Roatán Institute of Deep Sea Exploration, 197, 200–201
Roatán International Airport, 188
Roatán Marine Park Office, 201
Roatán Museum and Institute of Marine Sciences, 195
Roatán Shore Tours, 197
Roatan Zoo & Island Adventure, 197
Rogue's Gallery (Trujillo), 185
Roli's Place (Omoa), 150
Rollins Air, 162
Rosalia Temple (Copán), 122
Roseate spoonbill, 290
Royal Caribbean, 277
Ruins and archaeological sites
Copán, 118–123
El Puente, 130–131

S

Sabor Cubano (Tegucigalpa), 76
Saenz, San Pedro Sula, 95
Saenz buses, Tegucigalpa, 63
Safety, 276–277
Olancho, 254
in the wilderness, 39
Sailing, Lago de Yojoa, 108
Sambo Creek, 166, 172–174
Sami Airlines, 235, 246, 250, 267
San Antonio, 182
Sand flies (no-seeums), 226
Sandy Bay (Roatán), 194–199
Sandy Bay & West End Marine Park, 33
San Jose de los Colinas, 113
San Juan, 142
San Manuel de Colohete, 141
San Marcos de Caiquín, 141
San Marcos de Colón, 87
San Miguel Plus, 63
San Pedro Sula, 92–105
accommodations, 99–102
banks and ATMs, 96
getting around, 95
getting there, 94–95
hospitals, 96
Internet and call centers, 96
nightlife, 104–105
orientation, 95
outdoor activities, 98–99
police, 96
post office, 96
restaurants, 102–104
shopping, 99
sights and attractions, 96–98
visitor information, 96
water, 96
San Pedro Sula International Airport, 94
San Pedro Zacapa, 111
San Sebastián, 141
Santa Bárbara, 111–112
Santa Fe, 182
Santa Helena, 214
Santa Lucía, 4, 80–81
Santa Lucía Serpentarium, 80
Santa María, Catedral de, 114
Santa Rosa de Copán, 131–134
SATH (Society for Accessible Travel & Hospitality), 271
Scarlet macaw, 289
Scarlet-rumped tanager, 290
Scooters, Roatán, 190
Scorpion bites, 270
Scuba diving, 37–38
Cayos Cochinos, 179
Guanaja, 230, 231
Roatán, 193, 200
Utila, 219–220
Seasons, 25
Sea Turtle Conservation Project (Plaplaya), 239
Sea turtles, 293–294
Plaplaya, 239
Semana Santa (Holy Week)
Comayagua, 26, 114
Santa Rosa de Copán, 132
Sendero la Cascada (La Tigra), 77
Sendero la Mina (La Tigra), 77
Sendero las Plancitos (La Tigra), 77
Sendero Principal (La Tigra), 77
Senior travel, 277
Shark diving, Roatán, 192–193
Shopping
Roatán, 192
Trujillo, 183
Utila, 223
Sierra de Agalta National Park, 253, 257
Siguatepeque, 116–117
Single travel, 277
Skyservice (La Ceiba), 162
Smoking, 277
Snake bites, 270
Snakes, 292
Snorkeling, 37–38
Cayos Cochinos, 179
Utila, 219–220
Soccer, San Pedro Sula, 98
Soccer War, 19
Sol de Maya (Copán Ruínas), 130
Southern Honduras, 46, 82–91
suggested itinerary, 58–59
South Shore Canopy Tour, 36, 196
Souvenir El Buen Amigo (La Ceiba), 167
Spa and yoga retreats, 41
Spa Ixchel (near Copán), 124
Spanish conquest, 14–15
Spanish-language classes, 41
Copán Ruínas, 124
La Ceiba, 167
Roatán, 199
Santa Lucía, 80
Tela, 157
Utila, 216
Spas and yoga retreats
Copán Ruínas, 123–124
Pico Bonito National Park, 176, 177
Yoga's Garden Spa (Tegucigalpa), 75
Spirit, 265
Spooky Channel (dive site), 193
Sports and outdoor activities. ***See also*** **Active vacations;** ***and specific activities***
Brus Laguna, 247–248
Copán Ruínas, 123–124
Guanaja, 228–230
La Ceiba, 166–167
Roatán, 192–193, 200–201
San Pedro Sula, 98–99
Tegucigalpa, 75
Trujillo, 182–183
Utila, 218–220

STA Travel, 278
Stingray Point (dive site), 220
Street food, Tegucigalpa, 72
Student travel, 277–278
Study programs, ecologically oriented, 44
Sundowners Bar (Roatán), 205
Sun Jam Festival (Water Cay), 26
Susmay caves, 259–260
Sustainable Harvest International, 44
Sustainable tourism, 28–30
Suyapa, 64

T

Tabacos Hondureños S.A. (Santa Rosa de Copán), 132
Tabyana (Roatán), 196
Tabyana Tours, 197
TACA, 60, 265
  La Ceiba, 162
Taca Regional Airlines, 60
Tawahka people, 251–252
Taxis
  Copán, 117
  Isla del Tigre, 89
  Lago de Yojoa, 105
  Roatán, 190
  Sambo Creek, 172
  San Pedro Sula, 95
  Tegucigalpa, 64
  Tela, 154
Tayra, 287
Team Marin Fishing, 38, 247
Teatro Nacional Manuel Bonilla (Tegucigalpa), 75
Tegucigalpa, 60–81
  accommodations, 66–69
  banks, 65
  currency exchange, 65
  drugstores, 65
  emergencies, 65
  getting around, 64–65
  hospitals, 65
  Internet access, 65
  laundry and dry cleaning, 66
  layout, 63
  neighborhoods in brief, 64
  nightlife, 75–76
  outdoor activities, 75
  police, 66
  post office, 66
  restaurants, 69–72
  safety, 66
  shopping, 75
  side trips from, 76–81
  sights and attractions, 73–76
  suggested itinerary, 58–59
  telephones, 66
  visitor information, 63
  water, 66
Tela, 153–162
  accommodations, 157–160
  getting around, 154
  getting there, 154
  nightlife, 162
  orientation, 154
  outdoor activities, 157
  restaurants, 160–162
  shopping, 157
  sights and activities, 155–157
Tela Chamber of Commerce, 155
Tela Express, 95
Telephone, La Ceiba, 165
Telephones, 278. *See also* Hondutel
Temperatures, 25
Termas del Rio (near Gracias), 136
Terminal Metropolitana de Autobuses (near San Pedro Sula), 95
Thermal springs
  Aguas Termales de Azacualpa, 111
  Balneario Aguas Termales (near Gracias), 136
  Glenda's Paradise Hot Springs Resort (near Sambo Creek), 172–173
  Termas del Rio (near Gracias), 136
Three-toed sloth, 287
TICA, 95
Tica Bus, 63, 266
Time zone, 278
Tipping, 278
Toads, 291
Tocontín International Airport (Tegucigalpa), 60, 62
Toilets, 278
Tolupan people, 12, 262
Toto Tours, 273
Tourist information, 278–279
  Gracias, 135–136
  La Ceiba, 165
  La Esperanza, 143
  Omoa, 151
  Puerto Cortés, 148
  Roatán, 190
  Santa Rosa de Copán, 131
  Tegucigalpa, 63
  Tela, 155
  Trujillo, 181
  Utila, 216
Tourist Police
  La Ceiba, 165
  Tela, 155
Tranquila Bar (Utila), 226
Transportes Discovery/Aurora, 255, 257
Transportes Mi Esperanza (Choluteca), 86
Transportes Rivera (Comayagua), 113
Travel Buddies Singles Travel Club, 277
TravelChums, 277
Travel CUTS, 278
Traveler's checks, 274–275
Traveler's diarrhea, 269
Travel insurance, 272
Travesia, 150
Trees, 295
Treetanic Bar (Utila), 226
Trinidad, 113
Tropical illnesses, 269
Tropical Rez, 197
Trujillo, 180–185
Truxillo Disco (Trujillo), 185
Tun Club (Copán Ruínas), 130
Turaser, 173
Typhoid fever, 269
Tzolkin Calendar, 18

U

Uncommon Adventures, 38
Underwater Paradise, 197
Underwater Paradise (Roatán), 201
United Kingdom
  consulate, 272
  customs regulations, 271
  passports, 276
United States
  customs regulations, 271
  embassy, 272
  passports, 276
USIT, 278
Utila, 214–226
  accommodations, 220–223
  getting around, 216
  getting there, 215–216
  nightlife, 226
  orientation, 216
  outdoor activities, 218–220
  restaurants, 223–225
  shopping, 223
  sights and activities, 216–218
  Sun Jam Festival (Water Cay), 216
  visitor information, 216
Utila Dive Center, 220
***Utila Princess II* (La Ceiba), 164**
Utila Water Sports, 40, 218
Utila Whale Shark Research, 219
Utopia Dive Village (Utila), 220

V

Valle de Angeles, 4, 77–79
Vertigo (dive site), 231
Viana, 95, 164
Viana Clase de Oro, 63, 268
Victor Emanuel Nature Tours, 36
Villa Elena Country Club (near Tegucigalpa), 38, 75
Village Trail loop, 245
Violet sabrewing, 291
Virgen de Suyapa, 76
Visitor information, 278–279
  Gracias, 135–136
  La Ceiba, 165
  La Esperanza, 143

Omoa, 151
Puerto Cortés, 148
Roatán, 190
Santa Rosa de Copán, 131
Tegucigalpa, 63
Tela, 155
Trujillo, 181
Utila, 216
Volunteer and working trips, 41–42, 44
Cayos Cochinos, 179
northern Honduras, 172
Volunteer Honduras, 41

W

Waihuka Adventure Diving (Roatán), 192–193
Walpaulban Sirpi petroglyphs, 243, 244
Walpaulban Tara, 243
Wampusirpi, 251
Water, drinking, Tegucigalpa, 66
Water Cay, 218
Waterfalls
Big Gully Waterfall, 229
Chorros de Babilonia, 258
La Chorrera (near Yamaranguila), 145
Pulhapanzak Falls, 107–108
Waterparks, San Pedro Sula, 98–99
Wave Gallery (Roatán), 201
Weather, 25
Websites, 278–279
West Bay (Roatán), 205–207
West Bay Beach (Roatán), 196, 205
West End
Guanaja, 230
Roatán, 199–205
Western Honduras, 46, 92–145
Whale Shark and Oceanic Research Center (Utila), 218, 219
Whale sharks, 293
White-faced monkey, 288
Whitewater rafting, 42
Pico Bonito National Park, 175
Río Plátano, 244
Wildlife watching, 286–295. *See also* Butterflies
Arch's Iguana Farm (Roatán), 208
best, 7–8
bird-watching, 35–36, 288–291
Jardín Botánico Lancetilla, 156
Lago de Yojoa, 108
La Muralla National Park, 262
Macaw Mountain (Copán Ruínas), 123
Parque Nacional Capiro y Calentura, 182
Parque Nacional La Tigra, 76
Pico Pijol National Park, 262–263
Refugio de Vida Silvestre Guaimoreto, 182
Río Plátano Biosphere Reserve, 242
Cayos Cochinos, 178
La Mosquitia, 240
Refugio de Vida Silvestre Punta Izopo, 157
Refugio Nacional de Vida Silvestre Cuero y Salado, 166
Río Plátano Biosphere Reserve, 242
Roatán, 197
Sierra de Agalta National Park, 257–258
Utila, 217–218
Wind and kite surfing, 42
Wind Surf Honduras, 42, 198
Windsurfing, Roatán, 198
Wings, 36
Wonderland (San Pedro Sula), 99

X

Xukpi, 40, 123

Y

Yaba Ding Ding (Roatán), 192
Yamaranguila, 145
Yaragua, 40, 123
Yaragua Tours, 122
Yellowman (Tela), 162
Yoga's Garden Spa (near Tegucigalpa), 41, 75
Yoro, 262–263
Yuscarán, 82–84

Z

Zacapa, 111
Zizima Eco Water Park (San Pedro Sula), 98–99
Zona Viva (San Pedro Sula), 105

Accommodations

Airport Hillton (Guanaja), 232
Bahía de Omoa, 151–152
Bananarama (Roatán), 205–206
Banana Republic Guest House (La Ceiba), 169
Barefoot Cay (Roatán), 209
Bayside Tela, 158
Blue Bahia Resort (Roatán), 198
Brisa (Punta Gorda), 213
Brisas del Lago (Lago de Yojoa), 109
Cabana Lana (Roatán), 206
Cabaña Mirador El Rosario (Parque Nacional La Tigra), 77
Camino Maya (Copán Ruínas), 126
Casa Alemania (Trujillo), 183
Casa Calico (Roatán), 201
Casa Cangrejal (Pico Bonito), 177–178
Casa Colibri (Yuscarán), 84
Casa de Café (Copán Ruínas), 126–127
Casa del Arbol Centro (San Pedro Sula), 101
Casa Kiwi (Trujillo), 184
Casa Real (Santa Rosa de Copán), 132–133
Casa Rosada (Copán), 125
Casa Verde (Pico Bonito), 177
Cay View Hotel (Roatán), 192
Cesar Mariscos Annex (Tela), 158–159
Clarion Hotel Posada Real (Copán), 125
Clarion Hotel Real Tegucigalpa, 68
Clarion Los Proceres (San Pedro Sula), 99
Coco Bay (Omoa), 152
Cocolobo (Roatán), 201–202
Coco Pando Resort (La Ceiba), 168
Coco View Resort (Roatán), 209
Crowne Plaza (San Pedro Sula), 99–100
D&D Bed and Breakfast (Lago de Yojoa), 110
Deep Blue (Utila), 220–221
Don Udo's (Copán Ruínas), 127
El Cafetal (Danlí), 85
El Cortijo del Lago (Lago de Yojoa), 109
El Gran Samaritino (Puerto Lempira), 251
Estancia El Pedregal (Trinidad), 113
Fantasy Island (Roatán), 209–210
Finca El Cisne (near Copán), 125
Finca Las Glorias (Lago de Yojoa), 108–109
Flamingo's (Omoa), 152
Fronteras del Caribe (Travesia), 150
Fuego del Mar (Roatán), 213
Fundación Ecologista HR Pastor (Buenos Aires), 98
George & Ginger's Clearwater Paradise (Guanaja), 231
Gran Hotel Colonial (Santa Bárbara), 112
Gran Hotel Paris (La Ceiba), 168–169
Gran Hotel Sula (San Pedro Sula), 101
Grissy's (Tela), 159
Guacamaya B&B (San Pedro Sula), 101
Guancascos (Gracias), 137

Hacienda San Lucas (near Copán Ruínas), 125–126
Half Moon Cay (Guanaja), 230
Hilton Princess San Pedro Sula (San Pedro Sula), 100
Honduras Maya (Tegucigalpa), 67
Honduras Shores Plantation (Tela), 158
Hostal J.B. (La Campa), 140
Hotel America, Inc. (Comayagua), 115
Hotel Bellavista (La Campa), 140
Hotel Bonsai (Choluteca), 87
Hotel Boquerón (Juticalpa), 255–256
Hotel Cabañas Los Pinos (La Esperanza), 144
Hotel Canadien (Sambo Creek), 173
Hotel Casa Grande (Comayagua), 115
Hotel Centro (Puerto Cortés), 148–149
Hotel Cesar Mariscos (Tela), 159
Hotel Christopher Columbus (Trujillo), 183
Hotel Ciudad Blanca (Brus Laguna), 248
Hotel Copantl (San Pedro Sula), 100
Hotel Costa Azul (Puerto Cortés), 149
Hotel El San Carlos (El Puente), 131
Hotel Elvir (Santa Rosa de Copán), 133
Hotel Finca El Capitan (Gracias), 137
Hotel Gran Central (Tela), 160
Hotel Gualiqueme (Choluteca), 87
Hotel Hedman-Alas (Tegucigalpa), 68
Hotel Honduras (Juticalpa), 256
Hotel Juan Carlos (Catacamas), 260
Hotel La Esperanza (Danlí), 85
Hotel La Estancia (Brus Laguna), 248
Hotel Linda Vista (Tegucigalpa), 68
Hotel Mango (Tela), 160
Hotel Meyling (Catacamas), 260
Hotel Miller (Guanaja), 232–233
Hotel Mina (La Esperanza), 144
Hotel Mi Palacio (Gualaco), 261
Hotel Mirador de Amapala (Isla del Tigre), 90
Hotel Molina Real (La Esperanza), 144
Hotel Moskitia (Palacios), 239
Hotel Nuevo Boston (Tegucigalpa), 68–69
Hotel O'Glynn (Trujillo), 184
Hotel Olas del Mar (La Ceiba), 169
Hotel Palace (Yoro), 263
Hotel Papabeto (Catacamas), 260
Hotel Playa Bonita (Tela), 159
Hotel Playa Negra (Isla del Tigre), 90
Hotel Plaza Copán (Copán Ruínas), 127
Hotel Plaza San Martín (Tegucigalpa), 67
Hotel Plaza San Pablo (Siguatepeque), 117
Hotel Posada del Angel (Valle de Angeles), 78–79
Hotel Posada del Centro (Juticalpa), 256
Hotel Real Camino Lenca (Gracias), 137
Hotel Río Tinto (Palacios), 239
Hotel Rose (Jade Seahorse; Utila), 222
Hotel Santa Lucia Resort, 81
Hotel Santa Maria (Comayagua), 115–116
Hotel Sherwood (Tela), 159–160
Hotel Telamar (Tela), 158
Hotel Villa Bíosfera (Brus Laguna), 248
Hotel VIP Copán (Santa Rosa de Copán), 133
Hotel Vuestra Casa (Siguatepeque), 117
Hotel Yu Baiwan (Puerto Lempira), 251
Humuya Inn (Tegucigalpa), 68
Iguana Azul (Copán Ruínas), 127
Infinity Bay Spa & Resort (Roatán), 206
Isabella Boutique Hotel (San Pedro Sula), 100
Island House (Guanaja), 231–232
Island Life Tours (Jade Seahorse; Utila), 223
Jungle River Lodge (Pico Bonito), 178
La Aurora (La Ceiba), 169
La Ensenada Beach Villas and Resort (Tela), 157–158
Laguna Beach (Utila), 221
Laguna Vista (Jade Seahorse; Utila), 223
La Posada de Belssy (Copán Ruínas), 127–128
La Posada del Lago (Lago de Yojoa), 109
La Quinta (La Ceiba), 169
La Quinta Bay Hotel (Trujillo), 184
Las Cascadas (Pico Bonito), 176–177
Life's a Beach Villa (Jade Seahorse; Utila), 223
The Lily Pond House (Roatán), 202
The Lodge at Pico Bonito, 176
Los Jicaros (San Pedro Sula), 101
Los Pinares (Puerto Lempira), 251
Mango Inn (Jade Seahorse; Utila), 222
Marble Hill Farms (Oakridge), 211–212
Marina Copán (Copán Ruínas), 126
Mariposa del Mar (Roatán), 213
Marriott Tegucigalpa, 66
Maya Key (Roatán), 196
Mayan Princess (Roatán), 206
Maya Vista (Tela), 160
Mayoka Lodge (Roatán), 198
Metrotel Express (San Pedro Sula), 101–102
Nautilus Resort (Guanaja), 232
Nightline Cabins (Jade Seahorse; Utila), 221
Omega Lodge (near El Naranjo), 178
Palma Real Beach Resort (near La Ceiba), 169–170
Palmetto Bay Plantation (Roatán), 210
PANACAM Lodge (Lago de Yojoa), 109–110
Parrot Tree Plantation (Roatán), 210
Pawanka Beach Cabañas (Belén), 241
Paya Bay Beach Resort, 214
Plantation Beach Resort (Cayos Cochinos), 180
Portal del Angel (Tegucigalpa), 66–67
Posada de Don Juan (Gracias), 137–138
Posada Las Orquideas (Roatán), 202
Posada Mi Antigua Casa (La Esperanza), 144
Quinta Real (La Ceiba), 168
Raista Ecolodge, 241
Real InterContinental (Tegucigalpa), 67
Real InterContinental San Pedro Sula, 100
Reef House Resort (Oakridge), 212
Roli's Place (Omoa), 152
Santé Spa (Roatán), 210–211
Seagrape Plantation Resort (Roatán), 202
Sueño del Mar (Roatán), 202
Sueños de Mar B&B (Omoa), 152
Sunset Villas (Roatán), 203
Tamarindo Hostel (San Pedro Sula), 102
Terramaya (Copán Ruínas), 126
Tranquility Bay (Trujillo), 183–184
Turquoise Bay (Roatán), 211
Utila Lighthouse, 222
Utila Lodge, 221–222
Utopia Village (Utila), 221
Villagio Verde (Roatán), 203
Villa Helen's (Sambo Creek), 173

Villa on Dunbar Rock (Guanaja), 230–231
Villas del Agua Caliente (Gracias), 138
Villas del Sol (Puerto Cortés), 149
Villas del Valle (Valle de Angeles), 79
Villas Pico Bonito, 177
West Bay B&B (Roatán), 206–207
West Bay Lodge (Roatán), 207
West Peak Inn (Guanaja), 232
Yamari Savannah Cabañas (Brus Laguna), 248–249
Yat B'alam (Copán Ruínas), 127

Restaurants

Albert's Café (Puerto Cortés), 149
Aqui Pancha (Omoa), 152–153
Arrecifes (Tela), 161
Arte Marianos (San Pedro Sula), 102
Beach Club San Simon (Roatán), 207
Bella Italia (Tela), 161–162
Besos (Roatán), 203
Bite on the Beach (Roatán), 207
B.J.'s Backyard (Oakridge), 212
Blue Bahia Beach Grill (Roatán), 198–199
Bohio Bar (Puerto Cortés), 149
Bundu Café and Bakery (Utila), 225
Cactus Restaurant (Comayagua), 116
Café Del Valle (Valle de Angeles), 79
Café Honoré (Tegucigalpa), 70
Café San Rafael (Copán Ruínas), 128
Café Skandia (San Pedro Sula), 104
Café 1331 (Tegucigalpa), 72
Café Welchez (Copán Ruínas), 129
Cannibal Café (Roatán), 203
Carnitas N'ia Lola (Copán Ruínas), 128–129
Casa Castillo (Comayagua), 116
Casa Romeo's (Roatán), 208–209
Celeste's Island Cuisine (Roatán), 207
Cesar Mariscos (Tela), 161
Champa Kabasa (Sambo Creek), 174
Chef Guity's (La Ceiba), 171
Churasqueria Momo's (Copán Ruínas), 129
Comedor Caballero (Santa Fe), 182
Comedor y Pupuseria Mary (Copán Ruínas), 129–130
Costa Azul (La Ceiba), 170
Crepes (San Pedro Sula), 103–104
D&D Brewery (Lago de Yojoa), 110–111
Deriva Enoteca (San Pedro Sula), 102
Deriva Enoteca (Tegucigalpa), 69
Don Quixote (Santa Lucía), 81
Driftwood Café (Utila), 225
D'Var Resta & Playa (La Ceiba), 170
Earth Mama's (Roatán), 203
El Anafre (Valle de Angeles), 79
El Cafetal (Danlí), 85
El Delfin (Tela), 160
El Faro de Victoria (Isla del Tigre), 91
El Fogon (La Esperanza), 145
El Patio (Tegucigalpa), 69
El Pescador (Tela), 161
El Picante (Utila), 224
El Portal (Gracias), 138
El Portal (Valle de Angeles), 79
El Portal de las Carnes (San Pedro Sula), 103
El Torito (Choluteca), 87–88
Entre Pisco y Nazca (San Pedro Sula), 102–103
Entre Pisco y Nazca (Tegucigalpa), 69–70
Espresso Americano (La Ceiba), 171
Espresso Americano (Puerto Cortés), 149
Evelyn's BBQ (Utila), 224
Expatriates Bar & Grill (La Ceiba), 170
Fine London Pub (Tegucigalpa), 70–71
Flamingo's (Santa Rosa de Copán), 133
Foster's (Roatán), 204
Fronteras del Caribe (Travesia), 150
Furiwa (Tegucigalpa), 71
Gino's (Tegucigalpa), 71
Gio's Restaurant (Roatán), 209
Gota de Limon (Comayagua), 116
Graham's Place (Guanaja), 233
Guancascos (Gracias), 138
Hacienda San Lucas (Copán Ruínas), 128
Harbour House (Utila), 224
Hasta La Pasta (San Pedro Sula), 104
Hole in the Wall Restaurant (Jonesville), 212
Hungry Kiwi (Roatán), 199
Indian Wok (Utila), 225
Jade Seahorse (Utila), 224
Jalapeños (Valle de Angeles), 79
Jenny's Lusty Lizard (Roatán), 192
Jim's Pizza (Copán Ruínas), 130
La Cacerola (Tegucigalpa), 72
La Casa de las Abuelas (Valle de Angeles), 79
La Cumbre Restaurant (Tegucigalpa), 69
La Hacienda Lenca (La Esperanza), 145
La Palapa (La Ceiba), 170–171
La Piccola (Utila), 224
La Pirata (Utila), 225
Laura's Bakery (La Ceiba), 171
Lenca Maya Restaurant (Santa Rosa de Copán), 133
Llama del Bosque (Copán Ruínas), 130
Los Coco's Bar & Grill (Trujillo), 184
Luces del Norte (Tela), 161
Mamma Mia (Tela), 162
Manati (Guanaja), 233
Mangiamo (Roatán), 207
Mapak Almuk (Brus Laguna), 249
Merendero del Centro (Trujillo), 184–185
Merendero Emilia (Brus Laguna), 249
Mesón Casa Blanca (Santa Bárbara), 112
Meson de Don Juan (Gracias), 138
Mexi Treats (Guanaja), 233
Munchies (Utila), 225
The Mystic (Trujillo), 185
Naturaleza Restaurant (Lago de Yojoa), 111
Nau Lounge (Tegucigalpa), 70
Ni Fu Ni Fa (Tegucigalpa), 70
Nobu (Tegucigalpa), 70
Noodle Shack (Roatán), 204
Ooloonthoo (Roatán), 204
Opalaca's (La Esperanza), 145
Oregano (Juticalpa), 256
Pinocchio (Roatán), 204
Pizza Pizza (Santa Rosa de Copán), 134
Pizzeria Italia (San Pedro Sula), 104
Playa Dorado (Trujillo), 185
Plaza Típica Coracts (San Pedro Sula), 104
Porcao y Pizza House (Tegucigalpa), 71
Portal La Leyenda Café Bar (Santa Lucía), 81
Punto Italia (Omoa), 153
Pupuseria Universitaria (La Ceiba), 171
Rancho Mexicano (Danlí), 85
Restaurante Acuarion (Choluteca), 87
Restaurante Don Udo's (San Pedro Sula), 103
Restaurante El Muelle (Gualaco), 261
Restaurante Fisherman's (Omoa), 153
Restaurante La Casona (Santa Bárbara), 112
Restaurante Miluska (Santa Lucía), 81
Restaurante Vicente (San Pedro Sula), 104

Rinconcito Graciano (Gracias), 138–139
Rincon Danlídense (Danlí), 85
Rojo, Verde, y Ajo (Tegucigalpa), 71
Rosalin (Tela), 161
Sabor Cubano (Tegucigalpa), 71–72
Scapate (Omoa), 153
Sueños de Mar (Omoa), 153
Sushi Itto (San Pedro Sula), 103
Taco Taco (Tegucigalpa), 72
Tapadero's (Puerto Cortés), 149–150
Ten Nepel (Santa Rosa de Copán), 134
Thompson's Bakery (Utila), 225
Tío Rico (Choluteca), 88
Tong's (Roatán), 204
Tortas y Mas (Tegucigalpa), 72
Twisted Tanya's (Copán Ruínas), 128
Veleros (Isla del Tigre), 91
ViaVia Copán (Copán Ruínas), 129
Villa Real (Comayagua), 116
Wine & Tapas 188 (San Pedro Sula), 103
Zotz (Santa Rosa de Copán), 134